THE FEMINISM OF

CHARLOTTE PERKINS GILMAN

WOMEN IN CULTURE AND SOCIETY
a series edited by Catharine R. Stimpson

The Feminism of Charlotte Perkins Gilman

SEXUALITIES, HISTORIES, PROGRESSIVISM

Judith A. Allen

UNIVERSITY OF CHICAGO PRESS
Chicago & London

Judith A. Allen is professor of history and gender studies at Indiana University.

The University of Chicago Press, Chicago 60637
The University of Chicago Press, Ltd., London
© 2009 by The University of Chicago
All rights reserved. Published 2009
Printed in the United States of America

18 17 16 15 14 13 12 11 10 09   1 2 3 4 5

ISBN-13: 978-0-226-01462-3 (cloth)
ISBN-13: 978-0-226-01463-0 (paper)
ISBN-10: 0-226-01462-2 (cloth)
ISBN-10: 0-226-01463-0 (paper)

Library of Congress Cataloging-in-Publication Data

Allen, Judith A., 1955–
  The feminism of Charlotte Perkins Gilman :
sexualities, histories, progressivism / Judith A. Allen.
    p. cm. — (Women in culture and society)
  Includes bibliographical references and index.
  ISBN-13: 978-0-226-01462-3 (cloth : alk. paper)
  ISBN-13: 978-0-226-01463-0 (pbk. : alk. paper)
  ISBN-10: 0-226-01462-2 (cloth : alk. paper)
  ISBN-10: 0-226-01463-0 (pbk. : alk. paper)
  1. Gilman, Charlotte Perkins, 1860–1935. 2. Gilman,
Charlotte Perkins, 1860–1935—Political and social
views. 3. Feminists—United States—Biography.
4. Feminism—United States—History—19th century.
5. Feminism—United States—History—20th century.
I. Title. II. Series: Women in culture and society.
  PS1744.G57Z56 2009
  305.42092—dc22
  [B]
                        2008055265

♾ The paper used in this publication meets the
minimum requirements of the American National
Standard for Information Sciences—Permanence of
Paper for Printed Library Materials, ANSI Z39.48-1992.

FRONTISPIECE. Portrait of Charlotte Perkins Gilman,
London England, ca. 1896 (The Schlesinger Library,
Radcliffe Institute, Harvard University 177-325-14).

For Bette Allen (1930–2008)

& Kay Daniels (1941–2001)

Feminism is a term applied to what was previously known as "The Woman's Movement," and still earlier, as "Women's Rights." That Movement, in its largest sense, consists in the development of human qualities and functions among women; in their entering upon social relationships, instead of remaining, as has been almost universally the case, restricted to the sexual and domestic. It is in large part individual and unconscious, but it is also increasingly conscious and organized.

Charlotte Perkins Gilman, "Feminism" (1908)

CONTENTS

ILLUSTRATIONS

Charlotte Perkins Gilman (1860–1935) has fascinated me for several decades since my honors dissertation on Australian feminist Rose Scott (1847–1925). I found Scott leading a discussion of Gilman's feminist classic *Women and Economics* (1898) in 1899, as secretary of Sydney's Women's Literary Society. While enthusiastic, Scott expressed reservations about Gilman's reform Darwinist intellectual framing of "the Woman Question," particularly Gilman's use of animal-human comparisons.

Yet Scott's intellectual engagement with Gilman continued. Miles Franklin (1879–1954), author of the 1901 novel *My Brilliant Career*—immortalized in Jane Campion's 1981 film starring Judy Davis and Sam Neill—wrote to Scott about Gilman from Europe. Franklin recalled Scott's gift of Gilman's poetry book, *In This Our World* (1893). From this, Franklin reported, she had learned "the man-serving" nature of so-called civilized culture. As important, Franklin concluded from Gilman's work that a new hopeful path forward for women lay ahead.

Why was Franklin writing to Scott about Gilman just then, in 1913, on the eve of events that would dramatically change women's movement prospects? Because she had recently met Gilman, in Franklin's capacity as coeditor of *Life and Labor*, the journal of the Chicago-based Women's Trade Union League, to which Gilman contributed. Franklin had shared a hotel room with Gilman at the June 1913 Budapest international woman suffrage congress. Astounded at the then fifty-three-year-old Gilman's intellectual and physical vigor, Franklin described her vaulting over chairs, performing somersaults in a display of athletic strength and gymnastic skill. While in Budapest, Franklin attended a suffrage ball. There she danced with Gilman's second husband, George Houghton Gilman (1866–1934). To her bemusement, he and Mrs. Gilman's secretary won the best-looking couple award: "I was brimming over to think," in the rural vernacular of her youth, that the husband "of the boss cocky feminist could win a beauty prize."

Here Franklin concurred with the internationally widespread view that Gilman was the preeminent feminist intellectual of America's Progressive Era. The American press of the 1910s repeatedly identified three great feminist theorists: South Africa's Olive Schreiner, Sweden's Ellen Key, and Gilman. Though Franklin promised that Gilman, who wished to meet Scott, would be in Sydney on a 1914 lecture tour, it was not to be. The outbreak of European hostilities suspended Gilman's travel plans. Like Scott and other feminists, Gilman began the war years in a pacifist stance, identifying war as the ultimate "masculism" and the naked exercise of a male sex instinct. Scott here joined Jane Addams (1860–1935) and feminist pacifists worldwide in the Women's Alliance for Permanent Peace. Like Addams, Scott endured disrespect, public castigation, mail censorship, and internal security surveillance. She emerged from the war disillusioned and distanced from women's movement activity. Appalled at the sexualized jazz age flapper, it seemed that interwar women betrayed the vision of 1890s leaders like herself.

Though Gilman shared many of Scott's views, differences warranted further exploration. By 1916, Gilman was closing her monthly journal, the *Forerunner* (1909–16) on a distinctly bellicose note. She attacked Germans and rebuked the lack of patriotism among "our foreign residents." Living a decade longer than Scott, interwar Gilman seemed increasingly, and for twenty-first-century feminists, embarrassingly, preoccupied with race, ethnicity, nativism, eugenics, and population.

After her death in 1935 Gilman was forgotten for several decades. Then 1970s feminist scholars rediscovered and celebrated her in projects stretching into the 1980s and beyond. Yet, across the 1990s, Gilman became a more problematic figure. If she asked some of the right questions, critics held that her answers amounted to an ignoble legacy, contaminated by class bias, racism, ethnocentrism, and anti-Semitism. Gilman's legacy thereby became useless to antiracist, postcolonial, anti-globalization, and "third-wave" feminists today. Only for the politically comatose and theoretically lethargic could Gilman remain a feminist heroine.

What for me began long ago as a fascination with comparing Gilman to international feminist counterparts like Scott became increased interest on several fronts, with this book as the result. First, Gilman formulated a distinctive reform Darwinist feminist theory in the fin de siècle. Her theory, partly embedded in the emerging American social sciences, offered a radical challenge to the reformist initiatives of the early twentieth-century women's and progressive movements. These elements merited deeper exploration than existing scholarship yet provided.

Second, aspects of commentary on Gilman—hereafter referred to as "Gilmaniana"—had become progressively more intriguing. In particular, a highly politicized canon of Gilman commentary emerged, as well as shifts in the historiography of the Progressive Era, which was the context for her work as a feminist public intellectual. These invited searching appraisal. My relocation to the United States in the early 1990s provided me with the chance to examine rich primary sources by and about Gilman, as well as comparable sources related to her peers, contemporaries, predecessors, and successors within American feminist theory and politics. This research, especially during two years of sabbatical leave (1992–93 and 1999–2000) as a research fellow at the Schlesinger Library on the History of Women in America, reconfigured my own position as a historian reader of Gilmaniana, the vast bulk of which has been literary and textual in emphasis.

Third, this local and comparative research on Gilman convinces me that analysis of sexuality, and its discontented fin de siècle historicities, anchored her key feminist insights. This needs more emphasis than is usual in Gilmaniana today. For Gilman, analysis of women's oppression within reform Darwinism involved scrutinizing the evolution of sex differentiation itself, and its metamorphosis across human stages of savagery into the then-present world of male supremacy. Gilman called it "androcentric culture"—with prostitution, intemperance, and war its current hallmarks. This particular intellectual framework made her a feminist theorist without precedent in her own historical context; Elizabeth Cady Stanton, with her speculations as to an earlier "matriarchate," was the nearest peer. Gilman's focus on transforming the forms of desire, and the terms and genres of then-prevailing heterosexuality, generated the narratives and strategies for which she is today best known— from the 1892 short story, "The Yellow Wall-paper," to her advocacy of "baby-gardens" and kitchenless homes.

With these three distinctive areas of emphasis emerging from my research, it seemed time to address Gilman and the Western feminist canon. Ironically, it was initially in conversation about other projects that Susan Bielstein and Catharine R. Stimpson encouraged me to write *The Feminism of Charlotte Perkins Gilman*. I here examine Gilman's feminist thought and projects in the context of the influences she absorbed and rejected from her Progressive Era culture, and conclude with an appraisal of aspects of current Gilman scholarship. Twenty years of teaching Gilman's feminist theory, in both history and interdisciplinary gender studies frameworks, convinces me that adequate understanding of her specific context is crucial for making her contributions intelligible.

Like any project long in the making, *The Feminism of Charlotte Perkins Gilman* is the result of assistance from many people. No significant work is other than a collective effort. My debts for the genesis of this study of Gilman's feminism are dense and numerous. Not all of those who have contributed may be aware of it. I have been most fortunate in the inspiration, encouragement, and advice of many people. Without Heather Radi at the University of Sydney, I might never have heard of Rose Scott (through whom I discovered Charlotte Perkins Gilman), much less imagined becoming a feminist historian. She taught me much about feminism, politics, and the cultural battle against "the colonial cringe." Barbara Caine's contribution as teacher, mentor, and colleague has been crucial, her nuanced research an exemplary model for grasping the complex comparative historicity of feminism. For her insistence on the critical importance of comparative historiographies and cultures, as well as many lessons along the way, my doctoral supervisor Jill Roe has my deepest thanks, not least for her battle against my earnestness, an admittedly incomplete endeavor. My parents, Bette and Len, and sisters, Cathryn, Margaret, and Deborah, always smiled gracefully on my various goings and comings.

At the Schlesinger Library, with the largest collection of Gilman's papers, I record my heartfelt appreciation to many friends and colleagues for their interest, assistance, and many acts of kindness over the past seventeen years of preparation of this book. Wendy Thomas, then public services librarian, was simply astonishing in her command of resources and avenues I should try. Her generosity with time and brainstorming were way beyond the call of duty, making the project so much better than it otherwise might have been. She and many other superb Schlesinger Library staff have my admiration and gratitude. Here I especially thank Jacalyn Blume, Kim Brooks, Diana Carey, Joanne Donovan, Anne Englehart, Marie-Helen Gold, Diane Hamer, Sarah Hutcheon, Pat King, Jane Knowles, Sylvia McDowell, Eva Mosely, Debbie Richards, Ellen Shea, and Susan Von Salis. I also thank Mark Brown and Tim Engels of the John Hays Brown Library, Brown University; Phyllis Andrews of the University of Rochester Library Special Collections; Barbara Grubb of Bryn Mawr College Library's Special Collections; Becky Cape and Joel Silver at the Lilly Library, Indiana University; and Peter Blodgett of the Huntington Library for access to their Gilman-related collections and those of her relevant peers. For invaluable assistance, efficiency, and care in various phases of the manuscript's development, then Indiana University students Lisa Boehm, Brian Carr, Donna J. Drucker, Kyle McLauchlin, and Julie L. Thomas, as well as Harvard University students Nora Connell, Annalise Nelson, and Carmelo Rose, have my deepest thanks. This book has been extremely well-served by the professionalism, experience, generosity, and fine judgment of many staff of the University of Chicago Press. Here I particularly thank Yvonne Zipter for her keen perception and awe-inspiring editorial work, which immensely clarified the meaning and effectiveness of the text and brought calm wisdom to many aspects of the often-complex scholarly apparatus entailed in a project of this kind. I greatly appreciated her warmth and constructive vision — it was a true pleasure to work with her. Anthony Burton, Carol Saller, and Chris Westcott provided astute advice and rapid feedback needed in the various stages of the book's processing and production, making my tasks so very much easier. Megan Marz contributed lightning marketing insights and implemented impressive strategies to ensure that the book reached those most likely to appreciate it, and I thank her for all her efforts as well as her patience with my many shortcomings.

Historians of feminism and feminist theorists from several fields have guided my way, both in concurrence and debate; and here I owe a special debt of gratitude to Lucy Bland, Nancy F. Cott, Ellen Carol DuBois, Linda Gordon, Sally L. Kitch, Laura Levine Frader, Philippa Levine, Karen Offen, Carole Pateman, and Susan Ware. Meanwhile, Gilman scholars have been nothing but generous, thoughtful, interested, and encouraging. For opportunities for intellectual exchange, and to explore tangents outside this book or to develop earlier versions of arguments elaborated here, I thank Gail Bederman, Cynthia J. Davis, Catherine Golden, J. Michael Hogan, Jill Rudd, Val Gough, Mary Armfield Hill, Joanne Zangrando, and Denise D. Knight. I especially thank Ann J. Lane for her insightful and challenging responses to my earlier efforts to unravel Gilman's theorizing about sexualities.

A quarter century of friendship with philosopher Elizabeth Grosz has provided enormous inspiration toward this book. No one could have had a better sounding board and critic while writing a book on an American feminist theorist, especially one engaging so creatively with Darwinism, sexual evolution, temporality, and corporeality. Meanwhile, my bio-psychologist colleague and friend, Kinsey Institute associate director Stephanie A. Sanders, was invaluable in my grappling with aspects of evolutionary theory so central to Gilman's concept of human history and feminist prospects. More important, I owe a great debt to Steph for challenging my default humanist assumptions, which, at times, imperiled Gilman's audibility. And Michael McGerr's wisdom, deep expertise and technical wizardry proved indispensable, while his friendship and wit buoyed me throughout the writing process.

Indiana University has given me a superb community of scholars with whom to exchange and learn over many years. For all their encouragement I especially thank Laurel L. Cornell, Carol Greenhouse, M. Jeanne Peterson, Wendy Gamber, J. Scott Long, Chana Kai Lee, Michael Grossberg, Rosemary Lloyd, Susan Williams, and Liana Zhou. Meanwhile, in Britain, Canada, and Australia, colleagues and friends offered great assistance and encouragement as I completed the manuscript; here I thank Kelly Boyd, David Churchill, Jim Cronin, Andy Davies, Laura Levine Frader, Philip Graham, Sam Harris, Ian Henderson, Julia Horne, Cath Kevin, Mary and Michael Kinnear, Rohan McWilliam, Sam Nightingale, Pat Thane, Selina Todd, and Chris Waters.

I greatly appreciate Paul H. Hardacre's welcome hospitality during the Huntington Library research for this project. He was altogether "swell." Helen Hardacre was my coconspirator in adventures of the 1990s and early 2000s—immigration not the least of them. Her example made me better than I ever could have been without her—and so, as always, I thank beloved "Sveta." Her expertise and experience grounded the formative stages of this project, while her astute reading of several drafts hugely improved it. Always, her advice has proved indispensable. I have never deserved her, as I have always freely owned. Stephen Garton, with whom I "grew up" as a historian, has been companion, friend, and touchstone in my traverses from social to cultural history projects, as well as moves across nations, regions, and contexts. He has never let distance disconnect us, and he knows how much he has my gratitude, admiration, and love.

My fellow "low Anglo" and unassimilated immigrant, Peter Bailey, has given me so much across the past two decades, and not only *his* London, great jazz piano, pedantry as art form, and "parasexuality and glamour." He makes life make sense— always has. Some debts can never be repaid. He "put me in the air" and, miraculously enough, kept me there till this was finished. Always, he urged a portrayal of Gilman as humane/human, despite all about her that seems alien today. If I have not fully succeeded, it is due to my own limitations.

Finally, my mother Bette Allen always set the example of perceptiveness, shrewd intuition, and what I call her "fighting adaptation," while preserving core principles. By her own scholarly example, she instilled a great love of studying history when I was too young to quite realize. I thank her for continuing to ask about Gilman in our long phone calls between Bloomington and Sydney and wish she were still here to review this book. Without fanfare, she was the strongest and bravest person I've ever known. And the late Kay Daniels bequeathed gifts that endure: the endless excitement of archives documenting the rich historical intricacies of sex differences, sexuality, and gender; and her devastating methodological and epistemological insights, delivered with sharp wit and twinkling eye. She exemplified courage and integrity in the face of injustice, challenging others to make a difference, whatever it cost. She inspired a generation of feminist historians, and we miss her terribly. I dedicate *The Feminism of Charlotte Perkins Gilman* to them both.

Bloomington, 2009

INTRODUCTION

The opposition to Feminism . . . diminished in volume but increased in intensity with the steady success of the movement. As in all ages, people willingly believe all evil of a thing they fear and hate, so the Woman's Movement has been accused of the worst intentions and results. As each forward step was made and the dreaded change became an established fact, without the alleged evil results, the charges were transferred to the next demand, and today we find . . . extension of the franchise to women charged with the same evils long ago attributed to their having a higher education or the chance to earn their livings. The latest and highest form of Feminism has great promise for the world. It postulates womanhood free, strong, clean, and conscious of its power and duty.

Charlotte Perkins Gilman, "Feminism" (1908)

CHARLOTTE PERKINS GILMAN was the most significant Western feminist theorist of the period 1890–1920. Her most important contribution to feminist theory was *Women and Economics: A Study of the Economic Relation between Men and Women as a Factor in Social Evolution* (1898). It was translated into seven languages and sold steadily, generating its ninth edition by 1920. Gilman held that heterosexuality had become the means by which men subjected women through an economic dependency naturalized as the outcome of female sexual functions. Human societies perverted evolution, exaggerating sex differences in cultural patterns later called "gender," but which she called "androcentric culture." These patterns retarded women by confining them to "sex work." Sexual relations had to transform for women to contribute to the human race's progress—"race work." However warranted, though, a "human" world would not inevitably supersede an androcentric one. Rather, it would require struggle for (and within) feminism itself and Progressive Era reform politics.[1]

Hence, Gilman became a renowned feminist involved in the era's signature campaigns. These included woman suffrage from the 1880s, the abolition of regulated prostitution from the 1890s onward, and legalized birth control in the 1920s and 1930s. Gilman's admirers called her "the Dean of American feminists," while detractors named her "the high priestess of feminism." She was dubbed "the ablest woman in the United States. . . . Whatever she says is bound to be listened to. . . . She is the Bernard Shaw of America; or should we say that Bernard Shaw is the Charlotte Perkins Gilman of England?" This is the first systematic book-length study of the intellectual tenets of Gilman's distinctive contributions to early twentieth-century Western feminist theory and politics and of the dialogue between her feminism and Progressive Era reform culture. The tasks of this introduction are several: to outline briefly the book's objectives, to present an initial assessment of scholarly literature relating to Gilman, and to offer a concise account of the organization of this study.[2]

Gilman was a Protestant New Englander, living for varying periods in Massachusetts, Rhode Island, California, Illinois, New York, and Connecticut. To earn her living as a lecturer and editor she traveled across the United States, particularly in the West, Midwest, and the South. Moreover, on multimonth European trips in 1896, 1899, 1904, 1905, and 1913, she addressed woman suffragists, socialists, and other reform audiences in exchanges with key intellectuals and reformers. Descended from reformers, she was grandniece of abolitionist Harriet Beecher Stowe (1811–96), suffragist Isabella Beecher Hooker (1822–1907), and great-granddaughter of orator and cleric, Lyman Beecher (1775–1863).[3]

The American press covered Gilman's discourses more fully—critically and otherwise—than any feminist theorist to date. The British press, too, reviewed her favorably, praising her "exceptional ability" and "great courage" and extolling her *Women and Economics* for its "originality of concept and brilliancy of exposition." Hailed as an instant classic, reviewers held that it surpassed all ruminations on "the Woman Question" since John Stuart Mill's magisterial *The Subjection of Women* (1869).[4]

The designation of Gilman as the preeminent transatlantic early twentieth-century feminist theorist rests on several contributions. First, she was a feminist theorist insofar as she identified women as a sexed group, subjected or subordinated by, and in the interests of, the men of their cultures. Second, she provided a theoretical account of the origins and causes of women's "sex subjection"—today more typically called "oppression." Third, she undertook specific analysis and "thick description" of the operation of this "sex subjection," criticizing its usual justifications. Finally, she devised reform proposals designed to end women's subordination.[5]

Her theoretical works were many and impressive, including *Women and Economics* (1898), *Concerning Children* (1900), *The Home: Its Work and Influence* (1903), *Human Work* (1904), and *The Man-Made World; or, Our Androcentric Culture* (1911), the latter praised by the otherwise unfriendly *New York Times* as a "remarkable book and her best work ever." Moreover, her monthly journal, *Forerunner* (1909–16), serialized her other multichapter nonfiction treatises "Our Brains and What Ails Them" (1912), "Humanness" (1913), "Social Ethics" (1914), "The Dress of Women" (1915), "Growth and Combat" (1916), and "Studies in Social Pathology" (1916). Her favorably reviewed interwar treatise, *His Religion and Hers: A Study of the Faith of Our Fathers and the Work of Our Mothers* (1923), however, was no bestseller. Meanwhile, remaining unpublished was her long-reworked and variously titled manuscript on ethics. Finally, her autobiography, partly written in the 1920s, and reworked as she was dying from breast cancer, was published posthumously under the title of *The Living of Charlotte Perkins Gilman* (1935), as was her "The Right to Die," the last of nearly 1,500 nonfiction articles and chapters she had published since 1883. In these works she stressed needs for economic independence and emancipation from domestic work to end the intimate and erotic dimensions of "sex slavery."[6]

Gilman grounded her feminist theory in evolutionary and historical analyses of sexuality attending to the historical causes and operation of women's subjection. Evolutionary biology, archaeology, and ancient human history convinced her of the historicity of sex differentiation itself. In her ruminations on sexual relations she sought "a biological basis" for fighting women's subjection. Distinct from previous contributors to "the Woman Question" she made feminist theory a force within Progressive Era politics and culture by relating sexuality and sexual relations to contemporary debates. The ground she broke here profoundly influenced fellow campaigners.[7]

Gilman's feminism requires systematic study within its own historical and discursive context, by immersion in her terms of reference, and with attention to her thought as a whole. Her preoccupations included elements unrelated to feminism—at least as readers might understand feminism today—including, for instance, reform Darwinism, Nationalist and Fabian socialism, eugenics, and immigration restrictivism—elements that inflected her particular feminism. Her influence, in turn, ensured that some of these elements acquired feminist reconfigurations.

Of necessity, this study of Gilman's feminism assimilates a wide range of sources and media. These include her own extensive correspondence and that of others pertaining to her work; her draft writings, publications, lectures, notes, and other miscellaneous writing; and contemporary assessments of her work. Important insights, too, emerge from studying Gilman alongside peers such as Jane Addams, Lester Frank Ward, Edward Alsworth Ross, Upton Sinclair, Ida Tarbell, William I. Thomas, Olive Schreiner, and Ellen Key, among others.

The project of this book differs from those of historians of the Progressive Era. There is no need to retread the ground they have broken with such insight. Instead, this study seeks enhanced understanding of feminism within the wide spectrum of progressive politico-intellectual concerns. Historians of Progressivism are positioned best to judge the fuller significance of Gilman's feminism for narratives of the era's mentalité. It is neither my intention nor competence to resolve increasingly vexed debates about Progressivism. Can the era of Gilman's theoretical work any longer be called "Progressive" at all, in view of the patent flaws of noted reformers usually characterized as Progressive? Ultimately, historians may jettison the very notion of "the Progressive Era," dismissing it as a misleading, overunifying, conceptual dead end. Alternatively, "Progressivism" may become just one strand in a contradictory historical moment characterized in quite different terms—as some new research suggests.[8]

Whatever the future understandings of this period, feminist theory, as part of what to date has been called "Progressivism," remains underestimated, warranting firmer location within an array of early twentieth-century reform impulses. Such work requires comprehensive and context-sensitive analyses of the work of the era's most significant feminist theorist, who determinedly called herself a Progressive. This study offers a representative exposition of three elements of Gilman's feminism and career as a public intellectual. First, her sexuality-centered theories, and evolutionary history analyses of androcentric culture, receive exegesis. The implications of her theoretical corpus impel, second, an exploration of her contributions to her era's feminist theory and politics. The third element traced is the way her venerable stature as feminist intellectual involved her in Progressive Era reform initiatives.

Central to all three elements of this study of Gilman's feminism was her highly original account of human sexual evolution. She repudiated male conjugal rights, prostitution, and "sexual slavery," but did so without the erotophobia sometimes attributed to her by presentist commentators. Important also was Gilman's dichotomous contrasting of "sex work"—labor ascribed by sexual characteristics and performed, usually by women for men, both in pair bonds and individual families—and "race work"—work derived from common human characteristics and benefiting the human race collectively. Her focus on work matched her socialist concerns, dating from her days working and living among Californian socialist and Nationalist followers of Edward Bellamy (1850–98) in the early 1890s and, more enduringly, from her cordial ties with Fabian socialists in America and overseas. Socialists' backwardness on the so-called Woman Question disappointed her and led her to expound, instead, a revolutionary concept of work as originally "maternal" and, thereby, reviled within androcentric culture.[9]

Reform Darwinism shaped her canonic feminist contribution. Its tenets need stipulation, especially in relation to the theory of sexual relations advanced by her admired contemporary, founding sociologist Lester Frank Ward (1841–1913). She retained a distinctive, if not unique, reform Darwinist feminist framework long after its foundations were challenged by new developments in late Progressive Era and interwar science. That framework continued to shape her standpoint within feminist debates of the 1920s and 1930s, notwithstanding the mistaken claim that she ceased to work on feminist issues after World War I. Though adapting to changing contexts for feminist issues—debating woman suffrage with its enemies until the 1920s, and pondering birth control in the war and interwar decades—her basic analysis bore great consistency in forty years of her public intellectual career. Even so, as a working lecturer, writer, and editor, she assimilated new themes from her context, some of which challenged her longstanding theoretical oeuvre.

If Gilman occupied a preeminent place both within Progressive Era feminism and Western feminist theory, she presents a problem for would-be taxonomists. She repeatedly refused the title "feminist," arguing that "feminism" should be retitled "humanism." Hence some commentators refrain from calling her a feminist. Yet her resistance to being so labeled forms a part of the fascinating story of, what Nancy F. Cott terms, the American "birth of feminism" in the 1910s—a birth that from the outset involved sectarian disputes. Historians trace "feminism" as originally French, from the 1880s, and promptly exported. Derogatory in tone, ridiculing those seeking women's equality and autonomy, initially, it was not its adherents' chosen self-description. Only slowly obtaining Anglophone currency, reformers embraced feminism in a generational shift prior to World War I. Gilman's uncertainty about the term matched other peers, such as Rose Scott in Australia. Even in the interwar period, now acclaimed feminist theorist Virginia Woolf (1879–1941) evaded such self-labeling, while French feminist Simone de Beauvoir (1912–85) also dismissed earlier feminists.[10]

Gilman's feminism itself, then, remains elusive. Lack of systematic study of her feminist theory, compared with other key U.S. theorists and reformers, cannot be for want of sources. She left a prodigious corpus from childhood until 1935, two-thirds of it nonfiction, comprising treatises, theoretical expositions, parables, sermons, lectures, articles, reports, reviews, and essays. Perhaps due to Gilman's disavowal of the term, no book-length interrogations have yet charted the career-long totality of her complicated feminism as a sexual politics and philosophical discourse, understood in relation to other feminist theorists. Nonetheless, her theoretical writing on the origins, causes, and maintenance of women's oppression by and largely "in the interests of men" compels analysis, as does her feminist political work, including her engagement with Progressive Era reform agendas, domains explored in this three-part book.[11]

SINCE MY CENTRAL objective is to illuminate and characterize Gilman's feminism within its Progressive Era context, an initial discussion of relevant scholarship and commentary is appropriate, clarifying more exactly the contribution of this study to existing work. The prevailing literature on Gilman warrants loosely chronological analysis, beginning with the pioneering work of historian Carl N. Degler in the 1950s and 1960s. Following that, a comparison of women's liberation movement–inspired literary critics and biographers of the 1970s and 1980s with commentators from various nonliterary fields on Gilman fiction and nonfiction proves useful. Finally, more recent work warrants brief initial scrutiny, with a fuller discussion of the current strand of Gilmaniana interrogating intense debates since the 1990s over Gilman and class, race, ethnicity, and eugenics, particularly as contributed by advocates of new race history, whiteness studies, third-wave feminism, and antiracism in the last chapter.

Historian Carl N. Degler's 1956 and 1966 readings of Gilman both appeared in the wake of widely lauded postwar feminist texts: the 1953 English translation of Simone De Beauvoir's *The Second Sex* (1949), with its existentialist feminist theory and interdisciplinary analysis of women's oppression, and Betty Friedan's *The Feminine Mystique* (1963). These postwar feminist texts fired public debate about housebound, suburban, economically dependent (and as critics have noted, white) women seeking careers. Degler contrasted both Beauvoir and Friedan unfavorably with Gilman, questioning their originality, rhetoric, and strategies.[12]

Though Gilman was forgotten by the 1930s, Degler reintroduced her "as a sociologist and a social critic," and one who predated Beauvoir by decades in proposing strategies for women's emancipation. He implicitly deprecated the latter's originality. Long before the French feminist called woman "the Other," Gilman denounced women's relegation to sex-differentiated inferior sex roles, holding paid work to be liberating on the assumption that "women were human beings." In favorable contrast with Beauvoir, Gilman, never "shrill or ill-tempered," willingly gave "man" due credit for "historical activities on behalf of civilization," wisely refraining from the "philippic against men that appears in some feminist literature." She even exonerated men "from having selfishly kept women in a low status," arguing neither for women's superiority nor their "complete similarity to men."[13]

Degler contended that Gilman, because temperamentally unsuited to office holding and organizational leadership, gave no "attention to that limited goal" of woman suffrage—a cause that he held deflected attention from broader 1910–20 questions about "women in modern industrial society." Others have subsequently repeated his mistaken claims of Gilman's distance from the suffrage campaign. Although suffrage did not revolutionize women's position, many had feared it would, not least the antisuffrage societies targeted in Gilman's suffragism.[14]

Though Degler's Gilman was a moderate, relative to Beauvoir and Friedan, he still damned her with faint praise. If sharp, cogent, and lucid, her *Women and Economics* was an unoriginal and merely "pseudoscientific" reform tract. Degler read her out of context and not as a serious theorist. He called her "Mrs. Gilman" rather than simply "Gilman," congruent with his references to other theorists, such as Freud, Marx, Veblen, and Ward. If he judged prescient her emphasis on wives' paid work within egalitarian marriages, the sex division of domestic labor remained intractable, despite her plans for paid services and kitchenless houses. With sex equality still unrealized by the 1960s, Degler cast Gilman as a weak prophet, predicting change but mistaking its details.[15]

Gilman's significance reemerged after 1970 for a newly revitalized feminist movement. She became known through either feminist literary criticism or social science scrutiny of Degler's edition of *Women and Economics*. Renewed attention stimulated biographies, scholarly commentary, edited anthologies of essays, and the collection or reissuing of some of her immense oeuvre between 1980 and century's end.[16]

Most conspicuously, nearly three-quarters of Gilmaniana addresses Gilman's thirteen-page short story, "The Yellow Wall-paper." It was first published in 1892. Republished frequently since the mid-1970s, this critical attention by feminists has relocated Gilman's story into the mainstream of American literary criticism.[17]

Her 1915 utopian novel *Herland* has become the next greatest focus of literary Gilmaniana since the 1980s. Its republication in 1979 was followed by its originally serialized sequel, "With Her in Ourland" (1916), reissued in 1997, though in the latter case by two sociologists. Moreover, feminist scholars have analyzed Gilman's other short stories, novels, and plays, including the hitherto unpublished 1929 detective novel, *Unpunished,* finally published and edited in 1997.[18]

Literary critics have annotated and provided commentary on Gilman's diaries, letters, lesser-known fiction, and even the early artwork by which she supplemented the family income, both before and after marriage in the 1880s. Meanwhile, Gary Scharnhorst compiled an immense 1985 bibliography of known works by and about her up to that point. Since then, a Charlotte Perkins Gilman society has emerged, holding regular conferences and publishing a newsletter, constantly updating the bibliography of Gilmaniana. Typically, these works assume rather than systematically analyze Gilman's feminism.[19]

Understandably, the mainly literary scholarship in Gilman commentary has created her scholarly profile more as a literary figure than as the social scientist that was her own self-description, particularly throughout the work judged by her to be most important during her lifetime, *Women and Economics* (1898). Gilman was a founding member of the American Sociological Association and was often invited to participate as conference delegate, panelist, and reviewer. In 1898, *Women and Economics* made her known for the remainder of her feminist career as a sociologist, philosopher, ethicist, and social critic, producing some fiction on the side. By 1998, however, Gilman had become a feminist novelist and poet who produced some nonfiction.[20]

Yet Gilman herself consistently repudiated "art for art's sake" and declined the title of "poet," treating fiction as a medium for her feminist message. Sociologist Mary Jo Deegan rightly dubs her didactic fiction "sociological literature" or "literary sociology." With most Gilman scholarship emanating from departments of english and modern languages, sociologist Michael R. Hill regrets that such academic work often omits "Gilman's core sociological purpose and persona."[21]

Instead, literary scholars appraise mainly her fiction, along with some of her nonfiction, through paradigms current within feminist literary criticism and cultural studies. Since the 1990s, this has generated sustained critiques of her work in terms of contemporary U.S. debates related to race, racism, ethnocentrism, eugenics, anti-Semitism, and nativism. This work warrants careful appraisal in relation to the totality of Gilman's career. As such, it anchors the final chapter of this book.[22]

While Gilman's nonfiction is addressed in Gilmaniana, sustained analyses by scholars outside literary and cultural studies are relatively sparse, compared to prolific literary criticism of her fiction. Nonliterary scholars generally approach her nonfiction texts as instantiation of particular disciplinary concerns, rather than making Gilman herself their central focus. Thus, sociologists ask whether Gilman's associations and endeavors were sociological enough to justify her self-designation as a sociologist. Philosophers wonder if her pragmatism was enough like John Dewey's to make her a philosopher. Historians and philosophers of science scrutinize her appropriation of sociologist Ward's gynaecocentric theory to blend reform Darwinism and the Woman Question. Scholars of religious studies compare her critique of androcentric religion with works by feminist critics Elizabeth Cady Stanton and Matilda Joslyn Gage. Urban studies and material history scholars examine links between her architectural reform plans and other female planning reformers. Socialist theorists and economists wonder if her proposals for commodifying domestic labor and child care, allowing women, like men, to "work and love too," in fact were bourgeois.[23]

Some recognize Gilman as a sociological pioneer—even supplementing Gilman's own titles in reissues of her work to include the word "sociology," even though, like other founding sociologists, such as Ward, she worked outside academic institutions as a public intellectual. Depicted both as an influential outsider and as a marginal insider of Progressive Era intellectual life, her stature as an author, editor, lecturer, and commentator denied while at the same time permitted Gilman much. She was a "New Woman" of the urban intelligentsia, vividly chronicled by Christine Stansell, of the kind employed in "journalism, book publishing, acting, or advertising."[24]

Gilman's ongoing relevance, or prescience, noted in other work, is a key element of this nonfiction commentary. Her valorization of women, for instance, matched then-current "biological and socialist principles." Yet by connecting "the evolution of sex differences" with sexual economics, she here anticipated current feminist thinking. Philosopher of science Ann Palmeri showed that Gilman spoke in the newly "meaningful language of economics, anthropology, sociology"—social sciences now grounding feminist claims, surpassing formerly privileged individualism with the categories "culture" or "society" as collectivities. Gilman transformed feminism into "a theory of social evolution and political reform."[25]

Other feminist scholars have similarly praised Gilman's contribution to their various fields. The cogency of each individual rationale for addressing these particular aspects of Gilman's work may be clear enough from the perspectives of these various fields of knowledge. Indeed, Gilman can apparently seem to be all things to all analysts. Her collected titles include architectural feminist, material feminist, socialist feminist, radical feminist, pragmatist, environmentalist, pacifist, militarist, social philosopher, economist, ethicist, theist, theologian, educationalist, and humanist. While any of these designations might make sense within these scholars' particular projects, the very particularity of each one obscures any theoretical totality in Gilman's corpus. Consequently, Gilman the philosopher becomes difficult to reconcile with Gilman the urban planner or with Gilman the theological reformer. Yet, such commentary tends to detach Gilman's nonfiction from its historical, intellectual, and ultimately political moorings. The effect is to disaggregate Gilman's oeuvre. Each piece of work so analyzed loses its original historical framing within the totality of her theoretical contributions.[26]

Even allowing for totalizing theories being decidedly out of vogue these days Gilman's supposedly prophetic contributions become dizzyingly diverse. By conceding some sex differences, for instance, Degler likened her to Margaret Mead, Erik Fromm, and Erik Ericksen, "who linked sex and character." Deegan saw Gilman's gift to feminism in her critique of masculism in reform Darwinist sociology, in terms that were "insightful, timely, courageous, and . . . brilliant," as well as "often humorous." Dolores Hayden found Gilman's legacy in broadened constituencies for domestic reform. Meanwhile, literary critics Sandra Gilbert and Susan Gubar called Gilman's case for "female-centered spirituality" a foreshadowing of contemporary feminist critics Rosemary Radford Ruether and Mary Daly. More programmatically, Karen Stevenson praised her promotion of dress reform, short hair, women doctors, vegetarianism, exercise, and pacifism. Further, Jane Upin saw Gilman as an innovative philosopher who anticipated urban studies' gurus Jane Jacobs and Lewis Mumford. In addition, Gilman presaged Michel Foucault's concept of power, Susan Bordo's notion of "locatedness," Nancy Fraser's theories of cultural transformation, Richard Sennett's discourse of the urban "self/other" divide, and Susan Moller Okin's usage of the public sphere/domestic sphere dichotomy."[27]

Unanchored from her larger framework, houses with kitchens, cooking, or architecture, for example, themselves can appear as causes of women's oppression in this work. Gilman's plans for freeing women from household labor, permitting paid work, served her reform Darwinist theory urging that women needed to contribute to "race work," hence human progress. This entailed a reorienting heterosexuality to take account of its historical evolutionary grounding in reproduction and to evince more respect for women's "natural" desire for coitus less frequently than men's. Her ebullient later feminist admirers probably would refuse such reform Darwinist objectives.[28] Innocent of this dissonance, they stress her strategies for ending symptoms of women's oppression, ignoring Gilman's theory of the causes of that oppression informing these specific amelioration strategies.[29]

The very disparateness of those she allegedly anticipated precludes an accurate grasp of her theoretical impact in her own time. For the reader seeking to understand Gilman's feminist theory these approaches to her nonfiction remain too selective. This study then seeks to provide greater context and integration for the diverse elements of Gilman's feminist theory.

IN ORDER TO place Gilman's unique and sexuality-centered feminism into the fullest context of her a career as a Progressive Era public intellectual, this study delves deeply into the work this career involved. Principally, Gilman's contributions were writing, publishing, reviewing, and advocating reform. Most of this work was nonfiction—much of it journalistic—and remains, so far, little examined. *The Feminism of Charlotte Perkins Gilman: Sexualities, Histories, Progressivism* has three parts, each with four chapters.

Beginning her public intellectual career from the late 1880s, after colliding with conjugal duties and the Byronic sexual expectations of a bohemian artist husband—the subject of chapter 1—her critical inquiries converged on vexed zones of heterosexual relations. These concerns received complex impetus from the problems and dynamics of her years as separated wife, single mother, and divorcée between 1888 and 1900, especially as entailed in her intense relationships with women and men, addressed in chapter 2. Her resulting theoretical writing engaged with reform Darwinism to forge a fascinating relationship between "sexuality" and "history"—connections she interrogated through Gilded Age debates in ethology, anthropology, ancient history, and most of all, sociology, via Lester Frank Ward—issues examined in chapter 3. The outcome was Gilman's legacy of feminist classics, especially *Women and Economics* (1898), which explores the origins and evolution of women's subordination, as well as its operation and maintenance through institutions like dress, the home, motherhood, religion and war—and which is the focus of chapter 4.

Concerns with sexuality in women's historical subjection propelled Gilman's engagement with feminism, the subject of this book's second section. Contrary to other accounts, Gilman accorded a central role to woman suffrage and citizenship in liberating women from "sex work" in order to permit their contribution to "race work." Her fierce battle against organized antisuffragism is the subject of chapter 5, providing grounds to recast readings of Gilman's relationship to politics and public reform. Meanwhile, her reactions to the new term "feminism" and to others also called feminists, notably Olive Schreiner and Ellen Key are explored in chapter 6. The criticisms Gilman received for her own feminist stances are highlighted in chapter 7, as are a range of responses to her lectures and writings from the newspaper press and the general public. Moreover, her proposals to end women's subjection inspired her most optimistic writing, and chapter 8 situates these within her quest for "a human world," the rationale for feminism. Here though, she noted obstacles to her dreams of a gender-minimizing society in new sexual mores influenced by sexology and psychoanalysis, as well as changing paradigms in natural and social sciences.

The final part of the book explores Gilman's embrace of Progressivism in a feminist hope for a reformed polity, shared by both sexes. The issues of "vice," venereal diseases, and "white slavery" engaged her in the abolitionist campaign against regulated prostitution. These issues anchor chapter 9. Yet vice reform was but one issue that Gilman addressed as a progressive feminist public intellectual. On the lecture circuit, and as an editor, journalist, and publisher, she addressed sex parasitism, "masculism," sexual economics, birth control, eugenics, motherhood, pacifism, food adulteration, humanism, and Progressivism itself. Chapter 10 examines this public intellectual work in its incarnations as lectures, journal editing, and reviewing the work of other intellectuals, reformers, and cultural producers and critics. In chapter 11 I consider the claim that an embittered and marginalized Gilman abandoned feminist causes and disappeared after World War I, an assertion that collapses in the light of her books, articles, speeches, and correspondence, 1917–35. Her particular feminist work on immigration restriction, and on the central interwar feminist issue—birth control—at the behest of Margaret Sanger, absorbed her energies to the end, despite terminal illness. Finally, chapter 12 interrogates the exponentially enlarged strand of Gilmaniana today centered on the critique of Gilman's racial and ethnic discourses, held by some to disqualify her as either a feminist or a Progressive in light of the elements of her feminism charted in earlier chapters.

In the decades between her first publication in 1880 and her last in 1935, profound shifts propelled the intellectual development of feminism, engaging Gilman even as the term itself became embattled. If the study of feminism itself has become relatively neglected in current United States women's history, as Gerda Lerner reported with concern in 2003, a detailed examination of Gilman's feminism may contribute usefully, and perhaps inspire scholars toward further explorations. Gilman mediated crucial exchanges between feminism and Progressivism. If some of her stances are offensive today, the challenge is to understand how they infused her Progressive Era reform Darwinist feminism. If sexuality is indeed "to feminism as work is to Marxism," then Gilman's concerns with sexuality addressed its historical, evolutionary, political, and ethnic impacts. These concerns framed Gilman's feminism, and hence the terrain traversed in this study.[30]

PART ONE

Sexuality & Subjection in History

SATURDAY, MAR. 4, 1893. The essential indecency of the dependence of one sex upon the other for a living is in itself sexual immorality.

Charlotte Perkins Gilman, Diary

GILMAN'S IDENTIFICATION of women's subjection as a sexed group was framed in historical and evolutionary terms. Throughout adult life, her personal history stimulated much troubled analysis of more general patterns. Relevant here were her material statuses and options as daughter of a mother who had married into the reformer Beecher clan, only to be abandoned by their descendant, her feckless husband, Frederic Beecher Perkins. Consequences lay in the precarious material circumstances of her upbringing and young adulthood. Gender bias in favor of her brother ensured that Gilman was denied university education. Yet her professionally and personally unsuccessful brother, Thomas Adie Perkins, left families whose members Gilman eventually supported.

For a decade, Gilman was the unhappy wife of an impecunious and heavily indebted Bohemian artist, water colorist Charles Walter Stetson (1858–1911). Then, after several years as a divorcée traveling and trying to earn her own living, she again became a wife, this time for thirty-four years to a New York attorney of modest means and prospects, her cousin George Houghton Gilman. Crucially, she was the mother of one child, a daughter, who resentfully experienced her mother's ambitions beyond domesticity as rejection. Gilman also supported her daughter Kate's family financially, as well as the widowed second wife of her first husband, her friend Grace Ellery Channing Stetson (1862–1938), whose care of daughter Kate permitted Gilman's career as a public intellectual.

These kinship dynamics highlighted the themes of marriage, reproduction, economic dependency, and independence along sexed lines, starkly exposing the frequently dysfunctional operations of culturally prescribed masculine and feminine domains. Gilman, and women all around her, faced serious and unjust obstacles when they needed to support themselves and their children. Their world declared this to be the task of husbands and fathers, in her family a duty often honored in the breach.

The familiar constitution of male sexual identity as husbands and fathers, through the notion and practice of "conjugal rights," inspired some of Gilman's most searching scrutiny within her and her acquaintances' lives and for human cultures generally. The exercise of these asymmetrical "rights" seemed inherently coercive, yet equally axiomatic, in understandings of men as a sexed group. When doctors told her father that his wife would die in the event of another pregnancy, his conjugal rights effectively ended. He departed, no longer able, or willing, to husband. This event precipitated the impoverishment of Gilman's upbringing, the children consigned to the care of the parent least able to provide for them financially, their mother. Hence, sexuality, and sexed erotic rights, fatally intertwined with the (mal)distribution of material resources. That Gilman coined the characterization "sexuo-economic" testifies to the unmistakable links she saw between the erotic and the material. Side effects of such links gravely inflected her own life.

Moreover, a faulty theory of ovulation, the reverse of the current mid-cycle theory, was extolled by experts throughout the Progressive Era, only receding in the 1930s. Even with the declining rates of childbearing led by those of her race and class, conception, pregnancy, abortion, and birth strongly coordinated with the male exercise of conjugal rights. Cultural toleration of men's resort to prostitution, furthermore, could also associate conjugal rights with syphilis, gonorrhea, birth defects, and infant and maternal mortality and morbidity. The young Gilman, Gilman in her prime, and the late Gilman, continually asked how these human arrangements had emerged and developed. She was perplexed by the needless suffering they caused, their inefficiency, and their fatal stunting, not only of the sexes but of meanings for sexuality itself as well. The weight of evidence suggests a remarkable consistency, lifelong, in the preoccupations she explored, and positions she marshaled, to explicate the nature of androcentric sexual dynamics.

Yet not all women with her personal history of these matters arrived at her particular interrogation of the historicity of women's subjection in its specifically sexual dimensions. A profound and thoroughgoing engagement with reform Darwinist theory added a critical element in the path Gilman took toward a "world service" defined not by the familiar, even respectable, womanly dedication to philanthropy but by the intellectual labor of the theorist, ethicist, and sociologist. From a self-education in leading works of ancient history, anthropology, law, science, and religion, she reached the optimistic conclusion that sexuality had not always caused women's historical subjection. The problems she had encountered in romance, courtship, marriage, and family lives were outgrowths of provisional, circumstantial historical developments. They could be altered and, hence, were neither inherent nor the only paths humanity could pursue.

The importance of this historical interpretation of sex subjection through sexuality, or erotic relations, cannot be overemphasized in charting the genealogy of Gilman's feminist analysis. For if women's oppression and sexuo-economic dependency were natural or God-given, then resignation would be the only sane prospect ahead. But the intellectual cutting edge of her era, that is, the newly emerging social sciences, convinced her that, to the contrary, the present situation of the sexes was a monstrous distortion or hijacking of natural evolutionary patterns. Corrective intervention was

FIGURE 1. Portrait of a
young Charlotte Perkins
Gilman, 1875–77, by H. Q.
Morton (Providence, R.I.)
(The Schlesinger Library,
Radcliffe Institute, Harvard
University 177-325-2)

not only possible, it was necessary if humanity was to make the progress it could and should. This insight grounded her feminism.

This first part of the book explores both the personal history and evolutionary theories informing Gilman's diagnoses of what ailed the sexes in what she came to call "androcentric culture." Instead of university education, at age seventeen Gilman secured a scholarly reading list from her estranged librarian father. He recommended works on the origins of patriarchal societies, primitive marriage, and sexual customs, framed in dialogue with Darwin's *Origin of Species* (1859) and *The Descent of Man* (1871)—outlining sexual selection in insect, reptile, bird, and mammal species and in man. Gilman became a reform Darwinist, along with many peer intellectuals, while retaining Lamarck's thesis of inheritance of acquired characteristics. According to Lamarck (1744–1829), if humans altered their environment, changing the attributes of any given group, then these changes transmitted to their descendants.

Lamarckianism underlay much philanthropy and Reconstruction period social policy, with its optimistic prognosis on the enduring impact of cultural improvements among variously disadvantaged communities. Gilman soon applied it to sexual issues, inspired by the suggestions of reform Darwinist sociologist Lester Frank Ward. She reckoned that most negative consequences of androcentric conditions—especially the toxic aspects of prescribed femininity—could end through carefully designed strategies and innovative social practices.

The triumph of Weismann's germ plasm theory, refuting Lamarck's hypothesis, eventually discredited the reform Darwinist intellectual framework of her feminist theory. Yet she retained this framework long after Weismann, Mendel, and the scientific paradigms resulting in genetic and highly deterministic explanations became orthodox. Her adherence to theories extolling the historical naturalness of female sex selection and sexual periodicity partly resulted from her own experiences of sexual identity, desire, erotic relations, and the impact on women of prevailing sexual relationships, contracts, and institutions.

Chapter 1 examines her personal experiences and contemplation of love, marriage, sexuality, reproduction, and motherhood, as well as her developing rage against disenfranchisement, economic dependency, and conjugal duties. These directly informed the feminist analysis she advanced from the 1890s until the 1930s, as did her pursuit of separation, divorce, new relationships, relinquishment of child custody, and remarriage, addressed in chapter 2. The third chapter explores the intellectual underpinnings of the reform Darwinism that she grafted onto the feminist analysis of sexuality and sex subjection inherited from forebears like Margaret Fuller and John Stuart Mill and, especially, through the work of Lester Frank Ward. Chapter 4 examines the key texts and treatises through which Gilman outlined her own diagnosis of women's oppression and her rich descriptions of the operation of androcentric culture, with its abundant "masculist products," including world religions and warfare.

CHAPTER ONE

Desires, Matings, and Couples

Only one girl of many. Of the street.
In lowest depths. The story grows unmeet
For wellbred ears. Sorrow and sin and shame
Over and over till the blackened name
Sank out of sight without a hand to save.
Sin, shame, and sorrow. Sickness, & the grave.

Only one girl of many. Tis a need
Of man's existence to repeat the deed.
Social necessity. Men cannot live
Without what these disgraceful creatures give.
Black shame. Dishonor. Misery & Sin.
And men find needed health & life therein.

Charlotte Perkins Gilman, "One Girl of Many" (1884)

SEXUALITY WAS central to Gilman's feminism. If the term "sexuality" itself was a future category, designating erotic life, practices, customs, and identities, she constantly addressed sexualized institutions and meanings. Her earliest verses concerned the two central sexual contracts, marriage and, as in "One Girl of Many," prostitution, both published in early 1884 just before her wedding to Stetson. Gilman analyzed the rise of androcentric culture through the sexual subjection of women, advancing, thereby, distinct perspectives on "the sexual"—its past, present, and desirable future in a human world. Her views of sexual subjection had diverse origins, drawn not only from her own erotic life but also from her contemporaries' debates about sexuality.[1]

In this first chapter, I examine Gilman's intimate young adult relationships as they inflected her feminist theories, centering on her courtship, marriage, and separation from Stetson. In addition to biographies, most commentary on her personal life is found within literary Gilmaniana, dominated by her much reprinted short story, "The Yellow Wall-paper" (1892), a text often read as autobiography, recounting her 1887 month of "the rest cure," a prepsychoanalytic treatment for depression. Scholarly readings are diverse. Many adhere to Gilman's later stress on the rest cure in her leaving both husband and conventional motherhood—that is, to the neglect of the conjugal context for Gilman's rejection of her marriage. The intimately sexual impetus for her feminist analyses in her troubled relationship with Stetson needs attention. More than the rest cure, her difficulties with Stetson precipitated her arrival at feminist discourses on heterosexual relations, prostitution, reproduction, and birth control. If today her sexual thought seems foreign, hastily presentist rejection of her thinking as prudish needlessly obscures the core and founding impact of "androcentric" sexuality within her feminist theories.[2]

Resting the Rest Cure

For many years I suffered from a severe and continuous mental breakdown tending to melancholia—and beyond. During about the third year of this trouble I went . . . to a noted specialist in nervous diseases, the best known in the country. The wise man put me to bed and applied the rest cure, to which a still good physique responded so promptly that he concluded there was nothing much the matter with me, and sent me home with the solemn advice to "live as domestic a life as far as possible," to "have but two hours of intellectual life a day," and "never to touch pen, brush, or pencil again as long as I lived." This was in 1887. I went home and obeyed those directions for some three months, and came so near the border line of utter mental ruin that I could see over. . . . I wrote *The Yellow Wallpaper* . . . and sent a copy to the physician who so nearly drove me mad. He never acknowledged it.

Charlotte Perkins Gilman, "Why I Wrote 'The Yellow Wallpaper'" (1913)

Gilman retrospectively constructed her treatment with the rest cure as the turning point of her life. Her recollection of near insanity at being denied an intellectual life impelled her to act. "The Yellow Wall-paper," which centered on a woman's subjection to the rest cure—discussion of which dominates Gilmaniana—dramatized her case for radically altering her life. Many scholars are mesmerized by the mid-twenties Gilman subjected to Dr. Silas Weir Mitchell's 1880s rest cure and by the thirty-year-old author of its chilling fictionalization.[3]

The story is a first-person account of a new mother and wife of a doctor installed in the nursery of a New England mansion rented for the summer for the rest cure—that is, isolation, nutrition, sleep, and no exercise. With her sister-in-law Jennie caring for the baby and household, and husband John's tender commands whenever home from "town," the narrator becomes intensely introspective. Obsessing about the sulphurous stained wallpaper dominating the derelict upstairs nursery to which she is confined, she becomes convinced that the paper moves, that its bulbous shapes represent eyes and faces, infants and women, that finally a woman is imprisoned in it, trying to escape. The unnamed narrator's progression into paranoia and derangement, marked by her locking the door and frantically attempting to tear off the wallpaper to free the woman behind it, is met by husband John forcing the door open. He faints at the sight of his demented wife crawling round and around the perimeter of the nursery.[4]

As a riveting Gothic, Poe-like tale of Victorian marriage and madness, scholars frequently read Gilman's "The Yellow Wall-paper" as autobiography, her "rest cure" with Dr. Mitchell central in feminist readings of Gilman. Susan Lanser suggests that American feminist literary criticism launched itself through analytical canonization of the story and, thereby, of Gilman. Nor was such recognition undue. Her sensational tale about medical science, misogyny, and women's struggles to be cultural producers and critics is also a terrifying narrative of horror and madness, providing ample justification for its place in the American literary canon.[5]

Literary critic Elaine Hedges rightly notes, though, that changing readings of Gilman's story map shifts with changing feminist preoccupations. Initial commentary stressed its critique of patriarchal medicine, personified in the unnamed narrator's patronizing husband, John, taken as Dr. Mitchell. If some read the woman's descent into madness as resistance to domination, others regret resisting patriarchal oppression only at the price of madness. Meanwhile, psychoanalytic critics hold that Gilman's mother's inadequacies traumatized Gilman's own maternity. Unequal to baby Kate's demands, Gilman resented the vampirish extraction of all her waking energy by the small and noisy creature. Thus, the poor narrator of "The Yellow Wall-paper," relieved of the infant and now herself infantilized, is locked in a nursery and confined to a nailed-down bed, where she is fed. The yellow of the wallpaper symbolizes infantile urine projection, venting rage at her mother. For some critics, Gilman explored desires, rejection, and anger with her male relatives for their sex privileges and cruelties. Moreover, others reject the speaking position assumed by the narrator and presented to the sexed reader, while a further body of critics frame their interpretations in the light of current concerns with race, ethnicity, postcolonialism, and sexual diversities. Recently, some have urged moving critical focus onto Gilman's much less unconscious and more material protest against "the yellow press."[6]

Commentary on the vast corpus of literary criticism here is beyond the scope of this study, but two features of it matter for understandings of Gilman's feminism: first is the tendency to read the story in relation to Gilman's biography and second is the assumption that the rest cure and Dr. Mitchell's treatment of her fundamentally grounded Gilman's bid for emancipation and a career. These features repay scrutiny alongside other women's experiences of the rest cure and alternative interpretations of Gilman's biography and self-representation.

SCHOLARS COMMENTING on "The Yellow Wall-paper" often take its key elements as the genealogy of her feminism, ignited by the rest cure. During her unhappy childhood and adolescence, in which she moved constantly with her brother and mother from house to house of relatives, kind friends, and cooperative living experiments, her abandoned mother aggravated Gilman's misery by becoming a repressive, controlling, and bitter sole parent, frustrating her daughter's ambitions and assigning her relentless domestic work. With bleak teenage years in Rhode Island relieved only by student gentlemen callers, the highlight of young Charlotte Perkins's life was her intimate friendship with Martha Luther, to whom she wrote passionate lover-like letters, so much so that she later speculated on the scandal they might cause if ever discovered. Then, with Luther's marriage to Charles Lane in 1882, the bereft Gilman allowed the attentions of one suitor, the painter Stetson, to end in their May 1884 marriage, against her better judgment.[7]

The birth of a child came just over nine months later, followed by her complete mental breakdown. Her distress dominated the marriage, leading her, in April 1887, to Dr. Mitchell's rest cure in Philadelphia. The supposedly misogynist doctor prohibited any further intellectual life, at least according to Gilman's retrospective 1913 and 1935 accounts. In those portrayals she invited readers to understand this prescription as the cause of her near madness, proving that she was unsuited to the conventional domestic life represented by that month-long medical treatment. The rest cure, and rebellion against it, unleashed her path to independence and feminism.[8]

Gilman rarely mentioned "The Yellow Wall-paper" relative to her other work. Since in her lifetime *Women and Economics* (1898) was easily her most acclaimed work, its popularity led to interest in all other works by Gilman. So along with her 1893 poetry collection, *In This Our World,* her gothic short story, too, was republished. But, apart from a short 1913 note in her journal the *Forerunner*, "Why I wrote 'The Yellow Wall-paper,'" and a few later letters, it is Gilman's 1935 autobiography that depicts the rest cure as the launch or turning point for her career. Her heroism in surviving to contribute so much to feminist theory elicits commentators' admiration and identification and, thereby, a somewhat uncritical acceptance of her account, a tendency noted by Denise D. Knight.[9]

Literary canonization of "The Yellow Wall-paper" led to feminist debate over Mitchell and the rest cure. Initially, Mitchell was cast as a hostile sadist seeking to confine intellectual and otherwise "uppity" women. Yet scores of educated women sought his treatment. If he expected that most women would be wives and mothers, evidence shows that he supported patients making other choices. The cure was first formulated for Civil War veterans, thus not originally a misogynist treatment. Admittedly though, as Jennifer Tuttle demonstrates, the male version of treatment could involve the quest for lost or diminished manhood by sojourns into cowboy fantasies at Western ranches, while women restored their domestic femininity.[10]

Other activist women had contrasting experiences with Mitchell's "rest cure," including, according to Gilman, two of her female Beecher relatives. He also treated Jane Addams, founder of Hull House. Addams mentioned her 1880s treatment in terms rather different from Gilman's:

> The winter after I left school [1882–83] was spent in the Women's Medical College of Philadelphia, but the development of the spinal difficulty which had shadowed me from childhood forced me into Dr. Weir Mitchell's hospital for the late spring, and the next winter I was literally bound to a bed in my sister's house for six months. . . . The long illness inevitably put aside the immediate prosecution of a medical course, and although I had passed my examinations credibly enough in the required subjects for the first year, I was very glad to have a physician's sanction for giving up clinics and dissecting rooms and to follow his prescription of spending the next two years in Europe.[11]

Mitchell also treated Harriet Russell Strong (1844–1926), a Californian feminist, suffering from a degenerating back condition and marital problems for several months in 1886. Harriet Strong praised Mitchell for restoring her health and vigor, which grounded forty more years of feminist public work. She was but one of many women for whom rest, and removal from the domestic circumstances of the breakdown, offered relief in a prepsychoanalytic era. This treatment could enhance their sexual-politics bargaining position in conflicted marriages.[12]

The principally literary focus of most commentaries on "The Yellow

Wall-paper" gives scant attention to Gilman's use of both Dr. Mitchell's rest cure and the writing of the story three years later to justify her subsequent actions to critics, relatives, and friends. If feminist literary scholars "launched" themselves, vindicating their efforts through the story, the same may be true of its author. For everything she became, and for which she was denounced in the Californian and New England press — "an unnatural mother," divorcée, "libertine," essayist, lecturer, reviewer, political delegate, scholar, novelist, poet, and more — Gilman needed a persuasive explanation. She bore an undiminished grudge against "yellow journalism," which targeted her with unfair publicity during her separations and final divorce from Stetson.[13]

The rest cure itself is overemphasized as the genesis of Gilman's feminism and work as a public intellectual. A month of "agreeable treatment," as she later described the regime at Mitchell's practice, arguably was minor among the factors that launched her feminist career. Compelling evidence warrants putting the rest cure to rest.[14]

In what Carolyn Heilbrun has labeled a "moratorium," Gilman called a crisis, a halt to the path her life was supposed to follow with marriage to Stetson. Her advance letter of explanation of her case to Dr. Mitchell and her 1935 autobiography carefully omits admission of tension, arguments, emotional violence, cruelty, or other marital offenses, either on her or Stetson's part. Later she claimed that one momentous fact hijacked her life's direction: her mind broke at age twenty-four and was never in full repair again. A victim of fate, she was a dutiful, self-sacrificing victim, finally persecuted by the rest cure. With regret, as she explained to her readers, she was compelled to terminate her marriage and individual motherhood. This depiction understates the extent of Gilman's active agency and resistance at the time. She was an ambitious and creative woman caught on the wrong side of her culture's customary sexual division of labor. When writing her autobiography in the 1920s, a frustrated Gilman, deprived of the audiences and readers that she had enjoyed since her thirties, sought safe scapegoats for the constraints on her life's achievements.[15]

At the same time, once Gilman's divorce was final in 1894, Stetson married her close friend, Grace Ellery Channing and the couple took custody of the child, which permitted Gilman to pursue her peripatetic 1894–1900 lecturing career. In 1911 Stetson died in Italy as a poor, but increasingly celebrated American artist. Meanwhile, Channing-Stetson's raising of Kate substantially made Gilman's career possible, and she continued in a pivotal role in Gilman and her daughter's world. Later living alone in New York, Channing-Stetson became financially and emotionally dependent on Gilman and her new husband, George Houghton Gilman. Moreover, by the 1930s, Kate, who had replicated her birth mother's pattern by marrying an impecunious artist, also relied on her mother and stepfather. Unmistakable tension existed between all parties involved during the thirty-four years of Gilman's second marriage and her public fame. Gilman needed to explain her decisions, to reconnect, first with her daughter and, then, her grandchildren. These ongoing relationships checked any negative public account she might have given of Stetson's contribution to her 1880s breakdown. Indeed, she deflected attention from their 1884–87 conjugal conflicts, recorded by each of them at the time.[16]

Hence, Dr. Mitchell and the rest cure functioned in Gilman's narrative as justification for her abandonment of marriage and embrace of the career of social reformer and public intellectual in the Beecher family tradition. Her claim that Mitchell instructed her to abandon entirely intellectual, scholarly, or professional life was intended to enlist readers' admiration at her resistance. By whatever means necessary, she had to fulfill her destiny as a writer and reform advocate, even at the sacrifice of relinquishing custody of her daughter. One biographer notes that Gilman "used" her confrontation with Mitchell to "begin her liberation," by allowing her "to deny her father's power sufficiently to be able to heal herself." However, in view of Gilman's completion of her first book during this period of dramatic psychological collapse, Knight asks directly whether she was really as ill as she later claimed she had been. Ironically, as Ann J. Lane reports, once Gilman finally left Stetson for Pasadena, her recovery strategy was rest.[17]

"That Early Error in Mating"

> I counted up, subtracting my working time from the rest of the time, and that early error in mating cost me twenty-five years of not merely hopeless idleness, but black misery. . . . Slowly I recovered. It has been several years now since the recurrence of that blackness.
>
> Charlotte Perkins Gilman to Zona Gale, 1 December 1934

Marriages dominated Gilman's adult life, with only eight years unmarried between 1884 and 1934. As her formative heterosexual relationship, her marriage to Stetson threatened her desire for a life of "world service." He opposed her aspirations for a nondomestic life; and he did so intimately, insistently, and uncompromisingly, particularly once she embraced "the Woman Question." A watercolorist influenced by Tonalist, Barbizon, and Pre-Raphaelite movements, obsessed with the female nude in allegorical,

FIGURE 2. Formal portrait of Charles Walter Stetson, 1880 (The Schlesinger Library, Radcliffe Institute, Harvard University 2005-M125-1-35)

mythical, or landscape settings, Stetson added to his bohemian and Byronic persona some key tenets of German Romanticism. He insisted on the necessity of frequent sexual outlet for artistic creativity, yet also extolled "Victorian" ideals of the permissible activities of his wife and the future mother of his children.[18]

Both Stetson and Gilman left diaries of their courtship, marriage, and deteriorating relationship, as significant for divergence as for common ground. So far these accounts remain underanalyzed by Gilman scholars, despite their editors' insightful and erudite achievements. These diaries permit contrast with Gilman's later narrative of her younger life. Read together, these texts provide a historical precedent for the "paired reports" used, for instance, in postwar relationship counseling, often disclosing irreconcilable perceptions of parties involved. Periods of crisis, depression, sleeplessness, and constant crying reported by Gilman, for example, Stetson described as contented, or at worst, much improved, which shows his denial and idealization of the situation.[19]

The conjugal context of Gilman's breakdown is surprisingly underexamined. She later insisted on the innocent good intentions of her first husband, attributing her problem to a "brain disorder" that made the conventional adult female path lethal. Should scholars believe Gilman's absence of reported anger with her first husband? Even those scrutinizing Stetson somewhat critically tend to accept her portrayal of him as an enduring supporter, their trials just the gender dynamics in Gilded Age marriages of their class and region—nothing personal.[20]

Yet not all such wives and mothers lapsed into insanity; neither did Gilman's premarital pain and suffering cause mental breakdown—nor the marriage of her first love, Martha Luther, nor her rejecting father, nor her cold and manipulative mother. Stetson's love was another matter. Why was marriage to this romantic artist the occasion for Gilman to spiral into depression?[21]

An exception among scholars here is Denise D. Knight. She analyzes "The Yellow Wall-paper" as expressing rage against Stetson. He had followed her to Pasadena in 1888, moved into her house, and attempted reconciliation until early 1890. By deflecting criticism away from Stetson, and onto that "wise," arguably straw man Dr. Mitchell, Knight's Gilman thereby avoided "confronting the vulnerable part of herself that had voluntarily submitted to a marriage of servility against her better judgment." Moreover, not only in "The Yellow Wall-paper" but also in other Gilman short stories of the same period, rage and a series of charges of marital wrongs are leveled, covertly, at the character representing the husband. In his idolatry of lover, wife, and home, the archetypal Gilman husband was restraining, smothering, cold, and condescending. He policed his wife's every contact, forbidding her to read poetry and other books of which he disapproved, his wife a virtual prisoner unable to secure nondomestic existence. Yet he was often out late or stayed "in town," implying infidelity. Gilman's feminist concerns drew diversely on her own recorded experience. She recoiled, not erotophobically but specifically, from the costs of conjugality as they unfolded with this particular man.[22]

DURING THEIR courtship, Stetson portrayed himself as poor and anguished. He flirted with wealthy female patrons, lusted after attractive young models, pondered past affairs, while pursuing a reluctant lover who, as Lane aptly puts it, "talks and writes ceaselessly about her passion for him but her higher commitment to some untried mission."[23]

Yet Gilman's conflicts could not deflect Stetson from self-absorption. Within weeks of meeting her, he asserted his inherent artistic sexual needs, as well as his previous history with lovers Annie Angell and Nellie Sandford: "Charlotte, if you knew that so short a while ago I whispered those three words to—would you despise me?" Like a starving man receiving bread, when he professed love to Gilman's predecessor it was because of the "animal love she gave fully." Yet he was not, he said "ashamed of what I did: I am not a 'gay Lothario' or a 'Don Juan.'" He was entitled to the erotic life of a professional artist. Still, this ran counter to conduct expected of an unmarried Baptist minister's son who yet dined daily with his aged impoverished parents.[24]

He was frustrated not only that prudish respectable single women declined to sit for him as nude models, but that husbandly jealousy withheld from him, too, wives of his acquaintance. Hence, only "low women" could be enlisted. He resented dependence on them and their fees. He recorded his great, even graphic, familiarity with their bodies: examining the face and figure of one applicant to be his model, he noted that though "a harlot," there was no evidence of it except in her eyes and lips. "The nipples" however were, in his view, fuller than they otherwise would be, but because she was only eighteen years old "her breasts are that beautiful erect kind, not flabby as in most women." He made detailed appraisals of almost every premenopausal woman he encountered, particularly prospective models. Of an exotic "Oriental-looking" model, he wrote with frank enjoyment: "There was one pose that she took—a man who could paint it and make it real would be immortal and a great benefactor. Oh it was lovely!" Insisting he was not aroused in the least by the "harlots" whose naked breasts, limbs, and poses he described in such sensuous detail, he was outraged when a male patron referred a young woman to him, on the condition that he promised to have no sexual congress with her.[25]

Pleased that Gilman would model for him, he praised her lack of prudery, marveling at the skill and passion of her kisses and caresses. Though trying "to celebrate and glorify the 'soul delight' and 'god-like joy'" of sex, Mary Armfield Hill holds that he was oblivious to his own objectification of women. His purpose, to capture in his work female beauty and "the purity of the sexual relation," would draw a solid bond between "his love and his art," as did all great painters. Through erotic indulgence, his muse would save him from further lapses into temptation and vice. Regular intercourse ensured not only spermatic health but freed the mind from distracting desires, leaving it fit for creative work. Coitus, then, was an artistic aid. He urged Gilman to submit to her desires (for him), in order to do better work. After all, she was an artist too. Hence, she should marry him.[26]

Yet she resisted. Her reservations about marriage long predated her May 1884 wedding to Stetson. Across 1882–83, Gilman and Stetson battled over love, marriage, and gender norms. He sought to defeat her insistent yet ill-defined conviction that she was destined for "world service," despite her avowed love for him and her frank admission of erotic arousal. She did not believe that conjugal love could combine with the work she felt called to do. Only two weeks after they met, he dramatized their conflict as a dialogue, which he urged her to read:

> "Were I to marry[,] my thoughts, my acts, my whole life would be centered on husband and children . . . I must be free."
>
> "I can think of no good plans which true love ought to or would hinder."
>
> "Oh, on the simplest of physiological grounds I know that a love begun should be consummated: and consummation would mean relinquishment of all my plans—and perhaps it would feed the side of my nature which I am holding in check. I am pretty evenly balanced, animal and spiritual. Were I to give up—I fear I should give all up and become of no more use than other women."
>
> "Marriage need not rob you, would not rob you."[27]

Gilman told him she wished he were a woman. Perhaps she was here wishing, at least subliminally, that their relationship could become homosocial (as had been the one with her girlhood friend Martha Luther) rather than heterosexual. She saw that Stetson's version of heterosexuality threatened her hopes for nondomestic work—"race work" as she would later put it. In short, she feared that the strength of her erotic desires for him would enslave her.[28]

In a two-year negotiation with Stetson over what he would expect of a wife, Gilman insisted that she would not become a proficient cook or house cleaner. Instead she would support herself, one of their main disputes. He pitted childbearing against her dreams of economic independence. Asking if he would not mind if she supported herself, he replied that he "should rather support her; besides if she bore to me, she would have little time to earn for herself," unless, perhaps by writing, "in which case I should not object. Then she smiled."[29]

His Byronic persona greatly troubled Gilman's mother, Mary Perkins. She railed against his immoral nudes, wishing to end the romance and accusing them of indulging in unspeakable lusts. Then, in October 1882, she visited Stetson in his studio, telling him that her daughter was aflame with sexual passion, that they should marry immediately, and then board in rooms at her home to prevent their lapse into vice. His debts and professional obligations obstructed immediate marriage, but still Gilman was under great duress to submit.[30]

As resistance, she suggested they live separately except when "the erotic tendency was at a maximum," a proposal to which Stetson gave a chilly response. Instead, he proposed uncompromising expectations of wife, mother, and home. His parental home—in which he and his family were poor, ill-nourished, visited by illness and stress—inspired his compensatory dreams for the ideal mate, lover, companion, and mother of his children. He even had named their four as yet unborn children, in the spirit of German Romanticism: Sigmund, Katharine, Gottfried, and Hildegarde. Their erotic life was to be more or less constant, which he insisted was natural and "healthful."[31]

Were she to insist on rejecting his love for dreams of a public career, he would be doomed to loneliness, unable to love another. Moreover, he ruminated on seeing prostitutes or a mistress, if Gilman would not marry him, and he insisted she read these diary entries. Not only did he write of Annie Angell's visits to his studio, begging him to resume their relationship, but Gilman had actually seen Angell there when visiting his studio herself in May 1882 and immediately departed.[32]

On 22 May 1883, Gilman finally agreed to marry him. A week earlier Stetson had ventured in his diary that she felt too sure of him. This was signaled, he believed, by her asking for time to resolve her conflicting impulses. So, the only thing "that will teach her what my love is—is to lose me." His unhinged emotional state here emerged in his musing on suicide, "which would be to add unnecessary misery," an interesting note in view of the number of gunshot suicides by male relatives and friends of Gilman's acquaintance. The next day, on 16 May, he learned that the *Atlantic Monthly* had rejected some of his sonnets, of which he wrote in his diary, "Oh well, it matters little." Then he visited Gilman with an ultimatum: if she did not agree to marry him, he would go immediately to Europe, resettling there indefinitely. Once more, she asked for "one year's grace." He tearfully told her to burn his rejected sonnets; and amid his distress, she consented.[33]

Elated, Stetson made her a promise, later to become a bone of contention between them. If art did not pay, he would quit, so devoted would he be to their marriage as husband and breadwinner. In return, she must undertake nothing competing with her mission as wife and mother. Scandalized that she was proposing to read Walt Whitman's *Leaves of Grass,* he made her promise not to do so. Why? He explained in his diary, which, once again he asked to her to read. He did not want her to think that "all men are such animals as Whitman describes them. I wanted her to find love and sexual relations something so holy and lovely that it goes into some hidden place to enjoy its holiness rather than stands in the market place and cries up the odor of its perspiration, the action of its phallus, the hairiness of sweating breasts—and all the Whitman delicacies. . . . I wanted her to

FIGURE 3. Portrait of Charlotte Perkins Gilman as a young woman, 1884, by G. L. Hurd (Providence, R.I.) (The Schlesinger Library, Radcliffe Institute, Harvard University 177-325-4)

have learned that man could be delicate and tender before she read of such slaughter-house rankness." He advocated nudity in art, full sex education, and a frank approach to sexuality but put in wholesome terms, "not filled with the gore and odor of semen."[34]

Gilman felt increasingly diminished before Stetson's will, impressed on her in constant letters, evening and Sunday visits at her home, and her daytime visits to his studio. Her diaries described blackness, fog, humiliation, inferiority, guilt, and pain. She declined friends' invitations to visit the Museum of Anatomy, "because she thought about it, and deemed I would not want her to go," a development he reported with deep satisfaction. Expert knowledge of anatomy on his part, in contrast, was a professional necessity. Discussing obstetrical instruments with a doctor friend, however, he shuddered with revulsion at the thought of Gilman ever having a male physician. His "Love" would have a woman physician. If he had money enough, he would found a midwifery training institution for women, so that no male accoucheur, a specialty to which he confessed himself "rabid against," would ever have the opportunity to touch the parts "only a lover should rightly control." An obstetrician, however good and virtuous, could not be trusted by the husband to remain chaste in thought. Stetson did not notice, however, that questions just as easily could be asked about his mental chastity, while contemplating his carefully chosen naked women.[35]

In the months before their May 1884 wedding, Gilman published two poems, "In Duty Bound," a critique of women's confinement in marriage, and "One Girl among Many," an indictment of men's demand for prostitution. These texts did not auger well for her adjustment to her new husband's idea of marriage. Following their wedding, unresolved conflicts intensified. Gilman was frustrated and bored by wifely duties. She missed exercise at the local women's gymnasium and social life. Hurt by Stetson's sexual rejection when she tried to initiate conjugal relations, she tearfully wrote: "Am sad— last night and this morning. Because I find myself too affectionately expressive. I must keep more to myself and be asked, not borne with." If Stetson sought marriage primarily as a legitimate outlet for his sexual desires, in practice he did not extend the same courtesy to his bride.[36]

Meanwhile, to his delight, he promptly impregnated Gilman, his "prayers that the child might come" answered. Rather than joy, she reported daily sickness and poor sleep, oppressed by the never-ending pile of dishes to be washed and meals to be cooked. The couple debated the marriage/prostitution link, while she, increasingly depressed, put herself to bed. Her diaries read as a rehearsal for the rest cure: "Feel sick and remain so all day. . . . Do little all day but rest. . . . Mean to work tomorrow. . . . A really sick day, the worst I remember for years. . . . Dismal evening . . . unable to do anything and am mortally tired of doing nothing. . . . Great expectations of work today. Sick twice. . . . To bed, still prone." She slept and slept, with and without the cat, living in bed. A visit to a woman doctor disclosed a displaced backward uterus, "fixed with instrument, inserted cottons, bitter medicines. . . . Begin to take enema!" At someone asking Stetson if Gilman was growing large, she wrote furiously, "Confound her impudence!"[37]

Yet, during her fall 1884 emotional deterioration, Stetson wrote: "She seems full of reverent and sweet expectancy since she has felt the movement of that new life in her fair clean body. . . . All the intense motherliness of her nature seems in flower. . . . Life together is quite what I thought it would be—even better!" Then Kate's birth, more exhaustion, anger and depression as the grim reality imposed itself—she could not combine reading and writing with motherhood and wifehood.[38]

Childbirth escalated the couple's long-brewing crisis over conflicting visions of love, sexuality, and marriage. With some postnatal domestic help,

Stetson lamented that Gilman completely broke down, no longer doing domestic work or much childcare. Instead, she stayed in bed. At first there was no family support. Stetson's mother was an invalid, while Gilman's mother was caring for the family of her brother, Thomas Perkins, in Utah, only returning when Kate was five weeks old. With Mrs. Perkins moving in, temporarily, to care for the baby, they leased a larger residence in August 1885. Stetson, meanwhile, found that he had to help with housework, retarding his art.[39]

Hence, he fiercely resented Gilman's angry railing at her loss of strength, joy, and usefulness through marriage. Her wish to "rush from our sweet life . . . into the world to rid it in one fell swoop of all evil, pain and the like," he called "a monomania." Neglecting their happy little family, "she would convert the whole world." Perhaps influenced by his Providence friend and art lover, Dr. Knight, Stetson attributed his wife's ambitions to "some uterine irritation." Ominously, he admitted that "she has grown very dissatisfied with me. I think at times she feels hatred of me." He dismissed her reports of crying all night, "for I heard none of it." In his estimation, he was the true victim: by relieving his "fault-finding" wife of all responsibility "so that she might work," he was cramped and unexpressed, "degraded to a mere instrument of money getting." In the midst of this conflict, he wrote of his patron, Mrs. Cresson, and her envy of Gilman in having his love, to which he responded that he "could almost wish myself two, that I might rightly give her one to love her and to love." Around this time, he completed a painting, "In Grief," casting Charlotte in profile as a goddess in classical garb sitting slumped over a table, head on arm, weeping.[40]

The war between them escalated. Gilman did anything to escape the house, her worst days those spent in childcare alone at home. Stetson anticipated a future without his peevish wife endlessly ranting about "some insolvable moral problem." Despite their woes, he noted that Kate was well, and "thrives, vampire-like on her mother's blood"—a revealing characterization. Gilman tried to resume reading and writing, went to the library, and envisioned a new career. Stetson responded contemptuously to her desire to adopt the Beecher career of a social reform preacher: "My darling wife thinks now that she shall someday preach—sermons about health, morality, and the like—from the pulpit on what you will. . . . Leave mother—Leave child—leave all and preach. . . . Go. God help you!" Despite his hostility, she wrote articles and poems, which he criticized as didactic and unaesthetic.[41]

Against his pleas of debts and unsold paintings, Gilman departed for Pasadena in late October 1885 to visit her friend from art school days, now resident there, Grace Ellery Channing. Mary Perkins again came to stay to care for her granddaughter. Gilman did not return until late March of 1886. Her gain in better health and spirits rapidly declined as she resumed conjugality, and her "share of the burden that comes to us." Soon she was as melancholy as ever. In mid-1886, they "talked of the possibility of another child," and he described her as "resigned, or nearly so, but quite unhappy still." Presently, he claimed that Gilman was a hypochondriac. Yet he reported an operation performed by Dr. Keller (who had attended Kate's birth), involving an overnight stay at the doctor's home. Perhaps this was a gynecological treatment or, possibly, a miscarriage or an abortion.[42]

Meanwhile, Stetson's ongoing devotion to the female nude meant that he broke his promise to give up art, if unprofitable, in order to fulfill his breadwinner part of the patriarchal matrimonial bargain. He was in debt for thousands of dollars, unable to pay the family coal or gas bills. Still he continued, self-indulgently, his nonpaying profession. Bitterly, Gilman recalled his making her abandon public service dreams for the homemaker part of their bargain. She seethed with anger and resentment toward him.

Aggravations

FRI. DEC.31ST 1886 But I certainly have lost much of my self-abandoning enthusiasm and fierce determination in the cause of right. Perhaps it is as well for the ultimate work done. I do not feel so. I feel in some ways lowered — degraded — a traitor to my cause. But I am not sure, it may be a lingering trace of the disordered period just passed. When I know myself to be *well* in all ways I can better judge.

FRI. MARCH 18TH 1887 I don't go to gym., because I want to write some paragraphs for "The Amendment." Walter goes to Club, and takes the key as usual.

SUN. MARCH 20TH 1887 Bad day. Getting to the edge of insanity again. Anna and Aunt C. call. Put K. to sleep and feel desperate. Write my "column" though.

The Diaries of Charlotte Perkins Gilman

In most accounts, untreated postnatal depression was the cause of Gilman's spring 1887 breakdown and her repair to Dr. Mitchell's care. Baby Kate was two years and one month old on the day that her mother despairingly departed for Philadelphia. Several factors emerging between her return from the five-month sojourn in Pasadena and winter/spring 1886 should be considered as at least as significant in her April 1887 crisis. Just over a month after her return from Pasadena, Stetson recorded that he "left her with her head on the lounge in the most dejected condition." He then followed this with an account of a conflict between them of the previous afternoon. Two of his artist friends had called to take Stetson sketching. Gilman, who he admitted was also an accomplished artist, wanted to join them, clearly seeking some company, an outing, and a chance to do some creative work. Stetson would not permit it, recording her keen disappointment not to go. His reason was "because I *knew* the men would think it an intrusion and not feel so free. It seemed to hurt her disproportionately." Hence her dejected state, which he noted without analysis.[43]

More tellingly, she began to work for the state's woman suffrage referendum in the period immediately before her departure for the rest cure. Her suffragism exposed the heavy constraints that her marriage and motherhood imposed on her freedom to participate in political work and debate. It epitomized her protest and precipitated her breakdown toward its articulation. On 6 October 1886 she had attended her first woman suffrage convention, with important consequences.[44]

Three days after the convention, Gilman's heightening feminist consciousness led her to attack Stetson's lascivious nudes, the essence of his art and, arguably, the cause of their debts and poverty. Of the afternoon of 9 October she wrote: "Criticize his pictures, one so harshly from a moral point of view that he smashes and burns it. I feel badly; and after some tears he comes home with me." Though Stetson made no mention of her criticisms, Charles C. Eldredge, the curator of an exhibition of Stetson's paintings, notes that even during their courtship Stetson had worried "that Charlotte seemed to care little for his art." Her criticisms intensified, met with retaliations, so that "further assaults followed in a pattern which severely tested both partners."[45]

Her objections here should not be misunderstood as prudery toward visual representation, as some critics inferred. She had herself been Stetson's model, most recently for his "Eve," even amid her plain distress over their situation. Always, she stressed the importance of healthy sexual love being wholly free and without coercion. Thereby, she found indecent the dependence of one sex on the other for its living, making marriages like her own immoral. This sexual-economic nature of the marriage contract, and of the other sexual relation of which her husband constantly discoursed—prostitution—outraged her so much precisely because she did see the joyous possibilities of erotic life. Stetson's art celebrated the way economic dependency distorted sexual life, turning women into the overeroticized objects for the male viewer. It angered her that his nudes naturalized degraded forms of heterosexuality.[46]

Later that month, while visiting family and friends, she argued with her cousin, Robert Brown, when he dismissed her suffragism: "Robert makes an ass of himself by his loudmouthed contempt of women's rights and other justice. It is hard to be despised by men such as that." But this was the same man, a relative, with whom she had partnered in a little painted card advertisements business, who she might have hoped understood her aspirations and cared for her. Her heightened awareness of misogyny around her, like his, and the husband and fellow artists who could not feel "so free" if she joined their sketching party, led her to seek intellectual reinforcement and deeper knowledge of women's situation. The very next evening she began "Ode to a Fool." She also wrote an article on dress reform, while from November 1886 until January 1887 she began systematic reading on women at the Public Library. She carefully recorded all her readings, sometimes with brief comments on them, such as "Read article in the Forum on Woman Suffrage by Higginson," and "read Charlotte Yonge's 'Womankind.' A weak book." Stetson at first tried to make this a mutual pastime conducted at home, by bringing home such books for her, and even reading them to her while she sewed or painted.[47]

Meanwhile, some nights while he went to his club or to dinners with fellow artists, she visited friends to discuss politics. In this period prior to the rest cure, she became involved with dress reform activists, suffragists, and other women's rights reformers. This included Miss Oldfield and dress reformer Dr. Mary Walker, the couple from whom she collected her loaned *North American.* Her New England family background and friends with these same commitments ensured such links. In January, she began another dress reform article, "A Protest against Petticoats," an interesting resistance to Stetson's ridicule of the often trousers-wearing Dr. Walker as "nonsexual" and her dress reform ideas farcical, after Walker and Oldfield had visited the Stetsons in late November. Trying to do housework and childcare in the ridiculous dress of the period, Gilman had slipped and fallen with Kate in her arms, probably down some stairs, "bumping her head and slamming my knees," leaving her shaken and nervous.[48]

She was at large on other fronts as well. For instance, she visited a young couple, the Smyths, whose thin sick little baby "will be a cripple." Later, she spoke with Mr. Smyth alone "about his baby." Perhaps signaling what lay ahead, Gilman wrote in her annual New Year's Eve review of the year past that, as quoted in the epigraph above, "I feel in some ways lowered—degraded—a traitor to my cause." Soon after, she reported feeling "desperately out of place among a lot of young mothers."[49]

Before long, Gilman's loving husband was annoyed. Though with the 1887 New Year, she had happily recorded starting the full course of woman rights reading and had started to write an article on sex distinctions, all this suddenly stopped upon finishing Margaret Fuller's *Women in the Nineteenth Century*. Now she was reading her Uncle Edward Everett Hale's books, while her writing tackled a funding appeal for the women's gymnasium. She reported feeling "very draggy," "doleful," and "useless" by late January. The explanation emerged in her 5 February note that "I had left off my course of reading for two weeks to oblige him," meaning her husband. His diary omitted his ban on "woman question" reading. Stetson did record, however, his discontent with this reading, which he found made her cheerless, giving her "a heavy feeling in her head before going to bed." So impatient was he with her feminist concerns that one early February evening, he saw that "Charlotte was . . . ready to discuss ad infinitum the woman question. . . . I basely proposed, rainy as it was, to go to call on her mother. . . . Charlotte has been so absorbed in the woman question—suffrage, other wrongs, that she has tired me dreadfully with it. I have tried to conceal from her how tiresome it is because she means so well. But it *is* tiresome."[50] So she tried talking with others who were actually interested. Her pleasant February 1887 visit to friends aroused his irritation when he learned that she "went to talk about reform." Evidently, he exploded, overloaded with reform talk, and thus "fretty and annoyed." Admittedly, "I spoke rather harshly to her," but surely, he repeated, "it does get tiresome?" He did try to show interest in her ideas, but it all seemed "a wee bit unhealthy and feverish."[51]

Following the expiry of the ban, Gilman read more and more feminist material, and accepted suffragist editor, Alice Stone Blackwell's request that she write a suffrage column. Tellingly, she addressed women's sexual exploitation in marriage: "Mr. and Mrs. Smyth call, and we get them to stay to some dinner. Have a good talk with Mrs. S. She is 'another victim.' Young and girlish, inexperienced, sickly; with a sickly child, and no servant; and now very sick herself. Ignorant both, and he using his 'marital rights' at her expense."[52] Knight aptly describes this 20 February 1887 note on Mrs. Smyth as "commiseration." In Gilman's later writing, infant sickliness alluded to birth defects from venereal diseases, rebuking wives' abuse by hitherto promiscuous and/or unfaithful husbands. On an earlier visit to the couple, her mother had ventured that the Smyths' infant was likely "a cripple," she and her daughter concurring as to the cause—and Mary Perkins was no feminist. Amid Gilman's feminist politicization and revulsion against conjugal coercion, she returned to the gymnasium. Stetson, in turn, began spending evenings at his club, studio, or elsewhere, Gilman's diary often recording, "Walter late," and "Walter takes the key as usual." He meanwhile noted in his diary that Charlotte was unhappy: "Secretly, I think the gymnasium is a little too much for her," with all her other commitments. Though hitherto rejecting the idea that "women are very curious creatures," holding them reasonable, no more whimsical than men," events of late with his difficult wife made him reverse his stance.[53]

Her intellectual investment in the suffrage issue increased. At the end of February 1887, she visited *Woman's Journal* editor Blackwell, who probably urged her to assist further the Rhode Island woman suffrage referendum petition campaign. Certainly, Gilman attended more to its progress thereafter. Frustrated at her inability to participate fully due to her duties as wife and mother, her toddler's ill-health made her feel literally imprisoned. Kate had a cold and would neither sleep nor stop crying unless constantly held. This led Gilman in turn to have her own "crying fits," eventually feeling "all used up." Yet she wrote some paragraphs for "The Amendment," by awaking early, even if sleep-deprived from the baby's nocturnal wakefulness. She felt better when sleeping in the spare room, but the baby "howls for me in the night; won't let her father touch her." Early in March, she again talked with Mrs. Smyth, "like a mother," possibly about voluntary motherhood and resistance to conjugal subjugation.[54]

By late March 1887, just a month before leaving for Philadelphia, Gilman reported that she had cut "out a lot of suffrage articles." Her days were spent circling enviously, and increasingly excitedly, the suffrage work of other local women, including parlor meetings to discuss "W.S.": woman suffrage. She admired the vast work women undertook at "W.S. headquarters," much of it distributing tract parcels, at a cost of three hundred dollars for the postage alone. In this work, she met a Miss Brown, who she liked, noting that she "has had nervous prostration." The next day, "Miss Brown sews and I read to her and talk a lot—read suffrage articles aloud." In the evening, presumably while Stetson was at his club, her friend Jim Simmons joined them: "Talk about politics and W. Suffrage."[55]

Meanwhile, on another husband-free evening, Gilman had "a deep talk with Miss Brown." Soon after, in early April, she again met Miss Brown, "who says 40 women are ready to go to the polls Wed. and distribute ballots and influence votes. I don't see my way clear to do that, and am not

FIGURE 4. Charlotte Perkins Gilman, spring 1887, by G. L. Hurd (Providence, R.I.). Inscription (verso, in pencil): "This is what my 'breakdown' did to me" (The Schlesinger Library, Radcliffe Institute, Harvard University 2005-M125-14).

able now, either." Yet on 4 April, she took Kate to "the mass meeting this afternoon. Tell some of the girls things about our laws they didn't know before. Stay late talking."[56]

In contrast with her excited suffrage engagement, "a miserable night and day" followed, her state "approaching frenzy." Jim Simmons called and calmed her against becoming "hysterical." The following day: "We all ride down to get the election results. *Woman suffrage defeated,* as I expected. Miss Brown stays all night."[57]

Arguably, this decisive spring 1887 suffrage defeat symbolized the intractable nature of male power governing her own and other women's lives. Gilman became both despairing and enraged. From 7 April until she left eleven days later, she recorded her steadily worsening state of mind, with phrases like "bad again," "worse," "exhausted," and "weak." Friends and relatives other than her husband arranged the treatment, primarily the Diman family who provided one hundred dollars "to send me away to get well." Meanwhile, for the remaining week before departure, she moved into her mother's with Kate, leaving Stetson to sleep and breakfast alone. The tense dynamics between Gilman and her mother underscored the intensity of her marital clashes: staying with her mother was now preferable to being at home before leaving for treatment. Cousins and friends brought her farewell books. On the day she left, she penned the last diary entry she would make for nearly three years, until she had finally openly separated from Stetson in January 1890. Her final words were to him, which recalled Stetson's courtship custom of writing diary entries for her instruction:

> I am very sick with nervous prostration, and I think with some brain disease as well. No one can ever know what I have suffered these last five years. Pain, pain, pain, until my mind has given way. O'Blind and cruel. Can *love* hurt like this? You found me—you remember what I leave you—O remember what, and learn to doubt your judgment before it seeks to mould another life as it has mine. I asked you only a few days before our marriage if you would take the responsibility entirely on yourself. You said yes. Bear it then.[58]

Assured by his friend, Dr. Knight, that she was "simply hypochondriacal," Stetson rather sullenly bowed to relatives and other friends' urging that she go. Whatever Gilman claimed was the matter with her, he was convinced that she was exhausted from her efforts at mental and physical "self-culture" that she carried to perilous extremes. And whatever she had done to herself, he accused her of making him "miserable for four or more years." He reassured himself that he had "said very few impatient words to her, very few." Regretful that he had married her, he reverted to his courtship pattern of bemoaning trials to his bodily "virtue," of conjugal deprivation, "all the while surrounded by warm beings who could love me I think."[59]

Preeminently, though, he steeled himself against Dr. Mitchell's authority. Gilman wrote from Philadelphia to report that Mitchell held that she could not "live at home—that is the long and short of it"—because she had "a most unfortunate temperament, with a graft of hysterical disorder of the mind." From Stetson's Philadelphia patron, Mrs. Cresson, a woman manifestly jealous of Gilman, the report was even bleaker: Gilman "was doubtless really insane at times and that he [Mitchell] never had but one other such case, and that of a lady with the same blood in her veins"—a reference to her Beecher relatives. If Gilman was a victim of "periodic insanity," Stetson faced a "deadly abyss of grief" at the hereditary risk to their daughter. By contrast, Mitchell calmly wrote to Stetson that, while Gilman's case was of "profound interest," it was too soon to judge. That hers was merely a one-month treatment suggested that Mitchell by no means, however, regarded her as seriously mentally ill.[60]

If Gilman's condition meant change on her return, to "give her whatever freedom she wants," Stetson resentfully noted: "I scarce know what it can be more than she had for she has had a bed to herself," excused from housework and much childcare by her dramatic breakdown. The rest-cure treatment improved Gilman's bargaining position, as he angrily recognized, yet he still resisted any leverage she might have gained. As she journeyed home in summer 1887, he met her boat in New York and took her promptly to their stateroom on the overnight steamer to restore marital relations, extolling his plan for her to resume all her marital duties after a two-week vacation together.[61]

Before long, he complained that his art was suffering from curtailment of his full conjugal rights. Meanwhile, his wife was back to crying, he noted without any apparent insight, which she began to do on retiring to bed with him. Thus, he specially noted times when she "went bravely to bed without crying." Disturbingly, he reported that she regaled him "with talk of pistols and chloroform," apparently threatening at least suicide, if not also murder? Without his usual editorializing, his account here was almost cool, as if quite used to these tirades and threats, taking them as just more strategies to distance him and to evade her conjugal duties and responsibilities.[62]

By July 1887, he held that her moods seemed so senseless that "it looks as if the actor inside her plays a part." When facing "the flow tide of her distemper," having "a good deal to say about insanity," the minister's son "got a little impatient and took the name of God." His post–rest cure private writings, then, vented his belief that her "madness" was an elaborate performance to escape marriage and him.[63]

Amid these tempestuous conditions, Gilman had a pregnancy scare in September 1887, suggesting that Stetson used coercion, at least if he admitted that she did not desire coitus with him. And he did seem to admit this, more and more preoccupied with his sexual needs, self-pityingly parading his fidelity, even when his wife "loves him little and wants him not at all." Constantly tempted, he held that Gilman's sexual withdrawal justified resort to a harlot or a mistress, for "my soul needs the feminine to complete its work." When he told her of the willing women in his life, Gilman called his bluff on this territory from their courtship: she urged separation, divorce, and, in the interim, a mistress "if she be clean," until he could find a new wife who could make him happy.[64]

Her reference to women being "clean" meant free from venereal infection. The incredibly high rates of male contraction of venereal diseases in the period before penicillin were well known, especially with widespread tolerance of men's resort to prostitution. Gilman's concern here should not be thought prudish or undue. Eldredge reports that in spring 1888, after the Brown University commencement march through Providence, Stetson "sought the company of his old friend [Dr.] Knight and the two agreed 'that the patriarchal system of wives and concubines seemed nearer the truth than modern monogamous marriage.'"[65]

THE PARALLEL accounts of the troubled Stetson/Gilman marriage strongly suggest sexual issues, then, in Gilman's "madness," desertion, eventual divorce, and contributions to feminist theory. The feminist critique of "men's conjugal rights" was then current throughout the international Western feminist canon and formative in her quest to end intimate life with Stetson. In his theory of artistic creativity, he combined an insistent bohemianism and zealous prescriptions for erotic naturalism with older notions of hydraulic spermatic build-up and release. His hybrid male sex right assertions were difficult to withstand.[66]

Stetson was a committed "masculist," a term Gilman distinctly coined and popularized in the early twentieth century for men opposing woman suffrage and women's rights—men, like Stetson, who found them "tiresome." Even the admiring curator of Stetson's exhibition highlighted his "obsessive treatment of female figures," in emotionally charged situations, as symptomatic of unusual repression and the "greater than average turmoil which marked his professional and private lives." Even though the couple's intimacies remain elusive, Hill conjectures that sexual experiences infused Gilman's growing discontent, even though, by Stetson's own account, she was by no means "cold or unapproachable." By the end of 1887 she was adamant. She would no longer be his wife. She would go West.[67]

CHAPTER TWO

Longing, Leaving, Loving

One thing that makes me hold you very near is that you knew me—me before I died. Truly— wasn't I strong and of good promise? It is hard to keep faith in one's self—through the long years—when your brain goes back on you and there's no one to corroborate your memory.

Charlotte Perkins Gilman to
George Houghton Gilman, 16 June 1897

A DECADE after the rest cure and her decision to leave Stetson for California, Gilman still spoke in dire terms about her twenties and early thirties. Her admissions to Houghton ("Ho") Gilman, who would be her husband for the first third of the twentieth century, reveal how she understood her path to *Women and Economics* (1898) and her feminist public intellectual career in its wake. She "died" as she put it, via a "brain-sinking melancholy," starting fourteen years before. Thus, she dated her "good honest disease" from mid-1883, approximately the time Stetson finally wore her resistance down to accept his oft-repeated marriage proposal.[1]

Obviously, Gilman's own sexuality stands to illuminate her feminist theory, with its concerns with sexual patterns across human evolution. Erotic, romantic, and emotional experiences of the decade between her 1888 departure from Rhode Island to California and her 1897 reconnection with her first cousin Houghton Gilman profoundly informed the feminist theory advanced in *Women and Economics*. As a single mother, she was in more direct poverty than ever before. She lived in a ten-dollar-a-month Pasadena cottage, attempting to meet expenses from writing, lecturing, and private art tutoring. Her husband followed her there, refusing to accept her ending their marriage. Hence, she spent her first eighteen months away from Rhode Island resisting reconciliation, addressed in the first part of this chapter.

Once Stetson returned to his mother's deathbed in 1890, Gilman acknowledged their estrangement. Thereafter, new relationships and political engagements became crucial, notably with San Francisco *Call* journalist Adeline E. Knapp (1860–1909). Knapp provided considerable financial support. She encouraged Gilman to move to Oakland with daughter Kate and mother Mary in September 1891, where Gilman enlarged her political engagement with the socialism of the Nationalist movement and related women's organizations. There also, Gilman nursed her terminally ill mother, who had breast cancer, the disease that would eventually also end Gilman's life. She also finally secured a divorce in 1894. Scholars speculate about Gilman's intimacy with various men and women during this period—notably, Knapp, Harriett Howe, Edwin Markham, Eugene Hough, and, in Chicago in 1895–96, George O. Virtue—speculating as to the "true" nature of Gilman's sexual desires and orientations. Although much of her theoretical focus stressed sex complementarity, sex equality, and heterosexual dynamics, some scholars cast her as a closet (and perhaps at times "out") lesbian. Her loving, romantic, and at times melodramatic correspondence with women suggests sexual contact for some readers, as did her charting of loved ones' menstrual periods and writing of suggestive poetry. The second part of the chapter reviews these issues in the period from separation from Stetson to her reacquaintance with Houghton Gilman in 1897.[2]

Her cousin provided her a unique love, which is charted in the third part of the chapter. In him, she found not only receptiveness and warm responses but also, for the first time, a companion, friend, and eventually lover, who engaged her intellectually and facilitated the unfolding of her theoretical work. Biographers cast him as a retiring modest support figure of establishment credentials and conservative outlook, hardly a likely life partner for the firebrand socialist and feminist Gilman. He even is cast as an "androgynous" character, implicitly qualifying any erotic or conjugal relationship between them via presumed heteronormative criteria. This seriously underestimates his critical and intimate contributions to Gilman's greatest work, *Women and Economics*, and to her later theoretical corpus. He had an earnest stake in its successful design, articulation, completion, and reception. An exploration of their relationship then concludes the chapter.[3]

Resisting Reconciliation

> She [Grace] advised me, and now advises Charlotte, to insist on an immedi-
> ate separation—not a divorce of the final legal sort, but truly a separation . . .
> to leave Kate with her mother and me. . . . But I am the chief sufferer in all
> this. . . . She [Charlotte] has, it seems, always been gladder to be away from me
> than with me. . . . Illness was a large excuse, but she has been so much better of
> late that I need hope no longer that health will make her care more for me and
> my work and such love as I can give her. . . . [Father] asked me if she was trying
> to get a "separation" from me, which of course meant a divorce. I . . . said that
> I saw no signs of it and if she did, she really need not take so much trouble
> and . . . expense.
>
> *Charles Walter Stetson, diary, 6 August 1887, 15 June and 17 September 1888*

Grace Ellery Channing kept in constant contact with the Stetsons across
1887–88. She facilitated their initial separation, arranging a seaside summer
for Gilman, Kate, and herself in Bristol, Rhode Island, where they collabo-
rated on the play, *Noblesse Oblige.* As Knight discovered, Gilman published
her first book in 1888, long obscured by the listing of the author's name as
"Mrs. Charles Walter Stetson." It was called *Art Gems for the Home and Fireside,* consisting of forty-nine prominent painting reproductions with narrative analysis for each. At minimum, this publication raises doubts about
Gilman's later claim that she was too mentally ill during this period to do
productive work. Meanwhile, with Channing's help, Gilman sold an aunt's
bequest of some Connecticut property to settle her debts. Then she packed
to depart for Pasadena.[4]

Gilman's current best friend wished to marry Stetson. He visited Bristol
uninvited, making bitter outbursts, "until he drove his estranged wife to
the brink of madness." Though the twenty-six-year-old Unitarian minister's
daughter was expecting a marriage proposal from a curate (only to be disappointed), Channing mediated far from disinterestedly between the volatile
couple. Trying to "convince the heartsick Stetson that the cure lay in separation," she meanwhile fostered Gilman's long-desired quest for an independent career. Simultaneously, Channing blamed Gilman for the breakup,
describing Stetson to her concerned parents as very lovable.[5]

At the end of summer, Channing told him of her love, prematurely it
seems. Cynthia J. Davis shrewdly reads the Stetson-Channing-Gilman triangle. To have a further act in this heterosexual triangulation plot, the scene
had to shift.[6]

FIGURE 5. Studio portrait of Grace Ellery Channing, ca. 1888 (The Schlesinger Library, Radcliffe Institute, Harvard University 2000-M125)

In October 1888, Gilman separated from Stetson, taking her daughter to Pasadena. Stetson followed in December after selling paintings to fund his trip. He told Providence friends that Channing now encouraged his plan, seeking to secure for him a commission for the decoration of the new Pasadena opera house. Further, she promised portrait commissions, including one of herself. Stetson "vigorously pursued a prospect of reconciliation," despite guilt about abandoning his aged parents in Providence. If conjugal life temporarily resumed, its terms remain uncertain. His presence may have checked scandal and aided the lonely and unsettled Gilman's lecturing and writing career. The pressure of his "love," however, again led her into demented outbursts.[7]

As the Stetsons' dynamic deteriorated, Channing intervened. She arranged a studio for Stetson in her parents' house, and from April 1889, the Stetson threesome began dining at the Channings. Stetson and Gilman were fully estranged by summer's end. Yet Stetson nursed Channing through a fall illness and painted her bedecked with passion vine flowers, hinting at intimate comfort on the rebound. Though Stetson's art biographer, Eldredge, found Gilman's apparent approval of the new romance curious, her biographers report her relief.[8]

Still hoping for reconciliation, Stetson resisted his parents' pleas to return. Finally, leaving at the start of the new year for his mother's Providence deathbed, Gilman announced their open, final, and irrevocable separation. Channing comforted Stetson, joining him en route to Europe in fall 1890. They agreed to marry, him filing for divorce on the grounds of desertion. From summer 1893, Stetson and Channing cohabited, awaiting the divorce.[9]

This solution cost Gilman dearly. Her friendship with Channing, from the late 1870s, had eased the loss of Martha Luther and crises with Stetson. Perhaps Luther and Channing were partly interchangeable in her emotional landscape. They permitted her to express intense passion, desire, and love, without the smothering and dangerous difficulties of Stetson's version of heterosexual eroticism. Hereby Gilman expressed her resentment of Stetson, for he could take Channing as she could not. As Gilman wrote to Channing, "How awful to be a man inside a woman's body and not be able to marry the woman you love! . . . *I* want you — *I* love you — *I* need you myself."[10]

In bidding for Channing, if only inchoately, Gilman divined a crucial shift. With Channing choosing Stetson over herself as an intimate, the two women's previous relationship deteriorated. Gilman grieved the impending loss of Channing to Stetson. She sent her extravagantly passionate letters like those to Luther in the early 1880s. Biographers and critics contend open lesbianism risked the very career she struggled to establish. Nonetheless, she sought deliverance from abject aspects of female heterosexual positioning. Self-consciously, she took the man's (her father's?) part — in seeking a non-domestic career and identity — implicitly portraying herself as the "invert," by which Havelock Ellis, and other sexologists, explained same-sex attraction in this period.[11]

Whatever distance imposed by the new dyad, circumstances ahead required rapprochement to secure needs — the divorce, raising Kate, and from 1911, widow Channing Stetson's desperate financial needs. Indeed, contingencies shackled the two women firmly together. Still, an ever more conservative Channing resented Gilman.[12]

Did Stetson ever relinquish Gilman? Even as he and Grace waited on the divorce, Stetson did Gilman's portrait after the style of Rossetti and the Pre-Raphaelites with the signature flowing copper-auburn hair and tiny smile. His caption read: "To Charlotte — In memoriam — Walter 2nd May. '91." Davis asks whether Stetson ever fully transferred his affections to Channing. Just prior to his 1894 remarriage, he professed undying love to Gilman and criticized Channing's invalidism and inefficiency as making her

FIGURE 6. Copy by G. L. Hurd (Providence, R.I.) of a portrait of Charlotte Perkins Gilman by Charles Walter Stetson, 1858–1911 (1891). Inscription: "To Charlotte—In memoriam—Walter (?) 2nd May. 91" (The Schlesinger Library, Radcliffe Institute, Harvard University 177-325-7).

unfit to raise Kate. He reassured Gilman that Kate remained loyal to her biological mother, despite Channing's efforts to replace her in the child's affections.[13]

Stetson and Gilman's dynamics remained suspenseful from 1890 until she moved to Oakland in 1891. At first Gilman undertook creative projects with Channing. Once Channing and her mother departed for Rhode Island, Gilman's mood plummeted. Loss of daily intimacy turned her to writing poetry, short stories, and nonfiction articles and lectures. She wrote "The Yellow Wall-paper," with all its coded rage against John, the protagonist's controlling confining husband, six days after Channing left. Almost immediately, she began another gothic tale, "The Rocking Chair." Then she addressed "the maternal instinct" in the article "The Divine Right of Mothers." As well as caring for Kate, who she was finding "really naughty," she also was trying to earn money from writing and art lessons. In addition, she felt obliged to cheer the temporarily wifeless Dr. Channing, who came to dinner bearing Channing's letters. Often he would just come to call, though Gilman wrote of him, he "tires me to death."[14]

Lonely, tired, and sad, Gilman gradually started going to meetings, such as that of the Social Purity Society, which inspired, for example, the novelette *A Fallen Sister* (1890), an antipolygamy letter, and other contributions.

FIGURE 7. Adeline E. Knapp (1880s) from Frances E. Willard, *Occupations for Women* (Cooper Union, NY: Success Co., 1897), 288.

This connected her with statewide networks of local women, including Harriet (Hattie) Howe, and generated press coverage. Lecture opportunities soon followed.[15]

Once Channing confirmed the stability of her and Stetson's commitment, Gilman resumed writing to both of them, and to Stetson alone about Kate, work, and their mutual "growth" from separation. He lamented the complete financial failure of his latest exhibition. She sympathized. With Channing soon gone to Europe, in early 1891, he wrote Gilman lonely long letters. Illness led him to stay at his friend Dr. Knight's—she added "Much better so than had I been there."[16]

Several new lectures for Nationalist party audiences secured good crowds. In early 1891, her uncle, the Nationalist writer Edward Everett Hale, and her cousin, artist Ellen Day Hale visited Los Angeles and San Francisco. They attended her lectures, reporting on her great impact and rising fame. Of her uncle she wrote: "I am so *glad* to have him." By early 1891, her "increasing prospects and Walter's new success" cheered her. Literary critic and writer Gertrude Atherton had requested a photograph of Gilman and secured her invitation to speak in San Francisco at the "1st Semi-Annual Convention of the Pacific Coast Woman's Press Association" (PCWPA) in March 1891. The Hales attended, too, and her estranged father called on them and finally met his granddaughter. Gilman noted that there was no "emotion among us." A friend took Kate to a nearby ranch, freeing Gilman to lecture and network by day and read "The Yellow Wall-paper" to her relatives by night. After presenting her paper, "Sex Distinction," she gratified her fans with an evening of recitation from her published works, "I being a sort of baby lion." Gilman and Kate stayed on through April and May due to lecture opportunities emerging from the convention. Her father arranged a month-long legal contract giving her "fifty dollars a lecture," as she wrote to Channing and Stetson, describing her "new and brilliant prospects." Most gratifying, for the first time, she had enough money to dispatch some debts and help her mother. In response to all this sudden largesse, the impecunious Stetson offered to find an Eastern publisher for her poems. She sent him a group of thirty-three.[17]

With the success of her dress reform lecture, in which she used as a prop a dummy in the shape of Venus de Milo, she was profiled in the newspapers and was pleased to go downtown to see a "lithograph in all the windows, 'The Eminent Lecturess.' A fine portrait too from the *Cosmopolitan* photographs." Her social purity interests proved interesting to PCWPA members. She presented an evening reading titled "The Economic Dependence of Women in its Relation to Immorality." This was on the night of 11 May 1891. The next day: "Call from a Miss Knapp."[18]

"Two Devoted Women Friends"

DECEMBER 3, 1891 Home with Delle [Adeline] and Mrs. Parker and Miss Whelan, two devoted women friends, who work in the city, and have gone back and forth every day for ten years.

Charlotte Perkins Gilman, diary

Gilman freely admitted her love and hopes for her relationship with Knapp in her diary. Born in Buffalo, New York, also in 1860, Knapp was a journalist with the San Francisco *Call,* as well as a sometime teacher, novelist, and environmentalist. A keen equestrian, Knapp took Gilman riding. Soon, the latter recorded landmarks in their relationship in her diary: "Go and lunch with Miss Knapp. I love her. . . . I feel better, thanks to Miss Knapp." Two days later, "get boat and circulars and 5:30 boat, Miss Knapp also."[19]

Several days later, Knapp stayed the night. The next day Gilman wrote "A wretched night, only made bearable by Miss Knapp's tender helpfulness." Three other friends were present also for dinner the night Knapp stayed, one of them Dr. Kellogg, who attended to Gilman's daughter Kate's food poisoning, the cause of the "wretched night." Tender helpfulness was just what the doctor ordered.[20]

Once Gilman returned to Pasadena in June 1891, the two women corresponded most days, until in September, Knapp undertook to cover Gilman's expenses for a year so that she could write, if she moved to Oakland, bringing mother and daughter with her—at a stroke alleviating Gilman's poverty and housing difficulties. From mid-September until early February 1892, the quartet resided in two rooms in one boarding house: "I have a lovely room with Delle & mother one with Kate." Knapp was fond of Kate, taking her riding—Knapp's horse was called "Pussie"—and on picnics with other friends' children. Gilman and Knapp played chess, discussed Nationalism, called on literary and journalist friends, and spent time outdoors and pleasant evenings, Gilman often sewing for Knapp, especially her riding breeches. Through Knapp, Gilman met Kate Field, in whose journal she had placed some of her significant early articles.[21]

How should the Gilman/Knapp relationship be understood, and with what significance for Gilman's feminist theory? The evidence adduced for understanding their relationship as openly lesbian warrants scrutiny. It consists of Gilman's diary entries, her charting of Knapp's menstrual periods, an 1891 poem dedicated to Knapp, and Gilman's 1899 letter to her fiancé discussing her own 1891 letters to Knapp. In her later autobiography, she used the pseudonym "Dora" for Knapp, while describing the relationship with Martha as "love not sex," without such a caveat about "Dora." While Gilman's earliest references were to "Miss Knapp" or "Miss K." from their first meeting 12 May 1891, on 15 June she concluded the day's entry with "Write to my love." Thereafter, she called her "Delle" or the nickname she coined for her, "Delight." "My girl comes" she wrote of Knapp's arrival from San Francisco to visit her in Pasadena 14 July 1891. Six weeks later she wrote: "Am very lonesome for Delight."[22]

Yet, she still often referred to her as "Miss Knapp" in her diary. Prior to their moving into coresidence in Oakland in September 1891, they exchanged letters on an almost daily basis and sometimes more—the practice of a social world before telephone, e-mail, and other electronic communication. That she charted with an "X" not only her own menstrual periods but also those of Knapp, adds, in Knight's view, "fuel to the speculation that they may, in fact, have been sexually intimate."[23]

In fact, Gilman tracked Knapp's menstrual cycle only four times (between mid-August and late December 1891) during the twenty-two months in which they shared not one but two Oakland residences. She ceased this charting before they moved to the second boarding house in February

1892. Gilman keeping this record for the last months of 1891 may have signaled initial erotic intimacy, but one that soon ended without this change interfering with coresidence for a further eighteen months. Significantly, Gilman also tracked her own periods because she hypothesized a correlation between menstruation and her experience of debilitating depressions, sometimes speculating that she had a brain disorder. Gilman also frequently described Knapp as "not well," "rather uncomfortable," "in a wretched state of health," and indeed was "unwell a large part of the time"—Gilman often had to nurse Knapp in the mornings, and may have suspected a similar menstrual correlation. Perhaps after four records, she solved the question.[24]

An 1899 letter to her fiancé Houghton Gilman may be stronger evidence of an erotic relationship with Knapp. Should Knapp ever publicize Gilman's letters to her, he might be embarrassed at their expression of "the really passionate love I had for her. I loved her, trusted her, wrote her as freely as I write to you. I told you I loved her that way." She speculated as to others who "could make things very unpleasant for me if they tried," a reference to the ill-feelings remaining from her California days. Though she was "not sorry for nor ashamed of my life," such letters would be a gift for hostile newspapers: "Revelations of a Peculiar Past. Mrs. Stetson's Love Affair with a Woman. Is this 'Friendship?' and so on." This was like her 1882 thought to Martha Luther about outcomes if their passionate love letters were discovered: "What horrid stuff these letters would be for the Philistines— lock 'em up and sometime we'll have a grand cremation." Gilman asked her fiancé: "Dear Heart. Am I a woman you ought to marry? Are you willing to give such a mother to our Son—or daughter? Are you sure you have understood when I told you 'All'?"[25]

Such questions suggest two matters. First, their betrothal signaled that neither she nor he held that her relationship with Knapp defined an essential same-sex erotic orientation that thus posed an obstacle to their marriage. Second, her concern was reputation, what others might make of this passionate same-sex relationship in retrospect. Possibly, this reflected heightened and increasingly pathologized discussion of women's same-sex relationships, for instance in response to the 1892 Memphis slaying of seventeen-year-old Freda Ward by nineteen-year-old Alice Mitchell, much framed by Ellis's theory of inversion.[26]

More prosaically, she told her fiancé she had loved many people. What she meant by "love" and "that way" in Knapp's case may have several readings liable to presentist interpretations. Given that Knapp became a notorious antisuffrage polemicist and, at least according to Gilman, appropriated

FIGURE 8. Formal group portrait of Charlotte Perkins Gilman, her daughter Katharine (*right*), with two other women (Adeline E. Knapp [*right*], and Harriet Howe[?], [*left*]) and children, ca. 1892, Trestle Glen Ferrotype Gallery, Oakland, Calif. (The Schlesinger Library, Radcliffe Institute, Harvard University 2005-M125-1-21).

her literary work, as well as using violence, foul language, and strong drink, and, in addition, slandering Gilman far and wide, retrospective embarrassment about their period of "housekeeping" together had diverse elements. In Knapp's 1899 antisuffragist tract, she specifically ridiculed several of Gilman's key arguments in favor of woman suffrage and attacked national leader Carrie Chapman Catt, by then a self-admitted Gilmanite, for promoting them. Gilman's "'new' best friend," as it were, "had soured on her hands," Gilman ended her 1935 account of Knapp by noting her own shame, "that I should have been so gullible, so ignorant as to love her dearly."[27]

Meanwhile, Gilman used "love" liberally to describe relationships with both women and men during the period of her association with Knapp. Only a couple of weeks after her 15 June 1891 diary entry of "Write to my love," referring to Knapp, she wrote of a visit by Mrs. Johnson, a Los Angeles friend, "I love her a little, and freshen her up some I think." Only a week after first writing of Knapp as "my love," and receiving letters and photographs from her, Gilman wrote of the evening of 23 June: "Read poetry to Hattie in the evening and make love to her." Gilman again referred to Knapp in terms of love in her autobiography in which she minimized key personal issues: "Harder than everything else to me was the utter loss of the friend with whom I had hoped to live continuously. She certainly did love me, at first anyway, and had been most generously kind with money." Significantly, she noted that her "return was mainly in service, not only in making a home for her, but in furnishing material for her work."[28]

Whether they had a physically sexual relationship or a romantic "Boston marriage," Gilman's relationship with Knapp, and its deterioration, profoundly affected her life in Oakland and San Francisco during 1891–94. How long they shared a room and bed is unclear. In their first months together from September to December 1891, Knapp cheerfully comforted Gilman when hurt by Channing's accusations over delays with the divorce. By later December, Gilman's "hysterics" and anxiety peaked over her mother's illness, and again Knapp cared for her.

Whatever the cause, Gilman and Knapp's relationship deteriorated from early 1892, marked by cryptic diary clues. Their growing alienation became palpable when, in February 1892, they moved to a larger boarding house. There Gilman soon assumed the management. She and Knapp had their own separate rooms. Eventually there were eight boarders, mostly women in various kinds of ill-health, including her mother, who was diagnosed with terminal cancer.[29]

An important factor in the stress between Knapp and Gilman was Gilman's objective position. Once she resided with Knapp, her domestic work burden dramatically increased, at the expense of writing and the time and freedom to call on professionally useful contacts. Indeed, Gilman served Knapp, kept house for her, sewed for her, nursed her through frequent illness, especially in the mornings, crossed the Bay to collect Knapp's papers and assignments from the newspaper office, and even wrote for her. The impact on Gilman's time to write and lecture for a living was considerable, in turn keeping her dependent on Knapp's largesse, repaid by "service." As an indebted single mother, Gilman's downward spiral resulted in a life dominated by the task she detested above all among the primitive home industries falling to women: cooking. With Gilman's later estimate that family cooking tasks took a full six hours a day, it was small wonder that with eight ill women to feed, Gilman became "hysterical," and had fits of what she called "wretchedness," exactly as she had when married in Providence. When well, Knapp did chores like fixing up her own room, putting up pictures, and sometimes cooking, feeding, and bathing Kate. Knapp's relative economic power, professional salaried status, and access to travel and recreation may have led to Knapp's infidelity or disloyalty of some kind, or perhaps Gilman's jealousy. Then, Knapp's promotion to house editor of her newspaper in March 1892 reduced her domestic contributions. From just that point until March 1893, Gilman nursed her mother, who refused pain relief, while at the same time becoming distressed by negative press over the Stetson divorce proceedings. While facing the demands of this grave duty and running a boarding house, Gilman was trying simultaneously to write, lecture, and, thus, earn a living. She developed understandable anxieties over also properly caring for Kate, noting she would "get used up."[30]

In this decidedly overdetermined context, Gilman mentioned Knapp being "uncomfortable" in March 1892. By September, Gilman referred to Knapp either as perennially ill or problematic, the same month that Gilman's Nationalist party friend, Harriet Howe, also moved in. With Howe's permanent presence in the house, Gilman started to focus on Knapp's difficult behavior. Gilman's October diary entry reading "Delle goes on some trip" hardly struck a companionable or lover-like tone. Meanwhile, the negative publicity attending the Providence court's denial of Stetson's divorce petition by Christmas week led Gilman to more "hysteria." Hence Howe and Knapp cooked the Christmas 1892 dinner. Estrangement marked Gilman's 1892 New Year's Eve diary review: "great and constantly increasing trouble. Poverty, illness, heartache. My last love proves even as others." Knapp may have kept her distance, or perhaps even other company, for Gilman to note: "Delle home to supper" on one January night.[31]

One possibility is a romantic triangle. Hill contends that with Gilman's neediness, especially while caring for her dying mother and her own daughter, as well as the boarding house work, Gilman, Knapp and Howe formed a tense ménage à trois, with no love lost between Howe and Knapp. Equally, Howe, who penned a negative account of these days in the boarding house, might have been concerned about Kate's domestic exposure to a drunken, uncontrolled, and indiscreet Knapp, with contentious divorce proceedings in progress, and considerable pressure on Gilman from Stetson and Channing.[32]

Temperamentally though, Lane maintains that Knapp was difficult, "independent but not well-bred," with vulgar habits, rough language, and hard drinking," while the position of a woman reporter at the time was on "the edge of respectability." With a tendency to be possessive, insecure, jealous, and given to abusive scenes, Knapp aggravated Gilman's problems, leaving their relationship "traumatic" and "destructive." That Gilman's circle of friends and confidantes expanded as a result of her impressive publications of the 1888–92 period and that invitations to join key in committees, clubs, and movements increased perhaps heightened their tensions. Knapp was an outsider to Gilman's world of Nationalist and feminist politics, as well as to literature and theory, making Gilman the mentor. Neither intellectual nor reformer, others' esteem for Gilman led to Knapp's place in groups with

FIGURE 9. Informal portrait of Charlotte Perkins Gilman and Grace Ellery Channing, standing outdoors. Inscription (verso): "GEC and CPS taken in Oakland" (February 1894?) (The Schlesinger Library, Radcliffe Institute, Harvard University 2005-M125-1-26).

which she had no sympathy, Gilman coaxing her toward feminist and socialist articulations. Before long, Knapp would resist and repudiate them. In an 1893 review of Californian literature and journalism, Ella Sterling Cummis Mighels depicted Knapp as a latecomer, captured by her own personal prejudices, "the apostle of her own pet theories." By contrast, Gilman was "a real genius in her line," with an indefinable "fascination," producing work full of "beauty, integrity, honesty, and sincerity."[33]

Meanwhile, men of all marital statuses visited throughout the period of Knapp's residence with Gilman, some also remaining overnight. If some were comrades, others were more serious suitors, presenting situations arousing Mrs. Perkins's disapproval. In particular, socialist Eugene Hough was a regular caller, reader, and escort, one of many prominent radical political and literary figures. As well as inferences that Gilman and Knapp were lesbian lovers, commentators also surmise that Gilman had romantic relationships with one or more of these men.[34]

Knapp went to the Philippines on assignment in early 1893, leaving Gilman to deal with the death of her mother on 6 March. Afterward, she awaited Knapp's 5 April return, with the words "I wonder?" For her to write "Sleep with Delle" on the night of Knapp's return suggests this had ceased to be their practice. Perhaps "absence made the heart grow fonder," temporarily. Soon though, it was "hard times with Delle," who finally agreed to leave on 14 May, Gilman adding, "I have so desired since last August and often asked her to." It remains unclear how or why Knapp wrote Gilman a note two days later: "I left Mrs. Stetson's house for Mrs. Stetson's good, my ill temper and unreasonable conduct having rendered it impossible for her any longer to endure it. I would have remained had not my remaining sense of decency driven me away." Yet Knapp did not depart mid-May, beyond a brief sojourn nearby. Indeed, Gilman and Kate took horse rides and went to the theater with Knapp across summer 1893. In mid-June, Gilman collected Knapp's pay, extracting rent in advance up to 5 July. This eased a financial crisis, since Gilman just borrowed ten dollars to stop gas disconnection.[35]

Hence, Knapp lingered on, making unwelcome nocturnal visits to Gilman's room, "she with her affection." Knapp's antics across June–July had the whole house in an uproar, Gilman writing the articles "Drinking Women," "The Saloon and Its Annex," and "The Nationalization of the Liquor Traffic." Knapp was also now inseparable from a Mr. Wetmore. Gilman and Howe thwarted Knapp's efforts to install him and a Mrs. Poulson in the house. As Knapp departed with her goods mid-July, Gilman noted that "her behavior has been such as to gradually alienate my affection and turn it to indifference. It is a great relief to have her go." Soon after, Knapp called with Poulson, asking Gilman to explain why she would not give back the note quoted above on Knapp's reasons for leaving. Calling the episode very painful and depressing, Gilman wrote an evocative poem, "The Wolf at the Door," the next day.[36]

Knapp continued to initiate attention-getting incidents. She soon took the kitchen table and chairs, flaunted her relationship with Mr. Wetmore by making evening calls with him to the house a couple of times a week, abused Gilman for behaving like a servant girl with Wetmore, disputed ownership of the book *Arabian Nights,* and seemed to be everywhere Gilman went in Oakland, always trying to drive her home in her buggy, or going to San Francisco to accompany her on the ferry across the Bay in a pattern that to-day might be called "stalking." Channing visited in February 1894 to move along arrangements for Gilman to file for divorce in California, the Providence courts having rejected Stetson's petition on the grounds of suspected collusion between the estranged Stetsons. Interestingly, Gilman then re-corded no further calls from Knapp and Wetmore. By the time Knapp left, however, Gilman owed her $800 (almost $20,000 in 2009 values). As a jobless single mother, living lecture to lecture, article to article, this debt weighed heavily, not least due to a March 1894 letter from Knapp, shortly after Channing left, addressing her as "My dear Mrs. Stetson." Knapp re-minded Gilman that she had put her horse up as collateral for a $100 loan

($2,582 in 2009 dollars) from a Louise Smith, but "I have never been able to repay it, and it is running at 10% interest." The horse now was not worth "half that sum," and "I am earning almost nothing," so Knapp claimed that she feared she would have to relinquish her beloved horse: "I need not tell you how hard that would be for me." Had Knapp been fired or resigned her post at the *Call* after the end with Gilman? Soon after, she would resign her membership of the PCWPA, which may suggest as much, and explain her financial pressure on Gilman. Certainly she knew Gilman's straightened circumstances. What she offered Gilman was to acquit the entire debt Gilman owed her if she would "devise some way of lifting this responsibility." Then Knapp admitted that Smith was not requesting anything, concluding that she would rather dispose of her mare (to resolve the debt) were she worth $100 "than mention this matter to you, but I see nothing else to do." This letter dramatized for Gilman the leverage her debt continued to give Knapp over her. The temptation to accept Knapp's offer and remove all further claims can only have been forceful.[37]

Gilman noted receiving two declarations of love within two days in March. Her constant companion was becoming Eugene Hough. A warm presence in her life since the end of 1892, he was a great admirer of her lectures and writings, as well as an escort, reader, and friend, who assisted her with everything from laying kitchen linoleum to talking through problems and fears, especially in the acrimonious aftermath of her and Knapp's estrangement. Once Gilman filed for divorce in February 1894, his attentions intensified. He would be a possible candidate for one of these declarations of love.[38]

The other is more difficult to guess. Hill narrates Gilman's complex attraction to socialist poet and educator, Edwin Markham. Meanwhile, a married woman doctor friend from the Ebell Society—Dr. Knox—called the same day Gilman recorded these romantic developments, 20 March 1894. She "offered to lend me money to get out of here," meaning the financially burdensome boardinghouse. It must have been tempting, not only with the pressure from Knapp but also with the regular payments demanded by the divorce lawyer.[39]

Yet Gilman did not accept a loan from Dr. Knox, though she did receive some smaller loans from two other friends. This may suggest that Knox's largesse came with other complications. Was this the other declaration of love? Perhaps after the experience with Knapp, she did not wish to again assume obligations to a professional woman, while remaining herself without a clear profession or salary. Meanwhile, such money she borrowed at this point in 1894 was not for repaying Knapp. Ultimately, not until after she published *Women and Economics,* did she start repayment, beginning with an initial payment of $25.00 (about $670.00 in 2009).[40]

WITH THE APRIL 1894 press announcements of the Stetson divorce decree, Gilman called it "a slight matter now that it's done." More significant in the wake of the decree, she made three crucial changes across the late April to early June period. To end the daily stress of poverty and a life dominated by housework, she undertook the editorship of the PCWPA's journal, the *Impress,* on a probationary basis. Second, to better facilitate this work, and end the Oakland boardinghouse grind, with its proximity to Knapp and related complications, Gilman moved across the Bay to downtown San Francisco. Third, and the most critical factor permitting the two other decisions, she made the painful decision to send nine-year-old Kate back East to live with Stetson and his soon to be new wife.[41]

From her earliest courtship conflicts with Stetson, Gilman had feared that the probability of motherhood in marriage would preclude the "world service" to which she felt herself called. Her almost immediate pregnancy confirmed her worst fears, her despair and resentment thoroughly impeding any joy in motherhood. At an intimate level, Gilman found the child's needs variously draining and dismaying, imperiling her own precarious sense of self. Whatever the bonds of love, under Gilman's circumstances of poverty and frustration as a young adult, mother and child had conflicting interests. Gilman's selfhood could appear as established only at Kate's expense—as loudly shrilled by Gilman's critics—while Kate's rights and expectations of a conventional white, middle-class childhood in a two-parent home could be delivered only with the frustration of her mother's desperate desire for a nondomestic existence.[42]

At best, the life Gilman made during 1888–94 had been a compromise with these warring elements. So long as Mary Perkins lived with them, there was back-up childcare, though this was costly given Perkins's conservatism and disapproval of Gilman's aspirations. With Perkins's death in 1893, removing a key stability figure in Kate's life, the emotional and daily care burden fell back onto Gilman, at the very time her lecturing, publishing, and editorship opportunities began to expand. All these activities required space, time, and attention. Then, the departure of Knapp and subsequent estrangement removed another key figure from Kate's world.[43]

Knapp's letter about the debt—making her the veritable "wolf at the door"—escalated Gilman's already acute anxiety about Kate's welfare and the kind of care she could give her. The logic of debt acquittal demanded paid employment; but this collided with maternal duties, in a world with-

FIGURE 10. Charlotte Perkins Gilman and her daughter Katharine, Pasadena 1891 (The Schlesinger Library, Radcliffe Institute, Harvard University, 83-M201, carton 8, folder 228)

out childcare facilities and other provisions for working mothers. Gilman had doubted her capacity to manage single motherhood, wondering even in 1890 if Kate would not fare better with Stetson, and a possibility that recurred to her once he and Channing became a couple. Other events confirmed her doubts about Kate's well-being under her care and impelled her toward the April 1894 solution.[44]

In January that year, in an after-school childcare mix-up, eight-year old Kate was lost for several hours. She went walking with neighborhood children, before returning home after dark, just as frantic mothers called the police. The panic and anxiety left Gilman "used up." Children are not altruists, and this child resented the passing parade of caretakers while her mother worked. Meanwhile, Kate had various episodes of food poisoning, poison oak stings, and other childhood calamities that threw her mother into grief, guilt, and self-criticism. A saddened Gilman became increasingly aware that, alone and without a domestic partner, she was unable to properly care for her—at least not in the way that Kate herself, and others, expected—and also undertake her chosen paid work.[45]

Compared with her own unstable circumstances, Gilman believed that Kate's father and Channing could, at least in the short term, offer more stability. She had thought so for some time, but this childcare incident propelled her to entreat Channing and Stetson to assume Kate's daily care and custody. So, with the divorce impending, she relinquished Kate's custody to the soon to be married Stetsons. Kate's grandfather, Frederic Beecher Perkins, accompanied her on the train back east in May 1894. This decision was to have major consequences in both Gilman and Kate's lives. It also had marked ramifications for the body of feminist theory that Gilman developed, influential down to the present, in the areas of working mothers, childcare, birth control, and the sex division of labor, discussed in later chapters.⁴⁶

FOR HER REMAINING time in San Francisco, Gilman believed she was the target of a slander campaign by an aggrieved Knapp. Some of it took the form of anonymous letters, which had begun in June 1893, as well as unsavory rumors circulating within their small world, brought to Gilman's attention by Howe and others. Shortly after Kate departed, Gilman moved downtown and began as editor of the *Impress*. As noted above, Knapp tendered her resignation from the PCWPA, which, according to Gilman, occasioned lengthy discussion in the committee early in June 1894. Moreover, fellow members said that they were "glad to see me looking better." Soon after, Gilman received another anonymous letter, around her thirty-fourth birthday, this one including a copy of the *Impress,* with errors marked throughout. She immediately identified this as Knapp's doing. Its receipt led Gilman to feel "badly—go down town to borrow that money," without success. Friends like Hough offered her comfort and advice. On 19 July, she noted another committee meeting dealing with "complaint of a slanderous member and serious action decided." The next day she "went to 'Town Talk,' but 'no proof.'" Next, she visited a Mr. Clement (perhaps an attorney) concerning "another unpleasant letter," followed by a "good talk" with Hough. A few days later she returned to Clement about "another hateful letter."

The odds that Knapp sent them was underlined by Gilman's next step: she called on Louise J. Smith, Knapp's creditor. Evidently, Gilman discussed with Smith the deterioration of her and Knapp's relationship, including the note Knapp "wanted me to give her" back, admitting her deplorable treatment of Gilman, the grounds on which Knapp was asked to leave the boarding house. Smith chose "to have it remain as it is," not requiring further surety on Knapp's loan, hence making it no longer a pretext for Knapp to harass Gilman.⁴⁷

Did this strategy work? It is difficult to say, since shortly after this exchange in late August 1894, Gilman again ceased her diary, resuming again not until January 1896, when she had been in Chicago several months. Retrospectively, she referred to the increasing difficulty of her time in San

Francisco as *Impress* editor, fleeing as a heavily indebted failure. For this, she blamed malicious press criticism of her gender transgressions, which cast her as a libertine and an "unnatural mother," slanders she attributed to Knapp. Her 1935 autobiography charged that Knapp had a neurological disorder: the violence, drunkenness, lies, and "literary vampirism" originated in a brain abscess. Knapp certainly died prematurely—in 1909 at the age of forty-nine—so it is possible that Gilman had postmortem knowledge of such a disorder. Or her attribution here may just have been a Progressive Era explanation of conditions that medical specialists today might call borderline personality disorder aggravated by alcoholism.[48]

Her relationship with Hough briefly intensified after her divorce became final in April 1894, though by July she wrote of him: "More talk. Alas—he will not do." This happened amid the crisis over the letters (from Knapp?) and the financial pressure and emotional distress they caused Gilman. Hough's visits continued though. With the diary stopping in early September, resuming only again in 1896 when she was based in Chicago, it remains unclear how this attachment resolved itself, if at all. In her autobiography, she referred to him as a friend "to this day." Gilman ended this California period by accepting Jane Addams's invitation to base herself at Hull House in Chicago from mid-1895.[49]

There she had a brief infatuation or romance with a settlement coworker, George O. Virtue. She recorded long walks and long talks, exchanging Valentines and books of shared interest. Like Hough, Virtue admiringly attended her many lectures and escorted her home, passing pleasant time together. Whereas most of her and Hough's common causes related to socialism, Gilman and Virtue discussed "the woman question." He gave her a book, *The Rights of Women*.[50]

Her diary is the only source of evidence about Gilman's relationships with Hough and Virtue. After long encounters with them, the recording of which may signal attraction, she soon after reported emotional distress. In July 1894, after she concluded that Hough would "not do," for several days she reported feeling "goodfornothing," "badly" and "low." Similarly, after Valentines and long intensive talks with Virtue, and perhaps other exchanges, she reported a very "bad day." In March 1896, her admired friend and settlement house coresident, Helen Campbell (1839–1918) evidently remonstrated her: "feels badly about my behavior. I know that my behavior is my condition—that I am not well."[51]

It is unclear what the issues were here (Was Campbell jealous? Or was Virtue married or engaged?), but Gilman spent a week with her Chicago doctor, weeping and fearing the onset of melancholia. She lost her appetite, her mind "a heavy, dark grey." With continued talk, she rapidly recovered. Yet a further romantic walk with Mr. Virtue ended with her and Campbell once again talking "late," and soon the same pattern: "A bad day, nervous physically—intensely so toward night. Cannot bear the children even." Somewhat recovered, she again had an evening walk with Virtue in early April 1896, just before leaving for a lecture tour in New York, Hartford, Boston, Kansas, and Iowa. Whatever her hopes here, after a "nice talk," she wrote "I guess it's out of the question." Their contact revived in July 1896 when she stayed with him and his sister in Bedford, Iowa, prior to departing from Chicago for London to the International Socialist Convention. There, for her thirty-sixth birthday, he gave her a book of poetry. They corresponded during her lecture tour in England and Scotland until November.[52]

In England, she met socialist and feminist celebrities, greatly enjoying August Bebel, Edward Carpenter, Ramsay McDonald, George Bernard Shaw, May Morris, Beatrice and Sidney Webb, and many others. She traveled to Newcastle and Glasgow, investigated municipal development, and spoke outside shipyards and factories in support of unions and industrial organization. Yet Gilman experienced terrible recurrences of depression while away, most seriously at her London base, when she felt "very small," rather than when on the road busy with lectures. Even traveling though, receipt of Virtue's letters agitated her. Writing replies seemed to exhaust her available energies, leaving her empty and downcast. The relationship does not seem to have resumed with her return to the United States.[53]

Perhaps attractions to these men recalled the dark days of her marriage, her associations of heterosexual involvement with confinement, self-abnegation, loss of identity, and hence the obstruction of constructive work. She sought to analyze and propose solutions to women's subjection in sexual relations. Unless and until she could secure very different terms, sexual involvements spelled trouble, conflict, and emotional breakdown. Though Gilman was in no sense erotophobic and was both attractive and attracted to potential lovers, she recoiled from these risks to her precarious identity. Such self-preservation yielded loneliness and depression for her, but experiences since marriage made her fear the alternatives more.[54]

"O Elegant Youth of New York"

I told him [Stetson] I was a polygon.—that he met a certain facet or facets but not others. If I tied myself permanently to these—cutting off others—I could not function properly. You meet a score to his one—you "cover" me more satisfactorily than any man I ever saw—but . . . I'm a world critter—

FIGURE 11. Formal portrait of George Houghton Gilman, April 1897, Fredericks (New York, New York). Inscription (verso): "Cousin Charlotte, Here's looking at you. George Houghton Gilman, April 1897" (The Schlesinger Library, Radcliffe Institute, Harvard University 2005-M125-1-40).

absolutely no personal relation can cover my life.... Part of me, part of the time—that's all you'll get darling.

Charlotte Perkins Gilman to George Houghton Gilman, 6 March 1899

Cousin Houghton provided Gilman with an unprecedented relationship, which she here recognized, comparing it with the inadequacies of that with Stetson. On returning from England, Gilman acquired another home in the boarding house of her father's second wife, Frankie Johnson Beecher, from late 1896. The need for legal advice (on an unpaid lecture fee) led her to her cousin's Wall Street law office in March 1897. Two days later she recorded "Houghton Gilman calls. Like him." She had lost contact with this younger beloved cousin since the early 1880s. Amid dinners, tours, and visits to her father, Houghton arrived "rather late, and spends the evening up stairs with me. Delightful time. Get very friendly."[55]

They met around her meetings and activities with Fabian socialist Prestonia Mann and visits with Elizabeth Cady Stanton and daughter Harriot Stanton Blatch, and various lectures Gilman gave in New Jersey, Brooklyn, and Philadelphia, before she departed for a Midwest lecture trip in May. Even when they did not have an evening outing together, he would visit her after dinner, and they would spend it privately in her room. Their contact soon resembled a courtship—at least once she overcame her ambivalence about expressing her erotic attraction toward him: "To think that I had really as good asked you to kiss me. . . . It makes me ashamed . . . this is the worst piece of road since England."[56]

After the end of her relationship with Stetson, acknowledging attraction to men was discomforting for Gilman, as seemed the case with Hough and Virtue. Her younger cousin would break this pattern. He was an admiring confidante, a loyal friend, an intellectual sounding board, a research assistant, a translator, a teacher, an editor, and a critic, as well as a joyous lover. By the time they had agreed to marry, he also acted as her therapist, exploring with her the unresolved pain of her early adulthood.[57]

Through her letters to him, she registered and analyzed her experiences in new terms. To him, Gilman explained that keeping busy had become essential to her mental health to avoid pondering painful recollections. Though she did not keep his letters to her, her responses indicate that he addressed the extensive content of her painful memories and emotions with ever greater detail, to judge from her responses to his observations and questions. She wrote him lively, humorous, speculative, and exploratory letters, gradually confronting the painful zones in her relationships, while he particularly explored her views of marriage, motherhood, sexuality, and creative work. Gilman's relationship with him arguably impelled her to narrate, and then analyze, the genealogy of her own development into a self-described "wreck" and "failure" unable to sustain any intimate life. He challenged her self-representation, making their courtship an argument about past, present, and future. With him, she reviewed her previous loves, while he urged her to generalize beyond her own case.[58]

Once she resumed her extensive spring 1897 lecture trips, their letters became more intense. Like her letters to other intimates, quite normal among white women in the period, those she sent to Houghton Gilman also were long and emotional. One possibility is that through writing—letters, diaries, poems, articles, notes, and thoughts—she constituted an otherwise fragile sense of self. As she put it to him, "paper is freer than speech, especially when you want to talk to a most elegantly polite person and are mortally afraid you'll shock them." Her excuse for writing to him was "that I like to. I like you—and I'm lonesome—and you treat me well—and so I pour out volumes."[59]

Crucially, her loving cousin helped her to redeploy her most painful experiences into insights informing thinking, writing, speaking, and theorizing. The ruminations that produced *Women and Economics* were inseparable from their remarkable relationship more generally. It was as if by working out the problems with which she long wrestled, in collaboration with him, she was able to design the book which would influence feminist theory for generations. In other words, before she could fully embark on the intimate relationship that they both desired, she had to repair or resolve "that early error in mating." This meant that she needed to establish her own work and to set terms for domestic life preempting subjugation for either her or him. We might rethink the masterpiece *Women and Economics,* casting it as their prenuptial agreement. The issues between them that it addressed had to be resolved before they could consummate fully their love. Much of their correspondence negotiated terms by which she might be willing to wed, documented in Hill's superbly edited collection of Gilman's almost daily letters to him, until their wedding in Detroit on 11 June 1900.[60]

In order to fully engage with her intellectual and political framework, her cousin undertook extensive reading outside his own legal and classics training—especially anthropology, economics, and sociology—conducting two daylong workshops with her in the August 1897 design stage of the book. He wrote her "fat frequent epistles" as she drafted the manuscript in September–October in friends' and relatives homes. Pleading mental impairment from her fourteen years of woe, she had him read books she needed to master for her great treatise, for instance: "Talk to me of *my* book by Mr. Ward. . . . Why man it may be years before I am able to read such a book! Maybe never." In response to her urging, Cousin Houghton read avidly, argued, and generally engaged actively between her approaches and his own, evidently to their mutual benefit. Most important, he helped her to both conceptualize and unapologetically articulate the obvious: that she was a theorist, an intellectual, with important contributions to make. She then understood that in many previous settings, she had experienced the "cheerful condescension of the contented practical person for the theorist." Hence, she embraced the identity of thinker—of "social philosopher," whose best expression would always be in writing. It was the task of those committed to "progressive changes in personal relations who could do it first to make connections and establish what ought to be done, and then to suggest the steps that should be taken." In this theoretical work, she was imbued with a "sense of the oneness of the human race."[61]

They together honed the draft, both intuiting that the successful completion of this project somehow would permit their love the open, social, and everyday existence that, by 1898, both plainly desired. At the heart of this project was resolving or exorcising "the dark brown taste" in her mind, which she dated from her agreement to wed Stetson and which recurred when in proximity to him. In view of Houghton Gilman's contribution to the content of her intellectual work and the facilitating of her career as a public intellectual, there are grounds to reconsider biographers' portrayals of him. Her biographers find him a rather odd spouse choice for her: conservative in intellectual outlook, and neither an intellectual soul mate nor a notable Progressive reformer. It is true that her early letters urge him to think in wider and more social and collective terms. She suggested he might bone up on the literature on municipalization, which she first encountered in Glasgow in 1896 among the Fabians. She teased him for his disposition, which was less socialist than hers, his greater willingness to accept the world as it was, while she sought to reform or improve it. In her depressions, which recurred at regular intervals, she suggested that his political and ethical differences from her would prove intolerable to endure in a marriage.[62]

In response, he evidently suggested that perhaps she should marry someone more politically and intellectually radical than himself. In a flash she wrote of other loves, providing perhaps more information that he may have wanted. She had earlier mused—in September 1897—that all might be well if she became "rich and famous" and "my Englishman should turn up and fill that side of things." This suggested that she had a romance when in Britain in 1896, unmentioned in her diary. Now, in mid-1898, she elaborated:

> There are, it is true, two other men in the world who would be glad to marry me at any minute—but I do not love them—they don't count. They are more suitable in age, and they agree with me in my ideas—but they don't compare with you. The last man I loved—and I think I would have married, did not love me. No men have loved me since—or—O yes, there was one more that I might have married—I had clean forgotten him. Three since 1893, none since 1895—till you came. . . . There was no one on the horizon except slowly dying image of the past—I did honestly love that good man, to a degree. . . . I was steadily struggling out of existence the thought of the last—it cost a good deal too and backing down anew to the prospect of life without personal love, until you came.[63]

Not surprisingly, Gilman's loving young fiancé did not exactly find reassuring this prospect of suitors in waiting and several more appropriate admirers in Gilman's recent past. He again suggested that she should marry someone better suited to her interests and temperament. It is unclear how upset he was by all this, but she promptly replied: "Be rational," insisting that no one could compare with him for understanding, sympathy, tolerance, and above all freeing her to come and go as she needed without demanding housekeeping.[64]

This was the linchpin of their unique partnership for her. Not only did he offer her companionship and a happy home life, he would "care for my work and help me do it." He did care for her work and he did help her do it.

His wide culture and education were support resources he bestowed on her. In fact she projected that with the aid of his "scholarly criticism and cultivated taste" she could compensate for her deficits, her "later works" much enhanced by inoculation "with a college education!" She always referred to *Women and Economics* as "our book," while she equally regarded all her subsequent works of nonfiction as joint work.[65]

To his doubts that he could fully satisfy her, she exclaimed, "Darling, you satisfy wants I didn't know I had." He made her as happy as had her only true previous love: Martha Luther. In fact, she often called her love for him presaged only by that early relationship. She admitted that "I have loved many people, in various ways, mostly because they needed it, but sometimes from other causes. As to men folks I have told you of my having taken them in chapters mere chapters begun and ended piecemeal. But with each instance there were heavy disadvantages—things that of course, one loving, loves to bear with and understand." But, like Martha, with him, there was nothing to bear with or make allowance for, a fact she regarded with wonder. She also admitted her greed: "I want all kinds of love and lots of it." Indeed, with her much prized honesty, she did not spare him. She did not think he needed to fear that she would ever love "any one else better. Of course, no one can swear to the future." Her praise of him could be quite qualified, and she fully admitted that another man "might come much nearer to my work, my thought." While he certainly sympathized with her personally, she did not find that they thought "in the same lines by nature." She did not expect him to become a "socialist proper" but hoped he would embrace her "organic" theory of social development.[66]

Her lecturing career required regular travel, which she urged him to accept: "We mustn't let any ancient instincts get the better of my present necessities"; "Isn't it funny how we reverse every established program! There you sit and here I go and come"—again relishing the "man's part." She wrote *Women and Economics* while negotiating a very different kind of intimate relationship with him than with Stetson. Preeminently, she knew that dependency and confinement to domestic duties impaired her creativity and caused complete emotional breakdown: "Our problem dear is not the marriage but the housekeeping. . . . We must try to live like two friendly bachelors in apartments." They would reside in "flats" and pay for their meals. Determined to design a life permitting the "world service" contribution, to which she felt called, she would not do housework. Writing, editing, lecturing, and related activities would earn her bread. Their relationship would be one of love and companionship, uncluttered by mercenary motives and hypersexualization. In their apartments they would have "a room apiece"—though he could come into hers when he was "good . . . and that is all the time."[67]

Her epistolary banter with him (and evidently his with her) was overtly sensual. Often, she asked him to make love with her by letter when on the road and missing him. Much to her delight, he presented the passion of his sexuality, not "either to plead or to demand," which was likely a reference back to Stetson, but rather as something tender and exquisite to be read "beneath and behind." She confessed that she liked "to feel the force and fire of it—as a woman must." The erotic agency and pleasure she experienced with him was joyous. It allowed her sharper analysis of the sexual problems in her previous marriage specifically and, more commonly for women, along the continuum between coercion and manipulation. Further, she recognized that their passionate attraction combined multiple needs and goals, blending or smudging rigid demarcations, him fulfilling even her "never satisfied longing for mother love!" while also allowing her to take the initiative normally reserved for men in pursuing their courtship. In a joke referring to his relative political conservatism and questionable progressivism, she jibed that a "more persevering and progressive kisser I never saw." She urged him to "talk to *me*—me; blame me, scold me, make fun of me, make love to me—I want to *feel* you—*hard*."[68]

Anticipating reduced odds of conceiving at her age, she still was intermittently enthusiastic about their having children. She wrote:

> I sort of grieve to have you speak of "the children" so confidently. You know it is a slim chance and at best—so very slim. Please don't hope it too much . . . it is really unlikely you know. . . . If we didn't there would be consolations. I should insist on thinking that the combination would not have been a wise one—great risk of poor products; and that it probably would have upset my health again; and that I could remain freer to be your lover, companion and friend; and that I should not age so soon—O I'd think of lots of comforts if it didn't happen.[69]

That she married a close relative, a hitherto unmarried younger man of thirty-three, with whom doctors advised against childbearing on genetic grounds, is telling. As first cousins, convention forbade reproduction, as Gilman noted when they were courting. Although she sometimes wished for another baby, she more often told him that probably, for her, the demands of motherhood and a life as a creative intellectual were incompatible. Meanwhile, she informed him of medical advice that her periodic depressions would likely lift considerably after age forty-five, or menopause. This meant that experts classified what she called her "sinking brain malady" as grounded in the menstrual cycle, in a world before supplemental hormones and more sophisticated gynecological research were available. At times, thereby, she feared that her whole biological "womanness" was somehow afflicted.[70]

These ruminations recalled her "early error in mating" and her sadly "thwarted motherhood." Her interaction with Houghton also allowed her to express some of her negative feelings about Stetson, as well as her difficulties relating to the Stetsons, as a couple, and as Kate's chief caretakers. Evidently, her cousin expressed criticism of Stetson's painting. She replied that there was "a good deal of justice in what you say"—adding that she was "no ardent admirer of C.W.S.—his works—never was." More tellingly, despite her claims of no ill feelings toward Stetson, she admitted that she took "base delight in little digs," enjoying that Stetson saw her career prospering happily. Moreover, she was mightily amused when a newspaper report speculated as to whether CWS might be related to Charlotte Perkins Stetson? More bitterly, Gilman told her cousin that Stetson's portrayal of her to their daughter revealed "an absolute talent for saying things hatefully." Meanwhile, on being met at the train by the Stetson trio on Christmas Eve, 1899, she wrote: "Dear Me! What a disagreeable looking man he is! Isn't it funny how one can go through things and come out *absolutely*—as if never in."[71]

This visit with the Stetsons at Christmas 1899 revealed tensions and resentments of which Gilman had hitherto been unaware. Grace Channing Stetson, as Kate's stepmother, asserted that Gilman's successes had been won very much at Grace's own expense—a resentment on Grace's part exacerbated by the fact that she had recently suffered a miscarriage. News of the miscarriage caused Gilman great distress. She also had to recognize, however, that fondly nostalgic as she was about Grace, disapproval and incomprehension of Gilman's path ahead on Grace's part foreclosed regaining their former intimacy. When told of Gilman's wedding plans, Channing Stetson was quizzical, since Gilman left Stetson ostensibly because she could not "stand 'the relation,'" by which Channing Stetson took to mean heterosexual coitus itself. Gilman could hardly stipulate to Grace, of all people, the realization she could make with her fiancé: that the problem had been in the form of conjugal rights exercised by Grace's current husband. Stetson still stood between them.[72]

Ambivalence, too, that emerged in her dynamics with her adolescent daughter could be trusted to Houghton as to no one else. Indeed, to him alone did she outpour her grief over her own "thwarted" motherhood: "I can't even let myself go toward Katharine, for the simple reason that it hurts so. And pain, emotional pain, means madness." Letter writing to Kate was

FIGURE 12. Portrait of
Charles Walter Stetson,
ca. 1900 (The Schlesinger
Library, Radcliffe Institute,
Harvard University PCI-
154-1)

stressful, while even hearing children in adjacent apartments or in the street could cause her great and mournful distress. Yet when she was alone with Katharine, such as on a long summer vacation at Cold Spring Harbor in June 1898, she became disturbed and downcast. She groped toward insight: "How can I be unhappy while Katharine is with me? I'm sure I don't know. It is all foggy and dark somehow—I can't think it out. . . . It is sort of dreadful someway. . . . I guess it brings up things—makes old wounds ache." She described Kate as watchful and sharp-eyed, and how she sought privacy and distance from Kate, recoiling from how she "swarms all over me. . . . It almost seems as if the child were trespassing." Gradually Gilman reached the painful realization that her feelings for Katharine could not compare to her love for Houghton. Perhaps Kate could only remind her of Stetson and the traumatic decade as his wife—she certainly looked just like him. Gilman put it bluntly: "As far as personal happiness goes you are more to me than my child—far more. I don't need to say anything about that. You know." She also confronted continuing social disapproval for having relinquished daily custody of Kate to Stetson in 1894. She visited old Pasadena neighbors at Christmas 1899, who she had "foolishly supposed—friends" only to be "violently slapped in the face. . . . It's the 'unnatural mother' racket—the same old thing."[73]

Marrying her cousin when she was forty years old, Gilman lived with him for thirty-four years, until his death from a sudden stroke in 1934. Apart from *Women and Economics,* the best known of the other theories, urgings, and proposals that Gilman made related to sexuality belong to the period of this second marriage. The Gilmans mainly were part-time parents of Kate, who principally lived with the Stetsons abroad, until she married Pasadena artist Frank Tolles Chamberlin in 1918. By all accounts Gilman's marriage to Houghton was a happy one and made Gilman a permanent resident of New York City, residing on its Upper West Side until Houghton Gilman's joint inheritance of his family's Norwich, Connecticut home in 1922, where they then lived until 1934. Gilman rarely, if ever, mentioned him, even in her autobiography. Most insights about him emerge from her letters to him in the period of their courtship.[74] Other mentions of him remain in the distinctly biased letters between various Stetsons—Charles, Grace, and Katharine—in the context of disapproving of Gilman's nondomestic post-1900 life, construing her as selfish and inconsiderate of his husbandly needs. These accounts should be read cautiously and skeptically.

COMPLEX AND difficult personal conflicts over sexuality, conjugal rights, and erotic subjugation in marriage, as well as sexual exploitation from prostitution to sexual harassment, appear to have formed a steadily accumulating impetus to Gilman's feminist analyses and reform. Gilman's pervasive concern with prostitution and venereal disease were notable in her earliest public lectures and writings, during the years of separation before her divorce proceedings across 1892–94. Moreover, whatever the true nature of Gilman and Knapp's relationship, what is not in doubt is the crucial lesson that Gilman learned about the poisonous impact of economic marginality and dependence for adult women. Some of the problems in her interactions with Knapp, and the ways in which indebtedness and economic support curbed Gilman's creative freedom and independence, were completely identical to those she experienced in marriage. Heterosexuality was not necessarily, then, or of itself, the origin of women's oppression. Rather, women's oppression derived from heterosexuality's seemingly universal, and all but inextricable, entanglement with economic contracts—like marriage. The same dynamics could be present in any relationship in which one creature got its food, its means of living, from another. In such relationships, social and psychical subordination emerged in accord with the material facts. Her indebtedness to Knapp demonstrated this most painfully, ending any simple sense that a loving relationship with a woman could be necessarily a magic bullet or an antidote to problems of sexual-economic relations with men.

Perhaps these reflections account for her at least considering the possibility of a better kind of heterosexual relationship—one in which she did not obtain her living from the man. The men she met, however, most of whom were connected with socialism, Nationalism, literature, and Progressive urban reform, all proved problematic in their sexual dynamics and modus operandi—in different ways. Her visits to Britain led her to meet celebrity political men, "advanced," "funny all the time," even inspiring, yet men no less, European in values that could make them more problematic for a woman seeking to be free of what she would soon call "masculism." She returned from Britain partly relieved, even if carrying a smallish torch for someone she called her "Englishman."

By 1898, one momentous result of her reflections was *Women and Economics*. Her relationships and their dynamics—and most particularly, the experience of economic marginalization through dependence within marriage and through separation and single motherhood—set the stage for the classic feminist analysis of that text to emerge. Thereafter, across the period of her second marriage, Gilman elaborated her theory of "social motherhood," as opposed to mere individual motherhood. She developed increasingly critical views of erotic issues in women's lives across the Progressive Era, though interpretations of them are not straightforward. Representations of Gilman's sexual persona range widely, from on the one hand, a "heathen goddess" of uninhibited libido and erotic experimentation to, on the other, a repressive Victorian prude, hostile to the ebullient erotic mores of the jazz age and liberalized early twentieth-century sexual behavior. Since elements of her feminist thought sought limits on men's erotic prerogatives, some commentators infer that Gilman was hostile to heterosexuality, having instead lesbian erotic orientation or identity. The unevenly suggestive but inconclusive evidence here warrants continued debate. Analysis of sexual elements of Gilman's background and experiences of love, courtship, marriage, motherhood, separation, possible same-sex partnership, and domesticity then prove imperative for understanding her emergence as a feminist theorist.[75]

It is equally clear, however, that those experiences would not alone, and of themselves, have generated the classic *Women and Economics*. Her indignant 1898 description of the relations of the sexes and women's humiliating degradation takes much of its intelligibility, dynamism, and contingency from the framework Gilman adopted for it. To understand Gilman's feminism requires analysis of reform Darwinism, the approach she sought to carry her analysis. This means exploring her indebtedness to, and criticisms of, a key intellectual of the 1880s and 1890s, a founding father of academic sociology in America—Lester Frank Ward. Gilman's appropriation of his theory of gynaecocracy and androcentrism proved momentous in an original, and to that point unrivaled, articulation of the problem of women's oppression.

CHAPTER THREE

Gynaecocracy and Androcracy

Sex was a later development, with
a further purpose. There was
something to be done by the real Life Force
besides live and multiply. The big business . . .
was growth, development, evolution . . . sex was
an indispensable element of race progress, and
has not ceased to operate in human variation
and civilization. Its introduction through the
segregation of the male element, and its gradual
attainment of race equality allowed variation
and selection previously impossible. . . . The
other line of change, through natural selection,
was still wider, but whatever the source of a
modification, it was transmitted through the
functions of sex.

Charlotte Perkins Gilman,
"Sex and Race Progress" (1929)

SINCE ANALYSIS of sexual relations animated Gilman's feminism, accounting for their origins was a critical axis of her feminist theory. Key
portions of her work were historical, insofar as she scrutinized change over
time and within particular cultures and historical settings. Her evolutionary and genealogical inquiries accented change and development, characterizing human life as centered on transformation and improvement. History
proved vital to her efforts to challenge—preferably end—male dominance
over women. She located women's subjection in "the sex relation itself."
Had she conceived of that relation as inherent and unresponsive to changed
environments, then hers would have been a counsel to despair, her contri-

bution to feminist theory fading into obscurity. To understand the social, psychic, demographic, and thus evolutionary consequences of sexuality, she explored the historicity of shifts in sexual patterns, dynamics, and meanings. Engaging with contemporary theorists, she outlined a history of sex itself and the human epochs marking its development. Appropriating two terms from sociologist Lester Frank Ward, "gynaecocentric"—woman-centered—and "androcentric"—man-centered—she situated these characterizations within the evolutionary past, in the quest to free women and achieve a "human" world.

Gilman sought a biological basis for feminism in reform Darwinist terms. A key feature of androcentric culture was men's constant demand for coitus, as the "human" norm, overturning millennia of female-initiated and reproduction-related sexual periodicity among *Homo sapiens*. She endeavored to use Darwinian zoology and theories of sex selection to mandate women's renegotiation of conjugal sexuality, reduce unreciprocated sexual demands, and thereby, institute voluntary motherhood. Men's enslavement of women was an ancient history transformation. Progressives widely believed that, previously, women controlled industry, produced wealth, and were fully human and independent. For her, the cause of the hypothesized defeat of her sex was "sexuo-economic." Men, uselessly hunting uncertain prey and otherwise naturally lazy and parasitic, faced an economically precarious world. Eventually, they jealously realized that nonhunting women—working as agriculturalists, artisans and manufacturers—enjoyed prosperity and predictable sustenance. Men participated in, then appropriated, women's industries, advancing them into their modern industrial forms over thousands of years but forcibly excluding women.

Posing the emergence of sex itself (and thus of sex differentiation) as a historical event, Gilman held its purpose as species' organic strengthening or diversifying of themselves.[1] She sought an evolutionary account of the emergence of sex differentiation and, yet, a critique of male dominance as now harmful. Seeking to ameliorate women's subjection, she held that humans—the only species capable of culturally altering evolution—erred in maintaining women's economic dependence on men in sex subjection.[2]

Her claims here depended on an account of history, origins, and progress. If she could not persuade her readers and audiences that, at one time, women were free and independent, how could the case for women's humanity, free from sex slavery, be advanced? She needed historical evidence. With an account of eras when "mothers ruled the world" and an explanation of later male domination and female subordination, she built a platform from which to denounce androcentric culture and urge a "human world"—the quest she urged others to join.

This was a crowded field of contemporary contention. Sifting through competing theories was complicated. Gilman honed arguments and stances in direct and indirect dialogue with earlier scholars and peer luminaries in arriving at her distinctive position. The most central of these was Ward. Due to his importance to Gilman, a detailed examination of his theories of sexual relations forms the first part of the chapter.

His "gynaecocentric theory," explaining the rise of androcentric culture, addressed an explanatory gap in Darwin's theories. Presenting male sex selection as a given of human evolution, Darwin overlooked the need to explain this key human difference from other mammals in his *The Descent of Man and Evolution in Relation to Sex* (1871). Conversely, Ward held that women's selection of stronger, larger, smarter, and more handsome mates led to human encephalization and rationality. Males sought constant rather than periodic coitus in line with their narrow evolutionary function as fertilizers. Motivated by their developmentally belated discovery of paternity, they subjugated women through rape and violence, installing male sex selection, with all its dire consequences.

That Gilman was strongly influenced by Ward's work is beyond dispute. Gilman, however, complained that it was not a seamless one-way transfer of Ward's ideas to her but, rather, he should have been citing her work and influence on him as well. The fact that recognition between them could even become an issue bespeaks an ironic outcome: during the Progressive Era, Ward was the esteemed authority, yet Gilman became better known and, arguably, more influential. By appropriating his work, she acquainted a sizable reading public with him. The debts between them, then, were complicated, explored in the second part of this chapter.

Ward's theory of women's subordination and Gilman's initial embrace, then qualifications, of it places the nature of her critique of women's situation within a clearer Progressive Era intellectual context. The task of the final part of the chapter is to clarify the distinctive elements that she introduced into disputes about nature, history, sexual relations, and gender dynamics. In particular, she disputed Ward's evolutionary claims for rape and sexual violence—with, as its corollary, a depiction of women as victimized—and his neglect of economic motives in hypothesizing men's imposition of androcentric culture. Her interest in historicizing sex, itself, within human sexual arrangements, underlay all her theoretical work.

When Mothers Ruled the World

> Without going into any of the fine calculations of historians as to the centuries of human growth, I would simply state that some agree on about eighty-five thousand years. They assign sixty thousand to savagery, twenty thousand to barbarism, and five thousand to civilization. . . . These facts . . . show for how long a period, in proportion, women reigned supreme; the arbiters of their own destiny, the protectors of their children, the acknowledged builders of all there was of home life, religion, and later, from time to time, of government.
>
> *Elizabeth Cady Stanton, "The Matriarchate, or Mother-Age" (1889)*

Until the historical moment when men took over, mothers ruled the world. Human tribes centered on the needs of mothers and children. Men's relationships to mothers and children were transitory, their sexual access granted periodically and at the will of women. Female sex selection related to fertility and impregnation; otherwise, women refused male advances. Mothers created homes, furnishings, agriculture, and all known early industries. This was Gilman's view of human history. Elizabeth Cady Stanton—a prominent feminist forebear to whom Gilman was often compared—appropriated these matriarchal theories toward feminist ends. Her 1889 speech entitled "The Matriarchate" exemplified her approach. Men, leading the unstable, often improvident lives of hunters and warriors, grew "jealous of women's comfortable home life" and "began little by little to make their aggressions, and in time completely dominated woman." Its marker was the "permanency of sex relations" instead of the earlier female-chosen periodicity.[3]

Contemporaries debated the details of this female preeminence and subsequent subjection by men. Intellectual and popular contributors to discussion of formerly woman-centered human civilizations continued well into the 1920s and 1930s. Gilman was hardly alone in engaging with such ferment over history and evolution. Hypotheses of earlier matriarchal societies proliferated in the second half of the nineteenth century, notably with Jacob J. Bachofen's *Myth, Religion, and Mother Right* (1861) and Lewis Henry Morgan's *Ancient Society* (1877), identifying matriarchy as the linear predecessor of patriarchy.[4] Theorists' speculations led to further works exploring a hypothesized earlier world of female rule. Eliza Burt Gamble, Jane Christie Johnstone, Catherine Gasquoine Hartley, Otis Tufton Mason and Anna Garlin Spencer were some of the turn-of-the-century contributors to debates about the power and position of ancient women.

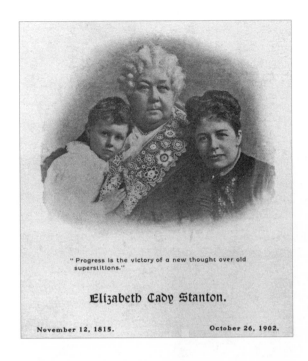

"Progress is the victory of a new thought over old superstitions."

Elizabeth Cady Stanton.

November 12, 1815.   October 26, 1902.

FIGURE 13. Elizabeth Cady Stanton, her daughter, grandchild (Catt: 2.2.3c, Carrie Chapman Catt Collection, Bryn Mawr College Library)

None of these scholars—drawing as they did on anthropology, archaeology, folklore, and ancient history—matched Ward's more nimble and diverse multidisciplinary deployments, however, which they themselves acknowledged.[5]

Born in 1841 as the tenth child of a poor Illinois farming family, Ward had negligible schooling and worked as an agricultural laborer. He married a shoemaker's daughter, Lizzie Caroline Vought, in 1862, before enlisting in the Civil War. Their only child died in infancy. Doggedly seeking a veteran's civil service post in Washington, DC, then taking advantage of night college for civil servants at Columbian College (later George Washington University), Ward pursued education, self-improvement, and his aim to be a wealthy respectable professional.[6]

He earned the Master of Arts in natural science at the age of thirty-one in 1872. Suddenly, his beloved wife died of appendicitis, also in 1872. Within the year he married a young New York City widow, Rose Simons Pierce, who devoted herself to advancing his career. Under the patronage of Major John Wesley Powell, Ward eventually became head paleobotanist with the new U.S. Geological Survey. He also developed the new field of American sociology, publishing numerous articles and books from the 1880s onward. From the 1890s, he became a key consultant on *Webster's Dictionary,* president of the Institute International de Sociologie in 1903,

FIGURE 14. Lester Frank
Ward in the Union Army
(John Hay Brown Library,
Brown University Library)

and then of its counterpart, the American Sociological Association in 1905. Finally, beginning in 1907, at the age of sixty-six, he became Brown University's first chair of sociology until his death in 1913.[7]

Anthropologists and scholars of ancient society had long debated the existence of early matriarchal, matrilineal, and matrifocal societies. Ward, however, judged the prevailing literature hopelessly awash in presentist biases. Its scholars failed to see the significance of their own findings, since they lacked both larger critical theories of human social and sexual development and sure grounding in the context of natural history. Here he specified John F. McLennan (1827–81), Sir John Lubbock (1834–1913), and Jacob J. Bachofen (1815–87) as scholars who failed to provide deeper interrogation of the anthropological, folkloric, and institutional evidence.[8]

Heated later-nineteenth-century debates about matriarchy derived from British imperial encounters with such societies in southern India. Scholars contended that patriarchal family forms were primeval, and natural, while matriarchal forms were merely exaggerated excrescences. Others maintained that matriarchal societies were temporary and functional for evolving patriarchal ones, during times of demographic diversification, when paternity became uncertain. Still others held that matriarchy persevered even when paternity was understood.[9]

FIGURE 15. Lester Frank Ward, ca. 1880 (John Hay Brown Library, Brown University Library)

Ward challenged earlier accounts with a bold theory of human society as originally mother ruled—later he called this "gynaecocentric"—wherein female-initiated sex selection determined parenthood and heredity. Prehistoric men ended gynaecocentric culture, banding together and forcibly establishing androcracy—man-centered culture with male-initiated sex selection determining population attributes. Unlike previous scholars, Ward postulated a progressive future to follow androcracy, through ending women's subordination, with monogamy based on mutual sex selection.[10]

More precisely than predecessors Ward theorized the means by which male domination was established, with its consequences for women. "The woman question" bothered Ward from the start of his career, "the place of women in civilization" being one of his "favorite questions," addressed "again and again."[11] At the age of thirty, he published an indictment of prostitution, likening women's status to slavery and attributing to religion the sexual double standard: "It was this Biblical sanction that perpetuated chattel slavery a thousand years longer in Christendom than it otherwise could have existed, and still perpetuates it, and it is this alone that is now perpetrating sexual slavery." Ward's analysis of women's oppression intertwined with anticlericalism, abolitionism, and a championing of science against theology and superstition. The indissolubility of marriage (except by death or proven adultery) fed demand for prostitution by imposing a lifelong contract on inexperienced young people initially blinded by romance.

The double standard of sexual morality stigmatized women failing to comply with "intolerable conditions" in marriage, while unhappy homes made "the wife an object repulsive to the man's embraces." The former furnished prostitution's supply, the latter its demand. Ward concluded that the blame for "this foul subject, reeking with loathsome disease" lay with the church "whence it originated and where it legitimately belongs."[12]

By the later 1870s, he had become a reform Darwinist, believing in the hereditary transmission of culturally and behaviorally acquired characteristics. In 1881 he published the article "On Male Sexual Selection," in which he argued that human males had wrested the power of sex selection from women. Men so acted due to brain development—encephalization—and the rise of rationality and imagination, causing corollary changes in human female sexual behavior. The male had constant rather than periodic sexual desire. He appealed "to woman's imagination and to her reason," learning ways to excite women erotically "at times when pure instinct forbade it." This basic mismatch between the sexes—one governed by sexual periodicity, the other by constant and indiscriminate desire—set the conditions for prostitution "naturally." The male was "able to secure submission at such times in exchange for other favors which he could confer and of which she ... stood in great need," even outside estrus periods. Compared to his blaming the church for prostitution a decade earlier, this was a significant shift.[13]

In his landmark text of 1883, *Dynamic Sociology,* Ward argued against all forms of sex divisions in industry, leisure, or politics. Sexual integration in all spheres of life stood to reduce men's definition of women in solely sexual terms and to foster equal rights and responsibilities. Sex equality could end the fiction that women required men's protection in all activities. Hence Ward integrated the subjection of women into his analysis of social organization and evolution.[14]

He remained concerned with prostitution. Indeed, it had a genealogical function. If man's appeal to woman's imagination in an attempt to evoke desire for coitus failed, then his appeals to "reason" had a pecuniary or mercenary inflection, as he took advantage of her other "more constant and less capricious desires," offering them in exchange for her submission "to his embraces." Moreover, he "lavishes upon her endearing epithets, gratifying her pride and her conceit," following with "those material gifts and advantages which he knows will constitute the strongest temptation." Thus, women submitted despite nature still "withholding impulse," material gifts retaining a central place in overcoming woman's "natural periodicity." He maintained, in Lamarckian fashion, that "the constant exercise of these influences on woman" ultimately resulted in "radical differences between human species and the lower animals, proportional to degree of social organization and material prosperity." One dramatic result was reproductive differences between humans and other mammals, caused by the disconnect between estrus and female sexual activity. This became a marker of male instead of female sex selection, which subverted women's natural sexual and reproductive biology.[15]

Ward admitted "scarcity of scientific data" on these physiological changes, advocating investigation of comparative ovulation, menstruation, and sexual physiology. Such data could chart the impact of sexual subjection on women's bodies, exemplifying how "a purely psychological phenomenon" had caused "a complete revolution" in women's sexuality. Menstruation became, under male sex selection, a "laborious and debilitating process by which women, even of the lower races, develop their ova." Ward doubted that evolutionary ancestors found themselves to be "under such a 'curse.'" Retention of female sex selection would have resulted neither in malignant menstruation nor in "radical and sweeping" bodily changes. The present "painful process" was due to the "excessive attention of the male sex." While still to be proven, his was "an attempt at rational explanation, certainly superior to the current theological one," meaning the "sin of Eve" portrayal of female menstrual and reproductive travail.[16]

Women's loss of the "scepter" of sex selection wrought consequences beyond modification of female corporeality. Their enslavement unleashed an array of "sexuo-social" inequities in duties, education, and rights, while their impractical, embellished dress gratified their sexual masters. Women performed the bulk of domestic labor as well as the lowest status nondomestic labor refused by men. Denied equal education and career opportunities, women everywhere were "destitute of both intellectual energy and aspiration." They lacked men's legal, suffrage, and citizenship rights, while sex divisions of labor and resources fostered female dependence, heightened by rape and violence, installing male sexual selection. Polygamy, marriage, prostitution, and other forms of female degradation followed. Such degradation flowed from men's wresting from women the right of sex selection, a victory "for male indulgence."[17]

Following *Dynamic Sociology,* Ward became a favorite of woman rights advocates. In 1888 he published "Our Better Halves," based on his "Sex Equality" talk at Washington DC's Six O'Clock Club. There, the audience included Elizabeth Cady Stanton (1815–1902) and Susan B. Anthony (1820–1906). In homage to the latter, he quipped that he would speak neither of "philanthropy nor philandry, much less of their opposites, misanthropy, misogyny, and misandry, for the last of which terms the synonym 'Miss Anthony' is now in common use." Human history was a "prolonged struggle on the part of man to escape the tyranny of woman." Males, originally puny fertilizers evolved to provide reproductive diversity, were eaten by cruel wives, as with spiders, or as drones treated contemptuously by queen bees, or as mayflies allotted but one day of mating, only to die of starvation. Then female birds became "so capricious and fastidious that they would have nothing to do with men unless they had some peculiarity that they imagined to be pretty . . . a crest of feathers, some bright gaudy color, long handsome tail feathers . . . or strong beaks or spurs that they could fight with." Because females selected the biggest and strongest, males acquired "great strength, size and fighting power. Then women began choosing mates for "sagacity. . . . Ah! What a mistake! Slavery is incompatible with intelligence," men soon using cunning to empower themselves. At some point "woman was compelled to surrender her scepter into the hands of man."[18]

Ward later called "Our Better Halves" the first "authorized statement of the gynaecocentric theory." Though incomplete, it offered a simple, compelling proposition. Far from natural, women's present inferiority was the result of the ending of female sex selection and its replacement by male sex selection among humans, a state of sexual relations "widely abnormal, warped, and strained by a long line of curious influences, chiefly psychic." Males provided "variability and adaptability." However, the attempt "to move the whole race forward by elevating only the sex that represents the principle of instability, has long enough been tried." Instead he insisted that "the female sex is primary in both point of origin and of importance in the history and economy of organic life. . . . Woman is the unchanging trunk of the great genealogic tree; while man, with all his vaunted superiority, is but a branch. . . . Woman is the race, and the race can only be raised up as she is raised up. . . . True science teaches that the elevation of woman is the only sure road to the evolution of man."[19]

These arguments popularized his twenty years of work on the woman question. Criticizing evolutionary anthropologists' theories of matriarchy and patriarchy, Ward hypothesized an ancient history of mother-centered cultures with large, strong females and reproduction-oriented sexual periodicity governed by female sex selection. Judging the prevailing matriarchy/patriarchy literature lacking, he theorized that parenthood and heredity were originally determined in human society by female sex selection. Outlining the rise of man-centered culture with the forging of population attributes by male sex selection, he advocated ending women's subordination and the establishment of true monogamy based on mutual sex selection.[20]

Ward's account of the subjugation of women and the rise of androcentric culture continued to evolve. In *Psychic Factors in Civilization* (1892), Ward offered a natural history of the emergence of sexual differentiation itself. The near universality of female superiority in nature led him to reiterate that "the female is the principal sex." She alone continued "the race," except that in the higher forms, where "she usually requires the aid of a fresh element derived from the male to cross the stock and renew the vitality of the offspring." Without such an intervention of some "extra-normal influence," therefore, he held that "female superiority would have been found to be universal in the animal kingdom." What was the "extra-normal influence" in play? With human sensory development—especially heightened senses of sight, scent, and taste—came "the dawn of the esthetic faculty." Females prized male partners for beauty, size, and strength. These qualities aided males in circumventing rivals, and "heredity did the rest." Ward hypothesized that females had, through these romantic and esthetic choices, made males larger, stronger, more handsome, and, in order to fend off rival suitors, smarter than their ancestors.[21]

In *Pure Sociology* (1903) and *Applied Sociology* (1906), Ward elaborated his analysis of sexual differentiation and dynamics. Chapter 14 of *Pure Sociology* has garnered scholarly attention as the most complete statement of his "gynaecocentric" theory, where he more precisely explained how female subjugation replaced the ancient natural order of female-initiated sex selection, the stage he called "gynaecocracy." He dubbed the new stage "androcracy," with the adjective "androcentric" describing its cultural formations, philosophy, and customs. These made "the female secondary in the organic scheme," rendering complete the "subjugation of woman," preeminently by depriving her of any voice in sexual selection.[22]

Further considering the "extra normal influences" by which females romantically selected larger, stronger, and smarter mates, Ward identified a process of increasing encephalization, contending that enlarged brain mass produced reason. Rationality in turn permitted men to defeat instinct in pursuit of other desires: "It is instinct which, throughout the animal kingdom below man, maintains female supremacy and prevents the destruction of animal races. But with man, reason begins to gain the ascendant over instinct. . . . Increased brain mass became a secondary sexual character . . .

that success in rivalry for female favor became more and more dependent on sagacity, and that this led to brain development." He also believed that, with regard to the brain, "a disproportionate share of the increment acquired went to the male," though he did not explain why this should be so. In essence, male brain development permitted men "to violate the restraints of instinct and inaugurate a regime wholly different from that of the animal world out of which he has developed."[23]

Unfortunately, men's ascendancy over the animal kingdom occurred prior to the evolution of sympathy, sentiment, or morality. Thus, man employed superior force violently and cruelly, "exacting from woman whatever satisfaction she could yield him." He ventured: "The first blow that he struck in this direction wrought the whole transformation. The aegis and palladium of the female sex had been from the beginning her power of choice. This, rational man set about wresting from woman . . . and for the mother of mankind all was lost."[24]

Unlike his earlier descriptions, Ward's periodization here was sudden, rapid, and decisive. The fact that, by this stage, males were in all probability larger and stronger than females facilitated this transfer of power. Most human groups would succumb to this changed process of sexual relations. Even with these pace and timing caveats, Ward's account of this transition was one of violence and rape.[25]

A foremost androcentric indicator was the establishment and regulation of marriage. Marriage enshrined men's proprietorship in women, Ward noting that the woman still publicly agreed to obey her husband, but not vice versa, making it "simply an institution for the more complete subjugation and enslavement of women and children." Contravening nature's injunction that the mother "dictates who shall be fathers" and guards her young, the successor primitive family "was an unnatural androcratic excrescence upon society."[26]

The ancillary second element of Ward's explanation concerned men's use of rationality to rise against women. He contended that early man deduced the connection between coupling and reproduction, discovering, literally, his own fatherhood. Now no longer willing to permit women to control offspring completely, men violently seized mothers and children, instituting marriage and families via violent sexual abuse of women: "The passage from the gynaecocentric to the androcentric state was characterized by the loss of . . . chivalry and respect for the preferences of the woman. . . . In discovering his paternity . . . man also discovered his power. . . . He began to learn the economic value of woman . . . exacting not only favors but service from her."[27]

Ward's paternity hypothesis for men's androcentric dominance over women more resembled the imagined scenarios of classical political theory—Hobbes's "state of nature" or Rousseau's "social contract"—than empirical sociological description. Of course, Ward could demonstrate neither the precise moment that some man or men made their paternal realization nor exactly what caused it, beyond its general encephalization framework. Yet, the fact that "primitive" peoples existed in the Progressive Era, still unable to make the causal connection between coitus and pregnancy, confirmed his faith that the discovery of paternity was both an evolutionary and epistemological matter.[28]

It remains unclear why Ward stressed paternity suddenly in 1903. Not merely one factor among many, the hypothesized discovery of paternity now became the precipitation of male violence and then "the enslavement of women . . . and a long train of horrors." Describing the days of primitive polygamous hordes, the strongest men seizing and capturing as many brides as possible, weaker men consigned to celibacy and slavery, he held that these processes greatly diversified and strengthened the hereditary stock of early human groups. Indeed, Ward was preoccupied with male violence and its species effects.[29]

Appropriating Lester Frank Ward

Woman's natural work as a female is that of the mother; man's natural work as a male is that of the father; their mutual relation to this end being a source of joy and well-being when rightly held, but human work covers all our life outside of these specialties. Every handicraft, every profession, every science, every art, all normal amusements and recreations, all government, education, religion; the whole living world of human achievement: all this is human. That one sex should have monopolized all human activities and called them "man's work," and managed them as such, is what is meant by the phrase "Androcentric Culture."

Charlotte Perkins Gilman, The Man-Made World; or, Our Androcentric Culture *(1911)*

Ward published his magnum opus, *Dynamic Sociology* (1883), when Gilman was twenty-three. It is unlikely that she read or was even aware of it during her twenties. She may have read *Dynamic Sociology* after becoming interested in his ideas in "Our Better Halves" (1888). Regarding the significance for his analysis of women's oppression to Gilman's work, Ward used a sculptural analogy. He had merely blocked out the statue from the slab in rough strokes, telling his sociologist nephew-by-marriage, Edward Alsworth Ross

(1866–1951), that he would have to "finish it up." Then "you come along and touch it up with a fine-pointed chisel." This tribute was generous, yet distinctly ambiguous. For her part, though publicly deferring to Ward, Gilman told her fiancé George Houghton Gilman that she had not read Ward's most important texts prior to beginning *Women and Economics* in 1897. Significantly, she insisted on the originality of those of her arguments likened to Ward's, in order to undercut charges that she was a mere disciple: "I wrote the brood Mare long before I met Ward. I've been thinking those things—and much more—for many years."[30]

Scholarly consensus is that Gilman turned to Ward to address the intellectual and political problem of accounting for women's subjection. Actually, she was selective in her approach to his theories, evincing disquiet about some of his central precepts. Instead, she substituted hypotheses about human sexual development significantly different from his, addressed below. Still, Ward remained a significant presence in her work. Hill speculates that "Ward may have been pleased (or was he annoyed?) that, at least through Charlotte's work, his ideas would reach a far wider audience than they otherwise would have," noting the seven printings and multiple language translations of her most famous work, *Women and Economics* (1898), compared with Ward's *Dynamic Sociology* (1883), which sold only five hundred copies across ten years.[31]

Commentators provide a mixed portrayal of Gilman's and Ward's relationship. Hill depicts Ward as Gilman's lifelong mentor, their relationship mutually admiring, though she also cites counter evidence: "Ward only reluctantly acknowledged her support and that after considerable prodding." Gilman considered herself to be his longtime, but unacknowledged, defender. Lane judges Gilman's claim "that Ward's philosophy was hers first as an adolescent" as overblown—the debt to Ward clear throughout her work, some texts such as *Human Work* "essentially paraphrasing" him. Clearly, Ward's hypothesis that women were "the race type" grounded most of her theoretical work. Nonetheless, Lane insists that Gilman "went beyond Ward's theories to envision a fully structured, cooperative, socialized world." Describing Gilman's admiration of Ward, Maureen L. Egan credits her with carrying out original developments "of Ward's theory of an early matriarchic period in human history."[32]

Perhaps consequently, Ann Palmeri attributes Gilman's unwarranted obscurity to her borrowing "from Lester Ward many of the ideas that buttressed her claims about the female half of the species"—ideas subsequently discredited by scientific skepticism about evolutionary thought. Meanwhile, Mary Jo Deegan sees Gilman as vastly influenced by Ward, yet "Ward generally failed to acknowledge Gilman's brilliant nonfiction works in his writings." Deegan's reading, however, disputes Wynn Allen's claim that Ward gave Gilman, who she characterized as an elitist, "a sense of belonging to a vanguard of intellectuals."[33]

If Gilman is supposed to have been a Wardian, such inconclusive commentary suggests that there is a need for closer scrutiny of Gilman's and Ward's complex relationship of identification, exchange, and disavowal. Themes evident in their relationship were influence and originality, recognition and respect, education and sex discrimination, gender and professional status, and competing trajectories in the history of science. The Gilman-Ward correspondence, in relation to their correspondence with others and to their writings, can illuminate more precisely the significance of Ward in Gilman's theoretical corpus.

Ward's criticisms of earlier participants in the matriarchy/patriarchy debates of the era interested Gilman, especially given the privileged place of such earlier works in her librarian father's suggested reading list. These texts presented a closed and seamless worldview casting the rise of patriarchy as both inevitable and progressive. Women's subjugation emerged as a marker of "civilization." His list made her well-prepared her for Ward's critique of early anthropological theories of matriarchy and patriarchy, for such a past offered no comfort for a young late-nineteenth-century feminist.[34]

Gilman first praised Ward's Lamarckianism in her journal, *Impress,* in 1894, and began an admiring friendship with him, at his initiation, in 1895. Her acclaimed evolutionary poem "Similar Cases" caught his attention. He wrote her in Chicago at Hull House while she was staying there with Jane Addams. Seeking further copies of her 1893 poetry book, *In This Our World,* he invited her to meet him at home during the upcoming 1896 Washington, DC, woman suffrage convention. She was "exceedingly proud" of his interest in her poetry, as he had used her verses in an 1896 attack on the theories and arguments of Benjamin Kidd (1856–1916), in a lecture "pitching into Kidd the obscure." She anticipated a mutually amiable alliance: "I felt like the stone in David's sling—supposing said stone too had a grudge against the giant!—and chuckling as it sped." Urging her to come "unfettered by duties," he told her that he was "counting on a charming visit." Listing guests to be assembled in her honor, he wanted "a good talk with you myself," a great honor for "your appreciative admirer."[35]

Hence, Ward forwarded her his pamphlets, article offprints, and reviews, educating her on debates in reform Darwinism and sociology. She constantly asked for more: "Can't you get Dr. Baker to send me the pamphlet you spoke of? 'The Ascent of Man'? I want so much to see it." Would he please send his review of Veblen's *Theory of the Leisure Class* (1899)? Mentioning her friendship with his nephew by marriage, Ross—Ward's principal professional confidante—she thanked him for his review of Ross's books. She spoke of her other social scientist friends such as Professor Earl Barnes (1861–1935) and Alfred Russel Wallace (1823–1913). In Ward's 1897 article "Collective Telesis," he cited her as an authority on irrational human resistance to imagining reformed future societies, through her "remarkable poem . . . Similar Cases."[36] As the foremost Progressive academic critic of women's subjection, Ward naturally fascinated Gilman as the author of the era's most acclaimed work on "the woman question." That she should be eager to secure his support, friendship, and even respect cannot be surprising. She confided to Ward her history and vulnerabilities, especially the insecurities of her position as an autodidact. In 1900, she requested from him sociological sources to supplement a new Italian edition of *Women and Economics,* her publisher seeking her "authorities" list: this recalled her 1878 request to her estranged librarian father for a list of authorities for self-education.[37]

At nineteen years her senior, the authoritative Ward could have approximated a father figure to help legitimate her aspiration to theorize and challenge women's oppression. She offered herself as both petitioner and disciple: "I think I have advanced nothing that conflicts with your teaching—have I? So if you'll tell me some of the best authorities on sociological development . . . who do not disagree with you—they will serve the desired end." She did not wish to appear to have invented her facts "as well as propounded an especial theory."[38]

Often she wrote Ward deferential or self-deprecating letters, a response he seems to have prompted in many women. Apparently, he had charged Gilman with being unfamiliar with his work. Her response, however, would have been not exactly flattering to a scholar expecting a close, appreciative reading: "Did you really think I did not know your books? I own the *Dynamic Sociology* and mean to have the 'Psychic Factors' some time. And you should hear me refer other people to them!!" Gilman repeatedly explained that her mental difficulties obstructed serious study, confining her reading to only the more journalistic and brief of his works. In response, he persistently explained that work pressures prevented him reading hers.[39]

Wishing to discuss many subjects with him, she minimized her own work: "I've been writing a scrap of a thing on 'Man as a Factor in Social Evolution' and another on 'The Persistence of Primitive Tendencies in the Domestic Relation'"—probably early drafts of her text, *The Home: Its*

Work and Influence (1903). Had he seen her new book, "'Concerning Children'? It is comparatively slight and uneven, a book of essays."

Her deference halted, however, with Ward's 1903 publication of *Pure Sociology,* with its 126-page chapter on sexual relations, setting forth his "gynaecocentric theory":

> We bought *Pure Sociology* at once—I already have the *Dynamic Sociology*—and I pitched into that Woman chapter first because you asked me to tell you what I thought of it. . . . Now I am trying to arrange with some big magazine to write an article on that tremendous theory of yours—it ought to be popularized at once. Will you tell me if anyone else is doing it anywhere? And what in your judgment would be the best place for such an article?[40]

Here she jettisoned the disciple for aspiring manager. By 1904, she had worked as editor of several journals and magazines, as well as regularly placing her own work out for publication in a wide array of periodicals. Although lacking his academic credentials, her hard-won negotiating skills could assist in publicizing his theories.[41]

Indeed, she enthusiastically extolled Ward's thesis to readers of the suffrage newspaper *Woman's Journal.* Under the title "Apropos Prof. Ward's Theory" (1904), she outlined his view of woman as the "race type" and the rationale for man's existence purely to provide a variance in reproduction. As a variant, man also was little more than an enlarged parasite. Prior to enslavement, woman was the "advanced, industrial animal . . . unique in the animal kingdom." Modern civilization came from men's appropriation and development of women's industries, while excluding women from industrial advance, "making them more and more dependent." The question of how this change had come about required closer attention to counter those convinced that the present patriarchal order was natural, God-given, and without variation across the history of humans on Earth.[42]

Her desire for his recognition, however, was not satisfied by publicizing him. She sought his acknowledgment of their shared mission on "the woman question"—implicitly, that she was his peer. Five years after *Women and Economics* (1898), her response to Ward's success with *Pure Sociology* manifested anxiety, if not jealousy: "I was a little grieved in reading your statement that no one had taken up your theory—for I had stoutly defended it in my book *Women and Economics.* But perhaps you didn't consider that book of sufficient importance to mention. Or perhaps you haven't read it. I instructed the publishers to send you advance sheets of it—so sure was I that you would be interested, but evidently I overrated your interest."[43]

He had indeed received a personal copy of *Women and Economics* (1898) from Gilman; and thereafter he laid somewhat greater emphasis on economic factors in his prescriptions for ending androcentrism. While he contended that the monogamic era of sexual relations based on mutual selection and romantic love taking root in the Progressive Era could abate androcentrism, it had not resolved "the almost complete economic dependence of woman upon man." From the gynaecocentric to the androcentric state, "man ... began to learn the economic value of woman ... exacting not only favors but service from her." Economic motives even paralleled sexual access as motives in women's subjugation, noting that human uses and assessments of available resources were fatally flawed by adherence to androcentric philosophy, which amounted to wasting the talents and potential contributions of half of the population—women—simply on the ground of sex. He continued to ponder the unsolved aspects of his own and other theories of androcentric culture across the 1900s. In 1910, he critically reviewed Annie Porritt's essay "Woman as a Metonymy," calling it ahistorical and unwarrantedly ignoring economic factors. Yet his extensively referenced texts failed to mention Gilman's bestseller, lending support to Gilman's 1903 charge that he had not yet read it.[44]

Ward saw Gilman as a poet, whose creativity provided grist to his mill, an admired creative artist. Indeed, he often confided to his female correspondents that he had no such creativity himself and greatly admired this gift, this genius, in others. Though sending Gilman copies of his articles and reviews, he did not see her as a peer contributor to sociological theory. Gilman, by contrast, expressed very different expectations of their relationship. She met his every request for evaluations of his published work. He sought such feedback on *Pure Sociology* (1903), especially from feminists and female reformers. In early 1904, Gilman responded:

> [I] want to tell you what I think of your Gynaecocentric Theory. You asked me to let you know. I think it is the most important contribution to the "woman question" ever made—(not excepting my own beloved theory)—and therein of measureless importance to the world. Moreover I mean to make it the recognized basis of a new advance in the movement of women.... I am to make it the subject of my address ... in the International Congress of Women held in Berlin in June. I am preparing a very impressive article on it which I hope to bring out in the *North American Review*.[45]

Moreover, she stressed reviewers' neglect of his theory: "It is a continuing surprise to me to find so little recognition of this great theory of yours in the reviews of your book or any other place." Maybe there were good reviews "in this country" that she had not seen? She implied that her role could be crucial in securing his rightful recognition: "I want to make the people feel what a great work you have done in this one thing—to say nothing of all the rest of your work." In the same vein, she wrote him a few months later that: "I have made known your name and work . . . in the great international gathering at Berlin to thinking women of a score of nations."[46]

Still seeking his recognition, she kept sending him her nonfiction work, with the added lure of her tireless promotion of his work. For instance, in summer 1904, after her return from Berlin, she gave a lecture in Brooklyn titled "The Mother's Duty" and "rested the argument on your gynaecocentric theory. . . . My publishers have sent you my new book—*Human Work.* It is the biggest thing I've undertaken—too big to be done properly by my weak head."[47]

Her own enhanced reputation intensified her quest for Ward's recognition. By 1904, as America's most acclaimed feminist theorist, she had published five books, numerous articles, reviews, short stories, and poems and was a feature page editor of the venerable suffrage magazine, *Woman's Journal.* In the New York woman rights circuit she was "feeling her oats." Just as she had tried to attach herself to Ward's coattails, he associated his ideas with hers, in more popularized versions of his theories of sexual relations. Thus, in his 1906 article, "The Past and Future of the Sexes," he cited Gilman, though still confining his references to her poetry: "The only person who, to my knowledge has clearly brought out this cosmological perspective, not merely in things human, but in the vast reaches of organic evolution, is a woman." His footnote was her poem, "Similar Cases." This mollified Gilman somewhat: "I am grateful to you for the most complimentary reference in your *Independent* article; which I prize the more now that you have sent it to me." But it was not enough. Again she railed against his nonrecognition of her as a social theorist:

> As you may know I have been preaching your doctrine, with specific reference to you and *Pure Sociology* ever since it was known to me. By the way, I was grieved to see in *Pure Sociology* that you have not read my *Women and Economics* or if you have you did not notice my explicit reference [page 171] to your *Forum* article of 1888, because you say that to your knowledge no one has ever advocated your theory; and I've done my humble best at it, in lecture, book, and article these many years.

She laced this complaint with assertions of her own loyalty against the army of detractors in their midst, citing others' criticisms, writing that all her "biological friends scoff at you, and say you have not the facts to rest the theory on—that they know no instance of a creature with the tiny transient male—the first stage of detached existence." Pressing her knowledge of his critics, she noted that "Mr. Holt has three replies which he calls 'withering.' I don't think they'll 'wither' much; and the matter needs wide and thorough discussion." Her mention of "Mr. Holt" concerned a symposium that Henry Holt (1840–1926), editor of the *Independent,* tried to publish in 1906. Ward was chagrined because Holt gave his work, without permission, to three professional rivals and critics: G. Stanley Hall (1844–1924), Edmund B. Wilson (1856–1939), and Franklin Giddings (1855–1931), proposing to publish their critiques with Ward's article, inviting him to reply to them. Ward refused, calling Holt's actions "a breach of professional ethics." He later wrote of this incident as "particularly objectionable," since the article had been for a popular journal, hence "bald and devoid of facts or evidence in support of a theory opposed to popular ideas." Consequently the critics Holt had assembled could easily discredit him by the usual "atomistic, myopic method by which all great truths have always been attacked."[48]

Gilman's softened her unwelcome reference to his critics with "I hear that you have been called to the Chair of Sociology at Brown. Power to your elbow!" Ward's 1907 appointment to a long-sought academic post only accelerated her demands for his recognition. Moreover, aspects of his account of the sexes continued to bother her. Though she had already sent him the book that she regarded as her most important, *Human Work,* in 1907 she sent it again, this time with passages marked, evidently no more confident that he had yet read it than he had her earlier nonfiction works: "I truly think it will interest you to see how largely I have followed the same lines of thought you have covered so much more fully; and that one or two points may have fresh suggestions perhaps." She again declared that improved health now permitted her at last able to read his earlier books since "except for the Phylogenetic Forces—in *Pure Sociology*—and some of the shorter papers you were so kind as to send me—I have not really read you at all." Reporting on her and her husband's reading of Ward's 1906 text, *Applied Sociology,* she noted that unlike her, Mr. Gilman had "read all the others."[49]

That a female intellectual denied higher education because of her sex might be competitive and resentful when the glittering prizes came to men like Ward is not surprising. Any such feeling would have been heightened when the institution honoring him was the one shadowing her Providence adolescence and young adulthood, supplying her first suitors and yet locking her and all other women out—Brown University. Viewing his good fortune, she could only reflect that, after all, she was a Beecher, one of the most famous public intellectual families in American history. Hence her good wishes on Ward's Brown appointment have a discernable edge, full of caveats: "I hope you are enjoying as you ought the Himalayan heights you have won—the glorious view—the light—the clear stimulating air; and best of all, the sure knowledge that this big job is for us all and will be reached by all. That is the real happiness—it does not much matter if only a few of us know you are there."[50] It was ironic that Ward should be the focus of such ambivalence or passive aggression. Hardly the entitled scion of academe or other learned professions or with hereditary wealth—the background of so many of the white male university faculty members of the period—his poverty was formative, his education hard won, and professional success elusive and belated.[51]

Gilman's bid for his recognition evoked apologies and appeasing gestures: teaching obligations confined his reading to materials illustrating social science for his "greedy young students," all else becoming vacation reading, a pile that, he assured her, her book would top. To soften the message that he judged her contributions to be summer reading, he rewarded her assertions of their common ground with: "Of course we think alike," reporting that he commended her book to his educational sociology class. Even so, he kept her significance as stubbornly poetic: "To show the similarity of your point of view and mine I read them your 'Flagstone Method,' . . . to their amusement. . . . Thank you very much for sending it to me."[52]

Gilman, whose *Women and Economics* vastly outsold all Ward's books, jealously guarded her own reputation for originality. Ward's rigid "art-versus-intellect" dichotomy had insulted her because he relegated her to the role of an artistic mouthpiece for his ideas, implicitly casting her as a mere popularizer rather than a theorist. Hence, her admiration for Ward was ambivalent, due to the fear that her own contribution might disappear in the shadow of her famous contemporary. In 1895, her use of the metaphor "the stone in David's sling" had expressed her delight at being judged useful to the Great Man. As their relationship unfolded, alongside her growing fame, she increasingly resented being treated as merely his bullhorn. Ten years and many publications later, no longer a mere stone, to extend the metaphor, she regarded herself as David's peer with her own slingshot. Moreover, having faithfully had his work cited by and having been brought to the attention of her huge audiences by

Gilman, Ward incurred a debt to her. Perhaps he had become a stone in her slingshot.[53]

Sexual Violence or Mother-Service?

> I have read your book. I could hear my own voice all the time. But of course, it was not an echo. It is pitched much higher than I can strike and differs also entirely in timbre.
>
> *Lester Frank Ward to Charlotte Perkins Gilman, 9 February 1907*

The tension detectable in the Gilman-Ward relationship would have little significance had their contributions on "the woman question" been identical. Her difficulties with his preeminence, and her autodidactic dependence on him as an authority, became complicated further by substantial disagreement between them over theorizing "the overthrow" of gynaecocentric culture. Her increasing skepticism after she read, and reread, Ward's *Pure Sociology* renders doubtful any claim that Gilman was an uncritical Wardian.[54]

Despite her reputation as a follower, Gilman challenged Ward's periodization, causality, and hypothesis of a violent androcentric overthrow of gynaecocentric culture. According more agency to women than Ward had, her alternative hypotheses featured economic causes. Thereby she objected to his theory of women's subjugation. By subversive revisions, she exceeded the role of disciple. In particular, she hypothesized the emergence of voluntary matriarchal polygyny, from which the worst of androcentric male characteristics resulted in an unintended side-effect.

Though her specific criticisms of his ideas culminated in 1907–9, their different explanations of the origins and causes of women's subjection were already clear with *Women and Economics,* and probably before she had read beyond Ward's "Our Better Halves" (1888). Despite her admiration for him, she judged Ward's explanations of women's oppression inconclusive. For Gilman, the cause of the women's hypothesized subjection was "sexuoeconomic," a phrase that she appears to have coined. Ill consequences of male sex selection anchored her case for women's independence and citizenship. Notwithstanding their forcible monopoly of women's industries, males were inherently work averse, choosing the path entailing the least effort, wherever possible. She speculated that "it occurred to the dawning intelligence of this amiable savage that it was cheaper and easier to fight a little female and have it done with than to fight a big male every time. So he instituted the custom of enslaving the female." Women, no longer free, could no longer feed their young or themselves. Indeed, the man, the father, found that slavery had its obligations: "he must care for what he forbade to care for itself, else it died on his hands." Hence, both "slowly and reluctantly" he acquired the duties of the breadwinner, fulfilling in his own person "the thwarted uses of maternity."[55]

Elsewhere in *Women and Economics,* Gilman described the "subjection of women" as involving "the maternalizing of man." This was, she argued, the silver lining in the otherwise "disease-, sin-, and evil-studded era of mightily overgrown sex passion" caused by male dominance. Secluded ownership of erotically accessible women forced men to provide and improve, men assuming "the instincts and habits of the female." Of course, however, this outcome was not men's motivation; rather it was "because of sex-desire the male subjugates the female. Lest he lose her, he feeds her, and perforce her young." This economic focus in analyzing the origins of women's subjection was Gilman's and not Ward's. For him, economic dependence for women was a consequence, not a cause, of androcentric culture.[56]

Gilman recast woman's admittedly painful and "long years of oppression" as a merely "temporary subversion" of her initial superiority, leading to the positive outcome of man's slow rise to "full racial equality with her"—note here her use of "racial" to mean human race. Originally "merely a temporary agent in reproduction and of no further use," or "merely a fertilizing agent," males could contribute more to race improvement if they equaled the already highly developed parent, the female. Thus, their enhancement to race equality required women's economic dependence to make man "the working mother of the world."[57]

Briskly gliding over the consequences of patriarchal oppression, she declared: "Women can well afford their period of subjection for the sake of a conquered world, a civilized man." She described women's historical enslavement in order to announce its passing: "And now the long strain is over, now that the time has come when neither he nor the world is any longer benefited by her subordination." She challenged the assumed naturalism of male dominance, casting it as a phase, leading to a present in which it was no longer constructive for "the race."[58]

Gilman explored adverse effects of male sex selection, especially in altered female secondary sexual characteristics—the whim of male choice. The "proprietary family" flouted nature's intent that men compete to be chosen by women as mates. "The man, by violence or purchase, does the choosing" instead, and she added, "he selects the kind of woman that pleases him. Nature did not intend him to select; he is not good at it. Neither was the female intended to compete—she is not good at it." Thus, men were freed from the "stern but elevating" effect of sexual selection. They just bought a woman or took one by force. Meanwhile, the natural selection that formerly elevated women now required only that she please prospective masters—merely the average intelligence, strength, skill, health, or beauty of the "house servant" or "housekeeper."[59]

On the consequences of men becoming the sex selectors, Gilman's and Ward's critiques converged, as they did on the character of male erotic desire. The sexes' desires pointed in opposite directions, yet with a ghastly symmetry. Under the gynaecocratic regime, females enlarged males into equality from their status as dependent parasite. By contrast, male sex selectors reduced females into inequality as dependent parasites. Females sought to make males more like themselves—to their cost—while males, once equal to females, sought to make the latter less like themselves—to their benefit.[60]

Despite their convergence on sex selection, Gilman ignored Ward's paternity hypothesis, advancing instead her economic and maternity-centered version of the story. In resisting the causal status attributed to the discovery of paternity, she also declined the comparable claims of those revered mid-to-late-nineteenth-century founding fathers of anthropology who were so palpably wedded to it—including those authorities recommended by her father. Insofar as her explanations centered motherhood and its economic activities, she rejected man-centered accounts of sex selection, finding the role they accorded sexual violence particularly troubling. In Ward's account, women's esthetically motivated equalization, through sex selection, of originally inferior males, was the last piece of female agency. Thereafter, men dominated. Gilman did not believe that women would have submitted to the violent transformation Ward described. In *Herland,* the women of the imagined Amazonian country, when confronted with such a threat from the men remaining after a deadly war, rose up and slaughtered their would-be oppressors. Moreover, in *His Religion and Hers* she rebuked contemporary feminists who assumed that ancient man "with a club . . . suddenly rose up against his female and subjugated her by . . . force." Ward's idea that ancient sexual patterns were "instantaneously changed and inverted by one man—or one generation of men" was absurd.[61]

She referred to the ending of gynaecocentric culture as "The Overthrow." Yet, against Ward's assertion that it was purposive, she wrote: "As to the Overthrow: Not telic. Not sudden. Not a conquest by man. Ward's suggestion unsatisfying." She ventured that "peace, plenty, beginnings of wealth, considerable industry" were the good conditions of "the matriarchate," leading to an excess of women, eventually "human matriarchal polygamy," where "able, industrious, productive" female groups maintained one male, who, valued for scarcity, "kept in comparative idleness by a group of industrious women, and overindulged sexually, became proud, sensual, lazy and cruel. All this slowly and gradually introduced and produced by cumulation. No literature."[62]

Hence, her theory was gradualist, insisting that "the change" occurred between the earliest appearance of savage humans and the beginnings of recorded history. She contended that the change happened more or less simultaneously in all races and places on earth. The cause was not discovery of the fact of paternity but, rather, the extension of motherhood centered on service. Beyond "natural" periodic coitus related to reproduction, cohabitation with mothers began to have added attractions for primitive men—economic attractions. Men, too, might claim maternal care. Thus, women's capacity for human service lay "at the root of our great race tragedy, the subjugation of the female." Contrary to Ward's raping and battering savage man in the vanguard of androcentrism, however, subjugation eventuated "not by any act of cruelty on the part of man but the increasing desirability of woman's services." With brief life expectancy, the age gap between a woman's oldest child and her current lover might be narrow; thus, the extension of her "mother-service" to the latter happened easily and unconsciously, as he "slipped into more and more dependence on her services." Androcentric man "first took advantage" more of motherhood than of sex.[63]

Motherhood originated women's industries, services, and usefulness and was itself synonymous with women's sexuality, prior to "the overthrow." Gilman provided a woman-centered account, certain that the shift to male-dominated culture arose through mutual economic negotiation. She neither endorsed nor repeated Ward's theory of female enslavement as the exercise of men's hyperdeveloped rational faculties, overcoming natural instincts, and the discovery, through such rationality, of paternity, which unleashed father right, and, thereby, male sex right. Women's subordination was not a planned undertaking, a pitiless, and rational, assertion of paternal control. Androcentrism did not derive from men's hypothesized realization of fatherhood; nor did rape and force establish it. Gilman rejected apocalyptic accounts of the rise of androcentric society.[64]

As such, she did not engage Ward's racialized account of interracial rape, sex/race differences, and lynching. In *Pure Sociology* (1903), he argued that violent rape originated and underlay marriage, as an unconsciously registered response to a biological call to strength and diversity within the human species. His "philosophy of rape as an ethnological phenomenon" entailed generalizations concerning so-called "miscegenation" and lynching. Without explaining how or why it should be so, he stated baldly that women of all racial groups would accept mates of a racial group they perceived as superior to their own and reject those of a group judged inferior, while men of all groups would have sex with women of any other group.[65]

In evolutionary terms, Ward contended that this meant that the racial "elevation" of African Americans would occur only through white men impregnating black women. Those black men seeking sex relations with white women, including by rape, did so in response to a biological imperative to enhance their racial stocks. Equally, the outraged community who lynched the black offender responded to an unconscious and unarticulated imperative to protect their own race from degeneration. Gilman's silence on this aspect of Ward's theories was as deafening as it was on his paternity hypothesis concerning the origins of "the overthrow" of women.[66]

In 1908, still seeking his engagement with her "fresh ideas," Gilman acquainted Ward with her alternative theory of "the overthrow," leading to "the complete extinction of those races most violently androcentric, as well as the visible decadence of so many others." She asked him to imagine another explanatory scenario:

Assume a matriarchal settlement under exceptionally good conditions. . . . Assume an excess of females. . . . Having now good conditions and surplus females, the male becomes increasingly valuable. The dominant females, already the industrial power and used to tribal communism, now establish a voluntary polygyny agreeing to maintain one male to each small group of females. If this were done, the male being now supported by the group of females and held in high esteem, is in a position to develop naturally, the excessive indulgence, cruelty, pride, etc. which would so lead to the more injurious effects of unchecked masculine rule. This hypothesis seems to me simple and genetic—requires no telic process, no determined action.

She concluded her hypothesis cheerily with a shorthand version: "Good conditions—excess females; excess females—male at premium. Male at premium—females establish polygyny. Polygyny—over-development of maleness. Predominant maleness—androcracy. Androcracy—the world as we have it . . . 'How's that?'"[67] Interestingly, she retitled "matriarchal polygamy" as "voluntary polygyny"—initiated by women, with very different sexual politics implications. Always puzzled as to how previously dominant women could have been overthrown, it seemed plausible to speculate that "from a peaceful promiscuity with matriarchal dominance to a voluntary polygyny—the females agreeing to share rather than compete—seems to me a very possible step. And polygyny produces the characteristics which lead to further masculine dominance." No letter survives revealing any written response from Ward to her hypothesis. From 1908 onward, however, his circumstances were changing, making him even less likely to engage with her ideas.

Ward's attention to his various female correspondents, including Gilman, declined after he went to Brown. Soon he became estranged from his invalid wife, who returned to Washington, D.C. He became singularly absorbed with Mrs. Emily Palmer Cape, a wealthy, Columbia-educated forty-five-year-old lumber merchant's wife, also a feminist, suffragist, artist, and writer, mainly of children's fiction. Cape proposed that she become his biographer and the editor of a twelve-volume compilation of his lesser-known writings, published since the 1870s, which eventually would come to be titled *Glimpses of the Cosmos.* They secured a publisher and set to work.[68]

This partnership absorbed Ward's final years, to the dismay of family and friends. His biographers contend that rumors of an extramarital affair cannot be proved beyond doubt. Cape invited him to stay at her marital home while her husband traveled abroad in 1910, the base from which Ward taught summer school at Columbia. When the next summer he visited Ross at the University of Wisconsin at Madison, Cape let adjacent rooms in Ward's boarding house.[69]

What was the nature of Cape and Ward's interaction? Like many of Ward's lonely, bored, or frustrated female correspondents, Cape wrote him affectionate, flirtatious, flattering, revealing, and above all self-deprecating letters declaring him to be the new center of her universe. It seems he responded encouragingly to such declarations. His anxious preoccupation with his standing among feminists, suffragists, and woman rights advocates—perhaps partly provoked by Gilman's criticisms—was evident in Cape's letters. She criticized famous Progressive Era women. For instance: "I heard Jane Addams (of Chicago) speak at the 'colonial club' the other day and I wondered then why such women did not give forth more of the real Root of progress—the forming of character . . . into people, to leave the education actually bring by degrees a new generation forth, and not only give the older people work and trades."[70] He confided critically to her about various suffragists, for instance, about two hours reluctantly spent with Mary Gray Peck, friend and biographer of suffragist Carrie Chapman Catt: "What a treat your last letter was! I thoroughly enjoyed it—and laughed out loud as I read of Miss Peck, for my impressions of her were the same; but *she* is so pleased with her little bunch of 'ego' that it [is] almost comical, yet I fear two hours would have buried poor small me."[71]

Reporting that she had "sent for several of the books you let me see while

I visited you that beautiful day," Cape mentioned Gilman: "I find too the poetry book: "In This Our World" by Mrs. Stetson I can buy, so I shall read again and learn 'our poems': — the one you read me, and I so liked on Evolution; how fine 'the horse' was!" If Ward did not acknowledge Gilman to her satisfaction, he evidently portrayed her as enough a part of his milieu for Cape, seven years Gilman's junior, to react.[72]

Cape characterized Gilman, along with other social scientists, as an unoriginal paraphraser of Ward's foundational theories: "All that Mrs. Gilman has written I see not only saturated, but well embroidered with your books. Her 'Concerning Children,' the strength of the words she uses in her evolutionary and biological hints, are but sifted through her clever, brilliant method. It is good and I admire it very much, but I feel so deeply what you have awakened people to. Thomas, Cooley, Ross even — how you have given, given to each one!"[73] With such methods, Cape detached Ward from his contemporaries, including his friends, admirers, and acquaintances, by demonstrating that their commitment to him and his ideas paled beside her own. Ward and Gilman appear to have exchanged no letters after spring 1911, the last an invitation from her to stay when he was in New York. Ward died from a sudden heart attack in 1913 at the age of seventy-two. When Cape claimed he appointed her as his literary executor and authorized biographer, Ward's female relatives scotched this plan by destroying his voluminous and revealing personal diaries and refusing Cape's claims. Her appeals to Ross to intervene on her behalf altered nothing.[74]

Gilman's *The Man-Made World; or, Our Androcentric Culture* (1911) might have suggested a full reflection and integration of Ward's concept of "gynaecocracy" superseded by "androcracy." With its fulsome dedication to Ward and prominent title use of his term, "androcentrism" also might suggest that Gilman operated as an unquestioning disciple: "This book is dedicated with reverent love and gratitude to Lester F. Ward, Sociologist and Humanitarian, one of the world's great men; a creative thinker to whose wide knowledge and power of vision we are indebted for a new grasp of the nature and processes of Society, and to whom all women are especially bound in honor and gratitude for his Gynaecocentric Theory of Life, than which nothing so important to humanity has been advanced since the Theory of Evolution, and nothing so important to women has ever been given to the world."[75]

She endorsed the essential Wardian finding that "the female is the race type, and male, originally but a sex type, reaching a later equality with the female, and, in the human race, becoming her master for a considerable period." Urging, however, that the results were by no means "an unmixed good," these conditions now needed to end. For our "androcentric culture is ... a masculine culture in excess, and therefore undesirable." Indeed, she declared that the fact that one sex should have monopolized all "human activities, called them 'man's work,' and managed them as such, is what is meant by the phrase 'Androcentric Culture.'" Ward's theory provided the basis to undo androcentric damage, permitting women's full inclusion in race development. This gynaecocentric theory had to account for the rise of androcentric order against the dictates of nature. Gilman relied on recognized authorities for the genesis of man-centered culture, though she at no point engaged Ward's paternity hypothesis, advancing instead an economic and maternity-centered version of the story.[76]

Other writers engaging with Ward directly rejected the discovery of paternity as an explanation for male dominance. University of Chicago sociologist William I. Thomas agreed with Gilman, seeing the origins of the shift to patriarchal societies as women's accelerating economic value to their communities. Probably Gilman also agreed with Catherine Gasquoine Hartley's rejection of this Ward hypothesis. Though indebted to Ward, Hartley disbelieved his conclusion "of the passive character of the female" and theory of the paternal recognition genesis of father-right. Instead, like Gilman, she found the cause of male domination to be men's recognition that in women there was the chance for property and services, in Gilman's terms. Hence, it was not due to the recognition of fatherhood; rather, women's kin beginning to see in them exchange value for "obtaining wives for themselves, and also the possibility of gaining worldly goods, both in the property held by women, and by means of the service and presents that could be claimed from their lover." Strict supervision of female sexuality and "alliances" ensued.[77]

WHEN WARD DIED in 1913, Gilman presented a measured tribute. His legacy would be his books and arguments, most especially for women, for whom "he should stand as the greatest light ever thrown upon their abnormal condition and its results to the world." She recalled a sociology meeting, where most delegates presented specialized, fragmented studies: "Ward rose to his feet, a towering figure, broad, massive, with a noble head that wore the kindness of large wisdom. He admitted the value of the local measures, but added 'I confess that nothing deeply interests me in social improvement which does not apply to the whole human race.'"[78]

Though later critics held Gilman's feminism flawed in its embrace of Ward's subsequently discredited Lamarckian theory of sexual relations, she always resisted aspects of his evolving account of women's subjection, especially its ironic man centeredness and disempowering stress on male violence. Unquestionably, his account of the consequent regime of andro-centric sexuality following women's loss of sex selection resonated power-fully with her. It authorized her quest for ending sex slavery pertaining in all known societies.[79]

Beyond this, however, a key sticking point emerged between them. De-spite his reform Darwinist commitment to human intervention to secure the best evolutionary outcomes, on the matter of the sexes Ward accorded the prime agency to men. Indeed, he seemed to expect women to be satis-fied by pinning their hopes for the future on men's evolution of roman-tic love, tenderness, and chivalry toward women. On this crucial matter, the differences between him and Gilman were strategic and political, yet grounded in a key analytical divergence on the demise of gynaecocentric culture and the establishment of androcentric rule of men over women.

In vain, she tried to engage Ward on their theoretical and interpretative differences. Much hinged on their disagreement, especially in view of their respective reputations as authorities on the woman question. Not for Gil-man the Arthurian, courtly, and gracious (if belated) recognition by men that women could be partners in the full range of human activities. Instead, she sought a more materially grounded rationale for both men and women to embrace change. She exhorted both sexes to see that the economic de-pendence so far hallmark of androcentric society was a provisional and only functional stage affecting the "human" evolution of men. That stage was over, and its continuance had become a potent threat to human progress. For the good of the human race, men had to give up their power and con-trol, and women their dependence and parasitism. Then sexual relations would cease to be toxic.

Armed with this theory of the origins of sex oppression, Gilman still faced the challenge undertaken by any serious feminist theorist. She had to convince her contemporaries that these causes led to outcomes that were disastrous, not only for women but also for men and children. Much of her work described outcomes she identified as critical in women's oppres-sion. She sought to persuade her audiences and readers that human sexual arrangements and sexed attributes were, variously, degrading, inefficient, dangerous, inhumane, laughable, pathetic, unjust, and just really foolish. Her descriptions carried a strong diagnostic element — practice must follow theory, problems must generate solutions.

CHAPTER FOUR

Sex Slavery, Home Cooking, and Combat

Mrs. Gilman, mind you, told those women that they were being held . . . in shackles like slaves, that present day conditions from the feminine viewpoint were as bad as serfdom in Russia. . . . The time had come for them to "stop cooking for John." Disparaging the so-called "home cooking" Mrs. Gilman said that women tied down to their homes could not hope to compete with experts and specialists. . . . "I am the first heretic," she asserted, a note of interrogation in her voice. There was a sullen murmur, and an angry glint in many eyes which said as plain as shouting that she no longer was alone: "Do you think home dressmaking is the best?" asked Mrs. Gilman. "No!" came the reply, alarming in volume and spontaneity, from every corner of the room. "Do you think that home millinery is the best?" "No!" The door which had been left open a crack, closed suddenly, and the window curtains swayed to and fro. "Then why is home cooking the best?"

There was no answer, and Mrs. Gilman smiled.

"Mrs. Gilman Swats Home Cooking Idol,"
New York Times, *12 March 1914*

IMBUED WITH her powerful sense of the historicity of human sexual arrangements, Gilman used the written and spoken word relentlessly to expose the injustices and inefficiencies of androcentric culture. She investigated and often dramatized the dire situation of women and children. A key element of her feminist theory legacy was her richly detailed analysis of masculinity, men's practices, and thereby the maintenance of male supremacy. Her diagnostic analyses shocked, disturbed, and provoked her audiences to revise conventional assumptions about men and women, the sexual division of labor, and the "naturalness" of sexed institutions.

Seeking both recognition of the Wardian insight of "woman as the race-type" and progress toward the "human world" of mutual sex selection and partnership in advancing humanity—"race work"—she exposed the high costs for all of androcentric rule of men over women and children. At its door, she laid prevailing sexual patterns in the morbid state of "the sex relation itself" and the excessive sexualization of women, manifest, for instance, in women's restrictive and sex-enhancing dress. Corporeal consequences included not only painful menstruation, as Ward noted, but also the general size, strength, and fitness of women's bodies.

Thus, she protested at prescribed femininity with regard to health, nutrition, work, leisure, and fashion since they reflected the expectation that women did only "sex work" rather than standing alongside men in "race work." Unlike other species with both sexes feeding themselves and developing the same skills, humans progressed only through the male line, confining women to personal and domestic service to individual men and families. Apparently enormous sex differences obstructed the case for women's cultural equality. For women, this was the minimum requisite for a "human world." As she was formulating her arguments for *Women and Economics* with her future husband, Houghton Gilman, she wrote: "Why man—if there was only so much work in the world (which isn't true) and just so much wages to go with it, it would be better for man and wife each to do half a day's work and get half a day's wage than for him to do all the work and she none—him to get all the money and she none. They'd have just as much money as now and have spare time to see each other in!"[1]

To denaturalize androcentrism, Gilman confronted its supporting assumptions and truisms with counterevidence from male and female existence and challenged the organization of the world around men's needs and interests. Her key targets were the home and its primitive industries, especially home cooking, motherhood, and childcare. Their features derived from the sex relation itself. Beyond androcentric femininity, however, she launched a reform Darwinist feminist denunciation of exaggerated male combativeness, which made modern societies relentlessly competitive, aggressive, and individualistic. Androcentric history became a litany of wars, conquests, slavery, and imperialistic imposition on others, all attended by cruelty and the darkest of motives. Not warfare alone but everyday life in war and peace shared these features because constitutive of masculinity itself. Combat attained eroticized overtones, aiding the oversexualization of men, with hideous consequences for women and girls. Moreover, far from mitigating these warlike tendencies of androcentric cultures, world religions all too often assumed a causal role in frightful sectarian wars or else rationalized violent missionary colonization of pristine indigenous cultures. Even God, constructed as a patriarchal father, would not escape Gilman's critical scrutiny.[2]

"The Sex Relation Itself"

> Yet it is not easy for the average "feminist" to admit the parasitism of women, with its accompanying abortion of social faculties. In the new recognition of the initial superiority of the female, and her continued advantage up to the early stages of our human culture, it is hard to reconcile that essential superiority with the inferiority produced by parasitism . . . the fact of female superiority ought not to blind us to her similar degradation when ceasing to use the constructive capacities of her race and getting her living through the sex relation, legal or illegal.
>
> Charlotte Perkins Gilman, "Parasitism and Civilized Vice" (1931)

Gilman contended that the sex slavery of women anchored androcentric culture. With marriage as their principal or only means of livelihood, the word "wife" defined a wageless menial domestic worker, preeminently responsible for all phases of meal preparations for her husband and children and for all the other household chores associated with the family group's living arrangements. While legally obligated to provide "conjugal rights" to her husband, any "wife" courted discipline, or even divorce, by neglecting household or conjugal duties. Meanwhile, for most women, "home and happiness, reputation, ease and pleasure, her bread and butter, all must come to her through a small gold ring. This is a heavy pressure."[3]

Following the abolitionists among her ancestors, Gilman drew analogies between sex subjection of women in marriage and chattel slavery. She called conditions consigning the majority of adult women to unpaid forced erotic and menial labor "sex-slavery." With marriage the only sexual relationship not stigmatized in Judeo-Christian cultures and, simultaneously, the prescribed livelihood for women, Gilman argued that "the sex relation itself" had been made the altar of women's subjection. For, on becoming "wife," the full force of androcentric prescriptions pressed most harshly on women. As discussed in previous chapters, Gilman did not believe that these features were inherent in heterosexuality but that historically they had been made so. Of course, numerous wives also undertook paid labor, especially and of necessity, women of the urban poor, racial, and ethnic minorities and, of course, women widowed or abandoned by their husbands, as was her mother. This further work rarely relieved them, however, of the household duties falling to wives in higher classes. Appallingly unequal pay for working women ensured that their paid work often enough supplemented family income, though without providing economic independence for working class and poor wives. Meanwhile, working wives had far less time for the time-consuming tasks of housework and childcare, even if still undertaking them at the expense of health and longevity.[4]

Citing the zoological truism that food supply most significantly modified any animal, Gilman contended that man becoming woman's feeder had consequences that had once been functional but were now lethal. Man literally became woman's environment, modifying her:

> We are the only animal species in which the female depends on the male for food, the only animal species in which the sex relation is also an economic relation. With us, an entire sex lives in a relation of economic dependence upon the other sex, and the economic relation is combined with the sex-relation. The economic status of the human female is relative to the sex relation. Since women obtained food "through the sex relation," their best interests and standards of living depended upon the effective and constant stimulus of that relation.

Thus, Gilman observed, women had become "oversexed," their sex differences from men morbidly exaggerated, resulting in an "intensification of sex-energy as a social force," producing vice and disease in its wake. Since males had seized sex selection from females to establish androcentric culture, men's sex function thereafter predominated, defeating the purposes of natural selection:

> Natural selection develops race. Sexual selection develops sex.... When then, it can be shown that sex distinction in the human race is so excessive as not only to affect injuriously its own purposes, but to check and pervert the progress of the race, it becomes a matter for most serious consideration. Nothing could be more inevitable, however, under our sexuo-economic relation. By the economic dependence of the human female upon the male, the balance of forces is altered. Natural selection no longer checks the action of sexual selection, but cooperates with it.[5]

Using sex differentiation to confine women to sex-associated activities, at the pleasure of the domineering male possessing them, led sex to have a "deteriorating" effect on "race progress." Women's seclusion was enforced by the savage male seeking to mate on demand, so that "the mate becomes also the master" for the first time in human history. These exaggerated sex functions went beyond their natural and intended limits, with "the two great evolutionary forces"—natural selection and sexual selection—rather than checking one another, "acting together to the same end; namely to develope [*sic*] sex distinction in the human female."⁶

Prehistoric men chose the easiest option of selecting smaller, weaker women to subdue and mate. Thereby, hitherto larger, stronger female forebears, differentiated from their male peers only by genital-reproductive systems, quite literally became extinct. They failed to reproduce themselves. Instead, women had become weak, cowardly, delicate, insecure, and manipulative, all marking what Gilman called "excessive sex distinction," manifest in "the body of woman." Reform Darwinism held that localized factors and distinctive environments caused different ethnic groups to evolve at different rates. Viewed at any one moment, variations marked different human groups. Thus, in the evolution of these excessive sex distinctions, Gilman noted that the women of some groups were more exclusively confined to "sex work" and exercise of "sex functions" with less access to race work alongside men than others. Certain androcentric institutions marked this dramatically: the harem, purdah, the bound foot, veiling, the open buying and selling of women—all characteristics that appeared to mark cultures closest to the earlier human stages of barbarism and savagery. Reform Darwinists like Gilman, Ward, and others sincerely saw in this theory a scientific account of manifest differences between the peoples of the world. It is, of course, now all too clear how this account seamlessly imposed the hierarchically differential bodies, politics, cultures, and ethical dispositions that became the stuff of negative eugenics and racial theoretics. Meanwhile, the Lamarckian legacy in reform Darwinism meant that its adherents believed that acquired characteristics transmitted to descendents. The democratic process of inheritance meant that successor males paid a price for so confining women, with female weakness and smallness being passed on and retarding, in effect, the people as a whole. Hence, Asian and Middle Eastern cultures, whose conditions historically had enabled men to be able to confine women most comprehensively, showed also the most evolutionary impact of androcentrism, while cultures with circumstances and environments in which total female seclusion was impracticable showed less impact of female bodily weakness and "excessive sex distinction." Here she described the

Germanic tribes as characterized by less sex distinction and implied more marked androgyny than other human groups.[7]

Women's oppression produced their parasitism on men, marked in women's self-presentations and the sexual identity they adopted in the sphere reserved for them, the home. This marking of women as sex parasites had its origins in their ancient enslavement: "In spite of economic waste, each man thinks himself entitled to one whole woman to wait on him. . . . It is the fact of that ancient usefulness, and the persistence of its value in the still useful consortium which so complicate the constitution of parasitism among women. . . . Leaving any direct or indirect service aside we come to the real basis of women's parasitism, the sex relation . . . for this alone is the 'gold digger' of all grades maintained by the male."[8] She had developed these arguments in the 1890s, and as she explained to Houghton Gilman, most economic theories, including socialism, were flawed by blindness to the collective impact of these dynamics. In her earliest blueprints for *Women and Economics,* she noted that "men as individuals tend to socialize industry as naturally as they have socialized warfare or government. But where there [*sic*] sex-instinct comes in there remains individualism. By putting the sex relation on an economic basis—by making it a sex-characteristic of our species that the male 'support' the female, we have brought all the ferocity and belligerence of sex combat into the field of economic competition. . . . Men, single, organize as naturally as bees. Men, married, individualize on the instant."[9] She received positive responses from progressive reformers with whom she discussed her sexuo-economic theories in advance of writing *Women and Economics,* notably from Jane Addams, with whom she spent two days in July 1897.[10]

Gilman's critique of wives and mothers' economic dependence in her lectures encountered audience resistance. In 1915, a questioner asked her if it was not true that poor women generally received the husband's salary to manage "as best she can," while the woman of more means received a spending allowance. Was not Gilman exaggerating to suggest that there were "a large percentage of women who have to wheedle and beg for their clothes?" She replied:

> I have known some very rich women, so called, who had to ask for car fare. I know one . . . her husband was a rich man, and he paid her bills generously and never gave her any money. They were going to a church fair. Now, it is no good going to a church fair unless you have real money. She wanted some to spend and he said, "Nonsense, tell me when you want anything and I will get it for you." That woman became very much enraged. She waited until her husband was conversing with a group of friends and neighbors, and then she went over to the group and said to a man who knew her and her

husband well, "Will you lend me five dollars, I have no money?" ... And the husband quickly produced the five dollars. ... It was an object lesson he never recovered from. It is true that a great many women do have to ask and tease.

She added that allowances were the exception and that generous men much preferred to gift money, resenting any claim that granting an allowance implied. With such concrete examples of the ramifications of androcentric sexual arrangements, she challenged contemporaries who justified these same arrangements.[11]

She told audiences that the most evil consequence of women's economic dependence was in the exaggeration of

all those faculties and methods by which they continually seek to attract and please the other sex. A good woman, healthy, vigorous, clean, reasonably handsome woman is sufficiently attractive as a woman without piling on top of that all the arts and inventions attainable in order to increase the power by which she makes her livelihood. It has a bad influence on the race for either sex, and especially the mother sex to have to use that great distinction, for motherhood to have to use it as an occupation, as a business, as Ida Tarbell has so infelicitously called the "business" of being marketed.

Here she referred to antisuffragist journalist and historian Ida Tarbell's popular text of 1912, *The Business of Being a Woman*. To Gilman's horror, this influential public intellectual, with whom she at times shared public platforms, sought to renaturalize the very sexual economics that Gilman sought to discredit by insisting, instead, that love and sexual relations ought not to be a business: "That relation should be entirely free from any taint of economic advantage. Love and money do not belong together, and it is the greatest source of the greatest evil in humanity that love and money may have been forced together by the dependency of women."[12]

Lopsided androcentric culture deployed only half of human attributes in politics, industry, religion, art, and education, with the lamentable consequences of war, competition, prostitution, and women's weakness and vanity. Indeed, ignorant women's stagnation at a primitive evolutionary stage created a chasm between the sexes. With captured women's forced submission to constant sexual relations, too many births resulted, providing incentives for unpalatable birth control choices such as abortion. Moreover, dependent wives endured infidelity, whether with prostitutes or others, and consequently suffered venereal diseases and birth defects: "A servile and dependent womanhood cannot be educated or strengthened to the purifying of our race from this pathological condition."[13]

In garments whose main purpose is unmistakable to announce her sex; with a tendency to ornament which marks exuberance of sex energy, with a body so modified to sex as to be grievously deprived of its natural activities; with a manner and behavior wholly attuned to sex advantage, and frequently most disadvantageous to any human gain; with a field of action most rigidly confined to sex relations . . . the female of genus *Homo* is undeniably over-sexed.[14]

Gilman constantly noted the impact of such sexual economics on women's bodies, particularly with regard to dress. Conventional sex-distinguishing dress partly functioned to secure women their parasitic livelihoods. Whereas in other animal species, the decorative male competed with other males for females, androcentric culture reversed nature, forcing women to prettify and compete. "In the human species alone the female assumes the main burden of sex-attraction, on the simple and all-too-evident ground that in the human species alone the female depends on the male for her living." Such sex advertising was a crude perversion, indeed an unsexing of women since they thereby adopted a natural male distinction. If sex distinction were working normally, she contended that "women would demand in men a rich variety, a conspicuous impressive beauty. The world would throb and brighten to the color music of Nature's born exhibitor, the male." By contrast, while women with their war paint, beads, and feathers had become male in their sex attraction behavior, males had become female with their "contented serviceable obscurity" in appearance. Essentially, this was an intersex transfer in terms familiar in Veblen's *The Theory of the Leisure Class* (1899). The gorgeous male raiment in human history belonged to men who did not have to work. In an era "where work and manhood are coterminous," a man exhibited his prosperity on his woman. So women, degraded from their high estate, "the choosing mothers of the world," had become "the exhibitors on approval."[15]

The human purpose of dress should be protection, comfort, modesty, and functionality. Good dress should be simple, durable, and well-constructed from high-quality materials. Instead, dress eroticized women's bodies. Men proclaimed their investment in eroticized dress by ridiculing dress reform, which typically deemphasized erogenous zones and freed women's respiration and limbs for freedom of movement, as "unsexing" women. Walter Stetson did just this in his mocking dress reformer Dr. Mary Walker. Since feminine dress advertised women's availability for parasitic sexual contracts, dress reform women, symbolically at least, made themselves unavailable.[16]

Sexualized dress was an industrial necessity for women in androcentric cultures. Gilman observed its primitive, even "savage" qualities, whether in hairstyles, hats, jewelry, or cosmetics, all newly commodified in the early twentieth century. Whereas once, only prostitutes "advertised" themselves through adornment, increasingly all women adopted these standards. The distinctions between women trading sex for a livelihood and other women thereby became blurry. Dress was also a means of women's unnatural competition among themselves to be partners in sexual contracts with men. Mindless, wasteful, ever-changing fashions carried this unfortunate human reversal of nature to absurdity, without sound aesthetic judgment.[17]

In "The Dress of Women" (1915), Gilman distinguished women's dress from men's in a number of critical respects. While men's clothing was most determined by physical conditions—their occupation, the climate, or their social class—women's clothing "is most modified by psychic conditions. As they were restricted to a very limited field of activity, and as their personal comfort was of no importance to anyone, it was possible to maintain in their dress the influence of primitive conditions long outgrown by men . . . the dress of women is still most modified by the various phases of sex distinction." So clear was the sex-distinguishing symbolism of dress that every anxious little boy madly sought his first trousers to proudly exhibit "the fact that he is a boy."[18]

Unlike men's clothes, adapted as protection for various occupations, the daily dress of wives and mothers engaged in housework and childcare consisted of the long full-skirted dress in a cotton print pattern. Dresses absorbed grease during meal preparation, becoming highly flammable around the wood fires used for cooking, unlike men's coarser-woven work clothes. Saturation from laundry water and floor and wall washing made dresses damp and uncomfortable, especially when hanging sheets in winter winds. Long dust-dragging skirts impeded the frequent bending and standing required to do housework, as well as climbing up and down stairs, especially with a baby in tow, resulting in many accidents. Surely housework and childcare warranted the wearing of trousers? Gilman extolled the excellent tunic and pantsuits of Chinese women, noting that even the woman of harems, with nothing to do beyond erotically serving their masters, wore trousers.[19]

Highlighting cross-cultural examples of the crippling foot binding of Chinese girls and the "veiling and muffling of women in various Eastern nations," Gilman concluded that customs and patterns in woman's clothing showed "more visibly, more constantly than any words, how exclusively she is considered as a female; how negligible has been her relation to society as a whole." Indeed, the injury inflicted by women's dress was its dual function of magnifying sex and limiting women's social development, their clothing accounting for the much vaunted "feebleness of women," their "slowness, awkwardness, weakness, tottering inefficiency." Her cross-cultural and historical comparisons played on common biases. Assuming readers would readily follow her condemnation of misogynist and barbarous ancient Greek, Chinese, and Middle Eastern markings of femininity, she turned the tables, insisting that in "what we fondly call civilized countries" women were just as retarded by clothing and related customs—particularly by the triad of the corset, the skirt, and the shoe.[20]

The long skirt pressured legs, limiting motion, while women's shoes tortured feet, especially on long walks. Gilman particularly reviled high-heeled shoes and boots, producing the archetypal pelvic-tilted, undulating feminine walk, rendering the walker incapable of a vigorous stride. Moreover, the endlessly plumed hat incensed her as impractical, ugly, or absurd, the ultimate symbol of women's enslavement to arbitrary changes of fashion.[21]

Finally, the corset critically anchored Gilman's exposé of women's dress. By contriving the smallest possible waist (at great cost to the health of the internal organs, muscles, and bones), the corset emphasized the breasts and hips, sexualizing, and in Gilman's view, dehumanizing. "Put on a corset, even a loose one, on a vigorous man or woman who never wore one, and there is intense discomfort" since it pressured the muscles and constrained all movement of the trunk, while "the stomach is choked, the process of digestion interfered with." She denounced the manipulations of fashion houses:

> those whose high mission it is to decide the size and shape of a woman's body . . . have given us first the "straight front" corset, and then the amazing object . . . which runs from waist to knee, almost; which binds up hip and abdomen with steel, bone, and elastic; and seems to serve principally as a supporting framework for a rigorous and complicated system of gartering. . . . If any man will solemnly fasten himself to one of these elaborate devices, and then try to pursue his customary avocations, he will feel at once, the mechanical disadvantage resultant.[22]

The corset example illustrated something broader about human capacities to accept "the most disadvantageous conditions, and fail to notice them." If her immediate concern was excessive sex distinction marked through such tortures as the corset or high-heeled shoe, the propensity of human groups to find unnoticeable "glaring evils" was her more general conclusion. Thus, in *Women and Economics,* her analysis took the corset and the shoe as marking human "racial habits" of leaving absurd or evil practices unchallenged to which groups had become inured. She immediately followed the examples of corset and dress details with that of chattel slavery, "an unchallenged social institution from earliest history down to our own day among the most civilized nations of the earth. Christ himself let it pass unnoticed. The hideous injustice of Christianity to the Jew attracted no attention through many centuries." She added that humans readily criticize the customs of nations other than their own, while fiercely resenting "the charges of the critic" against their own traditions. Under these circumstances, conditions appearing timeless and transcultural were least likely to attract criticism, and Gilman insisted that "the sexuo-economic relation is such a condition. It began in primeval savagery. It exists in all nations," and any criticism of it was unpardonably "offensive to many," as shown by the hostility met by abolitionists and feminists. Nowhere were local manifestations of that hostility louder or so symbolically laden as the rebuke of dress reformers among feminists.[23]

Consonant with women's dress, all phases of women's lives reflected "the sex relation," however unrealistically. Little girls played with dolls, prematurely encouraged to confine their play and imaginative development to their specific sex and reproductive functions. Adolescence was the short era of apprenticeship for the business of matrimony, succeeded all too soon by the hard labor and difficult negotiations of marriage and motherhood. But besides these functions, generally completed by age forty, androcentric culture had no honorable or productive roles for women who might live three or four more decades beyond the period of those responsibilities. They were expected to be invisible, pliant old ladies, defined as dependents of their sons in widowhood, caring for daughters and daughters-in-law in their grandmotherhood.[24]

Vexed Sexed Sites

> For each man to have one whole woman to cook for and wait upon him is a poor education for democracy. The boy with a servile mother, the man with a servile wife, cannot reach the sense of equal rights we need today. Too constant consideration of the master's tastes makes the master selfish . . . the constant universal cause of "food diseases": that every man has one whole woman to cook for him. He has for so long confounded the two that the words "Wife" and "Cook" are almost synonymous to him. The dependent woman has this business of cooking as the one main way in which to show her love, to fulfill her service; and—alas! Secure any special concessions she desires.
>
> *Charlotte Perkins Gilman,* The Man-Made World *(1911)*

Gilman wrote the bulk of her prodigious theory and its outworking between 1898 and 1923. This quarter of a century's work involved important shifts in her longstanding concern with the impact of women's economic parasitism and "civilized vice." Her most celebrated publication, *Women and Economics,* had assaulted the corporeal contracts of marriage and prostitution squarely. The happily married Gilman undertook scrutiny of institutions, sites, and cultural identities central in maintaining and manifesting women's dependence and subordination. Having rearranged the terms of her own marriage to permit her to "both love and work," she promoted the ennobling effects of "human work" for all women. Hence, she mercilessly condemned those institutions and beliefs preventing women's access to human, nonfamilial work. Androcentric economic dependency barred half the human race from "race development" on the grounds of sex. Particular targets were the home and its key industry, home cooking.[25]

Gilman's criticisms of "the home" have received considerable attention in the context of her utopianism. Her designs for "kitchenless" houses fascinate feminists and theorists of a range of persuasions. Yet the strongest element of her analysis of the home was a chilling description of it as the "racially" retarded primitive wife/mother's prison. Of course, for "about eight million" wives of all races and ethnicities in paid labor, the home could not have the precise significance Gilman gave it. Nonetheless, the main claim she advanced applied to many domestic units of her period:

> The home has not developed in proportion to our other institutions, and by its rudimentary condition it arrests development in other lines.... The two main errors in the right adjustment of the home to our present life are these: the maintenance of primitive industries in a modern industrial community, and the confinement of women to those industries.... Much that we consider essential to... home and family life is not only unnecessary, but positively injurious.... What is a home? The idea of home is usually connected with that of a family, a place wherein young are born and reared, a common shelter for the reproductive group.... Wherever the mother feeds and guards her little ones—more especially if the father helps her—there is, for the time being, home. This accounts at once for the bottomless depths of our attachment to the idea.

Therefore, the true basis of the primitive state of the home, and of women's existence within it, was "the sex relation" itself, entailing the mastery of men bodily over women. While to men out in the nondomestic world, "home" first means mother—adding, "as it does to all creatures"—it emphatically means also "his own private harem—be it ever so monogamous—the secret place where he keeps his most precious possession." Holding "the woman" and "the home" synonymous "gives the subtle charm of sex to man's home ideals."[26]

Nonetheless, men avoided homes as much as possible, experiencing

FIGURE 16. Portrait of Charlotte Perkins Gilman at age forty-three, 1903 (The Schlesinger Library, Radcliffe Institute, Harvard University 2005-M125-1-9)

"culture shock" transiting from men's to women's domains. Later Gilman put the problem baldly: by consorting with women—"lesser" creatures—men demeaned themselves or, in the language of imperialists, "went native" through sexual and domestic relations with their trivial, gossiping, insular, and small-minded stone-age housewives and coparents. Although men had caused and demanded this retardation of women, they then had the temerity to blame women for the ills of the world, indulging in misogyny. If a common result was "the bickering which is so distinctive a feature of family life," another, superficially "pleasanter" but "deeply injurious to the soul," was the purported "affectionate dominance of the strongest member of the family," subordinating all household members.[27]

Gilman directly connected the stagnation of the home, and its industries, to the "arbitrary imprisonment" of women there, another outcome of men's ancient subjugation of women. Excluding women from industries they had originally founded, each man asserted the right to his own private harem with a woman dedicated entirely to his service. With the world left to men, nondomestic activities became "exclusively man's province, and 'the home' exclusively woman's." Working narrowly only for her own immediate family, the housewife became parochial and conservative.[28]

Yet the home functioned neither efficiently nor well. Home industries were wasteful and unhygienic, best demonstrated by cooking. Lacking professional training, ignorant housewives bought and served their families adulterated food, in meals displaying no grasp of nutrition. Ill-fed and hungry men frequented bars and taverns compensating with intoxicating stimulants. Small-scale single family purchasing meant that the housewife could attain none of the economies of scale that cooks could secure for large institutions. Wives often paid at least twice as much as restaurants or hospitals for the same goods or inferior ones.[29]

Womanhood stagnated in home industries centered on meal preparation for individual male breadwinners. If the childcare and housework tasks confronting the nine-tenths of American wives without servants constrained time available for cooking, Gilman estimated that "even the plainest of home cooking must take up a good proportion of the day. The cooking, service, and 'cleaning up' of ordinary meals, in a farmhouse, with the contributory processes of picking, sorting, peeling, washing, etc., and the extra time given to special baking, pickling, and preserving, take fully six hours a day. To the man, who is out of the house during work-hours, and who seldom estimates women's work at its true value, this may seem extreme, but the working housewife knows it is a fair allowance, even a modest one."

Thus she gave a central place to food purchasing, cooking, the serving of meals, and clean-up afterward as a paradigmatic instance of what ailed the conventional home. Cooking was highly significant as a sexed, conjugal encounter. Feeding was associated with the mother, but even in homes without children, the wife cooked the food the man provided and served it to him. Cooking was the most grinding and inescapable part of wifehood. She called wife and cook coextensive, even synonymous. Despite the obvious efficiency and significant savings inhering in professional cooks paid by communities of families, the male sex right of "our historic period" included not only the notion of "conjugal rights" but also the designation of each man's woman as his private cook. Indeed, since most people were too poor to keep servants, "most mothers spend their days mainly in the kitchen, most children grow up with the unavoidable conviction that the principal business of life is to get dinner." Such a sexualized distortion of a human activity like cooking under androcentrism was a horrible testament to women's subordination.[30]

Noting that the ultrafeminized woman became ultraconservative in the home with its crude familiarity and lack of individual privacy, the widening gulf between the sexes was one of its consequences, inimical to resolving conflicts. Indeed the home itself produced conflicts of interests between the sexes: "The mother—poor invaded soul—finds even the bathroom door no bar to hammering little hands. From parlor to kitchen, from cellar to garret, she is at the mercy of children, servants, tradesmen, and callers. So chased and trodden is she that the very idea of privacy is lost to her mind; she never had any, she doesn't know what it is, and she cannot understand why her husband should wish to have any 'reserves,' any place or time, any thought or feeling, with which she may not make free." Moreover, the home wasted its inhabitants' money, time, and strength by over a half of its economic value—making it highly inefficient.[31]

This definition of the mother as cook injured the child rearing from which "the home" supposedly derived much of its rationale. A mother could hardly devote correct and undivided attention to the training and character building of her children. She was too consumed with the pressing task of ensuring the timely tabling of breakfast, dinner, and supper for her demanding breadwinner. Even if she could do two things at once, the small divided-room structure of homes made children invisible while cooking, unless she kept them with her in that dangerous environment. Therefore, burns and other frightful kitchen accidents often resulted in infant mortality and injuries. Children fell down stairs and off chairs, ingested poisons, and broke bones with great regularity. The home was not a safe environment. Despite the sentimental verbiage about the sanctity of the home for child nurture, Gilman asked the reader to recognize that in androcentric culture the child was the lowest priority. The wife was unable to properly care for her children with the multiplicity of primitive home industries simultaneously required of her, unpaid and usually unaided. Children came a poor second. The results were plain to see. The discourse of maternal instinct obstructed much needed reforms in child culture. Gilman thereby sought what we could term the "denaturalization" of motherhood, especially the dogma of "the maternal instinct":

> If there were an instinct inherent in human mothers sufficient to care rightly for their children, then all human mothers would care rightly for their children. Do they? What percentage of our human young live to grow up? What percentage are healthy? . . . What percentage of our children grow up properly proportioned, athletic and vigorous? Ask the army surgeon who turns down the majority of applicants for military service. What percentage of our children grow up with strong, harmonious characters, wise and good? Ask the great army of teachers and preachers who are trying forever and ever to somewhat improve the adult humanity which is turned out upon the world from the care of its innumerable mothers and their instincts. Has maternal instinct evolved any method of feeding, dressing,

teaching, disciplining, educating children which commands attention, not to say respect?

Her answer, of course, was that leaving child rearing purely to instinct had disastrous results. Only the intervention of health and education professionals had wrought any notable improvement in the otherwise "disgraceful level" of care "generally existent" from untrained motherhood. "Of all the myths which befog the popular mind . . . this matriolatry is the most dangerous."[32]

Most so-called natural mothers performed maternal duties poorly. As mothers, in our present culture "we" were pathetically unfit, inadequate, ignorant and untrained. She lambasted the fabled maternal instinct as once perhaps sufficient for rearing the "thick-skulled baby" of the cave era, but completely insufficient for infant inheritors of twentieth-century human progress. Here we see how pervasively the reform Darwinist account of differential evolutionary development infused her analysis. Such comparisons, of course, are found highly offensive by her readers today, as discussed further in chapter 12. Yet, for Gilman, appeals to instinct only excused women's smugness, laziness, or ignorance. Such appeals also helped opponents of women's higher education. Far from instinctual, Gilman contended that motherhood was a skilled business, needing appropriate training, remuneration, and respect. For children to contribute to human progress on reaching adulthood, mothers had to develop their own humanity fully. To rear children correctly, mothers needed to understand history, sociology, biology, ethics, and other branches of knowledge. Countering essentialist rhetoric, she insisted that the future of the human race required investment in mothers as professionals. In short, progress required "the unnatural mother," an echo or reference back to the 1890s charges against Gilman herself, as an old friend slapped her face and shunned her for sending her daughter to live with the child's father and stepmother.[33]

Under present conditions, mothers could not or would not meet their children's needs. Disrespecting their children, they regarded them as wills to be dominated and trained to submit without question. A good child, from a mother's viewpoint, was one whose care could be compatible with cooking and other home industries. That ideal child would be pliant, submissive, and undemanding. Hence, mothers resented intelligent, creative, and curious children as a drain on their time and energies, often treating them with savage cruelty and arbitrary injustice. Mothers such as these were quite incapable of teaching children sound ethics or right conduct. Yet the mother typically resented any intrusion by other experts into the care of their child, terrified "lest her child should love some other person better than herself." This fact "shows that she is afraid of comparison—that she visibly fears the greater gentleness and wisdom of some teacher will appeal to the young heart more than her arbitrary methods."[34]

In her priorities, the "natural mother" gave mothering an incidental status. The home, and her identities within, centered on the duties of the conjugal contract, as specified by her master. This choice went back thousands of years, having its origins in the ancient enslavement of women. The modern result was patently absurd. Gilman often used the device of reversals to denaturalize such conditions, to enlist the sympathy of audiences. In a 1915 speech criticizing the assortment of primitive industries thrown together in the home, she asked men in her typically forceful style:

> suppose you were left a widower with a couple of small boys, suppose you wanted those boys brought up at home, suppose you wanted to engage a tutor for your boys, you would want that tutor to be not only a scholar but a gentleman, would you not? You would want him to teach them their lessons and also teach them morals and manners and general good behavior. Would you think it good business to engage for a tutor a man who was by profession a janitor and have him keep on janiting [sic]? Would you think it possible for any man you paid to take care of your children to at the same time take care of a house, be a cook, be a chambermaid, be a nurse, be all of them? It is not possible for mothers to rightly fulfill their work while they practice at the same time that combined and chaotic group of industries which goes on inside the sacred circle of the home. If you started a kindergarten, a nice place to teach little children, would you add to that a restaurant and a laundry at the same time . . . so that when people ate they could hear the children and smell the wash? Would you then let lodgings overhead and think people would enjoy sleeping in that combination?

She concluded her analysis of housework and childcare duties expected of the average untrained wife and mother with a simple assertion: "I claim that the industries of a single home are too much for one woman." Noting the increasing reports of nervous breakdowns among women, insanity especially prevalent among farmers' wives—perhaps the most isolated and cruelly overworked women of all—she called for drastic changes in women's lives. Sex slavery was the lot of women in androcentric culture, marked by the dysfunctional and toxic state of marriage, femininity, the home, motherhood, and child rearing. Finally, Gilman characterized some pervasively negative features of this androcentric culture in terms of its masculinity. She would call the dominant gendering of the culture "masculism," especially the urge to combat.[35]

War as Androcentric History

> It does not suit women to have their men kill each other. In the man-made world, the women have to bear misfortune just because the men like the glory of fighting. History is made up of the exploits of men, never of women. . . . As long as the women of the world are kept inferior to men, so long as freedom and education [are] . . . kept away from them, that is why we have war. This means the limit of every civilization. History should be the story of our racial life. Men have made it the story of warfare. The growth of the world is made by the arts, the sciences, the trades and crafts and professions, religion, philosophy, and not murder.

Charlotte Perkins Gilman, "War and Women" (1917)

Born during the Civil War, aware of the Crimean and various African and Indian wars of the British Empire, to say nothing of America's imperialist Cuban, Philippines, and Mexican entanglements, Gilman gave combat a central place in her analysis of androcentric culture. The Great War sharpened her account of war as fundamental to androcentric politics, economies, cultural values, and distributions of resources. Her reform Darwinist and Ward-influenced account of human sex differences and women's subjection readily accorded combat profound significance but led to stances on particular wars distinct from those of Progressive Era pacifists, who did not share her theoretical analysis of androcentric culture. It is worth examining the terms in which she analyzed war and combat, especially during the 1914–17 period, when issues arising from the European war, which the United States joined in April 1917, had a great impact on her writing and thinking.[36]

For Gilman, war was the ubiquitous outcome of androcentric culture. As a male sex instinct, useful for providing females with the best mates through intermasculine combat, fighting had eliminated weaker males in prehistoric conditions. Alongside erotic desire and self-expression, combat was one of the three chief male sex traits. It had become, however, a primitive excrescence in civilized cultures, in which females no longer had the ancient right of initiating sex selection. It was enlarged and maintained beyond both its natural and historical limit. Sadly for humanity as a whole, "men, with their unavoidable sex prejudice in favor of their own primitive and limited process of combat, have misinterpreted the whole record." In support of this misinterpretation, an entire cultural discourse extolling the benefits of struggle, pain, and overcoming enemies permeated all aspects of androcentric culture. Man's "innate sex prejudice" displayed itself in the conventional "theory of combat," which held that "only under the stimulus of opposition are the faculties developed," with war or opposition functioning as a "spur to action." The values of cooperation, collective and harmonious work received short shrift beside the glorious thrills of individual battle and triumph over others, who could then be used, exploited, or destroyed. In *Women and Economics,* she described these fundamental differences between the sexes: "The belligerence and dominance of the male is a sex-distinction . . . . the tendency to fight is a sex-distinction of males in general: the tendency to protect and provide for, is a distinction of females in general."[37]

By contrast, progressive growth, combining the best contributions of both sexes in a "human world," was the real business of human life; yet its prospects were stymied, even prevented, in conditions of war. Undue male dominance led to this sex instinct to combat being generalized as "human" and worshiped as normal and natural. The political apparatus of war wrestled with other priorities, often successfully securing resources for shipbuilding, munitions, and the subjugation of foreign peoples, over critical domestic goals for education, infrastructure, and medical care.[38]

Her analysis of war by no means treated war as a special and extreme case. Rather, Gilman demystified the specificity of war by placing it alongside a whole host of aggressive masculine behaviors and practices, on a continuum. Mass world war occupied the most extreme point, but she included other violent or coercive practices deriving from competitiveness, such as greed, jealousy, hatred, or cruelty, as all stemming from the male sex instinct to combat, now wreaking havoc in a modern world. The breadth of her continuum was striking. She included lynching of African Americans, the "color bar," imperialism in developing countries and adjacent territories, attempted genocide of native Americans, school playground bullying, college hazing or initiation trials, corporeal punishment, dueling, newspaper press sensationalism, corrupt corporations, inflated national pride, crime, wife beating, and enforced conjugal rights, and the sexual coercion or seduction of females in work environments—later called sexual harassment. She contemptuously refuted the sentimental axiom that man was woman's "natural protector." At a suffrage debate in 1903, she observed that men did not care for women beyond those of their immediate family: "Did you ever think that the natural protector of women is the one thing on earth that she is afraid of more than anything else, more than she is of lions or crocodiles or bears? A man once said to me: 'Any true man will escort a woman at night and protect her.' I turned to him and asked: 'Protect her from what?'"[39]

So "normal" were these forms of aggression in this "combat-poisoned race mind of ours" that to oppose them courted charges across quite another continuum. Critics risked being called unrealistic or utopian or mawkishly feminine or else treasonous, disloyal, "un-American." Moreover, Gilman maintained that, far from being cordoned off into a discrete masculine realm, the combat instinct deeply inflected sexual relations of all kinds. It had an erotic charge and dire eugenic consequences for populations. In 1914 at New York's Astor Hotel, she addressed these themes, as recounted here in a *New York Times* report:

> "War has been defended by men, because its defenders were men," continued Mrs. Gilman. "Its glories were masculine. Through long association throughout the centuries the pain of war has become associated with the pleasure of love, to which it was usually a preliminary. For uncounted ages struggle and pain were the accompaniment of masculine desire. That accounts for the stern, rugged rapture of war to men. Yet war has been more harmful to the human race than to any other race of animals; for while animals merely fight to kill, man alone not only kills, but wipes out entire civilizations. Moreover, the men who go to war are the fit. They leave the unfit, the old and weak and defective at Home to breed the next generation."[40]

Again here, her reasoning was inflected by the reform Darwinist tenet of differentiation. Just as male sex selection meant the capture of the slowest, smallest, weakest women, so needless artificial wars eliminated not the weakest men, as did natural selection, but the strongest and best, thereby weakening the human race.

The glorification of the male sex instinct to combat provided a key cause of women's subjection in androcentric culture. All forms of male combat devastatingly affected women, yet women were not involved in relevant decision making. No one sought their consent, yet wartime authorities expected their service and support. Militarists and pronatalists thunderously asserted women's obligation to breed "cannon fodder." Otherwise, they were to knit socks for men at the front and divert their domestic skills to support war efforts. She connected women's lack of citizen rights, especially suffrage, to the proliferation of pointless, horrifying global war. Moreover, she contended that a world with economically independent women, contributing equally to human "race-work" in all spheres, would be a world unwilling any longer to go to war. After all, elimination of the weak by the strong through combat did nothing to improve, grow, or develop the victor's characteristics. The effort used for fighting opponents could have been used to solve problems and improve each nation.[41]

She insisted that the broader cultural enshrining of competition, whether in economic, educational, or cultural life, was nothing more than another instance of generalizing as "human" men's specific sex instincts to combat. Except in defense of their young, females showed no combat instinct. It was a male sex characteristic. With regard to industry, she insisted especially vehemently that sex combat had "no place in an economic system." Moreover, sex combat, in the form of "competition, introduced into business, has been a discordant jarring note all through our civilization. One reason why the other half of humanity should be introduced into the business of the world is because they, the women, lack that instinct of sex combat and have instead an instinct of growth."[42]

To Gilman, military life seemed to enhance the worst features of androcentric culture, exacting both direct and indirect cruelty on women. All-male communities begat misogyny, violence, and a veneration of death. Men's self-indulgent masculism was a sex distinction, driving them to kill one another in so many trivial and tribal disputes. In ancient times, when women were workers, and could sustain themselves, men were unnecessary to their livelihoods. "One husband and father went a long way," in polygamous circumstances, having mainly sex variation functions. In the contemporary world, however, where women were economic dependents, men's catapult of the world into war was an unmitigated disaster: "The natural masculine qualities of rivalry and combativeness, unmodified by feminine qualities have maintained in society an insistent competition with its ultimate expression in war; while the over development of sex, inevitably resultant from the use of it by men allowed by her economic dependence, has produced most injurious conditions in that field."[43]

If these were Gilman's general theoretical positions on the significance of combat and war within androcentric culture, she saw the First World War as a worsening instance of these deeper patterns. While she "came out" as a pacifist in 1916, it was obvious that she could not particularize this war in the way that many other pacifists did. To such contemporaries, her stances were at least disappointing, if not truly vexing. She criticized America's excessive neutrality and isolationism, urging national leaders to adopt a higher profile in efforts at international arbitration and other efforts to end the war, short of becoming a combatant. Praising the Ford Peace Expedition, a privately funded deputation of distinguished Americans to Europe aiming to further peace talks, she fiercely attacked press denigration of these efforts. Yet, annoyingly for pacifists, she did not believe that the round of petitions and letter writing that they advocated had any practical value whatever in the quest to end this particular war. She urged the creation of international councils and other such structures that might work to prevent war on this scale from ever happening again. While the present war presented women with opportunities for organizing, its primary effect was to bring forth tragedy. For instance, much discussion focused on the sex imbalance resulting from the shocking casualties among marriageable European men:

> For every man killed some woman is left husbandless, some children unborn. We cry out upon women for restricting the birthrate, but how can we keep it up without marriage? And how can we marry without men? Is it expected of women that they bear children out of wedlock, or reintroduce polygamy? . . . Are they to be silenced with prating of "motherhood," and "home duties," when each of those buried men has taken with him to the grave a woman's hopes? . . . If we repudiate forever that ancient status of polygamy; if we repudiate also that convenient last resort of all "unemployed women"—prostitution, then what shall women do?

Gilman ventured that these women could do worse than work, serve mankind, and engage in social motherhood, rather than individual motherhood, but it was "a greater thing to love mankind than to love a man. It is a greater thing to love all children than to love one's own."[44]

The First World War forcibly raised the injustices of women's economic dependence. Gilman's attention directly turned to demographic questions, especially sex ratios and marriage markets. Though her fictional husbandless women went out West (explored in her novels like *The Crux* [1911] and other fiction), European countries, at least, faced the prospect of a generation of marriageable women who would not have the option of choosing monogamous marriage and motherhood on any terms. In considering their options in a 1914 article reflecting on soldier mortality so far on European battlefields, Gilman anticipated the world of women depicted in *Herland* (1915). For Herlanders, the desire for motherhood in the absence of men (due to war and volcanic eruption) was resolved by the development of parthenogenesis. What did Gilman suggest for real women adversely affected by war?

> Out of this great army of women whose personal hopes are even now being buried on those red European fields, will rise a new spirit, a spirit of world motherhood. They should organize, forming huge bodies of united women, strong in mutual support. War-widows, and war-maidens, all bearing a common grief, strengthened by a common purpose, uplifted by a common hope. The hope of Europe, the hope of the world, lies ever more in its women. What men have not done, they must do. Where men have failed they must succeed. The bitterness, the discord, the jarring hatreds, the greed and dishonesty, the pride and ambition of previous civilizations they must

forgo—outlive forever. The history of the past is a history of men's fights. Let the history of the future be a history of women's service.[45]

In 1914, Gilman condemned the war as "masculism at its worst." Yet men could not make war without women's tacit support. Gilman urged that women ostracize bellicose, warlike men. Their aggression needed to meet disapproval and stigma from women. When her public speeches advanced these claims, she often encountered misogyny or woman-blaming audiences. For instance, in 1917, one questioner asked: "Isn't it the fault of women that men are so brutal because if women brought men up right they would not be so brutal?" She replied rapidly, indignantly: "When one party of the two is bigger and stronger, and wiser than the other, has behind him all religion and government, the whole power and management of the world; when throughout history he has treated the other party with contempt, and then when he does wrong, goes and blames the woman for it, [it] is about as mean a thing as could be done."

Not satisfied, another heckler demanded of her: "Isn't it true that such a great sovereign as Queen Victoria could have prevented the great war with the Boers?" Adamantly, she replied: "No one woman can prevent war. I said that when all women are sharing a half of the power with the men, the women will be able to accomplish what they desire. Not woman alone, not man alone, but the two together, then war will cease." But when a third questioner asserted that, "in regard to war and women, is not it true that women in the warring countries are just as much at fault to prolong the war which is raging?" she retorted: "Suppose you saw twenty-five million women all out desperately engaged in carrying on war, and the men left at home, suffering from the effects of a war, not desired by them, never made by them, but made by women. Would you say the men were to blame for it? Never! You would not say they are as much to blame. They do not want it. It's man's game. How can you hold women responsible? They are trained in the dogmas and doctrines of this man-made world, and they cannot help it at present."[46]

Gilman did not see any contradiction between her stated pacifism and her steadily enlarging dismay about German aggrandizement, national character, and atrocities. She had visited Germany in 1904, and while greatly admiring many features of its culture and achievements, she found its misogyny unmistakable. In 1906 she had reviewed Otto Weininger's hostile philosophical diatribe against women and femininity and, on later occasions, drew attention to the misogyny and masculism of Nietzsche, Schopenhauer, and other German philosophers. Sharing the horror of ordinary

FIGURE 17. American delegates to the International Congress of Women on board the S.S. *Stoordam*, including Jane Addams, holding up a large "Peace" banner, 1915 (The Schlesinger Library, Radcliffe Institute, Harvard University A39-261-1)

Americans at the sinking of the *Lusitania* and other American ships and the accelerating German aggression toward Belgium and France, she favorably reviewed Owen Wister's 1916 article, which hypothesized a gradual corruption of the German character and nation over a couple of generations, as background to the present conflagration. Further, she denounced H. L. Menken's praise of a misogynist German novel, ending with "Mr. Mencken does not belong in America."[47]

Once the United States entered the war in April 1917, she ceased pacifist protest in favor of work in international arbitration to prevent future wars. Conflicts over pacifism divided the Greenwich feminist luncheon club to which she belonged—the club Heterodoxy—whose ardent pacifist members included Crystal Eastman, Rose Pastor Stokes, and Elizabeth Gurley Flynn. When feminist journalist Rheta Childe Dorr resigned over the club's pacifist orientation, Gilman soon followed, though she reestablished her connection again in the 1920s. In her bitter autobiography she wrote of Heterodoxy that she found it "interesting for a while, but when the heresies seemed to center on sex psychology and pacifism, I wearied of it." But many members were friends who she respected. When the federal government's draconian wartime security act—which resulted in the imprisonment and eventual deportation of anarchists like Emma Goldman and Ben L. Reitman—was used against fellow Heterodoxy member Stokes for simply speaking against the war and capitalist interests fostering it, Gilman wrote to the attorney general protesting the ten-year sentence and begging for clemency, if only to protect the rule of law.[48]

If war was offensive for its glorification of violence and death, these tendencies were, in Gilman's view, directly fostered by androcentric religions. She identified death, suffering, punishment, and authoritarianism at the heart of all world religions. The Christian version involving Heaven and Hell, with its burning fires, seemed to her particularly obnoxiously framed around masculist values. Androcentric religion had winners and losers, rewards and admonishments, errors and retribution, and a general aura of competition so congenial to men. She maintained that all world religions "overestimated death and underestimated life." Moreover, the "dominant masculinity in the evolution of religions" was instanced in the "guileless habit of blaming women for the sin and trouble of the world."[49]

Nowhere was this religious masculism clearer than the stimulus it had provided historically for war and imperialism. Gilman's fictional character Ellador, the woman from the all-female country Herland, articulated these observations about the connections between religion, war, and attempted genocide. In the name of religion, men committed more wars, murders, and atrocities than in any other cause. Ellador had hoped that Christianity would be better than other religions on this score—but instead, its record of proselytizing at sword and gunpoint disturbed her greatly. She instanced the deterioration of the Hawaiians under American occupation, regaling her husband Van indignantly:

> "The missionaries came and—interfered. Now these natives and owners of the land are only 15 per cent of the population. . . . They are dispossessed and are being exterminated."
>
> ". . . I didn't do it—you're not blaming me, are you?"
>
> "Did not—America—do it?" she asked quietly. "And do you care at all?" . . .
>
> "We wanted to Christianize them—to civilize them," I urged rather sulkily.
>
> "Do you think Christ would have had the same effect on them? And does civilization help dead people?"

More practically, Gilman believed that most organized religions perpetrated reactionary values that ran counter to an ethic of progressivism. Stoicism in the face of suffering caused by injustice, fatalism about poverty, disease, inequality, oppression and misfortune, all these were the daily hallmarks of world religions. Thus, teasing her fiancé about taking his father to Church on Sundays, she jibed that if everyone did so "you would see the world wag backward pretty fast if we all went to the church of our fathers continually."[50]

IN HER ANALYSIS of the androcentric practices and institutions of her culture, Gilman stressed women's dress, the home, the mother, child rearing, war, and religion. Underlying her criticisms of each was her overarching identification of the dependent parasitic position of women in relation to men. The sex relation itself had evolved into being the rationale for this situation. Home was an unhygienic, poorly designed, and tastelessly decorated prison, established for the private cooking of men's meals by his dependent untrained helpmate. It was inimical to the proper care of children.

Women's "sex work" had to be reduced, replaced by their contribution to "race work." Gilman frequently discussed strategies for admitting women to work that aided human progress by redefining cooking, shopping, housecleaning, laundry, and childcare as amenable to professionalization. But these strategies were not ends in themselves. These areas of work and service must become independent of women and sexuality. By insisting on the historicity and contingency of androcentric mores and institutions, she held that their viability was over. Humanity could progress only by using women's intelligence and resourcefulness, leading Gilman to seek women's rights. After over half a century of its being classified as "the woman movement," a critical transformation was underway. The American political context for Gilman's analysis, discourses, activities, and proposed strategies came to be known as feminist.

PART TWO

"As to Feminism"

When we consider the woman movement of the last hundred years, four books stand out in English literature as milestones in its intellectual progress— Mary Wollstonecraft's "Vindication of the Rights of Women," John Stuart Mill's "The Subjection of Women," "Women and Economics," by Charlotte Perkins Gilman, and Olive Schreiner's "Woman and Labor."

"Woman's Growing Revolt against 'Coercive Marriage'" (1914)

A complete and self-consistent social philosophy is what Mrs. Charlotte Perkins Gilman offers as no other woman can. And she furnishes it to her hearers in a stimulating, convincing form that is entirely her own. . . . You will not regret dedicating the time to mastering Mrs. Gilman's message because hers is probably the most brilliant woman's mind of this country, and while she looks far forward in her thinking, her good sense and knowledge of human nature dominate. She is a sane and wholesome feminist with faith in her sex.

Mary Hutcheson Page to Mrs. Parker, 10 March 1917

GILMAN'S FEMINIST analysis led her, almost inevitably, to focus on women as a political constituency. She identified women as an interest group in the polity comparable with African Americans, Native Americans, and organized labor. This approach emerged logically enough from the historical and evolutionary analysis of women's situation centering her contribution to Western feminist theory. Their disabilities, as a sex constituting at least half the population of most androcentric cultures, acted to retard human progress—race work, as she called it. The undue and prolonged empowerment of the formerly puny male fertilizer furnished little hope that men would voluntarily end, or even reduce, the worst features of androcentric culture. She recognized that women, as the great losers in the present regime, would need to mobilize to challenge existing cultural and economic patterns if her reform Darwinist feminist objectives to maximize human progress were to be realized. Humanity could not continue to proceed at only half the rate of which it was capable, by developing only one of its sexes—ultramodern industrial man. For this was a man who insisted on mating with a woman retarded to "Stone Age" level.

This general account of sexual asymmetry in social evolution formed the cornerstone of Gilman's oft-repeated explanation of her focus on women's rights and, eventually, feminism. Students of her full career may smile at a degree of suspected disingenuousness here. Her diaries show, quite decisively, a deep engagement with the Woman Question and "the Sex Question," long predating her specific conversion to Ward-inflected reform Darwinism. Her distinguished paternal family had long leadership within women's rights advocacy, especially of woman suffrage. This was hardly a legacy she would repudiate. Yet Progressive Era rejuvenation of American state and national-level suffrage campaigns, in close dialogue with British, Continental European, and Australian counterparts, rendered both suffragism and the associated advocacy of "feminism" contentious in public debate.

Gilman's intellectual and strategic explanation of her work for women's rights warrants scrutiny. Despite moments of distancing herself from the appellation "feminist," she was deeply invested in the progress of the woman suffrage cause specifically, and feminism more generally. Her objective was to secure a human world in which sex was a much less determining factor in shaping options and opportunities of both men and women.

Thus, the second part of the book investigates her work for, and engagement with, the feminism of her era. An important initial task is to disprove the claim that Gilman had no significant interest in, or commitment to, the cause of woman suffrage. Chapter 5 explores her extraordinary profile as one of the loudest and ablest voices advancing the suffrage cause. Her particular genius in rebuffing antisuffragist and misogynist rhetoric demands close attention, as do her expectations as to the political possibilities for a democracy comprising women as citizens with at least some sex-specific interests and needs.

Woman suffrage was straightforward compared with the matter of feminism. Gilman expressed seemingly contradictory sentiments about feminism, at once disclaiming it for herself and, yet, vigorously defining its parameters, purposes, and implications. Chapter 6 charts her vexed relationship with this vibrant new political philosophy in its American incarnation in the 1900s and 1910s. With her precommitment to reform Darwinism as the grounding for analysis of sex subjection, she could not accept analyses made in the name of "feminism" that ignored what, for her, were indispensable grids of intelligibility for advancing the cause of women and humanity. Yet for all the nuances she attached to her relationship to this vexed new political category, contemporaries did not hesitate in identifying her as one of the most significant public faces of feminism. Indeed, her critics, examined in chapter 7, called her the "high priestess of feminism."

For all her angst about feminism as a political label and affiliation, there is no question that the world Gilman passionately outlined and urged her peers to pursue, her "human world," was a world fundamentally shaped by feminist principles. Her inspiring vision for that world collided with contemporary realities, including attacks on women workers, new understandings of women's psychology and sexuality, and deep cultural resistance to women reducing or abandoning their confinement to "sex work" in favor of "race work." Chapter 8 appraises Gilman's feminist political objectives and the reform vision driving her challenge to what she famously called in 1911 "our androcentric culture."

CHAPTER FIVE

Woman Suffrage, the Antis, and Masculism

The Suffrage question stands loud in front and quite rightly so. In a democratic country there is no full equality without political equality. The economic independence of women advances rapidly both in theory and fact; it need make no public appeal except where the law interferes, and there it joins in the demand for suffrage.... There is no phase of women's work that does not need the assistance of political freedom.

Charlotte Perkins Gilman, "As to 'Feminism'" (1914)

GILMAN WAS passionate about woman suffrage, the preeminent struggle of the woman rights movement of her day, using pen and voice to advance "the cause" in many ways. She was a regular contributor to the venerable suffrage weekly, *Woman's Journal,* from the 1880s to 1916, becoming one of its feature editors in 1904. As noted previously, her first husband, Stetson, found her endless obsessing on this cause tiresome, partly blaming her political and intellectual work for ending his conjugal sexual regime.[1]

Citizenship was central to Gilman's theoretical schema for moving women from a primitive, privatized domestic relation to "the race" into a social relation, able thereafter to evolve as men had. Moreover, as editor of *Impress* (1894–95), and a contributor to many other journals thereafter, she called the ballot critical to the human progress of women.[2]

As such, woman suffrage had an analytically critical place in Gilman's most important theoretical treatise, *Women and Economics* (1898). There she assumed suffrage advocacy to be an obvious marker of the growing unrest among women, no longer willing to be parasites, dependents, living through their sex functions alone. That unrest had cost its advocates dearly for half a century, yet a new spirit animated their perseverance—and here she specifically named Elizabeth Cady Stanton, Susan B. Anthony (for whom the Nineteenth Amendment was eventually named by enfranchising women), and Dr. Elizabeth Blackwell, as well "as all the women who have battled and suffered . . . forcing their way, with sacrifices never to be told, into the field of freedom so long denied them—not for themselves alone, but for one another." This work was vital, despite all the ridicule, for the women "who follow and climb swiftly up the steps which these great leaders so laboriously built may do the new work in the new places."[3]

It was while editing *Forerunner* (1909–16) that Gilman's strongest prosuffrage sentiments emerged, beginning its publication the same year as the visit of English militant suffragette Emmeline Pankhurst. Some American suffrage leaders resented Pankhurst's efforts at fundraising for the English movement, when the American struggle remained to be won. Behind this apparent isolationism for many was an objection to suffragette militancy. By contrast, Gilman, who sat on the podium with Pankhurst in Carnegie Hall, felt a close connection to British suffrage developments, partly due to her several lecture trips and friendships there for more than a decade. This was a bond that she shared with Elizabeth Cady Stanton's daughter, Harriot Stanton Blatch, who Gilman met on her travels in England and who was a major force in regenerating the U.S. suffrage movement after 1910. Gilman served on the board of Blatch's suffrage society and spoke under its auspices in New York.[4]

Acclaimed as the leading U.S. feminist theorist of the era, Gilman was also read and discussed by women around the world. She saw her own influence on a younger generation of activists and theorists. For instance, after she wrote in warm praise of London-based actress, playwright, and suffragette, Cicely Hamilton (1872–1962), for her popular feminist text *Marriage as a Trade* (1909), and sent her a gift—probably a signed copy of *Women and Economics*—Hamilton replied: "My own work owes so much to you that I am glad to know that you are not ashamed of your follower." In 1913, Gilman spoke in London on a platform as an invited guest of Emmeline and Christabel Pankhurst in a crowded hall infiltrated by police and surrounded by hostile men of the general public.[5]

Her most distinctive contribution to "the cause" was to identify and debunk misogynist antisuffragist forces. Publicly she advanced the suffrage cause by exposing the "masculism" and backward reactionary thinking involved in antisuffragist discourse of the period. Defending the mission and objectives of woman suffragists, she mercilessly ridiculed those she called "the Antis." She excoriated those she called the "masculists," her name for the usual male opponents of woman suffrage, including liquor, vice, and gaming interests, but also those "Women Who Won't Move Forward"— female collaborators publicly opposing enfranchisement of their own sex, affirming the legislators ranting that "true" women disdained the vote.[6]

For Gilman, the intensity of public opposition to women's enfranchisement heightened the urgency of analyzing masculinity. Violence toward suffragettes revealed that the sexual contract obtaining in so-called "civilized" societies was based on female coverture and compliance, any deviation unleashing what contemporaries called "the brute in man." Her own version of reform Darwinism and reservations about Ward's theory of women's enslavement by violence made her dread the prospect of sex war. When addressing men and masculinity she sought to defang the brute, playing on men's pretensions to "civilized" (and even racialized) notions of superiority over more barbaric peoples believed to oppress women more flamboyantly.[7]

Though some suffragists fixated on the vote as an end in itself, Gilman insisted that wherever enfranchised, women had secured progressive results. Hence, like Rose Scott in Australia, she emphasized women's uses of their vote. Gilman sought to empower women, denouncing the ills of a manmade world and engendering confidence both in women and right-thinking men that women could enrich the democratic process and the polity.[8]

Enfranchisement: "A Foregone Conclusion"?

The [woman suffrage] parade was really superb; it was a great pleasure to march up Fifth Avenue, so wide and magnificent, with rank upon rank of spectators the entire way. . . . The estimates range all the way from 8000 to 20,000. . . . Roofs, windows, steps, sidewalks—and much of the street was solid humanity. . . . It was a surprise to everyone, I think—in its magnitude and dignity. . . . Charlotte was just ahead of me among the writers. . . . [She] looked remarkably beautiful—in white.

Grace Ellery Channing-Stetson to Edward B. Knight, 5 May 1912

Gilman's support for woman suffrage should be so obvious as to require no comment. Yet scholars contend that she was unenthusiastic about woman suffrage, based on a few primary sources, most citing a July 1890 letter she sent to her politically conservative girlhood friend, Martha Luther.[9]

She wrote, "I'm glad you have seen the sense in equal suffrage," suggesting a recent conversion on Luther's part. This sentence followed a paragraph chiding Luther for criticizing feminist Olive Schreiner's classic 1883 novel, *The Story of an African Farm:* "I do perceive between us more abysmal gulfs than I had thought. Are you just where you were when we parted, or have you grown to be an integral part of the present social world, and content therein?"—a world that Gilman sought to change. After this accusation, Gilman sought reconciliation in words that have been read as deprecation of the cause: "I never was a very ardent suffragist, it has long seemed such a foregone conclusion that I can't get at all excited over it. But it is vitally essential." Situated after both the Schreiner passage, and her praise of Luther's change of heart, this treatment of woman suffrage sought to minimize personal differences between them. The last sentence however—"But it is vitally essential"—is little quoted by those claiming Gilman's indifference to the suffrage struggle, who stress also her absence from major suffrage organizations, her impatience with compromise, and her declining the role of the "team player."[10] Yet it is plain that Gilman maintained her commitment to a cause whose achievement was anything but a foregone conclusion.[11]

Another source for claims of Gilman's indifference to the suffrage issue is a disparaging comment in her autobiography, much of which was written in the 1920s at the height her alienation from the new generation of women: "The basic need of economic independence seemed to me far more important than the ballot; though that of course was a belated and legitimate claim, for which I always worked as opportunity offered," adding the caveat that she did not think it was "as important as some of its protagonists held." Notwithstanding this hindsight remark, for many contemporaries, Gilman and woman suffrage were inextricably linked. After the Nineteenth Amendment passed in 1920, she was hardly the only suffrage advocate later disappointed with its only modest impact on the body politic.[12]

Woman suffrage work was mandatory for Gilman, whose Beecher relatives held office in the movement and were widely quoted in suffrage pamphlets, manifestos, and handbills.[13] Gilman had her own journey, though, toward understanding the canon of earlier analyses of the women's cause underpinning Progressive Era suffragist rhetoric. Hill reports that, just prior to Gilman's May 1884 marriage to Stetson, the bride-to-be read John Stuart Mill's, *The Subjection of Women* (1869). Attending her first woman suffrage convention in fall 1886, Gilman devoted that winter to works on women's status, including Margaret Fuller's *Women in the Nineteenth Century* (1851), even having Stetson read it to her of an evening, as noted in chapter 1.

From 1886 until her final separation from Stetson in 1888, she lived in separate quarters within the marital home, abandoned corsets and high heels, accelerated her workouts at the Providence gymnasium, and declined housework in favor of writing. In spring 1887, Gilman began writing the woman's column of the Providence *People,* addressing dress reform, fitness and health, the economic independence of women, courtship and marriage, and, as we have seen, an ultimately defeated local suffrage referendum so consequential in her April 1887 "breakdown." Meanwhile, Ward's "Our Better Halves" (1888), and his ongoing 1890s and 1900s essays and books posing women's subordination as a contingent and historical event, greatly influenced Gilman's analysis of sex differences and political possibilities, as discussed in chapter 3. Although her evolutionary poetry had captured Ward's attention, she had also published her early rebuke of the widespread antisuffragist claim that women did not want to vote, in the form of the poem, "Women Do Not Want It" in her 1893 collection, *In This Our World.* Here she both named and delegitimized male collective violence and coercion with sarcastic humor. Such tender consideration by men withholding the burden of suffrage from women! Did men always so agreeably only give women what they desired?

> Have women always wanted what you gave to us before?
> Did we beg for scolding bridles and ducking stools to come?
> And clamor for the beating stick "no thicker than your thumb"?
> Did we seek to be excluded from all the trades that pay?
> Did we claim the lower wages for a man's full work today?[14]

From the mid-1890s, her lecturing and writing garnered national attention. With publication of *Women and Economics,* reviewers called Gilman's treatment of "the Woman Question" the most significant landmark since Mill's treatise.[15] For the suffrage movement, which supplied her with many contacts and lecturing venues, she accepted discounted fees. Susan B. Anthony was so impressed with Gilman's suffrage advocacy that she arranged for her to speak at the 1896 hearing of the National American Woman Suffrage Association before the House of Representatives Committee on the Judiciary, in Washington, D.C. There she displayed her signature reform Darwinist approach:

> For unnumbered thousands of years women have suffered from repression and it has hurt them and hindered them and interfered with their development.... Every kind of creature is developed by the exercise of its functions.... And to bar any part of the race from its development is to carry along with society a dead weight, a part of the organism which is not living,

organic matter, which is a thing to be carried instead of to help. To give suffrage to this half of the race will develop it as it has never been developed before.[16]

Gilman advocated woman suffrage because men did not represent women's sex-distinct interests, a claim long used to justify male-only suffrage. In a spirited 1903 public debate at New York's Outlook Club, she reminded the audience that voters and legislators represented "certain vested interests." Any well-informed person could identify among Congressmen "sugar men, iron men, railroad men, wool men, Standard Oil men . . . who represent business interests." Every class of citizens needed the suffrage, since classes have different interests and "cannot be represented by another." The prevailing political coverture of women was a "survival of a patriarchy" and one that injured the body politic by bequeathing a class of disenfranchised citizens, contributing to "indifferent ignorance, apathy, a lack of public and civic spirit." Thereby, as wives and mothers, women retarded "the growth of men." She even made the startling statement that women fared worse in civilized democracies—"the only kind of a government where all men rule over all women"—than in past forms of government, which at least allowed queens to rule.[17]

Moreover, men stood to benefit from female enfranchisement. Indeed, woman suffrage "has its advantage to women in that it adds to her humanness; to the man in that it gives him a full-grown and equal friend, instead of an angel, an ideal, and a cook." The *Brooklyn Eagle* reported on Gilman's "strong talk on Woman Suffrage delivered last night before a large audience at the Queensborough Real Estate Exchange, Jamaica," as a campaign founded by Stanton more than fifty years before, a measure aiming to "raise the woman from an exclusively feminine position to a human position." Gilman asked listeners to recognize that:

> Five per cent of man is purely masculine, 5 per cent of the woman is purely "feminine," said the speaker, "while the other 95 per cent of us is human." Woman suffrage is not an attempt to make women masculine, but to humanize them. Women have their sphere as mothers, and the privilege of voting will not take that away; but outside of their purely feminine functions, they have their race function. Writing is not masculine or feminine, but a race, a human function. And so is language and religion and voting. Women were once only domestic servants. They are now taking up every kind of work and their interest is as broad as humanity.[18]

Once she edited her own journal, *Forerunner,* her suffrage commentary expanded and intensified. Considering the topic of "Woman and the State," she observed that women's increasing discontent about their political inequality had become "the most prominent issue of 'the woman question' in England and America," noting that the activity of the "militant suffragists" had "forced it upon the attention of the world." And in her lecture "Women and Democracy" she called disenfranchised women "subcitizens," who constituted "a huge inert class, distributed evenly throughout society, acting as a general check to the orderly development of government." Such limiting of women had evil if unconscious effects on democracy, threatening the health of the state. It would be Simone de Beauvoir in 1949 who would develop this crucial theoretical insight—that women's dispersal throughout the polity was unlike the situation of other oppressed groups. For Beauvoir, this dispersal was an obstacle to their political mobilization. For Gilman's reform Darwinism, this same dispersal across all other social groups was the contagion of their retardation throughout androcentric culture.[19]

Men exercised social functions like citizenship appropriate to modern cultures; women by contrast, used social functions "proper to the tribal stage .... an abnormal and injurious condition." Refusing to have sex reduced to analogy with other disenfranchised groups, she contended that if the non-voting population constituted a separate race, as did African Americans, "we should have only the anomaly of a subject race in a democracy," while if it constituted a separate territory, "like an Indian Reservation, we should have only the anomaly of a subject country in a democracy." In the case of women, however, "constituting as it does half the population of the democracy itself, it constitutes an anomaly without parallel." Women's disenfranchisement not only fossilized their access to power, but also constrained their thought and functioning as full members of the human race. The suffrage movement meant that the female half of democracies "who have been preserved in our midst, each one encysted in her prehistoric domestic envelope, shining dimly there like a fly in amber, is now in process of a sort of new birth." Voting women would emerge onto the public stage as new human beings.[20]

Closer acquaintance with the "militant suffragette" movement in England during her conference and lecture trip in 1913 heightened Gilman's impatience with women's ongoing disenfranchisement: "Here in England I am meeting many of those much discussed people, 'The Militants,' and many suffragists of other brands as well. I find in the militant ranks ladies of birth and breeding, of brains and scientific attainment . . . as well as [a] large body of 'just workmen'—working women, housewives, and eager young girls. Their devotion, their courage, their earnestness, is most impressive. Also their conviction of the rightness of their methods."

FIGURE 18. Men's League for Woman Suffrage March in 1915 Parade (Catt 5.10.2c., Carrie Chapman Catt Collection, Bryn Mawr College Library).

As to the contention about militant methods, she reported that some of the "outrages" attributed to them were "as deliberately planned as any military maneuver," while others mere individual acts attributed to the militants. Meanwhile, other acts attributed to the suffragettes were the work of "mischievous boys" or men with criminal intent doing damage, blamed on the movement "by the simple process of leaving some of their literature about." For instance, a man set fire to his own lumberyard, "with a view to collecting the insurance, and leaving a copy of *The Suffragette* stuffed into a wall on the premises to serve as an aniseed bag. It did so serve at first, but he was later discovered—with a false beard." She praised the diversity of cooperating suffrage organizations, including those with men as speakers and organizers, or entirely constituted by men, "the country fairly blossoming with them." The American public was unaware of "how hot and imminent the question is over here. In our big wide land, with its many states, we forge along in comparative peace . . . steadily advancing in spite of delays and set-backs. Here the whole progress of women seems to be massed against this one point, and with reason. Able women have given up their work to win this tool, this weapon, this necessary means of working. With that . . . all will be easier."[21]

If the "militants" impressed Gilman, her support for them in turn inspired other feminists otherwise skeptical about militant methods. Such

FIGURE 19. New York City 1915 Suffrage Parade (Catt: 5.8.3, Carrie Chapman Catt Collection, Bryn Mawr College Library)

was her international reputation as a feminist theorist that her association with the Pankhursts and their colleagues enhanced the reputation of the Women's Social and Political Union (WSPU)—the militant branch of the British suffrage movement. Her larger account of women's subjection and its redress convinced women hearing or reading Gilman of the agency they might have ahead, once enfranchised. One glimpse of Gilman's impact on audiences emerged from letters sent home by Bessie Rischbieth (1874–1967), a prominent Australian philanthropist and feminist who was visiting London in May 1913. Advised to hear Gilman, she found that "she was speaking from the platform of the WSPU," the Pankhursts' militant suffragette organization, "this great theatre ... pretty well crammed ... the doors outside were swarming with police." She found Gilman's central argument completely convincing, that "we have erred in emphasizing *sex* as we have made women economically dependent on man," praising Gilman for speaking "so logically, with such zeal and knowledge." Since Australian feminists had achieved both state and federal suffrage by the early years of the century, without militancy, they were apt to be indifferent or even opposed to such methods. Hence, Gilman's clear support of the suffragettes had a profound impact on Rischbieth and, through her, on other Australian feminist leaders.[22]

European suffragists, too, extolled Gilman's influence. Rosika Schwimmer asked her to address the International Woman Suffrage Congress in

FIGURE 20. N.Y. Street Meeting: Charlotte Perkins Gilman Speaks (Catt: 5.14.1d, Carrie Chapman Catt Collection, Bryn Mawr College Library).

June 1913 in Budapest, believing that Gilman could galvanize Hungarian enfranchisement single-handedly, for "there is no friend of our cause in Hungary, who would not feel disappointed if the greatest woman of our movement would not stay with us." Gilman did attend, and there she met Australian feminist writer Miles Franklin, author of the novel, *My Brilliant Career* (1901) and coeditor, with fellow Australian, Alice Henry of *Life and Labor,* the journal of the Women's Trade Union League, headquartered in Chicago. Their warm meeting resulted in later contributions of Gilman to the trade union journal. Franklin observed to Australian feminist Rose Scott that her peers often compared Jane Addams and Gilman; but like her friend Floyd Dell, Franklin believed that politically and philosophically Gilman surpassed Addams: "She is incomparably the greatest American woman alive.... I refer to a vivific force who promulgates new thought, who changes the ideas of her generation ... Jane Addams has a wider fame but I don't think of her in the same street with Mrs. Gilman.... Jane Addams uses other people's minds ... and is very cautious ... whereas Mrs. Gilman is as bold as a lioness and never hesitates."[23]

This 1913 meeting, full of enthusiastic younger women like Franklin, further convinced Gilman that suffrage work was ennobling and empowering for women worldwide. Thrilled by its high caliber, she praised the growing breadth of a movement that now represented all but five "civilized states." No longer confined to "the mere demand for the ballot" or to the litany of "women's rights and wrongs and all that beating of the air where solid argument is opposed to sentiment and tradition." Now so much had

FIGURE 21. Susan Fitzgerald of Boston, Mass., speaking at a suffrage street meeting (Gilman left back seat) (Catt: 1.3.2c . Carrie Chapman Catt Collection, Bryn Mawr College Library)

been achieved that "one wondered at times if this was a suffrage congress, a peace congress, or a social purity congress." Why? Because of the range of issues debated. For Gilman, the meeting convinced her that suffrage was "no longer an academic question, or a general claim of 'the ennobling influence of women.'" Instead, women had "definite objectives," more and more convinced that the ballot "is necessary to the achievement of those purposes." Suffrage was becoming ecumenical, enlisting all elements of the heterogeneous "woman movement," hitherto working in relative autonomy. "The Cause" anchored the delegates' discussions of diverse goals. Gilman found that another benefit of the 1913 congress was seeing women voters from various states and nations. It was one thing "to hear endless talk of woman suffrage as a potential benefit—or calamity—and quite another to know of the accomplished fact—and see the calm and pleasant faces of women who are full citizens, yet remain women."[24]

Gilman conveyed this upbeat and unified portrayal of the suffrage movement in spite of its long history of rivalry and strategy disputes. She considered these historical differences as considerably less important than dialogue and unity. Hence, on the pages of *Forerunner* she praised the pioneering work of *Woman's Journal* of Boston, the key activity of one movement faction led by Lucretia Mott/Alice Stone Blackwell, as opposed

FIGURE 22. Nathan and her party, including Charlotte Perkins Gilman, on the steps of the de Megyeri Villa, 1913 (The Schlesinger Library, Radcliffe Institute, Harvard University A57-v.11-3)

to the Elizabeth Cady Stanton/Susan B. Anthony wing. Calling it once "the only Voice of the Woman's Movement in this country if not in the world," and recalling her thirty-year association with it and its "lovely" founder, she rejoiced that it had become again "the official organ of the unified national suffrage movement" and a great source of news for progressive women. In the absence of radio and television, this journal permitted women across the United States to keep informed of their fellow suffragists' work, through correspondence, conference reports, and exegesis of arguments.[25]

Yet Gilman always honored the venerated Elizabeth Cady Stanton as well. So Gilman never made the mistake that Anthony was the 1848 Seneca Falls pioneer of the movement (a frequent supposition that incensed Stanton's daughter, Harriot Stanton Blatch), when Stanton and Anthony only met in 1851. Still, she praised "Aunt Susan" Anthony's fine work at Berlin and London meetings, while treating her unpopular successor Anna Howard Shaw (1847–1919) with respect, despite their considerable philosophical differences. Meanwhile, Gilman's cordial relationship with Shaw's successor, Carrie Chapman Catt, did not obstruct her working with Catt's nemesis, Blatch, on deputations, platforms, and committees. Indeed, she found Blatch intellectually and politically "very advanced," admiring her greatly when meeting her in London in 1896. It was Blatch's suffrage organization for which Gilman most often spoke; while intriguing photographs place Gilman prominently at the scene of major suffrage events—a woman suffrage garden party in evening dress, a banquet to honor Elizabeth Cady Stanton's birthday centenary on 30 October 1915 at the Astor Hotel (which Catt refused to attend), and addressing a large crowd in Union Square from a car driven by fellow members of Blatch's Women's Political and Social Union. Gilman served on suffrage delegations, wrote for suffrage newspapers, addressed meetings, raised money, traveled to conventions, supported comrades through 1910s reverses, testified before Congress, and skewered misogyny obstructing women's advance.[26]

Suffrage, then, was anything but a foregone conclusion, hence Gilman's active engagement with this key feminist issue of her adulthood. She saw the domain of public discourse as her best contribution to "the cause" as international momentum multiplied its enemies. Gilman marched forward to take the fight to them.

Dissecting Antisuffragism

"No, there's one thing worse, much worse . . ."

"What's this horror?" I asked. "Prostitution? White slavery?"

"Oh no," she said, "those things are awful, but a sort of natural awfulness. . . . No this thing is—*unnatural!* I mean—the Antis."

"Oh—the Anti-Suffragists? . . ."

"Van, if you want one all-sufficient proof of the degradation of women, you have it in the anti-suffragist!"

"The men are backing them, remember," I suggested.

"Of course they are. You expect the men to oppose the freeing of women, they naturally would. But the women, Van—the women themselves—it's unnatural."

With a sick shudder, she buried her face in her hands.

Charlotte Perkins Gilman, *"With Her in Ourland"* Forerunner 7 (November 1916): 294.

The war on the "Antis" permeated the pages of Gilman's *Forerunner.* Antisuffragism, as an organized political movement was a "reaction formation," much like employers' organizations emerging in reaction to organized labor in the 1890s, as outlined by historian John Rickard. "Anti" organizations mushroomed after major forward movement by the suffrage cause, such as the reunification of its various factions into the National American Woman Suffrage Association in 1890.[27]

Gilman identified three Anti groups as most formidable locally in New York and in the greater New England region—the Association Opposed to the Further Extension of Suffrage to Women, which she called "the most prominent and influential of the three reactionary societies," the Massachusetts Anti-Suffrage Committee, and the Public Interests League. They combated suffragists' state by state referenda campaigns between 1908 and 1917. She called these female antisuffragists "Reactionary Women" (as distinct from progressive women) who believed that their previous complacent inertia now stood imperiled by the multiplication of admirable "New Women." Jane Addams, Olive Schreiner, Maria Montessori, and others of their caliber provoked reactionary traditional women into "malign activity." The Antis petitioned, lobbied, raised funds, wrote letters, and held drawing room and larger public meetings, all urging that any further extension of woman suffrage would be a disaster, based on its dire track record in states foolish enough to have enacted it to date.[28]

Most despicable in Gilman's view was the process by which Antis attempted to discredit and defame individual suffragists, including Gilman herself. Antis ridiculed suffrage campaign efforts and consistently minimized pro-suffrage sentiment, counting only formal members of suffrage societies, "and claim for themselves the entire remaining population." Worryingly, the Antis had influential allies, such as the *New York Times* and public intellectuals such as Ida M. Tarbell. Gilman denounced them in her poem, "On the Anti-Suffragists," published in the *Woman's Journal* in 1897, and continued to ponder them until the 1930s in her nonfiction concerning interwar polities retaining women's disenfranchisement.[29]

Historians offer a fascinating composite portrait of "the Antis." Superficially, antisuffragists seemed similar to suffragists. Most were white, Protestant, married, middle-aged, and if not rich then certainly not poor. Women in both groups often employed servants and engaged in philanthropy and social service. The significant differences were that suffragists included higher proportions of college-educated professionals and members of reform-oriented Protestant denominations than did the Antis.[30]

Antisuffragists asserted that the sexes were separate but equal. Women could not vote because men and women belonged in separate spheres. Women could not be soldiers, thus they should not vote. Besides, direct franchise was unnecessary, since they used "feminine influence" on enfranchised men. Directly voting would "unsex" women, making suffrage a wholly unwelcome burden on already hardworking womanhood. Moreover, "the wrong kind of woman" would dominate a newly feminized electorate, enlarging undesirable elements and overwhelming any of the supposedly noble influence brought to politics by more respectable women. Arguably, Antis protested against the modernizing urban womanhood so visible in cities like New York, Chicago, and Boston by the 1910s. If enfranchised, women's soft-hearted, inexperienced, and impractical natures would result in disastrous political orientations in American politics—anarchism, socialism, and even Bolshevism.[31]

Indeed, many of the Antis' arguments asserted the business and class interests of their husbands and families, interests that combined with the inchoate fears of well-to-do Anglo-Americans in the wake of the failures of post–Civil War Reconstruction. These same anxieties in others engendered Progressivism and reform work. Undesirable women voters were the urban poor—including prostitutes and sexually promiscuous working-class women—as well as African Americans, ethnic and culturally cohesive minorities, such as Irish Catholics and Jews, and most alarmingly, the growing tide of immigrants in Northeast and Mid-Atlantic cities. To the chagrin of the Antis, the Roman Catholic Church in these regions also thundered against woman suffrage. Also, many male immigrants firmly opposed suffrage, clear in the crucial 1915 New York referendum. These were not allies the Antis wanted.[32]

Gilman had her character Ellador from *Herland* comment to her sociologist husband, Van, on immigrant men's complaint that the American home lacked authority: "Of course they do. Your immigrants, naturally, understand democracy even less than you do." Suffragists like Blatch, distinctive in her understanding of the importance of working women's votes and of working-class organization for suffrage, reacted to the same indications of immigrant male antisuffragism with total outrage. She appalled her colleagues with intemperate denunciations of such men's right to suffrage on the basis of sex in spite of their ignorance, much as her abolitionist mother Elizabeth Cady Stanton had denounced the preference given to African American men over women of all races in the Fourteenth Amendment in 1871. These were bitter wounds still unresolved across two generations of suffragists. But ethnically prejudiced responses prevented some suffragists from noticing that the Antis hardly made common cause with voting immigrant men.[33]

Moreover, if immigrant men were unwelcome allies to the mainly Protestant and culturally conservative Antis, so was the "liquor interest," as well as those whose investments included gaming and prostitution. Gilman promptly exposed these strange bedfellows, with Antis featuring in her prose articles, poetry, novels, and dramas. She connected Antis and the enemies of Progressive reform—the food adulterers, the corporate monopolists, the corrupt local politicians, and the slumlords. Simultaneously, she portrayed suffragists as allies of reformer doctors, scientists, educators, sociologists, single careerwomen, and innovative, entrepreneurial businesspeople.[34]

Her criticisms of antisuffragism, then, highlight the centrality of woman suffrage to her vision of social ("unnatural") motherhood and the advance of women to "human" status. As late in her career as 1929, a decade since the Nineteenth Amendment, she fathomed Antis as evidencing deep and irrational responses to changes in women's position.[35] Meanwhile, the Antis portrayed Gilman as a libertine simply because of her widely discussed criticism of traditional, untrained, instinctive motherhood. This recalled the 1890s stinging newspaper attacks on her as an "unnatural mother" when she divorced Stetson and surrendered custody of her daughter: "Mrs. Charlotte Perkins Gilman, member of the Congressional Union, has shed this light on feminism: 'Human beings believe that their duty is far outside of merely being mothers, even a kitten could be a mother.'"[36] In turn, she portrayed Antis as pathetic and comical figures. Whereas previous and prevailing Antis were reformers—those seeking abolition of smoking, saloons, the segregation of prostitution into tolerated red-light districts, and so forth—the antisuffragists "of painful prominence are Anti-virtue. They are opposing a well-known good. They wish to prevent people from doing right." Under the heading "A Cry from the Depths," Gilman mocked the Antis' public appeal for money for their cause. Since they consisted of "wealthy ladies," to wit, "ladies belonging to wealthy men," Gilman was especially amused by their unwillingness to commit their own or their husbands' money to their "glorious" cause, appealing through the press for funds because "'preferable to the methods of fairs, rummage sales, collections from the unwary at public meetings, etc., used by the suffragists.' This is as amusing an instance of the Attitude as could be asked."[37]

Had compulsory voting prevailed, the ferocity of Anti opposition might have been somewhat intelligible. To the Anti objection that low, illiterate, and vicious women would vote rather than the good and intelligent, Gilman replied that the former women were hardly prominent among suffragists and were unlikely to "at once rush forward" when women were enfranchised. To the view of combat as the gateway to citizenship, she held that if once it vouchsafed community survival, force long since ceased to define the citizen as therefore male.

Most ridiculous and insidious of Anti arguments was the claim that "women do not want it." No important reform had ever hinged on the demand of the majority of those to be affected, whether the issue was chattel slavery, child labor, removal of legal discrimination against married women, or any number of other reforms. Indeed, part of the suffrage case was that their disenfranchised status fostered women's ignorance, apathy, and disconnection from public and civic life, making it unlikely that a majority could be mobilized to show desire for the vote before they had actually won it. At best, to insist on demand from a majority of women was disingenuous. At worst, it was a cynical plan to retain the status quo: Gilman called Antis "Anti-Democratic Government."[38]

More than undemocratic, Gilman judged most Antis to be dull, illogical, and ineffective. Mercilessly, she exposed their mistakes and faulty assumptions. With Carrie Chapman Catt's gift to the New York suffrage campaign from Mrs. George Howard Lewis of Buffalo following an anti-suffrage meeting, Gilman reported that Lewis was so "impressed" by their arguments that, "she forthwith bestowed on the work for Suffrage the sum of $10,000" (which is over a quarter of a million in 2009 values). Meanwhile, New York Antis saw Katharine Bement Davis's appointment as commissioner for corrections and Ella Flagg Young's to state commissioner of education as proof that women could secure public office without needing the ballot. Suggesting this was not their finest intellectual moment, Gilman asked was not a fundamental Anti objection to enfranchisement "that 'politics will take women away from the home?' Just voting does not take women away from the home: they must mean holding office, surely. Yet here they approve of women in office—in political office—and say it is an argument against giving the ballot to women!"[39] Meanwhile, Gilman joyfully reported the Chicago Public Librarian's finding that clubwomen had declining demand for fiction, offset by "works on sociology and civics … a clear comment on the ancient Anti argument that women do not know enough to vote. They can learn, it appears."[40]

As the suffragist frequently debating antisuffragists, Gilman lamented the "peculiar emptiness and causelessness of the 'Opposition to the Extension, etc.'" She held that the only sound basis for antisuffragism would be proof that enfranchisement caused damage or social degeneracy. New Zealand, Australia, Finland, and the American West afforded no such proof.[41] Moreover, Antis erroneously attributed to woman suffrage political corruption, when "the corruption charged is common to manhood suffrage everywhere."[42] Gilman also tackled the petty criticisms leveled at suffragists, including those who attacked the planning and execution of massive suffrage street parades. Men could have parades related to sport, trades unions, warfare, and secret male societies, but ridiculous Antis claimed that women could not do so for any cause.[43]

If mainly uneducated Antis were easy targets for Gilman, antisuffragist public intellectuals like Ida Tarbell required different responses. Tarbell's books, *The Business of Being a Woman* (1912), *The Uneasy Woman* (1911?), and her other widely discussed essays on women and girls naturalized women's sex specificities as essentially market commodities, for which the smart woman made the best deal. The analogy with prostitution here appalled Gilman. Such degraded concepts of womanhood were unworthy of such an intellectual, while for "so clear-headed a woman" to make such statements was "a keen disappointment to a sincere admirer." Tarbell's claim that paid work with economic independence, citizen rights, and legal equality would "unsex" women, making them unattractive to men and doomed to spinsterhood, assumed a grim present basis of male/female domestic and family partnerships. Her claim that to be a suffragist courted exile from "society" earned Gilman's sharp rebuke: being "a suffragist is not like being a leper—or a pauper—or excommunicated. There is nothing about the belief itself to cut off the believer from her kind; and make it impossible to invite her to dinner."[44]

CRITICIZING FELLOW women pained and disappointed Gilman. By contrast, she fully unleashed her anger on misogynist men, characterizing their efforts to resist women's rights as "masculism." Even before the revival of suffragism in the 1910s, she had alerted readers to the surge of misogyny in prominent books, a notable example here of Otto Weininger's *Sex and Character* (1906). She called his text a fully concentrated and dogmatic articulation of the "ultra-masculine view of women" as psyche-less, ugly and amoral corruptors of man's nobility, who should be eliminated through men's voluntary celibacy. She associated this young German philosopher's views with the ancient patriarchies of Europe but sensed a particular intensification in Germany, a theme to which she would return during World War One. With the term "masculism" she was seeking a fuller vocabulary to characterize men's collective political and cultural actions on behalf of their own sex. Titling a 1914 public lecture series at New York's Astor Hotel, "Studies in Masculism," she complained that the printer objected to the word and attempted to change it.[45]

Despite an unfriendly press, she specially targeted "masculist" authors and purveyors of negative views of women. Renewed suffragist momentum fueled extreme misogyny, for instance, Warren Fite's savage 1913 review of nine recent texts by women, "The Feminist Mind," in the *Nation*, which she found simply appalling. Noting that only Ida Tarbell and Ellen Key met his approval, he reduced the diverse others to one question: Did they demonstrate the intelligence that would justify women's enfranchisement?

Of course, he held that they did not, for women occupied "an indeterminate position between men and children," failing to mature as men did. Fite offered "a rather confused dissertation on that old theme of world-wide popularity—the inferiority of women ... the universal conviction among men that the female sex as a sex is a lower form of life than their own." She observed that misogynists typically knew only young women through work, from the home, and in "society," with the exceptions of their own mothers and aging wives, accounting for Fite's characterizing of feminine minds as adolescent. Moreover, men "have a wider acquaintance with girls of a lower class than their own, than have women with lower class men." Here she meant the dominance of workplaces by young female shop assistants, apparel makers, servants, restaurant employees, factory laborers, cleaners and launderers, secretaries, typists, clerks, and other service occupations. Yet, lady settlement workers associating with "poor boys, might find a somewhat similar basis of opinion as to the limitations of men's minds." The whole discussion was trivial and unscientific.[46]

Gilman also defended suffragists abroad. Once press and other public attacks on feminism erupted with British militant suffragette activism in the 1910s, Gilman vigorously confronted their enemies. She denounced much publicized English "masculists," including Grant Allen and H. B. Marriott-Watson, as well as other misogynist English criticism of the militants which had been reprinted eagerly in New York newspapers. She was especially indignant at the suggestion that only women's economic and social dependence checked men's "natural" propensity for violence toward women— "the brute in man." In suffragism, women violated the boundaries of their separate sphere, inviting "natural" male responses to women's militancy, including the assaults, rape, harassment, and denigration suffered by the suffragettes—mirrored, by suffragette accounts, in state administered torture and forced feeding in prison. Such violence was justified, according to Sir Almroth Wright and Professor William Sedgwick, as set out in the *New York Times*. She characterized Wright's "Militant Hysteria," as "an unusually frank exposition of combined sex and professional prejudice. Dr. Wright does not like women, except in one relation; as friends, equals, possible competitors, he finds intellectual intercourse with them 'repugnant'; and as a medical man, dealing continually with morbid phenomena in feminine psychology, he likes them still less. The submissive married woman, he accepts as a necessary evil; for the unmarried woman or the unsubmissive woman anywhere, he has not words to express his abhorrence."[47]

Gilman refuted this "brute in man" alibi across 1912–13, reflecting her earlier resistance to essentialist and fatalistic accounts of male violence in

Ward's theories. Self-consciousness led to emancipatory action by nations, peoples, classes, and races. Why should this not be true for sexes? No group had ever freed itself without protesting, demonstrating, and indeed, fighting on its own behalf. When had women signed a compact with men saying that they would never fight for their interests? She dismissed claims that women were naturally "pacific" and "nurturing," thus acting unnaturally in the fight for suffrage. Surely, the hunting and fighting prowess of many female mammals, like the lioness, were legendary. Gilman contended that combativeness for its own sake was a masculine sex trait, but that lionesses fought not for their own sake but to feed or protect their young. The vote was just one example of nourishment and protection in an advanced civilization with which women could feed and protect their own. Citizenship was a basic tool of the "social motherhood" she postulated as the true evolutionary goal of "the larger feminism." In fact, suffrage was such a crucial remaining step that proper analysis of feminism and its desirable development depended on removal of this obstacle. Until then, it was understandable that suffrage was the focus of the Woman Movement and feminist engagement.[48]

In this context of antisuffragist outbreaks, Gilman found the *New York Times*' antisuffragism and its withering ridicule of suffrage activities extremely annoying. The venerable newspaper served as a mouthpiece for outraged masculinities. She identified a shift from previous years when "the rise of the Equal Suffrage movement, while treated even-handedly, if without sympathy," gave way to a more virulent antisuffragism. Thus "I was wholly unprepared for the painful shock caused by reading the opening passages in the March number of these articles." By 1915, she likened its editorials to the deep ocean sea serpent in a Rudyard Kipling story, "A Matter of Fact." Making the analogy, she wrote:

> A huge gray unknown Thing, a vast and loathly Serpent, with a blind white Face—an Eyeless Face—thrown up from those black regions where no light ever came. . . . There has been a similar appearance lately in the *New York Times*. Here we were, sailing along as on a summer sea. . . . Then we realize some terrible commotion—an upheaval as of submerged mountains—and then appears before us in all its ghastly conspicuity, the blank white face of something made to live only in darkness, something cast up from the utmost depths, something dating from a part of primeval antiquity—a Leading Editorial against Equal Suffrage.

She described the editorial as "long and sinuous, limbless and finless as serpents are, mere billowy repetition of undulating curves and blind—

blind as a clam." Happily, she reported, this "prehistoric proclamation" evoked outraged protest and "a feeble handclapping," the following week's letters to the editor running to six pages, wherein those pro-suffrage outweighing Anti at a ratio of 7 to 2, despite the *New York Times*' evident deference to the Anti cause. Gilman could not resist noting that "those upholding equal suffrage were well-known names and some noted ones, while the opposition could boast only such long appended titles as "President, National Association Opposed to Woman Suffrage," and "Chairman, New York State Men's Association Opposed to Political Suffrage for Women," as well as merely anonymous letters. She declared such debate healthy, with the next two Sunday papers forced by response to give still more space to pro-suffrage letters, reminding readers of suffrage progress, since not long ago "both the weight of numbers and of power would have been preponderantly against, and the few supporters would have been laughed to scorn. Times have changed—but not *The New York Times*."[49]

She anticipated that eventually the newspaper would shift; indeed just one year after the unsuccessful New York 1915 suffrage referendum, antisuffrage rhetoric significantly diminished. To cheer dispirited colleagues like Blatch, Gilman wrote that, far from defeated, the movement was not even discouraged. Reporting on a *Woman's Journal* analysis of the New York referendum vote, the affirmative vote was larger than the number of state votes cast for either Taft or Roosevelt in the 1912 election. That almost half the male voters supported it was the remarkable outcome of the poll, a most significant change in public opinion. Comparing the fund-raising trends for the "pro" and "anti" sides of the referendum proved most revealing. The suffragists amassed $106,967.91 ($2,214,040 in 2006), the Antis $61,300.46 ($1,268,921 in 2006). However, members themselves donated or worked to raise very different proportions of these totals: among suffragists, two-thirds ($66,987.53—$1,386,528 in 2006) from members' work and contributions, compared with only $9,585.00 ($198,392 in 2006) or 16% of the Anti fund. In other words, the liquor, vice, gambling, and allied interests bankrolled the Antis.[50]

With each successful state referendum, she rejoiced and then gravely stated the task ahead for women voters. Under the heading "Ten States Free Now," she wrote: "That historical joke, the Association Opposed to the Extension of Suffrage to Women, has its field of effort again restricted by the election of 1912. Four more states have decided that women are people. There are now ten free states in our union, ten states where democracy can be justified, as compared with the rest of our androcracy."[51]

Nonetheless, the state-by-state referendum strategy gradually unraveled in favor of a focus on a federal constitutional amendment, notably after the 1915 New York defeat. If longtime state campaigners like Harriet Burton Laidlaw remained committed to state referenda, the *New York Times* identified Gilman as a founding member of the Constitutional Amendment League, the body seeking an amendment of the federal constitution. If pursued again in New York, however, Gilman predicted success, as it was under Carrie Chapman Catt's leadership in 1917. Hence, Gilman reminded readers that "within fifteen years the same *New York Times* went on record as denying and ridiculing the success of flying machines. It has never apologized for its later change of front, nor will it when, in a few more years, we may read on its neat pages pleasant comment on the 'Commendable Work Done by Women Voters.'"[52]

The terms in which Gilman criticized antisuffragism, then, establish beyond doubt the importance of woman suffrage to her vision of advancing women to "human" status. In her war on the Antis, Gilman rose to her rhetorical best, loyal to and fiercely defensive of her fellow women, certain of the contribution a female electorate could make to Progressive social reforms.

"Something to Vote For"

The first duty of womanhood is motherhood, but I don't mean to say that it should also come last. Modern motherhood requires for the good of children government care and protection. She needs the ballot more than for any other purpose that she may do her duty by her children.

"'The Extension of the Suffrage to Women': Subject of an Interesting Debate before the Outlook Club Last Evening" (1903)

It is the extricable masculinity in our idea of government which so revolts at the idea of women as voters. "To govern: that means to boss, to control, to have authority, and that only, to most minds. They cannot bear to think of the women as having control over even their own affairs; to control is masculine, they assume."

Charlotte Perkins Gilman, The Man-Made World *(1911)*

An important element of Gilman's suffrage work was her effort to move beyond the struggle for votes alone, toward the difference to be made by enfranchisement, inspiring and galvanizing women around political issues, with the example of women's actions in places like the western states and various countries where women were fully enfranchised. To this end, she often employed fiction. Her one-act play "Something to Vote For" (1911) was an important text illustrating her blending of suffrage advocacy, rebuttal of the Antis, and the articulation of a Progressive reform program beneficial to women and children. The play addressed a fundamental connection between women and children, nourishment, and more particularly, milk and its quality, as part of the increasingly commodified food supply in urban capitalist culture.

Women voters would be especially concerned about food distribution and quality. Men, hitherto dominating manufacturing, dealing, and distributing food, fought, "man-fashion" with competitors: "lies, dilutes, adulterates, artificially preserves, fills the market with poor products." For men, food was merely a commodity to sell. For women, however, "the consumer, the purchaser, the preparer, the server," food was, above all, nutrition. Hence, "woman suffrage then must inaugurate effectively a 'Mother's Party' for the success of their political interests—its platform to be Peace, Purity, Health, Economy, Education."[53]

The play was set at a meeting of an avowedly antisuffrage women's club, which embarrassed its newest member and guest speaker, the proudly voting Dr. Strong of Colorado. The topic of the day's meeting was pure milk, and other speakers included Mr. Billings, the boss of the Milk Trust, a milk inspector Harry Arnold, and a poor Irish American woman whose infant son died of a milk-borne disease. The feature was to be a demonstration test of the purity of Mr. Billings's sample milk. Billings, a man with ambitions for national office, was courting the wealthy young widow who was president of the club. Both Dr. Strong and Harry Arnold knew milk sent to poor areas was impure—infected with bacteria—and adulterated with starch additives and water. Billings's test sample was one of the high-quality and more expensive bottles of milk distributed among the wealthy. So Dr. Strong replaced it with a sample of the local grocer's store. Then she marked a $100 bill with a red ink line and asked Billings, in front of the lady president, to change the bill for smaller ones. She did this certain he would try to bribe the milk inspector (once he realized which variety of his product was being tested), and she asked Arnold to accept the marked bill if it was offered. Sure enough, Billings made the bribe. The bereaved mother told the heart-rending tale of her son's death from diarrhea caused by impure and adulterated milk. To Billings's horror, Arnold's cloth strain test for bacterial deposits and an iodine test turned the starch-adulterated milk bright blue, while the cloth became marked with dark brown sediments. Billings left in disgrace, and the president, formerly an Anti, declared: "Now we see what our 'influence' amounts to! Rich or poor, we are all helpless together unless we wake up to the danger and protect our homes! To protect our children! To protect the children of the poor! I'm willing to vote now! I'm glad to vote now! I've got something to vote for! Friends, sisters, all who are in favor of woman suffrage say Aye!" They all did.[54]

Adulterated milk was symbolically significant as well. For women to partake of race work, motherhood could not impede their full political participation. Milk supplies permitted others to feed toddlers and older children when their mothers were at work, while also being the foundation of "delicate cookery" for the feeding of children, the sick, and the elderly, tasks that often fell to women. An impure milk supply, injurious to health or just unreliable in quality, was a grave indictment of androcentric business. Women had to take action.

Theodore Roosevelt's 1912 Progressive Party and presidential candidacy encouraged Gilman to enumerate for her readers reforms that she hoped to see enacted in a "human world" with full adult suffrage, preeminently those involving woman suffrage and protective labor laws. Measures not specifically about women, however, also needed women's influence and opinions. She approved of Roosevelt's proposals for preferential primaries for presidential election years, election of U.S. senators by popular vote, a Corrupt Practices Act applicable to primaries as well as elections, public disclosure of campaign contributors, and, of great interest to suffragists, simplifying the process of amending the constitution. In the sphere of public welfare, she supported his call for strengthened pure food laws, a national health department, a minimum wage, and social and industrial justice for wageworkers, including insurance and old age pensions and the eradication of child labor. Gilman also noted his sudden opportunistic conversion "from a lukewarm academic admitter of women's 'technical right' to the ballot—when they wanted it, to a hot advocate of the immediate necessity of giving the vote to women—because he wants it!"[55]

Gilman stressed "the work before us." Women voters had direct interests in educating, protecting, beautifying, and cleansing all areas of life—interests that should imbue in them a strong sense of "the things we want to vote for." Appraising the record of women as voters in the "free states," she held that wherever women voted they improved the conditions of children, promoted equal pay for women, prevented candidatures of "notoriously immoral men" for public office, and in all cases sought altruistic legislation of social benefit. She concluded that woman suffrage "has improved women."[56]

The means for women voters to exert influence were complicated. Gilman's thinking on this evolved across the 1910s and 1920s, partly in response to antisuffragist criticism. On the one hand, she believed that women had distinctive interests and experiences as a sex that men neither represented nor understood. Proper reforms and just provisions hinged on their self-conscious sex solidarity, rather than their simply replicating the male vote. By this logic there could be a woman's vote, a platform for women, candidates favored by women, and even political parties for and of women. Gilman wrote and spoke eloquently on these possibilities, attracting the ire of many public commentators, not least the Antis.[57]

Yet Gilman was ambivalent on the issue of sex-determined politics. Abhorring the artificial sexualization of women exaggerating feminine attributes at the expense of their "race qualities," she denounced essentialist expectations that women would be a politically unified group, when this would never be expected of men. On this trajectory, then, she rejected the view of women as a distinct electorate, insisting instead on their common humanness with men, entitling them to the ballot—a sufficient ground itself. Hence, at times she disputed the need for a woman's platform, a woman's party, or other sex-specific political apparatuses. In 1915 she wrote: "The wise and understanding majority of suffragists have never advocated a woman's party, or even a woman's platform. Their claim to the ballot is on general human grounds. . . . It is by no means the suffragists who assume the rights of women to be opposed to the rights of men. . . . We do not want any Woman's Party, unless there should be a solid massing of men against some just and necessary claim of women."[58]

Nonetheless, a women's party emerged all too soon. After the failure of the 1915 New York Referendum, Gilman, like so many of her suffragist peers, rapidly changed gears to focus on a federal constitutional amendment. She used the pages of *Forerunner* to make a spirited case for the logic of the new federal focus, since Eastern states' advance was being "checked by a wall of 'states rights.'" She warned suffragists to be suspicious of legislators' willingness "to relegate the suffrage workers to the old effort in individual states" because it was well-nigh impossible due to state constitutions.[59]

Mary Ritter Beard (1876–1958) and Florence Kelley (1859–1932) prepared a pamphlet entitled "Amending State Constitutions: A Study of State Constitutions Which Lack Suffrage Amendments," and Gilman reproduced it in full in the *Forerunner.* They demonstrated that the state-by-state method was slow, cumbersome, and often hopeless. Some states required any amendment to be proposed by three-quarters of the members of each House and ratified by three-quarters of electors in the state as a whole and two-thirds of those in each county. Others required a majority of votes by all qualified electors of the state. Yet this majority rarely registered, much less voted. Moreover, Beard and Kelley raised forcibly the immigrant question. Alien males, they reported, could vote in most states in between six and twelve months of residency, by undertaking to naturalize. It seemed that legislators valued "the votes of these brand new aliens" far more "than the wishes of the women. That foreign vote in the Middle Atlantic states is a very considerable proportion." They concluded that "our women ought to realize exactly what they are up against in this single state work, and so realize the necessity of concentrating on the Federal Amendment." The only way for all American women, enfranchised or not, to obtain the vote was to bond together and work for the federal amendment to protect all of their rights.[60]

In endorsing the mission of the Congressional Union, Gilman loudly proclaimed that the preeminent issue for new female voters in enfranchised states was securing the federal vote for their fellow women for "that active body of suffragists who would have this question of political justice settled once and for all by Federal Amendment." Hence, women voters from the "freed states" formed a new party, The National Woman's Party, calling its first convention in Chicago during the same week as Republican and Progressive party conventions. Its single objective was securing suffrage for those remaining disenfranchised. Eventually, with the Nineteenth Amendment ratified, they could turn to securing the Equal Rights Amendment.[61]

The new Woman's Party was immediately attacked by the *New York Times*. Gilman trounced the editor, "who is so earnest an opponent of equal suffrage, that he has allowed his feelings quite to overmaster his intellect again." She found misrepresentations and double standards in the editor's "horror" at the "threat" and "political blackmail" entailed in organizing the women's votes and lobbying for change. Yet the National Woman's Party proposed nothing beyond ordinary voter rights, the "perfectly honest, open and usual method of organizing a group of voters to enforce desired legislation by their voting power." Such a method was not "blackmail—and that editor knows it." To the editor's charge that woman suffrage would divide politics along sex lines, Gilman cried "nonsense," for the present distinction "which gives men the ballot and denies it to women makes in politics a division along sex lines—an arbitrary, unjust, unwise, and most mischievous division. As fast as women are enfranchised that division is obliterated." Once again, she insisted on attention to the record: "In the free States men and women do not vote in separate and opposing groups. There is no indication that they will. This Woman's Party, with its massed vote, is not an effort to set women against men." What the National Woman's Party did was to urge women voters to vote against the party administration that refused to enact woman suffrage. In so doing, "they would be joining millions of men who vote similarly for similar reasons." She insisted that nothing showed that the women's vote "is in any way inimical to the interests of men."[62]

Gilman maintained that the importance of this new women's party could not be overestimated in marking the final passing of women's isolated helplessness. Its distinctive objectives of challenging the willingness of the political parties to add woman suffrage to their platforms did not mean the new party worked against the interests of men. Rather, it worked in a democratic fashion using the tools of democracy. Three months before the November 1916 elections, she urged that:

> If in that time the Democratic Administration should refuse to advance this measure, to distinguish sharply from the Republican position, then it would be quite fair to oust the Democrats, not on the ground that the Republicans were better, but that full opportunity was given for a change of heart before the election, and it was not made. If this was done successfully, and clearly attributable to the women's vote, they will have established their effectiveness so thoroughly that no subsequent administration will lightly oppose them, and the Republicans, though now indifferent, will see the light before another election.[63]

Gilman reported excitedly on her visits to equal suffrage states, going to the polls with now voting friends. She was especially fascinated by political candidates' discomfort in addressing female voters. The only previous relation such men had with women had been domestic, social, or sexual. They had no experience soliciting women as voters. Flattery failed as did aggression or condescension. According to Gilman, only showing women voters respect made candidates viable as politicians and men of character.[64]

ON 15 FEBRUARY 1920, Gilman presented the eulogy at the memorial ceremony for the centenary of the birth of Susan B. Anthony, whose bust was unveiled in the Metropolitan Museum of Art. The *New York Times* described the one hundred gathered suffrage veterans as happy "in the belief that the woman's suffrage amendment will soon be ratified." Gilman said: "Miss Anthony's work for woman suffrage was at a time when that work meant the sacrifice of all else in life. She cheerfully paid the price. Here in her native state we gather to commemorate her centenary."[65]

With the Nineteenth Amendment finally enacted, revisionism quickly appeared in public commentary, with accelerating interwar criticism of postsuffrage women. Gilman defended, evaluated, and reiterated her own vision for positive social transformation. She debated enemies of suffragism until the end of the 1920s. Her observations about both suffrage and feminism appeared on the pages of 1920s journal articles, as well as in chapters that she contributed to anthologies of "advanced" thinkers on sexuality and morality between 1924 and 1931. It is clear then that Gilman closely engaged with the postsuffrage moment. She rebutted frequent criticisms that suffrage had either no effect on public life or only negative effects, noting that the "steady push for legal equality was long and hard, and is by no means ended." Citing continuing state-level legal disabilities for women, she noted that campaigns met "opposition not only from men, but also from that small, unique, and historically comic group, the 'Anti-suffragists.'"[66]

From her newlywed days as a Providence suffrage columnist, until her final years in Norwich, Connecticut, as president of the local chapter of the League of Women Voters, Gilman worked as a suffrage intellectual and advocate. Contemporaries both for and against the measure unmistakably saw her as the Progressive Era movement's most able thinker and formidable speaker on behalf of "the cause." Her zealous and uncompromising suffragism often cost her, incurring anger, ridicule, and ostracism, but she paid the price willingly. She did at times moderate the message on this issue in order to secure other objectives, but this should not have led, as it has, to the view that she ranked the matter low in priority relative to other issues, such as women's economic independence. Instead, both economic dependency and political disenfranchisement attested to women's subjection in androcentric culture. She had to challenge all aspects of that subjection. Enfranchisement and citizen rights form a crucial dimension, then, of Gilman's feminism.

CHAPTER SIX

Debating Gilman's "Feminism"

I abominate being called a feminist.

Charlotte Perkins Gilman to
Grace Ellery Channing Stetson, 21 August 1929

IN SO PROTESTING to Grace Ellery Channing-Stetson, Gilman was responding to the news that a publisher who was considering her final nonfiction book manuscript, "A Study in Social Ethics," wanted to meet the era's "leading feminist." The publisher was hardly alone in judging Gilman America's preeminent Progressive Era feminist theorist. Contemporaries ranked Gilman among the world's three foremost feminists—the other two being South African Olive Schreiner (1855–1920) and Swede Ellen Key (1849–1926). Such acclaim continued long after the publication of Gilman's most famous book, *Women and Economics* (1898). In 1922, when Carrie Chapman Catt (1859–1947) was asked to name America's greatest women, she placed Gilman first, her many books "read by all classes of people"—books Catt credited "with utterly revolutionizing the attitude of mind of the entire country, indeed of other countries, as to woman's place." Gilman figured prominently in 1910s and 1920s book-length appraisals of feminism, reactions to her ranging from glowing praise to astringent denunciation. Even her fiercest critics, however, concurred on her preeminence and influence.[1]

Most of her contemporaries ignored Gilman's attempts to distance herself from the title "feminist." Indeed, seasoned campaigners asserted that Gilman made more women feminists than any single peer. Even younger Progressive Era women who disagreed with her so identified Gilman with feminism that they doubted their own feminist convictions. Meanwhile newspapers covering her public lectures consistently called Gilman a feminist.[2]

With her deep involvement in suffrage and women's struggles for citizenship, how can we best understand Gilman's efforts to distance herself from the term "feminism"? Is it problematic for Gilman scholars and historians of feminism to classify her as a feminist when she specifically and repeatedly refused this characterization? One way to answer this question is to place her disavowal of feminism in its own discursive context. Even as she ostensibly distanced herself from classification as a feminist, she energetically wrote about feminism and publicly spoke in ways that linked her name with it from the 1910s onward. She defined and characterized feminism during the unstable years of the American debut of the term. This involved her in criticism of well-known (though very different) commentators on women, such as Ida Tarbell and Ellen Key.[3]

Gilman's critiques disclosed her investment in international conversations about feminism. Though refusing the term for herself, her analyses of feminism demonstrated loyalty to the concept, amid ambivalence and disquiet. It may be that Gilman on feminism becomes comprehensible only through exploration of debates about this new term and the costs of association with it. A notable feature of the history of feminism is the frequency with which those identified as its most profound exponents have similarly distanced themselves from the label "feminist." These have included Australia's Rose Scott and Miles Franklin, England's Virginia Woolf and Viola Klein, France's Simone de Beauvoir, and America's Margaret Mead and Ruth Benedict, to name a few. Understanding criticisms of feminism in specific contexts is crucial for any study of this political philosophy.[4]

Disclaiming and Deprecating

The Social philosophy of Charlotte Perkins Gilman is better known and appreciated in Europe than in her own country as is so frequently the case with American thinkers. . . . She is called a feminist, one of the three outstanding names among them—Olive Schreiner and Ellen Key the other two. But Mrs. Gilman disclaims the term. . . . Her works are translated into Italian, Dutch, Russian, German, Hungarian, Swedish, and Japanese and read from New Zealand to Norway. She is widely known as a feminist, but deprecates the term, claiming that her interest is in humanity and in women only because their previous debasement has retarded upward movement of us all.

"Charlotte Perkins Gilman" (1915), lecture circular

Even those modern protagonists of women whom we call "feminists" find some difficulty in proving equality; much more, superiority in women, as we know them.

Charlotte Perkins Gilman, "Feminism and Social Progress" (1929)

Although the term "feminism" was widely used in the last decades of her life, Gilman still often put it in quote marks, as if it remained unfamiliar or unacceptable. She spoke of feminists as "them"—feminism and feminists were objects of her analysis—rather than part of an "us." Her dislike of the term was well-known among her friends and peers, as reflected here in writer and confidante Alexander Black's 1922 portrait of Gilman: "I have avoided calling her a 'feminist' not merely because the word is foolish, but because her emphasis on women has been the stressing of an outstanding imperative in a scheme as wide as life rather than either a class complaint or a specialist infatuation." Black implied that feminism was narrow, faddish, and rhetorically objectionable, assuming Gilman's accord with his sentiments. Alternatively, while warmly praising Beatrice Forbes Robertson Hale's 1915 text, *What Women Want,* Gilman included feminists as one reader constituency: "Even the sturdiest Feminist will find refreshment in the vivid summary of the nature, the achievements and the hopes of that great movement."[5]

Why did Gilman "disclaim" and "deprecate" the title feminist? Across the 1910s and 1920s she advertised her disdain for the term in lecture publicity and other self-description. Though often noting her nomination as the most significant feminist of the era, she expressed her preference for the term "humanist." Women's subordinate status from centuries of dependent domestic seclusion as house servants deprived social evolution of half of humanity's contributions. Advancing humanity as a whole required a temporary focus on making womanhood equal, fit, and independent. Women needed attention simply because their social, economic, and cultural retardation obstructed human progress. On this purportedly conditional basis, she supported women's movement causes, including woman suffrage. Her stated quest was for what she called, "a human world," one in which sex was irrelevant to the right to participate and contribute to the advance of "the race."[6]

Such a contingent endorsement of woman suffrage understated the intensity of her suffrage commitments. Acutely aware of negative portrayals of feminism, Gilman worried that the Antis' strategy of treating suffragism and feminism as synonymous would harm the cause. While suffragism was part of the platform of demands of avowed Progressive Era feminists, the reverse did not follow. By no means did all suffragists support other feminist demands. For instance, political and cultural liberals, across party lines, supported women's enfranchisement to correct an anomaly for the United States as a democracy, without necessarily subscribing to the view that women, as a sex, were systematically and unjustly subjugated by men. Temperance activists of both sexes, many without a trace of feminist belief, supported votes for women believing (correctly) that, thereby, they could secure Prohibition. A perception of suffrage as synonymous with feminism, then, could alienate crucial support for the ballot. Hence, Gilman sought, at least on some occasions, to sever the rhetorical connection between them. For anyone to propose that any states so far had enfranchised women because of feminism was absurd, and she characterized the Antis' efforts to tar suffragism by association with feminism as attempted "terrorism."

> "Feminism," a name full charged with looming horrors, is alleged to be the real wolf under the—comparatively—sheepish clothing of the suffrage movement. Then one looks back at the long line of plain and pious women who have heroically upheld "the cause" for so many years; then one thinks of the honest housewives of New Zealand and Australia, the sturdy Finns, the serious able women of our great West, the millions of these new voters in many countries; and one smiles at this little group of misguided ladies [the Antis]. . . . Do they think that the mad tendency toward "Free Love" is really what actually governs the great mass of American wives and mothers who uphold the equal suffrage movement? Do they think at all?

Note that she did not dispute the linguistic slide from feminism to free love in the antisuffragist position, here allowing (at least implicitly) the Antis claim that feminists were free love advocates and urban Bohemians, thus completely unlike the plain female voters of frontiers and settler societies. By ridiculing the Antis' efforts to connect suffragism and feminism in these terms, Gilman implicitly accepted this characterization of feminists, acquitting the good pioneer voters of such aspersions. Arguably this implication was no accident.[7]

It is a powerful testament to the ferocity of the period's antifeminist rhetoric that disassociation of suffrage from feminism seemed a more viable strategy than challenging antifeminist assumptions and prejudices more directly. The press regularly pilloried feminism, knowingly and humorously exaggerating its claims, objectives, and tactics. Feminism made great—sometimes sensational—copy. Under titles like, "Men Are Worried," unsigned articles proliferated in popular antifeminist discourse: "We are coming to believe of late that the subject of feminism is rather the deepest, most vaguely vague, dense, occult question that ever added bald territory to a man's scalp. We believe it to be the most alluring proposition that ever found its way to a front seat in the American forum." What was the ground for alarm? The author claimed that once upon a time, feminism consisted of goals a man could live with, such as his wife keeping her maiden name. Then it seemed women did not care to marry, "but took him on trial for a time, just as she would a phonograph." Suddenly, wives wanted men to wash the dishes and "take care of Fido while she goes to the office." If this was a glimpse at feminism, men were becoming uneasy about it. Worried by a melodramatic account of antisuffragist Mrs. Martin's claims that feminism "is the process of putting father out of business, deposing him as the breadwinner and political representative of the family and rendering him unnecessary," reducing him to the status of a "tomcat," the author concluded that it was time for a committee to determine if feminism means anything "so horrid" for men. If so, "it's time to begin drilling and arming, as they do in Ulster."[8]

Yet just as Gilman seemed to distance herself from feminism, and certainly to uncouple it from suffragism, elsewhere she defended it, condemning antifeminists as malicious reactionaries. Indeed, as discussed above, she treated antifeminists and antisuffragists as broadly synonymous, even as she resisted others eliding suffragism and feminism. So, in a 1914 article, she denounced "the present outburst of anti-feminist literature and oratory," in which men's strong feelings about women and their proper activities and domains overwhelmed any number of facts, "like a bull in a China shop." It was amusing, she observed, to see the male obsession with the sex qualities of "woman" and their prejudice "as to the importance of her femaleness," women having no other measurable qualities aside from femininity.[9]

Meanwhile, in 1911 when 10,000 women marched in the second woman suffrage parade in New York City, and half a million others lined the streets, the *New York Times* orchestrated a great masculist backlash, in a Sunday editorial conspicuously exhibiting blindness and "caution, squirming under a desire to be offensive." Extremist critics of the British militant suffragettes, such as Sir Almroth Wright, received extensive coverage, as mentioned in chapter 5. Wright held that the quest for suffrage extinguished femininity and the chivalrous compact between the sexes. Suffragists had only themselves to blame for the violence inflicted on them everywhere suffrage militancy emerged. Denouncing not only Wright's misogyny but also his unoriginality in recycling tired old masculist myths about the sexes, Gilman charged that he was apparently as "unacquainted with the world's great mass of anti-feminist literature as with its new feminist literature." In this context at least, she acknowledged the gravitas of the literature of feminism.[10]

Between her championing of the suffrage movement, which led to her disavowal of negative associations with feminism, and battling popularized antifeminists, which conversely led her to defend feminism, Gilman clarified her ambivalent stance. She was articulating a definition of feminism in accord with her own intellectual framework, one antithetical to divergent tendencies frequently associated with the category "feminism" in the polysemous phase of its United States emergence. While she loudly resisted masculist and antifeminist rhetoric of the period, she worried that others, who called themselves feminists, advanced arguments unable to withstand the assault. She did not wish to be associated with their positions. A crucial element, then, of Gilman's work with the category "feminism"—which for her was both problematic and irresistible—was to debate its parameters, meaning, and significance. Expanding its definition, she identified sectarian disputes from the outset of the currency of feminism. The shorthand for her position became "the *larger* feminism." Prevailing forms of feminism seemed narrow or superficial, her project less a repudiation of feminism than an attempt to improve it.[11]

In the Heterodoxy Club, founded in 1912, she engaged with other feminists. The club of self-proclaimed feminists, which included artists, writers, and political activists, met every other Saturday in Greenwich Village, where its members debated sexuality, psychoanalysis, socialism, pacifism, birth control, and anarchism. Gilman attended until early 1917, thus seeming to seek, rather than avoid, the company of feminists. Just as Gilman minimized the extent of her engagement with woman suffrage in her later autobiography, she also understated her involvement with fellow feminists and her interest in Heterodoxy, which she portrayed as becoming tedious with too much talk of sexology and pacifism. Instead, it is clear from evidence of the club's feminist analysis and advocacy that its members greatly admired and adopted Gilman's approach.[12]

For instance, Heterodoxy member Margaret Currey and her partner, bohemian writer Floyd Dell, were followers of Gilman's ideas, especially their implications for reconfiguring intimate and domestic life. And Miles Franklin, writing to Rod McMillen, editor of Sydney's *Stock and Station Journal* in 1912, described her friend Currey as "a Vassar graduate and a Gilmanite among many other up-to-date things." Gilman's theories were named for her—"Gilmanism"—as were their advocates: "Gilmanites." In 1948, over a decade after Gilman's death, Franklin reminisced with Currey

FIGURE 23. Portrait of Fola La Follette, 1918–20 (The Schlesinger Library, Radcliffe Institute, Harvard University: A25-73VO 71)

about getting "the glorious CPG ready for a lecture" in a hotel room, wishing that her intellectual idol or else a worthy successor might challenge the Kinsey report of that year. No peer had produced a corpus of theoretical work on women's subjection to compare with hers, feminists judging this contribution more essential than work for particular campaigns and movements. For contemporaries, Gilman the person was indistinguishable from her writings. If she did not place herself at the center of feminism then, other feminists placed her—and her work—there.[13]

In view of this recognition and influence, it was not surprising that in 1914, at New York City's Cooper Union, Gilman appeared as part of a public panel on feminism. Her copanelists were fellow Heterodoxy members: Marie Jenney Howe, its founder; journalists and writers, Rheta Childe Dorr and Beatrice Forbes Robertson Hale; women's labor activist, Rose Schneiderman; Fola La Follette, daughter of the 1924 presidential candidate, Robert La Follette; and writer Nina Wilcox Putnam. The lengthy report of this event in the *New York Times* carried the headline: "Feminists Ask Equal Chance: Leaders in Movement Discuss 'Breaking Into the Human Race' at Cooper Union: Wants Sex Fences Cut Down."[14]

The reporter called the speakers "six of the country's leading feminists." More tellingly, in Howe's introduction to the panel, she called each panelist, including Gilman, "a practical liver of her own feminist theories." In pure Gilman-speak, Howe announced feminist objectives as the recognition and development of women's human qualities shared with men. According to the *Times:* "The world, she said, was human, and women wanted to be human, not merely emotional, personal, feminine creatures. . . . We're sick of being specialized to sex. . . . We intend simply to be ourselves, not just our little female selves, but our whole, big, human selves." Dorr spoke on women's right to work and economic independence, Schneiderman on age discrimination against female workers and their right to organize industrially; and La Follette addressed married women's right to keep their own name and urged the abandonment of the title "Mrs." Marie Jenney Howe explained that fond as she was of Frederick C.—her husband and New York's popular secretary of customs—she did not care to be named Mrs. Frederick C. Howe, here part of the ethic of feminists "living out their principles in practice." Hale, a mother of twins, gave an address titled "The Right of the Mother to Her Profession" and took up the much debated proposal for "mothers' pensions." Nina Wilcox Putnam offered a stinging critique of fashion, asserting women's right to ignore it. Gilman spoke last, on "home industries," and the right of women to specialize, her persistent advocacy since *Women and Economics* and *The Home,* both over a decade old. Gilman enhanced this feminist meeting with her presence and intellectual profile.[15]

Later, she articulated her reservations about her classification by others as a feminist. She thought contemporary feminists did not address the background and historical components of women's subjection often enough: "The feminist movement of which recent decades have been so full, is but of the moment; back of it, still going on beneath it, and all around and behind it, lies the unbroken influence of ages of over-sexed subjugation. . . . The change is deeper, more important, than any mere feminist imagines. It is not the attainment of that first poor purpose, 'equality with men.' Heaven help the world if women could reach no higher than that."

Feminism needed to bring more than equality to women: it also needed to extend their power and agency to secure the much-needed "human world." Her resistance to classification as a feminist originated in her conviction that the term did not capture the totality of her arguments and preoccupations, only some of which directly concerned women. She held that her particular reasoning about women made sense only in the light of other nonfeminist discourses—especially reform Darwinism, Nationalism, Fabian socialism, and increasingly, eugenics. Moreover, she worried that thinkers of many political and ideological stripes were awkwardly grouped

FIGURE 24. Rev. Marie Jenney Howe
(Catt: 2/5/3c, Carrie Chapman Catt
Collection, Bryn Mawr College Library)

together under the label feminism, when their divergent viewpoints precluded much common ground. Once promulgated, there was such a genuine attractiveness and currency about the term. Unfortunately, it obscured significant differences between those also committed to other and incommensurate political and philosophical positions. In seeking a "biological basis for feminism," Gilman's stance diverged from those also called feminists who were unconcerned about biology, evolution, eugenics, reproduction, sexuality, and population development.[16]

In fact, Gilman's truth claims for biological and evolutionary bases for feminism made neglect of these factors by those claiming authority on the Woman Question intolerable to her. Hence, the word "feminism," at least as other feminists understood it, amounted to a misreading of her position. She did not like all of the company kept by feminism. To claim the concept fully—and to allow it to claim her person and her work—she wanted control over its boundaries and meanings. This became especially urgent as feminism gradually developed via paradigms different from those informing her reform Darwinist rationale.[17]

Her reservations about being called a feminist also may have been image management, necessary to keep viable her living as lecturer and editor. As a lecturer, writer, and publisher, her prized economic independence hinged on public credibility and reputation, making her especially vigilant about the label feminism. For the general public, feminism and suffragism were synonymous—the latter the most visible woman movement campaign of the period. She could not afford to represent herself as too far from "main street" and still maximize fee-paying audiences in cities and towns all across America. On the lecture circuit, Gilman received feedback directly from agents that suffrage advocacy would lose her audiences in some locales. Worried men forbade their wives going to lectures that might raise difficult questions and ideas.[18]

Notwithstanding the stigmatizing effect of the label feminist, it had one pleasant association. As noted before, the figure Gilman admired most was Olive Schreiner. If the label feminist put her in the same sentence as her idol, this could be a thrilling downside. Her dream was to produce work as good as Schreiner's. Biographers report that in her lonely nomadic years on the lecture circuit during the 1890s, her traveling bag always contained, alongside Walt Whitman's *Leaves of Grass,* her copy of Schreiner's *Dreams* (1890). The allegory from that work, "Three Dreams in a Desert"—on the "past, present, and future of woman"—profoundly influenced Gilman's thinking, particularly Schreiner's posing women's subjection as a historical event rather than an eternal necessity, the subject of the first "dream":

> And I said, "Why does she lie here motionless with the sand piled round her?"
>
> And he answered . . . "Ages and ages long she has lain here, and the wind has blown over her. . . . But . . . older than the oldest book, older than the oldest recorded memory of man, on the Rocks of Language, on the hard-baked clay of Ancient Customs, now crumbling to decay, are found the marks of her footsteps! Side by side with his who stands beside her you may trace them; and you know that she who now lies there once wandered free over the rocks with him."
>
> And I said, "Why does she lie there now?"
>
> And he said, "I take it, ages ago the Age-of-dominion-of-muscular-force found her, and when she stooped low to give sucker to her young, and her back was broad, he put his burden of subjection onto it, and tied it on with the broad band of Inevitable Necessity. Then she looked at the earth and sky, and knew there was no hope for her; and she lay down on the sand with the burden she could not loosen. Ever since she has lain here."

Schreiner's vision of the historicity and contingency of women's sex oppression accorded with the writings of many contemporary thinkers and

FIGURE 25. Olive Schreiner
(Catt: 6.5.3c. Carrie Chapman
Catt Collection, Bryn Mawr
College Library)

scholars postulating an earlier matriarchal or gynaecocentric era with independent laboring women free of patriarchal institutions. Gilman particularly endorsed the thesis of the second of Schreiner's dreams: namely,
that the duty of "Woman," allegorically coming out of the desert, was to
renounce all present comforts, to ford the dark and dangerous river to freedom, in the interests of the whole human race following her. This inspiring
call to service and social reform was the same mission Gilman embraced
and urged on her fellow women. In her call for a "human world," Gilman
shared Schreiner's critique of women's current social and psychological fos-
silization and her call for them to reclaim their rightful places as cocreators
of human society.[19]

Logically enough, reviewers and readers compared Schreiner's *Woman
and Labour* (1911), addressing women's economic independence and reconfiguring sexual relations, to Gilman's *Women and Economics* (1898),
though both wrote unaware of each other's projects. Parts of Schreiner's
text, written across the 1890s—its full publication delayed by the Boer War
and subsequent destruction of much of the original manuscript—were
published in *Cosmopolitan* in 1899. Gilman herself saw great similarities,
but she did not feel that Schreiner owed her an acknowledgment. In 1899
she confided to her fiancé, George Houghton Gilman, that she believed
that with *Women and Economics* and other work, she could stand as equal
to Schreiner. Urging that he read Schreiner's "fine" November 1899 *Cos-*

mopolitan article on the Woman Question, she noted that Schreiner's "power as a writer is great—but I don't see that after all she is saying more than I do. But she says it splendidly and it 'carries' far and wide." Scholars have held that there was no contact between them and that Schreiner was unfamiliar with Gilman's work. However, this proves misleading since Gilman also wrote to Houghton Gilman from California, in early 1900: "Another letter is a charmingly appreciative one from an English lady ... and she says in it that Olive Schreiner knows and admires my book—thinks it the book. I am proud: I have so long and deeply reverenced her."[20]

By the later 1920s, Gilman no longer deferred to the South African. In 1930, when psychologist and cultural critic Samuel D. Schmalhausen ventured that Gilman was "the first sociologist in America to discuss adequately women's parasitic psychology (under our social system), following the illuminating work of Olive Schreiner," Gilman retorted: "My 'Women and Economics' was published in 1898, Olive Schreiner's 'Woman and Labor' after the Boer War. She was one of the greatest women of the age, far greater than I in literary power, but unless you refer to the suggestions in 'The Story,' of An African Farm and the far-reaching vision of her 'Dreams,' my work on the economic dependence of women and its results antecedes hers." By publication dates, *Women and Economics* unquestionably predated *Woman and Labour*. However, Schreiner's 1899 *Cosmopolitan* articles appear verbatim in her 1911 text, sustaining her claim that the fuller work was completed by 1899, probably earlier. More remarkable is the extent of shared analysis between these almost simultaneously written texts from such different cultural contexts. Had Schreiner's full text survived and been published in 1899—particularly those chapters on the evolution of sex, human social development from primitive to savage, to semisavage, and eventually industrialized "civilized" forms, the retardation of women's status through loss of productive labor and enforced dependence, the critique of the home and primitive unpaid domestic labor, and observations on marriage, prostitution, divorce, and eugenics—their similarities would have been called astonishing.[21]

Being called a feminist alongside Schreiner, then, was a happy result of the paradigm shift involved in the new label. The term signaled a new grid of intelligibility through which Gilman's readers could debate and understand her and Schreiner's work. If Schreiner had been her only other peer, Gilman might have tolerated the new term "feminist." But Ellen Key was another matter.

Defining and Reviewing "Feminism"

It is doubtless true that besides her love a woman may have a calling in life. But the profound distinction between her and man is at present this: that he more often gives of his best as a creator than as a lover—while for her the reverse is nearly always the case. And while the man is appraised by himself and others according to his work, woman in her heart values herself—and wishes to be valued—according to her love.

Ellen S. Key, Love and Marriage *(1911)*

Ellen Key glorified motherhood, urged payment for mothers, and explicitly opposed Gilman's goals of paid work for wives and the transformation of domestic work, cooking, and child culture into public, valued, and well-recompensed work. Unsurprisingly, Key aroused Gilman's ire. Thoroughly essentialist in her conceptions of sex differences, commentators called Key's *Love and Marriage* (1911) the bible of European feminism and sex reform. Key repudiated Gilman's focus on women's economic independence, woman suffrage, and the working mother. Moreover, she warned that "new women," excelling in science or industry, would lose the sympathy and sex attraction of their men, eventually forced to endure unnatural celibacy, barrenness, and loneliness. In Key's world, Nature made opposites attract and the best marriages were those in which woman devoted themselves to sympathetic furthering of the man's endeavors. Indeed, avowed antisuffragists and critics of feminism typically attacked Gilman's proposals using Key's language and concepts.[22]

Gilman reviled Key's collusion with those antifeminist critics who supposed that women professionals necessarily neglected their homes and families. This assumption rested on another, namely, "that the home must always be a group of undifferentiated industries as it has been for so long, and that the woman must do both kinds of work at once." Here, of course, Gilman alluded to her broader program of reforming household design, marketing, food preparation, cleaning, childcare, education, and urban planning. Thereby, homes could become places of companionship and rest, not the unhygienic sites of primitive industries performed by untrained wives and mothers. Men and women could thus and equally "work and love too." Far exceeding a critique of the sexual division of labor, which fifty years later led to working women demanding men's equal participation in household and family work, Gilman rejected the very idea that households should perform such work at all. Instead, skilled labor and professions

FIGURE 26. Mrs. Ellen Key (Catt: 6.7.3f., Carrie Chapman Catt Collection, Bryn Mawr College Library)

should develop to perform these essential but presently unpaid forms of social labor.[23]

Key's text *The Woman Movement* (1912) was a diatribe against American feminist challenges to women's status. Over and over, Gilman's was clearly the approach Key targeted when criticizing "American" tendencies within feminism. Gilman already saw in old European cultures the reactionary mores of intransigent patriarchy, potentially "clogging" the progress of American women through the unfair influence of "backward" immigrant men voters. Hence, Key's denigration of American developments, using Gilman as exemplar, only inflamed Gilman's antagonism.[24]

With feminism becoming more entrenched in public dialogue, Gilman sought to separate herself, and her reputation, from Key. In fact, Key did likewise, distinguishing herself from Gilman, who she claimed exemplified "amaternal [*sic*] feminism." Meanwhile, Key's undue exaggeration of sex differences and sentimentalized depictions of motherhood and womanliness earned Gilman's epithet of a "feminine feminist," failing "to recognize that the distinction of species is far larger than the distinction of sex. Our humanness is a quality common to both sexes," and the evil was that women were confined "to the exercise of sex faculties only—however nobly developed, and denied the exercise of the human ones."[25]

Most fundamentally, Gilman rejected the essentialist maternalism entailed in Key's staking biological motherhood as the ground of women's rights, though she did not disparage the important work of motherhood. However, to require this experience to define all women's lives, and worse, to assume that adequate child rearing required nothing more than maternal instinct, caused human misery: "What I do deny absolutely, is that the individual mother is, or ever can be, all sufficient as an educator of humanity.... Mother love does not give human understanding. Ellen Key beautifies and extols an ideal Mother who is all-wise and unfailing in intelligent tendencies. Not all women are such—or ever can be."[26]

By contrast, she called those who sought to minimize sex differences rather than celebrate or enlarge them "human feminists," evidently including herself. She continued this argument about the varieties of feminism in her fiction. In her 1916 story, "Her Overhearing," Eleanor Moreham seeks to marry reluctant bridegroom, artist Hugh Talbot. Among her friends: "the newest and most 'intriguing' ... were feminists of the more ultra-feminine kinds. Their theory of feminism was to be as female as possible, openly, frankly, quite unashamed. Men they considered rather in the light of necessary evils, agreeable as lovers, but undesirable as husbands; children, to their minds, seemed rather a proud expression of womanhood than members of the family or the state. They were willing to have children when they chose, but the fathers thereof were to be considered from a eugenic standard only."[27]

In her criticisms of Key, Gilman registered discomfort about Key being designated, by contemporaries, as a feminist as significant as Schreiner and, therefore, as herself. This discomfort led her to announce the need for all to recognize that feminism was not one monolithic political and philosophical domain. Instead, she charted the diversity of feminism:

> What is now so generally called feminism is not only a thing quite outside the Suffrage question, but also a movement in more than one direction. There are two schools of Feminism, not only distinct, but opposed. The one holds that sex is a minor department of life; that the main lines of human development have nothing to do with sex, and that what women need most is the development of human characteristics. The other considers sex as paramount, as underlying or covering all phases of life, and that what woman needs is an even fuller exercise, development and recognition of her sex. There are, of course, all shades and degrees of opinion on the subject, but these two are quite distinct.[28]

While Gilman here did not classify herself as representing any variety of feminism, clearly her approach fitted the humanist feminist category, perhaps illuminating her assertion that she was a humanist, advocating that humans should no longer be specialized by sex.[29] In other words, her very definition of "humanism" and designation of herself as a humanist depended on adherence to the former "sex-minimizing" strand in the earlier articulation of American versions of feminism. Even in this early articulation, she registered the movement and its philosophical development as already fractured into new and different strands. Her sex-minimizing definition opposed women's sex parasitism, tacitly associating Key's position with a younger generation of women.

Moreover, Gilman's definition of "humanism" differed from its philosophical heritage as a position privileging human interest and perfectibility over theistic adherence. Popularized, this latter version could mean pursuit of the best interests of humans or humanity as a whole.[30] Criticisms leveled at Gilman, however, examined in chapter 7, revealed how political could be in the eye of the beholder—who was to determine the best interests of humanity? Such judgments could be quite prescriptive for women, evidenced when Gilman's self-declared humanist peers pitted their doctrine against her feminism.[31]

Gilman was not alone in raising objections to Key's claims and seeking to qualify the extent and terms by which Key was or was not to be recognized as an eminent feminist. For instance, in a widely reviewed book, *Feminism in Germany and Scandinavia* (1915), Susan B. Anthony's niece, Katharine Anthony, employed the dualism of "Anglo-American" feminism on one side, with the slogan, "Votes for Women," and on the other, "Teuto-Scandinavian" feminism, with the rallying cry, "protection of motherhood." Gilman's antagonistic response to Key's attacks, then, had a larger and more fundamentally philosophical anchor. As Anthony observed: "The overwhelming effect of Ellen Key's ideas in Germany, as well as in her own country, the passionate for-and-against which has raged round her as a center makes it hard to understand the extremely platonic attitude of English and American feminists toward the whole Ellen Key program. It is still true that the spirit of Susan B. Anthony guides the woman movement of this country to the exclusion of all foreign influence." Anthony fully reported the divisive effects of Key's 1896 attack on "the ruling ideas of the suffrage movement" and her associating it with the illegitimate and uncritical rush into men's occupations. Key suffered from "inconsistent thinking and deficient powers of correlation," according to Anthony, leading to "the liberal percentage of dross in Ellen Key's purest inspirations." Observing her lack of "associative discipline," her impracticality, and her isolation, "her genius

FIGURE 27. Portrait of
Katharine Anthony, ca. 1915
(The Schlesinger Library,
Radcliffe Institute, Harvard
University: A25-73vo-6)

and her incompetence together have made her the 'wise fool' of the woman movement."[32]

Gilman was not alone in praising Katharine Anthony's book for "the sparkle of admirable wit," but of course here her accolades were tinged with self-interest. Even Gilman's one-time Fabian socialist friend turned antifeminist critic, Prestonia Mann Martin, held that Key's thought showed disarray, so that "persons holding the most contradictory views on the woman question all look confidently to Ellen Key's books for support; and Ellen never fails them. To feminists she is a tower of strength; to anti-feminists a seer and a prophetess." Historian Mari Jo Buhle rightly notes that this dispute between Gilman and Key, "introduced many literate Americans to the basic tenets of modern feminism."[33]

Thus, Gilman partly resisted the label feminist to avoid being misunderstood. Being lumped together with Key, as if their causes were the same, vexed her considerably. While the differences between them are obvious, contemporaries often seemed oblivious to their irreconcilability. For instance, in 1913, feminist journalist Estelle Lawton Lindsay answered, in the *Los Angeles Record,* a complimentary correspondent urging Lindsay's feminist uniqueness: "No; you are mistaken. Charlotte Perkins Gilman is doing the same work and much more ably than I.... For what I know of the basic truths of life I am indebted to her, to the great Olive Shriner [*sic*], to Bernard Shaw, Lester F. Ward and Ellen Key." If pleased with the accolade, Gilman could only wonder how her own "basic truths" and those of Key could be juxtaposed intelligibly. Others, too, made strange bedfellows of their feminist idols.[34]

Alternatively, journalist and Heterodoxy member, Bessie Beatty, divided the feminist field between Gilman and Key in her account of a 1915 lecture by Gilman undertaking to define "feminism." Beatty portrayed Gilman as expressing "the feminist viewpoint on the economic independence of woman, on war, education, punishment, and most of the big problems to which women are more and more turning their attention." In contrast, "Ellen Key's feministic tendencies are directed chiefly to relations of men and women in the sphere of sex." This implied that sexual relations were not Gilman's concern, her attention instead "turned toward the economic relations of men and women, and it is on this subject that she has shown most brilliance." Perhaps Beatty was seeking to reconcile them.[35]

For Gilman, of course, the sexes' economic relations arose from their sexual relations. Hence, Beatty's artificial separation of Gilman from sexual relations misrepresented the whole rationale for Gilman's work. However, Beatty's separation of spheres permitted her to represent both Key and Gilman as feminists—one addressing the private sphere, one the public— without having to confront their diametrical opposition and critical incommensurability. This depiction may also reflect Beatty's and other younger feminists' inclination to find Key's free love message more congenial and familiar than Gilman's reform Darwinist quest to spare women from "oversexed" identities and overuse by men. As Cott notes, "By 1912 the feminists in Greenwich Village who used to read Charlotte Perkins Gilman were reading Ellen Key." This was despite Key's "very traditional gender ideas," according to historian Ellen Kay Trimberger, who contends that younger feminists used Key's ideas to support greater sexual freedom but ignored her more conservative stances. So Beatty and others promoted the parts of Gilman's message they could endorse: paid work, careers, public life, and commodifying housework and childcare—that is, Gilman's reform proposals—but not their sexual and evolutionary rationale.[36]

As one result of contemplating the image of her drawn by younger women like Beatty, Gilman came to associate feminist with the next generation of women—a generation who refused to heed her words with regard to free love and other topics. To her mind, this piecemeal acceptance of her ideas incomprehensibly narrowed and hollowed the possible span

FIGURE 28. Portrait of Bessie
Beatty, ca. 1910. Photo by Sarony's
(New York) (The Schlesinger
Library, Radcliffe Institute, Harvard
University: A25-73V0-11).

of feminist analysis. This was most apparent in the 1920s and 1930s, when
changed understandings of sexuality, which seemed inconsistent with her
ideas on reducing women's sex work and enhancing their race work, deep-
ened the divide between her and younger feminists. These younger women
did not intellectually and politically come of age under the influence of
reform Darwinism, as interpreted by Lester Frank Ward, as she had. Hence,
her intermittent description of herself as a humanist, rather than a feminist,
was more a rebuke and disagreement about erotic and sexual issues within
feminism than a mark of Gilman's abandonment of this philosophy and
movement to the Ellen Keys of the world.

Unquestionably, by the time of these disagreements, Progressive Era
sexual patterns and representations had shifted. Reaching adulthood in the
1880s, Gilman had negotiated the difficulties of adult femininity within
contemporary discourses. The urban New Women of the Progressive Era,
born in the 1880s and 1890s, became adults in the 1900s and 1910s, when
the word "feminism" first attained American currency. They deployed
discourses and options that had been unavailable to the young Gilman—
psychoanalysis, anarchism, Bohemianism, sexology and experiments in free
love, nonmonogamous relationships, and birth control. Literature, art, and

popular culture registered vividly these influences. Hence, Gilman's reform Darwinist analysis of women's sexual and erotic subjection during the 1890s at first challenged but increasingly was itself challenged by new understandings of sexuality—especially that advocating a clear separation between sexuality and reproduction.[37]

Even so, Gilman limited her implicit or explicit rebukes of younger feminists. As she constantly asserted, the future rested on the Progressive changes made by these same young women. She reserved her fiercest ire for reactionary women. This made her resistance to feminism ambiguous.[38]

If she worried about the meaning of "feminism" as a term including herself and Key without differentiation, she also drew attention to the phenomenon of male intellectuals claiming to be feminists speaking on behalf of the movement. Such men spread extreme, misinformed, or distorted versions of feminist theory and strategy. Englishman W. L. George was a case in point. He published an article in the *Atlantic Monthly* in 1913 that the *New York Times* promptly reprinted. While claiming to be a feminist, he described feminism as a movement seeking sex war and sex strikes, in order to end economic dependence and destroy world institutions built on male domination, including marriage. Proponents of free love, feminists intended to use the vote "to make women vote as women, and not as citizens; that is to say, they propose to sell the female vote en bloc to the party that bids highest for it in the economic field." Hating the child and motherhood, the feminist determined to take revenge on male society. Gilman found these claims alarming, especially when people read them in influential media, like the *Times:*

> This man who calls himself a Feminist and is published as its champion has contrived in this article to identify the movement with most of the present world's bugbears—Socialism, Syndicalism, Anarchy, and Free love, as well as a Sex-war, which seems somewhat incompatible with the latter. There is no way, of course, of preventing anyone who chooses saying what pleases him about Feminism, or about Socialism, or about Christianity. As a rule, however, those who carefully play upon deep-seated popular prejudices in arraying the worst features its worst enemies attribute to their subject, do not claim to be advocates, spokesmen, or champions.[39]

Prompted by these spurious debates over meaning, in 1914 Gilman offered a public lecture series available by subscription entitled "The Larger Feminism"—a title that epitomized her concern that prevailing feminist discourses needed greater span, range, and depth. Far from abandoning feminism, she challenged herself to define a feminism that she and others

FIGURE 29. Portrait of Clara Savage Littledale, 1914 (The Schlesinger Library, Radcliffe Institute, Harvard University: A157-2-5)

could embrace. Widely covered by New York newspapers, even the *New York Times'* often snide reporting offered almost verbatim transcription of these lectures once a week for many weeks, usually running to two full columns. This was a remarkable amount of coverage for an antisuffrage newspaper identifying feminists and suffragists as indistinguishable. It was the most coverage of a single feminist theorist's work ever documented in the *Times.* True to her reform Darwinist framework, and just a year since Lester Ward's death, she titled the first of these lectures "The Biological Bases of the Larger Feminism." Newspaper reportage of her lectures permits a detailed picture of her widely distributed arguments and strategies.[40]

Further insight into the currency of debates over feminism, as well as perceptions of Gilman as the period's preeminent feminist commentator, emerge from the daily 1914 diary of Clara Savage Littledale (1891–1956), a new Vassar graduate and women's affairs journalist at the *New York Evening Post.* On 4 March, she wrote, "went to Charlotte Perkins Gilman who talked on Feminism as everyone else is doing. 'I talk on Feminism Myself,' remarked a man, coming out. She has a lovely face but a harsh voice and I didn't like her especially." A month later, Gilman was lecturing again—this time, her "Masculism" series. Littledale wrote, "Heard Charlotte Perkins Gilman on 'A Male Civilization' and she made me furious. I dislike her manner and voice so much. She may have facts but that's about all she reveals to her audiences, and the conclusions she draws from them!!" She reviewed her day: "Sore throat, curse, and Charlotte Perkins Gilman. It made for a very nervy morning." Gilman's lectures drew large crowds and made news, however, so the young reporter found herself assigned to Gilman again the next month, this time as the featured Saturday story, her most extended article of the week. Gilman's voice as a definer and reviewer of feminism gave her considerable prominence during the early years of the First World War. Of course, these efforts only more firmly associated her name with feminism.[41]

The New Generation

> It is no great wonder that there is chaos among the awakening women. Take a cry like that for a "single standard of morality." It means two utterly contradictory things. For the Pankhursts it is assumed that men should adopt women's standards, but in the minds of thousands it means just the reverse. For some people, feminism is a movement of women to make men chaste, for others the enforced chastity of women is a sign of their slavery. Feminism is attacked both for being too "moral" and too "immoral."
>
> *Walter Lippmann, "The Woman's Movement" (1914)*

It was because she was widely regarded as her county's foremost feminist that Gilman had attracted criticisms. These attacks may have been a further reason for her distancing herself from the label feminist. She seemed to oppose free love, however, seriously alienating younger women, particularly feminists. Sexuality was the great divide between her and younger generations. Moreover, Gilman believed that Freudian claptrap had hoodwinked interwar women. She held that psychoanalysis was inimical to women's progress and the highest standing for monogamy, the sexual institution best serving women's "race" interests: "Another obstacle is that resurgence of phallic worship set before us in the solemn phraseology of psychoanalysis. This pitifully narrow and morbid philosophy presumes to discuss sex from observation of humanity only. It is confronted with our excessive development and assumes it to be normal. It ignores the evidence of the entire living world below us, basing its conclusions on the behavior and desires of an animal which stands alone in nature for misery and disease in the sex relation." If she resisted the cultural power of these contemporary positions she did not succeed in undermining them. In support of her alternative vision of sexual relations, she made a series of charges. Men now faced newly enfranchised women citizens who challenged hydraulic accounts of male sexuality and its need for constant indulgence, "more than women were willing to give." Hitherto, "feminine submission" resulted from "an imposing array of civil and religious laws," as well as women's economic dependence. With enfranchisement and all that it implied, women were becoming braver and more financially independent, no longer willing that "he shall rule over her." Thus, her previous master has no hold on her "beyond natural attraction and—persuasion." So men peevishly counterattacked, in part by advancing as a new orthodoxy the regressive mental straitjackets of psychoanalysis:

> Whereas in the past women were taught that they had no such 'imperative instincts' as men . . . now it is quite otherwise. All . . . worship of virginity, goes by the board, and women are given a reversed theory—that they are just the same as men, if not more so; our "double standard" is undoubled and ironed flat—to the level of masculine desire. Clothed in the solemn, newly invented terms of psychoanalysis, a theory of sex is urged upon us which bases all our activities upon this one function. It is exalted as not only an imperative instinct, but as *the* imperative instinct, no others . . . save the demands of the stomach. Surely never was more physical a theory disguised in the technical verbiage of "psychology."[42]

Gilman charged that psychoanalysis took the masculine to be the human, and as such was a bitter enemy of all efforts to deconstruct and reconfigure sexuality in what she called human terms.[43] She did admit that it reflected "the ingenious mind of man for thinking up a new theory to retain what the old ones no longer assured him." And despite her opposition, she understood how the feminist demand for equality could be taken by many younger women to mean equal sexual indulgence for women. This was merely "the same eager imitation of the previous master, which history shows in any recently enfranchised people." Women were showing that they could and would imitate "men's sex habits, in large measure."

In putting the matter this way, though, she gave short shrift to younger women's genuine attraction to newly eroticized cultural mores. Young urban women reveled in the erotic extensions of greater heterosocial ease afforded by the city. To them, Gilman's much extolled "humanness" meshed with equalitarianism, so that it seemed logical to demand the right to share in the full array of human experiences, including sexual ones, without penalty of the anciently unfair sexual double standard. The preferred single standard was one of equal sexual freedom for women. Thus, in a generational shift well underway before World War One, such younger women's conception of viable feminism combined "economic choice with heterosexual intimacy." This combination of priorities was well demonstrated in the life and experiences of feminists like Doris Stevens (1888–1963), taken

FIGURE 30. Portrait of
Doris Stevens (1892–1963),
1916–20, Ira L. Hill's Studio
(The Schlesinger Library,
Radcliffe Institute, Harvard
University A 140-15a-2).

by many historians of feminism to exemplify this shift of values around sexuality.[44]

Gilman knew the beautiful, vivacious, and college-educated Stevens through Heterodoxy, and after the Nineteenth Amendment, through the National Woman's Party, the Lucy Stone League, and other feminist organizations such as the International American Commission of Women. Stevens was committed both to a feminism indebted to Gilman's theories and to "the sexual revolution," including heterosociality, sexual experimentation, serial monogamy, divorce law reform, birth control advocacy, and psychoanalysis. For older feminists, such as New York suffrage movement patron Alva Belmont (1853–1933), Stevens's sexual involvements with men—including an open marriage and a long-term affair with a married man, who she subsequently married after divorcing her first husband—were unconventional if not unacceptable. Stevens had intensely loving same-sex friendships, yet she gradually internalized and expressed the homophobia that Leila J. Rupp identifies as a corollary of the male-defined sexual revolution of the 1920s, which Stevens was trying to reconcile with her deep feminist commitments. Like many urban women of the period, she turned to psychoanalysis as a tool to assist her to gain insight into her

FIGURE 31. Portrait of
Beatrice Hinkle, 1900–1905,
by Marceau (New York, N.Y.)
(The Schlesinger Library,
Radcliffe Institute, Harvard
University: A25-73v0-52)

own conflicting erotic needs and desires, as well as her intense difficulties
negotiating the versions of heterosexuality expected by men with whom she
was intimate. If she embraced sexual freedom in principle, it was a costly,
often painful quest.[45]

Stevens's experiences matched, to different degrees, those of other feminists of her generation. These included the actress Fola La Follette (1882–
1970), Beatrice Hinkle (1874–1953), Leta Hollingworth (1886–1939), Elsie
Clews Parsons (1875–1941), Crystal Eastman (1881–1928), Freda Kirchwey
(1893–1976), and many others aged fifteen to forty years younger than Gilman. Despite Gilman's later objections, psychoanalysis influenced these
feminists' understanding of feminism within Heterodoxy, even as they continued to admire Gilman's contributions. They embraced psychoanalysis as
a way to understand the elusiveness of emancipation from oppressive patterns of subjectivity, desire, dynamics, and meaning, matters unaddressed
by gaining either "equal" rights or the ingenious renegotiation of domestic and public worlds programmatically envisaged in Gilman's "human
world."[46] Indeed, among this generation of feminists, Hinkle was a remarkable Jungian psychoanalyst of prominent feminist men and women—including Max Eastman and Fola La Follette. As well, she was an avant-garde
feminist critic of Freud. She theorized masculine longing for and dread

of women, as it contributed to "the final problem of the feminist movement ... the psychic bondage of women to men." Her work helped her peers make sense of continued obstacles to feminist transformation of personal and sexual life.[47]

If Gilman's imagining of a human world so pivotally rested on men accepting conjugal moderation—if not Herlanderish temperance—these generational shifts challenged her optimism. Indeed, her impassioned diatribes against psychoanalysis, sexology, and sexual promiscuity—especially those behaviors requiring female birth control as their preconditions—showed her awareness of the chasm between her vision and the proclivities of her interwar contemporaries. How then to interpret Gilman's sexual thought?[48]

Her appropriation of reform Darwinism receives easy and justifiable criticism. Yet feminist scholars have been more attentive to her race and eugenic concerns than to the significance of her use of Darwinian zoology and theories of sex selection to mandate women's renegotiation of conjugal sexuality, reduce sexual demands, and institute voluntary motherhood. Unfortunately, presentist assumptions about sexuality powerfully inflect historians' contributions to the history of both sexuality and feminism in the United States, so that nineteenth-century feminist sexual thought often is characterized flatly as conservative, puritanical, and erotophobic. If, as Nancy Cott so cogently observes, feminists always face the contradictory stretch between contempt for existing forms of femininity and support for women as they are, Gilman lived a most acute form of this ambiguity. Yet she usually qualified any theories of women as generalities. Though disagreeing with younger women over sexuality and fashion, she held hope for the future in the new breed of wage earners and independence seekers. In fact, she reserved her most acid rhetoric for old-fashioned, conservative, ultra-feminine women, who retarded "the race" through their parasitic and unprogressive lives.[49]

Despite her disavowals, however, reports of her influence on feminism continued until the end of her life and beyond. In 1931, a California newspaper reported the launch of Mary Ritter Beard's book, *On Understanding Women* under the headline: "Power of Woman Is Told Audience: Civilization Is of Feminine Origin Asserts Mary R. Beard in Club Address." In the accompanying interview, Mrs. Beard "who admits to being a disciple of Charlotte Perkins Stetson Gilman, noted feminist," described women readers as responsive and men hostile to her exploration of previous historical contributions by women to culture and civilization.[50]

Feminists prominent in the waning years of the Progressive Era during the Depression and the New Deal voiced great admiration and indebtedness to Gilman. In 1920, Florence L. Cross Kitchelt (1885–1961), a leading suffragist, became Connecticut president of the League of Women Voters. She then worked on various law reform commissions and, by the later 1940s, was an activist in efforts to revive and have ratified the Equal Rights Amendment. She sent the editor of *Independent Woman* a file of papers and letters about Gilman, urging use of them in the paper, since "Mrs. Gilman, an author read with bated breath in my youth is barely modern today. It helps to know how far we have come. It is good for the young to know something of the early struggle." Even if her theoretical work was now untenable, the example of her life experience as a feminist was still worthy of commendation, a tip of the hat to a truly venerable foremother. Kitchelt had written to Gilman in 1897, prior to *Women and Economics,* on the subject of the position of wives, to which Gilman responded enthusiastically.[51]

Notwithstanding her distancing herself from feminism, it is important to explore ways in which Gilman connected feminism and Progressivism. Her formulations and theories influenced not only peers like Catt and Blatch but also thousands of unknown women and men, some of whom wrote eloquent letters to Gilman from across America and from countries like Sweden, Japan, Hungary, Australia, Germany, and India. She also inspired younger women to leadership in postsuffrage organizations, like Florence Kitchelt, Cicely Hamilton, and Mary Ritter Beard. Others more peripherally considering suffrage and feminism had strong views on Gilman, including journalist Clara Savage Littledale. Gilman had immense significance for generations of feminists, whatever she herself said about feminism.[52]

BY THE END of her life, Gilman seemed no longer to pit humanism against feminism, even though she certainly retained reservations about others called representative feminists, and occasionally indulged in curmudgeonlike sniping at their expense. In 1929, noting the challenge facing feminism in androcentric culture, she wrote: "The older, the more general, the more intimate in personal appeal a custom might be, the more universal and violent was the objection to changing it; and the movement of women which we call Feminism challenges a relation precisely the most intimate, general, and historically ancient of our race habits." Since this described precisely the mission she had embraced since the 1880s, Gilman seemed to recognize that the term "feminism" had come to stay. Even if she still adopted the role of commentator and appraiser of it, and even if she still might place quote marks around or capitalize the word, there was no real question of her being outside Progressive Era feminism.

Is it reasonable, then, for scholars to call Gilman a feminist, despite her disavowals? On the basis of her decisive intellectual work on suffrage and antisuffragism, on her definitions and critiques of peer feminists, and the place she occupied in Progressive Era critiques of feminism and feminists, the answer is "yes," even if this position disrespects some of her own words and wishes. Classifications of thinkers by theoretical orientations are tools, always externally and contingently imposed, to assist intelligibility and analysis. Apart from current redefinitions of feminism, Gilman's intellectual contributions to theorizing women's subjection meet all criteria for recognizable feminism in spite of, or even partly because of, the critiques they engendered.

Gilman's feminism was inflected by her ambivalent oscillation between pragmatic and utopian views of sexual contracts. She harbored uncertainty about the claims of feminism of her period, sometimes holding feminism as opposed to a more desirable state of humanism, the rightful successor of androcentrism. Yet her critiques of androcentric institutions, such as organized religion, military services, industry, prostitution, and the family, implied inexorable feminism—even if Gilman faced that implication only with difficulty.

CHAPTER SEVEN

"The High Priestess of Feminism"

I soon sat at the feet of the brainiest and most stimulating of nationally known leaders who for years had pioneered the most radical economic aspect of the woman question. Charlotte not only turned out books … she presented her facts in chiseled prose but, like all feminists I know, with devastating humor. She herself was a mistress of sarcasm, amusing as her lectures were peppered with ridicule and irony. She disliked the narrow word "feminism," her philosophy was rather based on what she called "Humanism."

George Middleton, These Things Were Mine: The Autobiography of a Journeyman Playwright *(1947)*

WHATEVER GILMAN herself said about the term "feminism," her contemporaries treated her as feminism's chief theorist and personification. As such, those invested in other political movements and intellectual positions commented, often critically, on her increasingly visible feminist contributions and stature. This chapter examines three kinds of responses to Gilman's designation as the "high priestess of feminism."

The first part examines would-be serious or scholarly discussion of feminism from the Progressive Era featuring discussion of Gilman in comparison with others such as Schreiner and Key. This includes close examination of texts by Fabian socialists, Prestonia Mann Martin and John Martin, conservative economist, Correa Moylan Walsh, and biologist Avrom Barnett. All featured criticism of Gilman's theoretical debt to Lester Frank Ward or skeptical responses to her accounts of sex differences and capacities. Most centrally, these critics represented the broader objection to Gilman's feminism: they took her to be minimizing the significance of sex differences and biological reproduction for the distribution of human resources and activities. These errors led her to propose reforms as naive as they were impracticable.[1]

The second task of the chapter is an examination of newspaper press and other periodicals' portrayals of and responses to Gilman's feminism. She began making local news with her earliest articles, poems, and talks in the 1880s. She began receiving national coverage by the early 1890s commensurate with her work among literary circles and Nationalists in California and her steadily enlarging lecturing itinerary after spring 1894, when Kate went back to live with Stetson and her new stepmother. Moreover, Gilman's move to Chicago to join Jane Addams, along with increasing association between suffragism and women's welfare causes thereafter, garnered additional press attention. The 1898 publication of *Women and Economics* cemented the press shift to assigning her to the "Woman Question," though journalists and editors did not significantly embrace the word "feminism" until around 1908 and after. With her European travels of 1896 and 1899, and the multiple language translation and distribution of *Women and Economics* thereafter, an international market of interest in her previous and subsequent work was established, manifest in print media reportage. The press had an inordinate influence in interpreting her work to contemporaries because of the extensiveness of the coverage. Gilman did not stand in some Olympian place. Whether fencing or deflecting adverse divorce publicity or defending suffragists against slander, press publicity bore heavily on her livelihood and mission.[2]

The final part of the chapter offers some account of personal and unsolicited correspondence Gilman received from the general public, usually in response to her feminist work. Sometimes, correspondents reacted to an article or book they had read, a lecture attended, a review of Gilman, or a criticism of her penned by others. Sometimes they wrote to harass and intimidate her. She was all too aware of the price radical advocates could pay in nameless hostility and ridicule. The enlarging scholarly analysis of gender and celebrity establishes most convincingly that women becoming publicly known elicits strikingly ambivalent responses that are not the usual experience of men as celebrities. Not least among critics of celebrity women can be their own relatives and friends, evincing resentment, jealousy, and bottomless criticism. More generally, the sexual double standard can make them "public women" in the gaze of some viewers, men of intensely patriarchal disposition being especially outraged to see a woman purporting to instruct the public on matters of ethics, sociology, economic reform, religion or, most offensively of all, men and women. Such elements were clear among unsolicited letters to Gilman from the public.

Ward's Fallacies and Naive Reformism

Her contributions on the economic evolution of women and of society are of the utmost value. . . . Like other writers of the day, Mrs. Gilman is wedded to evolutionism. But in spite of this her writing is pragmatic almost in every point. Mrs. Gilman's fundamental defect . . . is her unwillingness to admit that an appeal to private conscience is insufficient unless accompanied by a struggle to abolish class rule, with or without the consent of the ruling classes.

William English Walling, The Larger Aspects of Socialism (1913)

Gilman's one time Fabian socialist colleague, William E. Walling, regretted Gilman's closer association with feminism than socialism, animated, it seemed, through her adherence to Ward's reform Darwinism. As with other commentators on her profile as America's most eminent feminist theorist, he saw her evolutionary approach as a possible intellectual limitation but, as critically, an inhibitor of the revolutionary politics that he favored in 1913. If Gilman herself recorded her opinions, reservations, and disputes about feminism as it emerged and developed in U.S. political currency, her critics did the same. Her widely covered lectures generated responses by other lecturers, writers, and reviewers. One New York paper reported on the lectures of antisuffragist Mrs. John Martin (Prestonia Mann Martin), "who answers Mrs. Charlotte Perkins Gilman, the high priestess of feminism."[3]

Contemporary studies and critiques of feminism scrutinized Gilman's contributions. Floyd Dell opened his book Women as World Builders: Studies in Modern Feminism (1913) with a chapter on Gilman. He declared that, of all the women who represented feminism, Gilman should be considered first because, "from a superficial view," she was the most intransigent feminist of them all. Prestonia Mann Martin agreed, but for her this meant the threat of all women being burdened with the inefficient duty to vote. It was a nuisance, inflicted by suffragists like Blatch and Gilman. The chief business of women was to "make men who can do a man's work . . . without her interference. That's what they are there for. The suffragist is a weak sister, too weak to stand by her guns and hold a man to his." With this rigid sex division of labor, Mann Martin had no time for male suffragists like Dell who admired Gilman. Such men were "puling and driveling and howling for women to come and help him out of his political difficulties." Fit only

FIGURE 32. Floyd Dell, ca. 1926 (Sinclair Papers, Courtesy Lilly Library, Indiana University, Bloomington, Indiana)

either for an asylum for incompetents or bedrest "with a bottle of milk to suck," she rallied antisuffragists: "If there are any men left, let them stand by us in this fight against suffrage fury and folly."[4]

With this ferocity, Mrs. Martin and her self-described "humanist" and Fabian socialist critic husband John M. Martin turned on Gilman. Her preeminence made her the exemplar of all feminism's errors.[5] Their fundamental objection to Gilman's worldview, which they took to be authoritative and representative of all feminists, was her minimizing of the significance of sex differences and consequent advocacy of comparable lives for men and women. They called *Women and Economics* "one of the gospel books of Feminism," its erroneous thesis that "it is the traditional family, in which the father is head of the household and supplies the livelihood, which threatens women's degradation." Gilman assaulted the foundation of human society, a family, located between a working husband and a housekeeping wife.[6]

In their 1916 book, *Feminism: Its Fallacies and Follies,* the Martins repudiated Gilman's advocacy of economic independence for women through paid work. Her promotion of women's careers in the learned professions and salaried occupations for women was naive and elitist, ignoring the fact that most women's paid work was unregulated, low paid, and unhealthy—

usually factory, workshop, and office jobs. For most women, then, paid work could not supply true independence from men. Women's presence in the workforce flooded the market with cheap labor, driving down wages that male breadwinners could negotiate more skillfully to support their families. Thus, "men are sacrificed to the feminist doctrine." Under these circumstances, dependence within marriage furnished a far better quality of life for both sexes than attempted self-support by each individually. In the long run, then, feminists like Gilman did womankind a grave disservice. Moreover, Gilman's feminist ideas put the healthy expansion and advancement of "the race" at risk, as working women ruined their reproductive health. Worse still, Gilman's influential treatise, *The Man-Made World; or, Our Androcentric Culture* (1911), represented men as "either useless or malevolent," implicitly urging a woman's uprising in which "the drones will be slain, their corpses swept from the hive. . . . The feminist millennium will have arrived!" Her evident mission, they concluded, was "to alienate the affections of women from men."[7]

By contrast, for the Martins, the true "humanist" acknowledged and celebrated sex differences, arranging economic, social, and cultural lives in the different interests of the sexes, therefore enhancing the conditions of the next generation and improving humanity. Feminism and humanism, in the Martins' reckoning, were implacably opposed. Ironically, when dissociating herself from classification as a feminist, Gilman often claimed she was a "humanist." Clearly her concept of a "humanist" was significantly different from theirs. Indeed, "humanism" was a category contested by many progressive thinkers, subject, like feminism, to very different readings and definitions.[8]

Possibly anticipating controversy, the profeminist reform journal the *Survey* published advance excerpts from the Martins' book as advertising copy, eliciting what Gilman called "a deluge of condemnation." The editor defended his action as the exercise of free speech, whether or not the book was either "popular" or "valuable." The assertion of free speech missed the point of the readers' objections: namely, that "such a paper as we had supposed it to be should allow itself to be used in this manner." More fundamentally, the assertion that "the other fellow" needed a right to be heard used an honorable reverence for the first amendment slyly to advance covert antifeminism. For the implication was that feminist discourse had somehow become hegemonic, stifling alternative viewpoints. This Gilman exposed as insidious misogyny, mentioning the masculists she had reviewed during the suffrage renaissance:

Sir Almroth Wright, Otto Weininger, Mr. Everett P. Wheeler, might as well claim it. Chance to be heard! Chance! The world has heard nothing else since talking and writing began, and even today, the mass of sluggish-minded speakers and writers are still repeating these primitive views. One who claims that women are merely females; only so to be valued; and to be confined by law to the exclusive performance of their female function, if they show any signs of activity in other lines, needs no "chance to be heard." He has been heard.[9]

Further, Gilman wondered whether the *Survey* would have championed free speech by similarly printing lengthy advertising excerpts from publications "showing the necessity of prostitution"—it being distinguished by its fervent opposition to the so-called "white slave trade" and championing of the working classes and the poor. Was Martin proposing "a brilliant new idea . . . that woman's place is in the home"? From all the hullabaloo, one might think that an entire population "of triumphant 'Feminists,' 'unsexed,' 'denatured,' husbandless, childless, and triumphantly happy, were refusing to listen to him." She criticized Martin's work for its "ingenious unfairness in quotation," presumably referring to his treatment of her own writings, observing that it was "always such a pity to see a clear mind stooping to such a weapon." The Martins pounced on Gilman's conception of the home, masculinity, and work.[10]

Arguably, there was a personal bitterness involved in this Martin-Gilman collision. Gilman had been friends with the heiress Prestonia Mann before her marriage to Martin, often summering at her alternative socialist community in upstate New York with her daughter Katharine. As editor of the *America Fabian,* Mann had obtained several articles from Gilman in the late 1890s, and they shared many friends among the British Fabians. She saw Gilman as primarily as a socialist, given her work with the Pacific coast organizations, her early adulation of Bellamy, and her popularity with figures like George Bernard Shaw, H. G. Wells, and Sidney and Beatrice Webb. Gilman's enlarging profile as a feminist seemed to Mann a betrayal, while her English husband simply saw feminism as bourgeois, privileged, and class blind.[11]

What would cut deeper than the Martins' criticisms, however, was an attack on the theoretical foundations of her views—her Wardian framework. From a different framework altogether came Correa Moylan Walsh's criticisms of Gilman as "the foremost American feminist." This conversation had a very different register. Whereas the Martins were humanist socialists, the widely educated Walsh was a conservative economist, specializing in monetary policy, who also wrote imposing book-length critiques of both socialism and feminism in 1917. His book was an alarmist tract on the threat posed by feminism—and especially woman suffrage—to the United States, to its civilization in, its international stature, and its national well-being. Since Gilman was the most prominent American spokeswoman for feminism, perhaps Walsh found her more threatening than Ellen Key or Olive Schreiner, who were on different continents. His attack presented more rigor and intellectual depth than that of the Martins, providing a comprehensive, multidisciplinary interrogation of the historical origins of feminist claims.[12]

Four aspects of his critique of Gilman were especially significant. First, he claimed that her program amounted to the would-be masculinization of women and the feminization of men. Second, he insisted that the feminist goal of sex equality, understood as sameness or common humanness, was impossible, in a thoroughgoing rejection of theories of cultural socialization to account for differences between men and women. Third, he asserted that gynaecocentric, matriarchal, or matronymical theories of human origins, underpinning Gilman's challenge to the inevitability of patriarchy, were fallacious nonsense. And fourth, he criticized her proposed reconfiguration of heterosexual relations.[13]

Walsh called Gilman's economics-focused feminism nothing less than an attempt to apply the capitalist wage system to all women, ironically, at the very moment that socialists sought to abolish it. He criticized John Stuart Mill's 1869 claims that men have molded women's present characteristics:

Such a statement is itself an acknowledgment of some original difference between the sexes, by which men had a greater power to mould women than women had to mould men. This is, then, admitted to be no more than greater physical force in men, perhaps very slightly in excess at first, perhaps existing only at certain periods (when women were pregnant) of which men took advantage. They are supposed to have enhanced the difference in size and strength for their own selfish purposes, by selecting small and weak women for their wives, thereby diminishing the size and strength of their female offspring. "Man," says Mrs. Gilman, "deliberately bred the pretty, gentle, little type of female in his choice of a mate, for her sex qualities alone, because that timid type is the easiest to handle."[14]

Walsh contended that utopian socialist Edward Bellamy was the first to promote this theory of sex differences, maintaining that, in the ancient past, the sexes were equal in strength and size. Stronger men subjugated weaker women, and such unions dominated species reproduction. Stronger women and weaker men had no biological compunction toward each other, so their

characteristics died out: "If our ancestors descended from ape-like ancestors (why else talk of evolution?), this difference between men and women
began long before there were men and women—was original to our species.
Or, if our ancestors did not descend from ape-like ancestors, at all events . . .
how are the aping feminists, to explain this difference in size and strength
between the sexes in apes? In the same way?"[15] In one painful blow, Walsh
chopped Gilman, Ward, and all their feminist adherents at the root of their
critiques of androcentrism, hurling evolutionary evidence into their faces.
He insisted that all theories of an earlier period of female dominance or at
least sex equality were unproven, giving nearly twenty pages to a blistering
critique of Ward, "the prophet" of modern feminism. Ward's gynaecocentric theory, so influential on Gilman's thought and centered on women's sex
selection and its overthrow by the unnatural present state of androcentrism,
had "not a particle of evidence" in its support.[16]

Even if Ward had been correct, Walsh contended, he failed to prove that
the development of androcentric culture was not "a natural product of evolution." Women never ruled over anything but children. So-called mother
right was really father indifference during the "half-way stage between the
animal state and the fully human." At best, with their originating of such
industries as cooking, agriculture, and medicine, women advanced humanity from savagery to barbarism. According to Walsh, once men realized the
concept of paternity, they fought and defeated matronymy, bringing both
their children and mothers under patriarchal control with regulated marriage. Men took humanity from barbarism to civilization, inventing the
plough, the wheel, and gradually colonizing women's agriculture and hus-
bandry, all for the better.[17]

In the ten pages Walsh specifically devoted to criticism of Gilman, he
linked much of her thinking to Ward, while identifying her as a socialist
with a worrying penchant for natural history. In Gilman, he contended,
"we have a woman-made philosophy of history—perhaps the first . . . and
it is interesting. It is mainly inductive, going from the past trend of alleged
events to the future." His response to Gilman's assertion that economic dependence of women on men has enhanced sex differentiation to excess—
and her proposed reduction in the extent of such differentiation as a consequence of women securing economic independence—exposed the eugenic
pronatalism and masculist virilism underlying his entire antisuffrage text.
He called her proposed reduction in artificial sex distinctions a "movement
of assimilation, which has led other civilizations to decline."[18]

Since Gilman's proposals so prominently involved paid labor and socialized (or at least commodified) cooking and domestic work, Walsh

condemned them as race suicide: "Americans apparently are to leave the peopling of this hemisphere to foreigners; and if England wishes to fill up South Africa with white people, she must leave the job to the Boers—or to the Germans!" He also reached that conclusion because Gilman extolled friendship as the "new sex-relation," more interhuman than intersexual, confining female-initiated conjugality possibly "only at a season of rut." Comparing Ellen Key favorably with both Gilman and Schreiner, "nothing could be better," declared Walsh, than Key's denunciation of their "amaternalism" and her own stress "upon the unlikeness of men and women." Walsh was disturbed by any proposed alteration in existing male sex right, and his fear of feminist modifications of gender norms revealed his investment in stopping woman suffrage, female economic independence, and voluntary motherhood for white middle- and upper-class women. No specific evidence remains of any Gilman response to Walsh.[19]

Of all the critiques of Gilman as a feminist thinker, Walsh offered the most sustained attack on its Wardian and reform Darwinist foundations. Soon after, his critique was extended by another author. In 1921, Avrom Barnett sent his forthcoming book to Gilman for comment and perhaps feedback of some kind, out of curiosity for her response. In his text she found this description of herself: "Charlotte Perkins Stetson Gilman, perhaps the greatest American Feminist living." His text was a scathing critique of her and other feminists' use of Ward's "erroneous" theory of gynaecocentrism, androcentrism, and the evolutionary development of male dominance through sexual selection. To the extent that feminism appropriated such theories, now thoroughly discredited within the sciences, it was ill-conceived and fatally flawed. This young author launched a fullscale critique of all feminist authors influenced by Ward, naming Gilman especially but also other theorists and scholars, including: "Blanche Shoemaker Wagstaff, C. Gasquoine Hartley Gallichan, Jane Johnstone Christie . . . Professor W. I. Thomas and Scott Nearing." He asserted that feminists like Gilman, "in attempting to give their movement a 'scientific' basis, have committed all the atrocities of which the dilettante in science is capable . . . the older feminists' continual use of the unsound gynaecocentric theory of Ward, are representative."[20]

As one of the "older feminists" in question, Gilman's response was crisp and stubborn: "Whether the male was developed by sexual selection, by inheritance, or by mutation, does not touch the essence of Ward's Gynocentric [sic] Theory—which is that the female is the race type." Noting that whole feminist books and treatises had been "written with this theory as a basis," Barnett insisted that they offered a discredited theory of the emergence of sexual differentiation and male and female secondary sexual characteristics. Barnett claimed that Ward contended that males originated as a mere male organ, a puny parasite living on the female, hypothesizing further that:

> [she] develops suddenly a hyper-discriminatory instinct which impels her to choose for a mate only the largest and most prepossessing of her suitors. . . . But our never-satisfied female is not so easily made content. . . . The insignificant male must be improved, he must be made larger, stronger, more beautiful . . . and . . . she continues to select, and again and again to select . . . until a mate is produced who far surpasses her in color, strength, size, ornament, power of song, etc., etc.; in other words, in possession of the secondary sexual characteristics that she lacks.[21]

Thus, females unintentionally created—bred—a male able to subjugate them. This implausible theory, Barnett claimed, was adopted by theorists like Gilman and others without considering the enormous body of evidence and debate against it, detailed by Barnett in the bulk of his book. As such, Ward's theory, far from a gift, was an albatross around the neck of feminist theories of love, marriage, and the family, opening otherwise sound thinkers to ridicule and disrespect. Feminists shared the "pathologic ganglia in the Feminist psyche," their works amounting to rubbish jammed down the throat of an important social movement. "Nobody seems to realize" he lamented, "that Feminism neither has, nor requires, biological justification." Indeed, biology functioned within feminist theory as a wobbly "prop" and as "aimless potpourri."[22]

After reading his text, Gilman replied: "Thank you for sending me your book, 'Foundations of Feminism,' which I have read with much interest. . . . Your facetious personalities regarding the methods of study of a group of feminists weaken the work. To anyone who knows the persons mentioned you are shown to be quite ignorant of the facts alleged, and merely actuated by a baseless personal impression. In view of the careful and serious study shown elsewhere, this is a pity."[23]

In this letter she responded more to his critique of her personally than the elements attacking gynaecocentric theory. Ward was no longer alive to support and defend her, and Barnett prodded at her inability to go beyond the Wardian philosophy she had championed her whole public intellectual life. Undeterred by her response, Barnett replied further, insisting that she must recognize that the kind of reading of evolution and sexual selection she advanced (via Ward) on behalf of feminism was long-since refuted, with no place in mainstream biological theory. Perhaps he hoped that if he could change her mind on his terms, she could in turn adopt and promote his own theories, using a measure of her own remaining fame to support him. With publication of his critique, he resumed correspondence with Gilman about the fatal error feminism made in appropriating Ward:

> It is strange to read of the female being the race type. Why isn't the male equally typical of the race? And in asexual species what becomes of your race-type? In that case, you will answer with Ward, the organism is female so far as sex may be postulated for it at all. And my answer is—why postulate? Whatever may be the essence of the gynaecocentric theory, Ward certainly could not have developed it without assuming the truth of sexual selection. With sexual selection disproven, Ward's theory must collapse.... Feminists are the only ones who have exploited it, and I think that my "Foundations" proves that even this was unnecessary.

Nonetheless, he accepted that she might have grounds to object to his characterization of the famous feminist authors of the period and made the following admission: "Let me assure you that I have never met a single feminist writer. If I have burlesqued their methods of study, it is only because their results show a pretentiousness in science at least, that demanded such treatment. But, if I have erred in judging, I in turn, am being judged. I take this opportunity of expressing my admiration for your studies in the economic field which, after all, is the only one with which Feminism properly concerns itself." Even if her understanding of biology and evolution was flawed, at least her economic theory remained sound, although it may have remained so for Barnett precisely because it was outside his own expertise.[24]

Undaunted—but perhaps somewhat saddened—by such critiques, Gilman continued to refer to gynaecocentric and androcentric eras in her work across the 1920s. Yet one possible effect of these critiques of her use of Darwin and Ward was some loosening of Gilman's 1920s references to her long-held theoretical framework, at least in discussion of some issues, such as birth control, divorce and postsuffrage women's politics. Gradually, more contemporary intellectual paradigms challenged her. Even those she rejected, such as Freudian psychoanalysis and sexology, forced her to debate in different terms with her younger peers, such as her co-contributors in crucial 1924, 1929, and 1931 anthologies on sex, morality, and civilization.[25]

Gilman never announced an abandonment of the framework that had guided her entire intellectual career since the 1880s. It does, however, seem that the critique of her biological basis for feminism struck home. In her 1923 text, *His Religion and Hers,* already underway at the time of the Walsh and Barnett critiques, her use of Ward's reform Darwinist interpretation of sexual selection was a much paler, or at least a more tangential, version of this longstanding intellectual undergirding. It may be no accident that she published no further book-length theoretical treatises. She certainly wrote and kept publishing thereafter, but she did so in other forms, including a book on ethics, her autobiography, a detective novel, and numerous chapters and articles on women's situation, the occult, divorce, alimony, birth control, and fashion.[26]

Gilman's Press

> Being so universal a heretic it is much to the credit of our advance in liberal thought that my work has been for the most part well-received. The slowness and indifference of the public mind were of course to be expected, and its very general misunderstanding; the only thing I have to complain of in the way of ill-treatment has been from the newspapers, and even among them there has been much, very much of fair and helpful recognition.
>
> *Charlotte Perkins Gilman,* The Living *(1935)*

Gilman's 1935 characterization of much of the press coverage she received as fair and helpful is substantially accurate. The earliest press coverage of Gilman was brief and to the point, much of it lecture reportage. Scharnhorst reports forty-one articles on Gilman's 1890s lectures, eighteen for the 1900s, thirty-one for the 1910s, and three for the 1920s. These patterns partly reflect her residency and life cycle. The 1890s lecture reports matched her itinerant years living solely on her lectures, while the drop for the 1900s coincided with what Ceplair called "The Book Writing Years," when newlywed Gilman was based in New York City. The upsurge of her lecturing profile in the 1910s directly related to her work for the woman suffrage movement and the feminist Heterodoxy Club, as well as her promotion of works published in the *Forerunner*. Her 1922 retirement to Norwich Town, Connecticut, deprived her of immediate proximity to New York's lecturing opportunities. By 1930 she was seventy and, though still wishing to lecture, such invitations no longer materialized.[27]

Where the press was unfair, unhelpful, and downright offensive was in California in the 1890s. As discussed above, she fiercely resented the "yellow journalism" of the Hearst reporters hounding her over the several years of her complicated divorce and child custody upheavals in the 1890s. Thereafter, however, her work as a nationwide lecturer after 1894 and her extensive editorial and commentary work establishing her as an expert voice in the public arena was greatly facilitated by extensive press coverage. While newspaper coverage ranged from adulation to disparagement, especially on issues such as woman suffrage, Gilman attracted much press attention, assisting her pet causes and in making her living.[28]

The boon to scholars of ongoing digitizing of national and regional historical newspapers discloses more press coverage of Gilman with each new release or update. For this study, over a thousand separate and relevant newspaper and periodical items are identified so far for the 1880–1935 period. These findings considerably enlarge the picture of Gilman's national familiarity and salience. Hence, her own extensive clippings files in the Schlesinger Library represent just a fraction of the total coverage. Perhaps understandably, she did not weigh down her travels by retaining negative book or lecture reviews. Since several of the key newspapers of the period held avowedly antifeminist and at least antisuffragist stances, she was hardly likely to keep comprehensive holdings. Meanwhile, her distressing experiences with Hearst press tabloid-style reporting made her unlikely to hold that all publicity was good publicity.[29]

Apart from her divorce and remarriage, press coverage of Gilman so far available focused principally on three topics: her woman suffrage presence and work; her feminist claims and causes; and her proposed strategies and plans to end the confinement of women to "sex work." Beyond these themes, other more incidental coverage of Gilman acclaimed her birthday, her criticisms of various people or practices, and her comments on miscellaneous questions of the day. With her suicide in 1935, the press offered considerable discussion of euthanasia through obituaries and opinion pieces.[30]

The unfolding of these themes in press attention to her had a sequence. At first, reports framed her significance in relation to her family. Whether the report concerned her 1880s and early 1890s articles, poetry readings, or lectures, reporters tended to depict her qualification to intervene in public as almost hereditary. The blood of Lyman Beecher, her great grandfather orator, her uncle Henry Ward Beecher, and aunt Harriet Beecher Stowe transmitted both charismatic speech and writing.[31]

With her increasing publication in her own right, however, and especially after *Women and Economics,* her skills were more often treated as her own. She first generated national publicity shortly after she began to lecture and write in the Bay Area, especially under the auspices of the Pacific Coast Women's Press Association. Physical description of her person, not typical in accounts of men's lectures, opened the San Francisco *Newsletter* account:

A slight, delicate little woman, appearing taller than she really is by reason of her slender build, a clearly cut, sensitive face, a profile reminiscent of George Eliot, and eyes that are glowing coals of fire, brown hair parted in the middle and drawn down demurely into a coil at the back of the neck; a clear-toned voice, quiet motions, the living exponent of her theory that heredity, environment, and force of will make or mar the personal entity— that is Charlotte Perkins Stetson. Lyman Beecher was her great Grand-father; Edward Everett Hale is her uncle by marriage. Her husband is C. W. Stetson, a celebrated artist of Boston, who . . . has a portrait of his wife, clad in a costume of olden time. The figure, the pose, the accessories are all striking, but the face, with its deep spirituality, the intense earnestness of its look into futurity are what takes the picture out of the realm of portraiture, making it an inspiration.[32]

Beyond her appearance, the author reported that Gilman's personal-ity was "forcefully brilliant" and "not without the eccentricities of genius." Her literary friends told reporters that they feared she would give up fiction writing for political and philosophical causes, such as Nationalism, though interestingly, with no mention of women's rights or related matters. Yet this was not Gilman's weighting of her own concerns. Though often portrayed by later scholars as abandoning socialism in favor of the woman question, newspapers from the 1880s construct a Gilman who consistently stressed her concern with women and sexual relations from the beginning until the end of her feminist public intellectual career. Importantly, though, she saw any substantial improvement as requiring a concurrent transformation in resource allocation and economic production, a view shaping many of her proposed strategies.[33]

Interestingly, neither she nor her press said much at all about "The Yel-low Wall-paper," the work preoccupying scholars and thus reference works about Gilman today. The *Boston Investigator,* for instance, dismissed it as "very paragraphic and very queer generally," while the Chicago *Daily Inter Ocean* literary reviewer said that it read "like the scrappy reminiscences of an opium debauch." Instead, earliest Californian press accounts of her cov-ered the concerns she embraced once Stetson returned to Rhode Island in early 1890. These included social purity, prostitution, dress reform, women's economic independence, and childcare. Reporters described her lectures as "witty and very entertaining."[34]

With this profile, the Stetsons' various attempts at divorce became entic-ing news for early 1890s gossip columns. In particular, Stetson's remarriage to Gilman's best friend Grace Channing and the couple taking custody of ten-year-old Kate Stetson also occasioned much criticism of Gilman as an "unnatural mother." Meanwhile, the apparent cordiality among the three-some implied some dark deviance. Though this negative coverage perhaps lacked lasting impact, it established recurring themes and characterizations of Gilman. The accounts of her dress reform, physical fitness, and disdain for her husband's conjugal expectations, to say nothing of her temerity in believing she had a writing career to pursue, which sidelined marriage and motherhood, minced no words: "She appears to be a 'crank.'" She appeared "in public without corset, bootheels, and waistbelt." She had calfskin slippers made flat, without heels. Taking apartments inside the house, she left the conjugal bed and worked as a writer, when she was not exercising at the local gymnasium. Journalists often portrayed these more as personal peculiarities than as evidence of any wider cause in sexual politics.[35]

The publication of her magnum opus, *Women and Economics* (1898), generated demand for more substantive profiles of its author, with nearly thirty book reviews nationwide, as well as several overseas. Still, not all newspapers immediately associated Gilman with woman suffrage, women's rights, or feminism, in part because she did not always lecture on these topics. Helen Campbell, with whom she coedited *Impress* (1894–95) and with whom she visited Jane Addams and Hull House in 1895, reported in *Time and the Hour* that Gilman had fighting blood from both sides of her family dating back to "the Protectorate days in Old England to colonial battles in the New." Defining her as a socialist, an advocate for the "working man and working woman," rather than a women's rights or suffrage advocate, Campbell cast the just published *Women and Economics* as "Political Economy Stetsonized."[36]

In 1899, the antisuffrage and antifeminist *New York Times* reported the essence of her lecture for the League for Political Education as "that true progress and the social millennium could only be obtained by self-sacrifice for the good of all. . . . She would have every one stand with open arms to embrace the entire country, the entire world, and if necessary, sacrifice himself for the cause of humanity." The only reference to women was her criticism of them for "expecting too much from the men, who, after all did most of the hard work."[37]

Once she lived in New York, however, her activities soon sketched a principally feminist profile. Various newspapers' headlines reported her role in suffrage—for instance, a 1903 suffrage debate in New York City and a lecture on socialism in 1905 in Vancouver. Sometimes her suffragism received humorous coverage. For instance, a reporter for *Pictorial Review* told a story about a Gilman lecture from a society leader: "She came and she made a wonderful address, but dear me! She talked not only on suffrage, but on state care for mothers with children, and state care of the children themselves, and many other advanced views of the same kind. The women were simply shocked, and I am afraid I did not convert one. You see, they are so conservative. I had no idea that she would go so far."[38]

Most publicity about Gilman concentrated on what the *Boston Evening Transcript* called the most revolutionary aspect of *Women and Economics:* "The chapters on the Home and the new kind of home life which new conditions will make a necessity," a press focus that intensified with her book *The Home: Its Work and Influence* (1903). The *New York Times* reviewer described reading with delight her critique of the waste and inefficiencies of the current home, her "keen, incisive analysis" and "knife-edged criticism." He found her proposed solutions in commodified services and kitchenless homes "not a very appealing picture" because "there is something cold and shivery about Mrs. Gilman's vision of the home," unlikely to "be the family life of the future."[39]

Even such criticism only enhanced press interest in her as a feminist commentator. The *New York Times* is one indicator. It published articles mentioning Gilman once a year in 1900, 1901, and 1902, but thirteen times in 1904, twice in 1905, five times in 1906, and in 1907, six times in 1908, nine in 1909, and twice in 1910. Then, as the New York suffrage movement reignited and Gilman became a favored pro-suffrage orator, debater, and delegate—not to mention the author of the feisty and well-reviewed text, *The Man-Made World* (1911)—her name graced more reports and articles: ten in 1911, five in 1912, nine in 1913, and jumping to thirty-four in 1914, or one every eleven days. This reflected the impact on public discussion of her two six-lecture series in spring at the Hotel Astor—"The Larger Feminism" and "Studies in Masculism." Between February and May 1914, many New Yorkers must have had the sense of reading Gilman's arguments about women's subordination and feminism every time they opened the newspaper. In 1915, articles about or mentioning Gilman dropped back to twenty-three, once every sixteen days, followed by thirteen in 1916, four in 1917, one in 1918, three in 1919, five in 1920, and two in 1921. With her retirement to Norwich, Connecticut in 1922, the references to her thereafter primarily concerned books or articles she published, never more than five a year, a little more with obituaries and memorials in 1935 and after.[40]

Beyond the immediate New York press response to her lectures there, some of the extensive press attention to Gilman was the result of her regular lecture trips to the South, Midwest, and West. As a celebrity, she became local news, an article for each arrival announcing her imminence, then coverage of the lecture or lectures, often providing near verbatim reportage, then interviews with Gilman after her lecture(s). Moreover, syndicated articles about Gilman from New York, Chicago, or Los Angeles newspapers were reproduced in regional and local newspapers before and after her visits. Just as in New York, this coverage of her doings and sayings reached its greatest peak of intensity in the 1913–15 period. Partly, regional reporters characterized her as the preeminent feminist of the age. Ellen Key's attacks on her only heightened this aspect of her public profile. There was plenty of Gilman copy around, and it circulated widely outside the main metropolitan areas.[41]

In addition, these local papers featured articles on feminism, suffrage, and other sexual politics issues soon after her visits. Beyond her direct contributions within communities across the United States, her visits stimulated wider regional debate on the position of women. Hence, whatever Gilman's own reservations about the term "feminism," as noted by playwright George Middleton (in this chapter's epigraph), her presence nationwide hastened public familiarity with it. Cott correctly reports the later currency of feminism in the United States than in Britain and Europe, a lag permitting its portrayal as "foreign." Even so, it was increasingly discussed, and even before the 1910s. When American feminism was discussed, Gilman was never far away. [42]

Public Responses

I have just finished reading your "Women and Economics," and it has brought me the greatest happiness that has come into my life—I cannot express the feeling of relief and escape—The light you have held has altered for me the whole of life.

Dorothy M. Richardson, n.d., London

Letters to Gilman vividly demonstrate her stimulating and provocative effect. Readers sometimes simply wrote her fan letters; others sought clarification of her arguments. For instance, a group of Montclair, New Jersey, housewives had a reading group devoted to *Women and Economics*. Aspects of Gilman's arguments disturbed them: like Rose Scott, they rejected her use of animal analogies. They also feared that children would be "institutionalized" in the care of anyone other than their own mothers. They could scarcely imagine any other center of domestic life than the dinner table. Thus, Gilman's view that individual family members could seek privacy for their own activities smacked of "the tendency . . . to cover self-gratification with the mantle called 'self-development.'"[43]

Other wives and mothers expressed different views. In 1911, Patricia Cox from Buffalo, Iowa, wrote excitedly "I want you to know that you have a staunch Gilmanite way out here. . . . Some of the things you have said gave help at perhaps the most important crisis in my life . . . my two babes and I can work out our lives together in a way that we could not have before." From London, the avant-garde novelist Dorothy Richardson wrote that *Women and Economics* "has brought me the greatest happiness that has come into my life—I cannot express the feeling of relief and escape—The light you have held has altered for me the whole of life." Meanwhile, a male correspondent exclaimed that he was more influenced by *The Home* than anything he had ever read.[44] After reading an article on "Mrs. Gilman's idea of Homes without Housekeeping," an Indiana housewife wrote to the editor to request information about the location of such a home: "I think our town needs something of the kind and there are housekeepers that would be glad to occupy such a home as is described by Mrs. Gilman article if it could be carried on in a business like way." Elsewhere, her work converted a prosperous southern Yale-educated attorney: "I think Gilman, talk Gilman, read Gilman and act Gilman on all occasions." As a result, he had become a pronounced suffragist and more and more a socialist, determined to devote himself to social service, by way of a doctorate in sociology at the University of Wisconsin, notwithstanding intense parental disapproval.[45]

Other readers tried to implement Gilman's ideas and proposals. May Glenhauser of Tacoma, Washington, reported that, in April 1914, a group of local women had established "the Gilman Circle," dedicated to the study of human progress. By December, Glenhauser could report that the group gathered weekly, women and men, to discuss the *Forerunner* and to organize an approach to their legislators on various reform initiatives. They planned to organize

> into a small commercial and industrial body to prepare and sell fruit juices, food, and other useful products, all made by women and co-operate with the farmers. Through the Gilman Circle a large bundle of cheering Christmas cards were sent to the inmates of the State Prison. I saw many with quotations by C. P. G. . . . One of the members brought your "Prayer of the Modern Woman" with which we concluded to open our meetings. It will be the prayer of the Gilmanites . . . for a rapid widening and spreading of your sound and logical philosophy among all humankind.[46]

The term "Gilmanite" entered the vernacular. As mentioned earlier, Australian author Miles Franklin met Gilman while working in Chicago on the editorial staff of the Women's Trade Union League newspaper, *Life and Labor.* Gilman stayed with Margery Dell, one of Franklin's friends, who she called "a Vassar graduate and a Gilmanite among many other up to date things."[47]

From South Australia came the praises of the Kurrajong Club, a reading circle, which had just devoted an evening to discussing Gilman's poetry. Its secretary, Nellie S. Bowman, reminded Gilman that Australian women were already enfranchised and that her writings were influencing the first generation of voting mothers. Thanking her for the high ideals she had placed before them, voicing some of their "thoughts and longings," she asked whether Gilman would consider visiting Australia. In fact, she had considered it as early as 1898 and would do so again on the eve of war in 1913. Another correspondent, an economist, wrote in sympathy on the death of Gilman's husband in 1934, recalling that "I always feel a great wealth of gratitude to you, for it was through your influence that I became an habitual sociological researcher." In a similar vein, Emily E. Keel wrote in 1934 asking Gilman to autograph her thirty-five-year-old copy of *Women and Economics,* "for it transformed my way of thinking," noting also that on rereading Gilman's poetry book, *In This Our World* (1893), "it was extraordinary how little it was 'dated.'" Meanwhile, William Marion Reedy, publisher of the St. Louis newspaper *Reedy's Mirror,* wrote her that he read "every issue of the *Forerunner* with something very like avidity, and this is a thing I can't say of very many of the publications that come to my desk."[48]

A self-proclaimed "ardent feminist" admirer signed as "Box 34, Chicago" undertook a scheme to bring Gilman's ideas to the theater. She had taken a Gilman novel and converted it into a popular play and proposed that Gilman choose one of four "first class actresses," including "Miss Barrymore." She called Gilman's novels "not so much fiction and art as they are pure science—splendid antiseptic surgical operations upon some mental cancer of society, performed with the faultless skill and precision of which you alone of our thinkers are capable." Gilman regretted that the playwright's interest "in Feminism and Gilmanism" had led her/him to waste their time in dramatizing a copyrighted novel, adding that she certainly could not negotiate with a post office box![49]

Gilman also received her share of direct criticism from readers. In 1915, an indignant Kansas City shop assistant objected to a Gilman quote: "When the short work day and school day are done, all will be together in home," describing the long grueling day of the average working woman, as well as poor rates of pay, high rents and expenses, and difficulty with medical emergencies: "My purpose in writing you is this: you have the ear of the public. You are a leader in modern thought. You have influence. Why do not do something for us who leave home at 7:30 in the morning and get back if lucky, at 6:30 in the evening three hundred and seven days in the year. . . . We have no one to speak a word for us. We have not the ear of the public."[50]

More hostile letters serve to demonstrate the gender transgression Gilman committed by having a career as a public intellectual at all. G. C. Yearling, a forty-seven-year-old confirmed bachelor from Brooklyn, having read her *Harper's Bazaar* article "The Passing of Matrimony (1906)," wrote angrily to tell her that she was "entirely wrong." He reported that, though financially "well enough fixed" to marry and with "many and varied experiences with your sex," he had never met a woman he was willing to marry. No woman, especially if aged over twenty-five (!), would refuse "a good offer." While agreeing that marriage "is about played out," he rejected Gilman's critique in favor of another explanation: "It is because women are ceasing to be womanly. They are too mannish and we do not care for them any longer as wives . . . they have become too much like ourselves." With a thinly veiled misogynist threat, he added that it would be better for women if marriage did not die out, for otherwise men "would then take and use them by force to gratify their passions," here again, "the brute in man." Gilman could best serve her sex by urging them to prevent the passing of matrimony by becoming "womanly again."[51]

Like any public figure, especially one so prolific, Gilman received "crank" letters, some extremely nasty and, in the context, obscene. This 1909 epistle from Mayfield Georgia is an example. The man who wrote it—apparently a schoolmaster or principal—was furious at Gilman's criticism of Roosevelt in her *Good Housekeeping* article, "Why Are There No Women on the President's Commission?" He ranted:

> You are simply a blatant howling fool advocate of what you think is women's rights. . . . We do not want . . . vixenish and whorish suffragettes to rule over us, we shall not and will not have them. Roosevelt did right. A woman has no turn to seek for any commission. Her place is the home, her duty is to bear children to her husband and make home life happy. . . . Last year I served upon a board with five ladies? and five gentlemen. I had intercourse with three of these ladies. . . . This explains why so many women want to have further duties to perform . . . whenever and wherever a man comes daily in contact with a woman she is prostituted. . . . I ruined every lady teacher under me. St. Paul tells you . . . It is a shame for a woman to speak

(even) in public. The way of the harlot, old Charlotte, is hard. I am a woman suffragette hater.[52]

Such a letter was an index of the usually unmarked masculism that Gilman herself identified and named as such. While extreme, the letter disclosed the sexual politics stakes in her work, and the constraining discursive impact of misogyny on any feminist aspirations.

GILMAN'S WORK garnered diverse responses. Contemporaries grasped the significance of her challenge to existing social relations of the sexes and to the institutions enshrining an androcentric status quo. Scholarly and political critics of feminism placed her as the foremost American exemplar of the problem of a gender-minimizing orientation within feminism, seeking to demolish any intellectual grounding she had long claimed from reform Darwinism.

Meanwhile, the press, whether local, national, or international, evinced various responses. One was simply reportage. As feminism became increasingly associated with contentious suffrage referenda and cultural developments—from dress reform to pacifism, working mothers and utopian apartment design, free love and birth control—then Gilman could figure in several ways, whether as chief exponent of the issue in question or as critic or qualifier of widely supposed claims.

Moreover, letters from readers and lecture audience members (many from overseas) offered varying opinions about her portrayals of people and problems, attesting to the wide circulation of her texts and ideas. Whether happy or not, scholarly authors, journalists, editors, publishers, or members of the general public, those responding to her work then, were certain that she was having a profound impact on public opinion and policy debate. It mattered to applaud, dismiss, or denounce her and to set out the reasons for whatever course the commentator recommended. Gilman, truly, brought feminism home to America.

CHAPTER EIGHT

Toward a "Human" World

We must learn to study normal human life
as the outcome of the feminine nature, and to
see that many features we have assumed to be
natural to humanity are merely natural to masculinity, which is quite another thing. With the
opposite point of view we are quite familiar:
men assuming themselves to be the normal
human beings, deprecating the influence of
women as "feminine," objecting strongly to a
dreaded "feminization." The term "mascu-
lization," which is precisely as regular in form
and which describes a far more common
fact, we do not yet recognize.

Charlotte Perkins Gilman,
His Religion and Hers *(1923)*

IN HER EMBRACE of suffragism and her critique of forms of feminism
inattentive to reform Darwinism, Gilman constantly highlighted her vision of a "human world." This vision had two meanings: the quest for a
world that did not mistake male sex traits for universal human ones; and
a world whose culture and institutions valued characteristics, which were
denigrated currently as merely female, as in fact human. She quantified
elements of this vision. Ninety-five percent of men's and women's traits,
needs, and talents were shared in common, hence the mission of both sexes
should be to advance humanity. The sex-specific traits accounting for the
remaining 5 percent of each sex's "makeup" needed recognition in proportion to their presence and function. Under androcentric conditions, the
human commonalities of the sexes were eclipsed by overconcentration on

these 5 percent of sex differences. A human world, then, would not emerge without serious intervention into education, customs, and cultural meanings. Her reform Darwinist framework led her to imagine how evolution could be channeled and enhanced in positive directions. Her character Elador explained to her husband, Van, in the serialized novel, *With Her in Ourland* (1916): "'You could do it in about three generations,' she calmly replied. 'Three generations! That's barely a century.' 'I know it . . . 5 per cent in one, 15 in two, and 80 per cent in three. Perhaps faster.'"[1]

The central objective of feminism, namely, the ending of women's sexual subjection, would be the indispensable prerequisite for this human world to develop. Her goal was reformed heterosexuality—its substance, institutions, and consequences. She sought to snap the links between economic power and male sexual identities fundamental to women's oppression. Diagnosing specific ills of androcentric society, she proposed reforms of present arrangements, creatively describing worlds—human worlds—where these sexual economic links were broken.

Her theoretical work here concentrated on economic independence through education, paid work, and gainful occupations for women to eliminate the deprecated social identity of the "housewife." No woman should take her whole identity from homebound domestic servitude, entailed in diverse primitive industries, combined with childcare and conjugal sexual service. Nor should the identity of the "wife"—in the sense of a woman whose life was owned, was taken charge of, or belonged to a husband—subsume her other more unique interests.

Gilman envisioned alternatives. In a human world, food production, distribution, preparation, service, and postmeal clean-up would be social functions. In fact, they would be some of the most important functions, provided by well-paid professionals at every stage in the process. She similarly reevaluated home design and construction, agriculture, public planning, and environmental management. Parenthood would not obstruct a father's or mother's extrafamilial work, with progressive professional childcare and education available to all.

Under androcentric rule, Gilman contended that humanity progressed only through the male line. The human race was evolving at a pace only half that possible if both sexes contributed to "race progress." Women, confined only to "sex work," held back the species as a whole. Androcentric culture needed to recede, replaced by admitting women equally to industry, education, culture, religion, politics, the arts, and all other arenas. This cultural shift would enhance female contributions, bringing mothers up to speed for rearing ultramodern women and men. Only ending female specialization in privatized domesticity and related sex work would make women fully human. Hence human progress depended on their doing race work.

While denouncing the costs of women's sex slavery in primitive industries and degrading sex relations, Gilman faced an uphill battle to persuade her contemporaries as to how androcentrism might be ended and a "human" world begun. The prerequisite for such a world would be women's participation in race work as free and independent citizens, itself requiring their liberation from sex work—indeed, requiring the eradication of sex work in order to make a living altogether. In a "human" world, sex work would lack any rationale or attractions.

Fundamentally, then, her proposed transformations entailed challenging existing understandings of sexuality—its organization, institutions, and cultural representations—as well as related sexual divisions within labor and resources. Gilman advanced her schemes for erotic and sexual economics reform—with all the ramifications that followed—through many kinds of writing, especially on the pages of her own monthly journal *Forerunner* (1909–16) and in other journals and magazines. The novels *What Diantha Did* (1910), *Moving the Mountain* (1911), *Herland* (1915), and *With Her in Ourland* (1916) posed her most detailed visions of new sexual and reproductive arrangements required to anchor the new human world.[2]

By the 1920s, however, she recognized that powerful new discourses, with great popular currency, ran counter to her version of the reform of sexual relations. In particular, she blamed psychoanalysis and jazz age sexology for redefining women in newly sexualized terms, ones which co-opted the feminist demand for sex equality to mean that the healthy normal woman should "ape man and his amours." The urban flapper of the 1920s offered the spectacle of the femme fatale living promiscuously in the fast lane, imitating men's sexual freedoms, and using birth control. Gilman needed to revise her feminist case for reform, taking account of changing sexual mores, to convince this new generation of the need for a "human world."[3]

Diagnoses and Prognoses

In her five-minute whirlwind tour of "The Coming World," Mrs. Gilman described its essentials as first, a sufficient income for all to live a comfortable life, and secondly, a beauty replacing present ugliness—clean, healthy cities and fertile lands instead of present-day smoke-pits and miasma. In that day, she concluded, the world would be made finer and better by men and women, standing shoulder to shoulder, and co-operating without effort or strain to make the world the kind of place all wanted it to be. It could be such a place to-day, she added, if the two houses got together.

"Woman's Weakness Due to Education: Girls Do Not Belong to the Weaker
Sex Necessarily, Mrs. Gilman Asserts," New York Times (1914)

Gilman's main nonfiction texts were systematic diagnoses of what ailed androcentric culture and what stopped it from evolving into a human world. Thus, after Gilman sketched the undesirable features of human culture now abnormally distorted by outmoded sexual relations, she devoted the rest of each text to the future. She also advanced her diagnoses through an array of shorter articles and stories. Then she outlined the solutions needed to secure a human world.[4]

Her proposals for removing the category housewife, while mentioned in her books, were fleshed out in articles like "The Beauty of a Block," "Homes without Housekeeping," and "Applepieville." She demonstrated with drawings, photographs, and actuarial calculations how cheaply and beautifully collective apartment houses, with common spaces and professional cooking, cleaning, and childcare services, could operate in the large metropolis. Moved by the high rates of insanity reported among isolated rural farm women, she devised new arrangements of land, facilities, and services, conceptualized centrifugally like a big pie, permitting social contact and services for wives and children who could gather at the center.[5]

Gilman judged that the most substantial obstacle in women's advance to race work, and hence humanity's enhancement of "race progress," lay in their current confinement to sex work. So long as a culture portrayed a natural association between heterosexuality and women's work—designating women as cooks, cleaners, shoppers, sewers, and babysitters, permitting few alternative arrangements for these functions and services—then the main group of heterosexually active wives and mothers would have neither time nor scope to do anything other than the work of sex. This habit of associating women with "the home" had to cease if women were to have any hope of joining the race work of a human world, which would subvert prevailing sexual relations, patterns of sexual desire, and psychic dimensions of sexed identities. Contemporary configurations of the "sex relation itself" substantially generated much of women's all-consuming and all-confining sex work:

We cannot visualize a home in which no work is done, a home which will be a place of rest—for women! It seems a contradiction in terms. In simple outline, the prospect before us is this: that food will be purchased cooked; we shall order hot meals to be served to the family, instead of the present complicated distribution of ice, milk, bread, meat, vegetables, groceries, all the raw materials to be made up into consumable goods at home; while the work of cleaning, greatly reduced by the absence of a kitchen, will be done by trained experts hired by the hour.[6]

Gilman explored the possibilities of commercial catering in *What Diantha Did*. Diantha Bell is the dutiful daughter of a failed breadwinner and his frail New England wife. Diantha's father, the spoiled only son of an indulgent mother, has succeeded in being the undisputed head of his household, reluctantly moving his family to California in search of prosperity. The problem is that he has not succeeded in becoming the "head of anything else." Though approaching bankruptcy, he will not hear of his female relatives contributing economically to the household by working. Diantha's romantic relationship echoes this tension between gender and work. She and local grocer, Ross Warden, agree to marry. Six months later, she realizes that she faces a long engagement. It might be "six years or sixteen" before he can afford to marry. Custom decrees that Warden support his widowed mother and four able-bodied spinster sisters (two of whom are aged over twenty), until they have their own male supports. There is a sexual and eugenic subtext to Gilman's exploration of Diantha's dilemma. Late marriage, born of the notion that husbands alone support wives, widowed mothers, and unmarried sisters leads, inexorably, to men's demand for prostitution. Thus, venereal diseases often infect these lately married wives and their unborn children. Gilman's solution to this problem is that all able-bodied women can and should contribute to their own self-support. Then women and men would marry early for love alone, and prostitution, at least from this cause, would disappear.[7]

Against the wishes of both her own and her fiancé's family, Diantha moves to Orchardina, a male-dominated agricultural area. First, she works as a housekeeper for a woman architect, who desperately tries to juggle motherhood, marriage, and career. Diantha accumulates money, studies business theory, and resists pressure by her family and Ross to return to dependency. With her savings and the architect's backing, she opens a lunchroom for workers and a home-delivery catering business. She employs young women whom she thereby liberates from "live-in" domestic service and all its hazards in an exploration of sexual harassment. With his sisters' marriages, Ross finally sells his store and buys a ranch near Orchardina, expecting Diantha to give up her business to become his wife. She refuses. Once it is clear that she has other admirers willing to marry a career woman, Ross relents, without being altogether happy about the arrangement. They marry and have a child, while she continues with her business. Ross's tension ends when international journals praise her business, generating imitators. Admitting his mistake and prejudice, he becomes Diantha's supporter, and, naturally, they live happily ever after. Diantha was able to make her own decision as a human being, not as a sexed being, confined to sexed choices.[8]

The project of changing cooking greatly preoccupied Gilman. Prior to the increased momentum of the suffrage campaign after 1910, it was her proposals regarding this and related areas that drew the most contemporary reaction to her theoretical work. Cooking had to change. She admitted that there were not many Dianthas, that is, "women who would choose for a life work the profession of cooking. Because it is done by any and every body, at servant's wages, when not as a secondary sex function, it has not standing among women." However, she observed, in a good example of her characteristic wit: "Our great cooks, our highly paid and beribboned cooks, have been men. . . . Cooking is a science, an art, a handicraft, and a business. It requires the combined abilities of hygienist and dietician, of economist, craftsman, and artist. For our food service to find high praise in 'pies like mother used to make' is equivalent to a level of architecture wherein we lived in huts 'like father used to build.'" In the same vein, she proposed that the other primitive household industries be accomplished off-site, especially laundry, dressmaking, and related needlework. Bakeries already produced fresh bread for the household efficiently and effectively, replacing a task that consumed ridiculous amounts of energy, household by household. Family life had not ended because mother no longer daily baked the bread. The same possibility of saving time and energy existed for all the tasks of sex work that held women hostage and removed them from race work. As for cleaning, she calculated the time, effort, and cost to a given community when each household had one whole woman cleaning it, comparing this to the lesser cost of a collectivity, such as an apartment block hiring cleaners at good market rates to serve all of the households within it.[9]

With regard to childcare, Gilman proposed various forms of crèches, "babygardens," and daylong preschools, specially geared for the needs of working mothers. Again, fictional heroines exemplify the possibilities Gilman saw. Her proposals usually involved partnership and collaboration between professional women and mothers, who managed these costs. These proposals became controversial during the first decades of the twentieth century, critics accusing her of debasing motherhood, institutionalizing children, and turning the mother-child bond into a cold, instrumental relation mediated by strangers.[10]

Instead, her goal was nothing less than eradicating the remains of "the patriarchate." In urging men to sign on for change, she admitted that they would lose dominance. She urged on them the gains; men would lose a servant, a victim, a vampire, "horse-leech's daughters, crying 'Give! give!'" In return they would gain a woman more worth loving than they had ever known.[11]

Some of her earliest reform designs appeared in her 1911 serialized novel, *Moving the Mountain*. Set in 1940, in New York, a latter-day Rip Van Winkle, twenty-five-year-old John Robertson had been sleeping for thirty years, without physically aging, after an accident in Tibet. His younger sister Nellie traveled there to rescue him. On awaking, Robertson was amazed to learn that his nearly fifty-year-old sister had studied medicine abroad, worked as a doctor, then an academic chair, and was currently the president of a Michigan coeducational college. He was flabbergasted to find that, far from being the spinster her career path would have suggested in 1910, she had a loving husband, Owen, though not his surname, and two adult children, Hallie and Jerrold, who live independently in New York City apartments, working as a food inspector and musician, respectively. John feared that his society had evolved from one with "only a small proportion of malcontents" to an awful place "with strange masculine women and subdued men."[12]

New York had changed completely. It was all-electric, quiet, beautiful, efficient, unpolluted, and without slums, poverty, smoking, saloons, prostitution, gambling, advertising, cats, or dogs. Unemployment was nonexistent, and all adults worked at least two and, most often, four hours a day until noon or one o'clock for a full living wage, and all at work they found interesting and useful. Crime was virtually extinct, as were birth defects from venereal diseases. All immigrants were welcomed, trained, and Americanized. A new religion, described as a science of living and as ethics, replaced the old forms of patriarchal world religions.[13]

Lost brother John asked Nellie apprehensively if his native land has not adopted socialism. She answered affirmatively, but "that was twenty years ago. . . . We've got beyond it. . . . We understand better what Socialism meant, that's all. We have more, much more than it ever asked; but we don't call it that." These remarks reflected well the evolution of Gilman's socialist thought, from its Bellamyite origins in her 1880s–90s time in California among the Nationalists, through her later 1890s to early 1900s Fabian socialist influences from contacts in Britain and in New York. Her vision for

1940 in this 1911 novel addressed natural resources, work, and productivity. By then, she depicted rapid reforesting and soil improvement, fruit- and nut-tree farming along all major roads, with qualitative and quantitative output vastly increased. There were universally shortened working hours, while improved work conditions all but eliminated industrial accidents. In this new world, she explained, there was no labor problem, no sex problem, "no color problem." The whole beautiful world could be seen from airships gliding by, providing a moving view as if from a mountain top, hence the book's title. Learning that all school children had a year of travel abroad, the astonished John asked about its funding. Nellie explained that this investment in well-educated young people was simple, since no longer did government squander 70 percent of national investment on military preparedness.[14]

Living arrangements dramatically reflected the changed cultural priorities. Spare, spacious, dust-resistant, and comfortable homes had no kitchens. A professional food service replaced individual home cooking. Producers and manufacturers shipped in fresh supplies via underground monorails to basement kitchens. Residents supplied with menu lists placed phone orders by midnight the day before for lowest rates, and meals appeared automatically at their chosen mealtimes in the dumbwaiter in every dwelling in clean aluminum boxes. The used dishes and cutlery simply went back in the box the same way for cleaning.[15]

Admitting the food was delicious, John doubted that this service was cheaper than the old system of individual unpaid and untrained housewives. So, his food inspector niece Hallie did the calculations. Even among persons formerly employing cooks, the system of individual households was hugely wasteful: "Here were a hundred families, equal to, say five hundred persons. They hired a hundred cooks ... paid them something like six dollars a week, call it five on the average. There's $500 a week, just for cooks—$26,000 a year. Now as a matter of fact ... ten cooks are plenty for five hundred persons—at the same price would cost $1,300 a year." In fact, the new food service cooks received better pay—for instance, $3,000 for the most highly skilled chefs, two receiving $2,000, two $1,000, and five at $800. As a result, the cooks of these 500 persons—scientific artists 500 percent more skilled—received $13,000, exactly half the cost of the hundred much less skilled kitchen maids for individual families in the 1910 world John had known. Added to this saving on wages was the further savings on fuel, utensils, materials, altogether amounting to a meal provision for 80 percent less money than 1910 prices for higher-quality meals.[16]

Accompanying these domestic transformations, sexual and reproductive relations changed as well. Owen, Nellie's husband, informed John that

Ward's theory of women as the race type now framed male-female interactions: "A 'wife' used to be a possession," but now, "She does not belong to anyone in that old sense. She is the wife of her husband in that she is his true lover, and that their marriage is legally recorded; but her life and work does not belong to him. He has no right to her 'services' any more." Thus, when his daughter Hallie married, she would retain her career and certainly would not darn her future husband's socks or cook his meals. Girls and boys were raised identically.[17]

Moving the Mountain was Gilman's most detailed exposition of an imagined future incorporating the most urgently needed changes in sexual, social, economic, and civic relations. In their didactic discussions, all characters report that women becoming citizens amounted to a great cultural awakening. If suffrage underpinned the narrative momentum, Gilman stressed that changes were already in train. The matter was no longer hypothetical: women were embracing race work. Though an advocate, she was merely the prophet.

Race Work: Women Becoming "Human"

Real race progress, *which* has moved from a scant and meager, scattered and disconnected existence, to the present degree of racial and inter-racial organization, is as detached from sex influence as if it were a fourth dimension. . . .We find that social progress differing widely in degree and in rate of advancement among different races, but we do not find that they differ commensurately in sex development, or that sex is the acting cause of their progress.

Charlotte Perkins Gilman, "Sex and Race Progress" (1929)

Gilman sought to persuade her contemporaries that women would no longer perform only sex work—primitive, unpaid, and secluded home industries. Both women and men had to reclaim as human all the nondomestic "masculine" domains in androcentric culture. In no animal species, besides humans, did the sex work of females obstruct the "race activities" that they shared with males. Nor did female race activities injure sex activities, for "it is indeed through the demand on the mother for care and service to the young that much of the development of the species is due. But in humanity from the earliest times, we find a subject female, the property of the male, restricted to the lowest stage of industry, while the whole structure of civilization has been erected by the activities of men alone, freely using human powers long defined as masculine. Nothing is essentially masculine save such qualities and functions as pertain to the male."[18]

Gilman decried androcentric man's equation of human activities as male monopolies. In 1892, she sneered at the claim that women could "unsex" themselves through participation in activities that are human but called masculine. Never did such claimants hold that cooking or sewing "feminized" men. Beyond the minimal bodily differences organizing reproduction, many so-called innate sex differences were merely cultural exaggerations of masculinity and femininity, "derived from excessive sex-distinction wrought by women's economic dependence on men. We must explore 'human possibilities.'" This position informed her strategies for overturning women's exclusion from race work. As a corollary, she reexamined "human work" itself. Masculine proclivities dominated the paid workforce by emphasizing struggle, competition, and reward, distorting the true nature and origins of work. Again echoing Veblen's *Theory of the Leisure Class* (1899), she noted that androcentric cultures reviled work, men requiring major inducement to do it, those men of the highest status marking their position by idleness. Yet work originated in the social qualities that made *Homo sapiens* human.[19]

Gilman's first worker was the mother. The essence of work, beyond immediate feeding of the self—work on behalf of children—was altruistic, an expression of creative energy, accompanying human brain development. Not afflicted by the scattering, destructive, and combative urges of the sex-fertilizing male, woman, as the trunk of the human tree, originated work as an extension of motherhood. Here she used the most familiar American example of an indigenous preindustrial people to demonstrate sex differences in the relation to work, and she used the language of her era: "The humble squaw who drops corn in her stick-ploughed field" knew that "in time there will be fruit for her children." She needed no present benefit, motivated to see ahead, a result of neurological development. By contrast, her "lord, the noble Red-man, gallantly pursuing the buffalo, is acting merely as an animal, under direct stimulus of hunger and the visible beast before him. Being hungry, he hunts. Being fed, he does nothing. He can only act in the lower circuit of excito-motory nerves. But she, not hungry, makes the corn grow. She makes the tent. She makes the moccasins and leggings and beaded belt. She makes the dish and basket. She, first on earth, works, and she works for others." With such deep historical associations between women and work, she called comical the claim that women should not work. So, it was "more agonizing and more ridiculous for a woman not to work than for a man, because of her initial sex-tendency and her historic habits." Hence, "sparing" women from productive work could become intelligible only in cultures where male "protectors" perceived work negatively. No one despised work when it was performed by the free mother in matriarchal times.[20]

Only once men had enslaved women did contempt for work flourish as a characteristic of androcentric cultures. For Gilman and many of her peers, this ancient sex slavery provided the template for the other forms of slavery that followed, right down to the disgraceful and appallingly long-lived American version of chattel slavery. When, subsequently, men themselves enslaved other men in ancient wars, imperial expansions, and eventually, for instance in the European case, through feudalism, the negative associations of work spiraled. Thereafter, work was exacted through threat of banishment, bodily punishment, or death; then wage labor of modern democracies replaced punishment with reward as the incentive to work. Even though modern citizens could freely choose, at least compared with serfs or slaves, the threat of starvation remained for failure to work.[21]

Thus, work inherited entirely manmade, negative associations from these ancient patterns, making status and power for modern men expressed through possession of a parasitic wife who did no productive labor. Even poorer men forbade their womenfolk any truck with paid labor, as if an affront to their manhood. Men built the "pitiful enormity" of economically dependent womanhood and "admire it as a Chinaman admires the 'golden lilies' on his wife's shrunken shanks." By this, to modern eyes, ethno-culturally intolerant allusion to Chinese foot binding—though she did also criticize high-heeled Western women's shoes supporting "a flock of chiropodists"—she thereby suggested that those men denying women access to specialized work and independence were barbarians, comparable with the conventional Western assessment of Oriental culture: stationary, patriarchal, and ancestor worshiping, standard tropes in Progressive Era representations of East Asians. Gilman claimed that this backward situation was "already passing," echoing her previous argument in *Women and Economics,* namely, that women had endured a temporary era of androcentrism in order for formerly inferior men to be raised to sex equality with them.[22]

Gilman thought that forward advance now required both men and women to embrace specialized work based on their best inclinations, skills, and talents. While "work is essentially feminine in its origin," this implied neither a permanent nor necessary state but, rather, as it develops, work "frees itself wholly from sex limitations and becomes a social function in which men and women take part as members of society." The malleability of meaning showed that "women's work" once meant every kind of work, while "'man's work' is now generally supposed to include the harder and rougher, the higher and more difficult." These were arbitrary, sexed associations from an obsolete androcentric order, without "real foundation." Either sex could do modern work, which was without sex connotations. She reiterated the scientific case for the female being, rather than inferior, the more important of the sexes. The association of women with work need degrade neither. Instead, "the progress of the race is hindered by the arrested social development of women and by the over-development of sex resultant from their position. . . . Their freedom and further growth depend absolutely on the specialization of their 'domestic industries.'" In "Suggestions on Special Education for Women" (1933), Gilman proclaimed that women constituted "a newly liberated class . . . hitherto denied legitimate social relationship and development and now rapidly assuming them." In other words, despite the lingering effects of androcentrism, women were beginning to assume their proper share of race work. Therefore it was appropriate to rename motherhood as "a pre eminent social service instead of a minor department of housekeeping."[23]

Her concept of participation did not mandate sex neutrality, or androgyny, or the aping of men as the human norm, as some critics of feminism supposed. Gilman insisted that this new independent woman would make a great, new contribution to the world, namely, legitimate feminine qualities: "The feminine power is for growth, both in the rich fruition of physical motherhood, and in all the ensuing processes of nurture, which are the first of the endless steps of social growth. . . The really feminine contribution to our civilization is to spread and strengthen the cultivative process, to substitute a reasoned constructive effort toward social improvement for the unreasoned, often destructive processes of competition."

Gilman insisted that this change was happening as she wrote; women moved from domestic to social production over the shrieks of protest "far more lively than was aroused when the spinning wheel went to the mill." Resistance here protected "an iridescent web of sentiment about the sordid fact that practically half the citizens were house servants," an enjoyable situation for those served, who thereby preferred to think that "there was something in the very sex of women which endowed them at birth with magical skill in this kind of work, and an innate desire for it." Thus, women's status was to remain noncitizen assistants to male citizens, despite "this half of the people" being precisely as important as the other half "in heredity, in educative influence, and indirect effect on their community." Confining all women to wageless domestic service checked human progress by denying women participation in the project of race development: "As human beings, they vary as men do, have widely different tastes, abilities, desires. It is through this tendency to vary, that genius, talent, exceptional skill, appear; and these special gifts enrich and advance half the world. Half of this wealth and progress we have extinguished by holding half the world to one job. Conversely, the release of women, their entrance upon a whole range of human activities, promises large and swift advance."[24]

Before women could be admitted to race work, cultural understanding of work had to be liberated from historic masculine perspectives: "Work is human. It is not feminine, though women began it. It is not masculine, though men have taken it. But because men have kept women out of it for so long, it has shared the disadvantages of excessive masculinity. As a race quality, work means social service."[25]

Eliminating or reducing women's sex work and enlarging their race work were neither mere dreams nor fond hopes. In 1913, the issue erupted graphically in New York City when City Schools' Superintendent John Martin (soon to be Fabian author of an attack on Gilman, cowritten with his wife, Prestonia Mann Martin), and the Board of Education, attempted to fire married teachers who became mothers, with some infamous cases attracting public attention from 1913. The board had first tried to fire female, but not male, married teachers, until their action was declared illegal by the state Court of Appeals. Undaunted, the board persevered. If they could not maintain "an entirely celibate body of women teachers," as Gilman reported, they were determined to "at least prevent motherhood amongst them." The dismissals backfired. Defenders of the "teacher mothers" founded the League of Civic Service, undertaking to represent these embattled women with the city. Gilman became its spokeswoman, marshalling both pen and speech to repudiate the board's masculism. She skewered the board's action as a "piece of historic amusement," especially the assertion that it "is impossible to be a good mother and a good teacher." Insisting that the mother was the first and most natural teacher, the notion that a celibate nonmother was qualified to teach, but a sexually active mother was not, infuriated her.[26]

The New Woman was making modest inroads in teaching by 1910, despite derision from the Antis. For Gilman, teaching exemplified women pushing toward industrial specialization and away from general home trades, "one of the largest and most vitally important movements of the day." The board's effort to ignore this movement was foolish and wasted, for women were never going back: "They have definitely come out." Several episodes evoked Gilman's wrath. In a celebrated legal case, Mrs. Bridget Peixotto, a teacher with eighteen years of exemplary service to the city, was fired "because she bore a child." She appealed. In the board's defense, John

Martin declared teacher mothers impractical: "The mother while nominally holding the position which must meanwhile be filled by a procession of transient substitutes would really be present only for a month or two between successive periods of absence. Thereby the interest of thirty or forty children would be continually sacrificed to the avarice of the teacher."[27]

Gilman was dismayed. As her friend, schoolteacher Henrietta Rodman, noted, the teacher mother might have three children during a teaching career of thirty years on average. Gilman reasoned that leave without pay equivalent to one year in ten was surely not unreasonable, hardly "avarice." She ridiculed Martin's demographic fantasy of the "threatening deluge of teachers' babies, in unlimited procession . . . at eighteen month intervals." When challenged, the board classified Peixotto's action as "gross misconduct." An incensed Gilman joined five other feminist activists, including Fola La Follette, and met Mayor Mitchel as a deputation on 16 November 1914. Gilman spoke to the mayor on behalf of "the complainants . . . praising the Mayor for the stand he has already taken in advocacy of some modification of the present attitude of the school authorities." The *Times* noted, particularly, the inefficiency involved in firing experienced teachers, for the school and children, especially as these women would prefer to resume their profession than "do housework." Gilman concurred, observing that "one teacher who had taught ten years was worth more than ten teachers who had taught for one year.'"[28]

What was Martin's conception of women and conjugality? Much more contemptible was his serious misrepresentation of the assignments of teachers and pupils. Pupils did not stay with one teacher, year after year. Thus any "transient substitute" would have an equally transient roomful of children. More aggravating still, Henrietta Rodman was suspended and replaced by a substitute for writing a letter to the editor of the *New York Times* protesting the board's treatment of "teacher mothers." Rodman (1878–1923) was a schoolteacher and a socialist who organized the Liberal Club in Greenwich Village, as well as the Feminist Alliance, in 1912, devoted to developing and implementing practical reforms to the sex division of labor, many specifically based on Gilman's designs and proposals. She was also active in the Consumer's League and the Women's Trade Union League. Gilman denounced the two-year drama that followed Rodman's suspension.[29]

Informing her *Forerunner* readers about this ongoing fiasco in 1915, Gilman contended that the phony "gross misconduct" charged against Rodman, which resulted in a popular protest meeting, contravened her First Amendment rights. Gross misconduct as a ground for firing or suspension needed to be conduct related to the teacher's profession—teaching. All

FIGURE 33. Portrait of
Henrietta Rodman, ca. 1917.
Photo by Jessie Tarbox Beals
(The Schlesinger Library,
Radcliffe Institute, Harvard
University: PC60-134-8).

official and unofficial reports attested to Rodman's long experience and un-
questioned efficiency. Rodman's real offense was being a feminist: she had
"ideas of which they disapproved; she expressed them; she had married; but
she had kept her own name." With these salvos against the board generally,
and Martin particularly, the bitterness of Martin's attack on Gilman in his
1916 text, *Feminism: Its Fallacies and Follies* appears in a new light. His was
the paternalistic, not to say patriarchal, face of American Fabian socialism.

Moreover, it is probable that there was a personal element in the attack on Rodman and, hence, in Gilman's involvement. Prestonia Mann
had been an *American Fabian* comrade who tried to have Gilman become
editor in 1897. Gilman wrote to her fiancé from Mann's socialist summer
camp, Summer Book Farm, in 1897 where she holidayed with Kate. She described the routine of collective chores and meal making, her conversations
there with "Sister Rodman," and the ritual of Mann reading from various
luminaries—Ruskin, Darwin—to the assembly over meals. This socialist
vacation institution was famous and visited by Gilman admirers Floyd Dell
and Upton Sinclair, as well as many other writers and artists. Mann's marriage to English Fabian John Martin appears to have initiated the period of
estrangement between her and Rodman and Gilman, probably due to his
disapproval of their suffragism and advocacy of working mothers.

FIGURE 34. Group Photo at Summer Brook Farm with Gilman, her daughter, Katharine Beecher Stetson, and Prestonia Mann Martin (1897) (The Schlesinger Library, Radcliffe Institute, Harvard University: 2000-M125)

In the final analysis, the essence of the "teacher mother" episode was the struggle for maternity leave—still not universally recognized as a right in American workplaces, and decidedly meager compared with other industrialized nations. Praising European provisions in 1916, Gilman noted the teachers' case as but one example of localized opposition. Its rationale had to be "to prevent maternity" among working women, or to punish maternity, or else to prevent mothers from undertaking gainful occupations, "from working at anything for which they are paid." Noting that once upon a time the quest for gainful employment for women was confined to spinsters and widows, then young girls before marriage, married women sought paid work more and more "to meet family wants and preserve their own integrity." Wives and mothers "are becoming a permanent half of world workers . . . we shall inevitably change the brutal and foolish hardships now surrounding labor into such decent and healthful condition as shall be no injury to anyone." Moreover, Gilman held that, politically, mothers formed a collision with patriarchy that spinsters, widows, and "girls" did not. Since most women were wives and mothers at some point, until "mothers" earn their livings, "women will not."[30]

Just as in *Moving the Mountain,* the motivating force in reforming America had been women's citizenship and quest for productive labor and economic independence, so here Gilman similarly argued for a woman-led transformation of paid work and public policy provision. She did not advocate that women could or should simply be added to the labor force as it then existed. All her proposals for a human world presumed a postsocialist order in which humane conditions prevailed for all and in which increased efficiency and productivity would provide everyone with a good standard of living and shorter working hours.

Moreover, she advocated fundamental reexamination of standard assumptions about work, competition, productivity, incentives, capitalist profits, and the sex division of resources. By no means did she assume that women joining the existing workforce would revolutionize their situation. For a start, women's wages were hopelessly inadequate for their own or anyone else's support. She urged a complete reevaluation of the status and value accorded the socially important work women could do, as well as upgrading their access to training and career opportunities. In *Moving the Mountain,* John Robertson was astonished to learn that workers from top to bottom of the food production, preparation, service, and distribution occupations now earn generous salaries, the chief of the food inspectorate, for instance, earning as much as the president of Harvard University. That the novel should have such an emphasis is not surprising in view of her abiding preoccupation with food adulteration and the milk supply. She admired Upton Sinclair and his proletarian novel, *The Jungle* (1906), which profoundly radicalized her, a sentiment expressed in her warm correspondence with him.[31]

Critics accusing Gilman of insensitivity to class and race in her schemes for women's economic independence assume that the capitalist workforce would remain intact. Yet this was precisely what she insisted would have to change. In Gilman's future, there would be no more advertising executives, since advertising had ceased. The "yellow press," exemplified for Gilman by the Hearst newspapers, would be no more. Extinct also would be all highly paid, parasitic occupations, such as law, as all future work would contribute to the wider social good.[32]

Hecklers and aggressive questioners, including socialists, derided Gilman's views, observing that capitalism created competition enough among workers, without doubling it by adding women to lower average wages, and poisoning personal relations between the sexes. A self-proclaimed socialist, she replied by refuting the assumption that males had a god-given right to monopolize paid work. She also rejected the tacit presumption that there was only a fixed, finite amount of work available. Even if this assumption were true, however, social justice demanded that it be split evenly between men and women. There was work, important work everywhere: for instance, redressing the nationwide underdevelopment of roads and highways. The designation of some tasks as menial and low status, and others the converse, had everything to do with capitalist exploitation and urgently required reconfiguration.[33]

Obstacles

I think you show real breadth of mind in including such views as mine in your proposed book, the bulk of which I doubt not will be markedly different. Perhaps you will draw the line at my most disrespectful remarks about the "modern" views; but then, other of your chosen authors, including yourself, have been quite merciless toward what you consider fallacious.

Charlotte Perkins Gilman to Samuel D. Schmalhausen (1930)

Gilman was clear about her diagnoses of what ailed androcentric culture and equally certain about the advantages for women, and for men and children, of the human world she envisioned. Both sexes would contribute to the advance of the human race through work and development. Nothing suggested, though, that progressive change would just emerge voluntarily or inevitably. Indeed, her human world faced many real and present obstacles. Unless these were overcome, all the reform proposals she and others could devise would remain mere exhortations. Arguably, the implications of her analysis collided forcefully with alternative contemporary discourses regarding masculinity, sexuality, psychoanalysis, and women's sexual equality. To the extent that her reform Darwinist feminism became increasingly alien to a new generation of potential political actors and cultural critics formidable obstacles confronted the reality of a human world.[34]

Gilman was no stranger to controversies about her analyses. In particular, androcentric constructions of men's sexuality and the vested interests of their sexual politics, often enforced by violence, strongly obstructed a human world. World War One produced cultural conditions that heightened her sense of the obstacles facing progressive transformation of sexual relations. Her discussion of sexual negotiations in her 1915 serialized novel, *Herland,* conveyed gloom about prospects for change. The story centered on a South American country without men due to a war two thousand years earlier. It is discovered by three American men, Terry, Jeff, and Van—the latter, a sociologist, the narrator.

The two-thousand-year-old female culture had evolved, and gradually there developed parthenogenic reproduction, Gilman's fantasy here consonant with other early twentieth-century science fiction and related utopian and socialist fiction. First, one woman bore five daughters, each daughter bore five daughters and regeneration continued over time. In a few generations, the women had no further anxiety about reproduction. The women jettisoned the artificial patterns of femininity formerly demanded by men and became fully "human." One of the three male "discoverers from Ourland," Van later told the Herlander who would become his wife, Ellador, he had to revise his initial judgment that the women of Herland lacked femininity. He learned that what he had understood as feminine became culturally meaningless without "masculine" defined in polar opposite terms. These women were "People" first, then women. They wore short hair and fine, simple tunics with plenty of pockets. Moreover, they had no idea of flirtation, wiles, and the other sexualized attributes of women subjected to men. They were intelligent, observant, and articulate. Appalled by the men's accounts of practices and characteristics in "Ourland"— contemporary America—these women extolled a life-giving motherhood above all else. And they deplored violence, aggression, and exploitation in any form.[35]

Though this all-female society resulted from the Herlander women's slaughter of their would-be conquerors, former slaves, Gilman did not linger on this violence. Instead, she problematized men's violence, just as she had done so before, whether in Lester Ward's theory of androcentric genesis, masculist antisuffragists' "the brute in man," or justifications of the present world war. The attempted rape of Alimna by Terry, one of the three visitors from "Ourland," all of whom had married Herlander women, led to the expulsion of all three men from Herland. The most literal reading of the novel is that the probability of men changing was virtually nonexistent. A human world that was "bisexual," as the Herlanders termed it, faced one major obstacle: men's demand for constant rather than periodic sexual intercourse.[36]

If two of the three male visitors to Herland could not change, one, the narrator Van, tried to accommodate the wishes of his Herland "wife," Ellador: she had no desire whatever to engage in his idea of a "normal" conjugal relationship. She would countenance it only when, sometime in the future, her "great mother purpose" led her to the right time to reproduce. Initially, this strained their relationship, while they were still in Herland. Van explained that this was a general problem for all three men:

> The big point at issue between us and our wives was, as may easily be imagined, in the very nature of the relation. . . . These, as Terry put it, "alleged or so-called wives" of ours, went right on with their profession as foresters. . . . Of course, what we, as men, wanted to make them see was that there were other, and as we proudly said, "higher" uses in this relation than what Terry called "mere parentage.". . . [The Herlanders asked them,] "Among your people do you find high and lasting affection appearing in proportion to this indulgence?"

To this question, the male visitors had no satisfactory reply. Whereas the hypermasculine Terry complained relentlessly about his wife's withholding of his imagined conjugal rights, Van reflected on the cultural construction of masculine sexual desires in his experience of companionate marital continence:

> I found that much, very much of what I had honestly supposed to be a physiological necessity was a psychological necessity—or so I believed. I found . . . these women were not provocative. . . . You see, with us, women are kept as different as possible and as feminine as possible. . . . When, in spite of this, my hereditary instincts and race-traditions made me long for the feminine response in Ellador, instead of withdrawing so that I should want her more, she deliberately gave me a little too much of her society— always de-feminized, as it were. But this I soon began to find: that under all our cultivated attitude of mind toward women, there is an older, deeper, more "natural" feeling, the restful reverence which looks up to the Mother sex.[37]

Despite this representation of Van as willingly adapting himself to his wife's mores and beliefs, sexuality continued as a source of tension. In the 1916 sequel, "With Her in Ourland" Van made decisive strides toward the kind of erotic temperance extolled by Gilman as the condition for women's sharing a viable human world with men. He completely submitted to Ellador's wishes and accepted the full meaning of this revised form of social organization. Far from a partnership of equal exchange of discourses, some critics note Van's complete submission to Ellador, embracing her "seductive celibacy," so that while he does not inseminate her, she inseminates him with her thought. In espousing the joys of this new sexual arrangement, Gilman used the familiar device of having both Van and Ellador criticize contemporary American women as they found them in 1916. The excess of sex in Ourland women disappointed Van, lacking the humanness he found irresistible in his Herland wife:

> Persons, two Persons who love each other, have a bigger range of happiness than even two lovers. I mean two lovers who are not such companions, of course. I do not deny that it has been hard, very hard, sometimes ... but somehow the more I loved you the less it troubled me. Now I feel that when we do reach that union, with all our love, with all that great mother purpose in your heart and the beginning of a sense of father purpose in mine, I'm sure that it will be only an incident in our love, our happiness, not the main thing.[38]

Gilman lamented the fact that contemporary American "sexolatry" sneeringly regarded such unions as restrictive, advocating instead the health of "miscellaneous and continuous 'sex experience.'" She reiterated her charge that humans were the only species that had "separated sex from its universal purpose," privileging coitus for "a barren gratification" followed by "a rising tide of vice." Even beyond "Ourland," her human world demanded a new reconfiguration of coital and sexological discussion. Rather than men rising to women's moral and ethical standards, to most modern Americans, "equality" seemed to mean instead that women should "descend" to men's erotic norms. In Gilman's view, a major obstacle to building a human world was the cultural requirement of women's increased "sex indulgence," their imitation of men's sexual mores, and the resulting "race" consequences. She launched a critique, then, of "sexolatry" in the modern age.[39]

Her utopian writings of female worlds confronted the real-life intransigence of normative masculinities. Transformation could not take place without a separate feminist struggle after all. This view differs from usual readings of Gilman's utopianism as a symptom of her optimism as a reformer. But any feminist struggle—indeed, any "larger feminism" of which Gilman could approve—needed to take as its guiding principle the eradication of sex work, the full contribution of women to race work, implying women's reclaiming their humanness, a humanness so long distorted and repressed by androcentric demands. Only fully human men and women could build a human world—and she tried to envision these new people in creative explorations and critiques, whether in the fictional adventures of Herlanders and their romantic partners or her repudiation of Freudian imports into sexual politics. The possibility of more frequent heterosexual coitus being free of the likelihood of pregnancy was still remote in 1915, and even the birth control methods available had effectiveness odds drastically reduced by the faulty theory of ovulation prevailing into the 1930s, mentioned above. Put most literally, more coitus meant more babies or more abortions for average women, potentially, then, deeper ensnarement by sex work. This highlighted the critical feminist issue that effective birth control stood to become, but in 1915 when Gilman wrote *Herland,* such a prospect seemed truly utopian.

The need to shift toward the human world undergirded all of her visions. She was not, however, a dewy-eyed utopian, pointing the right path then righteously withdrawing from an uncomprehending and skeptical world. Gilman's inclination was always to pursue the implementation of positive change. This dictated her keen interest in feminist work toward legislative and policy reform. Hence, she embraced enthusiastically a critical engagement with the largest movement generating reform momentum of her adult life: Progressivism.[40]

PART THREE

Embracing Progressivism

Don't you think you have counted mainly on the literary and professional lecturing side of my life; and discounted the "reforming" department? I have shown you less of it, of course. Do you not see how close association— identification, with a life so alien to your own is going to jar upon you?

Charlotte Perkins Gilman to George Houghton Gilman, 29 March 1899

GILMAN DEVELOPED her sexuo-economic theories of women's oppression and relational dynamics with men in order to change them—indeed to revolutionize them fundamentally if she could. Hence, her narrative of the rise of androcentrism, and its dire evolutionary consequences, formed no mere academic rumination. It historicized and deessentialized the existing status quo, preeminently mandating a political and policy focus on the rights and activities of women. However complicated her engagement with feminism of the period, Gilman's deep investment in feminist interventions in the public arena was always clear, her defense and cherishing of that movement unmistakable, indispensable to her mission and purpose in "world service."

To work only for causes and reforms about women, however, would not address the larger auspices within which women's oppression and sexual relations currently transpired. Effecting real reforms for women, on Gilman's model, involved engagement with a complex of larger political and cultural issues. Oppressive dimensions of men's sexuality and sex supremacism found their expression in women's economic dependency on men, the primitive state of the home and home industries, and deleterious consequences of unchecked masculinity on public and private life. These problems interlocked and coordinated with others.

The cultural interconnectedness of such problems then belied any simplistic politics of magic bullets. So, critical as woman suffrage was, and would be, it alone could not deliver the range of challenges to androcentric culture prerequisite for the transformation of life that she envisioned, for instance, in the 1940 version of New York City, depicted in her serialized novel *Moving the Mountain* (1911). That human world was brought about through the eradication of the ancient, injurious, and parasitic features of androcentric culture and through the building and "growth"—often almost literally in the botanical or agricultural sense—of new structures, arrangements, customs, policies, and portrayals of men, women, and children.

Hence, Gilman's reform temper had both abolitionist and architectural/ agricultural dimensions, in fairly equal and interdependent coexistence. Abolitionism, of course, came almost naturally, as a Beecher family tradition. Like her famous Gilded Age forebears, she had no difficulty grasping politics aimed at rooting out corruption and injustice. The building and growth elements of her politics, however, drew on her profound commitment to reform Darwinism. She infused these elements with her belief in reform Darwinism's compelling narrative for a viable future world of "race progress" and enhanced human happiness set in accord with, rather than against, nature.

With these orientations and preferences, it was virtually inevitable that Gilman, as the most distinguished feminist theorist of the early twentieth century, would become a Progressive. Programmatically, the diffuse and, for a time, ubiquitous tentacles of Progressivism in American public life intertwined decisively with the feminist aspirations and reform agendas most directly commanding Gilman's dedicated energies. Gilman embraced Progressivism keenly, though as emerges in this final section of the book, neither uncritically nor without certain difficulties on specific matters. Since Progressivism was the greatest political reform era of her lifetime, her longer philosophical embrace of reform Darwinist feminism left her no choice but to engage as productively as possible with Progressive allies in change.

The four final chapters here chart that engagement. Gilman's intervention into Progressive Era campaigns concerning prostitution signal precisely the blend of abolitionist and architectural/agricultural sensibilities informing her distinctly feminist slant on competing policy trajectories of her warring contemporaries. Rhetorically, she made a powerful abolitionist case for the ending of the "sex slavery" of the prostitution contract. Yet her distinctive political focus on the demand for prostitution, that is to say, on the male client, epitomizes both her embrace and critique of typical Progressive approaches. Rather than merely tinkering with the management of the supply and profiteering from segregated urban prostitution, she sought nothing less than the construction of an erotically altered new manhood. Prostitution reforms then, as examined in chapter 9, illustrate the quality and limits of Gilman's embrace of Progressivism, in a highly contested domain of long and deep significance to women's rights and feminist movements before her.

In making such detailed and, some would contend, revolutionary interventions into politics and policy, Gilman forged herself a profile as one of the most significant public intellectuals of the Progressive Era. Applauded or reviled, she became a household name among the newspaper-reading public during the 1900s and 1910s, the heyday of the Progressive movement. Chapter 10 outlines the ways in which she worked as a public intellectual, especially the sense in which she wrote feminism into Progressivism in her work as a journalist, theorist, editor, and lecturer. Then, chapter 11 examines and revises claims that Gilman abandoned the cause of women after World War I and closing her journal, *Forerunner.* In fact, she battled relentlessly within the declining opportunities faced by a formally uneducated autodidact now in her sixties and seventies. She continued to interconnect the great political impulses of her lifetime, reform Darwinist feminism and Progressivism, even as both underwent profound transformations that she was, ultimately, unable to comprehend fully. Her controversial work on the themes of immigration restriction, eugenics, and birth control, the latter in collaboration with Margaret Sanger, exemplify the complexities of these connections and transformations.

Finally, chapter 12 outlines and evaluates the extent to which Gilman's embrace of Progressivism poses problems for scholars addressing Gilman's life, work, and legacy today. The influence of the "wave" metaphor in periodizing and characterizing feminism results in a highly rhetorical and extensive Gilmaniana centered in the humanities and, especially, literary criticism. Highly presentist in method and categories of analysis, this work is especially preoccupied with reading Gilman in the light of class, race, and ethnicity. Reconciling these approaches with evidence from Gilman's own Progressive Era context remains a serious challenge to this current scholarship.

CHAPTER NINE

Reconfiguring Vice

Man . . . has insisted on maintaining another
class of women . . . subservient to his desires; a
barren, mischievous unnatural relation, wholly
aside from parental purposes, and absolutely
injurious to society. . . . One major cause of the
decay of nations is "the social evil"—a thing
wholly due to androcentric culture.

Charlotte Perkins Gilman,
The Man-Made World *(1911)*

GILMAN EMBRACED Progressivism by integrating feminist axioms
within it, nowhere more clearly than in her analyses of prostitution. Reformers made commercialized vice and white slavery key targets of law and
policy revision, particularly during the 1910–16 period. Prostitution was a
signature Progressive reform issue, though typical interventions met only
some of Gilman's concerns. It encompassed her Progressive peers' key targets: bloated trusts, debt peonage in labor contracts, and bribery within the
corrupt political machine. These spotlighted the suppliers and profiteers
from the trade in flesh. Such perspectives displaced the late nineteenth-
century fascination with rescuing and reforming individual prostitutes.[1]

Yet both nineteenth- and twentieth-century perspectives mostly ignored clients, who were the most numerous group involved in commercialized vice. Estimates of clientage for a full-time prostitute in the period
ranged from a low of thirty to a high of 185 weekly, with highly variable
conditions, rates of pay, services provided, and professional costs. Remarkably, rather than attempting to tackle the salience of such a significant topic
in the history of men as a sex, historians of prostitution, social purity, and
social hygiene debate the extent of the trade, its degree of segregation and
professionalization, its legal and wider regulation. Clients were the major-

ity of those involved in prostitution, in whose interests it was regulated. Though clients vastly outnumbered prostitutes, they substantially have evaded historical gaze.[2]

By contrast, Gilman called prostitution an abomination of androcentric culture: women's economic dependency led them to exchange sex and sexualized services for room, board, and clothing. Though concurring with a tradition of feminist analogies drawn between prostitution and marriage, she insisted that economically independent monogamy ensured the best life for women. Thus, she sought to end "the social evil" not only by tackling suppliers—the preference of many Progressive Era reformers—but also men's demand for commercial sexual encounters.

Those seeking to end regulated prostitution adopted the name "abolitionists," drawing analogy between chattel slavery and sex slavery, in their aim to eradicate regulated and segregated prostitution.[3] If Gilman's ideal future entailed commercialized and professionalized provision of the services comprising "sex work," she exempted prostitution because she regarded it as uniquely injurious to humanity. Initially, then, her concerns aligned Gilman with abolitionists like Chicago's Jane Addams, the woman usually taken as the personification of Progressivism and with whom Gilman lived for a time in 1894–95. Gilman's particular proposals, however, exceeded the typical abolitionist framework, with one that was recognizably feminist. If Chicago had its "Saint Jane," most decidedly, Gilman was not New York's "Saint Charlotte"—for she saw both client and prostitute as enemies of all women, all children, and of the mission of the human race toward growth and improvement.[4] Situating Gilman's particularities as an abolitionist, however, is complicated by presentism in histories of United States prostitution and feminist sexual thought, which dismisses abolitionists in the shadow of the feminist "sexuality wars" over pornography and sex industries in the 1980s and 1990s. Abolitionists became, at historians' pens, class-blind and gullible fools, who were appropriated and marginalized by patriarchal social purity and social hygiene forces.[5]

Gilman's critique of prostitution combined several preoccupations distinct from those of peer abolitionists. The paucity of women's economic options produced the dependence that retarded them as a sex. The loss of female-initiated sex selection meant that, instead, women competed for male support, using feminine wiles and exaggerated sex differences. Men's right to purchase sexual mastery poisoned sexual relations in many ways. Blameless wives became infected with venereal diseases, thereby deforming the next generation with birth defects, dysgenically weakening "the race." The sexual asymmetry of the prostitution contract announced that sex was something disadvantageous that men did to women on demand. Even if not all women could be "bought," a sizable proportion had their price, a profoundly bleak prognosis for parallel forms of heterosexuality. There was no reciprocal equivalent to these androcentric dynamics.

Prostitution affected all women negatively; it epitomized, then, the evils of women's situation.[6] As one of the three great evils "most strictly due to our androcentric culture—war, intemperance, and prostitution," she noted that prostitution, with "its train of diseases," had the grave title of the "the Social Evil." References to it haunted her earliest lectures, as well as both *Women and* Economics (1898) and *The Man-Made World* (1911), her two most significant Progressive Era texts. Prostitution and venereal diseases inflected her novel *The Crux* (1911), published at the height of the Progressive Era's white slavery outcry, and pervaded numerous other Gilman fiction works. More specifically, as Janet Beer observes, the story "of sexually transmitted disease is one of the most powerful reiterations in Gilman's body of fiction." Meanwhile, these issues were central to many nonfiction publications, including one of her last, "Parasitism and Civilized Vice" (1931). To end prostitution, male demand had to cease, a precondition for a world with a "natural" mutually initiated erotic life.[7]

Androcentrism's "Social Evil"

> The personal profit of women bears but too close a relation to their power to win and hold the other sex. ... When we confront this fact boldly and plainly in the open market of vice, we are sick with horror. When we see the same economic relation made permanent, established by law, sanctified by religion, covered with flowers and incense ... we think it innocent, lovely and right. The transient trade we think evil. The bargain for life we think good. But the biological effect is the same. In both cases the female gets her food from the male by virtue of her sex relationship to him.
>
> *Charlotte Perkins Gilman,* Women and Economics *(1898)*

Gilman confronted arguments about the marriage-prostitution relationship in the first days of marriage in May 1884, jesting that her husband might pay her for her services. Stetson's intense anger in reply signaled a sore spot. As his premarital and marital diaries revealed, he had an occupational obsession with and considerable personal knowledge of prostitutes. His self-pitying narrative of Gilman's initial reluctance to marry him, despite her admiration of his "genius," then their sexual estrangement during her postnatal emotional breakdown and depression included a hydraulic account of male sexual needs, wifely conjugal duties, and justifications of the resort to prostitutes. Later, in an article on male erotic "excess," a sex characteristic to used to assert the inevitability of prostitution, Gilman disdained the very argument Stetson had put to her, namely, that men of genius had extreme libidinous development generating their particular needs which had to be understood. She disputed "the hasty deduction that such development was an essential concomitant of other power."[8]

In the articles and lectures with which Gilman supported herself, after separating from Stetson in 1888, prostitution loomed large. Her 1890 lecture "Causes and Cures" highlighted prostitution, in which she argued that concealment, keeping women protected, innocent, and ignorant of the possibility of venereal diseases, endangered everyone. Meanwhile, selective prosecution of prostitutes, but not their clients, was useless. The view that prostitution was inevitable, warranting official fatalism and resignation, was, for Gilman, "simply wrong" and "utterly mistaken," for "there is no physician who can deny the immeasurable extent of disease and death which have been brought upon us from this evil alone. There is no lawyer who can deny the immeasurable extent of crime and death which have been brought upon us from this evil alone. There is no minister who can deny the immeasurable extent of pain and death which have been brought upon us by this evil alone.... The evil exists—the evil is great. In one way or another we all suffer from it." Given the importance of prostitutes in the production of her estranged husband's art, the heat of her emphasis here is striking. In what ways had she suffered from it? Whatever speculations are possible, she was clear in affirming one claim usually judged to be utopian or naive by the so-called worldly: authorities could end prostitution, but only through changed conceptions of sexuality, creating conditions for ending prostitution, a project justified by the potentially great collective human gain.[9]

Her focus on venereal diseases steadily enlarged in her work on prostitution, noted in the press in early 1890s accounts of her lectures: "One of the leading causes ... to which the existence of the social evil is due is the ghastly ignorance in which men and women rear their children. Another cause was the preposterous dependence of women upon men for their support. A cure would be the equalization of the sexes and a purification of the environments of men and women.... Mrs. Charlotte Perkins Stetson is one of the advanced guard."[10]

By the time she published *Women and Economics* in 1898, she was engaged to Houghton Gilman, intending to pursue her dream of a married life combined with a career that could keep her economically independent.

Though she held to the longstanding feminist analogy between the two sexual contracts, her many references to prostitution condemned it, relative to monogamous love, the latter portrayed as the most highly evolved sexual relation.

For Gilman's reform Darwinist feminism, analysis of prostitution was critical to efforts to enhance women's economic, political, and cultural options. If evolutionary thought was to emancipate women, then would-be reformers needed to identify the odious features of women's situation as perversions of "nature," impeding the biological basis for human progress. Rather than "natural," Gilman contended that prostitution, and the economic dependence of women on men generally, monstrously distorted evolution and, hence, threatened ongoing progress:

> Some hidden cause has operated continuously against the true course of natural evolution, to pervert the natural trend toward a higher and more advantageous sex-relation; and to maintain lower forms, and erratic phases, of a most disadvantageous character. . . . That peculiar sub-relation which has dragged along with us all the time that monogamous marriage has been growing to be the accepted form of sex union—prostitution—we have accepted, and called a "social necessity." We also call it "the social evil." We have tacitly admitted that this relation in the human race must be more or less uncomfortable and wrong, that it is part of our nature to have it so.

Gilman gave a Lamarckian account of the prevalence of prostitution, holding that women's dependence in androcentric cultures heightened sex distinctions. Men called women "the sex," a chillingly accurate designation of female humanity's prescriptive raison d'être. By excluding women from waged occupations, men had reduced economic competition, compelling women to bargain only in one "trade," wifehood. As with workers in all oversupplied trades, wives faced the poor conditions and dispensability. Those women who failed to please men did not reproduce themselves, while those with maximum sex distinction, the hyperfeminine, or "overfeminized," were most prevalent, assured of perpetuation through mating. Hence, the physically smallest, frailest, and least vigorous of women became overrepresented in "the stock" of the human race. Their sons, the fathers of the next generation, inherited their characteristics, weakening the human species. This "breeding out" more vigorous strains of womanhood reduced female genetic diversity.[11]

Consequently, males stepped up their demand for prostitution due to artificially inflated erotic stimulus, through "excessive" sex differences. Not confined to their sexually "overused" wives, men's practices led to women's and girls' seduction, sexual assault, unmarried motherhood, and recruitment to prostitution. A culture enjoining single women to maximize excessive sex distinction, as their source of livelihood, made these hazards inevitable. Meanwhile, the double standard of sexual morality ensured that at least some women would always be available for prostitution, opening for all men, in the words of political theorist, Carole Pateman, the option of purchasing sexual mastery, without requiring reciprocal desire. Gilman noted:

> Where ... man inherits the excess in sex-energy and is never blamed for exercising it, and where he develops also the age-old habit of taking what he wants from women ... what should naturally follow? ... We have produced a certain percentage of females with inordinate sex-tendencies and inordinate greed for material gain. We have produced a certain percentage of males with inordinate sex-tendencies and a cheerful willingness to pay for their gratification. And as the percentage of such men is greater than the percentage of such women, we have worked out the most evil methods of supplying the demand.[12]

Humans reversed nature, then, with direct, literal eugenic consequences, engendering in turn an ever-increasing demand for prostitution. A connection between the economic dependency of the wife and the prostitute could be drawn in a variety of ways. Gilman claimed that in rural and agricultural contexts, a wife was a productive work partner in the enterprise. Therefore, men and women would marry young and exercise a sex attraction that was "natural" and "normal." In the industrialized cities by contrast—and she clearly referred to the Northeast and Mid-Atlantic—a wife was a consumer and nothing more. She lived on her husband. This led men to delay marriage until they could provide fully for their own consumer.[13]

Prostitution was a touchstone for Gilman's Progressive reformer peers not because of its constitutive place in androcentric culture but because it threatened the health of both population and the body politic. Despite frequent differences from them in analysis and motivation, Gilman often praised reformers' new legislative and policy initiatives affecting prostitution. She also evaluated publications depicting prostitution and venereal disease issues. Especially critical of works endorsing the double standard of morality, she condemned popular fiction, for instance, Josephine Daskam Bacon's *The Mortgage* (1913), as "so evil in its influence that one's pleasure in the well-conducted dialogue is lost in horror at its meaning." Bacon perpetuated the double standard: while a man was entitled to bring a debauched sexual history into marriage, any such lapse made women unfit to wed: "Now, nature may be praised or blamed for many things, but certainly not for this local, fairly recent, sociologically speaking, and quite obviously man-made doctrine, that women must be chaste and men need not. Nature shows no such distinction in any species. She does develop chastity, in the sense of faithfulness to one mate, in many of the monogamous creatures, but this chastity is for both."[14]

By contrast, Gilman applauded scientific studies of venereal diseases in relation to both prostitution and marriage. Praising Lavinia L. Dock's *Hygiene and Morality* (1910), Gilman liberally quoted Dock's estimates of venereal diseases rates, which corresponded with other authorities estimates in this period three decades before penicillin drastically cut infection rates. On syphilis: "She quotes from five to eighteen per cent of the population, varying in the different countries. Taking down the most modest estimate for ours and allowing for our population at 80,000,000—this would give us an army of 4,000,000 syphilitics at large among us—unknown to the public." Meanwhile, for gonorrhea, "a cause of sterility, blindness of babies, and all manner of surgical operations" and for "diseases peculiar to women, so common among innocent wives," Dock put infection rates at 75 percent for European men and 60 percent for American men.[15]

In a similarly adulatory review of a reissued edition of Dr. Prince Morrow's authoritative *Social Diseases and Marriage* (1904), Gilman wrote:

> We have allowed to . . . spread wide in the world, the most terrible of contagious diseases, and have carefully suppressed all knowledge of it! Fancy treating an epidemic of cholera in this way? Considering it improper to mention, to know the name of, treating the complaints of the cholera patient as a "sacred confidence," and falsifying the reports of death from cholera that the public be prevented from knowing their numbers. Suppose also cholera to be hereditary! This has been, up to the present time, the attitude of the world towards the most universal and most dangerous of diseases. . . . Modern bacteriology has shown the danger of the most common of venereal infections, hitherto ignored by its innumerable victims; and the peculiar horror by which clean, healthy brides, and the innocent children unborn, are often poisoned by the husband and father, has at last forced its way into our consciousness.[16]

Morrow observed that gonorrhea, so common in men, was superficial, localized, and quickly exited the male body. For women, by contrast, it was a seriously invasive, though hidden disease, "primarily localized within the deep parts . . . the germs being deposited in the uterine neck at the moment of ejaculation," with dire gynecological and obstetric consequences. New brides acquired diseases that might blight their babies or prevent conception from husbands unaware that premarital infections were still active; "in many cases it is the unfaithful husband and father who receives the poison from a prostitute in an extraconjugal adventure, carries it home and distributes it to his family." Matching Dock's estimates, Morrow contended that gonorrhea was "the most widespread and universal of all diseases in the adult male population, embracing 75 per cent or more," compared with a syphilis rate of between "5 to 18 per cent." He grimly accounted women's vulnerability to gonococcic infection, "destroying her conceptional capacity" and resulting in the need for surgical operations, producing "castrated women." Speaking of his practice at the New York Hospital, "fully 70 per cent of all women who come there for treatment were respectable married women who had been infected by their husbands." While in some cases, divorce or separation resulted, most wives were fatalistic about "the universality of masculine unchastity," seeing their fate as the "common lot of women."[17]

Under these circumstances, Morrow denounced state failure to impose any restrictions on men's liberty to poison their families venereally, underscored by the professional medical insistence on secrecy for the "spreader of disease." The American medical profession therefore colluded in this free rein permitted infected husbands. Doctors also prominently endorsed either European-style segregated and regulated prostitution or, else, more informal red-light districts in most cities. The Bridgeport Vice Commission summarized the typical regulationist position and then proceeded to criticize it: "Vice is one of the weaknesses of men; it cannot be extirpated; if repressed unduly at one point it will break out more violently and bafflingly elsewhere; a segregated district is really a protection to the morality of the womanhood of the city, for without it rape would be common and clandestine immorality would increase; when a segregated district is defined the women are brought within bounds, they are under police control and the danger of venereal disease, because of frequent medical inspection, is lessened or eliminated."[18]

Perhaps doctors had material interests at stake. They avoided giving offense "to a large class, a terribly large class of patients—a class which with its collateral crop of diseases in wives and children constitutes one of the mainstays of the profession." In other words, doctors risked financial loss if they disclosed their male patients' diseases.[19]

Gilman endorsed "the new widespread movement" for the abolition of segregation and regulation. Here she judged Dock to be convincing in the evidence of "not only the immense extent of this evil, but the fact that the large majority of its victims are unwilling ones." To this end, she accepted Morrow's invitation to address his 1910 conference on sociological aspects of venereal diseases, urging the need for compulsory premarital examination of men, rather than the obsessive focus on examining prostitutes. New Progressive Era injunctions against landlords of properties used for prostitution, notably in California—the advance guard of the "red-light abatement" strategies of desegregationists and abolitionists—also received Gilman's enthusiastic approval because they "attacked commercialized vice in a most effective way. It provided for a quick injunction against the owner of a house used for prostitution, a quick trial, and a quick abatement of the nuisance." The target here was not the prostitute, nor even the house manager, but the owner of the house, with stiff and effective penalties. She also noted Californian women's success in securing this legislation, confirming a similar link made by Dock: woman suffrage would be the key to abolition of prostitution. Prominent suffragist and feminist vice reformer Harriet Burton Laidlaw, too, stressed active suffragists' grasp of this heinous "political corruption and cupidity" making them "true and steady as the north star."[20]

Such reform zeal led to Wisconsin's pioneering 1914 provision for compulsory premarital physical examination, alerting young women "to the all-too-frequent dangers of matrimony. . . . If the suitor shuns the examination, the lady may reconsider her choice." The measure provided some disincentive to young men's "biological sins without discovery, and without condemnation." Wives afflicted with recurring venereal diseases "will no longer suffer in ignorance" and resent their suffering.[21]

Gilman's friend, socialist writer Upton Sinclair, author of the most celebrated proletarian novel of the era, *The Jungle* (1906), explored the problem in his 1915 novel, *Sylvia's Marriage*. Unapologetically didactic, the novel addressed "the terrible results of gonorrhea, as well as the danger of ignorance and the conspiracy of silence by which offenders are protected." Gilman took his text to be "a sincere and vigorous effort to expose a very real evil." Sylvia Castleman a sheltered Southern beauty had married, unwittingly, the wealthy Eastern womanizer, Douglas Van Tuiver. His mistress, a prostitute Claire LePage, had contracted gonorrhea from him. The birth of a blind baby girl began Sylvia's painful discovery that, as a friend explained, "the doctor told him to marry. That was the only way he'd ever get cured." This referred to the dangerous folklore that gonorrhea could be cured by marriage to a "clean" virgin. Other characters in the novel discussed the widespread incidence of gonorrhea, especially on college campuses, whose young men were oblivious as to its serious consequences. In a dispute with an older woman, shocked at Sylvia's campaign to inform young women of the dangers of venereal diseases, the narrator declared:

> I heard a college professor state publicly that in his opinion eighty-five per cent of the men students at his university were infected with some venereal disease. And that is the pick of our young manhood—the sons of our aristocracy. . . . They call the disease a "dose"; and a man's not supposed to be worthy of the respect of his fellows until he's had his "dose"—the sensible thing is to get several, till he can't get it any more. They think it's no worse than a bad cold; that's the idea they get from the "clap-doctors," and the women of the street who educate our sons in sex matters. . . . It's going on in every fraternity house, every "prep school" dormitory in America. And the parents refuse to know.[22]

Sinclair's novel fitted the Progressive Era exposé genre in fiction, attempting to warn young women and their parents of the dangers of men's immorality, venereal diseases, and procurement into white slavery. Eugene Brieux's "Damaged Goods" (1912) was perhaps the most famous example in drama. So closely was Gilman associated with such efforts that she was one of the original sponsors of the dramatization of François Coppee's novel, "The Guilty Man." A year later, she favorably reviewed Northrup Morse's *Peach Bloom* (1913), a play she described as dedicated to "the unnumbered thousands of girls who have suffered through 'Ignorance'" and exposing skillfully the "irremediable disaster to which young girls are exposed, and the idiotic policy by which we keep them in ignorance." She added that the reader was "not left curdled with horror, as in 'My Little Sister,' yet we have seen here the very jaws of the wolf." Here she referred to expatriate actor and militant suffragette, Elizabeth Robins's 1913 novel. It concerns two genteel but downwardly socially mobile daughters, lured by deception from the countryside to London by their rapacious dressmaker. The latter works as an agent for a Paris-based white slaver. The story ends in madness, premature death, and misery. Prostitution is not merely "a vice of men, but a business of men; a great, well-organized international trade; and further, that it is not only a matter of immorality, but one of the largest elements in our burden of disease."[23]

Gilman hailed the findings of Mrs. Alice Wells, a Los Angeles "plain clothes man"—a female vice investigator. An opponent of segregated prostitution, Wells quipped dryly that Los Angeles was as clean as any city could be "where women are prosecuted and men set free." Considering this, Gil-

FIGURE 35. Upton Sinclair, 1906 (Courtesy Lilly Library, Indiana University, Bloomington, Indiana)

man wondered at so many men's imperviousness to the fact that prostitution served them, dispensing shame, pain, disease, and sometimes death to women, and as such, "most women do not like it," recruited only by poverty and retained in the trade by "physical and social coercion." Demand still exceeded supply, and therefore women "are enticed away and ensnared into it and held as slaves." Without other sources of livelihood, "when they seek employment in this, their only means of support, they are arrested, tried, judged, and punished by men!"[24]

Here she alluded to an insidious aspect of prostitution: forced sexual service in brothels through kidnapping and violence. She insisted on the reality of coerced, commercial prostitution, designated by the term "white slavery." Other anti–white slavery reformers, like fellow suffragist Harriet Burton Laidlaw, protested the relentless campaign of vice interests, "The Vice Trust," to discredit as exaggerations all efforts to expose the traffic in women and girls. They insisted on the qualifiers "so-called" or "alleged" before the words, "white slavery," quibbling over exact estimates of the inestimable, in order to minimize "the misery, horror, and danger," and calling the reformer a "crude sentimentalist, a rank outsider." So appalling were many prostitutes' lives, that there were few willing women. Thus procurers and

FIGURE 36. Harriet
Laidlaw (Catt: 1.5.2a,
Carrie Chapman
Catt Collection,
Bryn Mawr College
Library)

panderers sought 50,000 girls annually to supply the American market, an
enterprise involving coercion, "shame, disease, and painful death; hence the
'White-Slave Traffic.'" Gilman particularly approved of Dock's contention
that woman suffrage would permit women to "reduce this evil," judging
from the record of states with adult suffrage.[25]

THERE IS NO question that Gilman understood the "social evil" as one
of the cornerstones of androcentric culture and, thus, along with suffrage,
a central issue in feminist reform.[26] She did not flinch before ridicule for
belonging, along with reformers like Addams, Laidlaw, or Kate Bushnell,
to a so-called sobbing sisterhood of cranks, in stressing the coercion, fraud,
or desperation that led girls and young women into the trade. Gilman re-
buffed the charge that abolitionism here denied the rational choices and
cool agency of savvy urban working-class women and snobbishly refused
working-class women the right to choose their "career path." That was
merely androcentric cant.

Deconstructing Demand

> We are the only race where the female depends on the male for a livelihood.
> We are the only race that practices prostitution. From the first harmless-
> looking but abnormal general relation, follows the well-recognized evil of
> the second, so long called "a social necessity," and from it in deadly sequence,
> comes the "wages of sin"; death not only of the guilty, but of the innocent.
> It is no light part of our criticism of the Androcentric Culture that a society
> based on masculine desires alone, has willingly sacrificed such an army of
> women; and has repaid the sacrifice by the heaviest punishments.
>
> *Charlotte Perkins Gilman,* The Man-Made World *(1911)*

Gilman saw the use of prostitutes as an integral feature of androcentric male
sexuality. That this demand was protected by law served the interests of
men with dire implications for all women—implications obscured, however, by widely accepted "worldly" and "realistic" portrayals of modern urban men.[27] She noted the regional skewing of sex ratios and marriage markets. With the prevailing hydraulic understanding of male sexuality, men
delaying marriage to an "unnatural" age led also to an artificially heightened
demand for prostitution. Men came to cities for better opportunities, but
their income would not at first permit marriage and family. Yet as their
income rose, so did their standard of comfort; as a consequence, young successful urban men postponed marriage into "the indefinite future" or abandoned "expectation of it altogether." Seeking only their own pleasure, men
found self-justification for indulging "the[ir] strongest native impulse" in
vice through hedonist philosophy.[28]

Her insistent focus on male demand for prostitution might seem at odds
with her Progressive reformer peers. They typically targeted suppliers—
procurers, panderers, white slavers, and landlords—rather than the men
providing the demand for "vice." Nonetheless some reformers did focus on
the client. Gilman was neither alone nor extreme in this concern; but her
reform Darwinist feminism transcended the analytic framework of peer
Progressives, as discussed below. An examination of varying approaches to
the client and demand by secular, religious, public health, and legislator
reformers—many of whom Gilman praised in the *Forerunner*—helps to
specify more exactly the distinctiveness of Gilman's feminist critiques and
proposals.

If some of her reformer peers analyzed demand, they cast it as the outcome of unsound structural, demographic, environmental, moral, or policy
factors, which they often claimed "artificially" stimulated demand. As such,

many reformers saw demand as open to reduction, if not eradication, by legal amendments and changed enforcement patterns. Indeed, some of them depicted male demand as a mere epiphenomenon, a provisional consequence of conditions amenable to Progressive reform, men simply the victims of undue influence. Alternatively, others portrayed men's demand as inhering in existing social relations of the sexes but alterable by will, decision, calculation, and other cultural disincentives.

Although Gilman's reform Darwinist feminist theory framework ascribed different explanations of men's demand for prostitution, this did not prevent her from being a powerful contributor to abolitionist critiques of state-regulated and segregated "vice," advocacy work comparable with her public intellectual campaigning against antisuffragism. Once again, however, she sketched a vision of alternatives to prevailing patterns of prostitution and sexual relations through novels and short stories, repaying some scrutiny, especially those she penned at the height of the various state enquiries into prostitution initiated nationwide, just before and during the first world war: *The Crux* (1911), "His Mother" (1914), "The Vintage" and "Cleaning up Elita" (1916).

GILMAN ADMIRED reformers who stressed the client, whether in medical, legal, or moral terms. Yet only some of her peer reformers directly addressed the nature and mutability of male sexual practices in their analysis of demand. Instead, many held that demand was entirely or largely the outcome of artificial stimulus by vice interests, who also victimized not only farm girls or peasant immigrant girls new to the city but also boys lured into seducing and "debauching" girls in order to hand them over to white slavers. So, while Jane Addams admitted men's responsibility for the trade in her Progressive classic, *A New Conscience and an Ancient Evil* (1912), she claimed that "twenty thousand of the men daily responsible for this evil in Chicago live outside of the city" and were "moral at home." In other words, it was the conditions these men encountered in the city that stimulated their demand, particularly womanless men, such as soldiers and immigrants. In Addams's stress on the analogy between chattel slavery and prostitution, however, she prioritized police corruption and political graft as targets for Progressive reform. Though noting that "the trade constantly demands very young girls," she declined analysis of male desire and demand, effectively naturalizing clienthood as part of male sexuality.[29]

Anti–white slavery reformer Kate Bushnell also contended that an element of this "artificial stimulus" of male demand was the segregation and medical regulation of prostitutes. A false sense of security resulted that incited men to vice and, thus, increased venereal disease rates. Also, the state forced all citizens to pay for this "security" by obliging prostitutes to submit to a gynecological examination, their genitals "manipulated by the doctor's hand until a discharge is secured for microscopical examination" for germs that might pose risk to men. Similarly, despite the prostitute's health certificate, "worthless except as false lighthouses to lure men onto the rocks," reformer J. W. Walton told the 1895 National Purity Congress in New York of the spiritual and psychical degradation and fear afflicting the "loose-living voluptuary." He urged men to embrace virtue as inherently, powerfully manly, drawing on its Latin root, "'vir'—a man."[30]

Religious leaders also addressed men's demand and their role as clients, through pleas to young men for alternative models of manliness, grounded in chivalry, restraint, self-mastery, and loyalty to their future or actual wife and children. Ernest Bell, an anti–white slavery crusader, addressed the client in a muscular and blunt fashion. Patrons needed to see that the white slave trade operated both "at their instance and at their expense," since the cost of the agents and procurers were passed on to the clients. Indeed, every dollar "that any man spends there makes him a stockholder in the white slave market and a partner in the traffic in girls." Speaking of Judgment Day, when the hired men, procurers, and "divekeepers" receive their final condemnation, he warned that the men "who support the hideous business [and] are the ultimate white slave traders" will be arraigned and punished beside their partners in crime for eternity.[31]

Further, in a novel approach to the client, the visiting Australian temperance suffragist Jessie Ackerman held that one-sidedness weakened most rescue work on prostitution:

> Why not begin missions to fallen men? Why not enter the houses of shame and try to rescue the men first? Why not build rescue homes for men? Why not form rescue bands and station them at well-known houses of ill repute in large cities to begin a mighty effort in the interest of outcast men? What is the Church doing for outcast men? Did Christ come only to save woman? Have Christians no duty toward debauched and degraded men? Save the fallen men and there would be no such thing in all the land as an impure woman.[32]

Whether principally religious or secular, Gilman's peer reformers argued that segregated vice areas, far from limiting prostitution, provided a particularly intense stimulus to client demand. Hence, they urged as the solution the punitive repression of stimulants, red-light districts, and white slave traders with their liquor sodden dives. Vice reformer Theodore A.

Bingham, for instance, declared that "the immorality of women and the brutishness of man has to be persuaded, coaxed and constantly stimulated, in order to keep the social evil in its present state of prosperity." Similarly, the nationally known vice commissioner, Clifford G. Roe, saw white slavery as the outgrowth of an artificially stimulated demand. He asked, "why not wage a relentless war against those who create the demand as well as those who make up the supply?" Seeking to target procurers, landlords, and pimps, he also urged that clients be punished not only by law but also by social ostracism. This might end forever the tendency of ambitious parents to arrange the marriages of their blameless daughters to upwardly mobile men "whose relations with the social evil were notorious." The sacrifice of girls "upon the altars of lust" must end.[33] And reformer Robert K. Massie asserted that commercialized vice sought to "overstimulate the sex instinct for gain ... powerfully and abnormally ... by the arts and devices" of prostitution proprietors. Here he included the slot-piano "with its cheap and trashy music, the indecent dance of the brothel, the sale of liquor, the steady pressure of the pimps and madams—all these things play their part to stimulate the demand." Unlike Gilman, Massie held that essentially "the demand is created by the sex instinct which is universal and ineradicable," a gloomy prognosis for any lasting reform, and like others, he naturalized demand as inherently grounded in male sexuality.[34]

Jane Addams, too, addressed demand as the outcome of artificial stimulus: hapless young men from monotonous dreary lives lured to vice "through alcohol and all vicious devices designed to stimulate the senses." Moreover, toleration of male demand engendered a slick but dangerous cynicism: "Thousands of decent men have developed a peculiar distrust of human nature, a cynicism which assumes that a certain proportion of men in every community will so inevitably violate the laws of chastity as to make the prostitute a social necessity and the free masonry among men in regard to her does much to lower the moral tone of the whole community."[35]

More challengingly, from a reform medical framework, Prince Morrow, mentioned above, dismissed all the usual causes of prostitution, stating that the "most essential cause, the *causa causans,* of prostitution is masculine unchastity." Lavinia Dock put the matter even more forcefully: "The doctrine of 'physical necessity' has been invented for men by themselves. And this has even been fortified by the positive teachings of prominent medical men.... It is evident that if unregulated sexual practice were really necessary for men, there could be no element of shame or wrong in it, and there could therefore, obviously be none for the woman, for no act that is physically necessary is wrong, no matter how primal it may be." For Morrow and

Dock, if prevailing conditions heightened male demand, it was not necessarily ineradicable. Indeed, medical reformers criticized their professional brethren who promulgated the fallacious claim that men should demand prostitutes for the good of their health, especially bachelors or men temporarily separated from their wives. O. Edward Janney argued that the inevitable diseases following exercise of this demand regularly drove men to suicide. The cause of these suicides was the realization on the part of infected men that they could not marry and father children. Otherwise, diseased men became mentally degraded, morally coarsened, and despairing.[36]

On a different trajectory, some secular Progressive reformers saw in the tolerance afforded to the client an unacceptable legal sexual double standard, threatening the just rule of law and democracy itself. The authors of the Honolulu Social Survey's *Report of the Committee on the Social Evil* (1914) stated forcefully that the policy of vice segregation and medical regulation known as "reglementation" impaired the liberty of only one of the two parties to commercialized copulation, the woman. They cited approvingly a Colorado Legislative debate on segregation: "A woman member of the House of Representatives opposed it on the ground that 'fallen men should be segregated the same as fallen women.' The introducer of the bill declared his willingness to insert such a section, 'But,' objected the woman, 'there would be no men left.' The House burst into laughter which lasted ten minutes. Just as the roll call on the measure was about to begin, the woman rose and said, 'Let him among you who is without sin cast the first vote.' Not one vote was recorded in favor of the bill."[37]

Here the Hawaiian commissioners identified the client as the political interest served by reglementation, the policy's object "to produce a cleaner feminine article for man's lustful pleasure," yet thereby unspeakably degrading the women affected. Alternatively, commissioners bluntly urged that premises be raided and "both the men and women captured dealt with according to law." Moreover, such men should be examined for venereal disease and treated "with enforced segregation if necessary. . . . In the case of a married man, notification of disease when present should be given to the wife with instructions for preserving the health of the family pending cure." Others concurred on the value of subjecting clients to inspection. Meanwhile, in 1912, Columbia University professor Edwin R. A. Seligman attacked the sexual double standard that protected clients in New York City policy. He directed his ire at official attempts to enact discriminatory laws and procedures under the mantle of public health. Proposed laws would permit forcible examination and detention for treatment of otherwise unconvicted women, but not men, found with venereal diseases, making them nothing more than efforts to secure "primarily, the health of the patrons, the health of the male sex." Similarly, members of the New York Reform Club proposed that prison terms for customers would reduce demand and counter the erroneous view that "the indulgence in vice is a necessity for men." If subjecting clients "to the public disgrace they deserve, many who perhaps are more foolish than depraved would fear to run the risk of entering brothels, and would thus be saved from both temptation and sin."[38]

THUS, GILMAN inhabited a crowded field of Progressive Era reformers focused on the client or demand side of prostitution. Many abolitionists of her acquaintance believed, as she did, that the elimination of prostitution was within their grasp, provided the necessary tools of political and economic change. Gilman and other abolitionists insistently highlighted the chaos generated by condoned male demand for prostitution and its official accommodation, even facilitation.

Just as Gilman had skewered the arguments of the Antis in the woman suffrage struggles of the Progressive Era, so with prostitution, she tackled forcefully the arguments of the regulationists. Among all those debating prostitution laws and policies, regulationists were the least inclined to scrutinize male demand, even in the limited terms of Gilman's peer abolitionists, instanced above. Instead, regulationists advocated universal segregation and regular compulsory medical examination only of prostitutes, usually portraying male sexual instincts as biological, inherent, and irrepressible, likely to cause social havoc if thwarted. Sometimes such advocates portrayed prostitution as a safety valve for womanless men, bachelors, and widowers, who might otherwise rape women and molest children.

Determined to challenge this widespread view of male sexuality underpinning the "oldest profession" portrayals of prostitution, Gilman penned a satirical short story, "Cleaning up Elita" (1916). She described a self-righteous town undertaking a revivalist campaign against vice. Through the voice of an Eastern sociologist guest speaker, Gilman mocked the superficiality and double moral standard of reformers, who would target the most visible forms of prostitution—that is, brothel inhabitants and streetwalkers—while leaving clients undisturbed. She had the guest speaker confront such hypocritical exercises with uncomfortable statistics. Noting that their town had three hundred prostitutes and fifteen thousand men, ten thousand of whom were husbands, the speaker pointed out that it "takes two to make a trade." The sociologist reported that each prostitute needed thirty men to make a livelihood, or a total clientele of nine thousand men. Even assuming that all of the five thousand single men "practiced evil courses," that made the other four thousand clients husbands. And these were conservative estimates: for if each of her patrons paid the prostitute only a dollar a month, the total payment for brief encounters might barely cover the high rents that "reputable gentlemen" charged prostitutes, not to mention the related expenses associated with the profession. So once the citizens had

"saved, cared for, and punished your three hundred women, what are you going to do with your nine thousand men?" There was complete silence. . . . "How are you going to check the constant demand of all these citizens for something the law forbids, for an indulgence which can only be met by the sacrifice of these miserable lives? Can you not see that if you are to 'clean up Elita' you must clean up your *men*? You women, wives, mothers, girls, and all of you, citizens—must bear and rear and educate a different kind of man."[39]

Interestingly, Ben L. Reitman (anarchist Emma Goldman's lover) later confirmed the data informing Gilman's argument. Reitman was a libertarian who saw a biological grounding of male demand. He sought sound public policy accepting natural male demand, against fairy tales like the so-called white slave trade, views Gilman would obviously reject. Yet in the process, he confirmed Gilman's estimate of husbands as a core client group.

In his 1931 account of thirty years as a medical practitioner for the underworld, a frequently imprisoned birth control advocate, venereologist and Cook County corrections officer, he reported some fascinating statistics on Chicago clients. Put bluntly, "men buy between fifty and one hundred million dollars worth of extramarital sex contacts a year," while the average Chicago male adult lived "an extra-legal sex life." The city was the venue for extralegal contacts numbering an average of 500,000 weekly, 2 million monthly, and 25 million annually. Yet men paying for sex overwhelmingly did so once a week. He reported that women in houses, the most numerous class of prostitutes in the business, each had 50–75 contacts per week, compared with thirty contacts each week for streetwalkers. His marital status breakdown for the clients in 500,000 weekly contacts was: 200,000 single men, 20,000 widowers, 3,500 divorcees, and 76,500 transients, leaving local husbands to account for the remaining 200,000.

Reitman calculated husbands at 40 percent, while Gilman figured them as 45 percent of prostitutes' clients. Such close estimates, despite their very different sexual politics regarding tolerated client demand, were remarkable. This widespread sexual practice of husbands, then, informed the wider critical case she made against the negative impact of clienthood on women, motherhood, and evolution in a world before penicillin.[40]

FIGURE 37. Dr. Ben L. Reitman, 1931 (Collection Senya Fléchine, International Archive of Social History, Amsterdam)

There would be no prostitution in a human world, a world to be brought into reality through Gilman's own feminist theories and principles. Her definition of feminism placed a central focus on responsible motherhood, postulating a "womanhood free, strong, clean and conscious of its power and duty. This means selective motherhood, the careful choosing of fit men for husbands. . . . This means a higher standard of chastity, both in marriage and out, for men as well as women. It means recognition of the responsibility of socially organized mothers for the welfare of children." Balancing expressions of desire within thoughtfully chosen marriages would eradicate prostitution by default.[41]

This evil institution not only potentially (if not actually) harmed all women but also harmed children, born and unborn, through inherited syphilis and gonorrhea. Gilman's short story, "The Vintage" (1916), explored the horrifying consequences of a man, Rodger Moore, marrying his beloved Leslie. His doctor warned that he remained syphilitic from a past infection, contracted in a "brief black incident in his past . . . long since buried." One frail withered son, followed by stillborns and miscarriages, was the outcome of their union. Leslie never knew the reason: "He had to watch it. He had to comfort her as he could . . . as her health weakened, her beauty fled from her, and the unmistakable ravages of the disease began to show, she did not know what was the matter with her, or with her children."[42]

Male clients and female prostitutes imperiled the vigorous motherhood central to Gilman's reform Darwinist feminist objectives. She exhorted mothers to take responsibility and blame for the perpetuation of prostitution. They should prevent prostitution by raising men with better values. This was the moral of one of her didactic short stories, entitled "His Mother" (1914), concerning Ellen Martini, a New England woman and estranged wife of an Italian, eventually widowed. By doting on her handsome son, Jack, she unintentionally raised a feckless rake. Mother and son became estranged when Jack seduced and abandoned a pregnant schoolgirl. Meanwhile "the girl slipped out of sight altogether, left the town, and people judged by the silence of her family that they knew nothing of her, or knew no good." As some atonement, Ellen devoted her life to rescue work among fallen women, becoming a probation officer specializing in the detection and prosecution of procurers. Then Ellen discovered that a procurer, responsible for the recruitment of several young women department store assistants whom she personally knew, was none other than her son Jack. He was one of those men who "lived on the earnings of fallen women, women whose fall they first bring about, and then carefully prevent their ever rising." One night, she learned that he was about to seduce his latest target. Sure enough, Jack brought the girl, after theater and supper, "drugged and half-conscious," to his lodgings, where Ellen waited:

> He laid the helpless form down on his bed, standing a moment with a sneering smile. Then, turning as he threw off his coat, he met the gray eyes of his mother.
>
> "Just in time, I think, Jack," she said calmly. "This one can be saved anyhow. But I doubt if you can.... If you were a leper, Jack ... I'd have to give you up. You are far more dangerous to society than that. I know your record now, for ten years back.... It's got to stop right here. As for this child— she's my girl now. I'll take care of her ..." His mother, with black stone in her heart above the grave of her young love, spent a long life in trying to do good enough to make up for her own share in his evil. Ellen repented for her poor rearing of Jack by expanding her mother instinct to protect white slavery victims. Jack, supporting himself through the trade, had no interest in repentance.[43]

Gilman's most sustained treatment of prostitution and venereal diseases was her novel *The Crux* (1911). The story is notable for its address of the impact of male demand not only on women but on the male body itself. Nine years ago, Morton Elder, a local boy, kissed Vivian Lane, now a twenty-five-year-old spinster of Bainsville, Rhode Island. Following his expulsion from school for a drunken spree in New York City, he went west. Distracted, Morton "changed occupations oftener than he wrote letters." A friend, Dr. Jane Bellair—one of the several female doctors significantly featuring in Gilman's fiction—persuaded Vivian, Morton's sister Susie, and their single friend, Orella, to return with her to Denver, Colorado, to run a boarding house. With a ratio of three men to one woman, in a gold-rush town, all women who wanted to could marry. Vivian's sixty-year-old grandmother joined them on the grand adventure.[44]

Here Gilman elaborated on the great potential she identified in male-dominated frontiers where wives were in short supply, enabling women to make favorable marriage terms with individual men. This made the American West particularly interesting to her, a frequent setting for her utopian feminist fiction as a place where prostitution could truly end. She incorporated Progressive historian, Frederick Jackson Turner's postulate that the frontier was a place of enthusiasms, innovation, and Progressive social changes, signaled by their early adoption of woman suffrage. It was in such contexts that a beginning could be made on ending prostitution.[45]

The novel's Denver boarding house was a magnet for womanless men. This atmosphere delighted the women, who recalled the humiliation of waiting to be chosen by arrogant New England boys: "Half a dozen boys to twenty girls, and when there was anything to go to—the lordly way they'd pick and choose! And after all our efforts and machinations most of us had to dance with each other. And the quarrels we had!" By contrast, in Denver, "they stand around three deep asking for dances—and *they* have to dance with each other, and *they* do the quarreling"—a scenario to make Lester Frank Ward smile. Other characters in the drama included Dr. Hale, Dr. Bellair's partner in the practice, a man who was bitter toward all women except "fallen ones." Lastly, there was Jeanne the cook, an enigmatic French woman, who was an ex-prostitute and madam with a retarded son, trying to give up "public life," yet "private life won't have her."[46]

One night, Morton Elder arrived from rural Colorado, having tracked Vivian to Denver, with the intent to pursue her hand in marriage. At a party, Vivian observed that he had changed: "He danced well, but more actively than she admired, and during the rest of the [first] evening [after he arrived] devoted himself to the various ladies with an air of long usage." Over the next few weeks, Vivian observed unhappily that he had a "too free manner, . . . coarsened complexion, a certain look about the eyes."[47]

Two of the older women noticed Morton's deteriorated complexion. He was seen crossing the street to Dr. Hale's house. Then Dr. Bellair found the laconic cook Jeanne at her door, urging Bellair to stop the romance— for the reunited couple had just announced their engagement. Jeanne said, "He has lived the bad life." Dr. Bellair replied, "Most young men are open to criticism." Jeanne would not relent: "He has had the sickness." Coralie, Anastasia, and Estelle, three young women in Jeanne's brothel, all became diseased after sexual intercourse with Morton, eight years ago. Jeanne continued, "I have heard of him many times since in such company." Jeanne pleaded: "You must save her. . . . I was young once. I did not know—as she does not. I married—and *that* came to me! It made me a devil for a while. Tell her . . . about my boy!"—Jeanne demanded, meaning his birth defects due to venereal disease.[48]

With her suspicions confirmed, Dr. Bellair confronted Dr. Hale, who refused to tell Vivian about his patient's condition. Thus, Dr. Bellair confronted Vivian herself, complete with the medical facts of gonorrhea and syphilis as she knew them: "They are two of the most terrible diseases known to us; highly contagious, and in the case of syphilis, hereditary. Nearly three-quarters of the men have one or the other, or both." She warned Vivian of the ills from contracting these diseases: stillbirth, miscarriage, birth defects, sterility, and early death.[49]

In a later conversation, Vivian's grandmother assured her that Dr. Bellair was knowledgeable and concerned because the doctor's estranged husband had infected her, rendering her sterile. The desire to help other women and prevent the kind of suffering that she herself endured had motivated Bellair's later entry into medicine. Reeling from the horror of it all, Vivian asked if the statistics were true. "Our girls are mostly clean, and they save the race, I guess . . ." replied her grandmother. "Remember that we've got a whole quarter of the men to rely on. That's a good many, in this country. We're not so bad as Europe—not yet—in this line." Consequently, despite Morton's "indignant" arguments, Vivian broke her engagement to him and, opening the kindergarten she dreamed of, became an acclaimed teacher. Professionally established with numerous gentlemen admirers, she eventually allowed the love developing between herself and the hitherto misogynist Dr. Hale to result in marriage, on the understanding that she would maintain her economic independence by continuing with her school.[50]

IN BOTH HER fiction and nonfiction treatments of prostitution, Gilman squarely faced the demand for prostitution and the effects of men's sexual practices on prostitutes, and all other women. Hating the evolutionary impact of the prostitute, she emphasized strategies to end the trade. She would not allow analysis of prostitution to be displaced onto the dynamics of class, ethnicity, or race. For her, it was always and finally about sex, with male dominance exceeding any distant natural boundaries to the detriment of evolution. Gilman also exhibited the optimism of other feminists of her era in that she saw nothing inherent, or inevitable, about existing sex relations. Therefore, she sought to intervene against prostitution, and the eugenic outcomes of male sex demand and female economic dependency, underlying the "social evil." She believed that prostitution could end within three generations.[51]

Ending Prostitution

This whole field of morbid action will be eliminated from human life by the normal development of women. . . . An intelligent and powerful womanhood will put an end to this indulgence of one sex at the expense of the other and to the injury of both. In this inevitable change will lie what some men will consider a loss. But only those of the present generation. For the sons of the women now entering upon this new era of world life, will be differently reared. With all women full human beings, trained and useful in some form of work, the class of . . . idlers . . . will disappear as utterly as will the prostitute. . . . No woman with real work to do, work she loved and was well fitted for, work honored and well-paid, would take up the Unnatural Trade.

Charlotte Perkins Gilman, The Man-Made World, or, Our Androcentric Culture *(New York, 1911), 247–48.*

Gilman proposed the complete elimination of prostitution. With the development of a human world, superseding androcentrism, all women and men would be partners in productive labor. Both the demand and the supply for prostitution would cease. Women's economic independence anchored Gilman's projection of new generations of men no longer believing that every woman had her price. In short, she refused any inevitability in men's demand for prostitution.[52]

The analytic significance Gilman accorded to prostitution intensified across her writing career, especially in the 1910–16 period of wider international and wartime concern about "the red menace" of venereal diseases. Moreover, some of her key associates during this period were active in attempts to suppress or eradicate vice districts in cities like New York and Chicago, providing her with reports of successful outcomes that made the idea of ending prostitution forever seem within reach. The Rockefeller-funded Bureau of Social Hygiene in New York, for instance, reported the significant effects of their pressure on police to enforce existing laws and end graft between 1912 and 1915. Praising Police Commissioner Woods, a 1915 bureau report cited a decrease in parlor houses (from 142 in 1912 to 23 in 1915), while it had become "exceedingly difficult for men to enter these houses unless they are personally known to the madam or one of the inmates, or bring cards of introduction." Meanwhile, tenement houses, hotels, furnished rooms, and massage parlors conducting vice had numbered 1,172 with 2,294 inmates in 1912, but by 1915 the figures were 482 and 771 inmates plus 140 "on call." This 60 percent reduction in vice resorts and 66 percent reduction in prostitutes, madams, and pimps made complete eradication look possible. As for saloons, whereas the bureau found prostitutes in 308 of the 765 saloons investigated in 1912 (40 percent), only 346 saloons remained in 1915, of which only 84 (24 percent) remained soliciting haunts. The bureau claimed to have eradicated the landlords of pimps and prostitutes, while identified prostitutes had dropped from 14,926 in 1912 to 3,689, only 24 percent of the 1912 workforce.[53]

Even commentators less sanguine about the odds of complete eradication still believed that Progressive reforms could materially reduce both supply and demand for prostitution. Proponents of this view stressed the need to end urban overcrowding, publicly fund wholesome recreation and amusements, improve conditions of waged labor, offer sex education with anti-vice campaigns for high schools and colleges, increase provision of hospital beds for those with venereal diseases, and indeterminately incarcerate "notoriously debauched" minors engaged in prostitution.[54]

It should be noted that Gilman's prostitution-disease focus also drew urgency from a local eruption of xenophobia and anti-Semitism. Annual Eastern European Jewish immigration to Gilman's Manhattan suddenly soared to approach 2 million by 1910. Women and girls formed 43 percent of the Jewish Poles, Lithuanians, Russians, and Hungarians, many arriving without relatives or friends. Moreover, Gilman's heightening interest in population issues, eugenics, sex ratios, marriage markets, and "race progress" propelled her to examine all factors supposedly deteriorating the American "stock." This ensured particular anxiety about birth defects and hereditary disabilities caused by venereal diseases.[55]

Why did Gilman, with her distinctive focus on work and economics, reject the view that prostitution was work like any other, no better, no worse, than other jobs that the sex division of paid labor in all known human cultures assigns to women? Such a position might have left intact her critique of economic dependence of wives on marriage. Given her concern about women's poverty and dependence, why did she take no joy from the probability that, at least during her "currency," the prostitute earned the highest wages available to women at the time? Her reform Darwinist feminism rejected any significant sense of sisterhood or solidarity with prostitutes. Making their livings through the artificial enhancement of sex distinction, sex attraction, and sex indulgence, these traits exiled women from "race development." Prostitution was the most intense, extreme example of this tendency toward excessive sex distinction. Though men were far worse in their demand for excessive sex indulgence, such indulgence did not keep them from race development because it was not their primary occupation. Hence, while they might morally fail, their work in other areas of social usefulness counteracted the significance of their vice. Women, cut off by their economic dependence on men from race development, had only the option of putting their intelligence, energy, and creativity into sex development. Hence, moral sin was judged more harshly and had greater significance for women. Her concerns about prostitution, then, need analysis in the framework of her feminist evolutionary arguments.[56]

Gilman showed a clear understanding of the systemic factors that led to women's recruitment into the trade. Nonetheless, she saw prostitutes, as a group—as an entity in sexual politics—as the enemies of women's advancement. They weakened the bargaining position of all women. They helped sex-indulgent men deteriorate "the race." War was evil because sex-segregated men used prostitutes and, on returning home, infected their sweethearts and wives, damaging generations to come. Prostitutes were the agents of all that was worst in men. They offered the most extreme example of the reversal of nature by which women exhibited sex-attraction plumage. In the frequent and needless changes called "fashion," prostitutes led the way, so as to please men's sex indulgent demand for variety. Their existence, especially in state-regulated forms, had hideous effects. As the Honolulu vice commission put it in 1914, "Where vice is most open, woman's lot is hardest. To maintain a stockade for fallen women where they are kept penned by law as slaves to man's lust constantly presents to men an argument for women's inferiority, lessens their respect for womankind, and tends to degrade the entire sex." In her concern about men's demand—its legal protection, cultural condonation, and consequences, potentially for all women—it is clear that Gilman was by no means alone.[57]

Gilman's proposed a reconfiguration of "vice," placing the focus on the male demand for prostitution. It was a trade, a living, for women, albeit an injurious and obnoxious one. For men, however, it was a recreational pleasure, a form of sexuality, dangerous for women, children, and "the race."

Her fiction was full of visions for a world preventing or eradicating prostitution. In the novel "Mag—Marjorie," Gilman saves the pregnant teenage servant Mag, seduced and abandoned by the doctor vacationing at her aunt's New England boarding house, from the almost inevitable fall into prostitution through the good offices of an older woman—a friend of the family. That woman ships her off to France, and, after the birth, places the baby in temporary foster care with a loving family and puts Mag through extensive Swiss education and work experience. Mag returns as Marjorie, an accomplished medical researcher and physician. She exposes her seducer, reclaims her child, and finds true love with a fellow doctor. In Gilman's futuristic novel *Moving the Mountain,* an ex-prostitute overcomes venereal diseases and becomes the loving partner of a reforming doctor, who previously lived the life of a libertine. Jeanne, too, the ex-brothel madam, is a key voice for saving Vivian Lane from danger in *The Crux.*[58]

Gilman held that practices presently classed as only trivial offenses needed sanctions, including seducing or procuring girls into prostitution, living off the earnings and related extortion from prostitutes, knowingly infecting a wife and "poisoning" an unborn child. Like other reformers in her milieu, she contended that the ballot would be essential for women to secure laws needed to eradicate prostitution. Some of her peers even identified prostitution as a key obstacle to that very enfranchisement. Henry B. Blackwell, Boston suffragist and reformer, contended that prostitution was the direct result of women's exclusion from public affairs. He saw male superiority affirmed daily, with men personally empowered by the trade in flesh. Men's contempt for women was inevitable since the polity declared women's opinion irrelevant to legislation and policy making. Meanwhile, their disenfranchisement produced in women a pervasive self-deprecation. Woman suffrage would cure sexual vice by organizing women as a class for self-protection. Like Gilman, he saw the "outcast woman" as the deadliest foe of the wife and children, taking as a given husbands as the core clients. Men would never move to eradicate prostitution. Only the input of women as voters could do that, ending forever the "useless and cruel raids of the police, who spasmodically arrest and make public, and degrade unfortunate women . . . while they conceal and exempt from arrest and punishment the male associates of these women."[59]

Once again, Gilman's views here matched eminent contemporaries. Still other reformers concurred with the conviction that prostitution could and should be eradicated. As the Honolulu vice commissioners contended, "prostitution never became established among primitive peoples. Indeed chattel slavery and prostitution are close parallels. Neither is a primitive human institution. . . . But chattel slavery has been abolished. There is no reason why prostitution should not follow the same road."[60]

Nor was this perspective only American. English suffragette Christabel Pankhurst held that male investment in sexual vice fuelled opposition to woman suffrage. When women were "politically free, and economically strong," they would not be "purchasable for the base uses of vice. Those who want to have women as slaves obviously do not want women to become voters." Pankhurst's famous cure for the social evil was "Votes for Women and Chastity for Men."[61]

Historians have judged harshly the effects of abolitionist attacks on vice infrastructure and "red-light abatement" laws as at best ineffective, and at worst damaging the poorest and most vulnerable of women involved, a bitterly ironic verdict against feminist foremothers. Not only did feminist reform efforts boomerang, leaving men exempt, but also efforts to abolish state-regulated prostitution had only short-lived success. World War I, with its "Red Plague" (venereal diseases) scare, was the occasion for the savage designation of prostitutes (elided with other sexually active women and girls) as public enemy number one.

Wartime and interwar conditions did not produce the results Gilman and other abolitionists hoped. Indeed, as David Pivar shows, fears of venereal diseases, "the white slave traffic, and degeneracy contributed to a triumph of neo-regulation after World War I." Competing medically dominated "neo-regulationists" undermined abolitionists' gains by prioritizing military efficiency, national security, and expediency. Moreover, feminist professionals inadvertently aided the criminalizing of sexually active women and girls through work with the Girls' Protective League in New York and the Federal Committee for the Protection of Women and Girls. The use of "preventative detention" made women, but not men, bear responsibility, with thousands of women forcibly examined, most incarcerated in federal facilities, measures that jettisoned women's but not men's civil rights.

Despite protest that this amounted to protection of soldiers rather than girls, and despite amounting to, for Gilman, a resurgent masculism in prostitution and venereal diseases policies, feminists continued supporting Progressive Era abolitionism. It was principally directed at the protective structures housing prostitutes and supplying clients. By forcing women into the arms of exploitative underworld pimps, prostitution was not eradicated. Rather, it became less visible and more professionalized.[62]

By the 1920s and 1930s, however, Gilman's focus widened from prostitutes and prostitution to the more generalized matter of modern postsuffrage women's increased "sex indulgence" and "aping" the sexual mores of men and the "race" consequences. She may have shifted gears at least in part due to the achievement of universal suffrage in 1920 and, in part, as a result of pondering the horrors and deep consequences of the Great War. Ironically, this enlarged concern finally diluted the earlier specificity of Gilman's version of the prostitution problem, her discussion was now enmeshed in much more general critique of the "sexolatry" of the modern age. In newly modern sex relations, money was not exchanging hands, at least not directly. Here Gilman stood on the brink of a recast analysis of sexuality. Embraced by many of her peers, this view extolled sexual expression, erotic experimentation, and the lifting of repressive and customary taboos. It claimed, in particular, to set women's eroticism free, thereby sidelining Gilman's lifelong theoretical corpus, her blend of sexual economics, and reform Darwinism, into extinction.[63]

By the time of Gilman's death in 1935, her dream that the prostitute might decline as a major figure in sexual culture might have seemed a reality, at least relative to her nineteenth-century prevalence, familiarity, and rhetorical currency. Yet this "passing of the prostitute" coincided, if anything, with a heightening of Gilman's concerns about "sex and race progress." For that passing melded with increased, not reduced, adherence to men's indulgence of lust on demand, a distortion of nature. Now all women, not just those set apart, were expected to meet these demands and, in the solemn dictates of popularized Freudianism, received the brainwashing message that it was natural, good for them, and met their own real desires, no longer unhealthily repressed. These developments threatened her long-predicted political unification of women as a sex against the menace of prostitution and forced sexual service to men.[64]

PROSTITUTION BEGAN its place in Gilman's work as a subject of sexual economics and masculine distortion of nature in libidinous excess. Like other abolitionists of her period, she had sought to end prostitution as prerequisite for changing men's sexual behavior to more resemble women's. She had not anticipated a recasting of male sexuality as human, a paradigm for women as well. If she began her theoretical career analyzing the prostitution-economics-disease connection, spotlighting men, she ended it confronting the prostitution-sexuality continuum—for women. These discursive developments sidelined the earlier feminist analysis of prostitution, as much in its categories and assumptions as in its substantive content. No one pretended that prostitution had disappeared or that it no longer had significance for feminist analysis. Changed understandings of sexuality, however, eclipsed prostitution's position as the emblematic institution of women's subordination. Other preoccupations moved to the fore in the era of the Great Depression.

Prostitution, as a target for eradication, was one dimension of Gilman's wider critique of androcentric sexuality. With the development of a human world, superseding androcentrism, women and men would be partners in productive labor, ending both supply and demand for prostitution. This central problem, then, deeply embedded her theory and language within Progressive Era debates. Her distinctive brand of abolitionism—a Beecher family tradition—drew an analogy between chattel slavery and sex slavery. If such an analogy would be controversial for many readers today, it is a measure of the urgently problematic contours of then-prevailing male sexuality and these discourses of erotic life naturalizing male demand for prostitution, irrespective of its profoundly negative consequences. For these reasons, Gilman sought her distinctive reconfiguration of vice, as a feminist Progressive.

CHAPTER TEN

A Progressive Era Public Intellectual

It is hard to be progressive, but glorious.

Charlotte Perkins Gilman,
"The Women Who Won't Move Forward" (1914)

GILMAN'S NAME was a household word during the Progressive Era. She supported herself on the lecture circuit and through writing and editing and was constantly called on to comment on events of the period. Even unsolicited, she wrote letters to the editor of newspapers like the *New York Times* on topics as great as that newspaper's misogyny and as small as chewing gum in public. After *Women and Economics* (1898) established her intellectual significance, further publications received close attention, especially *The Home* (1903) and *The Man-Made World* (1911). She commented on not only issues related to women but also other reform matters, popular manners, mores, and beliefs. Gilman was more famous than her mentor Lester Frank Ward or her friend, sociology professor, Edward Alsworth Ross. Her books reached hundreds of thousands, while her ideas, appropriated by many others—from novelist Upton Sinclair to journalists like Bessie Beatty—circulated widely.[1]

Newspapers and magazines gave Gilman extensive coverage as a public intellectual. Often the press in the countries, states, and towns she visited profiled her and gave verbatim reports of her lectures and interchanges with audiences. Gilman was a public intellectual without either an academic salary or any reliable source of private income. Quite literally, the public supported her living, or at least that was her goal. With the public a notoriously fickle employer, the poverty of her later years and the modesty of her bequests to her daughter and grandchildren were not surprising. Despite the difficulties of aging (discussed in chap. 11), however, Gilman battled that public for her living.[2]

To say that Gilman was a Progressive Era public intellectual is to claim that the substance and tone of her work belonged to the Progressive project. Just as her status as a public intellectual remains unexamined, Gilman's status as a Progressive remains unelaborated, for her work and thought find little space in scholarly writing on the Progressive Era. She resided for a time with the emblematic Progressive Jane Addams—the person regularly voted the greatest American during the period—in Addams's Chicago settlement house in 1894 and 1895. But Gilman jettisoned philanthropy to embrace the lonely and precarious path of the lecture circuit, a divorced woman preaching the gospel of "race progress." Overdrawn efforts to conjoin Gilman's and Addams's projects and philosophical stances have not dispatched the need for an elucidation of Gilman's distinct reform Darwinist feminist Progressivism.[3]

Her career as a lecturer, editor, and writer revealed her deep Progressivist commitments. Reform Darwinism, gynaecocentric theory, Fabianism, imperialism, eugenics, nativism, and anti-Semitism were all strands of Progressive Era discourse inflecting her thought. Her feminism both incorporated and challenged these discourses in various ways. Meanwhile, comments on her interventions from editors, journalists, readers, and members of the general public revealed her currency and impact on contemporaries.

On the Lecture Circuit

> Mrs. Stetson is a most brilliant and effective platform speaker. She speaks as she thinks, clearly, concisely, and in a perfectly straightforward and simple manner, but her utterances are always striking and she never fails to rivet the attention of her hearers. Last season she made a tour of the south and aroused more interest than any lecturer upon similar subjects . . . and her addresses in England last summer before the International Congress of Women and elsewhere attracted favorable notice from the best public in London . . . her gift of ready and eloquent speech seems inborn . . . developed by incessant labor.
>
> Oakland Enquirer, *untitled clipping (1900)*

Gilman embarked on the competitive yet temporarily lucrative public platform–speaking livelihood in the period of its heyday in the decades before the advent of radio and, later, television. Entertainment and edification circulated as public and widely reviewed events. Family background clearly shaped her choice of this option. More immediately, her personal crisis about her dependence on marriage for her living aroused her interest in the livelihood of lecturer and preacher. This crisis emerged soon after her 1884 wedding to Stetson, a crisis aggravated by pregnancy and the birth of her only child in 1885. During temporary separations from Stetson between 1888 and their formal divorce in 1894, Gilman repaired to California, attempting to support herself fully on the lecture circuit. Proud of her Yankee, abolitionist Beecher family heritage, and gifted with considerable public speaking talent, she took to the road more freely thereafter, spreading the gospel of social reform in the family tradition.[4]

Reports on her lectures often addressed the novelty of a woman preacher and podium speaker. One reviewer recalled her 1890 San Francisco lecture on dress reform, first propelling her to national attention. She dramatized the horrors of the tight-laced corsets prescribed for women of her class. On a stage decorated with a statue of Venus de Milo and a tailor's dummy, she produced an illustration of a racehorse with a corset around its middle:

> The whole bulk of the animal's middle body was squeezed into a narrow space within which no breath could possibly penetrate, while the outraged flesh bulged out at both the forequarters and hind quarters in a manner ludicrous beyond description. The audience recognized instantly the telling satire and roared its applause and Charlotte Perkins, then Mrs. Stetson was a made woman. Newspapers east, west, north and south copied the picture and those who saw it never forgot it or Mrs. Stetson. How we did laugh at that horse laced up in a corset.[5]

With her divorce final in 1894, the remarriage of Stetson to Grace Channing, and the newlyweds' custody of daughter Kate, Gilman gradually moved back from the West to the East Coast via paid speaking opportunities, as discussed in chapter 2. If her romance with her cousin finally drew her back to New York by the end of the 1890s, she resisted the gender convention that she should favor love over professional life, with her fiancé in no doubt of her priorities: "I wish you could have heard me last Sunday night. I never spoke better in my life. A full church. A big platform all to myself. And it came. It just poured in a great swelling river and all these people sat and took it in. . . . I forget everyone in the audience when I speak." So important was her professional identity that their wedding in 1900 was "on the road," in Detroit—not New York—because she had speaking engagements there. As discussed in chapter 2, she agreed to remarry only after negotiating wifely duties she would and would not fulfill. Though her earning power declined significantly in her later years, for portions of her adult life speech making was her living, literally, with consequent implications for her published work.[6]

FIGURE 38. Portrait of Charlotte Perkins Gilman on a poster, 1895 (The Schlesinger Library, Radcliffe Institute, Harvard University 177-5-10)

Between 1896 and 1900, Gilman presented an average of fifty lectures a year nationwide, her venues including universities, women's clubs, municipal leagues, religious bodies, and all manner of civic and community groups. Her lectures were fewer when writing books, and when she edited the *Forerunner* (1909–16). Once she finished a monthly issue, however, she took lecture tours before the next month's issue, using her fees to defray costs. After closing the journal and later moving to Connecticut, she resumed lecturing, managed by a Boston agency.

Her papers document her freelance lecturing in rich detail, including precise financial records. Writing in 1915 to an agent regarding a forthcoming Los Angeles tour, Gilman elaborates her fee structure:

> 1st. Yes, I could make a special trip, any time after Jan. 1st, but it would cost ten days travel and all of three hundred dollars. [$6,632 in 2009] I should want to see at least a thousand dollars [$22,477] engaged to do it.
>
> 2nd Yes I will take single engagements as well as "weeks," and rather think those are all I shall get this December. Terms are $100 [$2,582] for one lecture. For Socialists, or Suffragists . . . I will cut as far back as $50.00 [$1,105], and in some *especial* cases . . . for as little as $75.00 [$1,658], but *never state that*. . . . Other lecturers of my standing get $200.00 [$4,421]

and \$300.00 [\$6,632]. My present price is a fair one, and should be insisted on.[7]

She confessed to Houghton that "in the money making line, I can't seem to keep to it," in reference to her frequent agreement to travel and lecture for nothing more than her costs.[8] Her preference was to present six closely spaced lectures as a subscriber series, presented across one or two weeks. That so many women signed on for these series attests to the popularity of her mission to educate and improve her women listeners. These subscribers were women with enough disposable time and income to attend consecutively. Crucial in Gilman's lecture enterprises, then, was advance identification and solicitation of subscription audiences.

Her lecture subjects varied across her career. At first, her lecture topics sprang from her editing and political work, especially Nationalism, socialism, dress reform, women's health, the labor movement, and literary matters. Economic themes loomed large across the 1890s, culminating in *Women and Economics,* stressing both prostitution and marriage. By 1900, she offered three categories of paid speeches: "General Lectures," "Clubs and Parlor Meetings" and "Sermons." The issues she addressed most related to marriage, motherhood, children, and the home. Her focus sharpened by World War I, and she concentrated more on woman suffrage and citizenship, masculinity, feminism, war and peace, and international issues.[9]

Preparing her own publicity materials, Gilman lavished praise on her own published works. She also used written testimonials, accounts of her successful European tours, and comparisons of her own philosophy to that of other leading women thinkers of the day, such as Olive Schreiner and Ellen Key. Noting that her name headed a New York newspaper's list of the twelve greatest living American women, her publicity circular reported her designation as one of only four leading women "meriting the title 'great.'" Gilman's promotional self-description claimed, first, that she "has had an enormous influence upon American life" and, second, that her *Women and Economics* "utterly revolutionized" attitudes toward "woman's place" not only nationally but, thanks to European and Asian language translations, internationally as well. By 1925, her circular named Gilman's eight most significant published works—according to her—two fiction ("The Yellow Wall-paper" and *In This Our World*) and six nonfiction books. Although an agent managed her, she controlled her own promotion. When fixing an upstate New York trip in 1920, she wrote her agent:

> You asked for some publicity material, and with great distaste I have endeavored to manufacture some. . . . It occurs to me that something might be

done by asking a number of Syracuse women "What Mrs. Gilman Means to You?" That would make good newspaper stuff, and if you only asked friendly ones it ought to help the lectures. Then someone might make little funny or sharp extracts from my books or the *Forerunner,* call 'em "Gilman-isms," perhaps some paper would run a few. I'm not good at this publicity stunt, if I were I should be richer.... You see I am particularly anxious for you people to make a real success of this, so that I can convince other clubs that I am not an Expense Account only.... How about a sermon on the 3rd to get more folks roused up? I love to preach better than anything, have done it often.

These materials convey the deadly seriousness with which she approached her paid work. Her zealous self-promotion and vigilance over reputation signaled her intent to continue lecturing indefinitely, underscoring her deep fear of poverty. Accordingly, her handbills evinced her ambivalence about "feminism," a term which, as previously discussed, entered the American political lexicon in the 1910s. Noting her nomination as the most signifi-cant feminist of the era, she "disclaimed" this in preference for the term "humanist." She held that she stressed women simply because their social, economic, and cultural retardation obstructed human progress.[10]

Audiences nationwide received Gilman favorably. Women dominated Gilman's paying public—her natural constituency. She expected female audiences to like her, whereas men's approval surprised her, as she told Houghton in 1898: "I don't know why you should be so surprised about the women. Women are human and so am I; I know women best and care more for them. I have an intense and endless love for women—partly rever-ence for their high estate, partly in pity for their feebleness, their long ages of suffering." In North Carolina, she reported that "my welcome is among the women here. They like me much better than I expected." Yet if women were the audience for her hallmark critique of women's economic depen-dency and its disastrous ramifications, it was largely men's money that sup-ported Gilman. Often, her engagements were during men's working hours, at women's clubs and other cultural or civic bodies. Audience members usu-ally were wives using their husbands' funds to subscribe. Meanwhile, for evening lectures, when men might accompany their wives, Gilman had to appeal to at least some men. She was preoccupied with male audience mem-bers' attitudes toward her. When she won men over, she bragged unapolo-getically, as when she charmed a curmudgeon in St. Louis: "The Beecher reputation weighs heavily in my favor so far—which I had not expected. A big old man got up last night and declared that he felt himself 'in the grip of the mastermind of Henry Ward Beecher' and that now he was in favor of

FIGURE 39. Portrait of Charlotte Perkins Gilman, standing outdoors in front of a train, ca. 1900 Inscription (verso): "Taken on Seattle Suffrage trip by the editor of the Union (?) Signal. She said 'We got a splendid picture of you!'" (The Schlesinger Library, Radcliffe Institute, Harvard University 2005-M125-1-11).

women on the rostrum—though he never had been before." Similarly, she crowned her stay with a wealthy southern family, the Bordens, with the success of converting a rich old banker patriarch. His wife confided that he was reluctant to go—"had never heard a woman speak." Yet, he "sat through the whole thing with unswerving interest and has since been telling everyone to go and hear me with many praises." She said that another man, a lawyer, also reluctant to go said it was "the best address he had ever heard anywhere." Later she reported proudly that "the South loves oratory," despite disliking Progressive women, giving her much gratification "as a woman speaker." Audience enthusiasm left her exhilarated and optimistic about her potential to effect change, feasible because her husband accepted a nonconventional marriage. She was certain that normal wifehood, consisting of primitive home industries and Darwinian or Galilean greatness, could not coexist. With Houghton's cooperation, she happily ventured that the "human world" was on the horizon.[11]

Alternatively, men's disapproval discouraged and unsettled her; for instance, after a lecture in a southern town she noted: "I have met almost no men here and those I have, married and staid, show no signs of more than polite tolerance to an eccentric stranger." Another occasion was worse, when the women in the audience liked the lecture but the men

FIGURE 40. Gilman seated at desk, ca. 1916 (The Schlesinger Library, Radcliffe Institute, Harvard University 177-326-5)

did not: "I wanted the men to get a better feeling toward the women's movement—and I feel as if I had not succeeded at all—rather the other way." Audiences exposed her emotional vulnerability, challenging her confidence. Reporting on a disapproving audience, she observed that "some people like me, others don't. Your father don't your aunts don't," a reference to his family's dismay that their thirty-three-year-old Houghton marrying his divorced, forty-year-old first cousin, echoed in some of her comments: "Some people in our audience come up and shake hands and say nice things. Many more go out silent. How do I know what they think? . . . When I meet disapproval I feel that I am indeed a naughty girl and deserve all I get."[12]

Gilman's rattled responses to critical audiences highlighted the gender transgression involved in being a female public intellectual, an advanced thinker, presuming to educate her fellow women. With few white women having any higher education, and only a tiny handful having academic careers, Gilman's lectures functioned as adult education for women. Her own lack of higher education contrasted with some of her peers, for instance, Jane Addams. Meanwhile, as mentioned in chapter 5, Katharine Bement Davis (1860–1935), superintendent of New York's Bedford Women's Reformatory, and then New York commissioner for corrections, was one of the first female doctorates from the University of Chicago. Nonetheless, since adolescence, Gilman had mastered difficult texts, beyond the experience of

FIGURE 41. Portrait of the Gilmans, 1920 (The Schlesinger Library, Radcliffe Institute, Harvard University 177-326-18)

most women, constructing herself as a "forward-looking woman." This gave her enough of an edge over her audience to be preacher or teacher but not so much so as to alienate them.[13]

What did their subscription fees buy her audience members? Audiences heard early versions of her feminist theories, including a challenging rewriting of history, and alternative visions for human societies, without prostitution or venereal diseases and with professionalized home and family services. Rhetorically, Gilman denounced women's poor performance as household managers and mothers, a message that could seem unthreatening to breadwinners, husbands, and fathers, especially those of the business and professional classes, the core of Gilman's target female and mixed-sex audiences. With titles apparently criticizing women, men of even the most misogynist views might find themselves in, unexpected, agreement.[14]

Gilman's mainly female lecture subscribers heard early prototypes of her subsequent publications. The germs of most of her articles and books could be seen in her lectures long before publication. Through these she brainstormed new ideas or novel formulations of existing ones, reported on her reading, commented on current issues, or debated prevalent views. These speeches found new life on the printed page. Thus, much of Gilman's published writing has a spoken, conversational character. Like any effective speech, its passage through main points was lively, colored with graphic examples, amusing anecdotes, and other devices designed to maintain a listener's, more than a reader's, attention. Without an academic's or journalist's salary, affording her time and space to reconsider carefully, rephrase, and further research the more contentious themes of her lectures, she wrote speeches and articles very rapidly. With her genius for reconfiguring well-worked texts into new contexts, each piece seemed distinct and self-contained, a material aspect of her legacy as a public intellectual, pertinent to her nonfiction. Insofar as her publications drew on lectures, forging an unusually close relationship between her spoken and published words, her living though her pen was paid piece by spoken piece.

Overturning commonsense assumptions, scolding audiences, and seeking to instruct them via a higher authority, particularly science, Gilman's lectures pitted reason against passion or prejudice. Rather than simply conveying information to passive listeners, each talk established an audience goal, a revised interpretation for them to comprehend, a new or renewed commitment to a reform campaign. Moreover, her arguments allowed no conclusion but her own, though she permitted caveats on minor points after receiving questions from her audiences. She began her lectures conversationally, captivating audiences with anecdotes and examples. Once she engaged her listeners, she would reconfigure the advertised topic in startling ways. The trademarks of her lectures were challenge, confrontation, and even repudiation of her audience's conventional stance on the matter at hand.

Gilman usually featured animal analogies such as the corseted horse. Typically, animals emerged from the comparisons more favorably than human, a strategy to shame audiences into recognition of their own foibles. "Noble" animals—leopards, lions, horses, and gazelles—showed the human idiocy of "excessive sex distinction," by which men dominated industry, public life, and all other advanced human "race" activities, to the exclusion of women. Lacking common attributes, with only the bonds of sex and "whatever mutual delight" they might entail, immense evolutionary gaps separated the sexes. By contrast with the nimble leopard, where the distinctions of sex were "in their place," rather than artificially heightened as they were among humans, no obstacle prevented males and females of the species from working together, defending each other and their young, hunting and killing food, and climbing trees. Comparing female animals with women, she stressed the strength, skill, and prowess of female animals, exhorting women to cultivate these qualities and resources. If female cheetahs and leopards could participate equally in their species development, why not female humans?

So distinct had androcentric human cultures made the sexes, it was as if each sex was a distinct species, a race of its own. Unless altered, human marriage could not be a shared life. Mating men and women together made little race development sense. Such matches were like mating a lion and a sheep, an eagle and a hen, a clam and a salmon. Just as two hens have more in common than a hen and an eagle, two women had more in common than a man and a woman. While opposites might well "attract," retorted Gilman to the old adage, "like" kept, and bonded enduringly.[15]

Gilman offset positive animal analogies with other negative references to animals and animality. Criticizing women's forced submission to coitus on demand, Gilman characterized this as the "lowest" of animal instincts, contrasted with the higher state of "humanness." Since other cultural discourses portrayed women as closer to nature through reproduction, with men the custodians of mind, culture, and civilization, her feminist impulse was clear: she portrayed men as behaving like animals, thus closer to nature. Women had to elevate men into "civilized culture." In lectures on sexuality, "animal" was synonymous with rapacious masculinity. Meanwhile, humanness, as opposed to animality, implied a sexual order attuned to women's reproductive periodicity and voluntary motherhood. She vigorously advanced this feminist notion of human civilization, in which husband and wife were equally breadwinners and parents, notwithstanding the prevailing discourse of masculinity, animality, and nature. Perhaps as a reaction, the very male line that Gilman sought to represent as animalistic and uncivilized was being recast as the dynamic player in "racial" advance and higher civilization. At the very moment that her discourse demanded women's entry into the human world of race improvement and species work, the domain of animal instincts received recharacterization as both inherently manly and civilized. Once again, to her chagrin, women were shut out of participation in race progress. Such rhetorical developments influenced her Progressive Era lectures, becoming targets and points of refutation.[16]

As a public intellectual, lecturing centered her work. Skilled and widely traveled, she invested greatly in her lecturing and preaching career. It was a difficult, demanding path, not only as a woman making long journeys and securing accommodation and appropriate local arrangements—the business side of it—but, also, because of the intellectual work committed to the lectures themselves. She labored constantly at her reform Darwinist feminist theoretical corpus through speaking to her contemporaries. As her reputation solidified, published work and editing became more significant components of her work, especially in the 1904–16 period. Then the interplay between lectures and writing became more dynamic and reciprocal. A critical vector between these forms of public intellectual work emerged in her reviews of the work of others influential in Progressive Era politics, cultural production, and criticism.

An Editor's Desk

> To poison one man's food is wrong. To poison the food of the public is more wrong. To weaken and poison the public mind is worse, far worse. The results are not so instantly visible but do more harm. That is why a man who prints lies and lewdness in his newspapers is more wicked than one who puts benzoate in his canned goods. . . . The conditions of slavery, of ownership, of authority, with the dependence and submission of the owned, check the growth of ethics completely. This dominance underlies the despotism of officer, priest, and king, and still finds expression in the attitude of our captains of industry.
>
> *Charlotte Perkins Gilman,* His Religion and Hers *(1923)*

A major part of Gilman's work as a public intellectual involved editing journals, writing for journals, magazines, and newspapers, and exegetical reviewing of notable works of her period. Her first periodical writing and editing was the women's column for Providence *People* in 1886–87, then in California in the 1890s. Once her full-time work on the lecture circuit brought her eastward, her new journalistic and editing opportunities began. The impact of her favorably reviewed books—*Women and Economics, Concerning Children,* and *The Home*—intensified demand for shorter articles. Hence the placement of her work diversified from 1898 onward in journals and newspapers. Thus, by the time she took up residence in New York with her second marriage, she had considerable experience in editing, publishing, and negotiating the world of journals and newspapers.[17]

The great perennial among publishers of Gilman's work was the Boston-based *Woman's Journal,* edited and published by Alice Stone Blackwell, the daughter of pioneer suffragists Lucy Stone and Henry Blackwell. Gilman's first publication in this journal was in 1884, her poem "In Duty Bound," while her last submission was also a poem, "Woman's Hour," in 1916. She published regular nonfiction articles in between, 145 of them published during 1904 alone, the year she undertook editorship of one of the journal pages. Alongside the 1904 work for Alice Stone Blackwell's journal and after, she continued to publish in other journals of Progressive Era opinion—especially the *Independent,* which published twelve of her articles. Her increasing stature also ensured that she was called on by editors to comment on contemporary developments or controversies. She was an inveterate writer of letters to the editors of newspapers, most notably to the *New York Times.*[18]

The genesis of the *Forerunner,* according to Gilman, lay in rejection slips from publishers and editors. Across the 1890s and into the early 1900s, she placed her work readily enough with the radical press, such as *Impress, Woman's Journal, American Fabian,* and small publications of particular reform organizations. Her ambition, however, was to reach a wider Progressive Era reading public. After her bestseller *Women and Economics,* editors of journals and magazines certainly wanted to publish Gilman pieces. Yet her correspondence reveals a constant process of negotiation, not to say haggling over her content. Could she change the introduction? Could she write more generally, or better, on more cheerful subjects? Sometimes editors worked with her in an effort to construct articles along certain lines. It was clear that editors feared that their readers could not accept the short unvarnished versions of her general arguments, rooted in reform Darwinist assumptions, without the assistance of their own red pencils. Autodidact and somewhat dogmatic, Gilman did not take kindly to their revisions. She was a prickly contributor, insisting on professional and equal treatment, at all times. For instance, she replied irately to the proposed removal of a woman suffrage stanza from her poem condemning child labor solicited by a reform league newspaper: "Do not take a gift horse to the orthodontist. I am distinctly unwilling that my work should be altered by other persons, however superior their contribution may be." Hence, the publication process was full of tension.[19]

Unquestionably, her greatest contribution as a Progressive Era editor and reviewer was her own monthly journal, the *Forerunner* (1909–16). While much of its content touched issues addressed in previous chapters, particularly marriage, housework, paid work for women, woman suffrage, cultural misogyny, and prostitution, she also wrote articles on a broad array of other Progressive Era themes. Her monthly column, "Comment and Review," was especially notable for its critical discussion of Progressive Era books, plays, legal and policy changes, personalities, and issues. It provides a fascinating glimpse of what Gilman read, what excited her, and what bothered her in these key years of Progressivism in America.

In the *Forerunner* work, she highlighted Progressive Era social sciences, especially sociology. Her friend, Progressive Era sociologist, Edward Alsworth Ross, loved the *Forerunner,* telling her that what impressed him was "the freshness of it all—as if Eve could have visited our time, sized it all up and commended [*sic*] on it. It is a wonder that you keep your mind so unjaded. You must spend a lot of time in the parks." In 1906 the American Sociological Association invited her to offer a discussion/response to Ross's paper "Western Civilization and the Birthrate" at their annual meeting at Brown University. The committee sought her as someone familiar with "the effect of American conditions upon [the] fecundity of the immigrant." She gave a glowing review to Ross's *The Changing Chinese* (1911), and also to University of Chicago psychologist William I. Thomas's book *Sex and Society* (1907), "a clever book about women," illuminating the ancient origins of human emotions. His book's appeal to her was not least due to the manifest influence of Ward. Gilman noted that Thomas showed how, "in our long pre-social period we were accustomed to strong excitement, long hours of quivering suspense, mad rushes of blind fear, and orgies of wild triumph. Our nerve channels were like the beds of mountain streams, in dry warm-lands; lying shallow or even empty at times; and again roaring torrents. So that nowadays, on the paved levels of our civilized life, the well-graduated dribble of small steady feelings, the organism itself cries out for a change in the pressure." Other social scientists she praised included Ward, as well as Charles Ellwood, whose book *The Social Problem* (1915) had won high praise from his fellow sociologist, Ross. The journal also included Gilman's own sociological treatises on ethics and human society. She serialized these works in monthly chapter-length installments, just as she did her novels.[20]

Gilman explored theoretical and philosophical concerns, such as the culturally made problems of human evolution, especially disastrous cultural exaggerations of sex differences and sex divisions of resources and activities. The *Forerunner* also featured articles on practical social problems typical (and atypical) of Progressive reformers' concerns: animals in cities, sanitation, pure food supply, urban planning, financial waste, socialism, religion, air pollution, advertising, cremation, newspaper sensationalism, and many other related topics.[21] She endorsed the typical slate of proposed Progressive reforms in her praiseful reprint of Mary Johnson's poem "The Wise Housekeeper," outlining a platform of causes or practices to which she was committed and advanced through the *Forerunner*'s pages. These included the extermination of moths, rust, and mildew; the problem of spoiled children, child labor, and graft; and support for federal departments of health and eugenics, juvenile courts, an eight-hour workday, compulsory education, and international arbitration. As a frequent interstate traveler, she especially condemned the unfair, monopolistic practices of the large railroad trusts—the bad and extortionately priced food they offered a captive market, the lack of public facilities for passengers (such as cafeterias and sheltered waiting rooms), and the imposition of absurd and arbitrary rules.[22] For instance, when prohibited from playing solitaire in a waiting room of one railway, owing to antigambling regulations, she wrote indignantly to its superintendent, R. O. Johnson. Not only did he lift the ban, he wrote her: "These so-called soulless corporations are simply organizations of men who are just as human as any individual and your splendidly expressed letter certainly got under the skin of one of them in myself. I shall show your letter to Mrs. Johnson, a very ardent admirer of yours."[23]

Reviewing Friends and Foes

"Progressiveness"—This is a clumsy word, an ill-fitting name for the kind of behavior . . . at the highest for the human race.

Charlotte Perkins Gilman, "Pernicious Adam: A Study in Ethics" (1930)

In addition to promoting Progressive reforms, Gilman's review pages often praised or criticized new literature, especially in relation to sexual politics. She scorned masculist writers and critics for failing to see new options and identities for women. For portraying women in sexualized and misogynist terms, she lambasted H. G. Wells, Rudyard Kipling, Josephine Bascom, and H. L. Menken.[24]

Meanwhile, for boldly imagining men and women in new relations of equality and mutual respect, she applauded the playwright George Middleton, husband of suffragette Fola La Follette. Middleton's memoir recorded his delight in his friendship with key woman suffragists, including Gilman. She reported favorably on several of his plays of the *Forerunner* years, commending his "elastic breadth of view" and grasp of various aspects of contemporary feminism, rare among men. In his plays, female characters' humanity often triumphed over their maternity, showing "the growing humanness of women. They no longer relish having their sex nature, its weaknesses and strengths, continually played upon. They begin to see that Love is a different thing from Hunger and that women are not made to feed men as well as babies." Gilman loved Middleton's themes, which she took to promise rapid enlightenment: the daughter seeking economic independence, the wife breaking out of dependency, the mother resuming work. She concluded that a man grasping all this gave great hope for "feminist advance . . . the crux of the whole change in the position of women. They are beginning to specialize—the first step of civilization." In 1915 she applauded another collection of Middleton's plays, especially "The Black Tie," which she described as "a marvel of lightly indicated tragedy and injustice on 'the color line.'"[25]

Similarly, Gilman extolled the merits of novels that broke masculist molds. One of these was Leroy Scott's *Counsel for the Defense* (1912), replete with popular Progressive Era themes. In this, Katherine West, a modern woman, college-bred, independent, a lawyer by profession, had been working for New York's Municipal League. Her father, Dr. West, a typhoid expert, called her home to Westville, Indiana, to defend him against charges of bribery while overseeing construction of the town's waterworks. After losing the case, she uncovered a conspiracy to ruin her father, orchestrated by her disappointed suitor, a mayoral candidate seeking to privatize the waterworks for profit. A confession from one of his co-conspirators, after that man's wife contracted typhoid and Dr. West cared for her, reversed matters dramatically. With the local paper printing the confession, the scoundrel candidate was arrested, the father exonerated. West agreed to marry the editor of the radical paper, Arnold Bruce, on the condition that she would continue to practice law. The novel echoed Gilman's own fiction, when Arnold refused at first to consider Katherine continuing her profession after they are married:

> "But what you don't seem to understand is, that I have the same need, the same love, for work that you have. . . . I demand for myself the right that all men possess as a matter of course—the right to work. . . . I also demand the right to choose my work."
>
> "But don't you realize, in doing it, if you are successful, you are taking the bread out of a man's mouth?" he retorted.
>
> ". . . if you use that argument, then in doing my own housework I'd be taking the bread out of a woman's mouth."
>
> "Why—why—" he stammered. His face began to redden. "We shouldn't belittle our love with this kind of talk. It's all so material, so sordid."
>
> "It's not sordid to me!" she cried, stretching out a hand to him.

They resolved their negotiation in entirely Gilmanite terms, reminiscent of her characters, such as Ross and Diantha in *What Diantha Did* (1910), complete with the bride-to-be lecturing Arnold on the history of women's position among early man and evolutionary changes generating the women's movement. Calling Scott's book "a novel of the new age," Gilman ventured that it was well "in the interests of fairness and public impression that a book of this sort should be written by a man," especially one evincing, as Scott did, a "height and reach of a mind not bounded by the Himalayan walls of prejudice, the sea of immemorial tradition or the gulf of sex distinction"[26]

Another novel that Gilman reviewed enthusiastically was Henry Kitchell Webster's *The Real Adventure* (1916). Like Scott's novel, it involves the conflict in a relationship over a nonfamilial career and identity for the woman, this time set in Chicago. Unlike the young Katherine West, who declines marriage for a legal career, Rose marries the wealthy Rodney Aldrich at the age of twenty, giving birth to twins, too quickly to develop an identity other than mother. Discontentedly she realizes that "she had just one charm for her husband—the charm of sex. To that she owed her hours of simulated companionship with him, his tenderness for her, his willingness to make her pleasures his own. To that she owed the extravagantly pretty clothes he was always urging her to buy—the house he kept her in—the servants he paid to wait on her." Wishing to earn his respect as a career woman, she leaves Rodney and the twins for a theatrical career, eventually in costume design. In a tortuous plot involving pursuit, jealousy, another lover, and endless negotiation, Rodney finally comes to his senses: "Without knowing it, yielding to a blind, unscrutinized instinct, he'd wanted Rose to live on his love. He'd tried to smooth things out for her, anticipate her wants. He wanted her soft, helpless, dependent." Had he wanted her as a trophy, as her lover suggests, had he been "as bad as that?" Her professional success teaches him "that love, by itself, was not enough." Through independent work, Rose had won Rodney's friendship and respect, the ultimate prize. Not surprisingly, Gilman recommended this novel, as "amazing—and doubly valuable—because it is written by a man, thus proving anew" the capacity of these truths to transcend sexed subjectivity. Webster advanced "the new high standard of marriage, the demand for mutual love on an equal basis of human value, as well as the love which is emotional and physical, but lacks that element of respectful friendship."[27]

If Scott and Webster had clearly read their Gilman, so too had Upton Sinclair, whose novel about venereal disease, *Sylvia's Marriage* (1915), she reviewed favorably (as discussed in chap. 7). In the final chapter of Sinclair's classic Progressive Era novel, *The Jungle* (1906), the characters Maynard and Dr. Schliemann discussed the reading a good socialist needed to understand American conditions. Says Schliemann:

Allowing five to a family, there are fifteen million families in this country; and at least ten million of these live separately, the domestic drudge being either the wife or a wage slave. Now . . . consider one single item, the washing of dishes. . . . The dish-washing for a family of five takes half an hour a day; with ten hours as a days work, it takes, therefore, half a million able-bodied persons. . . . And note that this is the most filthy and deadening and brutalizing work; that it is a cause of anemia, nervousness, ugliness, and ill-temper; of prostitution, suicide and insanity; of drunken husbands and de-generate children—for all of which the community has naturally to pay. And now consider that in each of my little free communities there would be a machine which would wash and dry dishes, and do it . . . scientifi-cally . . . and do it at a saving of all the drudgery and nine tenths of the time! All these things you may find in the books of Mrs. Gilman.[28]

Similarly, in Sinclair's thinly disguised autobiographical novel *Love's Pilgrimage* about his ill-fated marriage to Meta Fuller, which ended in divorce in 1912, he presented a didactic passage in which the wife charac-ter, Corydon—portrayed as a nonintellectual millstone around the neck of her creative artist husband—sits reading a book, "Charlotte Gilman's 'Women and Economics'; she read it at one sitting and brought it to Thyr-sis, who thus came to understand the scientific basis of yet another article of his faith." In response, the hero husband Thyrsis then read Lester Ward, August Bebel, and Havelock Ellis, realizing that women "had not always been clinging vines and frail flowers and other uncomfortable things." In-stead, primitive women held their own, until the slavery and exploitation accompanying the advent of the leisure class made women appendages, men's property and household servants. Paraphrasing Gilman, he wrote: "For generations the male had selected and bred in her those qualities which were most stimulating to his own desires, which increased in him the sense of his own dominance. . . . So the woman became frail . . . her success by the only method that was open to her—by finding some male whom she could ensnare."[29]

If imitation is the most sincere form of flattery, Gilman's disapproval of Sinclair's book on account of its graphic, explicit details must have been painful for both of them. Gilman had previously read drafts of his unpub-lished work, and evidently he did not anticipate her reaction to his *Love's Pilgrimage* (1911). Gilman told him that though she ranked him a "genius," she objected not only to his unnecessary "explicitness of detail; but most extremely, to the publication of such intimate matters" about his wife, Meta. Moreover, she abhorred his depiction of sexual politics and use of her "hu-manist" feminism against his wife instead of on her behalf. He portrayed

Meta as too backward to transcend "sex work," retarding his making a full commitment to his art, advancing "race work." His efforts to educate her in socialist and feminist thought proved futile, as she pursued an ill-fated love affair with a minister, before a temporary reconciliation. Worse, Sinclair cast Meta as an animalistic woman who aroused primitive and violent erotic passions in her husband. He depicted their honeymoon floridly in overwrought language too metaphorical to arouse formal censorship but enough to offend Gilman as exploitative, the chapter, tellingly entitled "The Bait Is Seized." Here again was "the brute in man":

> He clutched her to him with a force that crushed her, that made her cry out. The soul of the cave-man awoke in him—he lifted his mate in his arms and bore her away to a secret place. . . . "Please, dearest, please! I'm afraid Thyrsis." But nothing could stop him now. She was his—his to do what he pleased with! And he would bend her to his will! The voice of his manhood shouted aloud to him now, and it was like the clashing of wild cymbals in his soul. . . . Before this they had been strangers; but now he would penetrate to the secret places, to the holy of holies of her being. . . . So all the chained desire of a lifetime drove him on. . . . The touch of her warm breasts . . . the pressure of her soft, white limbs—these things . . . turned a madness loose in him . . . And so it was that he wreaked his will upon her.[30]

There had been erotically charged conflicts between Gilman and her first husband recorded in their 1880s diaries, but unpublished in their lifetimes. They remained loyal to each other in public, even to the point of Gilman's untrue autobiographical portrayal of theirs as a viable marriage but for the complication of her own mental illness, as explored in chapter 1. Her own experience then might explain her negative reaction to Sinclair's public exposure of his marital woes. Much as the material feasibility of Gilman's career depended on her reputation among other intellectuals, she took no joy from this particular appropriation of her work.[31]

IN 1916, GILMAN ended *Forerunner.* Subscriptions had never paid for it. Subscribers widely lamented its demise. Totaling the journal's content of "seven novels (by which I definitely proved that I am not a novelist)!, and seven other books of considerable value . . . enough verse for another volume, and all the rest of the varied material," she entered a fallow period, for "I had said all I had to say." After she closed the *Forerunner,* she published only three articles in 1917 and two in 1918. Meanwhile, her regular drama, novel, and short story writing effectively ceased with the last issue of the *Forerunner,* with the single exception of her unpublished 1929 detective novel, *Unpunished*. Nonetheless, in 1919, the *New York Tribune* editors, always favorable to her views (unlike the *New York Times*), persuaded the now almost sixty-year-old Gilman to undertake a six-days-a-week syndicated column, published 17 March 1919 through 20 April 1920.[32]

As well as attempting to translate her longstanding concerns into this new medium, she also used this column to raise issues and to revise views that had not appeared in her other work. For instance, she presented the cases for and against Prohibition, provisionally supporting the measure, a position she would later repudiate. Moreover, in contrast to her earlier optimistic assessment of the contribution of evolution and eugenics to social analysis and policy, she offered a more sober perspective in the aftermath of world war. She observed that the evolutionary "survival of the fittest" often meant the proliferation of hyenas, alligators, "poison snakes and all manner of vermin" to say nothing of apples "small, hard and sour," instead of the "big red and yellow beauties we know." In fact, the best people on earth were often "the unfit," measured by the savagery of combat and war.[33]

Reflecting the increasing socialist disillusionment with the post-Revolutionary Russia, she indignantly rebuked race prejudice in Russia, asserting that such prejudice was entirely learned, with no inherent basis. She disdained a visitor's comment that in neither Russia nor England was there prejudice against Negroes; she noted that neither country had many people of African descent, while they nonetheless showed virulent prejudice against Jews and Indians, respectively, the English stigmatizing "intermarriage" with native women throughout its Empire. Meanwhile, she insisted on the entirely learned or cultural origins of racial prejudice against those white supremacists who would call it "natural" and "inherent." Addressing the American South, she observed that, "in the very hotbed of discrimination against negroes, our own South, we find that this 'deep-seated, born, ineradicable' etc. feeling does not exist in childhood." Such views provoked a chilly response from readers in Louisville, Baltimore, and other Southern cities that printed her syndicated column; and this was also the fate of her fierce denunciations of lynching. Earlier, she had agreed with the *Independent*'s horrifying account of a 1916 lynching in Waco, Texas, drawing readers' attention to the barbarity and criminality of hundreds of white people who had the temerity to claim they were more "civilized" than African Americans. And previously, in 1915, she had been a panelist and speaker at the annual meeting of the National Association for the Advancement of Colored People's meeting to present the first Spingarn Medal "for the highest Achievement of an American Negro," a panel she shared with W. E. B. Dubois, Moorfield Storey, Oswald Garrison Villard, William Pickens, and

Linden Bates Jr. In her fiction, too, she deplored the color line of Jim Crow America, mercilessly satirizing it in *With Her in Ourland* (1916). So, her interwar newspaper criticisms of racial bigotry and Jim Crow abuses continued her earlier positions but for a wider, much less sympathetic readership than her fifteen hundred *Forerunner* subscribers.[34]

Later, she judged this syndicated journalism episode a failure: "But alas! though I tried my best to reach and hold the popular taste, I couldn't do it, so after a year that effort came to an end. It was the only time in my life when I had a 'pay-envelope,' and that was most enjoyable." Thereafter she tried to depend again on lecture tours, converting some of her lectures into the remaining nonfiction publications of her career.[35]

Considering the audiences assembled nationwide for her lectures, the contribution she made as journal editor and reviewer of contemporary work, it is clear that Gilman had an immense impact on her contemporaries. Unquestionably, they constructed her as a public intellectual. Ellen DuBois rightly includes her among important politically influential social thinkers confronting "the fundamental political challenges of the age. Even without a vote, figures like Gilman pressured the nondemocratic Progressive Era state to diversify and modernize."[36]

Indeed, Gilman's opinion, often sought and often offered, addressed not only the situation of women and men but the array of reform controversies of the Progressive Era as well. After the heat and contention of the suffrage struggle, it is notable that the *Pictorial Review* dubbed her, in 1919, "the most sane of our feminists." For one who told friends that she rejected this term for herself, many such public references rolled into print with no protest from her. Contemporaries understood her to be—whether they approved of her interventions or not—a feminist public intellectual, and something of a celebrity at that.

CHAPTER ELEVEN

The Later
Gilman

I am afraid you are not well for I see no more
mention of your literary contributions to the
public.... Now, of course, if there was any
achievement in winning the vote for women,
it was collective.

Carrie Chapman Catt to
Charlotte Perkins Gilman, 6 November 1930

My last book, *His Religion and Hers* came out
in 1923. Every now and then I have an article
or bit of verse somewhere, but not often. The
modern taste does not enjoy my work, you see,
the "readers" are just out of college.

Charlotte Perkins Gilman to
Carrie Chapman Catt, 22 November 1930

GILMAN DID NOT age quietly. Commentators assert that she became
racist, ethnocentric, nativist, and even antifeminist with age. World War I
had convinced her of fundamental ethnic differences, with other peoples
at earlier stages of evolutionary development. Her earlier Lamarckian optimism about the transmission of culturally acquired traits gave way to a
starker if still reform Darwinism. The later Gilman held that the "fittest"
would not necessarily survive against competition from the overly fertile.
Decades of unrestricted mass immigration threatened American culture,
particularly its women. Ethnic differences caused war, witness Germany.
Meanwhile "excessive reproduction" stimulated belligerent imperialism. By
1920, immigrants and their children constituted a full 78 percent of Manhattan's population, prompting Gilman's turn to demographic questions,

along with other interwar scholars like historian Frederick Jackson Turner and sociologist Edward Ross. It is instructive to place the later Gilman's ethnic prejudices in context, since her views evolved. This chapter examines the later part of her feminist career, from the closing of the *Forerunner* in 1916 until her death in 1935.[1]

Commentary on Gilman's nonfiction from World War I and the interwar years has been sparse. Scholars prefer the younger Gilman, finding her later stances uncongenial. Her attacks on libertarian sexual mores, Freudian psychoanalysis, and initially, birth control can resemble the ranting of some prudish dinosaur. Naturally, scholars deplore her favoring of eugenics, immigration quotas, and Americanization of immigrants. Some even link Gilman to Germany's "final solution," exemplifying a metamorphosis of Progressivism into appeasement of fascism. Pitched against the masculist, antimaternalist "mongrel Manhattan in the 1920s," the later Gilman lost momentum, her cultural currency spent. Her satires on the flapper and unapologetic ethnic prejudices suggested that she morphed into a marginal cultural anachronism. Yet these assessments ignore Gilman's heightened interwar opposition to patriarchalism.[2]

Despite claims that she abandoned work on women and feminist issues, considerable evidence suggests otherwise. True, she was frustrated at being drowned out by Jazz Age feminism's priorities. She recalled longingly her fame in the 1910s and strove to galvanize her audiences to oppose the risks she saw to women's (and humanity's) progress from interwar sexual culture. Backlash against the Nineteenth Amendment she believed boded ill for women, as did problems of mass immigration—such as slums, poverty, prostitution, and corruption.[3]

It is timely to consider "the later Gilman" more productively and with more nuances. Racism, ethnocentrism, nativism, and anti-Semitism were not terms in which peers saw her positions. A challenge is to probe the relationship between problematic discourses and her central claims, grasping her use of them for feminist ends. This chapter considers the later Gilman's marginalization, providing an account of her feminist theory and public intellectual work, particularly her engagements with immigration debates that were as feminist as they were nativist. Her belated recruitment to birth control advocacy added a significant final note to the work of the most influential feminist theorist and advocate of her age.

On the Margins?

> I've had quite a number of articles out in the last year or two, some pretty good ones. The Autobiography I can see may not find a publisher on the ground of my antediluvian reputation. As one juvenile refuser [put] it, "Mrs. Gilman is not as well known as she was ten years ago."
>
> *Charlotte Perkins Gilman to Lyman Beecher Stowe, 16 July 1928*

Commentary typically portrays Gilman as the most influential Progressive Era feminist theorist up to about 1914–15, her irrelevance thereafter mirroring the decline of Progressivism itself. In 1956 Carl Degler asserted that she did not work on women's issues after 1920. Yet in the nineteen years between her 1916 closing of the *Forerunner* and the year of her death at the age of seventy-five, she published two books, forty-six nonfiction articles and book chapters, 310 newspaper columns, and sixteen poems, many of which addressed feminist issues. Most significantly, in 1923, she published the treatise *His Religion and Hers: The Faith of Our Fathers and the Work of Our Mothers,* her first book-length nonfiction text since *The Man-Made World* (1911).[4]

What was the sequence of her late career? Gilman temporarily rested from writing after the *Forerunner* until 1919–20, when, as discussed in chapter 10, she wrote a syndicated daily column for the *New York Tribune* in 1919–20. There she criticized postrevolutionary Russia, a position common among those, like herself, formerly known as socialists. Soon she would attack first Marxism, then Bolshevism for closing the American mind to any form of sensible socialist reform. Briefly, she also worked for a while in the National Woman's Party, before resigning in 1921 and joining the American Federation of Labor's Patriotic Convention. Like other well-known Republicans, she joined the Democrats' campaign for American membership of the League of Nations. In 1924, she joined the women's committee for Progressive Senator Robert La Follette's presidential bid.[5]

With few regrets, she left New York in 1922, since "one of the bitterest lacks in that multiforeign city . . . swollen rather than grown, is that freedom in friendship and neighborliness. People of similar tastes huddle in little local groups, narrower than villages, as in the vaunted pseudo-artistic settlement, Greenwich Village. Dwindling islands of earlier inhabitants cling to Murray Hill or some other spot and do not 'call' beyond certain limits."[6]

Moving to Norwich Town, Connecticut, early in 1922, she and Houghton ostensibly retired, coinheriting and coresiding in her husband's family home, with her uncongenial in-laws (Francis and Ellen Gilman). This arrangement proved to be a strain for all. Initially, though, her work benefited, for she completed *His Religion and Hers* that year, while by 1925, she had twenty new publications, many addressing interwar women's subjection. For instance, she deplored alimony for able-bodied childless women, for fostering the disquieting, misogynist theme of the gold digger in popular culture. She became president of the local chapter of the League of Women Voters; and by mid-decade, she debated modern sexual mores and birth control, especially in relation to feminism and psychoanalysis. By 1928 she had drafted her curiously selective autobiography, blending bitterness, rationalization, and self-aggrandizement. Of its 335 pages, 277 (83 percent) covered the 1860–99 period, minimizing her heyday in the Progressive Era and beyond. Eventually, she worked with Margaret Sanger, who in the early 1930s called her out for a last public campaign: the fight to repeal, once and for all, the ancient federal Comstock laws deeming distribution of birth control information to be obscene.[7]

More personally, Gilman felt compelled to earn into her sixties and seventies, partly due to pressure from an array of dependents. Her daughter Kate married (just as Gilman herself had done) a young improvident artist. Instead of son-in-law Frank Tolles Chamberlin being a support to Kate, "she is one to him," Gilman telling her cousin that the artist was "in a dangerous condition of nerve exhaustion—as real as broken bones, as well I know." Later she called her son-in-law "a dead weight," who Kate supported "by borrowing money!" Moreover, Gilman provided financial aid to her thrice-married unemployed brother, Thomas Perkins, and his ill and troubled family. Meanwhile, Stetson's widow lived alone in poverty in a small Manhattan apartment. Gilman assisted her in tense arrangements that disclosed resentments in the postdivorce relationship between them, an obligation made more onerous since the second Mrs. Stetson was now deaf, "old, heavily disabled, poor and alone." These dependents may have led Gilman to pursue unrealistic professional expectations. She lived her own longstanding theories: that women founded industries, that they were the world's first and hardest workers, and that work justified life. Above all, women worked to care for others. She certainly did.[8]

Unfortunately, maintenance of the drafty mansion soon depleted Houghton Gilman's reserves. Placing their grandchildren's welfare above their own comfort, the now vegetarian Gilmans grew their own food. By winter 1930, they decided that a cheap hotel was more affordable than their share of the heating bill. Meanwhile, Houghton Gilman had made personal loans to family and friends, which they had not repaid, as well as unwise secret investments not fully revealed to Gilman until his death.[9]

In 1934, Gilman wrote to writer Zona Gale, from her daughter's Pasadena home: "My husband is dead. . . . A telephone call, an accident, a fall in the street . . . he lay on the floor, at my feet, dead. Three dreadful months of sorting, poking, destroying, and giving away. . . . Then I came here to live and die. Because, for which I am grateful and strictly in confidence . . . the doctors give me but a year or two."[10]

With a 1932 diagnosis of inoperable breast cancer, Gilman decided that a year was enough. By then she despaired of ever publishing her study of ethics, which she judged her most important contribution to social theory, after *Human Work* (1904), on which she was "willing to rest my claim to service." It was "particularly important now . . . old bases of conduct wavering and new ones so weak." Here she referred to the changes of the 1920s and 1930s, which seemed to render her lifelong reform commitment unintelligible to new generations. If her ethics book stalled, publishers did want her autobiography, as she told Gale, asking for her help with it, "for the sake of the scrappy, imperfect, desperately earnest work I have done."[11]

The sadness of these words augments the impression of the late Gilman's marginality. For some, she had always been marginal, excluded from a central place in the intelligentsia and the women's movement, due to lack of higher education and poverty. For others, she became marginal in this period, her ideas old-fashioned, out of step, and her chignon and lace collars embodying a bygone era, beside the bobbed-haired, short-skirted flapper. Feminists now were college-educated, sexually libertarian, pro–birth control, and fragmented in many directions, arguing about such matters as the Equal Rights Amendment and international politics.[12]

In other ways Gilman was far from marginal. Certainly, she connected with current interwar celebrities and notable modern women. Figures like Amelia Earhart personified the era, breaking new barriers for women, asserting their essential humanness. Indeed, Gilman admired some younger "new women." She particularly commended the actor Katharine Hepburn (daughter of her friend, fellow suffragist and white slavery campaigner, Katharine Houghton Hepburn) — referring to her as "Katy" when praising her performance in the 1932 film, *A Bill of Divorcement*.[13] For some, however, Gilman's revulsion for women adopting men's sexual behavior signaled her marginality by the 1920s. Her ridicule of flappers demonstrated this: despite their avowed modernity, she mocked primitivism in women's "powdering their noses" on streetcars. Metaphorically, she wrote, this was the equivalent of men going to work with bows and arrows. With her caustic wit, she went beyond metaphor. Specifically, she objected to the flapper fashion of tight-banding the breasts flat and binding the hips, creating the

FIGURE 42. Portrait of Amelia Earhart leaning against a wall, 1934 (The Schlesinger Library, Radcliffe Institute, Harvard University MC451-6-6)

appearance of a straight drop from the shoulder to a knee-length hemline. For this "boyish" fashion disavowed the female body in "order Mammalia," expressing hostility to feminine and maternal functions.[14]

So Gilman's career-long interest in dress and fashion as sexualized androcentric institutions—reversing nature in ornamenting women—did not cease. If anything, the flapper era enlarged and revitalized that interest. She insisted that, contrary to the much-vaunted independence of modern women, they remained slaves to fashion, continuing to dress to please men, whether or not men reported themselves "pleased." Women were not "more foolish than they [men] were, but they show it more. We learn unsuspected weaknesses in their newly exposed characters, as we learn unsuspected anatomical errors in their newly exposed legs." Elsewhere she wrote of skin exhibited in public, stressing that she had no objection when appropriate, as at the beach; but on streetcars, "I have seen legs, yards of them one might say, with knee and thigh in full evidence, which so far from being desirable, were fairly repellent."[15]

In her lively and humorous commentaries, she certainly did not behave like a marginal old lady. In 1912, she had denounced the suggestion that proper aging for women was to sit knitting quietly in a rocking chair for twenty or more years. Good as her word, she continued as a public intellectual, commenting particularly on the status and situation of women.

Misogynist newspapers delighted in the spectacle of the modern woman attacked by a venerable feminist like Gilman.[16]

Moreover, in works like "Toward Monogamy," she called alleged sexual freedom a new form of erotic domination. The risks of unwanted pregnancies and venereal diseases remained high before correction of the prevailing faulty theory of ovulation in the 1930s, penicillin from the later 1940s, and the contraceptive pill from 1960. To Gilman, then, sexual libertarianism enslaved women. Knowing directly its bohemian version, Freudianism appeared, from her 1880s marriage to Stetson, to be as phallic worship reborn. Psychoanalytic injunctions against erotic repression may have reignited long-buried anger from her first experience of Stetson's erotic masculism. Though some simply classify her as a puritanical, repressive erotophobe, she was hardly alone in protesting psychoanalytical sexual politics.[17]

Despite her criticisms, Gilman always allowed that excesses were the understandable exuberance of a newly freed class. And always, she stressed that prospects for her long desired "human world" rested with young women—the Amelia Earharts and Katharine Hepburns of the world, the new generation. Against discourses disrespecting women's "humanness"— she reasserted her longstanding account of women as the first sex, the trunk of the human racial tree, and the collective necessity for making a human world.[18]

GILMAN'S MOST important publication of her later career, *His Religion and Hers,* addressed this new generation of readers. Her preface contained the bald statement that "religion is the strongest modifying influence in our behavior," expressing highest instincts and serving best advancement. Yet religions were responsible "for much evil." Androcentric cultures' religions universalized primitive male experiences and marginalized women's. Arguably, she used religion as a case study for analyzing the broader operation of androcentrism.

Centered on life after death, world religions deprecated life on earth. Preoccupied with self-expression, dominance, and combat, they cast the deity in a deadly struggle with an opposing nemesis—a devil or evil spirit— emphasizing death and tests of faith in the pursuit of virtue or enlightenment among worshipers. The hard demanding gods of world religions fostered grim contests to reach the afterlife. Dogmatism within and between religions led to frightful wars against heretics, heathens, or infidels. More innocents were killed in the name of Christianity than in other faiths; but most world religions had blood on their hands. Religion could be war by other means, "justifying hate and violence."[19]

Gilman's principal objection to the death-worshiping and life-deprecating character of world religions was the androcentric pattern of male supremacy and female subordination underpinning them. Female economic dependency and sexual slavery cojoined to exclude feminine perspectives from world theologies, while firmly barring women from most ecclesiastical hierarchies. Only by ending androcentrism and creating a truly human world might religions beneficially transform toward emphasizing life, growth, and human improvement.[20]

Religious androcentrism led to their obsessive concern with sex behavior. Most religions endorsed male sex interests in the control of wives and all unmarried women and girls. Excessive carnality and celibacy were equally absurd, unnatural, and masculist. She compared ecclesiastical celibacy with prohibition posed as the solution to excessive drunkenness, rather than temperance in all things.[21]

Ultimately, *His Religion and Hers* was an ambitious attempt to connect a critique of the primitive masculism of world religions to a feminist case against the subjection of women. Gilman restated the case for freeing women from "sex work" and fully incorporating their gifts in "race work." Her interrogation of religion was not theological. It arose, rather, from her critique of androcentric ethics. Since "the most powerful group of concepts governing conduct are those forming religion," human behavior mirrored religious institutions, preoccupations, and mores. That so much human behavior was bad proved that the governing human ideas were erroneous and injurious.[22]

Religions' death-centered concepts arose from the "fact that they have been introduced and developed by one sex only, the male, in whose life as a hunter and fighter, death was the impressive crisis." Though women were equally human, their capacities had "atrophied through long suppression," while economic dependence nullified their evolutionary power as selector of the best male for race improvement. The longevity of women's suppression ensured that "ultra-masculinity has interfered with normal social evolution." Here, Gilman retained Ward's position, even in the aftermath of scientific critiques of his gynaecocentric theory.[23]

Moreover, religions left intact the darker aspects of human behavior in the present world. Christian Europe had just proved exactly as warlike as "heathen" Europe in the past. Moreover, in the Americas, the taint of chattel slavery, modeled, Gilman declared, on the first slavery—woman slavery—weakened the slave and made the master, through long slaveholding, "proud, lazy, selfish, cruel, unjust." Little wonder, then, "that his early gods were all of these together." Meanwhile, Christian America had "maintained slavery after every other advanced people had outgrown it," as well as savagely perpetrating "the slow torturing to death of helpless prisoners, which we cover by the term 'lynching.'"[24]

Organized religions ignored human improvement. They failed to guide, owing to their despairing gaze at life on earth, preferring death and beyond. Static religions improved nothing since they accepted "man's original mistake in making a private servant of the mother of the race." Women needed life-promoting religions.[25]

If religion failed race progress, the cause was the same as that which Gilman had elaborated a quarter of a century before, in *Women and Economics* (1898). Despite objective changes in their position, women failed the human race, due to their "contemptible surrender to previously masculine vices and weaknesses." Here she did not spare younger women: "No prisoned harem beauty, no victim of white slavery, no dull-eyed kitchen drudge is so pitiful as these 'new women,' free, educated, independent, and just as much the slaves of fashion and victims of license as they were before." Given her passionate denunciation of slavery and its consequences, this criticism was harsh. As noted above though, she conceded that the "imitation of masculine vices" understandably attended women's release from masculine enslavement.[26]

Gilman wrote *His Religion and Hers* with force, confidence, and conviction. While most commentators appreciated *His Religion and Hers,* it remains underanalyzed relative to Gilman's earlier nonfiction works.[27] By the mid-1920s, Gilman's cumulative works since the 1890s identified her as a key exponent of humanist equalitarian feminism, minimizing gender differences, grounding analysis of women's subjection in material factors, and accordingly, mandating material cures. She remained an important voice for notable editors, such as Victor Calverton, Freda Kirchwey, Brownell Baker, and Samuel D. Schmalhausen, who invited Gilman to contribute alongside others with whom she had marked sexual politics disagreements. Her contributions all restated her earlier feminist stance but framed distinctly for 1920s readers.[28]

THE LATER Gilman believed transformed ethics to be prerequisites for altering androcentric sexual practices and gender patterns. Hence, her study of ethics became the major work of her later years. Initially titled "Pernicious Adam," she defined ethics as "the science whereby we may judge and measure morals, religion, and law. Contrary to its place within philosophy today as a humanities field, she insisted that ethics was "a social science," based on an understanding of both biological evolution and sociology. Encompassing many themes preoccupying her throughout her career, the text addressed diverse but familiar topics like venereal diseases, war, pacifism, temperance and prohibition, socialism, marriage, sexuality, motherhood and childrearing, and school hazing.[29]

Gilman always described "Pernicious Adam" as a work of general social understanding; yet throughout, she used gendered examples. When showing that even highly civilized cultures had unexamined flaws in their social ethics, she gave illustrations related to women's bodies:

> In modern Europe and America, Christian, civilized, believing our race to be made in the image of God, the unhealthy distortion of the "hour glass corset" has but lately passed and is even now returning. Our loudly boasting younger generation, standing proudly beyond the errors of their predecessors, has given us the spectacle of the "debutante slouch": an attitude reminiscent of a junk man's horse; of crippling high-heeled shoes which maintain a flock of industrious chiropodists; and as a crowning instance of blasphemy, the boyish form brassiere of the early 1920s. . . . What should we think of the intelligence of men who tried to imitate the mammary gland with a girlish form corset?[30]

She tackled erroneous ethical thinking in many areas, but none with more force than medical ethics related to venereal diseases. Appalled at physicians knowingly allowing young women to marry syphilitics, she rejected the privileging of patient privacy over the interests of general humanity. The later Gilman on this matter was as feminist as earlier interventions, decrying the suffering of wives and children due to medical loyalty to "the injurer." Meanwhile, morality for women in androcentric culture wrongly resided first in virginity, followed by chastity, as the litmus test of female honor. A maiden might be "a tale-bearer, a coward, a liar, lazy, and self-indulgent, without impinging in the least upon her honor." Once married, if she dared to stray, committing the infidelity so common among husbands, then her spouse's honor "established in the body of a woman" becomes imperiled. The husband "may commit adultery and leave the wife's honor untouched, but if she does it his honor is so implicated that the offender, meaning the man, may be justifiably killed on the spot, sometimes the woman also."[31]

Despite publisher rejections, she persisted, buoyed by encouragement from friends like Edward Ross: "There really is no satisfactory and popular treatise on ethics. . . . You have the gift of putting across the deepest and soundest ideas. Good luck to you." Characterizing her text as humorous and "no more irreligious than most thinking people are nowadays," she attributed publisher rejection to her "be-labeling" with reform causes—presumably woman suffrage, women's economic independence, reform of the home, food supply, house and urban design, pacifism and feminism. Thus, the ethics book never found its publisher.[32]

The work of the later Gilman showed both change and continuity with that of her early and middle career. She remained committed to historical and evolutionary explanations of women's subjection, as well as to materialist and economic solutions to free women from sex work and to allow them to contribute fully to race work. Yet she saw that changed concerns among women, as well as new twentieth-century mass communications technologies introduced inspiring possibilities. If some interwar gender relations and sexual patterns appalled her, she was also excited and elated. No enemy of the future, she gradually decided, however, that her long-sought human world stood threatened within the culture that had enabled women's greatest advance so far—her own country, America. The decisive move against unrestricted immigration in the waning years of the Progressive Era engaged her not only due to nativist sentiments, which she shared with so many fellow Progressives, but also due to her diagnosis of negative effects on women's advancement in the collapse of "American unity."

Defending American Stock

> It is a wonderful spectacle, the mingling of peoples that goes to make up our people . . . by the slow restricted process of physical inheritance, through the ceaseless intermarriage of all stocks . . . going on among us, with great results. . . . We complain too much of our low grade immigration, and are not sufficiently thankful for the value of the noble races who have come to us, of whom our best are made. . . . Coming here and entering our "institutions," all men become Americans, and that is how America comes to be the home of the world's swiftest growth.
>
> Charlotte Perkins Gilman, "The Making of Americans" (1904)

Gilman gradually became opposed to unrestricted immigration and the nonassimilation of immigrants across her twenty-two years of residency in Manhattan. Hitherto she had encountered anti-immigrant sentiments with impatient bemusement. For instance, in a lecture at Hull House in 1898 she criticized negative views of immigrants, since she saw in these new citizens great hope for renewing American democracy: "Take the immigrant question—look at it from the wider standpoint of progress in history—show that the thing to be noted is not the incidental disturbance caused by hasty assimilation of varied racial elements—but there is a land where all the nations of the earth can live together, compelled by the same free and enlightening popular spirit. Show that these 'lower classes' we so condemn as immigrants are healthier grafts upon our body politic than more highly specialized branches would be; and give facts to prove their rapid assumption of citizenship." Moreover, even in 1904 she asserted that the American fear that "foreign stock" will grow faster than native was "an amusing distinction—as if none were Americans save those whose foreign stock came over in a certain century, charter members as it were—all later additions inferior."[33]

How should Gilman's gradually more critical stances on unrestricted immigration be understood? First and crucial, her earlier approval of immigrants was predicated on assimilation. That is to say, she assumed that the historic and evolutionary evidence demonstrated assimilation and, by this, enrichment, enhancement, and strengthening of American population through healthy variation. Newman well-establishes Gilman's systematic ethnic assimilationism. In contrast with the intransigent older patriarchies found in many European cultures, Gilman believed that American conditions fostered a progressive new cultural synthesis, through assimilation and integration. She endorsed cultural infusions from immigration then, assuming the unquestionable Americanness of the outcome.[34]

By contrast, in 1915, after decades of unrestricted immigration, she suggested that the psychic basis of "American Unity" was at risk. Wartime conditions revealed apparent assimilation to be superficial; few foreigners would fight for America: "Even so long established residents as the Irish remain Irish—they are not Americans. They would willingly sacrifice the interests of this country, or of the world as a whole, for the sake of Ireland." The so-called melting pot hardly extinguished ethnic loyalties to countries of origin. As the 1920 census would show, of the 2,284,103 residents of Manhattan, only just over half were classified as born "native white" (54.6 percent), nearly two-thirds with foreign parentage, a further 11 percent with a foreign parent; meanwhile, the remaining 45 percent of the borough were themselves foreign-born. Gilman bemoaned hearing no English as she traveled about the city. Many other signs pointed not to American enlargement but to unassimilated ethnic enclaves.[35]

The second element of her shift against unrestricted immigration was the conclusion that unassimilated immigrants had specific ethnic characteristics made them inassimilable with the historic features of America's ethnic mix within a reasonably immediate timeframe. This conclusion stood in marked contrast with her optimistic analysis of prospects for African

Americans, which she pitted forcefully against Jim Crow "subjugationists," discussed below. Third, and most significant, she judged these inassimilable characteristics to be negative forces or obstacles to the advancement of women in America, the key to building a human world.[36]

Gilman's initial problem with unrestricted immigration was its scale. Cities were unprepared and ill-equipped to integrate properly all who wished to come. Adverse consequences ensued, and for all inhabitants, from immigrants remaining unassimilated. As graphically portrayed in critical novels, like Upton Sinclair's *The Jungle* (1906), she reiterated concerns over the ways in which slum landlords, employers, political factions, and providers of goods and services took advantage of non–English speaking immigrants. The ill consequences stretched beyond their neighborhoods. The toll in disease, exploitation, and impoverishment meant deteriorated conditions for all. Prostitution, sweated labor, unemployment, and homelessness were only the most obvious evils.[37]

Perhaps less dramatic, but of great concern to Gilman, were the attributes and habits of mind grafted onto American polity and culture from the various immigrant groups. Here she referred to patterns of religious observance, arranged marriages, seclusion, and male relatives' rigid control of women, reactionary patriarchal "honor" codes, female illiteracy, and daughters' exclusion from education even when available to them in American cities. At the very time that reformers secured a vision for girls' lives beyond domestic drudgery, "backward" concepts of womanhood and manhood imparted by unassimilated ethnic groups threatened fragile consensus about the need for modernization and "humanness" for women. Gilman saw little evidence of the most separatist of recent immigrants advocating women's admission to race work or the pursuit of a human world.[38]

In examining her stance on interwar immigration restriction, one must note the crucial distinctions in this period between "ethnocentrism" and "racism." The former meant the tendency to judge other ethnic groups negatively in the light of one's own (privileged) attributes and characteristics. "Racism" was not formally in use in Gilman's lifetime, but when first defined in 1935, it was "the ascription of inferior, negative characteristics judged innate, inherent, and inalterable, and thus which justified segregation, enslavement, or extermination." Some commentators ascribe both terms to Gilman, using them as broadly synonymous, or as too closely related to warrant much distinguishing. Others recognize that in her ruminations on American population characteristics she was little concerned with race, writing rarely about African Americans. When she did, more often than not she criticized their situation and treatment in Jim Crow America.

She criticized not forebears' prejudices against persons of color, but their blindness about more significant and incommensurable ethnocultural differences: "The noble spirit of our founders and their complete ignorance of sociology began the trouble. They honestly imagined that one kind of man was as good as another if he had the same opportunity, unless his color was different." Here she held that African Americans suffered wrongly and unjustly from white prejudice. African Americans did not, in her view, threaten or adversely impact either American polity or "American stock." By contrast, as becomes clear below, she identified peril to both polity and stock from Progressive Era immigration.[39]

WHAT DID Gilman write about African Americans? Her only publication (of a total of 2,157 in her lifetime) addressing African Americans' situations was "A Suggestion on the Negro Problem" (1908). On the Progressives' watch, Jim Crow white supremacy became secure from federal legal challenge and, thus, formed the first, and longest prevailing, racist polity of the twentieth century.

Gilman consistently criticized Jim Crow lynching, the color line, and the deplorable consequences of slavery. In 1916 she had the *Herlander* character Ellador denounce American white supremacy as "silly, wicked—and hypocritical." Nothing was more ridiculous than "Southern enthusiasts raving about the horrors of 'miscegenation' and then to count the mulattos, quadroons, octoroons, and all the successive shades by which the black race becomes white before their eyes." Herlander Ellador and her Ourlander husband Van argued about African Americans, he taking a defensive stance against her description of them as enforced aliens, insisting that "they are Americans, loyal Americans." Sarcastically roasting America's treatment of these "loyal Americans"—a tenth of the population denied citizenship, Ellador exclaimed: "You will let them serve you and fight for you—but that's all apparently."[40]

Unquestionably, Gilman's view of African Americans was assimilationist, entailing a judgment that all humans evolved but that different groups evolved at different paces under different conditions and stimuli. This reform Darwinist intellectual framework, which she shared with other Progressive Era social scientists (such as Edward Ross, Lester Ward, and William I. Thomas), abolitionists, and radical Republicans, militated against seeing many African Americans as currently equals of Caucasian Americans, despite her indignation about their unjust treatment.

Yet this same intellectual framework identified huge "advances" by African Americans relative to African peoples in Africa. Indeed, she stipulated that the gulf between the races after only fifty years since the end of slavery should surprise no one, given the denial of education under slavery, and the origins of many West African slaves. But she enjoined all to offer hope and assistance, due to the fact that "so many . . . in this brief time, have made such great progress." This same point was made by African American education-alists during the same period, who claimed that by the 1920s the achieve-ments of black Americans, in spite of drastic obstacles, were astonishing.[41]

Hence, Gilman's relative optimism about prospects for mutual coexis-tence and racial equality sharply distinguished her from many participants in contiguous debates on "the Negro problem." Nowhere here did she as-sert the immutable inferiority arguments of racist Jim Crow peers. Many of them decried education for African Americans due to their smaller brains, innate propensity to criminality, inability to achieve economic self-sufficiency and independence, and complete unfitness, ever, to vote or self-govern. For such "subjugationist" advocates, the best choices were con-finement to disenfranchised menial labor or, better still, exportation to re-colonize Africa. Others held that black Americans were so inferior that they were doomed to die out naturally and that, to this desirable end, whites need only ensure that laissez-faire neglect was state and local policy.[42]

In the face of Jim Crow denunciation of all plans to educate and "uplift" an allegedly permanent, backward underclass, Gilman's 1908 assimilation-ist proposal supported African Americans against virulent subjugationists. She suggested taking only those unable to self-support and enlisting them into an army of honorable employment and education, offering higher education for those able to benefit from it. Recruits would soon become self-supporting contributors to improvement and development. With su-perior teachers, managers, and supervisors, African Americans would "rise in social evolution," adding "millions to the value of the southern land." She goaded Southern subjugationists for ensuring that the South remained an "undeveloped country," suggesting that incapacity to implement her pro-posal, with its permanent benefits, would warrant a betterment scheme for those boasting their own superiority to African Americans.[43]

Her "developmentalist" proposal targeted Southern states, where in 1900 nearly 8 million residents included 90 percent of the nation's Afri-can Americans. Regionally concentrated, they formed almost a third of the Southern region's population, quite enough to rouse white "Redeemers" in the quest to thrust them decisively back into their imagined rightful place. A fresh brand of racism, "hysterical and harsh, proclaimed in legislature, country stores, and newspaper columns," animated these Jim Crow efforts, the specter of the "bestial New Negro" posed as a threat to white womanhood. So prevalent was this discourse that even Progressive, liberal publications like the *Nation* at times gave space to white southern viewpoints on the peril to their women posed by rapacious blacks.[44]

Indeed, the immediate stimulus not only to Gilman's "suggestion" but also to proposals by other commentators before and after hers was the escalating pattern of Southern interracial violence. She and fellow Progressives were shocked by the violence, torture, and annihilation of blacks at the hands of lawless whites. Collusive local Jim Crow authorities ignored atrocities, while studies found local police participating in one of every three reported lynchings. Frightening race riots and lynching in New Orleans and New York City (1900), Evansville, Indiana (1903), Atlanta, Georgia (1906), and Springfield, Illinois (1908), unleashed reform proposals of many kinds, including the foundation of the NAACP in 1909.[45]

Gilman's intervention here demonstrated Michael McGerr's finding that Progressives accepted partial or strategic segregation as a "shield" for protecting African Americans against wholesale murder. On the Progressives' watch, black disenfranchisement and segregationist policies were legalized state by state and ratified by a Southern-dominated Supreme Court. Many rationalized such deplorable measures as preferable to attempted genocide. In fact, Northerners were terrified of consequences should there be a mass influx from the South. From President Roosevelt down, a consensus evolved against federal intervention against Southern states' race-related decisions. A range of views about race obtained among Progressives, but the prevalence of neo-Lamarckian assimilationism permitted rationalization and acquiescence to Jim Crow segregation. Gilman and her peers believed that, thereby, lives would be spared to develop and progress, again called "uplift," embraced too by black leaders such as Booker T. Washington.[46]

Unquestionably, Gilman's 1908 *American Journal of Sociology* essay accorded with many prevailing Progressive believers in assumed then-present white superiority. If this is of course today unforgivable, in context it was worlds away from the racist proponents of inevitable black extinction by their inherent inability to survive. Her stance similarly departed from related but pseudohumanitarian racial policy, prominent, for instance, in Australian race relations history, of "smoothing the dying pillow" of Aboriginal Australians.[47]

Meanwhile, Gilman's 1908 "suggestion" was more interventionist than those proffered by most exercised Progressives since her scheme actually required Southern communities to take responsibility. They were to be accountable for the development, education, subsistence, health, accommodation, and welfare (for as long as necessary) of those African American inhabitants lacking independent self-support. Crucially, Southern states were to do so on a nonpartisan basis, to prevent this scheme from derailment by subjugationist administrations.

Given the framework here of shame, sympathy, anger, and fear over the various 1900s urban race riots, Gilman's readers did not see her suggestion as racial prejudice, unlike readers today, apt to impugn it as an instance of Gilman's obnoxious racism. For instance, her reviewer in the *Literary Digest* (1908) effectively promoted her "suggestion" by reproducing large slabs of it verbatim for readers unlikely to see the *American Sociological Review*, adding three comments.

First, however benign her motives, Gilman's "enlistment" would smack of the "enforced laboring" and "enslavement from which the writer is at such pains to distinguish it." Second, noble as was her important caveat that this provision be "kept out of politics," it was simply naive to think this likely or feasible in the South anytime "before the millennium." Hence, Gilman's scheme unwittingly risked deteriorating into "re-enslavement" in the hands of corrupt administrations. Third, by including only dependent and not self-supporting African Americans, Gilman then "admits at the outset that the 'problem' is one of status rather than of race." This latter specification accords with McGerr's characterization of Progressivism as fundamentally a class uplift project.[48]

Since Gilman proposed no such scheme for economically dependent whites in the south, however, her suggestion can appear racist to modern eyes. It is true that she did not write any "suggestion" on white Southern poverty, as Knight shrewdly observes. In 1908, however, her liberal and Progressive contemporaries did not make this objection. Perhaps this was because Southern whites monopolized or disproportionately benefited from all available forms of resource allocation—especially such education, health, housing, and welfare provision as existed. This unequal distribution was eloquently accounted for by African American peers whom Gilman admired, such as W. E. B. Du Bois and William Pickens. As Pickens put it, Jim Crow was "a contrivance to humiliate and harass the colored people and to torture them with finesse unequaled by the cruelest genius of the heathen world. . . . Jim Crow tortures the bodies and souls of tens of thousands hourly."[49]

More urgently, it was not poor and economically dependent whites who were targeted principally for lynching, murder, torture, and brutalization. It was vulnerable blacks who motivated Gilman's "suggestion." Their sufferings similarly inspired Jane Addams's polemic against "lily white" political parties, which excluded black interests from the democratic process. Equally, this concern animated Katharine Bement Davis's commendation of Du Bois's exposé of cultural and economic segregation of black Americans in Philadelphia. The considerable common ground between Gilman's stated assimilationist departure points and those proffered by Davis were striking. Davis contended: "1.The negro is here to stay. 2. It is to the advantage of all, both black and white, that every negro should make the best of himself. 3. It is the duty of the negro to raise himself by every effort to the standards of modern civilization and not to lower these standards in any degree." African Americans, then, did not threaten America or the feminist struggle for human status for women. If anything, it was indefensible "race prejudice" that, according to Gilman, threatened African Americans.[50]

BY CONTRAST, the later Gilman's concerns about immigrants were intense. In 1915, mourning the loss of wartime cultural unity, she wrote that "America draws no line but the color line, and there are many of us who would not draw that; but there are differences other than of race and color which give ground for serious consideration." She signaled that what is now called racism was despicable. The Jim Crow regime wasted resources in maintaining reprehensible racial bigotry. Alternatively, unrestricted immigration without assimilation presented serious dangers needing redress.[51]

Her concerns and rhetoric match historians' portraits of wartime and interwar anti-immigrant ethnocentrism. John Higham contends that Progressivism restrained and concealed declining American faith in unrestricted immigration. Declining Progressivism led even liberal editors to contend that excessive immigration generated no longer tolerable ills that imperiled democracy. The very concept of nativism was an American 1830s and 1840s coinage, anchored less in scientific evidence than in cultural representations. It was an intense opposition to "an internal minority on the ground of its foreign (i.e. 'un-American') connections," which translated into a "zeal to destroy the enemy of a distinctly American way of life." By the end of the war, Gilman was unquestionably motivated by nativism and "ethnocultural intolerance," as Higham and George M. Frederickson respectively define them.[52]

Yet feminist concerns also informed her steadily mounting criticisms of unrestricted immigration. Many immigrants, she observed, came from cultures more patriarchal than Progressive Era America. Sectarianism, too, informed her fusion of nativism and feminism, as she targeted Russian and other Slavic Jews and the Catholics of Italy and Ireland, prominent in the influx to New York and typical targets of anti-European nativism in the period. Her intemperate utterances further reflected her perception of potent threats to women's limited gains in the patriarchal character of these religions and cultures. Aghast at reports that "there are but 7 per cent native born of native ancestors" in New York City, she asked readers to imagine "Paris with but a fifth of its citizens French! London with but a fifth English—Berlin with but a fifth German." To this she added that one-third of New Yorkers were "Jews, and we know of the hundreds of thousands of Italians, Germans, and others."[53]

Also, she worried about demographic pressure from countries and cultures with unchecked birthrates. War was the ultimate masculism and the least auspicious framework for women's rights and truly progressive reforms. Gilman gave interwar nativism and ethnocentrism their most feminist face, making them feminist issues, forcefully articulated, along with her peers, in the context of interwar overpopulation anxieties. She used contemporary ethnic theories to buttress her critique of androcentrism. Ethnocultural intolerance enhanced the vigor and confidence of the analysis she pitched to her contemporaries.[54]

Differentiating between types of women's subordination, she wrote that "our use of sex has contributed to race progress a deteriorating influence. It can be roughly indicated that those peoples whose women are most completely denied freedom and growth remain the least progressive."[55] Here she introduced to prevailing scientific, ethnic, and evolutionary discourses her longstanding critique of sexual patterns and gender dynamics. Probably she thereby enlarged her reception as a serious thinker about contemporary problems, contributing to post-Progressive social policy debate. It was only scientific and accurate to acknowledge that all peoples of the world were at different stages of evolution.[56]

On this topic, Gilman cited modern scientific views. Historians of nativism trace the steady acceleration of new ethnic typologies from the turn of the century, reaching their 1910s apogee in the claimed superiority of the "Nordic" type over the "Alpine," "Celt," "Slav," and "Mediterranean." This so-called Nordic Spell appealed widely to academics, who wished to see ethnic differences analyzed on scientific bases. Physiological claims seemed stronger than the cultural tropes that were the usual stock of polemical eugenicists and Anglo-Saxon nativists. Higham identifies psychologists and geographers as examples of fields incorporating the Nordic ethos, giving it such authority that it was little wonder that a broad segment of educated opinion accepted racial nativism as "proved truths of science." Obviously, Gilman was no exception. Why would she be?[57]

Here, the earlier reform Darwinist tenet of evolutionary hierarchies due to differential rates of development became reconfigured by these supposedly scientific ethnic typologies that Gilman pushed forward. To expect, by fiat, that social evolution involved the even march of "all races to the same goal" was simply mistaken. Indeed, the "sea-weeds and mosses have not all become oaks and roses." Instead, she explained, evolution selects. If trying to improve corn, "you do not wait to bring all the weeds in the garden to the corn level before going on." The same applied to social evolution.[58]

As a result, just like Gilman, many public intellectuals abandoned their former sympathy for the plight of immigrants. The former Progressive reformer and journalist George Creel, for instance, began to denounce unassimilated immigrants as "so much slag in the melting pot." Indeed, the melting pot metaphor received unprecedented repudiation as a threat to democracy. Worse, its critics called it a hopelessly inaccurate characterization of the actual historical course of immigrant integration. Meanwhile, those earlier immigrant waves, which were relatively favored in new "scientific" ethnic typologies, joined the end-of-war uproar of the "tribal twenties." Scandinavian and German American groups asserted their own ethnic superiority in calls for ending or drastically reducing immigration. Proposed moratoria against "less desirables" ranged wildly, from as little as two and as much as fifty years.[59]

Gilman, however, did not participate in such moratoria or fixed-term immigration freezes. Instead, she wanted the entire rationale for unrestricted immigration rethought. As a socialist, she opposed the desire of big business for cheap labor in illiterate immigrants, as did trades unions. With ruthless Jim Crow exclusion of blacks from skilled labor with living wages, intense pressure and competition for jobs led some African American leaders to support restrictivism of various kinds, sentiments with which she sympathized. By 1920, according to Du Bois, even the beginnings of restricitivism, prior to the 1921 and 1924 immigration acts, had raised black men's and women's wages. Even more important, for women, "it has opened to them a sense of new avenues of earning a living," in a context in which high male unemployment obstructed marriages and thrust women and children into poverty. In such precarious circumstances, black support for restricting immigration becomes at least comprehensible, however deplorable the ethnocentrism.[60]

A further retrograde twang to interwar ethnocultural politics relevant to Gilman's interventions was a new virulence to anti-Semitism. Hitherto, historians contend that disparagement of Jews had blended within more general prejudice against southern and eastern European immigrants. Seemingly diverse press sources attributed the 1917 Russian Revolution to Jewish radicalism. Powerful interwar anti-Semitic propaganda spread from Czarist army officers to Henry Ford and the Ku Klux Klan, making anti-Semitism more distinctive, theorized, and mainstream than at any previous moment in American history. Despite her earlier condemnation of Christian prejudice against Jews, Gilman increasingly resented Jewish cultural separatism and refusal to assimilate into American cultural life. The more she contemplated and compared world religions, the more she blamed them for androcentric subjugation of women. On this count, Judaism seemed to be among the worst. In these views of the patriarchal character of immigrant groups and their threat to the hard-won and still unfinished project to secure equalitarian gains for women and girls, she was not alone. Rather, according to Thomas Peyser, this was a widely canvassed view among intellectuals like Ross and among the newspaper and magazine editors and their reading publics.[61]

Hence, Gilman increasingly highlighted ethnic specificity. If she had once dismissed the notion that superior peoples stood to be swamped by the inferior, war taught that "a conquering people is not necessarily superior to the conquered, and that social progress has been most seriously retarded by the destruction of more advanced societies by the less so." This accorded with the widespread "death of innocence" cultural nihilism found throughout early interwar European and American arts, letters, and memoirs. Gilman stressed barbarism toward women in some ethnic cultures. Hereby, she advanced nativist and American exceptionalist arguments that America was the best hope not only for women's advancement but also for all progressive change. These sentiments mirrored the markedly isolationist mood of interwar legislators and public opinion. She used gross and derogatory examples from "benighted" cultures. Only the most advanced civilizations and nations could position to end androcentrism—marked by the consignment of women to sex work—and move toward a human world, in which women and men alike shared race work. Here she invoked sex complementarity in the designation of both men and women in advanced cultures as superior to others, a point much discussed by her modern critics, addressed in chapter 12.

Conversely, she characterized other non-Western cultures as stagnant and brutal, effecting more extreme degradation and segregation of their women into what she termed "sex work." In other words, she sought to instruct contemporary Euro-American men on the costs of sex inequality by transcultural comparison. Thereby, she cast the dire implications of restricting women to sex work in ethnic terms, while imbuing ethnocultural antagonisms with sexualized dimensions.

Once again, however, her assimilationism meant that she did not claim that "backward" societies would never advance. On the contrary, social evolution meant that change toward more highly evolved forms was inevitable for all cultures, though it occurred at different rates. In the history of humanity, "savagery" had prevailed longest. Thus, postsavagery development was uneven. Some present cultures retained more features of savagery than others, revealing how presently civilized societies may once have functioned. For instance, men acting as women's "natural protector" was no more than fighting other men for their own possession of women, expressed most starkly in the harem of still savage societies: "In the veiled woman of the east, secluded, imprisoned, cut off from all contact with human life, we see the real climax of this much boasted 'protective instinct of the male'"[62]

Gilman's elaboration of the consequences of reform Darwinist discourses on the sexes and contemporary sexual relations was distinctive. Her sociologist friend Edward Ross entirely endorsed and was influenced by her views. He wrote to her in 1927 over the international controversy erupting when the American feminist doctor Katherine Mayo published *Mother India*. Mayo presented a sensationalized and horrifying account of Indian customs, such as child marriage and widow burning. Echoing Ward's earlier designation of India as the spiritual home of androcentric culture, Ross urged Gilman to skepticism toward Indian nationalist critiques of Mayo's book. His own book on overpopulation—*Standing Room Only?* (1927)—gave Mayo's descriptions "statistical expression." He denounced the oppression of Indian women, maintained by collusion between male British officials and male Indian leaders.[63]

A crucial part of Gilman's concern over immigration, then, was the now widely vaunted inassimilability of some immigrant groups. She tried to define "Americans" more exactly. Though a mixed people, she now contended that they were "mainly of English descent, mingled with the closely allied Teutonic and Scandinavian strains, of which indeed the English are compounded, together with some admixture of the Celt and Gael." These origins entailed a political disposition to "freedom and the capacity to get it." Added to these civic characteristics, these ethnic strains also had "a flexible progressiveness," as well as three attributes of the distinct American national character, namely: "inventive ingenuity, a patience and broad kindliness of disposition." Such ethnic features had positive implications for women. Here the feminist theorist she most admired, Olive Schreiner, strongly influenced her position on the ethnic origins of American national character.[64]

Schreiner identified historical and ethnic reasons for feminism emerging in northern Europe and its overseas settlements. Feminist leaders descended from "that old, Teutonic womanhood, which twenty centuries ago plowed its march through European forests and morasses beside its male companion." Moreover, Schreiner held that present feminist leaders had in them "the blood of a womanhood that was never bought and never sold; that wore no veil, and that had no foot bound." Those women had sexual companionship and equality in duty and labor with their men. It was still "the cry of the old, free Northern woman which makes the world to-day." Rhetorically, Schreiner posed the descent of Western feminist leaders from forefathers in a Teutonic memory, a logical outcome of ancestral emancipatory struggles: "We are the daughters of our fathers as well as our mothers. In our dreams we still hear the clash of the shields of our forebears as they struck them together before the battle and raised the shout of 'Freedom!' In our dreams it is with us still, and when we wake it breaks from our own lips! We are the daughters of those men."[65]

This view of Western European female ethnic heritage dovetailed with Progressive Era political theory that democracy originated in the Black Forest, spread among Teutons, Saxons, and Nordic peoples. Their disposition toward self-government became an "ethnic" characteristic in these portrayals. In turn, these peoples had a strong impact on American culture through early Dutch, German, and Scandinavian immigrants. This account matched the Nordic Spell accounts of ethnic hierarchy so popularized in America in the 1900s and 1910s.[66]

Gilman's experiences of a New York City with unrestricted immigration made her fear for democracy. Corrupt interests mobilized "ignorant peasants," who were enfranchised simply because they were men. Without the slightest understanding of Progressive Era reform issues in the public domain, the large so-called immigrant bloc could prove a retrograde force against feminist reforms. As discussed in chapter 5, suffragists widely attributed the failure of the 1915 New York referendum on woman suffrage to the immigrant vote. At the time, Gilman put the best face she could on the 1915 defeat. The fact that she and other public-spirited Progressive reformer women remained unenfranchised under these circumstances stung badly. It imported a sour and even bitter tone to subsequent references to immigrant men and politics. Suffragists recalled angrily enough chagrin at the Reconstruction polity's (at least ostensible) preference for African American men as voters on the basis of sex (however nominally, as it turned out, with the federally unchallenged reassertion of states' rights to racially restrict voting), rather than adult suffrage, including all women. Peyser perceptively notes that Gilman was horrified by ethnic hybridity or "the mongrelization of America," implied by America's "melting pot." Hers was a concern about politics, democracy, and the masculist state. Gilman also feared men's hybridization of women. In effect, she feared that ethnicity would trump sex, as it had before in American history, indeed in her lifetime.[67]

Hence, she dismissed the claim that immigration fostered democracy around the world and contributed special gifts to American life. Any country wanting a democracy can have one. No one can stop them. If they are not a citizenry interested in democracy at home, however, their immigrants might retard the development of the precious American democracy, which had finally admitted its women to full citizenship. Backward immigrants might "mix our physical stock and clog the half-grown 'body politic' with all manner of undemocratic peoples."

Gilman's interwar doubts about the great American experiment, when she declared some elements "inassimilable," greatly contrasted with her earlier optimism. This underscores, once again, the centrality of suffrage to her feminist political vision. Hence, it was feminist concerns, and reform Darwinist ones at that—her quest to secure women the means to end their evolutionary retardation through confinement to sex work and instead to contribute alongside men to race work and, thereby, to human progress—that underlay distinctively her convergence with other contemporaries opposing unlimited immigration. Gilman's nativist and assimilationist ethnocultural intolerance intensified in tandem with her investment in both feminism and Progressivism. It was for these reasons that the later Gilman joined other Progressives in seeking restrictions on unlimited immigration. Interestingly, her peer suffragist and feminist, Harriot Stanton Blatch, showed great and ethnocentric political alarm about the impact of voting immigrant men, a risk she did not perceive from African Americans. As more nuanced investigations of diverse Progressives emerge, it becomes even more apparent that views of race and those concerned with ethnicity and with population characteristics—as either positive or negative eugenics—did not yet constitute the species of unified worldview designated by comprehensive terms more common today.[68]

The later Gilman constantly assessed the implications of changing conditions for her longstanding reform Darwinist feminist analysis of women's oppression. Since reform Darwinism gave significance to aboriginality and ethnicity, her quest to end women's confinement to sex work led her to identify ethnic dimensions of the problem. Meanwhile, in her eloquent use of a public intellectual's bully pulpit, she asked her contemporaries to grasp the salience of sex distinctions for the great questions of the day. Her work lent a feminist slant to ethnocentric debates over unrestricted immigration.[69] Ironically, her priorities can seem reversed in her interwar work on birth control. Here it appears that her ethnic and demographic concerns contributed as much to her belated advocacy of birth control as feminist concerns.

A Reluctant Birth Controller

> During his [man's] period of supremacy he has so lavishly over-indulged this impulse that he has completely lost sight of its purpose, and now, with careful provision for birth control, he presents to the astonished mother of the world an urgent demand for a relationship wholly divorced from its reason for being, and yet which he calls "natural."
>
> *Charlotte Perkins Gilman,* His Religion and Hers *(1923)*

Gilman's conversion to birth control advocacy contravenes claims that her later years meant abandonment of issues related to women. The early and midcareer Gilman took at first a hostile then a skeptical stance, while the later Gilman gradually moderated her position toward a qualified support for legalized birth control. How the evolution of her thinking here unfolds on this matter is traceable through several publications from 1914 to 1932, as well as in her correspondence with birth control champions, Mary Ware Dennett (1872–1947) and Margaret Sanger (1879–1967), suffrage leader Carrie Chapman Catt, and Edward Ross. Indeed, she wrote more on this subject than on issues of race and ethnicity, yet Gilman scholars have said little about her views on birth control.[70]

Birth control highlights the historicity of feminism. Support for reproductive self-determination for women is often posed as a litmus test or a nonnegotiable criterion for judging anyone to be a feminist. Thus, scholars express dismay that historical forebears opposed birth control in favor of voluntary motherhood or reduced childbearing via conjugal continence or temperance—the right to say no to husbandly demands—in a context of monogamy. Even if sincere, such forebears were misguidedly shaped by repressive Victorian or Puritan attitudes toward women's sexuality, seeing sex as something men did to women, without admitting any equal urgency of female erotic desire. Forebears such as these disappoint successor feminists by stressing danger over pleasure in feminist sexual thought. Commentators today assert a different and arguably postwar "truth of sex." Understandably, they judge feminists of Gilman's ilk as failing to bequeath a liberating erotic theoretics for their feminist successors—voluntary motherhood without birth control being at best naive and, at worst, willfully prudish.[71]

Gilman's initial stance on birth control derived from her reform Dar-

FIGURE 43. Margaret
Sanger and sister, Ethel
Byrne, in Federal court,
ca. 1917 (The Schlesinger
Library, Radcliffe Insti-
tute, Harvard University
MC 444-149-3)

winist feminist framework. Events of the 1910s challenged her to revise her
stance. Some of her earliest references to birth control corresponded with
the 1914 New York furor over Margaret Sanger's prosecution for advocating
"practical methods of prevention" in her newspaper *Woman Rebel.* Sanger,
as quoted in the *New York Times,* said "that she considered Charlotte Perkins Gilman, feminist, a conservative and a reactionary, who had lost courage by obtaining too much publicity."[72] Here Sanger deplored the lack of
public support for her cause from feminist public intellectuals like Gilman,
neither addressing nor comprehending reasons for Gilman's position.[73]

Why would she? A generation away from Gilman in age, Sanger was
nineteen when *Women and Economics* (1898) was published. Though sharing Gilman's socialist convictions, Sanger was a member of the International
Workers of the World and embraced a "direct action" concept of politics.
Notwithstanding Sanger's rebuke, however, newspapers identified Gilman
among a group of suffragists, feminists, and club women called Sanger's
"friends." Among other things, these "friends" issued invitations to a large
dinner that Sanger would address, visited the courts for Sanger's appear-

ances, and petitioned the state to empanel a jury of women as her peers, claiming that she could receive no justice at the hands of an all-male jury. Some of those involved included Gilman's friends and co-workers Harriot Stanton Blatch, Mary Ritter Beard, Fola La Follette, George Middleton, and Elsie Clews Parsons.[74] Support for birth control, to relieve the misery of working-class wives overburdened with children, was becoming orthodox in Gilman's circles on feminist and socialist grounds, adjectives widely used to describe her standpoints.

What, then, were Gilman's objections and how did they change? She objected to parts of the case for birth control pertinent to sex subjection and her reform Darwinist critique of androcentric culture. She had repeatedly held that a hallmark of women's economic dependence in androcentric culture was their obligatory submission to men's demand for "constant indulgence," thereby retarding human evolution. She saw manifestos in favor of women becoming sexually more like men—involving assertions of male sexual practices as the "natural" human norm—as reactions against her well-known sexual thought. An obnoxious part of this sexual doctrine was to deprecate as almost "unnatural" the sequel to sexual impulses in other animals, the consequence most centrally affecting women: reproduction.[75]

Chary of free love advocates, she saw that "increased indulgence," urged by figures like the prolifically published Dr. William J. Robinson, rested on birth control. Otherwise, sexually emancipated women might bear twenty children apiece.[76] Gilman rebuked Robinson energetically, but why? Robinson portrayed coitus as "the expression of a perfectly natural instinct, an instinct indispensable to the perpetuation of the race, an instinct often irresistible and untamable." His sentiments were inimical to Gilman's denaturalizing of male sexual mores and behaviors. She resented the androcentric grandstanding of the male role in reproduction: "When will men learn that 'the perpetuation of the race' depends upon the woman's capacity for bearing children, not upon the man's capacity for enjoying himself?" More tellingly, if perpetuation of future generations were truly the rationale for "constant indulgence" of what she called "this originally periodic impulse," she noted dryly that, statistically, any father in twenty annual unions in the course of his spouse's reproductive years could comfortably achieve this object—as was the practice of other higher animal species.

Given what she had first called in *Women and Economics* the present "disordered and oversexed condition," she did offer a caveat: "I am not saying that there is no other claim to be made for this union quite aside from parentage." But she took issue with disguising such a claim as the quest for population continuity, as if it were imperiled. She detected a coercive misogyny lurking in Robinson's gratuitous characterization of unmarried, presumably celibate women as "angular, jaundiced, anemic, pimply, flat-chested and crabbed old maids," suffering from hysteria "in its thousand and one manifestations, from lack of sexual satisfaction." She rebuked this slander on the "surplus women" of war-torn Europe, noting the counter examples both of healthy, happy, attractive, unmarried women and of pathetically down-trodden wives: "It is unworthy of a scientific mind to let feeling so run away with reason."[77]

The heat of her reactions to Robinson suggests that this dispute threatened her central analyses. A year later she published a longer *Forerunner* article simply titled "Birth Control" on the strengths and weaknesses of typical arguments. Three seemed significant: economic pressure, women's welfare, and the desire for sexual freedom or what she called "free indulgence"—free that is, from pregnancy.

Against the first, she objected that humans determined economic conditions. For an intelligent humanity to accept arrangements that did not secure for everyone a fair standard of living, so that all could enjoy their families, was contemptible. And to renounce parenthood as an alternative to changing miserable conditions was appalling, a superficial palliative postponing the more basic need for socialist transformation. On women's welfare, the second argument, and Sanger's concern, Gilman conceded that women had to be able to say that, given limited means of support, they would have no (or no more) children. The third ground, pregnancy-free indulgence, provoked her main reply, since it was the most broadly endorsed of the three, yet for her the most objectionable. Despite the question of the "biological base—what is sex union for," she held that "practically everyone" now believed that, unlike in all other species, human (hetero) sexuality had a special psychological function, requiring constant exercise. Centuries of androcentric art, literature, music, and religions advanced this view. Yet Gilman called it flimsy and emotional. It caused a "disproportionate development of preliminary sex emotions and functional capacities, to the detriment of the parental emotions and capacities, and to the grave injury of the higher processes of human development."

Hitherto, Gilman had objected that androcentric culture's sexual patterns thwarted nature, manifest in periodic female sex selection prevailing in the nonhuman animal kingdom. Yet nature was precisely the ground appropriated by advocates of constant indulgence. Gilman instanced alcohol use and abuse in now noting that plenty of actions satisfied nature without being good, healthy, beneficial, or desirable. Moreover, she questioned the "height" of the allegedly higher function of constant sex—higher than mere reproduction? Since her antagonists on this topic invariably drew comparisons with hunger, food, and eating, she too used these examples. Agreeing that, beyond mere nutrition, food could provide hospitality, entertainment, and aesthetic pleasure, one "would hardly seek to justify a ceaseless gluttony, or even an erratic consumption of unnecessary food on those grounds."

Against "natural," she pitted "normal," recasting men's excessive erotic demands as "abnormal." Rather than serving these allegedly higher functions, "the visible sum of our shameful diseases, sufferings, poverty, crime, degeneracy" suggested that prevailing practices were based on "some wrong condition." If one child a year would be the result for each woman subjected to "natural" constant indulgence, "biological law" countered: namely, that "reproduction is in inverse proportion to individuation." For Gilman, the "individuation of women" was a contemporary reality and historic breakthrough. The woman movement and feminism were its visible signs. When humans achieved full individuation, perhaps they would crave union more "naturally," possibly only for brief annual periods, and, thus, even without "prevention," average birth rates would be two or three children per family.

That was all ahead. In the meantime, she conceded, women in difficult conditions had the right to refuse more than this average or to refuse to bear any—an important qualification of her general stance. She also deplored celibacy as abnormal and, presumably, did not believe that just because a couple had reproduced their two or three children, they would then become celibate. Indeed, she added that, "reputable physicians or other competent persons" should teach birth control methods.[78]

These significant concessions signal that her underlying objection was not to birth spacing or even prevention altogether, if that was women's choice. It was that birth control might become, if virtually compulsory, a masculist tool. Women's sexuality would be defined solely in androcentric terms. Birth control might aid men's instincts to undermine monogamy, just when she hoped that moves to end regulated prostitution might strengthen it in women's and children's interests. Normalizing an expectation of birth control might intensify andocentric erotic pressures on women and marriage contract's coerciveness as to sexual servitude. In evolutionary terms, monogamy developed in species for the benefit of the young needing the continued care of parents, not for the pleasure of constant sexual indulgence by one or both parents. She later described women's "weary disillusionment, an unromantic dutiful submission to an unromantic physical indulgence" as the erotic norm in most androcentric marriages.[79]

Her opposition, then, was less to birth control itself, than to its deployment by enemies of women's emancipation, who could reinscribe dependency and toxic forms of femininity on women—hence her caustic rebuke of Theodore Roosevelt's tirades about educated women's "race suicide." Just as she had rallied promptly to the defense of the suffragettes when under attack by the Antis in the 1910s, so she defended college-educated feminists and career women—the latter proving less likely to marry, and when they did, used birth control and bore fewer babies than other women. Lowering birthrates and death rates advanced civilization, and none contributed more than, as she put it, this "heroic generation of women who have grown faster than the men of their times could appreciate, and whose work has helped the world on."[80]

In 1922 Gilman took up her pen against psychoanalysis and in Sanger's own *Birth Control Review*. Its advocates vowed to combat "sexual repression" in the interests of mental health and civilization. Here she expanded her controversial objections to the rhetoric of some birth control advocates. Sharpened in fierce debates with younger intellectuals, she clarified her position in "Back of Birth Control": "Birth Control does not seem a basic measure at all, but one seeking to eliminate a consequence while leaving the cause untouched. It is no harm, it is doubtless doing good, but it is too popular with those who go on doing old evil with a new assurance. . . . For the crushed over-bred mother it would mean a vast improvement in her condition and that of her family. Long before men are able to outgrow this condition of excessive desire, they will be willing at least to restrict the consequences." If male power over women remained the context for this "excessive desire," Gilman baulked at the claim that birth control would permit the expression of "suppressed desires"—a "lingering echo" of the much longer pattern from early in the unwritten human history of "a world cult of indulgence"—man's gratifying his erotic desires "either in his household in peace; or anybody's household in war."[81]

Psychoanalytically authorized libertarianism, facilitated by birth control, pointed in exactly the opposite direction from Gilman's quest for women's emancipation. She sought reduced emphasis on sex functions, so that women might rejoin the human race and contribute to its progress. When "fully enslaved and held helplessly under dominant male tutelage," women had no options but to remain the objects of male use. She called for change since "the real trend of the woman's movement is away from the long abuse of this relationship." Though birth control spared women, especially the poor, from "enforced childbearing," she feared it left no cultural space for a female sexuality consistent with race progress.

Meanwhile, Gilman resisted the "inevitablism" and "economic catastrophism" of 1920s population explosion debates, whose participants exhorted women to affect "control," while exempting men's sexual prerogatives. She also found reference to the "menace" of women's reproduction by population biologist Raymond Pearl particularly irritating in pathologizing maternity. Yet she still insisted that women had the inalienable right to decide if conditions they faced militated against reproduction, to which no unwilling woman should be compelled. Since most "birth control" methods were barrier forms, and used in the context of a continuing faulty theory of ovulation, abortion remained a major form of birth control.[82]

English socialist-feminist birth controller and sex reformer, F. W. Stella Browne (1882–1955), wrote a rejoinder to Gilman, calling her a Puritan who would sacrifice "quite half the Art and Literature of the World in her dislike of sexual expression." Instead, insisted Browne, birth control was "the key to sexual liberty." Her response clearly stung Gilman, who made several later references to the unfair characterization of her objections to birth control as Victorian or Puritan. Rather, she implored women to recognize the treacherous nature of androcentric moral discourse. Once upon a time, all emphasis was on control of women by individual men; and women were told they lacked men's strong sex drives and "imperative instincts." Now, she pointed out, it is "quite otherwise. All that elaborate theory of female chastity, that worship of virginity, goes by the board, and women are given a reversed theory—that they are just the same as men, if not more so; our 'double standard' is undoubled and ironed flat—to the level of masculine desire."[83]

BY 1927, her emphasis had further shifted. Now applauding Sanger's demands for the protection of women, especially of the working class "on strictly feminist grounds," she regretted the injury to the birth control movement's reputation caused by those who advocated unnaturally excessive sex indulgence. Here she faced the pressing reality of the majority of women's situations, that is, that they lived in marriages. Husbands demanded conjugal rights and, by custom and belief, "needed" frequent intercourse for health, sanity, fidelity, and the stability their families. The earliest sex frequency surveys taken in the 1920s found average rates of marital coitus as three to four times a week in the couples in their twenties, two to three times in the thirties, one to two in the forties, and weekly to monthly with aging. Without birth control, then, wives had to capitulate to the "excessive breeding" so detrimental to race progress or submit to the risk of impairment and death from the "loathsome" practice of abortion, the prevalence of which in "Ourland" (that is, America in 1916) horrified the enlightened women of "Herland."[84]

Acknowledging all these factors, Gilman allowed that birth control was a "feminist" issue. Nonetheless, she held that prevailing feminist approaches to birth control were individualistic and emotional rather than social or collective in import. Thus she urged that an "active sense of social motherhood is desperately needed among the women of today, if we are to put a stop to war, to cease producing defectives, and to begin conscious improvement of our stock." She now outlined the importance of birth control for solving world overpopulation and generating peace, in order to broaden Sanger's feminist birth control advocacy. Just as she had urged a broader, multifocused woman suffrage movement in the 1900s and "larger feminism" in the 1910s, in the 1920s she advocated a larger birth control movement. The demand for birth control had to encompass world population control, world peace, and eugenics. She did not primarily support birth control as a woman's right, though she admitted the importance of freeing overburdened mothers from further suffering. At best, birth control was the lesser of other evils, already signifying women's disadvantage. Birth control was damage control. It was the disastrous state of the human sex relation itself that required fundamental change. For Gilman, birth control mitigated consequences rather than resolving the problem of androcentric sex relations.[85]

When in the late 1920s she advocated birth control, her reasons were neither libertarian nor in the feminist cause of erotic equality. She did not conceive the issue at an individual level. Instead, it was the question of the human stock—and through it, race progress—that moved her to active support for birth control. If there was no immediate prospect of the great mass of the population reducing injurious and excessive forms of sex indulgence, then the consequences stood to haunt the future of the human race. Filling America with peoples even less promising than the existing population posed an immediate threat to prospects for the transformations she desired. Birth control was one strategy to contain negative impact on hard-won gains for race progress. In the short term, then, birth control might be the only way to reduce the evolutionary menace of "the unfit" and the ill consequences of excessive sex indulgence. Therefore, she saw birth control as an obligation of the poorest and least fit of parents. They needed encouragement in this social responsibility. Archaic laws suppressing contraceptive knowledge must be overturned while the pernicious effects of backward religious prohibitions against birth control should be discredited.[86]

One of Gilman's central projects was to theorize population dynamics, human species history, sexual contracts and their biological consequences. The intensification of nativist, anti-Semitic, anti-immigrant, and ethnocentric discourses stimulated her to grapple with these problems. Indeed, a key part of her eugenically inspired conversion to birth control advocacy was connected to the horror of war and hopes for peace, as well as to concerns about immigration. As she explained in her 1927 article, "Progress through Birth Control," countries with unchecked birthrates would inevitably seek imperialist expansion. This posed Russia, China, and Africa as looming threats to world peace, as Germany had been.

She partly formed these views in dialogue with Edward Ross. His travels in China, India, and several other developing countries informed his alarmist position on the demographic necessity for birth control. He became close to Margaret Sanger and an indefatigable worker for her cause, a major theme in his correspondence with Gilman and other colleagues across the 1920s and 1930s. Ross was crucial in her conversion: "So, we are faced with a choice of three courses: shall we allow the unchecked increase of population, till all . . . peoples either mixed, or stratified in castes? Shall we allow that unchecked increase and fight continually for our places in the sun? Or shall we keep population within rationally chosen limits?"[87]

Even with her caveats, Sanger noticed Gilman's shift of emphasis. They met in 1931, and, despite Sanger having publicly criticized Gilman in 1914, she asked Gilman to help the cause. Sanger and co-workers believed they had the numbers to revoke laws declaring birth control materials and information "obscene," permitting instead medical dissemination of devices and supplies. She asked not only for Gilman's endorsement but also her testimony before the House Ways and Means Committee in 1932. Susan B. Anthony had asked this same favor thirty-five years before on woman suffrage. Gilman (by now diagnosed with breast cancer) was delighted to serve. She testified: "I wish any of you would for the moment use your imagination and think of what it is to the woman, either by coercion or compulsion or persuasion to have forced upon her, as it were, another life within her to carry, to bear, to bring forth, to nurse, when she does not want to. When she does want to she is free to. There is nothing to prevent her. The whole thing hinges on that; the woman who does not want more children must not be made to bear them." Just as Gilman's 1896 congressional testimony belied the claim that she was not significantly involved in the suffrage campaign, so here, her testimony confounds the claim that the later Gilman no longer concerned herself with feminist issues.

Sanger appreciated Gilman's contribution. Gilman replied that it "was a pleasure to be there and we both know that all this pressure steadily counts. Each succeeding 'failure' is like another wave for a rising tide." In the same year, Gilman published her last article on birth control, "Birth Control, Religion, and the Unfit":

> Personal is the protest of the woman, who after all is more immediately concerned in the matter of birth than the man. Must she, if worn, exhausted, usually tortured, often killed in the process, bear children regardless of her own wish or ability to the detriment of the entire family? Or may she choose, saying "Not this year" or "Not till we can afford it," or "Six is enough"? . . . Child-bearing is not so easy and painless as birth control. . . . It is for the women, bearers and rearers of children to decide on the numbers needed.[88]

Gilman attended further national meetings at Sanger's behest, significantly, the 1934 national convention of Sanger's Birth Control League, explaining to Carrie Chapman Catt that birth control was "a thing we've got to have if we are to ever have lasting peace." Sanger praised Gilman's 1934 convention speech as "an inspiration to many of us to hear you present and to hear you speak with your usual clarity and force." On the prospect of Gilman speaking at Smith College, Sanger observed that those "young things will have an ideal to live up to, as I had after I heard you speak for the first time years ago."[89] Thus, Gilman found in birth control a means of relieving population pressure within and beyond America, fusing her eugenic and feminist concerns.

NEW INTELLECTUAL positions disturbed Gilman's arguments connecting historical change, evolution, and human species progress with "abuse of the sex-function," causing species retardation and deterioration. This forced her to reconfigure her analysis. By the late 1920s and early 1930s, her analyses of sexuality and birth control as related to divorce, eugenics, and population issues had become difficult to reconcile with competing approaches. She remained preoccupied throughout her "later" period, however, by sex, sexuality, and related customs and mores, which pervaded whatever topic she discussed. Even on other matters, such as immigration or ethics, the impact on women and sexual relations undergirded the analysis.

Other constants were her openness to change and her interest in science and technology. To the end of her life she adapted to new opportunities and media. Seeing great didactic and ethical possibilities in film, she explored the possibilities of screenplay writing in 1921. Meanwhile, in 1933, learning of her cousin's Lyman's move into radio, she wrote him about "The Yellow Wall-paper": "Look here, I've had an idea! . . . Why wouldn't that make a

FIGURE 44. Portrait of Grace
Ellery Channing (1862–1937),
1915. Inscription (verso): "GECS,
S.F. 1915" (The Schlesinger
Library, Radcliffe Institute, Har-
vard University 2005-M125-1-31).

gorgeous monologue! Stage setting of the room and the paper, the four windows—the moonlight on the paper—changing lights, and movement—
and the woman staring. I could do it myself, in a drawing room and make
everybody's flesh creep; but I think it would make a real superior thing on
the stage. I thought Eva Le Gallieu—could she do it? I've met her. Perhaps
Kate Hepburn would consider it."[90] What an ironic intuition. With the
new generation's inattention to the large nonfiction oeuvre of her reform
Darwinist feminist analysis, she seized on the creepy 1892 story with which
she had entertained friends in evening readings in California so long ago.[91]

Even when Gilman was in her last months, suffering from shingles, lung
complications of her cancer, and unable to converse, she still wrote, remaining provocative, declamatory, and often very witty. To her cousin Lyman she
not only confided her suicide plans but also expressed her gratitude for his
financing Grace Channing Stetson's trip to Pasadena to be with her and her
daughter Kate at that critical time. She mentioned a Miss Seuter, a friend
of Grace's since 1876 and a "third mother" of Kate's, now sadly failing from
heart disease and also deaf. Describing the three of them there in Kate's
care, Gilman quipped that "we are a sorry bunch of old ladies!" Resisting to
the end, she added the caveat that had "this extraneous enemy not attacked
me"—referring to her cancer—"I should have continued to be a very agile

old party for some years yet." She arranged for Lyman to publish in *Forum* her final article, "The Right to Die," a few months after her death.[92]

She insisted that individuals had the right to decide when disease and disability made life unendurable. The right to control one's own life formed the core of the article and the record of "a previously noble life is precisely what makes it sheer insult to allow death in pitiful degradation. We may not wish to 'die with our boots on' but we may well prefer to die with our brains on." Wanting no funeral or memorial, and determined to engage with social and political topics, even after her death, Gilman arranged for this article's publication on her own suicide to provoke public debate. The *Forum* commissioned articles for and against, while old friends and admirers published letters defending her against detractors.

Anticipating the usual arguments, she spiritedly observed the hypocrisy in public prating about the sanctity of life if terminally ill people asked to be released from agony and disability, when no such concern had aided lives up to that point. In relation to murderous and unrepentant criminals, she found the anti–capital punishment argument for the sanctity of life especially trying when suddenly applied at the point of death to "a life neglected and corrupted from babyhood." Having nursed her own dying mother in 1892–93, she was keenly sensitive to the burden for adult daughters, especially those providing protracted hospice care. She determined to be no such burden on Kate, once it was clear that nothing more could be done to ease her own pain.

In 1883, her very first published article extolled bodily self-determination and the importance of women making their bodies fit and strong. Now, fifty-two years later, her final article again centered on corporeal autonomy, dignity and self-sovereignty. Her final words by no means sounded defeated or sad. She was battling to the end the sentimental old ideas and emotions preserved in "our mental attics," urging her peers to be progressive, humane, and efficient, reducing burdens not only on the terminally ill and permanently disabled but also on their female relatives.[93]

To know that Gilman died looking forward, still anticipating her beloved human world, wishing to fly, to preach in new media, to see modern women crash through all remaining barriers to their humanness mitigates somewhat the tragedy of the frustrations, poverty, and unpublished works of her final years. The later Gilman sought movement, embracing, as controversially as ever, the issues of the day affecting women and sexual relations. We can be sure she died with both brains and boots on.

In the winter of 1933, cousin Lyman threw Gilman a party with sixty guests, many young people. Standing on a box, as she recalled, she "discoursed for an hour or so," which made her very happy, relieving her misgivings that she was an irrelevance to the modern generation, "young things just out of College who had no use for any prewar stuff (unless bottled)"—wittily referring to newly available vintage wines with the recent lifting of Prohibition. She told Lyman that "I want so much to do something that our discontented young people will read. . . . One is no longer a dim memory but becomes a present, vital force."[94]

CHAPTER TWELVE

Gilmaniana Today

SATURDAY, 21 FEBRUARY 1891 [San Francisco].
Find that Uncle Edward and Nellie have arrived
at the Dexters.... Uncle Edward says—"You are
getting to be a famous woman my dear!" Says
"Similar Cases" is a great "campaign document."

Diary of Charlotte Perkins Gilman

GILMANIANA FLOURISHES today as never before. Since 1975, nearly
eight hundred publications and scholarly projects specifically have addressed Gilman's life or work, while hundreds more have referred to her in
other contexts—and this is a conservative estimate. Since 1995, regular international conferences address her work, while a Charlotte Perkins Gilman
Society newsletter documents publications, new primary sources, events,
and Gilman-related news. The next most studied earlier American feminist
is Elizabeth Cady Stanton, with about two hundred publications since 1975,
many centered on analysis of her rhetorical strategies and speeches. All the
signs are that Gilmaniana will continue unabated. Yet Gilman has never
been so controversial.[1]

Debate centers on the character of her work and its significance for
feminism today. The seeds of the current upsurge were sown during the
1970s and 1980s, when newly inspired feminist scholars, sometimes now
classified as "second wave" feminists, joyously claimed Gilman as their worthy ancestor. Their presentist portrayals have generated considerable debate with regard to Gilman's stances on class, socialism, race, eugenics, and
ethnicity. As a result, much Gilmaniana today is not only critical but even
hostile to the retention of Gilman in the feminist theory canon, many of
them penned by so-called third-wave feminists.[2]

This shift in approaches to Gilman is inseparable from wider shifts in
contemporary U.S. feminist theory and politics. Scholars commonly pe-

riodize feminism today in terms of the aforementioned "waves." Conventional typology casts the "first wave," incorporating woman suffrage and beyond, as slumped during the 1920s, to be succeeded by the second wave, of the Women's Liberation movement commencing in the late 1960s. In turn, this was followed by the "third wave," arising in the 1990s and still ascendant. This metaphor of waves proves problematic, not least because of the implied trough in between them and an oversimplified tidiness that mismatches a more complex history of overlapping theories and political priorities. Arguably, different typologies would better characterize debates within feminism. From its beginnings in the Euro-American political lexicon, feminism has been disputed, that between Ellen Key and Gilman in the 1910s but one example.[3]

Notwithstanding conceptual disadvantages with the wave metaphor, it is plain that the bulk of Gilman critics identify with either the second or the third waves. Insofar as Gilman became a so-called second-wave feminist icon, her fortunes today partly mirror those of second-wave scholars and activists in portrayals by third-wave critics. This latter stance is founded on denunciation of the failures and limitations of the second wave. Third wavers stress differences or the factors dividing women rather than "sisterhood" and common cause, finding the latter too often a smokescreen for the covert privileging of white middle- to upper-class heterosexual women's perspectives.[4]

From fields such as critical literary theory, new race history, whiteness studies, cultural studies of religion, postcolonialism, and antiracism, new feminist critics coming of age in the 1980s and 1990s question Gilman's place in any feminist canon. They find her almost criminally negligent on issues of class and, most notably, race and ethnicity. Contributions of this kind by scholars like Lanser, Peyser, Bederman, Hausman, Newman, Kaplan, Fessenden, Weinbaum, cited in previous chapters, have been widely discussed. Their work grounds the view that Gilman's feminism was inseparable from racism, and hence all discussion of her neglecting the significance of this crucial dimension will be fundamentally flawed. Questioning the terms for study of historical forms of feminism and feminist cultural production, they indict "business as usual" and apolitical Gilmaniana in literary studies, still by far the largest area of work on Gilman—dismissing much of it as collusive hagiography. Even those scholars attempting to both accommodate third-wave criticisms of Gilman and, yet, still attend to her life and work can dismay the former critics. This "accommodate and attend" strategy has been called the "mixed legacy" approach, the title of a Gilmaniana anthology on her work published in 2000. Critiques of mixed legacy approaches to Gilman often proceed, as did earlier praise, from presentist criteria, as elaborated below.[5]

In view of such contention, there is no longer much consensus on Gilman and, hence, on her significance for the history of American feminism. This stands in stark contrast to her stature thirty or forty years ago. This final chapter analyzes recent and politicized Gilman commentary and its impact for the subject of this book.

Waves and Waves of Gilmaniana

> There is much in her social philosophy which is valid today. . . . Her description of male experience as normative is one which feminists today continue to affirm. Gilman utterly rejected any suggestion that male dominance is natural. . . . The debt of Second Wave feminism to Charlotte Perkins Gilman is a profound one, one which we slowly repay as we continue to build upon her radical contributions to the first wave.
>
> *Maureen L. Egan, "Evolutionary Theory in the Social*
> *Philosophy of Charlotte Perkins Gilman" (1987)*

One explanation for the distinctive characteristics of Gilmaniana today is that earlier Gilman scholars often proceeded from 1970s and 1980s feminist concerns, as Egan's praise demonstrates. These scholars personally identified with Gilman as feminist prophet for current feminist issues. Hence, Gilman's prescience, that is, the extent to which she anticipated later feminist concerns, determined her increasingly canonic stature among these commentators.[6]

Many 1970s and 1980s feminist commentators praised her unreservedly: Gilman was "the early feminist most closely embodying the assumptions and aims of the contemporary women's movement," whose critique of taking male experience as normative, as Egan notes, "feminists today continue to affirm." By transcending the sexist biologism of her era, some called Gilman a prophet for later theories of gender socialization, conditioning, and cultural construction. Holding the sexes to be innately similar, her uproar against women's inequality resonates with feminists today, especially her recognition as well that "men were going to have to be a necessary element in the liberation of women." Gilman was among the first to highlight the sex division of labor, a still-debated feminist theory problem. She also highlighted the importance of "educating future generations to create a humane and nurturing environment."[7]

Prophetic again, she theorized "gender," before its feminist post-1970 usage, according to sociologists Kimmel and Aronson. Gilman also foreshadowed later feminist analyses of reproduction and the sexed body, according to cultural studies critics, linking them with prospects for women's emancipation. Presaging theoretical focus on "the body," Gilman defined the female body as a "product of both biological and social evolution," echoing contemporary feminist theorist Elizabeth A. Grosz's designation of the sexed body as the materiality of sex, showing that a "redefinition of 'biological experience' is not a new problem in feminist thought." However, feminist critics tended to value Gilman's significance by her likeness to current luminaries. Her anticipation of present feminist concerns proves to be a problematic basis for understanding Gilman's contribution to the history of feminist theory. It is less than helpful to have her cast as "prewriting" contemporary French feminist theorist, Luce Irigaray, or to view her concept of "the spatial" as enhanced in value by resembling that French philosopher, Michel Foucault. As third-wave feminist critic Seitler remarks, this work often suffered "from the much noted problem of presentism," whereby texts were treated as confirmations of contemporary feminism, proof "of the ongoing fight for liberation."[8]

Moreover, the publication of her extensive personal writings made Gilman the person all too familiar—an easy subject for reader identification. With her girlhood through many of her adult diaries, imaginings, notes, and letters painstakingly transcribed, annotated, edited, and published, Gilman can seem "knowable" and familiar in ways unusual for other theorists and intellectuals. This approach had some positive effects for 1970s and 1980s feminist scholarship and activism. Designating Gilman as a precursor or prophet, however, has led to the problem of overidentification, often signaled by scholars referring to her as "Charlotte," rather than "Gilman," as they would, and do, refer to "Freud" rather than "Sigmund" or "Ward" instead of "Lester." Of course, Gilman is not the first historically significant woman theorist to receive this treatment. As Frankel notes, scholarly devotees insist on addressing anarchist and birth control advocate, Emma Goldman (1869–1940) on a first name basis "deliberately inverting the once demeaning social practice of depriving women of surname formality or simply expressing a deeply felt sense of intimacy." The same problem can be found in work on Margaret Sanger and on many other feminists and politically active female figures. Nonetheless, the effect in earliest Gilmaniana keeps the focus on Gilman's personality and psychology rather than on her theoretical endeavors.[9]

Perhaps even more problematic than commentator identification with Gilman via presentist criteria has been its obverse. Especially since the 1990s, critics condemn Gilman for failing to anticipate current values and ethics. A sequel to previous overinvestment, then, has been denunciation of a Gilman found to have been incorrigibly mired in problematic discourses of her own era. She turns out to have been a Progressive after all—and just when revisionist historiographical scrutiny recasts its advocates as troubling if not downright retrograde. Her prolific published and private writings, which at first permitted admiring feminist identification, now fuel detractors' fierce denunciations. As a precursor for feminism, she becomes an embarrassing compendium of elitist, racist, anti-Semitic, nativist, and imperialist discourses to be exposed, denounced, and routed out. These discoveries, critics argue, mandate her downgrading in the feminist canon or, at least, a full exposé of the contamination in any current feminism indebted to her—recommendations both inquisitorial and epidemiological.[10]

Historians will find self-identified Gilman commentators from both second and third waves as standing in need of some correction. Their claims and arguments are distorted in varying degrees by presentism and a telling lack of attention to context and contingency. The problem of presentism, then, is crucial here for understanding the increasingly critical portrayals of Gilman newly prominent since the 1990s. "Presentism" here is meant in the classic historiographical sense, dated from about 1916 in the *Oxford English Dictionary* (but possibly in use in this sense since the 1870s), namely, "a mode of analysis in which present-day ideas and perspectives are anachronistically introduced into depictions or interpretations of the past," a mode whose inevitable distortions modern historians usually seek to avoid. An examination of criticism of Gilman with regard to class, socialism, race, eugenics, and ethnicity help to instantiate this problem in Gilmaniana today.[11]

Class and Comrade Gilman

> There's a hot breath at the keyhole
> And a tearing as of teeth!
> Well do I know the bloodshot eyes
> And the dripping jaws beneath!
> There's a whining at the threshold—
> There's a scratching at the floor—
> To work! To work! In Heaven's name!
> The wolf is at the door!
>
> Charlotte Perkins Gilman, "The Wolf at the Door" (1893)

Elitism is a central charge leveled by commentators and critics against Gilman. The evidence related to Gilman and class, however, proves to be complex. Critics have called her, variously, upper middle class, petit bourgeois, class biased, or class blind, refusing to see her as a socialist, charging that she failed to challenge either women's responsibility for "domestic organization" or "the hierarchy of social and economic class." Hayden, for instance, charges that Gilman's concerns fixed a conservative response to "the consequences of industrialization and urbanization" on the middle class, her reform proposals amounting to little more than a petit bourgeois solution to the "servant problem." Moreover, some claim that she carried the distinct cultural capital of her Beecher lineage, which she shamelessly paraded for all it could gain her. Gilman's alleged class prejudices seem ironic to one biographer, given her refusal to have male experience be universalized, while too often "universalizing her own."[12]

Alternatively, others stress Gilman's class analysis, identification with workers, and direct experience of poverty—"The Wolf at the Door"—and lack of higher education, first as the daughter of a single parent and, eventually, as breadwinner for assorted dependents. Indeed, so parlous was her situation in the early 1890s that one Christmas Eve, local socialists declared her destitute and offered assistance, as discussed in chapter 2. Rather than representing privileged white women, Lane noted Gilman's "abiding concern with the huge number of poor working women and men," whose situation she squarely blamed "on the well-off." She wrote fiction exploring more equitable distributions of economic resources and services. Moreover, she rebuked deterministic and fatalistic accounts of poverty, slums, and social problems of the economically marginal.[13]

Socialist and labor leaders called her a comrade. Her lectures and writings on socialism, including her prizewinning 1892 essay on the labor movement, and her work with the Bellamyite Nationalists of California, led to her warm welcome among British socialists on her European lecture tours, especially from the Fabian socialists H. G. Wells, George Bernard Shaw, Sidney and Beatrice Webb, William Morris, and his daughter May Morris. Prestonia Mann invited her to edit the *American Fabian;* and though she could not, she published a series of articles in Mann's journal. Socialist writer Upton Sinclair cited Gilman's theories favorably in his acclaimed novel *The Jungle* (1906). As shown in previous chapters, his later fictionalized account of his marriage and its breakdown portrayed the main character's wife seated in rapt attention, reading Gilman's *Women and Economics* (1898). Meanwhile, as earlier chapters also showed, most newspaper coverage characterized her as a socialist rather than a women's rights advocate until the suffrage movement acquired more prominence. With Gilman becoming one of suffragism's contentious public figures, her previously praised views about the importance of women's economic independence came under criticism as elitist, utopian, or myopically blind to the realities of working women's conditions. Alternatively, her much-discussed blueprints for changing work, home, culture, and customs clearly argued for a socialist transformation to improve dramatically both women's and men's working conditions.[14]

Part of the disquiet expressed by critics of Gilman's socialist credentials is the sense that she left behind the Californian Bellamyite Nationalist Movement and threw in her lot with the women's movement campaigns and the Progressive movement, both subsequently denounced as reactionary via various criteria. She did so because she believed that both movements had more serious prospects of affecting change in the world as it was and that both advanced feasible reform plans. By then, she preferred to infuse her ideas within Progressivism to improve human arrangements in the world as it was, since socialist mistakes reduced the chances of real impact on her most urgent concerns. With the Russian Revolution of 1917, she shared the disquiet of former U.S. socialists as the full details of the Leninist then Trotskyist phases in the formation of the Soviet Union gradually emerged. Along with other socialist revisionists, she deplored violence, coercion, backwardness, and the inefficiency of the regime. Unquestionably, Gilman became disillusioned, too, with the androcentrism of socialist movements and campaigns around her. This should not be confused with a procapitalist stance, however: it was rather that socialism, or at least, living socialists, had not fulfilled the promise of socialist analysis and beliefs.[15]

A somewhat wobbly leap is involved, however, in suggesting that this judgment about forms of socialism up to that point was tantamount to abandonment of all concerns about class inequality and poverty. Instead, she persistently criticized monopolies that unfairly exploited the public. The railroads were her frequent target since prevailing conditions were immensely relevant to her work as a traveling public intellectual. She also denounced slum landlords, ward bosses, exploitative employers, and ordinary people's inadequate access to fresh air, sunshine, nutritious food, education, and competent medical care, issues addressed in chapter 10. Religions were retrograde for encouraging fatalism in the face of poor worldly conditions, enjoining their flocks to passivity rather than protest, and for this she fiercely rebuked the various churches. So, despite her reservations about her era's socialist achievements, however, Wienen makes a compelling case for her stature as an important American Progressive Era socialist theorist.[16]

Ultimately, evaluations of criticism of Gilman as elitist or about the adequacy of her class analysis and socialist convictions depend on the criteria employed. On the one hand, if anyone ever employing domestic help at any point in their life is disqualified, then she becomes the class-blind elitist denounced by Hayden and Allen. And, then, with her, go Marx, Engels, and many others. On the other hand, if her fiction and nonfiction, her associates, conferences attended, and reputation mean anything, in their own context, then Gilman seemed markedly sensitive to issues of class and status and continued to be classified as a socialist. Her experience of poverty, however genteel, imparted lessons not forgotten. Of course, all those in poverty do not become socialists. Her contemporaries believed, however, that she was a perceptive and creative socialist writer, a friend and comrade of those struggling to end capitalist exploitation of labor.[17]

Were her peers deluded, deceived, or just plain wrong to think of her as a socialist, a supporter of labor, and one concerned for the welfare of ordinary people? Did they somehow miss the attributes leading some modern critics to call her elitist and class blind? Was being a Beecher descendent so decisive? Plenty of socialists hailed from families much more prosperous and prestigious than Gilman's family, Prestonia Mann being a case in point.

Gilman's reputation as a socialist, her friendship with socialists for much of her public life, leaves her critics today unimpressed. Despite the caveats outlined above, a consensus now prevails in the literature that Gilman became conservative and abandoned her original commitment to social class equality. This position would be more persuasive if it took more comprehensive account of the array of counterevidence from Gilman's own lifetime, whether her agonized prenuptial letters urging her fiancé beyond individualism toward her socialist convictions or the postcapitalist and fully collective futures sketched in her fiction of the 1910s.

Despite portrayals of Gilman as a failed socialist, one who refused the daily grind of assisting the poor when living at Hull House with Jane Addams in the 1890s, the contextual evidence is persistently contrary. More crucially, Gilman's analyses and strategies related to class, poverty, and socialism prove inseparable from her feminist analyses. The naturalization of women's subjection through economic dependence, generated through (usually) heterosexual relations, anchored androcentric culture. The fully "human world" would dismantle androcentrism; but for Gilman it was predicated on socialist transformation. From this central axiom, she never retreated. But she could not, thereby, support androcentric socialisms because they posed no significant challenge to the sexual bases of women's oppression.[18]

Gilman, Whiteness, and the Racialization of Feminism

> More recent, younger Gilman scholars, not surprisingly, focus more sharply on those flaws, particularly the racism, Anti-Semitism, and ethnocentrism, so prevalent as to be almost commonplace in her day, and so offensive in ours, although certainly not eliminated. She was able to reject and deny so many prejudices that we are impatient and unforgiving when she did not repudiate others.
>
> *Ann J. Lane, "What My Therapist, My Daughter, and Charlotte Taught Me While I Was Writing the Biography of Charlotte Perkins Gilman" (2000)*

> Gilman's disturbing ideals . . . haunt feminist self-conception, and promulgate the mistaken belief that it is possible for a feminism that does not account for the racialization of gender and sexual formation to be truly liberatory.
>
> *Alys Weinbaum,* Wayward Reproductions *(2004)*

Canonizers and critics alike have been vexed by Gilman's stances on racial and ethnic issues.[19] Despite efforts to recast her feminism in racialized terms, scholars remain conflicted about the evidence and its significance. This focus within Gilmaniana develops against a backdrop of debates within new race history, feminist whiteness studies, and related genres. To appraise this critical recent phase in Gilmaniana, some initial context points are pertinent. One issue is the proportion of her oeuvre concerned with race and ethnicity. Scholars provide diverse claims on this. Also, meanings of key terms used in critics' charges relative to Gilman's historical framework prove to be important.

How much of Gilman's work addressed race and ethnicity? Intense criticism of Gilman might prompt readers to surmise that these topics dominated her writings and lectures and the critical attention they received at the time. Neither proves to be true. Gilman published close to twenty-two hundred separate items and also wrote hundreds of unpublished lectures, sermons, platform, and parlor talks between 1883 and 1935. The topics of race, ethnicity, eugenics, and immigration restrictivism were the titles or clear content of fewer than twenty, none more than a few pages long, as discussed in chapter 11. Here she stands in some contrast with Progressive Era authors of treatises, journal issues, or novels negatively portraying African Americans, immigrants, and populations deemed "dysgenic."[20]

Furthermore, to the few explicit Gilman forays on these topics, fewer responses were published. For the most part, these even briefer pieces offered exegesis, caveats, or bemused jibes at her political naïveté. One looks in vain for contemporary antiracist or liberal attacks on her for offensive racial and ethnic views, or any sense that she even rated as a contributor of such views. Progressive Era African American leaders and intellectuals such as W. E. B. Du Bois, Anna Julia Cooper, William Pickens, and Ida B. Wells of necessity targeted racial subjugationists. Gilman was not among them. Instead, Du Bois, for instance, cited her work as useful for explaining how African American women had become "cheap labor."[21]

Gilman's absence from mainstream histories of Progressive Era race relations, racism, ethnicity, eugenics, and nativism is not a collective oversight by sexist historians. Rather, her slight contributions on these topics did not rate significantly or have an impact on contemporary debates and policies. Hence, some recent scholars' efforts to link her with major racial theorists and racist popularizers like Madison Grant or Lothrop Stoddard are unconvincing because ungrounded in the relevant discursive and rhetorical context.[22]

As for meanings of relevant terms, what was the currency and understanding of "racism" during the Progressive Era? It was not current as a single term conveying a comprehensive worldview during Gilman's life. She and her contemporaries used terms like "race prejudice" or "bigotry." Racism's founding 1936 meaning was "the assumption that psychocultural traits and capacities are determined by biological race, and that races differ decisively from one another, which is usually coupled with the belief in the inherent superiority of a particular race and its right to domination over others." George M. Fredrickson's more precise historical definition is that "racism exists when one ethnic group or historical collectivity dominates, excludes, or seeks to eliminate another on the basis of differences that it believes are hereditary and unalterable." These conditions prevailed in the Jim Crow South of the 1870s–1960s, the German Nazi regime of the 1930s and 1940s, and South African Apartheid in 1948–91/94, the three true racist political regimes of modern history so far.[23]

Consequently, Fredrickson rejects imprecisely overinclusive attributions of "racism," prevalent in recent decades. Intolerance, prejudice, bigotry, xenophobia, nativism, and discrimination were each historically distinct phenomenon, with differing textures, political purchases, and lived densities. While loathsome, they did not, in and of themselves, constitute "racism" in the Progressive Era and, in his view, should not be treated as synonymous with it. The element of belief in unchangeable, unbridgeable, and disadvantageous differences, which are then taken to mandate enslavement, genocide, or exclusion as official policy, anchors the distinctive historical meaning of "racism."[24]

While such racist beliefs were famously popularized in Jim Crow America by many public intellectuals, scholars, journalists, and other popular figures, these were not Gilman's beliefs. On the contrary, Lanser, Deegan, and Allen note that in a long career of many developments, her "strong theoretical commitment to racial harmony" and "unconventional support for interracial marriages" meant that, at times, Gilman offered striking criticisms of racial and ethnic features of Jim Crow America, specifically, the color line and antimiscegenation laws, as well as more generally condemning America's racist history. She publicly deplored literacy requirements directed against African American voters. As well, she reviled anti-Semitism as "the hideous injustice of Christianity to Jews," condemned lynching, and denounced the government's missionary imperialism in Cuba and the Philippines. In 1913 she pilloried environmental destruction, the doctrine of Manifest Destiny, and race pride among white Americans, retorting: "That we have cheated the Indian, oppressed the African, robbed the Mexican and childishly wasted our great resources is ground for shame." For the first part of her career, she rebuked short-sighted anti-immigrant prejudices, preferring Lamarckian Progressive reforms over eugenics for improving future generations.[25]

If "racism" has a historically precise meaning, it is not synonymous with other terms also often applied to Gilman. Scholars tend to elide "racism" and "ethnocentrism," though the latter is an older word, dating from 1900, as "a habitual disposition to judge foreign peoples or groups by the standards and practices of one's own culture or ethnic group." It was first used to describe warring Native American tribes. Clearly, these two characterizations had significantly different ramifications within Gilman's reform Darwinist feminism.[26]

Moreover, although her embrace of Progressive social science inevitably entailed a hierarchical classification of "racial and national development," Gilman declined the static determinism of other theorists. Instead, her optimistic faith in evolutionary progress through education and social consciousness sharply distinguished her from many prevailing cultural authorities, at least for much of her career. World War I left Gilman and many peer reformers deeply disillusioned, and some biographers contend that she embraced increasingly racist, ethnocentric, anti-Semitic, and nativist views in the interwar years of her sixties and seventies. Even so, Gilman does not appear to have ever rated in these terms for her peers.[27]

Successors, however, use "racism" and other terms in relation to Gilman more loosely and with less sense of their conceptual historicity, as presented by scholars like Fredrickson. Since around 1990, debates about Gilman's race and ethnic views have overshadowed those on class, though earlier commentators had noted and condemned them. Commentators now attach graver significance to amplified charges of racism and ethnocentrism against Gilman, reflecting current feminist concern with differences forged by ethnicity, culture, and sexuality. Initially the Gilman works at issue were her two serialized utopian novels (1915 and 1916), "The Yellow Wall-paper" (1892), and the two short nonfiction articles (1908 and 1923) concerned with race and ethnicity, respectively, as discussed in chapter 11.[28]

Recent scholars from literary, cultural, and American studies identify more and more of Gilman's texts as "racist." Even texts not about race, ethnicity, or eugenics—these include her letters, diaries, and youthful artworks—receive criticism for their implicitly racialized preoccupations and subtexts. Unlike earlier commentators lamenting Gilman's racial and ethnic lapses from her otherwise admirable ideas, literary critic Susan S. Lanser urges the inseparable interpenetration between feminism and racist ethnocentrism throughout Gilman's work. Her influential 1989 critique centers on Gilman's "The Yellow Wall-paper" (discussed above in chapter 1). Lanser portrays the story as a projection of "patriarchal practices onto non-Aryan societies," through an intellectual female subject "built on the repression of difference, manifest in an unconscious ethnocentric hostility to 'yellowness.'" Preeminently, she detects racialized preoccupations—from advocacy of white supremacy to opposition to immigration—throughout Gilman's writings and purports it was not just an aberration of her later years. Among historians of America and American studies scholars, Lanser strongly influenced three important critical essays by Bederman (1995), Peyser (1998), and Newman (1999), here warranting review.[29]

Bederman devotes a chapter to Gilman in her cultural history study of American Gilded Age and Progressive Era discourses of civilization and "manliness." She argues that Gilman displaced antifeminists' view that male supremacy and female dependence advanced civilization with the alternative view that white supremacy, built on racial bonds between white men and women, was the path to civilized advance. Gilman warned that heightened sex differences, characteristic of advanced societies, far from causing progress, contained the seeds of social degeneration and doom. According to Bederman, Gilman's "re-writing the civilization discourse was crucial to her success as a feminist theorist," but it was deeply flawed by being predicated on the "exclusion of nonwhite men and women," making Gilman's feminism "at its very base racist." Though Gilman "rarely made race the explicit focus of her analysis," it was riddled with "implicit assumptions about white racial supremacy," which inflected her arguments for ending the "sexuo-economic" relation, "the cornerstone of her feminist version of 'civilization.'" Though Gilman never specified "white races," Bederman claims that whenever she mentioned the terms "civilization," "women," or "racial advancement," Gilman meant white civilization, white women, and white racial advancement." So assumed was this race specificity that Gilman did not need to "specify which race she meant," for to say that she meant only whites "would be redundant." With a feminist program inextricably rooted in the "white supremacism of 'civilization,'" Gilman's proposal to end sexuo-economic dependence "would not merely confer on women sex equality": rather, it would bestow "full racial equality," as advanced Anglo-Saxons.[30]

Bederman also observes that Gilman reversed patriarchal discourse by taking women as the agents of a civilization to which violent and primitive men were peripheral. In effect, Gilman enjoined men to serve the advance of the (white) race by giving up the "primitive rapist" attributes used to found androcentric culture and instead to help minimize sex distinction, saving the race from degeneration, in common cause with white women and against lesser races. Based on evidence presented in chapter 3 concerning Gilman's resistance to this aspect of Ward's theory of "the overthrow of gynaecocentric culture," her efforts to marginalize rape-centered theories in favor of those foregrounding women's agency would appear consistent. But here she failed, says Bederman, because the masculinity of the primitive was increasingly romanticized by figures such as Theodore Roosevelt. "The brute in man" was being repackaged as consistent with advanced (white) male civilization, reinforcing or even heightening sexual differences. In other words, Gilman was witnessing a cross-race hybridization of masculinity, blurring the boundaries of race distinctions.[31]

Even Bederman's critics acknowledge her impact on Gilmaniana. Kimmel and Aronsen reject as overliteral Bederman's reading of Gilman's uses of "the race," countering that Gilman, like her contemporaries, used the term as shorthand for "the human race," as is plain in Progressive Era sociological texts, as well as periodicals and journals of opinion They are not persuaded by Bederman's inference that Gilman meant "whites only" whenever she mentioned "race," women, and civilization. They call Bederman's "grounded in racism" reading of Gilman's feminism "excessively politically correct," especially since Gilman paid little attention to race in her prolific writing and lecturing. Though she nonetheless drew on prevalent racialized examples and themes, Gilman also discredited "race prejudice" in her fiction, nonfiction, and public acts. Others, acknowledging the force of Bederman's reading, call Gilman's racism and ethnocentrism "inconsistent," bemoaning her simultaneous bigotry and enlightenment. Certain of her views, writes Fishkin, "belong in those moldy heaps we need to discard," while others appear not only relevant but also brilliantly illuminating. Moynihan, while regretting those of Gilman's racial and ethnic ideas found offensive today, notes uses and defenses of Gilman by African American leaders among her peers, including Du Bois and Julia Anna Cooper, as noted above. These complicate oversimple charges against Gilman for "racism." Were such figures likely to endorse a known race bigot?[32]

In response to Bederman's critique, some Gilman scholars now split the difference, citing the "mixed legacy" of Gilman, acknowledging Gilman's prejudices and errors, without jettisoning contributions that remain valuable. Some minimize more obnoxious traces, while others find hers a dismal record. Knight, for instance, itemizes prejudices and derogatory expressions throughout Gilman's public and private work, casting racism as a shadow that diminishes her legacy. Nonetheless, Knight still continues research on biographical and literary aspects of Gilman's work. Another approach is the contrasting of Gilman's "ethnocentric lapses" with both her feminist and socialist commitments. Scholars here observe that racism, ethnocentrism, nativism, and related discourses had no consistent unity in her lifetime, a fact making Gilman's apparently inconsistent assertions intelligible. Her feminism, then, was separable from other racialized discourses, even if at times they collided. Moreover, Deegan contrasts the tough presentist standard to which she is now held—just when feminists have reinstated her significance—with more lenient critical treatment of grave lapses by other theorists evincing misogyny, sex discrimination, and blindness, including Marx, Weber, Freud, and Durkheim.[33]

Critics are far from a consensus, then, on Bederman's claims about Gilman's racism and ethnocentrism. Some reject the view that Gilman's feminism was grounded in racism. Even if, for instance, the women in Gilman's *Herland* (1915) were of Aryan stock, Lloyd accords racialized analysis little role in Gilman's major works, particularly compared, for example, to Veblen's discussions of "Dolichos-blonds" and the like. While admitting her nativism toward immigrants, nonetheless, she declined biological arguments used by male peers to justify the oppression of immigrants, African Americans, and women. Similarly, rather than racism, Kimmel and Aronson find "an often virulent nativism" a far more significant factor in Gilman's thought, in which "her major . . . nemesis remained the Jews." Unlike in the Nazi regime, though, where anti-Semitism became genocidal policy and thus "racism" in Frederickson's sense of the term, it lurked among Progressives like Gilman as religious bigotry and cultural intolerance, what

Dinnerstein terms "genteel discrimination," as discussed in chapter 11. Alternatively, Johnson identifies Bederman's account of a Gilman weaving an ever-tightening web of white supremacy as part of an unwarranted politics of despair among historians writing about the Progressive Era and race. Despite these objections and caveats, however, Bederman's account is widely cited as authoritative in casting Gilman's feminism as a racist project.[34]

Literary critic Thomas Peyser also launches an important chapter on Gilman in praise of Lanser's inextricably interconnected racism and feminism approach: "We must take both the progressive and the reactionary in Gilman as part of a single package deal." He castigates Gilman scholars' efforts to separate these elements in her thought. Instead, he makes the argument that Gilman's heavily sociological efforts embracing evolutionary and historical arguments that differentiated the progress of races protested degenerate patriarchal homogenization of all women of all races as "the sex." In other words, for Peyser the most crucial "fact" about Gilman's feminism is her response to globalization in fear of "women's degradation," that is, "white women's degradation" by libertine and profligate men into a common rank with women of all other (inferior) races. Peyser maintains that a fear of hybridity haunts the totality of her work, leading her toward a "radically segregationist aesthetic" in pursuit of racial purity. He contends that her longing was for a united local culture keeping the world at bay.[35]

If Peyser's reading is compatible with Bederman's in terms of the stress on the racial/racist core of her feminism, Louise M. Newman makes these links even more explicit in her 1999 chapter on Gilman. She takes Bederman to have established conclusively that Gilman's version of the Woman Question was the struggle to secure Anglo-Protestant women's right to develop "those 'race' characteristics" they shared with white men," thus to assimilate women into white male social or civic public culture. These were the superior characteristics of rationality, citizenship, suffrage, professional competence, economic independence, and cultural authority. As such, these were (white) race characteristics, mistakenly and hitherto represented as exclusively masculine. Gilman's critique of patriarchy, then, relies for its power on refusing the patriarchal lumping together of white women and backward races, at the expense of the latter.[36]

Hence, Gilman's key contribution to feminist theory was to recast sexual difference "not as the touchstone of Christian civilization" but as a primitive survival of less evolved societies that blocked the ongoing evolution of white society. Newman notes that Gilman effectively dismantled her society's hegemonic association of (civilized white) "woman" with the supposedly natural and ineradicable sexual differences produced by woman's relegation to the home. The home, in fact, was primitive. Hence Gilman proposed that the solution to the problem of different races within America was to assimilate them to normative gender relations of male breadwinners and homebound dependent wives, thereby lessening race differences. Alternatively, the solution to the problem of excessive sex differentiation among whites was to free women from the home to economic independence, the racial equality of white women with white men of Bederman's formulation. Crucially, like other white Progressives, Gilman downplayed blackness, Newman notes, as a marker of permanent inferiority, any limitations able to be overcome through culture and environment. As such, Gilman would not, Newman deduces, have seen herself as a racist.[37]

Behind the apparent unity of approach among these three revisionist scholars, however, aspects of their often reductionist arguments prove irreconcilable, while they evince a sometimes startling parochialism, oversimplification, and neglect of the context for Gilman and other feminists' anxieties about the relative weighting of sex and race in the post–Civil War polity. As Newman concedes, abolitionist suffragists remained deeply bitter in the aftermath of their unexpected exclusion from suffrage but, more, the way the Fourteenth Amendment defined maleness as prerequisite for the voting citizen for the first time in American history. At a stroke, men, and ostensibly all men, became a political entity and interest group interpolated by the constitution. This male citizenry defined itself against women, all women, who became newly and specifically excluded. This creation of an aristocracy of sex, elevating "all men over all women," removed the common cause that had pertained between black men and women of all races in the former drive for adult suffrage. Moreover, it injected what Ellen DuBois calls a "strong element of race antagonism" into subsequent campaigns.[38]

For race had trumped sex, and not for the last time in American history. In their concern to impugn Gilman's alleged racism in her fear of the hybridization of all women by men, Peyser and Newman neglect the more striking fact of *men's* hybridization and its threat to Gilman's feminism. The Fourteenth Amendment, at least rhetorically and constitutionally, made men of all races and ethnicities a single political group. It was white men's viewing all women as "the sex," all equally unqualified for citizenship, irrespective of race, that permitted this outcome. It virtually preordained that excluded feminist theorists and activists' would be preoccupied with demonstrating that a mistake had been made and that corrective evidence advanced would have a racialized character. Moreover, Bederman demonstrates the cultural hybridization of American men across racial lines in the celebration of primitive brute masculinities, leaving little scope to doubt its implications for women. Sadly, the parochialism of an "America only" focus here misses the creative opportunity to ponder the sexual politics implications of exactly the same "manhood" stipulation on citizenship becoming enshrined as the electoral law of the land across the Australian colonies in the 1850s, and in the British 1867 Reform Act, one year before the U.S. Fourteenth Amendment. In other words, the sexing of voting was larger than the post–Civil War context, a fact of which U.S. suffragists, if not their historians, were all too aware.[39]

Nonetheless, Bederman's and Newman's accounts of Gilman's "racist feminism" and assimilationism receive warm praise and defense against detractors from third-wave antiracist and feminist whiteness studies critics, such as Weinbaum, Nadkarni, Fessenden, Hudak, Seitler, and others. While much of their work is creative, ingenious, and passionate, it is also mired in presentist criteria obviously unavailable to Progressive Era Gilman. Unwittingly, perhaps, some reduce Gilman to a mere cipher for current debates over race and ethnicity. For them, Gilman's feminism was a comprehensively reactionary, eugenic, white supremacist, and subjugationist worldview, making her racialization of feminism the chief, perhaps the only, feature about Gilman now worth studying. Gilman's efforts to transform domestic duties become "outsourcing," according to Fessenden, in her quest to merge the gendered spheres of home and world, shifting "the axis of subordination from gender to race." For antiracist critics with this approach, Gilman's feminism "cannot be untangled," then, without excavating the racist objectives it served. Fessenden finds debate over how Gilman might have meant "race" unimportant. Why? The very concept of "progress" has "always meant to be sloughing off the troubling, sticky remnants of outmoded religions and backward races." Hence, Gilman's narrative of progress is irredeemable, more of her malignant heritage.[40]

Antiracist critics portray Gilman also as a "eugenic feminist." Nadkarni claims that, by promoting "regeneration narratives" of social progress through a eugenic "white middle-class motherhood" and by deploring miscegenation and ethnic hybridity, Gilman racialized feminist language. Her project becomes the race-purified creation of a feminist subject who "guarantees the reproduction of the sovereign nation," her discourse then embedded in discourses of race. Hence, feminist scholars who fail to subject Gilman to antiracist critique reveal their investment in her legacy as a foremother in a "pure" feminist genealogy. Thereby, feminism today remains ensnared in "Gilman's race/reproduction bind," Weinbaum charging scholars with producing collusive "Gilman hagiography." They must recognize that her life's work was diagnosing and alleviating "the ravages on the

United States effected by wayward reproductions across racial lines," her priority "maternalist racial nationalism."[41]

Other critics see Gilman as seeking integration of feminism within cultural imperialism. Hers was an expansive project of outreach and aggressive assimilation of difference, "bringing Herland to Ourland," as Hudak puts it. Yet with Gilman's claimed horror of miscegenation and quest for eugenic purity (examined above), another line of criticism is that she retreated into exclusionary and isolationist nationalism. As Nadkarni puts it, "Gilman's imperial desires are thus undone by her need for racial purity."[42]

All this amounts to a significantly incomplete portrayal of Gilman's "life's work." Supposing it was accurate, what do these critics propose that feminists learn from recognizing Gilman only in these terms? Quite simply, the message is, as in the epigraph above, that it is impossible "for a feminism that does not account for racialization of gender and sexual formations to be truly liberating." The critical task becomes to show "how Gilman participated in a First Wave feminism that promoted racism as part of its overall program." The lesson from Gilman's errors is that there are no "colorless" bodies and that without an analysis of racialization, "the female body" will be constructed as white. This quest may be laudable and intelligible within the terms of current feminist debates. Unfortunately, however, this project proves to be not only unhistorical but also antihistorical when its advocates reject the historian's mission of investigating transformation over time and situating evidence in its own historical context.[43]

Unfortunately, many antiracist Gilman critics are unapologetic presentists. For some, such as Weinbaum and Fessenden, analysis that pays attention to historical context is suspect. They dismiss as special pleading of "historical exigencies" the efforts of other scholars such as Palmeri, Magner, Egan, Deegan, and Ganobcsik-Williams to place Gilman's Darwinian and hierarchically structured racial and ethnic thought in her own historical context.[44]

Fundamentally, to recharacterize Gilman's feminism as itself "racism," in the context of Jim Crow meanings, imperils the credibility of these antiracist critiques. This is because whiteness historian Newman, and those following her position, also represent Gilman as an assimilationist who demonstrated "the simultaneous emergence of feminist ideology and assimilationism, as two components of a culturally comprehensive racial politics." Proof lay in Gilman's stress on "Americanization" of immigrants and full education of African Americans, while objecting to Jewish separatism. These Gilman concerns do indeed support Newman's characterization of Gilman as an assimilationist.[45]

SIR THOMAS MORE invented the word "utopia" to describe the ideal state. In that state everyone was inspired by the divine spirit of God to be good. A single act of adultery was punishable by slavery and, if the adultery continued, death. More's writing career was cut short (as was More himself) when, in 1535, Henry had him beheaded.

CHARLOTTE PERKINS GILMAN, an early feminist, believed that all problems stemmed from cross-breeding: "The moral qualities of hybrids are well known." In her novel "Herland" (1915), a colony of Aryan women give birth, by means of parthenogenesis, to girls only. In this sexually and racially homogeneous society, there are no wars, no aristocracies, and no priests, and everyone is happy, happy, happy.

FIGURE 45. Edward Sorel, "Five Writers in Search of Utopia," *New Yorker* (December 24 and 31, 2007), 110

Yet if Gilman was an assimilationist, comparative race historians like Frederickson do not see Progressive Era assimilationists as racists. Their very advocacy of assimilation, which meant advance, or "uplift," conflicts with historical definitions of "racism." If advocates in racial and ethnic debates held that assimilation was possible—as Gilman did for most of her career—then cultural, religious, or ethnic intolerance might prevail but not racism, that is, the assertion of permanent, undesirable, and inferior characteristics justifying elimination or slavery. By Frederickson's lights, then, Newman has identified Gilman's assimilationism convincingly; and equally, she has undermined the case for reading Gilman as a racist in her own context, hence explaining Gilman's marginality in histories of U.S. racism.[46]

In the wake of revisionist antiracist insistence that Gilman studies must be anchored by exposé of her racialization of feminism, whether by eugenics or by other obnoxious discourses, some recent scholars and reviewers decline rather firmly. They maintain that unrelieved framing of Gilman by racism obstructs a necessary appreciation of her still considerable value for understanding the history of feminism. Such resistors see a predictable problem with revisionist accounts, such as those of "whiteness" and antiracist studies scholars, in that they tend to overcompensate. Arguably, this has been a persistent criticism of revisionist "new race history" and whiteness studies approaches to histories of Progressivism and the labor movement, among a range of other topics. The same limitation holds for much recent revisionist work on Gilman and race. Historian Peter Kolchin holds that Newman pushes "far beyond the sensible observation that most white feminists shared the racial prejudices common among whites in the late nineteenth and early twentieth centuries," in her reading of Gilman. By so doing, he regrets that Newman overgeneralizes and understates the range and complexity of feminist thought in arguing that racism constituted feminism, making it a racialized theory of gender oppression. He observes that such tendency to problematic overreaching is especially evident where scholars hail from fields in which the bulk of analysis centers "heavily on image, representation, and literary depiction." These are the very fields that have dominated Gilmaniana.[47]

Many historians contend that the idea of a naturalized racial hierarchy was pervasive and virtually uncontested throughout the United States during the Progressive Era and well into the early decades of the twentieth century. Despite present critical dismay at Gilman's racialized utterances and expressions of ethnic intolerance, she nonetheless clearly embraced a reform Darwinist framework throughout most of her career, stressing human agency to effect constructive change. Just like many of her social scientist peers, she attributed racial and ethnic differences to environment, opportunity, and cultural circumstances, positions that appalled Jim Crow racist subjugationists. And as her Beecher forebears combated chattel slavery, she, in turn, denounced Jim Crow as an immoral response to its consequences and aftermath.

If racism means a belief in permanent, inherent, unbridgeable, disadvantageous differences justifying treatment of peoples as segregated inferiors, slaves, or targets for extermination, then the charge of "racism" might express later feminists' disappointment in such a hitherto prescient foremother. But it is an inaccurate, loose, or blunt analytical instrument in this context, not yet explicating the force of these problematic discourses within Gilman's Progressive Era reform Darwinist feminism. "Racism" was unknown to Gilman as a concept: there is no evidence of it remaining in anything she wrote or received from others among her voluminous papers. She reproved "race prejudice," however, as defined by her admired peer, sociologist William I. Thomas. Her contemporaries used terms different from successors, not proceeding from any systematic combining of race, ethnicity, and positive accounts of cultural specificity, more typical in late interwar and postwar theories. Instead, they impugned bigotry, prejudice, or the color line in disaggregated ways, issue by issue, affected group by group. The need to coin terminology more overarching and systematic coincided, in the West, with the interwar rise of fascist regimes like Germany's, based on racialist rationales—hence the debut of the term "racism" at that time.[48]

THE PRESENT STUDY has offered a historical analysis of themes in Gilman's complex feminism in its own context. With Progressive Era racism entailing an essentialist and determinist discourse declaring progressive change impossible and justifying drastic, draconian, and permanent redress by the group judged the "superior" race, applying it to Gilman in that context is inaccurate. On racialized and ethnic discourses within Gilman's feminism, in its own historical context, however, there has been much to say, as offered above. Perhaps drawing these important distinctions can help to enhance the impact of historical analysis within Gilmaniana. History is certainly not the "master" discipline, but it is indispensable to a full and fair and careful account of Gilman's feminist significance. This is a plea neither to idealize nor to canonize her. It is just a call to frame her contributions as accurately as possible in and for their own place and period.[49]

NONE OF US can know the future of any scholarly field. In the case of Gilmaniana, however, it seems worthwhile to identify unresolved tensions

FIGURE 46. Rear view of Charlotte Perkins Gilman showing details of dress she made herself, 1896, London, England. Caption: "Claire James Hicks photos of me" (The Schlesinger Library, Radcliffe Institute, Harvard University 177-325-10).

and avenues that are less than productive in current discussion, perhaps toward encouraging helpful dialogue and advance our understanding of the historicity of feminist theories. Perhaps Gilman is doomed to disappoint, at least by some contemporary feminist criteria of worth. Why? She was a self-proclaimed Progressive, a reform Darwinist, and a proud Beecher descendent, as well as a white Protestant New Englander. She lived mainly heterosexually, and at times publicly espoused eugenics. She left traces of her privately displayed class and ethnic prejudices.

In fact more than disappoint, she is set to outrage exponents of some contemporary feminisms. If for today's readers, she was less admirable on ethnic issues, pacifism, and other matters than, say, Jane Addams, Gilman did write *Women and Economics* (1898), the starkly original and internationally acclaimed attribution of women's subjugation through economic dependency constructed through heterosexuality. For the reasons outlined above, Gilman did eventually support Progressive Era moves against unrestricted immigration. As also previously observed, like others, she did lose patience with the Marxist forms of socialist revolution of the interwar period. She was slow to advocate birth control as a feminist issue and, like Margaret Sanger, remained staunchly opposed to abortion. Whatever the truth of her private erotic life, she did not espouse free love, unwed motherhood, gay pride, political lesbianism, or transgendered identities. No doubt about it: Gilman's feminism little resembles its typical current forms, nor were her stances in general ones likely to be espoused by feminists today.

Is any of this really surprising? Unless one is interested in the historicity of feminism itself, for itself, studying Gilman's reform Darwinist feminism, replete with its differential development theories of races and ethnicities can only annoy, astonish, or disillusion us today. There is, of course, something of a scholarly industry in disillusionment with past feminist theorists for failing to reach our own insights on all manner of issues. Mary Wollstonecraft, Olive Schreiner, Virginia Woolf, and Simone de Beauvoir are just obvious examples in this regard from the Western feminist critical corpus. If foundation by denunciation appeals, they are easy marks. Given the grave intensity of current American racial and ethnic oppressions, that Gilman would receive fierce critiques might be expected. How helpful these can continue to be, at least in the prevailing forms discussed above, will be a judgment call for future scholars.

Arguably, feminists, of whatever stripe, can always derive enlightenment from studying feminists and feminisms of the past. Present axiomatic terms, whatever they are, have not always been privileged in feminist discourses. Comparison helps to identify more precisely present conditions of possibility and, especially, the discourses making current analyses plausible — with awareness of the contingencies in which they necessarily are embedded. Notwithstanding the sincere and serious criticisms discussed above, Gilmaniana will continue to flourish because Gilman's struggles to analyze and alter women's oppression through sexuality mattered to her contemporaries. Her words changed lives. The condescension (not to say condemnation) of any other feminist posterity does not gainsay her historical significance, her ingenuity, creativity, insights, and crucially, her closures and prejudices, as they unfolded among her own peers. If she failed us, and how could she not, she did not fail them.

CONCLUSION

GILMAN'S FEMINISM was a rich hybrid whose sources were correspondingly rich and various. She drew on a lifetime of experience and thought, stretching from the Civil War to the Great Depression; but her feminism found its most congenial context and clearest voice in the Progressive Era rather than in the 1890s or the interwar period. Later feminist commentators, galvanized by the potent slogan "the personal is political," have located the most formative influences on Gilman's feminism in her own earlier personal life in the Gilded Age. They concentrate on her family background and her painful experiences with marriage, motherhood, separation, single parenthood, divorce, and love relationships with both sexes, focusing on the evidence of her 1880s and 1890s diaries and the by-now ubiquitous "The Yellow Wall-paper" (1892). As this book has shown, Gilman's personal life—not least her direct experience of domestic oppression and poverty—was profoundly influential in her political and ideological formation. A consistent theme of her political rhetoric, however, was on the insignificance of personal or individual problems and solutions, compared with those of collective, social import—rhetoric that she adopted in the early 1890s in her work with Nationalism, socialism, and the labor movement but which became more forceful and explicit in the Progressive Era. Hence, her 1890 separation from Stetson, followed by attempts to live outside heterosexual family and relationship norms, then her divorce in 1894 amounted to individual remedies but no solution at all to the broader problems in androcentric sexual relations. Similarly, her 1900 marriage to a first cousin who actively supported her intellectual work, hence precluding childbearing, as well as her refusal to be a housewife again, solved aspects of her own but not other women's sex subjection.

Gilman sought to transcend individualism, the great incubus in American life, which Progressives struggled to redirect if not eliminate. Her *Women and Economics* (1898) conceptualized women as a collectivity with a distinct identity as a sexed social group, on a par with men as a sexed group. In this she worked in tandem with an accelerating impetus in Progressivism to build other active political constituencies—such as labor, immigrants, African Americans, and Native Americans—highlighted by such Gilman contemporaries as Jane Addams, Eugene V. Debs, Ida M. Tarbell, Upton Sinclair, Emma Goldman, Booker T. Washington, and W. E. B. Du Bois. These collective quests inspired Gilman to posit women as a distinct sexed group with particular needs and interests. They permitted her to shift the rationale for women's emancipation beyond individual rights and the constraints of a purely equalitarian reform program. Indeed work like hers did much to propel the American adoption of the originally French word "feminist."

Conceiving women as a "sexuo-economic" group, which she critically developed in exchanges with Lester Frank Ward and his gynaecocentric theory of the rise of an androcentric culture that enslaved women, her first avowedly political struggle was to write women's emancipation into socialist thought. In fact, the entirety of her feminist analyses presupposed a socialist transformation of work, economy, society, and culture as axiomatic for a human and, thus, postandrocentric world. Among her earliest glimpses of that future, her serialized novel *Moving the Mountain* (1911) charted her case for the intertwined nature of feminist and socialist transformation.

Yet unlike most socialists of her day, she believed that only with women as economically independent and enfranchised citizens could the socialist transformation be truly fulfilled. It was not a matter of choosing between them as two unrelated causes, at least in principle; but, in fact, socialist backwardness forced her to choose. Work to advance the female half of "the people" would have to proceed substantially without the blessing and assistance of masculist socialists, if women were ever to gain the power to contribute to the inauguration of a socialist, human world.

Dismayed by socialism's self-defeating masculism, she increasingly allied herself with the amorphous, yet more optimistic, Progressive movement. Later, after 1917, the violence of Marxist Communism disappointed her by its masculism, seeming to vindicate her earlier reservations. Revolutionary Marxists, she maintained, had tainted the more longstanding cooperative and evolutionary socialist tradition, destroying the careful work of many hands. They eroded prospects that Americans, exploited under free enterprise capitalism, would ever accept collective and state responsibilities for basic economic infrastructures and services.

Yet reform Darwinism, with its stress on both history and sexual relations, formed the true intellectual centerpiece of her critique of women's

FIGURE 47. Portrait of Charlotte Perkins Gilman, 1915–22 (Folder: Charlotte P. Gilman, The Schlesinger Library, Radcliffe Institute, Harvard University: AG 487a-1-1)

subjection and, indeed, of her feminist theory. Since such Darwinian-influenced approaches also anchored so many Progressive Era reform initiatives, Gilman's theories were both intelligible and admired across that era. Thereby, she advanced a singular theory of women's oppression through a profound critique of androcentric culture—a culture premised on an economically motivated male overthrow of periodic female sex selection. This overthrow had hijacked the correct path of evolution by distorting "the sex relation itself." Her rich descriptions of the dire consequences of androcentric culture encompassed such matters as the processes and character of cooking, housework, and childcare, the absurd—and often dangerous—nature of women's dress, and the attributes of men and masculinity, especially in combat and war, and the shaping of world religions.

Even as she coined "masculism" to characterize the sexual politics of androcentric cultural discourses, she firmly resisted essentialist claims for inevitable and unchangeable characteristics of men. She especially rejected fatalistic and causal accounts of male propensities toward violence and rape. Hence, she declined this crucial element of Ward's theory of the overthrow of gynaecocentric culture and the establishment of an androcentric one, predicated as it was on forcible rape and coercion. As her rueful correspondence shows, she attempted to debate her alternative economic theories of women's subjection with Ward, probably from soon after they met, and certainly after his 1903 *Pure Sociology,* but without success. Similarly, in the 1910s, she rebuked as utter nonsense the outbreak of antisuffragist rationalizing of institutional and crowd violence against suffragettes as their own fault for breaching the thin veneer of the sexual contract otherwise protecting women from "the brute in man." That such essentialist appeals to the "eternal male" could be used to perpetuate the undemocratic polity prevailing in most of the world was unspeakable. Not surprisingly, then, in her fiction and nonfiction texts, rape and other forms of male violence received their just desserts. The three explorers from Ourland were expelled from Herland in 1915 for attempted marital rape by one of them. She exposed and denaturalized rape at the height of international reports of war atrocities and outrages on civilian women and girls in Europe. In exactly the same period, she loudly condemned widely reported lynchings, unhesitatingly calling them cowardly atrocities. Her resistance to fatalistic acceptance of male violence as "natural" expressed a core optimism about men's capacity to change—to think and behave differently. Unless this was possible, there could be no foreseeable change to women's subjection.

More was at stake in her resistance to Roosevelt-like celebrations of, or at least tolerance for, male violence than feminist distaste or, perhaps, personal experience and traumatic recollections. The issue here was both analytical and strategic. Long ago, in the 1870s, the texts sent by her librarian father for her self-education extolled the rise of patriarchy by the defeat of matriarchal or matrifocal cultures as "civilized" and progressive. In their disappointment at Gilman's failure to reject these authorities' hierarchy of development approach to different races and ethnic groups, current commentators have overstated Gilman's general adherence to these works, missing her rejections and substantial qualification of their key claims. If men's violence was inevitable, inherent, and even evolutionarily anchored and "hardwired," as sometimes argued today, then there was no rationale for feminist struggle at all. Nothing could be done. Rather than accept the political paralysis implicit in such claims, Gilman redefined men's coercive sexual patterns as part of their self-interested expansion of their own preferences—a species of "role creep" in excess of any evolutionary mandate. As such, by depicting such patterns as chosen "preferences," she thereby made them contingent, volitional, and unquestionably cultural in origin. Here they belonged alongside the demand for prostitution, equally portrayed as "natural." Like her international feminist counterparts, she called the demand for prostitutes part of male supremacy. In her particular reform Darwinist terms, such demands were merely androcentric prerogatives, nothing more, though certainly nothing less. Men's violence then, directly and indirectly, was of critical significance within Gilman's feminism.

As solutions to the worst excesses of androcentrism, she contended that women needed to become citizens in order that their votes become valuable to ambitious legislators. Assuming a degree of common interests among women, the vast majority of whom did their own housework without assistance from servants, she reckoned that, as did antisuffragists, women would form a cohesive voting block. As half the population, if enfranchised, they could make or break political orientations and reforms, and influence, if not directly hold, the electoral balance of power. Because of the incorrect charge that she was uninvolved in the suffrage struggle and wrote little about it, previous Gilman commentary underestimates her passionate engagement with the signature feminist issue of the Progressive Era. A vocal and literary warrior for the cause, she became one of the best-known faces and voices for the suffrage side, regularly featured as the witty and articulate foe of the Antis in public debates. Taking the fight to the enemy and surgically dissecting antisuffrage and misogynist discourses of the 1910s energized and engaged her as had no previous cause. It was her work for the suffrage movement that gave Gilman her widest prominence and exposure, nationally and internationally.

Indeed, her deep investment in "the cause" was one source of her own ambivalence at being called a "feminist" from the 1910s onward. She wished to define her objectives in the largest and broadest way, the vote serving the wider pursuit of a human world and not an end in itself. Plenty of suffragists were not feminists, but feminists always supported enfranchisement. At times, then, she strenuously resented being labeled feminist alongside the likes of Ellen Key, who actually spoke against both the ballot and paid work for mothers. Yet, simultaneously, Gilman permitted herself to be described as a feminist. This was increasingly so as the term gradually "stuck" in the war and interwar years as a way of making intelligible a body of analysis, debate, and reforms concerning women's subjection and emancipation.

Gilman was taken to be the "Dean of American feminism" by antifeminist critics of many stripes—including her former friend, Fabian socialist Prestonia Mann. For Mann's Fabian socialist husband and New York school board commissioner, John Martin, Gilman was feminism's hated personification. Other critics excoriated the Wardian and reform Darwinist underpinnings of her feminism, hoping that once corrected, she would henceforth cease and desist. She did not. The conflict over feminism and Gilman made great press copy, while the task of covering her many lectures, both in metropolitan cities and smaller regional towns nationwide generated an astonishingly detailed and extended newspaper attention to her and the issues she raised. This media attention in turn generated letters to and about Gilman, both positive and negative, from the general public. Newspapers sneered over the scandal of her divorce and child custody arrangements and gloated over the eccentricity of her dress reform practices and woman rights causes. After *Women and Economics,* however, press stories referred to her as a socialist, a nationalist, a poet, a suffragist, an advanced woman thinker, or more clumsily, as "strong for women's rights."

Identifying collective feminist positions was difficult in the United States before the 1910s. There was no single word current in America that captured the array of her unfolding thought and proposed reforms, either in the 1890s or the 1900s. Though many of her 1890s lectures, articles, and fiction pieces concerned women and sex subjection, nothing she published before *Women and Economics* foreshadowed the density or sophistication of this stunning contribution. Works like this, and others by the likes of Cicely Hamilton, Olive Schreiner, Ethel Snowden, Anna Garlin Spencer, Katharine Anthony, and Harriot Stanton Blatch, highlighted the obvious need for accurate terminology to designate this body of political and philosophical discourse.

Throughout Gilman's engagement with suffrage and feminism, her mission remained the building of a postandrocentric world. She recast Darwinism to provide a justification for women's emancipation to "work and love too," to contribute to human species progress — "race work" — beyond the "sex work" half of humanity alone performed. For her "human world" to emerge, there would need to be wholesale and extensive reforms. Gilman stood for the eradication of prostitution, venereal diseases, and thereby many gynecological disorders, birth defects, and involuntary sterility. She sought the elevation of women's status through education, citizenship rights, paid work, domestic modernization, urban planning, childcare, dress reform, and legal equality. And she promoted pacifism, population control, and eugenics. Most crucially distinguishing her from other coreformers was her conviction that all such reforms were predicated on fundamental changes in male/female relationships and dynamics, especially with regard to sexuality.

Of all Progressive Era reform issues, prostitution most especially perturbed her; and here the personal as political clearly exerted leverage with Gilman. In this concern, she was exactly comparable with international feminist contemporaries and peers. Fundamental to androcentric culture, prostitution degraded humanity universally, inflicting specific injuries on innocent and guilty alike, often wreaking hidden and longstanding physical and emotional damage, as she may well have known at first hand. Its tacit toleration as a normal recourse for men dramatized the hydraulic justification of male sexuality that precipitated her father's desertion and her immediate family's subsequent impoverishment on medical advice that further pregnancies would kill Mrs. Perkins. Stetson used the specter of harlots—his nude models—to taunt and manipulate her erotically. Her frequent rumination on the genetic and physiological impact of "biological sin" may not have been entirely academic. Beyond Kate, conceived almost immediately after the wedding, Gilman had no further children during her first decade-long marriage, four or five years of which were in coresidence with an artist much impressed with exercising his "conjugal rights." His second wife suffered miscarriages and bore no children. Moreover, discourses naturalizing male demand for prostitution bore a queasy family relation to those rationalizing rape and other male violence toward women and members of other minority groups.

Gilman endorsed the proposed abolition of regulated prostitution in segregated redlight districts. Meanwhile, she stressed the male client as a political and discursive construction, refusing to leave him unmarked and naturalized by those pondering prostitution only in the framework of "the vice trust," municipal corruption, and urban machine politics. She anticipated a human world in which no woman would have the slightest reason to sell herself, but even more significantly, no man would desire to buy sexual indulgence.

A century before women's studies and the employment of married women in academic positions, Gilman made herself into a feminist public intellectual, earning a living as a lecturer, editor, and author. Whatever her ambivalence about the new term "feminism" itself, she persistently and effectively insisted that ending women's subjection could simultaneously advance Progressive reform. Beyond mere strategy, though, she held that the cause of advancing women and, thereby, building a human world to supersede an androcentric one was, itself, progressive. Besides their injustice, key forms of sex subjection led to corruption, inefficiency, and diseases, anathema to the progressive impulse, yet all amenable to Progressive reforms. Meanwhile, her critique of androcentric culture and its hallmark female economic dependency drew on key Progressive social science discourses.

Not only was Gilman a significant exemplar of Progressivism, her record and currency for at least twenty years of the period placed feminism firmly within the Progressivist agenda. Gilman's feminism, her life's work, can contribute to a recasting of the tangled debates on "Progressivism." Though historiographers note the ever more despairing characterizations of the era as conservative, reactionary, myopic, smug, and inhumane, her contemporaries found Gilman's to be a powerful and radical voice. Her *Women and Economics* (1898), *Concerning Children* (1900), and *The Home* (1903) were fitting curtain raisers for feminist engagement with Progressivism. Their compatibility with other intellectual reform classics of the fin de siècle— for instance, Veblen's *The Theory of the Leisure Class* (1899), Ross's *Social Control* (1900), Ward's *Pure Sociology* (1903), and Thomas's *Sex and Society* (1907)—suggested an exciting potential for conjoining "the woman question" and progress. As the Progressive Era proceeded, Gilman joined the most notable intellectuals of the period—including the historian, Frederick Jackson Turner, especially in the aftermath of the First World War—in characterizing what they held to be the deficiencies of American culture, including Jim Crow racial bigotry and unrestricted immigration. Since the specifics of her attacks on the irrationality, injury, inefficiency, and injustice of sexual institutions often struck raw nerves, whether among her own family and friends or within institutions like the then-antifeminist *New York Times,* such concurrence of other leading intellectuals and reformers decisively enhanced her impact and authority.

Yet prospects for her desired human world—outlined vividly in her series of futuristic fiction works—appeared imperiled from the 1910s and beyond by new discourses of human identity, personality, and sexuality. Her particular targets here were psychoanalysis and sexology, charging them with "sexolatry," "phallic worship," and "sex obsession." In sexualizing and masculinizing women under a "shallow guise of equality," these discourses stalled feminist challenges to androcentrism. Claiming to free women erotically, sexual libertarianism threatened Gilman's theoretical framework.

Her Progressive Era reform Darwinist feminism was caught between two discursive moments, formed after the Gilded Age's social Darwinist hegemony, but before the full impact of psychoanalysis and scientific sexology. Insisting on the desirability of human sexuality evolving toward mutually initiated, and thus likely more periodic sex relations, she remained skeptical about new, yet increasingly hegemonic, views of sexuality. Had she lived longer, she might have come to see them in different terms, standing as she did on the brink of a reanalysis of sexuality that extolled sexual expression, experimentation, and lifting (at least some) erotic taboos. Essentially, Gilman resisted the most popularized terms of the twentieth-century shift separating reproduction and sexuality—and valorizing the latter—as only further degrading women. She was not alone in this conviction. Later scholars dubbing such stances "conservative" or "puritanical" have shed little light on the implications of her interventions into debates on sexuality, gender, and reproduction for her larger feminist theory.

If a human world was the desirable successor to the androcentric era, 1920s and 1930s trends left her little hope of its advent. Moreover, the First World War unleashed a reinvigorated masculism hostile to feminist objectives, undermining the impact of the long-awaited enfranchisement of women. More problematic still was the massive influx of immigrant men from countries and cultures opposed to Anglo-American feminism, who, with full political rights, might organize to sabotage hard-won feminist progress, as many suffragists believed they had done during state referenda on woman suffrage. The influx of less progressive but fully enfranchised males furthered her sense of an imminent threat to women's still fragile new "personhood."

Meanwhile, though initially Gilman had not endorsed birth control as a feminist cause and a means toward voluntary motherhood, she later did so, but principally on eugenic, pacifist, and ethnocentric grounds. Her hesitation on this issue can seem especially incomprehensible to critics today. It is all too easy to forget though that the fin de siècle and interwar libertarian and sexological advocacy of the separation between heterosexual eroticism and reproduction was advanced ahead of reliable contraception and within a still prevailing but incorrect theory of ovulation. Thus in Progressive Era practice, the sexuality/reproduction separation could seem more honored in the breach, freer sexual expression for women all too often rewarded by the actuality of unwanted conceptions. With her mission to free women from sex work, her less than sanguine response to her era's birth control options was not visionary; but it was consistent and responsive to empirical experience. Most immediately, the outcomes for women proceeding as if the separation was already in place might be more children than desired or affordable, plunging the family or individual into hardship, dependent poverty, or perhaps loveless marriage. Since wartime and interwar rates of actual childbirths decreased, and yet maternal mortality rates increased, the gap or time lag between the discourse of the sexuality/reproduction separation and its actual feasibility was met by the ever-increasing resort to technically "criminal" but widely practiced abortion. This state of affairs simply deflected the problem; and failing any other solution, Gilman continued to hold that restraints on male sexual demands so often resulting in women's sufferings had to be central in feminist transformations. Under still prevailing conditions, she could not see then existing birth control methods as a mass solution for strengthening women's path out of sex work. So when she did come to support birth control in the 1920s, as demonstrated above, principally it was on grounds other than feminist ones.

Meanwhile and unquestionably, Gilman's feminist accounts of prostitution, sexuality, birth control, and eugenics were intelligible to her contemporaries in part due to elements they shared with Progressive Era ethnocentrism, anti-Semitism, and nativism. She sexualized unfolding interwar debates over immigration and American national identity to the detriment of those non-Americans whom she identified as threats to women's claims to race progress. In this she was entirely comparable with past feminists seeking to make the advance of women intelligible through prevailing discourses. Gilman's late nineteenth-century framework was one of Darwinist hierarchy of civilized development theories. Mary Wollstonecraft, over a century earlier, chided the sons of Enlightenment in France and England for their exclusions and confinement of women as thorough as those practiced by stationary "Mahometan" women of the seraglio or for binding women as surely as the Chinese binding of their feet.

DESPITE PLENTIFUL evidence of her accord with her era's reformers, Gilman's work also highlighted fundamental conflicts between Progressivism and feminism. Her critiques exposed the androcentric investments at the core of her era's most pivotal reform programs. Transcending conventional Progressivism, she contributed original and critical dimensions, destabilizing existing verities. Thus, while Gilman's work demonstrated integration of feminist theory within Progressive Era rhetorical paradigms, and its intelligibility within public debates, she also exposed the limits of certain Progressive tenets for feminist objectives. Hence, she ended her life unsure women's emancipation would be secured and a human world be born.

Nonetheless, with her innovativeness and creativity lauded by her peers, the Progressive Era Gilman was no isolated voice in the wilderness, incomprehensible or unappreciated in her time. Quite the contrary, the highs and lows of her career as a public intellectual registered, according to Gilman herself, in the extent of her public support. She measured that support by lecture fees, book royalties, magazine subscriptions, newspaper reports, invitations, and fan letters. Lacking either formal education or job security, she faced the lifelong need to support herself and other dependents. This constantly forced her to attend to the business side of her career, to its economic viability.

Lack of education made her overreliant on external authorities, like Ward, and defensive among mostly college-educated younger feminists.

Her perseverance in the face of these deficits marked the depth of her commitment to the quest for a human world. Yet the works she judged her greatest contributions to "world service"—*Human Work* (1904) and her "Study in Ethics" (variously revised 1928–1935)—were her most abstruse and theoretical texts, the former her greatest commercial failure and recipient of uncomprehending reviews, the latter unpublished. These two works shared another feature, though not one she acknowledged: unlike her other nonfiction works, they did not concern women, sex relations, home, and family, at least not ostensibly. It was as a commentator on these themes that she had a public, a market niche, at least for a time. That generally elated her but also frustrated her as she grimly perceived the boundaries of what she could achieve.

She confronted an early version of a problem identified by later feminist scholars. It was one thing to write about women or sexual dynamics as subject matter, whether as a fiery critique, a corrective, or an addition to existing knowledge, framed by feminist perspectives. It was quite another to write as a feminist on general subjects—on ethics, economics, or labor. As it happens, both *Human Work* and "A Study in Ethics" were thoroughly infused with examples, analogies, and materials related to women and sexual relations. Nonetheless, in an era of university expansion, with the increasing enshrinement of the doctorate as the entry level credential to write in any given specialization, it was becoming implausible for autodidacts like Gilman to present themselves as qualified to write philosophy, economics, or sociology. This was especially so by the 1920s and 1930s. In a world without professionalized gender or women's studies, she nonetheless achieved considerable authority. When she ventured beyond this terrain into established academic areas, she was politely ignored.

SOME OF THE most historically significant feminist analysts, by virtue of their specific purchase on contemporary life in their own era, have not worn well. The more integrated and effective within the discourses of their time, the less likely it is that they will withstand the application of presentist criteria by historians of feminism, an effect particularly apparent in Gilman commentaries. Few feminists today could canonize unreservedly those of her feminist preoccupations so absolutely of the now-compromised values of the Progressive Era. Of course not; why should they?

Still, there is much to learn from the historicity of feminist analyses and objectives like Gilman's. Understanding them within past eras and contexts brings into a sharp focus the specificities, conditionality, and provisionality of some present feminist theories and strategies. Perspectives, interpretations, and demands thought fundamental for any recognizable feminism can tumble when we find that the woman judged as the preeminent early twentieth-century feminist theorist not only did not share or endorse current concerns but at times flatly opposed them. Here is counsel against both false universals and dogmatically specific and time-bound definitions of feminism itself. For feminism, as much if not more poignantly than for other political discourses, location and contexts have proved critically determining and are, thus, essential coordinates for useful analysis.

This is not to say, however, that feminism cannot and should not be defined in expectation of being applicable to past eras, as well as our own. "Feminism" is not so variable, contrary to critics who would define it so elastically and contingently, as to leach it, in Cott's words, of any meaning at all. This is a mistaken judgment and certainly not one recommended by contemplation of features of Gilman's feminist concerns that are incomparable with those of later feminists. Instead, the extent to which Gilman's theories and preoccupations diverge from those of feminist theorists a century later is critical measure of historical changes in sexuality, sexual relations, and gender dynamics. The extent of change, the contingencies shaping political and ethical priorities for and within feminism, can be grasped perhaps most acutely by those struggling today to integrate fully feminism and antiracism. Gilman's differences from the present sexual politics status quo present a challenge to bring greater precision, contextual sensitivity, and explanatory prowess to bear on the matters of causation, change, and periodization for the history of feminism.

To the end of her career, Gilman sought to integrate feminism within mainstream, leading-edge movements and intellectual issues of the day, just as do feminists today. This led her increasingly to stress the constructedness of the masculine, the feminine, and sexuality. Although her reform Darwinism emphasized sexed attributes, she used historical analysis to make consideration of sex differences compatible with assertions of the commonality of human qualities and potentialities. She treated the artificial cultural elaboration and exaggeration of sex differences into gender markings as deeply problematic if and when they impeded progress. This did not mean that she sought some flat and bland androgyny. Instead, she worked to eradicate the tyrannies of what we now call gender. It is along that feminist trajectory that Gilman's feminism reaches across the decades, indeed, the centuries, to successor feminisms.

NOTES

All references to Gilman in manuscripts have the abbreviation CPG, while for her published works, "Gilman" is used. In consideration of space, in most cases, note numbers are placed at the end of the paragraph (or a succession of related paragraphs) in the text, and within notes citations are provided in order of matter mentioned in the corresponding paragraph(s).

INTRODUCTION

1. Gilman, "Feminism," unpublished notes (1908), Charlotte Perkins Gilman Papers (hereafter CPGP), Schlesinger Library Mss. 177/175. Throughout the notes, Gilman's name will be abbreviated to CPG for correspondence. See Gary Scharnhorst, *Charlotte Perkins Gilman* (Boston: Twayne, 1985), 55, and Scharnhorst, *Charlotte Perkins Gilman: A Bibliography* (Boston: Twayne, 1985), 99–101. Since 1960 *Women and Economics* has been reissued several times—for some details, see my "Select Bibliography," 439–40. See also Gilman, *The Man-Made World; or, Our Androcentric Culture* (New York: Charlton, 1911), 67, 144, 154, and 201–4.

2. Gilman, introductory remarks in "Women in Industry," 15 October 1915, Bureau of Vocational Information (1911–26), Records (New York City), 1908–32, 46–47, Arthur and Elizabeth Schlesinger Library of the History of Women in America (hereafter SL), Radcliffe Institute, Harvard University, Mss. M-34/45, 26; and see "Living Out of a Laboratory," *Evening Mail,* 12 March 1914, clipping, CPGP, SL 177/282/1.

3. On Gilman's Beecher family relatives, see Barbara A. White's illuminating study, *The Beecher Sisters* (New Haven, CT: Yale University Press, 2003); and Stephen H. Snyder, *Lyman Beecher and His Children: The Transformation of a Religious Tradition* (Brooklyn: Carlson Publishers, 1991).

4. For a valuable discussion of American and British press and periodical reviews of her work, see Scharnhorst, *Charlotte Perkins Gilman,* 55–56.

5. For fuller discussion of the feminist category "oppression," see Marilyn Frye, *The Politics of Reality* (Trumansburg, NY: Crossing Press, 1983), 1–16. See also Clifford Geertz, "Thick Description: Towards an Interpretative Theory of Culture," in *The Interpretation of Cultures* (New York: Basic Books, 1973), 9–10, 12–13, and 20.

6. See Gilman, *Women and Economics* (Boston: Small Maynard, 1898), Gilman,

Concerning Children (Boston: Small Maynard, 1900), Gilman, *The Home: Its Work and Influence* (New York: McClure, 1903), Gilman, *Human Work* (New York: McClure, 1904), and Gilman, *Man-Made World*—see the review of the latter, "Charlotte Perkins Gilman Puts Man on the Grill," *New York Times*, 15 January 1911, Sunday magazine, 14. See also Gilman's periodical *Forerunner* (1909–16), Gilman, *His Religion and Hers* (New York: Century, 1923), Gilman, *The Living of Charlotte Perkins Gilman: An Autobiography* (New York: Appleton-Century, 1935), and Gilman, "The Right to Die" *Forum* 94 (November 1935): 297–300.

7. See Judith A. Allen, "Charlotte Perkins Gilman, Feminism, and Progressivism," in *Rhetoric and Reform in the Progressive Era*, ed. J. Michael Hogan, *A Rhetorical History of the United States*, vol. 6 (East Lansing: Michigan State University Press, 2003), 427–69, esp. 428 and 440–43.

8. See, for instance, Michael McGerr, *A Fierce Discontent: The Rise and Fall of the Progressive Movement in America, 1870–1920* (New York: Free Press, 2003); Nancy Cohen, *The Reconstruction of American Liberalism, 1865–1914* (Chapel Hill: University of North Carolina Press, 2002); Daniel T. Rodgers, *Atlantic Crossings: Social Politics in a Progressive Age* (Cambridge, MA: Harvard University Press, Belknap Press, 1998); Leon Fink, *Progressive Intellectuals and the Dilemmas of Democratic Commitment* (Cambridge, MA: Harvard University Press, 1997); and Eldon J. Eisenach, *The Lost Promise of Progressivism* (Lawrence: University Press of Kansas, 1994).

9. See Janice J. Kirkland, "Mrs. Stetson and Mr. Shaw in Suffolk: Animadversions and Obstacles," in *Charlotte Perkins Gilman and Her Contemporaries*, eds. Cynthia J. Davis and Denise D. Knight (Tuscaloosa: University of Alabama Press, 2004), 87–102.

10. See Nancy F. Cott, *The Grounding of Modern Feminism* (New Haven, CT: Yale University Press, 1987), 1–16; Karen Offen, "On the French Origins of the Words *Feminism* and *Feminist*," *Feminist Issues* 8 (Fall 1988): 45–51, Offen, "Defining Feminism: A Comparative Historical Perspective," *Signs* 14 (Autumn 1988): 119–57, and Offen, "Feminism and Sexual Difference in Historical Perspective" in *Theoretical Perspectives on Sexual Difference*, ed. Deborah L. Rhode (New Haven, CT: Yale University Press, 1990), 13–20. See also Judith A. Allen, *Rose Scott: Vision and Revision in Feminism 1880–1925* (Melbourne: Oxford University Press, 1994), 235–237; Philippa Levine, *Victorian Feminists, 1850–1900* (London: Hutchinson, 1987), 14–16, 132–33, and 150; Virginia Woolf, *A Room of One's Own* (1929; reprint, New York: Harcourt, 1985), 103–7; and Simone de Beauvoir, *The Second Sex* (New York: Penguin, 1953), 271–73.

11. See Michele Barrett, *Women's Oppression Today* (London: Verso, 1980), 8–9.

12. For discussion of Friedan's race blindness, see Joanne J. Meyerowitz, "Beyond the *Feminine Mystique*: A Reassessment of Postwar Mass Culture, 1946–1958," in *Not June Cleaver: Women and Gender in Postwar America, 1945–1960*, ed. Joanne J. Meyerowitz (Philadelphia: Temple University Press, 1994), 229–62. See also Carl N. Degler, "Charlotte Perkins Gilman and the Theory and Practice of Feminism," *American Quarterly* 8 (Spring 1956): 22–23, and 36.

13. See Degler, "Charlotte Perkins Gilman," 38–39 and 31.

14. See Carl N. Degler, introduction to Gilman, *Women and Economics* (San Francisco: Harper Torchbooks, 1966), viii and xxix; Brian Lloyd, "Feminism, Utopian and

Scientific: Charlotte Perkins Gilman and the Prison of the Familiar," *American Studies* 39 (Spring 1998): 103; Thomas Peyser, *Utopia and Cosmopolis: Globalization in the Era of American Literary Realism* (Durham, NC: Duke University Press, 1998), 63; Michael S. Kimmel and Amy Aronson, introduction to Gilman, *Women and Economics* (Berkeley: University of California Press, 1998), viii; and Ann J. Lane, *To Herland and Beyond: The Life of Charlotte Perkins Gilman* (New York: Meridian, 1991), 8.

15. See Degler, introduction to Gilman, *Women and Economics* (1966), xxiii and xxxii. For critique of Degler's approach to Gilman, see Ann Palmeri, "Charlotte Perkins Gilman: Forerunner of a Feminist Social Science," in *Discovering Reality*, ed. Sandra Harding and Merrill B. Hintikka (Dordrecht: Reidel, 1983), 98.

16. See, for instance, Mary Armfield Hill, *Charlotte Perkins Gilman: The Making of a Radical Feminist, 1860–1896* (Philadelphia: Temple University Press, 1980); and Lane, *To Herland*. See also Sheryl L. Meyerling, ed., *Charlotte Perkins Gilman: The Woman and Her World* (Ann Arbor, MI: UMI Research Press, 1989); Joanne B. Karpinski, ed., *Critical Essays on Charlotte Perkins Gilman* (New York: G. K. Hall & Co., 1992); Catherine J. Golden, ed., *The Captive Imagination: A Casebook on The Yellow Wallpaper* (New York: Feminist Press, 1992); Val Gough and Jill Rudd, eds., *A Very Different Story: Studies on the Fiction of Charlotte Perkins Gilman* (Liverpool: Liverpool University Press, 1998), and Rudd and Gough, eds., *Charlotte Perkins Gilman: Optimist Reformer* (Iowa City: University of Iowa Press, 1999); and Catherine J. Golden and Joanna Schneider Zangrando, eds., *The Mixed Legacy of Charlotte Perkins Gilman* (Newark: University of Delaware Press, 2000).

17. See Elaine Hedges, afterword to *The Yellow Wallpaper* (New York: Feminist Press, 1973), 37–63; and Larry Ceplair, introduction to *Charlotte Perkins Gilman: A Nonfiction Reader*, ed. Larry Ceplair (New York: Columbia University Press, 1992), 3–4. See also Gilman, "The Yellow Wall-paper," *New England Magazine* 5 (January 1892): 647–56; and my bibliography here for examples of reprinting and anthologizing of this short story. For examples from the specialist commentary on "Yellow Wall-paper," see nn. 2 and 11–18 in chap. 1.

18. For the also considerable scholarly criticism of *Herland, With Her in Ourland,* and *Moving the Mountain,* see chap. 8, nn. 2, 12, and 38. See also Gilman, *Unpunished,* ed. Catherine J. Golden and Denise D. Knight (New York: Feminist Press, 1997); and Lillian S. Robinson, "Killing Patriarchy: Charlotte Perkins Gilman, the Murder Mystery, and Post-Feminist Propaganda," *Tulsa Studies in Women's Literature* 10 (Fall 1991): 273–85.

19. From Gilman's diaries and letters, see Denise D. Knight, ed., *The Diaries of Charlotte Perkins Gilman,* vol. 1, *1879–87* and vol. 2, *1890–1935* (Charlottesville: University Press of Virginia, 1994); Mary Armfield Hill, ed., *A Journey from Within: The Love Letters of Charlotte Perkins Gilman, 1897–1900* (Lewisburg, PA: Bucknell University Press, 1995). Collections of previously unpublished fiction include Gilman, *Herland,* ed. Ann J. Lane (1915; reprint, London: Women's Press, 1979)—and for several other editions of this 1915 novel, see my bibliography here; Ann J. Lane, ed., *The Charlotte Perkins Gilman Reader* (New York: Pantheon, 1980; reprint, Charlottesville: University Press of Virginia, 1998); Gilman, *With Her in Ourland,* ed. Mary Jo Deegan (Westport, CT: Praeger, 1997), Gilman, *Mag—Marjorie: Two Novels by Charlotte Perkins Gilman* (Forest Hills, NY: Ironweed Press, 1999), Gilman, *Benigna*

Machiavelli: A Novella by the Author of "The Yellow Wallpaper," ed. Joan Blake (Santa Barbara, CA: Bandana Books, 1994), Gilman, *The Crux: A Novel,* ed. Jennifer S. Tuttle (Newark: University of Delaware Press, 2002), and Gilman, *What Diantha Did,* ed. Charlotte J. Rich (Durham, NC: Duke University Press, 2005). Further examples of reissued Gilman nonfiction include *The Man-Made World,* ed. Mary Armfield Hill (Amherst, NY: Humanity Books, 2001), *The Home,* ed. Michael S. Kimmel (Walnut Creek, CA: AltaMira Press, 2002).

20. For instance, in Scharnhorst's 1985 estimate of Gilman's 2,157 items of published work, nonfiction dominated in a 2-to-1 ratio. By 1916, she had published all but fourteen short verses from her life's 678 fiction items, while her nonfiction work still totaled 366 items between 1917 and 1935. At no part of her earlier career—1880–1914—were fiction items more than a third of her output, while for her final twenty years she published almost solely nonfiction, except for some verse in 1930–35. This estimate excludes undated nonfiction items found in her papers, as well as numerous lectures, letters to newspaper editors, and interviews extant in Gilman's papers. Between 1883 and 1935, she averaged thirty published nonfiction items each year. Not only did she frame her most important treatises as sociological works, she denied any interest in art for art's sake, ascribing didactic purpose to her poetry, plays, novels, and short stories. For an indicative estimate of her publication genres and ratio patterns, see Scharnhorst, *Bibliography.* For her own sociological framing, see also Gilman, *Women and Economics,* 80, 95, 102–3, 105, 107, 143, 222, 241, 267, 295, 302, and 306.

21. See also Ann J. Lane, introduction to *Reader,* xxii; Mary Jo Deegan, introduction to *With Her in Ourland,* 2, 41 and 46–47; Janet Beer, *Kate Chopin, Edith Wharton, and Charlotte Perkins Gilman: Studies in Short Fiction* (Basingstoke: Palgrave Macmillan, 2005), 15; and Michael R. Hill, introduction to Gilman, *Social Ethics: Sociology and the Future of Society,* ed. Mary Jo Deegan and Michael R. Hill (Westport, CT, and London: Praeger, 2004), xv. On this issue of the sociological character of Gilman's fiction, see also Haley Salinas, "A Sociological Analysis of Charlotte Perkins Gilman's *Herland* and *With Her in Ourland,*" *Discourse of Sociological Practice* 6 (Fall 2004): 127–35. My study of Gilman's feminism here approaches the overt content and message of her fiction through historical attention to context and correlative evidence rather than in terms of its strictly literary qualities or through analysis of its literary criticism, so well explored elsewhere by distinguished literary scholars.

22. See, for instance, Tracy Fessenden, "Race, Religion, and the New Woman in America: The Case of Charlotte Perkins Gilman," *Furman Studies* 37 (June 1995): 15–25; Gail Bederman, *Manliness and Civilization: A Cultural History of Gender and Race in the United States, 1880–1917* (Chicago: University of Chicago Press, 1995); Peyser, *Utopia and Cosmopolis,* 63–91; Bernice L. Hausman, "Sex before Gender: Charlotte Perkins Gilman and the Evolutionary Paradigm of Utopia," *Feminist Studies* 24 (Fall 1998): 488–509; Louise Newman, *White Women's Rights* (New York: Oxford University Press, 1999), 132–57; Sandra M. Gilbert and Susan Gubar, "'Fecundate! Discriminate!' Charlotte Perkins Gilman and the Theologizing of Maternity," in *Optimist Reformer,* ed. Rudd and Gough, 200–216; Scharnhorst, "Historicizing Gilman: A Bibliographer's View," in *Mixed Legacy,* ed. Golden and Zangrando, 65–76; and Alys Eve Weinbaum, "Writing Feminist Genealogy: Charlotte Perkins Gilman, Racial Nationalism, and the Reproduction of Maternalist Feminism," *Femi-*

nist Studies 27 (Summer 2001): 271–302. For some of these themes framed in a more comparative context, see Mariana Valverde, "'When the Mother of the Race is Free': Race, Reproduction, and Sexuality in First Wave Feminism," in *Gender Conflicts: New Essays in Women's History*, ed. Franca Iacovetta and Mariana Valverde (Toronto: University of Toronto Press, 1992), 3–26, esp. 21–23.

23. See, for instance, Deegan, introduction to *With Her in Ourland*, 10–27; Jane Upin, "Charlotte Perkins Gilman: Instrumentalism beyond Dewey," *Hypatia* 8 (1993): 38–63; Charlene Haddock Seigfried, "Can a 'Man-Hating' Feminist Also Be a Pragmatist? On Charlotte Perkins Gilman," *Journal of Speculative Philosophy* 15 (May 2001): 74–85; Lois N. Magner, "Darwinism and the Woman Question: The Evolving Views of Charlotte Perkins Gilman," in *Critical Essays*, ed. Karpinski, 115–28; Frank G. Kirkpatrick, "'Begin Again!' The Cutting Edge of Charlotte Perkins Gilman's Gentle Religious Optimism," in *Critical Essays*, ed. Karpinski, 129–43; Dolores Hayden, *The Grand Domestic Revolution* (Cambridge, MA: MIT Press, 1981), 182–277, 202–3, Hayden, "Charlotte Perkins Gilman and the Kitchenless House," *Radical History Review* 21 (Fall 1979): 245; and Naomi B. Zauderer, "Consumption, Production, and Reproduction in the Work of Charlotte Perkins Gilman," in *Optimist Reformer*, ed. Rudd and Gough, 151–72.

24. See, for instance, Deegan and Hill's creative subtitle for Gilman's originally serialized "The Dress of Women" (*Forerunner* [1915]): *The Dress of Women: A Critical Introduction to the Symbolism and Sociology of Clothing*, ed. Michael R. Hill and Mary Jo Deegan (Westport, CT: Greenwood Press, 2002). Another example of editorial alteration of Gilman's work is Joan Blake's edition of Gilman's *Benigna Machiavelli*, in which she deletes Gilman's melodramatic expressions and punctuation, imposes nonsexist language, toning down "sexist remarks about 'boys'"—see Blake, introduction to Gilman, *Benigna Machiavelli*, 6–7. For these contrasting views, see Lane, *To Herland*, 19–20; and Polly Wynn Allen, *Building Domestic Liberty: The Architectural Feminism of Charlotte Perkins Gilman* (Amherst: University of Massachusetts Press, 1988), 171. See also Christine Stansell, *American Moderns: Bohemian New York and the Creation of a New Century* (New York: Metropolitan Books, 2000), 245.

25. Maureen Egan, "Evolutionary Theory in the Social Philosophy of Charlotte Perkins Gilman," *Hypatia* 4 (Spring 1989): 102, 106, and 111; Judith Nies, *Portraits from the Radical Tradition* (New York: Viking Press, 1977), 143; and Palmeri, "Charlotte Perkins Gilman," 115.

26. See, for instance, Deborah De Simone, "Charlotte Perkins Gilman and Educational Reform," in *Optimist Reformer*, ed. Rudd and Gough, 146. For an account of her "architectural feminism" slighting those parts of Gilman's work incompatible with this framework, see Allen, *Building Domestic Liberty*, 5 and 171–73. See also Mary Jo Deegan and Christopher W. Podeschi, "The Ecofeminist Pragmatism of Charlotte Perkins Gilman," *Environmental Ethics* 23 (Spring 2001): 19–36.

27. See also Degler, introduction to Gilman, *Women and Economics* (1966), xxiii; Deegan, introduction to *With Her in Ourland*, 32 and 49; Hayden, *Grand Domestic Revolution*, 202; Karen Stevenson, "Hair Today, Shorn Tomorrow? Hair Symbolism, Gender, and the Agency of Self," in *Optimist Reformer*, ed. Rudd and Gough, 219–42; and Upin, "Charlotte Perkins Gilman," 56.

28. Georgia Johnston, "Exploring Lack and Absence in the Body/Text: Charlotte

Perkins Gilman Prewriting Irigaray," *Women's Studies* 21 (1992): 75–86; and Upin, "Charlotte Perkins Gilman," 56.

29. See, for instance, Allen, *Building Domestic Liberty,* 103–18.

30. See Nancy Cott, Gerda Lerner, Kathryn Kish Sklar, Ellen DuBois, and Nancy Hewitt, "Considering the State of U.S. Women's History," *Journal of Women's History* 15 (Spring 2003): 146. And see Catharine A. MacKinnon, "Feminism, Marxism, Method and the State: An Agenda for Theory," *Signs* 7 (Spring 1982): 515.

PART I

Gilman's diary is archived in the Charlotte Perkins Gilman Papers, Schlesinger Library.

CHAPTER I

For reasons of space, individual diary and collected correspondence references are to page numbers in Knight and Hill's editions. The general chronology should be plain in corresponding portions of text above; where necessary, more specific dates are given. Gilman, "One Girl of Many" was originally published in *Alpha* 1 (February 1884): 15.

1. On the "newness" of the term "sexuality," see my "Frameworks and Questions in Australian Sexuality Studies," in *Rethinking Sex: Social Theory and Sexuality Research,* ed. R. W. Connell and Gary Dowsett (Melbourne: Melbourne University Press, 1992), 5–31, esp. 6–8 and 26–27; and for diverse approaches to the category "sexuality" by historians, see Stephen Garton, *Histories of Sexuality: Antiquity to Sexual Revolution* (London: Equinox, 2004), 1–30.

2. Full appraisal of the voluminous critical literary and cultural studies commentary on "The Yellow Wall-paper" is beyond the scope of this present study. For indicative examples of this rich strand of scholarship see Judith Fetterley, "Reading about Reading: 'A Jury of Her Peers,' 'Murders in the Rue Morgue,' and 'The Yellow Wallpaper,'" in *Gender and Reading: Essays on Readers, Texts, and Contexts,* ed. Elizabeth Flynn and Patricinio P. Schweikart (Baltimore: Johns Hopkins University Press, 1986), 147–64; Ellen Bassuk, "The Rest Cure: Repetition or Resolution of Victorian Women's Conflicts?" in *The Female Body in Western Culture: Contemporary Perspectives,* ed. Susan Rubin Suleiman (Cambridge, MA: Harvard University Press, 1986), 139–51; Diane Herndl, "The Writing Cure: Charlotte Perkins Gilman, Anna O., and 'Hysterical Writing,'" *NWSA Journal* 1 (1988): 52–74; Catherine J. Golden, "'Overwriting' the Rest Cure: Charlotte Perkins Gilman's Literary Escape from S. Weir Mitchell's Fictionalization of Women," in *Critical Essays,* ed. Karpinski, 144–58; Jonathan Crewe, "Queering 'The Yellow Wallpaper': Charlotte Perkins Gilman and the Politics of Form," *Tulsa Studies in Women's Literature* 14 (Fall 1995): 273–93; Jane F. Thrailkill, "Doctoring 'The Yellow Wallpaper,'" *English Literary History* 69 (Summer 2002): 525–66; Shawn St. Jean, "Hanging 'The Yellow Wall-Paper': Feminism and Textual Studies," *Feminist Studies* 28 (Summer 2002): 397–406; and Anita Duneer, "On the Verge of a Breakthrough: Projections of Escape from the Attic and the Thwarted Tower in Charlotte Perkins Gilman's 'The Yellow Wallpaper' and Susan Glaspell's 'The Verge,'" *Journal of American Drama and Theatre* 18 (Winter 2006): 34–53.

3. For representative discussions of Gilman's young adulthood and breakdown, see David Schuster, "Personalizing Illness and Modernity: S. Weir Mitchell, Literary Women, and Neurasthenia, 1870–1914," *Bulletin of the History of Medicine* 79 (Winter 2005): 695–722. And see, for instance, Mary Armfield Hill, "Charlotte Perkins Gilman: A Feminist's Struggle with Womanhood," *Massachusetts Review* 21 (Fall 1980): 503–26; Carol Ruth Berkin, "Private Woman, Public Woman: The Contradictions of Charlotte Perkins Gilman," in *Critical Essays,* ed. Karpinski, 150–73; and Hedges, afterword to *The Yellow Wallpaper,* 37–63.

4. Critics have debated whether the narrator is nameless or whether her name is "Jane," as argued by some psychoanalytic readers of the text—see Barbara A. Suess, "The Writing's on the Wall: Symbolic Orders in 'The Yellow Wallpaper,'" *Women's Studies* 32 (January–February 2003): 79–97.

5. See, for instance, Carol Margaret Davison, "Haunted House/Haunted Heroine: Female Gothic Closets in 'The Yellow Wall-paper,'" *Women's Studies* 33 (January–February 2004): 47–75; and Beverly A. Hume, "Managing Madness in Gilman's 'The Yellow Wall-Paper,'" *Studies in American Fiction* 30 (Spring 2002): 3–20. And see Susan S. Lanser, "Feminist Criticism, 'The Yellow Wallpaper,' and the Politics of Color in America," *Feminist Studies* 15 (Fall 1989): 415–41.

6. On her other works with these themes, see also Denise D. Knight, "The Reincarnation of Jane: 'Through This'—Gilman's Companion to 'The Yellow Wallpaper,'" *Women's Studies* 20, nos. 3–4 (1992): 287–302; Michelle A. Masse, "Gothic Repetition: Husbands, Horrors, and Things That Go Bump in the Night," *Signs* 15 (Summer 1990): 679–709; see Elaine Hedges, "Out at Last: 'The Yellow Wall-paper' after Two Decades of Feminist Criticism," in *The Captive Imagination: A Casebook on "The Yellow Wallpaper,"* ed. Catherine J. Golden (New York: Feminist Press, 1992), 324–27; William Veeder, "Who Is Jane? The Intricate Feminism of Charlotte Perkins Gilman," *Arizona Quarterly* 44 (Autumn 1988): 43, 48–49, 52–61; and Paula A. Treichler, "Escaping the Sentence: Diagnosis and Discourse in 'The Yellow Wallpaper,'" in *Feminist Issues in Literary Scholarship,* ed. Shari Benstock (Bloomington: Indiana University Press, 1984), 62–78. And see Sari Edelstein, "Charlotte Perkins Gilman and the Yellow Newspaper," *Legacy* 24 (2007): 72–92.

7. CPG to Martha Luther, 30 July 1881, in Charlotte Perkins Gilman (1860–1935), Letters to Martha Luther Lane, 1879–90, Rhode Island Historical Society Mss 437.

8. See Lane, *To Herland,* 225–56.

9. On Gilman's maternal ambivalence and contradictory stances, according to critics, see Juliann Evans Fleenor, "The Gothic Prism: Charlotte Perkins Gilman's Gothic Stories and Her Autobiography" in *Woman and Her World,* ed. Meyerling, 117–18; and Hill, *Making of a Radical Feminist,* 72. Allowing themselves to be too guided by Gilman's own selective commentaries on aspects of her life, scholars have missed key facts and Gilman's slants. See Denise D. Knight, "Charlotte Perkins Gilman's Lost Book: A Biographical Gap," *ANQ: A Quarterly Journal of Short Articles, Notes, and Reviews* 14 (Winter 2001): 27.

10. Ann Douglas Wood, "Fashionable Diseases: Women's Complaints and Their Treatment in Nineteenth-Century America," in *Clio's Consciousness Raised: New Perspectives on the History of Women,* ed. Mary Hartman and Lois Banner (San Francisco: Harper Torchbooks, 1974), 23–37; and Lane, *To Herland,* 111–17. See also Jennifer S. Tuttle,

"Rewriting the West Cure: Charlotte Perkins Gilman, Owen Wister, and the Sexual Politics of Neurasthenia," in *Mixed Legacy,* ed. Golden and Zangrando, 103–21.

11. Regina Morantz, "The Lady and Her Physician," in *Clio's Consciousness Raised,* ed. Hartman and Banner, 38–53; Jane Addams, *Twenty Years at Hull House* (1910; reprint, New York: Signet, 1961), 42. While Hill states in her 1980 biography that Mitchell had treated Gilman's great aunt, Catherine Beecher (1880–78), Knight suggests that one Beecher treated by Mitchell was Gilman's cousin, Georgiana Beecher Stowe, but that the identity of the other remains unclear. See Denise D. Knight, "'All the facts of the case': Gilman's Lost Letter to Dr. S. Weir Mitchell," *American Literary Realism* 37 (Spring 2005): 259–77, esp. 262, 272, and 275.

12. See Silas Weir Mitchell to Charles Lyman Strong, 10 October 1882, and Harriet Russell Strong to Charles Lyman Strong, 21 December 1882; and Harriet Russell Strong, "Business Training for Women," *Business Folio* 1, no. 1 (January 1895):1, Box 10/234 and Box 17, Harriet Russell Strong Papers, Henry E. Huntington Library, San Marino, CA. One of these activities was her founding of the Ebell Society—a musical appreciation group—whose events Gilman attended with her daughter in the early 1890s. Gilman and Strong became acquainted in the early 1890s through the Pacific Women's Congress, both presenting papers in May 1895 on the conference theme "The Home"; Strong's paper was titled "Domestic Duties" and Gilman's paper was "Organization in Home Industry"—see conference program, CPGP, SL 177/4/7, and diary entry, 31 October 1891, in Knight, *Diaries,* 2:480.

13. See Gilman, "From a Hearst Paper," *Forerunner* 5 (September 1914): 251.

14. Gilman, *Living,* 96.

15. See Carolyn Heilbrun, *Writing a Woman's Life* (London: Women's Press, 1981), 48–49; Lane, *To Herland,* 232–37, 317–19; Hill, *Making of a Radical Feminist,* 158–59; and Gilman, *Living,* 163. Hill contends Gilman unfairly blamed her deceased mother, Mary Fitch Westcott Perkins, for many of her problems, thereby omitting all the complexities, love, and interdependence of their relationship; see Hill, *Making of a Radical Feminist,* 153–54, and Gilman, *Living,* 318–24.

16. These include "Why I Wrote 'The Yellow Wall-paper,'" *Forerunner* 4 (October 1913): 271, published after Stetson's death, during the editing of his diaries of their courtship and marriage, 1882–88. See Mary Armfield Hill, *Endure: The Diaries of Charles Walter Stetson* (Philadelphia: Temple University Press, 1988), xxxviii–xxxix.

17. Knight, "Charlotte Perkins Gilman's Lost Book," 28; and see also Cynthia J. Davis, "Love and Economics: Charlotte Perkins Gilman on 'The Woman Question,'" *American Transcendental Quarterly* 19 (December 2005): 246. For further discussion, see Lane, *To Herland,* 123–24, 132, 180, 217–18, 221–22; and Mary M. O'Brien, "Autobiography and Liminality: Which Story Does Charlotte Perkins Gilman Choose to Tell?" *Women's Studies* 20 (October 1991): 37–50, esp. 42–44. And see Lane, *To Herland,* 142–43.

18. See Charles C. Eldredge, *Charles Walter Stetson, Color, and Fantasy* (Lawrence: Spencer Museum of Art, University of Kansas, 1982), 21–23 and 35–36.

19. See, for instance, Emily Hartshorne Mudd, Marvin Stein, and Howard E. Mitchell, "Paired Reports of Sexual Behavior of Husbands and Wives in Conflicted Marriages," *Comprehensive Psychiatry* 2, no. 3 (1961): 149–56; and Knight, *Diaries,* 1:300.

20. See, for instance, Hill, *Making of a Radical Feminist,* 120, 124, 128, and 145–47.

21. See Scharnhorst, *Charlotte Perkins Gilman,* 7–11.

22. Hill, *Endure,* xxxvi, xxxvii–xxxviii; Lane, *To Herland,* 102; Denise D. Knight, "'I am getting angry enough to do something desperate': The Question of Female Madness in 'The Yellow Wall-paper'" in *"The Yellow Wall-paper" by Charlotte Perkins Gilman: A Dual Critical Edition,* ed. Shawn St. Jean (Athens: Ohio University Press, 2006), 82–84, and Knight, "The Reincarnation of Jane," 296. For further discussion of the Stetsons' interactions and more skeptical treatments of Gilman's depiction of Mitchell, see also Marjean D. Purinton, "Reading Marital Relationships: The Wallpaper in *A Room of One's Own,*" in *The Pedagogical Wallpaper: Teaching Charlotte Perkins Gilman's "The Yellow Wall-Paper,"* ed. Jeffrey A. Weinstock (New York: Peter Lang; 2003), 97–103; and Michael Blackie, "Reading the Rest Cure," *Arizona Quarterly* 60 (Summer 2004): 57–85; and see Veeder, "Who Is Jane?" 59.

23. Lane, *To Herland,* 87.

24. Hill, *Endure,* 7–8, 48, 41, 163, and 247.

25. Ibid., 15, 49, 92, 25, 242, and 82.

26. Ibid., 82, 96, and 55.

27. Ibid., 149–50, 193–94, 32–34, and 44.

28. Ibid., xxx, 60, 169, 201, 55, and 213. Interestingly, recalling the incident in 1897, she reported to her cousin that "I told Walter once I wished he were a woman and it seemed to hurt his feelings. I can see why now but I didn't then" (Hill, *Journey from Within,* 99). Stetson records two such incidents in his diary, both quotations from her letters to him. In the first she had written in January 1882 shortly after they met, "I half wish you were a woman. I have a haunting dread that in this joy there may lurk some danger"; while the second read, "I don't like it. O why weren't you a girl! Why weren't you a girl! . . . I shun your eyes; I shun your touch—because I want them." Far from hurt, Stetson took these to be signs that "I have touched her heart and awakened her amorous desires." He found them "touching," not evidence that her basic erotic orientation was same-sex. See Hill, *Endure,* 29 and 44.

29. See Lane, *To Herland,* 85; and Hill, *Endure,* 69.

30. Hill, *Endure,* 111–12.

31. Ibid., 70, 144, 144–45, and 224.

32. Ibid., 48–49, 245, and 67.

33. Ibid., 184, 185, 186, 187, and 189. On men's suicides in her circle, see Denise D. Knight, "The Dying of Charlotte Perkins Gilman," *American Transcendental Quarterly* 13, no. 2 (1999): 137–59, esp. 142–46.

34. Hill, *Endure,* 201 and 202.

35. Knight, *Diaries,* 1:101–2, 149–50, 225–26, 244, and 246; and Hill, *Endure,* 202, 220, and 210.

36. See Gilman, "In Duty Bound," *Woman's Journal* 15 (12 January 1884): 14, and Gilman, "One Girl among Many," *Alpha* 1 (1 May 1884): 15; Hill, *Endure,* 27–29; Knight, *Diaries,* 1:277 and 286–87; see also Jane Lancaster, "'I could easily have been an acrobat': Charlotte Perkins Gilman and the Providence Ladies' Sanitary Gymnasium, 1881–1884," *American Transcendental Quarterly* 8 (March 1994): 33–52; and Lane, *To Herland,* 98.

37. Knight, *Diaries,* 1:324, 329, and 332.

38. Hill, *Endure,* 268.

39. Ibid., 264; Knight, *Diaries,* 1:277, 289, 295, 301, 298, and 296; CPG, diary, 1 September 1884, CPGP, SL 177/Box 27, vol. 19, 104; and Hill, *Endure,* 179–80.

40. Ibid., 279, 280, 281, 282–83 and 285–86; and see also Eldredge, *Color and Fantasy,* 43.

41. Hill, *Endure,* 297, 293, 290, and 291.

42. Ibid., 300–301, 306, 307–8, 309–10, and 322.

43. Ibid., 83 and 304.

44. Knight, *Diaries,* 1:348.

45. Ibid., 349. Later, she speculated that making visual art more "human" and less "ultra-masculine" would be very difficult, for the "ultra-masculine artist" was typically full of the "natural urge to expression of the sex"—see Gilman, *Man-Made World,* 85–86; and see also Gilman, *His Religion and Hers,* 74–77. See also Eldredge, *Color and Fantasy,* 42.

46. Hill, *Making of a Radical Feminist,* 208 and 201.

47. Knight, *Diaries,* 1:366, 351, and 370, and Knight, "'I could Paint Still Life as well as any one on Earth': Charlotte Perkins Gilman and the World of Art," *Women's Studies* 35 (July–August 2006): 477–81.

48. See Hill, *Endure,* 322–3; and Knight, *Diaries;* 1:371. Gilman noted that she liked Dr. Walker "but am not converted. She has no feeling for beauty in costume; thinks it beneath intelligent beings. She wears heels; and was to put to it for a reason when I attacked them. Her costume was old-fashioned, very. Short hair of course." (see Knight, *Diaries,* 1:355). See also Gilman, "A Protest against Petticoats," *Women's Journal* 18 (26 February 1887): 60. Later in her 1915 serialized treatise, "The Dress of Women," she cited exactly this common accident of women's primitive home industries. See discussion in chap. 4. And see Knight, *Diaries,* 1:369.

49. Knight, *Diaries,* 1:375–76.

50. Ibid., 368 and 373; and Hill, *Endure,* 331–32.

51. Hill, *Endure,* 332–33.

52. Knight, *Diaries,* 1:375.

53. Ibid., 366, 379, 359, and 374; and Hill, *Endure,* 331.

54. Knight, *Diaries,* 1:375, 374, 377, 378, 379, and 380.

55. Ibid., 381–82.

56. Ibid., 382.

57. Ibid., 383.

58. Ibid., 384, 385, 376, and 377; see, for instance, Gilman, *Crux* (1911), ed. Jennifer S. Tuttle (Newark: University of Delaware Press, 2002), 165; Knight, *Diaries,* 1:262, 311, 331–32, 373, 375, 381–82, 359, 369, 374, 378, 381, and 385.

59. Hill, *Endure,* 335.

60. Morantz, "The Lady and Her Physician," 42–43 and 51–52; and see Hill, *Endure,* 337, 338, and 339.

61. Ibid., 339 and 340.

62. Ibid., 342.

63. Ibid., 341 and 342.

64. Ibid., 351, 335, and 347.

65. For discussion of venereal disease rates in the period, see chap. 9. See Eldredge, *Color and Fantasy,* 46.

66. See, for instance, Lucy Bland, *Banishing the Beast: English Feminism and Sexual Morality, 1885–1914* (London: Penguin, 1995), 124–85; Sheila Jeffreys, "'Free from All Uninvited Touch of Man': Women's Campaigns around Sexuality, 1880–1914," *Women's Studies International Forum* 5, no. 6 (1982): 629–45; and see "Mrs. Gilman's Scorn Strikes 'Masculism,'" *New York Times,* 2 April 1914, 11.

67. Eldredge, *Color and Fantasy,* 106; and Hill, "Feminist's Struggle," 509.

CHAPTER 2

For reasons of space, individual diary and collected correspondence references are to page numbers in Knight's and Hill's editions. The general chronology should be plain in corresponding portions of text above; where necessary, more specific dates are given.

1. CPG to George Houghton Gilman, 16 June and 11 July 1897, in Hill, *Journey from Within,* 67 and 71.

2. See Lane, *To Herland,* 152, 228, 337–39, and 347–49; Hill, *The Making of a Radical Feminist,* 217–20, 218, and 297.

3. See Hill, *Journey from Within,* 25.

4. See Cynthia J. Davis, "The Two Mrs. Stetsons and the 'Romantic Summer,'" in *Charlotte Perkins Gilman and Her Contemporaries: Literary and Intellectual Contexts,* ed. Cynthia J. Davis and Denise D. Knight (Tuscaloosa: University of Alabama Press, 2004), 3–5; Gilman, *Art Gems for the Home and Fireside* (Providence, RI: JA and RA Reid, 1888); Denise D. Knight, "Charlotte Perkins Gilman's Lost Book: A Biographical Gap," *ANQ: A Quarterly Journal of Short Articles, Notes, and Reviews* 14 (Winter 2001): 26–29, 28; and Knight, "'I could Paint Still Life as well as any one on Earth,'" 475–76 and 485–89. And see Adelaide M. Kennedy, Jane S. Knowles, and Lucy Thoma, "Channing, Grace Ellery, 1862–1937, Papers, 1806–1973: A Finding Aid, Arthur and Elizabeth Schlesinger Library on the History of Women in America, Radcliffe College, OASIS: Online Archival Search Information System, Harvard University, 1985. The epigraph is excerpted from Hill, *Endure,* 348, 363–64, 365.

5. Davis, "The Two Mrs. Stetsons," 6–8.

6. See also, Hill, *Endure,* 347, 355, 363, and 366; Davis, "The Two Mrs. Stetsons," 8; and in Stetson's words, 27 August 1888: "Miss Channing says that she quite loves me, which means a good deal, coming from her" (Hill, *Endure,* 366).

7. See Eldredge, *Color and Fantasy,* 49; and Davis, "The Two Mrs. Stetsons," 8.

8. Eldredge, *Color and Fantasy,* 59.

9. Ibid., 59; Davis, "The Two Mrs. Stetsons," 8.

10. See CPG to Grace Ellery Channing Stetson, 3 December 1890, CPGP [Addendum], 1884–1935, SL Mf.6. See also Cynthia J. Davis, "The Two Mrs. Stetsons," 1.

11. For a useful discussion of these issues in the context of women's same-sex relationships, see Lillian Faderman, "The Morbidification of Love between Women by Nineteenth-Century Sexologists," *Journal of Homosexuality* 4 (Fall 1978): 73–90.

12. See Eldredge, *Color and Fantasy,* 52 and 58–59; Davis, "The Two Mrs.

Stetsons," 11. Typically Channing Stetson wrote (for *Harper's, Atlantic Monthly,* and *Saturday Evening Post*) stories of self-sacrificing dependent women nobly enduring the weakness of their partners and living and suffering happily ever after. Many were set in Italy and aimed at children—for instance, *The Fortune of a Day* (Chicago: H.S. Stone, 1900). See "Barbara A. White," in *Charlotte Perkins Gilman: A Study of the Short Fiction,* by Denise D. Knight (New York: Twayne Publishers; London: Prentice Hall International, 1997), 203–5. For a helpful account of their friendship, see Lane, *To Herland,* 150–52 and 137–49.

13. See the photograph by G. L. Hurd (Providence, RI, 1891), "Copy of a painted portrait of Charlotte Perkins Gilman," of the painting done by Charles Walter Stetson (SL 177-325-7/M8432); and Davis, "The Two Mrs. Stetsons," 2.

14. See Knight, *Diaries,* 2:427; Eldredge, *Color and Fantasy,* 106; and Scharnhorst, *Charlotte Perkins Gilman,* 41–42. See Denise D. Knight, "'With the First Grass-Blade': Whitman's Influence on the Poetry of Charlotte Perkins Gilman," *Walt Whitman Quarterly Review* 11 (Summer 1993): 18–29.

15. See, for instance, "Seek Health: Physical Education for Girls—Charlotte Perkins Stetson," *Los Angeles Times,* 6 March 1890, 7; "Social Purity: A Meeting to Be Followed by Organization," *Los Angeles Times,* 28 June 1890, 7; and "Woman's Nature: An Interesting and Instructive Address by Mrs. Stetson," *Los Angeles Times,* 27 July 1890, 7. See also Knight, *Diaries,* 2:417, 419, 421, 427, 428, 433, and 434.

16. Knight, *Diaries,* 2:432, 435, and 441.

17. Ibid., 421, 444, 446, 440, 442, 441, 450–51, and 453.

18. Ibid., 454.

19. Ibid., 455. The epigraph to this section is taken from ibid., 2:484.

20. Ibid., 456–57. Hill observes that, absent biographical studies, Knapp remains an enigma, often recollected by those portraying her negatively—for instance, Harriet Howe, "Charlotte Perkins Gilman—as I Knew Her," *Equal Rights,* 5 September 1936, 211–16. Knapp also moved to New York in 1897. She joined teaching expeditions to the Philippines and wrote a critical history of imperialism suffered by its people, praising its democratic leaders and its peoples' characteristics and customs. She also published well-received fiction and nonfiction, as well as editing a home magazine and running a girls' school, before dying in California in June 1909. The *New York Times* quoted a letter by Knapp, stating that she left journalism because "it does not offer a real career for a woman—the sacrifices are too great." She lived alone for extended periods in the desert, wrote books, "and did a lot of thinking." Her other publications included *The Story of the Philippines* (New York: Silver Burdett & Co., 1902), and *A Well in the Desert* (New York: Century, 1908). See "Adeline Knapp," *New York Times,* 26 June, 1909), BR402.

21. Knight, *Diaries,* 2:492. See, for instance, Gilman, "Two Races in One," "The Maternal Instinct," "The Bugaboo of Publicity," "The Illogical Mind," "Ought a Woman to Earn Her Living," "Masculine, Feminine, and Human," *Kate Field's Washington,* 5 November 1890, 69; 21 January 1891, 44–45; 25 February 1891, 119; 22 April 1891, 252; 26 August 1891, 136–37; and 6 July 1892, 6–7, respectively.

22. Knight, *Diaries,* 2:472.

23. Ibid., 461, 466, 472, 906, and 916.

24. Ibid., 479, 482, 487, 495, 502, and 513. Knight identifies the dates Gilman

charted for Knapp as 13 August, 6 and 31 October, and 24 December 1891. See Knight, *Diaries*, 2:916.

25. CPG to George Houghton Gilman, 7 March 1899, in Hill, *Journey from Within*, 246; and see Hill, *Making of a Radical Feminist*, 67.

26. See Carroll Smith-Rosenberg, "The Female World of Love and Ritual: Relations between Women in Nineteenth Century America," in *Disorderly Conduct: Visions of Gender in Victorian America* (New York: Oxford University Press, 1985), 53–76; Sheila Jeffreys, "Does It Matter If They Did It?" in *Not a Passing Phase: Reclaiming Lesbians in History, 1840–1985*, ed. Lesbian History Group (London: Women's Press, 1989), 19–29; Jennifer Terry, "Theorizing Deviant Historiography," *differences* 3 (Summer 1991): 55–74; Martha Vicinus, "Lesbian History: All Theory and No Facts or All Facts and No Theory?" *Radical History Review* 60 (1994): 57–75; Judith M. Bennett, "'Lesbian-Like' and the Social History of Lesbianisms," *Journal of the History of Sexuality* 9 (2000): 1–24; and Leila J. Rupp, "Toward a Global History of Same-Sex Sexuality," *Journal of the History of Sexuality* 10 (2001): 287–302. The scandal of Alice Mitchell's slaying of Freda Ward in Memphis led to rumination on women's unhealthy relationships across 1892 and into 1893, exactly when Gilman and Knapp's relationship soured. See Lisa Duggan, "The Trials of Alice Mitchell: Sensationalism, Sexology, and the Lesbian Subject," *Signs* 18 (Summer 1993): 791–810; and Lisa J. Lindquist, "Images of Alice: Gender, Deviancy, and a Love Murder in Memphis," *Journal of the History of Sexuality* 6 (July 1995): 30–61. See also "Eloped with Her Girlfriend," *Washington Post*, 18 March 1892, 4; "Alice Mitchell's Peculiar Insanity," *Los Angeles Times*, 19 July 1892, 1; "Thinks It Was Brain Love: Relations between Alice Mitchell and Dead Freda Ward," *Washington Post*, 24 July 1892, 1.

27. See Gilman, *Living*, 143; and see Adeline E. Knapp, *An Open Letter to Mrs. Carrie Chapman Catt* (New York: New York State Association Opposed to Woman Suffrage, 1899), 5, 6, and 8; Knight, *Diaries*, 2:592; Hill, *Making of a Radical Feminist*, 68, 74, 77, 81; Lane, *To Herland*, 78–79; and Hill, *Journey from Within*, 232.

28. Knight, *Diaries*, 2:465, 462; and Gilman, *Living*, 143 and 144.

29. Knight, *Diaries*, 2:468, 479, 485, 507, 512, 513, 531, 532, 534, 540, 541, and 542.

30. Gilman, *The Home*, 95; Knight, *Diary*, 2:506, 523, 529, 531, 499, 913, n.5; and Hill, *Endure*, 309 and 352.

31. Knight, *Diaries*, 2:498, 502, 507, 510, and 506.

32. See Hill, *Making of a Radical Feminist*, 204–5; Lane, *To Herland*, 173.

33. Knight, *Diaries*, 2:483; and see Ella Sterling Cummis Mighels, *The Story of the Files: A Review of California Writers and Fiction* (San Francisco: Cooperative Printing Co., 1893), 390–91.

34. See Lane, *To Herland*, 158, 164, and 176. Other men of all marital statuses accompanied her to and from events, staying to dinner or visiting later, sometimes staying over: Joaquin Miller, James Whitcombe Riley, Edmund Russell, Eugene Hough, Edwin Markham, Will Clemens, George McChesney, Charles Bowles, and Frank Carter. Others noted by surname in her diary included Messrs. Cohen, Andrews, Russell, Calkins, Worcester, Bamford, Griffes, Latimer, and Cridge—see Knight, *Diaries*, 2:503, 512, 513, 531, 533, 534, 540, 545, 553, 492, and 537.

35. See Knapp to CPG, 16 May 1893, CPGP 177/137; and Knight, *Diaries,* 2:538.

36. Knight, *Diaries,* 2:542, 541, and 545.

37. See Knapp to CPG, 11 March, 1894, CPGP 177/137. Lane is arguably more persuasive in reading this letter as pressure, than is Hill in taking it as proof that Knapp was relaxed about repayment. See Lane, *To Herland,* 174–75; and Hill, *Making of a Radical Feminist,* 203; and Knight, *Diaries,* 2:547, 585, 548, 549, 552, 553, 554, 555, 556, 557, 559, 560, 561, 562, 566, 569, and 570.

38. Knight, *Diaries,* 2:51, 572, 574, 575, 582, 591, 592, 593, 594, 595, 596, 597, 598, and 599.

39. See Hill, *Making of a Radical Feminist,* 217–20; and Knight, *Diaries,* 2:575, 579, and 582.

40. Knight, *Diaries,* 2:805, 578.

41. Ibid., 564–65.

42. Hill, *Making of a Radical Feminist,* 227–35.

43. Knight, *Diaries,* 2:574–75.

44. Hill, *Making of a Radical Feminist,* 226–27.

45. Knight, *Diaries,* 2:570, 571, and 581.

46. Ibid., 570, 583, and 585.

47. Ibid., 597

48. Gilman, *Living,* 143; and Knight, *Diaries,* 2:593.

49. Knight, *Diaries,* 2:586, 592, and 594. And see Gilman, *Living,* 143.

50. Knight, *Diaries,* 2:605.

51. Ibid., 609 and 613.

52. Ibid., 616, 632, 633, 634, 612, and 614.

53. Ibid., 603, 605, 609, 611, 614, 616, and 632.

54. Later, she would tell her cousin Houghton Gilman that she had three or four suitors in the period after Knapp left the boarding house. See Hill, *Journey from Within,* 146–47.

55. Knight, *Diaries,* 2:668. The epigraph comes from Hill, *A Journey from Within,* 245.

56. Knight, *Diaries,* 2:668–69; and Hill, *Journey from Within,* 114.

57. Hill, *Journey from Within,* 117 and 356–57.

58. Ibid., 42, 49, 249, and 298.

59. See, for instance, Kimmel and Aronson, introduction to Gilman, *Women and Economics: A Study of the Economic Relation between Men and Women as a Factor in Social Evolution* (Berkeley: University of California Press, 1998), liv; and Hill, *Making of a Radical Feminist,* 77, 79, and 81–84; Adrienne Rich, "Compulsory Heterosexuality and Lesbian Existence," *Signs* 5 (Summer 1980): 631–60; and Hill, *Journey from Within,* 80, 95, 336, 41–42, and 66.

60. Hill, *Journey from Within,* 663, 68, and 814. Cynthia J. Davis sees this process of theorizing and negotiation on Gilman's part as "contradictory" and hypothetical, since she had not yet come to practice what she preached. Yet somewhat more credit for Gilman's projection and analysis is warranted by the evidence. To make a comparison, famous English birth control advocate and sex adviser Marie Stopes (1880–1958), supposedly had not yet experienced the erotic ecstasy that she outlined as every wife's right. This hardly invalidates the quest outlined in her best-seller *Mar-*

ried Love (1918), often credited with revolutionizing interwar heterosexuality in Western cultures. The same holds for Gilman and *Women and Economics* (1898). See Davis, "Love and Economics," 245, 248, and 252.

61. Hill, *Journey from Within,* 49, 75, 77, 97, and 177.

62. Ibid., 336 and 143.

63. Ibid., 97 and 146–47.

64. Ibid., 147–48.

65. Ibid., 301.

66. Ibid., 148, 132, 207, 139, 140, and 143.

67. Ibid., 145, 149, and 156, 245, 175, and 344.

68. Ibid., 149, 51, and 192.

69. Ibid., 126, 128, 229, 231, 234–35, 293–94, 328, 380, and 142. In late 1899, when Stetson told her that he wished to take Katherine with them to Italy, indefinitely, Gilman wrote her fiancé, "I don't want her to grow up European. And O I want a new baby so. I want to begin again and have a fairer chance" (ibid., 335).

70. Ibid., 286.

71. Ibid., 149, 265, and 333.

72. Ibid., 341, 342, 346, and 350.

73. Ibid., 115, 44, 65, 160, 161, 212, and 249; and Knight, *Diaries,* 2:792 and 806.

74. Hill, *Journey from Within,* 149.

75. See Mary Armfield Hill, "'Letters are Like Morning Prayers': The Private Work of Charlotte Perkins Gilman," in *Mixed Legacy,* ed. Golden and Zangrando, 49–50; Gary Scharnhorst, "Historicizing Gilman," in *Mixed Legacy,* ed. Golden and Zangrando, 69; Kimmel and Aronson, introduction to *Women and Economics* (1998), xiii and liv–lvii; and Lane, introduction to *Gilman Reader,* xli–xlii; Degler, introduction to Gilman, *Women and Economics* (1966), xvii and xi; and Kessler, *Charlotte Perkins Gilman,* 69–70.

CHAPTER 3

Gilman, "Sex and Race Progress" can be found in *Sex and Civilization,* ed. Victor F. Calverton and Samuel D. Schmalhausen (New York: Macaulay, 1929), 109.

1. For an insightful feminist theory analysis of Darwin on sexual selection, see Elizabeth Grosz, *The Nick of Time: Politics, Evolution and the Untimely* (Sydney: Allen & Unwin, 2004), esp. 65–79.

2. Gilman, *Women and Economics,* 7, 23–28, 37–39, 141–42 and 225–37, Gilman, "With Her in Ourland," *Forerunner* 7 (November 1916): 296–97, Gilman, "Washtubs and Women's Duty: Is a Mother's Business Child Culture or Housework?" *Century* 110 (June 1925): 154–55, Gilman, *The Home,* 96–97, and Gilman, *His Religion and Hers,* 218–30.

3. See Aileen S. Kraditor, *Up from the Pedestal: Selected Writings in the History of American Feminism* (Chicago: Quadrangle Books, 1968), 144–45; and Sally J. Perkins, "The Myth of the Matriarchy: Annulling Patriarchy through the Regeneration of Time," *Communication Studies* 42 (Winter 1991): 371–82.

4. See Jacob J. Bachofen, *Myth, Religion, and Mother-Right* (1861; reprint, London: Routledge & Kegan Paul, 1978); Lewis Henry Morgan, *Ancient Society* (New

York: Henry Holt & Co., 1877); also see Rosalind Coward, *Patriarchal Precedents: Sexuality and Social Relations* (London; Boston: Routledge & Kegan Paul, 1983), 31–35 and 38–42; and Lester Frank Ward, *Pure Sociology: A Treatise on the Origin and Spontaneous Development of Society* (New York: Macmillan, 1903), 339.

5. See Eliza Burt Gamble, *The Evolution of Woman: An Inquiry into the Dogma of Her Inferiority to Man* (New York: Putnam's Sons, 1894); Jane Johnstone Christie, *Advance of Women from the Earliest Times to the Present* (Philadelphia: Lippincott, 1912); Catherine Gasquoine Hartley Gallichan, *Age of Mother Power: The Position of Woman in Primitive Society* (New York: Dodd, Mead, 1913); Hartley, *The Truth about Women* (London: E. Nash, 1913); Hartley, *Position of Women in Primitive Society: A Study of the Matriarchy* (London: E. Nash, 1914); Otis Tufton Mason, *Woman's Share in Primitive Culture* (New York: Appleton, 1894); Rosa Mayreder, *Survey of the Woman Problem* (London: William Heineman, 1913); Scott Nearing and Nellie S. Nearing, *Woman and Social Progress* (New York: Macmillan, 1912); and Anna Garlin Spencer, *Women's Share in Social Culture* (New York: Mitchell Kennerley, 1913).

6. For fuller discussion of his early life, see Sean H. McMahon, *Social Control and Public Intellect: The Legacy of Edward A. Ross* (New Brunswick, NJ: Transaction, 1999), 1–29.

7. Scott, *Lester Frank Ward*, 16. For additional biographies and studies of Ward's life and work, see Bernhard J. Stern, "The Liberal Views of Lester F. Ward," *Scientific Monthly* 61 (August 1950): 102–4; John C. Burnham, *Lester Frank Ward in American Thought* (Washington, DC: Public Affairs Press, 1956); Barbara Finlay, "Lester Frank Ward as a Sociologist of Gender: A New Look at His Sociological Work," *Gender and Society* 13 (April 1999): 251–65; and Edward C. Rafferty, *Apostle of Human Progress: Lester Frank Ward and American Political Thought* (Lanham, MD: Rowman & Littlefield, 2003).

8. Ward, *Pure Sociology*, 300 and 339.

9. Coward, *Patriarchal Precedents*, 20, 68–69; Ward, *Dynamic Sociology*, 1:657; and John Ferguson McLennan, *Primitive Marriage: An Enquiry into the Origin of the Form of Capture in Marriage Ceremonies* (Edinburgh: Adam & Charles Black, 1865), 165.

10. Among Ward's most important writings, see: "Darwin as a Biologist," *Proceedings, Biological Society of Washington, D.C.* 1 (1882): 81–86; *Dynamic Sociology*, 2 vols. (New York: Appleton, 1883); "Mind as a Social Factor," *Mind* 9 (October 1884): 563–73; "Genius and Women's Intuition," *Forum* 9 (June 1890): 401–8; "Neo-Darwinism and Neo-Lamarckism," *Proceedings, Biological Society of Washington, D.C.* 6 (1891): 11–71; *The Psychic Factors of Civilization* (Boston: Ginn, 1893); "Weismann's Concessions," *Popular Science Monthly* 45 (June 1894): 175–84; *Outlines of Sociology* (New York: Macmillan, 1898); "A Review of the Theory of the Leisure Class, by Thorstein Veblen," *American Journal of Sociology* 5 (May 1900): 829–37; "Social Darwinism," *American Journal of Sociology* 12 (March 1907): 709–10; "Eugenics, Euthenics, and Eudemics," *American Journal of Sociology* 18 (May 1913): 737–54; and *Glimpses of the Cosmos*, 6 vols. (New York: Putnam's, 1913–18).

11. Emily Palmer Cape, *Lester F. Ward: A Personal Sketch* (New York: Putnam's, 1922), 28–30; and Deegan, "Introduction," to *With Her in Ourland*, 1–57.

12. Ward, "The Social Evil," *Iconoclast,* 4 September 1871, reprinted in *Glimpses of the Cosmos,* 1:238–41.

13. Ward, "On Male Sexual Selection," *Transactions of the Anthropological Society of Washington* 1 (May 1881): 37–39, reprinted in *Glimpses of the Cosmos,* 3:75–76.

14. Ward, *Dynamic Sociology,* 1:642–47.

15. Ibid., 608–14.

16. Ibid., 651–63.

17. Ibid., 607–8 and 650

18. Ward, "Our Better Halves," *Forum* 6 (November 1888): 266–75, esp. 269–71; Ward, "Six O' Clock Club Speech" (1888), Ms. 90-23/ 8/171/4, Lester Frank Ward Papers [hereafter LFWP], John Hays Brown Library, Brown University [hereafter JHBL]; and Ward, *Pure Sociology,* 298.

19. Ward, "Our Better Halves," 268

20. Ibid., 274–75; and Ward, *Dynamic Sociology,* 1:614–19 and 649–55.

21. Ward, "Genius and Woman's Intuition," 401–8; and Ward, *Psychic Factors in Civilization,* 87 and 87–88. For discussion of Darwin's peers and successors' rejection and then neglect of this theory of female sex selection, see Kay Harel, "When Darwin Flopped: The Rejection of Sexual Selection," *Sexuality and Culture* 5 (December 2001): 29–42, esp. 38–39.

22. Ward, *Pure Sociology,* 292, 376, and 399. The *Oxford English Dictionary* credits Ward here with the first use of "androcentrism," listing precursor terms from the field of botany—"androdicecious" used by Charles Darwin in 1877 and "andro-hermaphrous" in 1888 in reference to flowers—and from a paper read at the Atheneum on 7 October 1893 entitled "Marital Relations," which referred to "androcratic government." In fact, this theory did not originate with Ward. One of its most influential exponents was Edward Burdett Tylor (1829–81), who made the period's most authoritative statement of this deduction and its ramifications. See *Oxford English Dictionary* 2d ed., s.v. "androcentrism."

23. Ward, *Pure Sociology,* 335–36.

24. Ibid., 353.

25. Ibid., 345.

26. Ibid., 292.

27. Ibid., 300.

28. Ibid., 335–36.

29. Ibid., 353, 350–51, 339–40, and 345. For further discussion of Ward's theories of women's oppression, see Clifford Scott, "A Naturalistic Rationale for Women's Reform: Lester Frank Ward on the Evolution of Sexual Relations," *Historian* 33 (November 1970): 54–67, esp. 58 and 62.

30. See Hill, *Making of a Radical Feminist,* 264–66. The epigraph to this section can be found in Gilman, *The Man-Made World,* 38.

31. See Egan, "Evolutionary Theory," 106; and Hill, *Making of a Radical Feminist,* 267.

32. Hill, *Making of a Radical Feminist,* 266–67; Lane, *To Herland,* 57, 277–79, and 231; Egan, "Evolutionary Theory," 104.

33. Palmeri, "Charlotte Perkins Gilman," 98; and Allen, *Building Domestic Liberty,* 43.

34. Hill, *Making of a Radical Feminist,* 265; Bederman, *Manliness and Civilization,* 126.

35. Gilman, "Editorial Notes," *Impress* 1 (June 1894): 1; Lester Frank Ward (LFW) to CPG, 28 December 1895, CPGP, SL 177/124; and Scott, *Lester Frank Ward,* 106. See Deegan, introduction to *With Her in Ourland,* 18, 20, and 21. Both Gilman and Ward objected to Kidd's "survival of the fittest" approach to social Darwinism and his embrace of Weismann's repudiation of Lamarck's theory of inherited cultural traits, evident in his *Social Evolution* (New York: Macmillan, 1894). See CPG to LFW, 1 January 1896, Ms. 90-23/ 23/10; and LFW to CPG, 13 February 1896, CPGP, SL 177/124. For further context discussion, see Mark Pittinger, *American Socialists and Evolutionary Thought, 1870–1920* (Madison: University of Wisconsin Press, 1993).

36. CPG to LFW, 18 January 1896, 10 February 1896, 18 April 1901, 22 July 1908, LFWP, JHBL 23/10, 28/8, 33/9, 23/10; Ward, "Collective Telesis," *American Journal of Sociology* 2 (March 1897): 815.

37. Cynthia J. Davis makes the interesting observation that Gilman always operated more as an aspiring editor than disciple of Ward's, his providing a theory that "she appropriated, enlarged and politicized." Davis sees Ward as more environmentalist and assimilationist than Gilman, with which I take issue below (see chap. 12). See her "His and Herland: Charlotte Perkins Gilman 'Re-presents' Lester F. Ward," in *Evolution and Eugenics in American Literature, 1880–1940: Essays on Ideological Conflict and Complicity,* ed. Claire Roche and Lois Cuddy (Lewisburg: Bucknell University Press, 2003), 75, 83. I thank Davis and Knight for helpful comments in 2001 on my own essay on Ward and Gilman, "The Overthrow of Gynaecocentric Culture: Charlotte Perkins Gilman and Lester Frank Ward," in *Her Contemporaries,* ed. Davis and Knight, 59–86. See also Gary Scharnhorst, "The Intellectual Context of Herland: The Social Theories of Lester Ward," in *Approaches to Teaching Gilman's "The Yellow Wall-paper" and "Herland,"* ed. Denise D. Knight and Cynthia F. Davis (New York: Modern Languages Association Press), 111–24. See Frederic Beecher Perkins to CPG, 15 October 1878, CPGP, SL 177/26. His suggestions included George Rawlinson, *Five Great Monarchies of the Ancient Eastern World* (London: J. Murray, 1862); William Boyd Dawkins, *Cave Hunting: Researches on the Evidence of Caves Respecting the Early Inhabitants of Europe* (London: Macmillan, 1874); George Grote, *A History of Greece* (London: J. Murray, 1862); Edward B. Tylor, *Researches into the Early History of Mankind and the Development of Civilization* (Chicago: University of Chicago Press, 1865); and John Lubbock, *Prehistoric Times, as Illustrated by Ancient Remains and the Manners and Customs of Modern Savages* (London: William & Norgate, 1865). And see CPG to LFW, 28 November 1900, LFWP, JHBL 90-23/28/8.

38. See Lisa Ganobcsik-Williams, "The Intellectualism of Charlotte Perkins Gilman: Evolutionary Perspectives on Race, Ethnicity, and Gender," in *Optimist Reformer,* ed. Rudd and Gough, 31; and see CPG to LFW, 28 November 1900.

39. Some of Ward's female correspondents became "regulars" with whom he exchanged considerably more correspondence than with the professional peers that preoccupied his biographers, most in the last twenty years of Ward's life (LFWP, JHBL 90-23/19, 20, 23, 24, 27, 28, 31, 33, 35, 37, 38, and reels 12–14). See also LFW to Joanna Odenwald Unger, 27 October 1903, LFWP, JHBL 90-23/30/1. Ward "had always

been a handsome and virile man" whose woman's rights advocacies "produced a group of women admirers" (Scott, *Lester Frank Ward,* 40). And see Judith A. Allen, "The Overthrow of Gynaecocentric Culture," 59–86.

40. CPG to LFW, 15 January 1901, LFW to CPG, 3 January 1907, SL, CPGP 177/124; and CPG to LFW, 3 January 1907, 15 January 1901, 30 June 1903, LFWP, JHBL 90-23/28/8.

41. By 1904, Gilman's work had appeared in over thirty regional, national, and international periodicals; see editor, *Philadelphia Saturday Evening Post* to CPG, 26 September 1899; Hamilton Holt [editor, *Independent*] to CPG, 31 May 1902; and Elizabeth Jordan [editor, *Harper's Bazaar*] to CPG, 10 December 1908—CPGP 177/128, 126, and 133.

42. See Gilman, "Apropos of Prof. Ward's Theory," *Woman's Journal* 35 (16 April 1904): 122.

43. CPG to LFW, 30 June 1903.

44. Ward, "The Past and Future of the Sexes," *Independent* 60 (8 March 1906): 547; Ward, *Pure Sociology,* 345; Ward, *Applied Sociology* (1906), 232; and Ward, "The Historical View of Women," *Independent* 68 (16 June 1910): 1326–28, reprinted in *Glimpses of the Cosmos,* 6:356.

45. See CPG to LFW, 20 January 1904, LFWP, JHBL 90-23/28/8/2.

46. See CPG to LFW, 3 June 1903, LFWP, JHBL 90-23/28; and CPG to LFW, 20 January 1904, LFWP 90-23/28/8.

47. CPG to LFW, 5 August 1904, LFWP, JHBL 90-23/28/8.

48. Ward, "The Past and Future of the Sexes," 541; CPG to LFW, 15 March 1906, LFWP, JHBL 90-23/28/8/1; and Ward, *Glimpses of the Cosmos,* 6:223–24.

49. CPG to LFW, 15 March 1906; and Ward, *Glimpses of the Cosmos,* 6:223–24; CPG to LFW, 15 March 1906; Hill, *Making of a Radical Feminist,* 277–79; and see CPG to LFW, 1 February 1907, LFWP, JHBL 90-23/33/9. Gilman wrote to Houghton Gilman in October 1899 that "I begin to realize that I can read a good deal more than I used. It does not seem to me so much, and I have more appetite for it." See *Journey from Within,* 304.

50. For criticism of Gilman's investment in her Beecher genealogy, see Weinbaum, "Writing Feminist Genealogy," 271–30; and see CPG to LFW, 1 January 1907, LFWP, JHBL 90-23/33/9.

51. For an account of the inadequate salaries paid to academics, see Carnegie Foundation for the Advancement of Teaching, *The Financial Status of the Professor in America and Germany* (New York: G. P. Putnam's Sons, 1908); and U.S. Bureau of Education, *Salaries in Universities and Colleges in 1920* (Washington DC: GPO, 1920).

52. LFW to CPG, 3 January 1907; and Gilman, "The Flagstone Method," *Saturday Evening Post* 172 (15 July 1899): 42.

53. See "Remarkable Literary Success of Mrs. Charlotte Perkins Stetson," *Oakland Post,* 1900; Olivia H. Dunbar, "Mrs. Gilman's Idea of Home," *Critic* 43 (December 1903): 568–70; Vernon Lee, "The Economic Dependence of Women," *North American Review* 175 (1 April 1903): 71–90; "Mrs. Gilman Arouses Hotbed of Discussion," *Brooklyn Eagle,* 29 February 1903; "'Men's Collective Brains Joint Organ of Thought': Mrs. Charlotte Perkins Gilman Tells How People Are Trained Not to Do

Things While the Girl Stands Still," *Toronto World,* 10 November 1904; "The Extension of the Suffrage to Women: Subject of an Interesting Debate before the Outlook Club Last Evening," unidentified newspaper clipping, 1903; "The Ideal Mother: Her Place in the World as Defined by Charlotte Perkins Gilman," unidentified newspaper clipping, 1903; "Editorial: Maternity Mixed with Housework," 20 June 1903, *New York Times,* 19 June 1904, 6; and Henry T. Finck, "Letter to the Editor: Do Women Protect Men?" *Times Democrat,* 8 December 1904, CPGP, SL 177/287/1 and 266/1.

54. Nor was Gilman the only skeptical reader of Ward. Harriot Stanton Blatch, suffragist feminist daughter of Elizabeth Cady Stanton, disputed his account of prostitution, female sexuality, and race relations. See Harriot Stanton Blatch to LFW, 23 June 1903 and 2 September 1903, LFWP, JHBL 90-23/27/11. The epigraph can be found in CPGP 177/124.

55. Gilman, *Women and Economics,* 125.

56. Ibid., 127,

57. Ibid., 128, 141, and 132.

58. Ibid., 134, 136, 138.

59. Gilman, *Man-Made World,* 41, 42, and 57.

60. Gilman, *Women and Economics,* 45, 46, 54, 55, 56, 58, and 59.

61. Gilman, *Herland,* 55; and Gilman, *His Religion and Hers,* 204

62. Gilman, "Notes on 'The Overthrow,'" 5 March 1908, CPGP, SL 177/336/vol. 24.

63. Gilman, "Sex and Race Progress," 109, 112; Gilman, "Washtubs," 153–54; and Gilman, *His Religion and Hers,* 206–7.

64. Gilman, "Notes on 'The Overthrow.'"

65. See Ward, *Pure Sociology,* 359.

66. Ibid., 360. Recent feminist commentators have been certain of Gilman's uncritical racism—often treating it as synonymous with "assimilationism"—but have assumed that Ward somehow stood apart from racialized thought, eugenics, and even racial and ethnic stereotypes. See, for instance, Penelope Deutscher, "The Descent of Man and the Evolution of Woman," *Hypatia* 19 (Spring 2004): 35–55; Minna Doskow, "Charlotte Perkins Gilman: The Female Face of Social Darwinism," *Weber Studies: An Interdisciplinary Humanities Journal* 14 (Fall 1997): 9–22; and Davis, "His and Herland," 83.

67. CPG to LFW, 6 November 1908, LFWP, JHBL 90-23/33/9, 6–7.

68. Cape was the first Barnard College "co-ed" to attend Columbia University classes. "Memories of New York's First Co-Ed; Although Allowed to Take Examinations at Columbia, Mrs. Emily Palmer Cape Was Debarred from Lectures," *New York Times,* 26 March 1916, X4. Also see obituary, "Mrs. Emily Cape, Artist-Author, 88," *New York Times,* 30 December 1953, 23.

69. Scott, *Lester Frank Ward,* 40–41; and Rafferty, *Apostle of Human Progress,* 277–83.

70. Emily Palmer Cape (EPC) to LFW, 15 February 1909, LFWP, JHBL 90-23/33/4.

71. See Mary Gray Peck, *Carrie Chapman Catt: A Biography* (New York: H. W. Wilson Company, 1944); and Peck, *The Rise of the Woman Suffrage Party* (Chicago:

M. S. Hartshorn, 1911). See also, EPC to LFW, 25 September 1909, LFWP, JHBL 90-23/32/15. Given both Peck and Catt's life partnerships with women, homophobia may underlie their disdainful remarks. See Leila J. Rupp, "Sexuality and Politics in the Early Twentieth Century: The Case of the International Women's Movement," *Feminist Studies* 23 (Fall 1997): 577–95.

72. EPC to LFW, 25 September 1909, LFWP, JHBL 90-23/33/4.

73. EPC to LFW, 4 November 1909, LFWP, JHBL 90-23/33/4.

74. See CPG to LFW, 23 February 1911, LFWP, JHBL 90-23/36/8; EPC to Edward Alsworth Ross, 24 April 1913, Edward Alsworth Ross Papers, reel 7, Lamont Library; and Scott, *Lester Frank Ward,* 40–41.

75. Gilman, *Man-Made World,* ii.

76. See Allen, "The Overthrow of Gynaecocentric Culture," 77–79.

77. See Hartley, *The Truth about Women,* 50 and 170. See Thomas's 1890–1900s articles on "primitive" society sex relations from the *American Journal of Sociology,* collected in William I. Thomas, *Sex and Society: Studies in the Social Psychology of Sex* (Boston: Richard G. Badger, 1907), 3–51, 123–46. See also Deegan, "Thomas and the Sociology of Women," in *Jane Addams and the Men of the Chicago School, 1892–1918* (New Brunswick, NJ: Transaction Books, 1988), 202–20; Ellsworth Faris, "W. I. Thomas (1863–1947)," *Sociology and Social Research* 32 (March–April 1948): 755–59; and Gisela Hinkle, "The Four Wishes in Thomas' Theory of Social Change," *Social Research* 19 (December 1952): 464–84.

78. Gilman, "Lester F. Ward Is Dead," *Forerunner* 4 (June 1913): 166.

79. See Palmeri, "Charlotte Perkins Gilman," 98. This evidence of Gilman's resistance to casting ancient savage man as an all powerful "primitive rapist" and evidence of her more gradualist and mutually negotiated account of the rise of androcentric culture provide grounds for some critical qualification of Bederman's influential narrative of Gilman's theory of female subordination. For more discussion of Bederman's approach, see chap. 12. See also her conference paper, "Naked, Unfettered, and Unashamed: Charlotte Perkins Gilman, Anti-Feminism, and the Figure of the Savage Rapist" (paper presented at the Second International Charlotte Perkins Gilman Conference. Skidmore College, Saratoga Springs, NY, 26–29 June 1997).

CHAPTER 4

1. Hill, *Journey from Within,* 83.

2. Gilman, "With Her in Ourland," *Forerunner* 7 (November 1916): 291–97.

3. Gilman, *Women and Economics,* 71. The epigraph for this section is taken from Gilman, "Parasitism and Civilized Vice," in *Woman's Coming of Age: A Symposium,* ed. Samuel D. Schmalhausen and V. F. Calverton (New York: Horace Liveright, Inc., 1931), 125.

4. Gilman, *Women and Economics,* 5 and 141–42.

5. Ibid., 5 and 37.

6. Ibid., 37 and 38.

7. Ibid., 44–46.

8. Gilman, "Sex and Race Progress," in *Sex in Civilization,* ed. Samuel D. Schmalhausen and V. F. Calverton (New York: Macaulay, 1929), 116.

9. Hill, *Journey from Within,* 70.

10. Ibid., 71.

11. Gilman, "Women in Industry," 26.

12. Ibid., 46–47 and 26–27.

13. CPG to Arthur Keller, 24 August 1924, CPGP, SL 177/149/1.

14. Gilman, *Women and Economics,* 53–54.

15. Gilman, "The Dress of Women," *Forerunner* 6 (May 1915): 134, 138, and 135–36.

16. See Gilman, "Why Women Do Not Reform Their Dress," *Woman's Journal* 17 (9 October 1886): 338.

17. Gilman, *Man-Made World,* 141.

18. Gilman, "The Dress of Women," *Forerunner* 6 (January 1915): 23 and 25, and *Forerunner* 6 (February 1915): 50 and 48.

19. Gilman, "The Dress of Women," *Forerunner* 6 (March 1915): 76–77 and 78–79.

20. Gilman, "The Dress of Women," *Forerunner* 6 (June 1915): 159–65.

21. Gilman, "The Dress of Women," *Forerunner* 6 (March 1915): 79.

22. Gilman, "Pernicious Adam: A Study in Ethics," unpublished typescript (1930), CPGP 177/227.

23. Gilman, *Women and Economics,* 78–81.

24. "Objects to Dolls," unidentified newscutting, CPGP, SL 177/282/1; Gilman, "Comment and Review" *Forerunner* 3 (December 1912): 336; and see Lillie Hamilton French, "Where Are the Old Ladies?" *Century* 84 (October 1912): 824–28.

25. Gilman, "Parasitism and Civilized Vice," 126. The epigraph to this section can be found at Gilman, *Man-Made World,* 42 and 66–67.

26. See Allen, *Building Domestic Liberty,* 62–76; Gilman, *The Home,* 20–21, Gilman, *Herland,* 48, Gilman, *The Home,* 15–16, 16, 22, and 22–23.

27. See Gilman, *The Home,* 145–46, 22, 30, 29, Gilman, "Parasitism and Civilized Vice," 121–22, and Gilman, *The Home,* 41.

28. Gilman, *Man-Made World,* 175 and 30.

29. Gilman, *The Home,* 134, 70–71, and 130–31.

30. Ibid., 95, 226, 22, and 136–38, and Gilman, *His Religion and Hers,* 29.

31. Gilman, *The Home,* 40 and 52.

32. Ibid., 72, 246, and 243, and Gilman, *Concerning Children,* 58–59.

33. See discussion of this in chap. 2, 69–71.

34. See Gilman, "Our Maternal Duties" (lecture, Oakland, 17 November 1891), CPCP, SL 177/166, 13 and 10, and Gilman, *Concerning Children,* 72–73, 72, and 136. For later controversy over her promotion of "the unnatural mother, that is, the trained mother," see "A New Conception of Maternity," *Current Opinion* 54 (March 1913): 220–21.

35. Gilman, "Women in Industry," 40–41 and 50.

36. To presentist historians of pacifism, Gilman has been at best contradictory and, at worst, a disappointment, compared for instance, to Nobel Peace Prize winner, Jane Addams. See for instance, Margaret Hobbs, "The Perils of 'Unbridled Masculinity': Pacifist Elements in the Feminist and Socialist Thought of Charlotte Perkins Gilman," in *Women and Peace: Historical and Practical Perspectives,* ed. Ruth

Roach Peirson (London: Croom Helm, 1987), 149–69, esp. 158–63. The epigraph to this section is from Gilman, "War and Women" (speech delivered in Union Square, New York City, April 1917), Maida Herman Solomon Papers, Schlesinger Library.

37. "Mrs. Gilman's Scorn Strikes 'Masculism': Lecturer Admits That Word, Like Some of Her Ideas, Is New: Deplores Too Much 'He': At His Door She Lays the Three Greatest Evils of the World, War, Drink, and the Social Evil," *New York Times,* 2 April 1914, 11; Gilman, "Growth and Combat," *Forerunner* 7 (February 1916): 49, and (March 1916): 77 and 78, and Gilman, *Women and Economics,* 41.

38. See Gilman, "Comment and Review," *Forerunner* 7 (September 1916): 251–52.

39. "'The Extension of the Suffrage to Women': Subject of an Interesting Debate before the Outlook Club Last Evening: Mrs. Gilman Holds That It Is Essential as a Safeguard and Guarantee of Justice—Mr. Finck Declares That There Are No Honors for Women in Politics," unidentified newscutting, annotated "1903," CPGP, SL 177/266/1.

40. Gilman, *Man-Made World,* 175–79; and "Mrs. Gilman's Scorn Strikes 'Masculism,'" *New York Times,* 2 April 1914, 11.

41. Gilman, "Growth and Combat," *Forerunner* 7 (March 1916): 77 and 76.

42. "Mrs. Gilman's Scorn Strikes 'Masculism,'" *New York Times,* 2 April 1914, 11.

43. Gilman, "Feminism or Polygamy?" *Forerunner* 5 (14 October 1914): 260, and Gilman, "Feminism and Social Progress," 123.

44. Gilman, "Feminism or Polygamy?" 261.

45. See Henry Ford, "Peace Not War," *Detroit Free Press,* 22 August 1915, reprinted in *The Peace Ship: Henry Ford's Pacifist Adventure in the First World War,* ed. Barbara S. Kraft (New York: Macmillan, 1978); and Gilman, "Feminism or Polygamy?" 260–61.

46. Gilman, "Masculism at Its Worst," *Forerunner* 5 (October 1914): 257–58. This foreshadowed British feminist Virginia Woolf's counsel to women a quarter of a century later, on the eve of the Second World War: that women must offer bellicose men indifference, withdrawal, disapproval, if war is to be prevented. See Woolf, *Three Guineas* (Harmondsworth: Penguin, 1979), 125; and Gilman, "War and Women."

47. See Owen Wister, "The Pentecost of Calamity," *Saturday Evening Post* 188 (3 July 1915): 3–5 and 26–29; and Gilman, "Comment and Review," *Forerunner* 7 (July 1916): 193.

48. Judith Schwartz, *The Radical Feminists of Heterodoxy: Greenwich Village, 1912–1940* (Norwich, VT: Victoria Publishers, 1986), 42; Gilman, *The Living,* 313; and CPG to Hon. Thomas W. Gregory [U.S. Attorney General], 9 June 1918, CPGP, SL 177/153.

49. Gilman, *His Religion and Hers,* 73–76, 42, and 43–44. These were long-standing Gilman concerns about religion discussed in tandem with ethics in *Man-Made World* and receiving comment shortly after its 1911 publication (see "Charlotte Perkins Gilman's Dynamic Social Philosophy," *Current Literature* 51 [July 1911]: 67–70, esp. 69).

50. Gilman, "With Her in Ourland," *Forerunner* 7 (April 1916): 97–98; and see also Hill, *Journey from Within,* 223.

PART 2

The epigraph to part 2, "Woman's Growing Revolt against 'Coercive Marriage,'" appeared in *Current Opinion* 56 (February 1914): 132; the letter from Mary Hutcheson Page to Mrs. Parker is archived in the Women's Rights Collection Papers, Schlesinger Library, 1633–1958, 2/76.

CHAPTER 5

Gilman's "As to 'Feminism'" originally appeared in *Forerunner* 5 (February 1914): 45.

1. For examples of her *Woman's Journal* suffrage-related articles, see Gilman, "Pungent Paragraphs," 28 (12 March 1887), 88; "Pacific Coast Press Notes," 22 (25 April 1891), 130; "The Washington Convention," 27 (15 February 1896), 49–50; "New England Anniversary Meeting," 27 (6 June 1896), 81, 184; "Why Great Women Are Few," 35 (20 February 1904), 58; "At the Convention," 35 (20 February 1904), 58; "Japan's Reserve," 35 (19 November 1904), 370; "This Also from the *N.Y. Times,*" 35 (29 October 1904), 346; "An Englishman on American Women," 35 (15 October 1904), 330; "World Peace and Sex Combat," 35 (8 October 1904), 322; "Over-Marriage" and "Impure Food," 35 (1 October 1904), 314; "Public Sins and Private Indifference," 35 (24 September 1904), 306; "The Refusal to Marry," 35 (17 September 1904), 298; "The Making of Americans," 35 (13 August 1904), 258; "Woman's Alleged Inhumanity to Woman," 35 (23 July 1904), 234; "Woman's 'Manifest Destiny,'" 35 (4 June 1904), 178; "The 'Double Standard,'" 35 (12 March 1904), 82. And see Hill, *Endure,* 331–32; and Ward, *Dynamic Sociology,* 1:647.

2. Gilman, *Women and Economics,* 144–45; "Editorial Notes" and "Equal Rights Women Endorse Candidates," *Impress,* 3 November 1894, 7; and the following articles by Gilman: "The Voting Mother," *Woman's Journal* 27 (20 June 1896): 1, "The Great Meeting of Women in London," *Saturday Evening Post,* 27 May 1899, 758, "Suffrage Work," *Woman's Journal* (5 March 1904): 74, "The Socialist and the Suffragist," *Life and Labor* 2 (February 1912): 61, "Are Women Human Beings? A Consideration of the Major Error in the Discussion of Woman Suffrage," *Harper's Weekly,* 25 May 1912, 11; "Why Nevada Should Win Its Suffrage Vote in November," *Out West* 8 (August 1914): 73–74, "Woman and the Ballot," *Marsh's Magazine* 1 (October 1908), 5 and 12, "Woman Suffrage Would Unsex Women" in *Twenty-Five Answers to the Antis,* ed. National American Woman Suffrage Association (New York: National American Woman Suffrage Press, 1912), 3, "On the Anti-Suffragists," *Woman's Journal* 28 (26 June 1897): 206, and "A Rational Position on Suffrage," *New York Times,* 7 March 1915, Sunday Magazine, 14. Reported accounts of her comments on suffrage include "Woman's Suffrage League," *Boston Advertiser,* 10 November 1897, 1; "Equal Suffrage Day at Mechanic's Fair," *Woman's Journal,* vol. 29 (5 November 1898): 357; "An Advancing Cause," *Current Literature* 36 (April 1904): 338–39; "Noted Woman Suffragist Speaks at the Alhambra," *San Francisco Call,* 17 July 1905, 6; and "Author Demands Woman Suffrage," *San Francisco Chronicle,* 14 November 1910, 1.

3. Gilman, *Women and Economics,* 167.

4. See, for instance, "Mrs. Pankhurst Has a Day of Triumph," *New York Times,* 30 November 1909, 5; "Mrs. Pankhurst: Something of the Personality of the Militant Leader of English Suffragettes," *New York Times,* 24 October 1909, Sunday Magazine,

6; and "Mrs. Pankhurst Gets Crowd," *Chicago Daily Tribune*, 26 October 1909, 9. For mention of Gilman in Blatch's organization, see Ellen Carol DuBois, *Harriot Stanton Blatch and the Winning of Woman Suffrage* (New Haven, CT: Yale University Press, 1997), 96, 105, and 233.

5. See June Sochen, *The New Woman in Greenwich Village, 1910–1920* (New York: Quadrangle, 1972), 26–28, 30, 32, and 44; Cicely Hamilton to CPG, 19 March 1911, CPGP, SL 177/150/3. Hamilton (1872–1952), a dynamic American expatriate actress, became a famous militant suffragette in London. She authored *Marriage as a Trade* (New York: Moffat, Yard & Co., 1909). She also wrote *A Pageant of Great Women* (London: Suffrage Shop, 1910), and cowrote, with Christopher St. John, *How the Vote Was Won: A Play in One Act* (Chicago: Dramatic Publishing Co., 1910).

6. Gilman, "The Women Who Won't Move Forward," *Physical Culture* 31 (February 1914): 126–28.

7. See Gilman, "'The Brute in Man,'" *Forerunner* 4 (December 1913): 317; and Bederman, *Manliness and Civilization*, 157–59. Gilman did not mean "masculism" to cover men *supporting* feminism, as suggested in Lucy Delap, *The Feminist Avant-Garde* (Cambridge: Cambridge University Press, 2007), 28.

8. For examples of Gilman's suffrage-related *Forerunner* articles, see: "As to Feminism," 5 (February 1914): 45; "A New Impulse in the Women's Movement," 5 (December 1914): 313; "A Platform for Women," 6 (January 1915): 6–7; "An Answer to the Antis," 2 (March 1911): 85–86; "Comment and Review," 3 (April 1912): 110–12; "Comment and Review," 3 (June 1912): 167–68; "Comment and Review," 4 (November 1913): 303–8; "The Biological Anti-Feminist," 5 (March 1914): 64–67; "Woman Suffrage and the Average Mind," 3 (June 1912): 148–53; "An Anti-Suffrage Meeting," 6 (February 1915): 51–52; "Masculism at Its Worst," 5 (October 1915): 257–58.

9. See, for instance, Aileen Kraditor, *The Ideas of the Woman Suffrage Movement, 1850–1920* (New York: Columbia University Press, 1965), 50, 102, and 120–21; Scharnhorst, *Charlotte Perkins Gilman*, 4; Hill, *Making of a Radical Feminist*, 261; Allen, *Building Domestic Liberty*, 29; Lane, *To Herland*, 184. Alternatively, see Deegan's introduction to *With Her in Ourland*, 37. The letter from Grace Ellery Channing-Stetson to Edward B. Knight quoted at the start of this section is printed in Hill, *Endure*, 22–23.

10. CPG to Martha Luther, 27 July 1890, CPG Letters, Rhode Island Historical Society; Mss. 437/33/3; and Ceplair, ed., *Nonfiction Reader*, 3.

11. See, for instance, Gilman's later *Woman's Journal* suffrage articles: "Shall Suffrage Clubs Work for Anything Besides Suffrage?" 35 (30 January 1904): 34; "What Shall the Suffrage Clubs Do?" 35 (19 March 1904): 98; "Suffrage Work," 35 (5 March 1904): 74; "Is the Woman Movement Slow?" 35 (30 July 1904): 74; and "Song for Equal Suffrage," 40 (13 February 1909): 28.

12. Gilman, *The Living*, 186–87. Many former suffragists disavowed their prior hopes for reform through woman suffrage in response to skeptics observing its failure to solve the world's ills. See also my *Rose Scott: Vision and Revision in Feminism, 1880–1925* (Melbourne: Oxford University Press, 1994), 226.

13. For instance, both Harriet Beecher Stowe and Henry Ward Beecher were among those quoted in *Eminent Opinions on Woman Suffrage*. Her great aunt, Isabella Beecher Hooker (1822–1907), was a suffragist and author of *A Mother's Letters to a Daughter on Woman Suffrage* (Hartford: Press of Case, Lockwood & Brainard,

1870), and Hooker, *Womanhood: Its Sanctities and Fidelities* (Boston: Lee & Shepard, 1874). Meanwhile her great uncle, Reverend Henry Ward Beecher, served as president of the American Woman Suffrage Association (see Hill, *Making of a Radical Feminist,* 14). Harriet Beecher Stowe denounced taxation without representation, holding that the state could "no more dispense with the votes of women in its affairs than in the family." Gilman, too, was quoted clearly connecting woman suffrage and Progressive Era reform issues: "Politics governs over the purity of the milk supply. It is not outside the home but inside the baby" (see NAWSA, *Eminent Opinions on Woman Suffrage* [Warren, Ohio: NAWSA, n.d.], 12, 29 and 42, in Frances Squire Boardman Potter Papers, "Suffrage Pamphlets," carton 2, vol. 33, SL 1441-B1-M126).

14. Hill, *Making of a Radical Feminist,* 119, and Hill, *Journey from Within,* 19. See also Gilman, "Women Do Not Want It," reprinted in *Current Literature* 36 (May 1904): 4.

15. Review of *Women and Economics* by Charlotte Perkins Gilman, *London Daily Chronicle,* 26 June 1899, CPGP, SL 177/300; and Scharnhorst, *Charlotte Perkins Gilman,* 9, 44–45, and 24–26.

16. CPG to Mrs. Williams, 20 June 1915, CPGP, SL 177/153; Knight, *The Diaries,* 2:439, 648, 655, 783, 829, and 832. See also House of Representatives, Committee on the Judiciary, *Hearing of the National American Woman Suffrage Association* (Washington, DC, 28 January 1896), 4–5.

17. "Women in a Democracy under Man's Dominion. Better Off in a Monarchy, Mrs. Gilman Tells Jamaica Audience What Suffrage Stands For. It is an Effort to Humanize Woman, Not to Destroy Her Distinctively Feminine Attributes," *Brooklyn Eagle,* 7 April 1910, CPGP, SL 177/266/1. Had Gilman been university educated, she might have published work here foreshadowing distinguished feminist political theorist Carole Pateman's concept of "the fraternal social contract" of modern civil democracies. See Pateman, "The Fraternal Social Contract," in *Civil Society and the State: New European Perspectives,* ed. J. Keane (London: Verso Books, 1988).

18. See "'The Extension of the Suffrage to Women,'" unidentified clipping, annotated "1903," CPGP, SL 177/266/1.

19. Beauvoir, *The Second Sex,* xxiv–xxx.

20. Gilman, "Woman and the State," *Forerunner* 1 (October 1910): 10; and Gilman, "Women and Democracy," *Forerunner* 3 (February 1912): 36.

21. Gilman, "Women and Democracy," 37, and Gilman, "Comment and Review," 4 (July 1913): 196.

22. Bessie Rischbieth to Olive Evans, 23 and 29 May and 19 June 1913, Bessie Rischbieth Papers, National Library of Australia, 2004/1, 7–10, and 9.

23. Rosika Schwimmer to CPG, 20 July 1912, CPGP, SL 177/152. See also Allen, *Rose Scott,* 221–22. For Dell's view, see Floyd Dell, *Women as World Builders: Studies in Modern Feminism* (Chicago: Forbes & Co., 1913), 23–25. Rose Scott had given Franklin a copy of Gilman's poetry collection, *In the This Our World* (1893) in 1901, shortly after they met. By the time Franklin met Gilman, she had admired her nonfiction feminist theory for some time, as Jill Roe demonstrates in her recent biography: in 1911, Franklin sent her mother a 1908 edition of *Women and Economics* (1898), "with instructions to read it carefully, and Aunt Lena too." Roe identifies Ward as a key philosophical inspiration for the editors of *Life and Labor,* who called Gilman

his foremost follower, and one immensely influential in Franklin's intellectual development. I thank Jill Roe for allowing me to read the manuscript for chapter 6 of her biography of Franklin, now published as *Stella Miles Franklin: A Biography* (Sydney: HarperCollins, 2008).

24. Gilman, "Comment and Review," *Forerunner* 7 (May 1916): 139; and Gilman, "The Woman Suffrage Congress in Buda-Pest," *Forerunner* 4 (August 1913): 204–5 and 205.

25. Gilman, "Comment and Review," *Forerunner* 3 (April 1912): 110.

26. See, for instance, Gilman, "Does a Man Support His Wife?" *Forerunner* 2 (September 1911): 240–46; Lane, *To Herland*, 333–34; Hill, *Making of a Radical Feminist*, 260–62; and DuBois, *Harriot Stanton Blatch*, 249.

27. See John Rickard, *Class and Politics: Victoria, New South Wales, and the Early Commonwealth* (Canberra: Australian National University Press, 1976), 167–203. Gilman's "With Her in Ourland," an excerpt of which opens this section, first appeared in *Forerunner* 7 (November 1916): 294.

28. Gilman, "The Women Who Won't Move Forward," 127.

29. See, for instance, Gilman, "An Answer to the Antis," 85–86, Gilman, "Woman Suffrage Would Unsex Women," Gilman, "On the Anti-Suffragists," Gilman, "Comment and Review," *Forerunner* 3 (April 1912): 110–12, Gilman, "Comment and Review," *Forerunner* 3 (June 1912): 167–68, Gilman, "Comment and Review," *Forerunner* 4 (November 1913): 303–8, Gilman, "Woman Suffrage and the *Woman's Journal*," *Forerunner* 7 (February 1916): 46, and Gilman, "On the Anti-Suffragists," *Woman's Journal* 28 (26 June 1897): 206.

30. This Protestantism link is stressed by some scholars. See, for instance, Tracy Fessenden, *Culture and Redemption: Religion, the Secular, and American Literature* (Princeton, NJ: Princeton University Press, 2007), 171–172.

31. For insightful discussions of antisuffragism, see Thomas J. Jablonsky, *The Home, Heaven, and Mother Party: Female Anti-Suffragists in the United States, 1868–1920* (Brooklyn: Carlson Publications, 1994); Jane Jerome Camhi, *Women against Women: American Anti-Suffragism, 1880–1920* (Brooklyn: Carlson Publications, 1994); Anne Myra Goodman Benjamin, *A History of the Anti-Suffrage Movement in the United States from 1895 to 1920: Women against Equality* (Lewiston, N.Y.: Edwin Mellen Press, 1991). For some critical contemporary analyses of this trans-Atlantic political phenomenon, see Bertrand Russell, *Anti-Suffragist Anxieties* (London: People's Federation, 1909–10), and Russell, *The Women's Anti-Suffrage Movement* (London: National Union of Women's Suffrage Societies, 1908). For useful perspectives on antisuffragism relative to other "antiradical" movements, see Kim E. Nielson, *Un-American Womanhood: Antiradicalism, Antifeminism, and the First Red Scare* (Columbus: Ohio State University Press, 2001).

32. See Jablonsky, *The Home, Heaven, and Mother Party*, 34, 19, 21, 42, 67–69 and 66–67.

33. See Gilman, *With Her in Ourland*, 52; DuBois, *Harriot Stanton Blatch*, 178–79; and DuBois, "The Radicalism of the Woman Suffrage Movement: Notes towards the Reconstruction of Nineteenth Century Feminism," *Feminist Studies* 3 (Fall 1975): 63–71.

34. These connections are clear in the plots and characters of Gilman's suffrage-

era novels—*What Diantha Did* (1910), "Moving the Mountain" (1911), *The Crux* (1911), *Mag-Marjorie* (1912), *Herland* (1915), *With Her in Ourland* (1916)—as well as in her many short stories and prose essays in the *Forerunner.*

35. Gilman, "Feminism and Social Progress," in *Problems of Civilization,* ed. Brownell Baker (New York: Van Nostrand, 1929), 128.

36. See "Raise 'Free Love' Cry: Antis in a Bulletin Quote the Views of Suffragist Workers," *New York Times,* 25 May 1914, 11. Alice Paul founded the Congressional Union in April 1912—see Jennifer L. Borda, "Woman Suffrage in the Progressive Era: A Coming of Age," in *Rhetorical History,* ed. Hogan, 358.

37. Gilman, "Answers to the Antis," *Forerunner* 2 (March, 1911): 74 and 77, Gilman, "Comment and Review," *Forerunner* 3 (April 1912): 112; and Gilman, "Comment and Review," *Forerunner* 4 (May 1913): 139.

38. For another reprinting of her poem, "Women Do Not Want It," see *Woman's Journal* 28 (23 January 1897): 30; see Gilman, "Answers to the Antis," 77.

39. Katharine Bement Davis (1860–1935) received her doctorate from the University of Chicago under the supervision of famed economist Thorstein Veblen. She worked first as superintendent of New York's Bedford Hills Reformatory for Women, where she implemented experimental "Progressive" prison reforms, before her appointment as the city's first woman to serve as commissioner of corrections. For an insightful discussion of her work and career, see Ellen Fitzpatrick, *Endless Crusade: Women Social Scientists and Progressive Reform* (New York: Oxford University Press, 1990), 92–129; and see also, Katharine Bement Davis, "Three Score Years and Ten," *University of Chicago Magazine* 26 (December 1933): 58–62. Ella Flagg Young (1845–1918) began teaching in Chicago public schools in 1862, also serving as a principal and a district superintendent. She completed a doctoral dissertation at the University of Chicago under John Dewey and went on to serve as superintendent of public schools in Chicago in 1909 and as president of the National Education Association in 1910. See John T. McManis, *Ella Flagg Young and a Half Century of the Chicago Public Schools* (Chicago: A. C. McClurg & Co., 1916), 173–74.

40. Gilman, "Comment and Review," *Forerunner* 5 (February 1914): 56 and 55–56.

41. Gilman, "A 'Debate' on Suffrage," *Forerunner* 6 (January 1915): 10.

42. In 1910, she rebuked antisuffragist Molly Elliot Sewall's most recent attack, "The Ladies' Battle," *Atlantic Monthly* 106 (September 1910): 289–303, in these terms. See Gilman, "Comment and Review," *Forerunner* 1 (December 1910): 25–27

43. Gilman, "Comment and Review," *Forerunner* 4 (March 1913): 84.

44. See Gilman, "Comment and Review," *Forerunner* 1 (June 1910): 24 and 24–25. For further discussion of this conflict between Tarbell and other feminists like Gilman, see "Ida Tarbell Answered," *Woman Voter* 3 (June 1912): 7–13, esp. 11–12; and "Is Woman Making a Man of Herself?" *Current Literature* 52 (June 1912): 682–84, esp. 682 and 684.

45. Gilman, "Dr. Weininger's 'Sex and Character,'" *Critic* 48 (May 1906): 414–17; and see "Mrs. Gilman's Scorn Strikes 'Masculism,'" *New York Times,* 2 April 1914, 11.

46. See Warner Fite, "The Feminist Mind," *Nation* 96 (6 February 1913): 123–26; and for Gilman's response, see "Comment and Review" *Forerunner* 4 (March 1913): 82 and 83.

47. "Mrs. Gilman's Scorn Strikes 'Masculism,'" *New York Times,* 2 April 1914, 11. See also Gilman, "Is Feminism Really So Dreadful?" *Delineator* 85 (August 1914): 6, Gilman, "As to 'Feminism'" *Forerunner* 5 (February 1914): 45; "What Feminism Is and Isn't," *Ford Hall Folks* 2 (April 1916): 1–2, 4; and "What Is Feminism?" *Boston Sunday Herald,* 3 September 1916; and Gilman, "Woman, the Enigma," *Harper's Bazaar* 42 (December 1908): 1193–97. See also Almroth E. Wright, *The Unexpurgated Case against Woman Suffrage* (New York: Paul B. Hoeber, 1913). For a discussion of government initiated force feeding of hunger-striking suffragettes in prison, see Schwarz, *The Radical Feminists of Heterodoxy,* 39 and 44–46. And see Gilman, "Comment and Review," *Forerunner* 4 (November 1913): 303.

48. Gilman, "Should Women Use Violence?" *Pictorial Review* 14 (November 1912): 11 and 78–79, Gilman, *Man-Made World,* 29, Gilman, "Teaching the Mothers," *Forerunner* 3 (March 1912): 73–74; and Gilman, "Feminism and Social Progress," 121.

49. Gilman, "Comment and Review," *Forerunner* 1 (June 1910): 24. See also Rudyard Kipling, "A Matter of Fact," in *Many Inventions* (New York: D. Appleton & Co., 1893; reprint, London: Macmillan, 1982), 163–81; and Gilman, "Comment and Review," *Forerunner* 6 (April 1915): 112, 111, and 111–12.

50. They had 633 donations of between $62 ($1,371 in 2009) and $235 ($5,195) per man. By comparison, the suffragists had 1,896 registered donors with an average donation of $17 ($376), 1,654 further donors averaging $5 ($311), and 1,024 donating $3 ($66) a piece. See Gilman, "Woman Suffrage and the *Woman's Journal*," 45–46. All contemporary figures rounded to the nearest dollar and calculated for the year 2009, using database "Measuring Worth.com." Gilman, "Comment and Review," *Forerunner* 3 (December 1912): 335–36.

51. Gilman, "Ten States Free Now," *Forerunner* 3 (December 1912): 336.

52. See, for instance, Gilman, "A Rational Position on Suffrage," *New York Times,* 7 March 1915, Sunday Magazine, 14; and Gilman, "Comment and Review," *Forerunner* 7 (August 1916): 223.

53. Gilman, "The Woman's Party," *Forerunner* 2 (November 1911): 291. The epigraphs to this section are "'The Extension of the Suffrage to Women': Subject of an Interesting Debate before the Outlook Club Last Evening," unidentified clipping, annotated "1903," CPGP 177/266/1; and Gilman, *The Man-Made World,* 151.

54. Gilman, "Something to Vote For," *Forerunner* 3 (June 1911): 153.

55. Gilman, "The New Party," *Forerunner* 3 (September 1912): 252.

56. She overstated somewhat the public and formal commitment of the progressives to woman suffrage. See DuBois, *Harriot Stanton Blatch,* 123, 144, and 195–96. For discussion of Roosevelt's reform agenda, see Edmund Morris, *Theodore Rex* (New York: Random House, 2001), 205–8, 258–62, 422–23, 435–36 and 506–9. See Gilman, "The Work before Us," *Forerunner* 3 (January 1912): 9. And see "Women in a Democracy under Man's Dominion," *Brooklyn Eagle,* 7 April 1910.

57. Gilman, "Comment and Review," *Forerunner* 1 (December 1910): 25–27; and see Allen, *Rose Scott,* 170.

58. Gilman, "Do We Want a Political Party for Women?" *Forerunner* 6 (November 1915): 385–86.

59. Gilman, "Obstacles to Suffrage by States," *Forerunner* 7 (August 1916): 215–16.

60. Gilman, "Addressing the New Voters," *Forerunner* 6 (June 1915): 165; and Gilman, "Obstacles to Suffrage by States," *Forerunner* 7 (August 1916): 215–16 and 216. Beginning a career as a public intellectual with the women's suffrage movement, Mary Ritter Beard (1876–1958) wrote books on American women, Japanese women, and American history, several with her husband, Charles A. Beard (1874–1948). Beard's publications included: *On Understanding Women* (New York: Longmans, Green, 1931), *America through Women's Eyes* (New York: Macmillan, 1933), *Woman as Force in History* (New York: Macmillan, 1946), and *The Force of Women in Japanese History* (Washington, DC: Public Affairs Press, 1953). Florence Kelley (1859–1932) wrote, edited, and translated works on socialism, labor, and industry, in addition to her work on suffrage. Kelley's own titles included *Modern Industry in Relation to the Family, Health, Education, and Morality* (New York: Longmans, Green, 1914), and *Some Ethical Gains through Legislation* (New York: Macmillan, 1914).

61. Gilman, "The National Woman's Party," *Forerunner* 7 (August 1916): 214.

62. Gilman, "Comment and Review," *Forerunner* 7 (August 1916): 222–23 and 223.

63. Gilman, "The National Woman's Party," 215.

64. Gilman, "Addressing the New Voters," *Forerunner* 6 (June 1915): 165–66.

65. "Eulogize Susan B. Anthony: Mrs. Charlotte P. Gilman Addresses Meeting in Honor of Her Centenary," *New York Times,* 16 February 1920, 15.

66. Degler influenced subsequent Gilman scholars in the view that Gilman ceased feminist work by the 1920s (see Degler, "Charlotte Perkins Gilman," 21 and 23). See, for instance, Gilman, "Toward Monogamy," in *Our Changing Morality,* ed. Freda Kirchwey (New York: Albert & Charles Boni, 1930), 53–66, Gilman, "Sex and Race Progress," 109–23, Gilman, "Parasitism and Civilized Vice," 110–26; and Gilman, "Feminism and Social Progress," 128.

CHAPTER 6

The letter that begins this chapter, from Gilman to Grace Ellery Channing Stetson, 21 August 1929, can be found in Charlotte Perkins Gilman (1860–1935), Letters, 1884–1935, Schlesinger Library Mf6.

1. "Charlotte Perkins Gilman, Author and Lecturer," February 1925, CPGP 177/ 10; "'America's 12 Greatest Women': Mrs. Catt Gives Own List of," *New York Post,* 5 June 1922, CPGP, SL 177/295/1. And see John M. Martin and Prestonia Mann Martin, *Feminism: Its Fallacies and Follies* (New York: Dodd, Mead & Co., 1916); Correa Moylan Walsh, *Feminism* (New York: Sturgis & Walton Co., 1917); and Avrom Barnett, *Foundations of Feminism: A Critique* (New York: Robert M. McBride & Co., 1921).

2. See, for instance, Edith Houghton Hooker, "Charlotte Perkins Gilman," *Equal Rights Independent Feminist Weekly* 1 (August 31, 1935): 202; and "A Feminist Revision of History," *New York Times,* 3 April 1914, 10; and "Feminist Dooms Home Cooking," *New York Tribune,* 12 March 1914.

3. Ida Minerva Tarbell (1857–1944) was a journalist most famous in the muckraking era with her publication of *History of the Standard Oil Company* (1902). She also wrote several other books on American business, Abraham Lincoln, and an autobiog-

raphy, *All in the Day's Work* (1939). See Mary E. Tomkins, *Ida M. Tarbell* (New York: Twayne, 1974). For Gilman's comments on Tarbell, see "Comment and Review," *Forerunner* 1 (June 1910): 24–25; "Miss Tarbell's Uneasy Woman," *Forerunner* 3 (February 1912): 33–37 "Miss Tarbell's Third Paper," *Forerunner* 3 (April 1912): 92–95; and "Miss Tarbell's Homeless Daughter," *Forerunner* 3 (May 1912): 120–21. Meanwhile, the Swedish author Ellen S. Key (1849–1926) published *The Century of the Child* (New York: G. P. Putnam's Sons, 1909), Key, *The Education of the Child* (New York: G. P. Putnam's Sons, 1912), Key, *Love and Marriage* (New York: G. P. Putnam's Sons, 1911), Key, *The Woman Movement* (New York: G. P. Putnam's Sons, 1912), and Key, *Rahel Varnhagen: A Portrait* (New York: G. P. Putnam's Sons, 1913). Her only biography was written during her lifetime: Louise Nystrom-Hamilton, *Ellen Key: Her Life and Work,* trans. A. E. B. Fries (New York: G. P. Putnam's Sons, 1913).

4. For debate about the timing and meaning of American feminism in comparative perspective, see Cott, *The Grounding,* 1–16, and Cott, "Comment on Karen Offen's 'Defining Feminism,'" *Signs* 15 (Autumn 1989): 204–5; Offen, "Defining Feminism," 143–52, Offen, "Reply to DuBois," *Signs* 15 (Autumn 1989): 200, and Offen, "Reply to Cott," *Signs* 15 (Autumn 1989): 207–8; Ellen Carol DuBois, "Comment on Karen Offen's 'Defining Feminism'" *Signs* 15 (Autumn 1989): 196–98; and see my "Contextualizing Late Nineteenth Century Feminism: Problems and Comparisons," *Journal of the Canadian Historical Association* 1, no. 1 (1990): 17–36, esp. 24–28.

5. Alexander Black, "The Woman Who Saw It First," *Century Magazine* 107 (November 1923): 42; and Gilman, "Comment and Review," *Forerunner* 6 (February 1915): 55. The epigraphs to this section are, respectively, "Charlotte Perkins Gilman" (1915), lecture circular, Charlotte Perkins Gilman Papers, Schlesinger Library, 177/153/1-2, and Gilman, "Feminism and Social Progress," 236.

6. When asked after a 1917 lecture "War and Women" to define "feminism," she tartly replied that feminism should be renamed as humanism and then declared herself a humanist. See Gilman, "War and Women," (lecture delivered in Union Square, New York City, April 1917), Maida Herman Solomon Papers, SL MC418/24/296/Questions, 2; and "Charlotte Perkins Gilman, Author and Lecturer," February 1925, CPGP.

7. Gilman, "An Anti-Suffrage Meeting," *Forerunner* 6 (February 1914): 52.

8. "Men Are Worried," unidentified clipping [1916?], CPGP, SL 177/295/2.

9. Gilman, "The Biological Anti-Feminist," 64 and 65.

10. Gilman, "Woman Suffrage and the Average Mind," 152–53; and Gilman, "Comment and Review," *Forerunner* 4 (November 1913): 304.

11. As articulated by Ellador, the Herlander visiting World War I America, this was the problem: "They seem like flies behind a window, they bump and buzz, pushing their heads against whatever is in front of them, and never seem really to plan a way out." See Gilman, "With Her in Ourland," *Forerunner* 7 (November 1916): 294.

12. At a 1915 lunch for Stanton, she sat with her fellow Heterodoxy members at the table closest to the camera: see DuBois, *Harriot Stanton Blatch,* fig. 21, "Elizabeth Cady Stanton Centennial Luncheon, October 30, 1915," between pp. 194 and 195.

13. Currey was also the partner of the Greenwich Village libertarian and bohemian writer Floyd Dell. See Stansell, *American Moderns,* 259; and see "Mrs. Charlotte Perkins Gilman: Miles Franklin—an American Letter," *Stock and Station Journal* 6

(December 1912), CPGP, SL 177/266/1. See also Miles Franklin to Margery Currey, 24 November 1948, Franklin Papers, Mitchell Library. Mss 364/22/249-50—again, I thank Jill Roe for this invaluable reference.

14. "Feminists Ask Equal Chance: Leaders in Movement Discuss 'Breaking into the Human Race' at Cooper Union," *New York Times,* 21 February 1914, 18.

15. Ibid., 18.

16. Gilman, *His Religion and Hers,* 82–83.

17. For a critical discussion of her concerns here, see Egan, "Evolutionary Theory," 102–19; and Magner, "Darwinism and the Woman Question, 115–28.

18. See Daniel Kiefer to William B. Feakin, 8 June 1914, CPGP, SL 177/139/2.

19. Scharnhorst, *Charlotte Perkins Gilman,* 12; and Olive Schreiner, "Three Dreams in a Desert," in *Dreams* (London: G. P. Putnam's Sons, 1890), 57–58 and 66–72. Gilman's diary entries of the 1890s were filled with notations about reading Schreiner to friends in the evenings, often moving them to tears. See, for instance, Knight, *The Diaries,* 2:442, 443, 448, 483, 567, and 716.

20. See, for instance, Joyce Avrech Berkman, *Olive Schreiner: Feminism on the Frontier* (St. Albans, VT: Eden Press Women's Publications, 1979), 26; and Ceplair, ed., *Nonfiction Reader,* 36; see also CPG to George Houghton Gilman, 3 November 1899, in Hill, *Journey from Within,* 308. On these articles, see Olive Schreiner, "The Woman Question," *Cosmopolitan* 28 (November 1899): 45–54, and "The Woman Question," *Cosmopolitan* 28 (December 1899): 182–92. An undated and unsigned letter to Gilman, probably after 1921, reports disparagingly on self-aggrandizing by Schreiner's husband, Cronwright Schreiner: "The man is almost inconceivable. Yet Olive Schreiner loved him. I think she was constantly mistaken in individuals, though rarely in human life" (CPGP, SL 177/149/1). But see also Hill, *Journey from Within,* 338. Other scholars often compare Gilman and Schreiner: see, for instance, Barbara Scott Winkler, "Victorian Daughters: The Lives and Feminism of Charlotte Perkins Gilman and Olive Schreiner," Occasional Paper in Women's Studies, no. 13, American Culture Program (Ann Arbor: University of Michigan, 1980); and Rosaleen Love, "Darwinism and Feminism: The 'Woman Question' in the Life and Work of Olive Schreiner and Charlotte Perkins Gilman," in *The Wider Domain of Evolutionary Thought,* ed. David Oldroyd (Dordrecht: D. Reidel, 1983), 113–32.

21. Samuel D. Schmalhausen to CPG, 19 June 1930; CPG to Schmalhausen, 23 June 1930, CPGP, SL 177/122; and see Schreiner, "The Woman Question" (November 1899), 53–54, Schreiner, "The Woman Question" (December 1899), 189–91, and Schreiner, *Woman and Labour* (New York: F. A. Stokes, 1911), ix, xi, and xiv–xvi.

22. See, for instance, Ellen S. Key, *The Morality of Woman and Other Essays* (Chicago: Ralph Fletcher Seymour Co., 1911), Key, *Love and Marriage,* Key, *The Century of the Child; Love and Ethics* (Chicago: Ralph Seymour Co., 1912), Key, *The Renaissance of Motherhood* (New York: G. P. Putnam's Sons, 1914), and Key, *The Younger Generation* (New York: G. P. Putnam's Sons, 1914). See Key, *The Woman Movement,* 158–61. Not only Gilman but Schreiner as well rejected Key's "opposites attract/like repel" view: "In the world of sex, kind seeks kind, and too wide a dissimilarity completely bars the existence of the highest forms of sex emotion, and often even the lower and more purely animal . . . The two sexes are not distinct species but the two halves of one whole . . . [they] resemble two oxen tethered to one yoke: for a moment

one may move slightly forward and the other remain stationary or move forward together . . . the males of to-morrow will be cast in the mold of the women of to-day" (Schreiner, *Woman and Labour,* 101–2). The epigraph to this section, from Key's *Love and Marriage,* can be found at 98.

23. Gilman, "Ellen Key," 37. For Gilman's extensive writings on these subjects, see Gilman, *The Home,* "The Beauty of a Block," *Independent* 57 (14 July 1904): 67–72, Gilman, "The Passing of the Home in Great American Cities," *Cosmopolitan* 38 (December 1904): 37–47, Gilman, "Standardizing Towns," *Forerunner* 6 (February 1915): 52–54, Gilman, "The Milkman and the Public," *Forerunner* 7 (November 1916): 285–86, Gilman, "A Summary of Purpose," *Forerunner* 7 (November 1916): 286–90, Gilman, "The Housekeeper and the Food Supply," *Annals of the American Academy* 74 (November 1917): 123–30, Gilman, "Applepieville," *Independent* (25 September 1920): 365 and 393–95, and Gilman, "Making Towns Fit to Live In," *Century* 102 (July 1921): 361–66. See also Hill, *Journey from Within,* 380.

24. See particularly, Key, *The Woman Movement,* 23–24, 31, 44, 55–57, 67–70, 79–80, 103–4, 126–27, 146–47n, 148, and 176–93. Gilman's explicit anti-European sentiment appeared in "Is America Too Hospitable?" *Forum* 70 (October 1923): 1985–86.

25. See Key, "Education for Motherhood," *Atlantic Monthly* (July 1913): 49–50; Gilman, "Ellen Key and the Women's Movement," *Forerunner* 4 (February 1913): 36. For further contemporary commentary on their diametrically opposed approaches to the nature and causes of women's subjection and, hence, their suggested remedies, see "Ellen Key's Revaluation of Woman's Chastity," *Current Literature* 52 (February 1912): 200–202, esp. 202; "Ellen Key's Reply to Her Critics," *Current Opinion* 52 (March 1912): 317–19, esp. 319; "Ellen Key's Attack on 'Amaternal' Feminism," *Current Opinion* 54 (February 1913): 138–39, esp. 138; "Charlotte Perkins Gilman's Reply to Ellen Key," *Current Opinion* 54 (March 1913): 220–21, esp. 221; and finally, "The Conflict between 'Human' and 'Female' Feminism," *Current Opinion* 56 (April 1914): 291–92, esp. 292.

26. Gilman, "Education for Motherhood," *Forerunner* 4 (October 1913): 271; and see "A New Conception of Maternity," 221.

27. Gilman, "Her Overhearing," *Forerunner* 7 (March 1916): 57.

28. Gilman, "As to Feminism," 45.

29. For an elaboration of this refusal of continued "specialization by sex," see Marie Jenney Howe, *An Anti-Suffrage Monologue* (New York: National Woman Suffrage Publication Co., 1912).

30. For historical examples and other conceptions of humanism in Gilman's era, see F. C. S. Schiller, *Humanism: Philosophical Essays* (London and New York: MacMillan, 1903); John S. Mackenzie, *Lectures on Humanism, with Special Reference to Its Bearings on Sociology* (London, S. Sonnenschein; New York, MacMillan, 1907); R. B. Haldane, *The Philosophy of Humanism: And of Other Subjects* (London: J. Murray, 1922); and Norman Foerster, *Humanism and America* (New York: Farrar & Rinehart, 1930).

31. See, for instance, Martin and Martin, *Feminism,* 9–11.

32. Katharine Anthony, *Feminism in Germany and Scandinavia* (New York: Henry Holt & Co., 1915), 4–5, 9–10, and 211–14.

33. See also Gilman, "Comment and Review," *Forerunner* 7 (May 1916): 140; and Martin and Martin, *Feminism*, 306–7. And see Mari Jo Buhle's insightful discussion of their dispute in her *Feminism and Its Discontents: A Century of Struggle with Psychoanalysis* (Cambridge, MA: Harvard University Press, 1998), 48.

34. "Letters to and Answers by Cynthia Grey," *Los Angeles Record*, 1 August 1913, CPGP, SL 177/295/1. Gilman annotated this clipping: "I think Estelle Lawton Lindsay was writing the Cynthia Gray [*sic*] letters at this date."

35. Bessie Beatty, "Would You Know Feminist Truths? Hear Mrs. Gilman," *San Francisco Bulletin*, 26 April 1915, CPGP, SL 177/7/8.

36. See Cott, *The Grounding*, 49 and 20; and Ellen Kay Trimberger, introduction to *Intimate Warriors: Portraits of a Modern Marriage, 1899–1944 — Selected Works by Neith Boyce and Hutchins Hapgood,* ed. Ellen Kay Trimberger (New York: Feminist Press, 1991), 12 and 34.

37. For compelling accounts of these generational shifts, Cott, *The Grounding,* 1–16; Estelle Freedman, "The New Woman," in *Decades of Discontent: The Women's Movement, 1920–1940,* ed. Lois Scharf and Joan M. Jensen (Westport, CT: Greenwood Press, 1983), 21–42; and Stansell, *American Moderns,* 225–338.

38. See, for instance, Gilman, "The Problem of the Unhappy Woman," *Beautiful Womanhood* 1 (October 1922): 10 and 64, Gilman, "Vanguard, Rearguard, and Mudguard," *Century* 105 (July 1922): 348–53, Gilman, "New Generation of Women," *Current History,* 18 August 1923, 731–37, Gilman, "Feminism and Social Progress," 138–41, Gilman, "Kitchen-Mindedness," *Forerunner* 1 (February 1910): 7–11, Gilman, "Parlor-Mindedness," *Forerunner* 1 (March 1910): 6–10, Gilman, "Nursery Mindedness," *Forerunner* 1 (April 1910): 7–10.

39. Gilman, "Comment and Review," *Forerunner* 5 (January 1914): 27.

40. See, for instance, "Adam the Real Rib, Mrs. Gilman Insists," *New York Times,* 19 February 1914, 9; "Mrs. Gilman Tilts at Modern Women: They Are Far behind Men as Human Beings, She Tells 'Larger Feminists,'" *New York Times,* 26 February 1914, 9; "Cupid Is Scorned by Mrs. C. P. Gilman," *New York Times,* 5 March 1914, 8; "Mrs. Gilman Swats Home Cooking Idol," *New York Times,* 12 March 1914, 8; "Mrs. Gilman Seeks Wider Motherhood," *New York Times,* 19 March 1914, 8; "Woman's Weakness Due to Education," *New York Times,* 26 March 1914, 10; and "Mrs. Gilman Calls Science to Witness," *New York Times,* 9 April 1914, 10.

41. See Clara Savage Littledale, "Daily Reminder, 1914," 4 March 1914; 4 April 1914; 8 April 1914; and 6 May 1914, Clara Littledale Savage Papers, SL A-157/1/ vol. 16.

42. Degler, "Charlotte Perkins Gilman," 32; Gilman, "Toward Monogamy," 59, Gilman, "Parasitism and Civilized Vice," 123, Gilman, "Feminism or Polygamy?" *Forerunner* 5 (October, 1914): 261. The epigraph to this section, Walter Lippmann, "The Woman's Movement," was published in *Forum* 52 (August 1914): 156.

43. Mary M. Moynihan deftly examines the elements of her argument in "'All Is Not Sexuality That Looks It': Charlotte Perkins Gilman and Karen Horney on Freudian Psychoanalysis," in *Her Contemporaries,* esp. 196 and 203–8, disputing the claim that Gilman's critique rested on a "horror of sex."

44. See Cott, *The Grounding*, 42 and 45.

45. See Leila J. Rupp's engrossing analysis, "Feminism and the Sexual Revolu-

tion in the Early Twentieth Century: The Case of Doris Stevens," *Feminist Studies* 15 (Summer 1989): 294–95, 302, 305, 292, 290, 303, and 300; and also Mary Trigg, "'To Work for Ends Larger than Self': The Feminist Struggles of Mary Beard and Doris Stevens in the 1930s," *Journal of Women's History* 7 (Summer 1995): 54–55. And see Doris Stevens, *Jailed for Freedom* (New York: Boni & Liveright, 1920), Stevens, "Wages for Wives," *Nation* 122 (27 January 1926): 81–83, Stevens, "Birth Control and Women's General Advance," *Birth Control Review* 10 (April 1926): 122–23, Stevens, "Is a Uniform Marriage and Divorce Law Desirable? Pro," *Congressional Digest* 6 (June–July, 1927): 203–5.

46. See, for instance, Ann G. Klein, *A Forgotten Voice: A Biography of Leta Stetter Hollingworth* (Scottsdale, AZ: Great Potential Press, 2002); Desley Deacon, *Elsie Clews Parsons: Inventing Modern Life* (Chicago: University of Chicago Press, 1997); and Sara Alpern, *Freda Kirchwey: A Woman of "The Nation"* (Cambridge, MA: Harvard University Press, 1987).

47. See Kate Wittenstein, "The Feminist Uses of Psychoanalysis: Beatrice M. Hinkle and the Foreshadowing of Modern Feminism in the United States," *Journal of Women's History* 10 (Summer 1998): 43, 45, and 49. And see Beatrice M. Hinkle, "Why Feminism?" *Nation* 125 (6 July 1927): 8–9, and Hinkle, "Woman and the New Morality," *Nation* 119 (19 November 1924): 541–43.

48. Gilman, "Toward Monogamy," 58, 58–59, and 63.

49. Magner, "Darwinism and the Woman Question," 121; Egan, "Evolutionary Theory," 11–13; Linda Gordon and Ellen DuBois, "Seeking Ecstasy on the Battlefield: Danger and Pleasure in Nineteenth-Century Feminist Thought," *Feminist Studies* 9 (Spring 1983): 17–38; Cott, *The Grounding,* 12–14; Gilman, "Toward Monogamy" 56, Gilman, "New Generation of Women," 731–7, and Gilman, "The Women Who Won't Move Forward," 126–28.

50. Unidentified clipping, CPGP, SL 177/295/1.

51. Florence L. Cross Kitchelt to Frances Maille, 1 August 1947, and Kitchelt to CPG, 1897, Florence L. Cross Kitchelt Papers, SL A-61/6/146 and 147.

52. See Lane, *To Herland,* 7; and Delap, *The Feminist Avant-Garde,* 84.

CHAPTER 7

The epigraph to this chapter—George Middleton, *These Things Were Mine: The Autobiography of a Journeyman Playwright* (New York: Macmillan, 1947)—can be found at 125.

1. See Allen, *Rose Scott,* 235–37; Woolf, *A Room of One's Own,* 103–7; and Beauvoir, *The Second Sex,* 271–273.

2. See Edelstein, "The Yellow Newspaper," 73–76.

3. See Rodgers, *Atlantic Crossings,* 66; and "Men Are Worried," unidentified clipping [1916?], CPGP, SL 177/295/2. The epigraph to this section—William English Walling, *The Larger Aspects of Socialism* (New York: Macmillan, 1913)—is at 365–66.

4. Floyd Dell, *Women as World Builders: Studies in Modern Feminism* (Chicago: Forbes & Co., 1913), 22. He judged Jane Addams a "lone eminence" in "imaginative sympathy," not militant, serenely reasonable, never sounding "the note of defiance,"

but therefore unable "to imbue the movement in which she is a leader wither her own spirit." See Prestonia Mann Martin, "Suffrage Sophistry," letter to the editor, *New York Times*, 31 January 1915; a year later she published another letter, this time urging that, if enfranchised, women should have the option of delegating their vote to a male voter of their choice. See Prestonia Mann Martin, "Proxy Voters for Women," *New York Times*, 31 January 1916, 8.

5. John M. Martin (1864–1936), Fabian socialist, political scientist, and sociologist, was born in England, educated at London University, and professor and lecturer at East London Technical College before marrying *American Fabian* editor, Prestonia Mann in 1900, and immigrating to New York in 1903. There he directed the League for Political Education and was a member of the city Housing Corporation and the Education Board. His publications included John M. Martin, *State Education at Home and Abroad* (London: Fabian Society, 1894), *The Workers' School Board Program*, Fabian Tract no. 55 (London: Fabian Society, 1899), and *Dictators and Democracies Today* (Winter Park, FL: Rollins Press, ca. 1935). Prestonia Mann Martin (1862–1945) was the author of *"The Most Important Question in the World": Is Mankind Advancing?* (New York: Baker & Taylor Co., 1910), and *Prohibiting Poverty: Suggestions for a Method of Obtaining Economic Security* (New York: Farrar & Rinehart, 1933). See also her letter to the editor: Martin, "Suffrage Sophistry," *New York Times*, 31 January 1915, XXI.

6. Martin and Martin, *Feminism*, 23

7. Ibid., 31.

8. Ibid., 110, 243–44, 36–37, and 205–8.

9. Gilman, "Comment and Review," *Forerunner* 7 (May 1916): 139.

10. Ibid., 139–40. John Martin and Gilman clashed over his opposition to married teachers' maternity leave (discussed further in chap. 8). And see Mrs. John Martin, "Feminism Makes Man the Drone in a Beehive," *New York Times*, 12 April 1914, Sunday Magazine 4.

11. Martin held that married schoolteachers' demand for maternity leave was the ultimate in elitist feminism. See "Married School Teachers," *New York Times* (15 November 1913): 10.

12. Walsh, *Feminism*, 74. Correa Moylan Walsh (b. 1862), New York economist, educated at Harvard, with university studies in Berlin, Paris, Rome, and Oxford, was a member of the American Economic Association, American Academy of Political and Social Science, the Royal Economics Society, the Royal Statistical Society, the American Mathematical Association, and author of several books, including *The Measurement of Exchange Value* (New York: Macmillan Co., 1901), *The Fundamental Problem in Monetary Science* (New York: Macmillan, 1903), *The Doctrine of Creation* (London: T. Fisher Unwin, 1910), *The Political Science of John Adams: A Study in the Theory of Mixed Government and the Bicameral System* (Freeport, NY: Books for Libraries Press, 1915), *Socialism* (New York: Sturgis & Walton Co., 1917), and *Feminism;* and *Four Kinds of Economic Value* (Cambridge, MA: Harvard University Press, 1926).

13. Walsh, *Feminism*, 33.

14. Ibid., 51.

15. Ibid., 51.

16. Ibid., 82

17. Ibid., 178.

18. Ibid., 181–182

19. Ibid., 184, 174, and 175.

20. Barnett, *Foundations of Feminism,* 37 and 73; and Avrom Barnett to CPG, 28 December 1920, CPGP, SL 177/142/2.

21. Ibid., 38–39.

22. Ibid., 47–48.

23. CPG to Avrom Barnett, 26 February 1921, CPGP, SL 177/142/2

24. Avrom Barnett to CPG, 6 March 1921, CPGP, SL 177/142/2. Barnett, *Foundations of Feminism,* 3, 4, and 72.

25. Her co-contributors in *Our Changing Morality,* ed. Freda Kirchwey (New York: Albert & Charles Boni, Inc., 1924) included Bertrand Russell, Elsie Clews Parsons, Floyd Dell and Beatrice M. Hinkle; while others in *Sex in Civilization,* ed. V. F. Calverton and Samuel D. Schmalhausen (New York: Macaulay Co., 1929), were Robert Briffault, Beatrice Forbes-Robinson Hale, Mary Ware Dennett, Judge Ben B. Lindsey, Smith Ely Jeliffe, Bernard Glueck, Margaret Sanger, G. V. Hamilton, and Ira S. Wile. Others contributing to *Woman's Coming of Age: A Symposium,* ed. Samuel D. Schmalhausen and V. F. Calverton (New York: Horace Liveright, Inc., 1931) were Alice Beale Parsons, Margaret Mead, Havelock Ellis, Lorinne Pruette, Dora Russell, and Rebecca West.

26. For full discussion of these, see chap. 11.

27. See Ceplair, *Charlotte Perkins Gilman,* 84–187; Gilman, *Suffrage Songs and Verses* (New York: Charlton, 1911), and Gilman, *Does a Man Support His Wife?* (New York: Charlton, 1911). The epigraph to this section—Gilman, *The Living*—can be found at 310.

28. See, for instance, "A Matter of Figure: The Dressmaker's Dummy Is Fearfully and Wonderfully Made," *Idaho Daily Statesman* 28 (20 May 1892): 3; "A Woman's Book," *Labor Advocate* 10, no. 41 (14 October 1899): 1; "Where Did Women Lose It? Mrs. Gilman Says All the Work of the World Was Started by Them," *Kansas City Star* 73, no. 3 (4 January1910): 1; "Brilliant Audience at Suffrage Meeting: Mr. Charlotte Perkins Gilman Greeted by Enthusiastic Crowd," *Lexington Herald* 43no. 308 (4 November 1913): 1; Charlotte Perkins Gilman, "What's Feminism?" *Sunday Oregonian* 35, no. 36 (3 September 1916): 2.

29. See Edelstein, "The Yellow Newspaper," 87–88.

30. See, for instance, "Authoress Kills Self," *Los Angeles Times,* 20 August 1935, A1–A2; "A Woman with a Will," *Los Angeles Times,* 10 November 1935, A6; "The Time... the Place... the Story," *Washington Post,* 20 August 1935, 1; "The Right to Death," *Washington Post,* 21 August 1935, 8; Alice Stone Blackwell, "Regarding Mrs. Gilman," *Washington Post,* 28 August 1935, 8; "Charlotte Gilman Dies to Avoid Pain," *New York Times,* 20 August 1935, 44; and "Mrs. Catt Defends Mrs. Gilman's Suicide," *New York Times,* 21 August 1935, 21.

31. See, for instance, "Of Famous Ancestry..." *Minneapolis Journal,* 17 November 1899, 7; Elizabeth Lee, "Charlotte Perkins Gilman the Apostle of Work for Women," *Montgomery Advertiser* 75, no. 305 (11 June 1904): 13.

32. "Charlotte Perkins Stetson," *San Francisco Newsletter,* 28 March 1891. Writer

Gertrude Atherton reported that Gilman lived in Pasadena devoting most of her time "to the literary work which is in increasing demand" ("Literary Development in California," *Cosmopolitan* [January 1891], clipping, CPGP, SL 177/266/2).

33. Certainly this was how critics of her positions saw her mission during her lifetime. For instance, see "The Social Purity Movement," *Los Angeles Times,* 26 July 1890; "Woman's Nature," *Los Angeles Times,* 27 July 1890, 7; "Woman and Home," *Los Angeles Times,* 25 December 1892, 12.

34. See "Magazines for January," *Boston Advertiser* 40 (6 January 1892): 6; and "Literary Notes," *Daily Inter Ocean* 282 (2 January 1892): 10. A "profile" in its "News From the Clubs" column reported briefly that "Charlotte Perkins Stetson spoke at San Francisco on 'Dress Reform,'" and 'Society and the Baby,'" *New Nation,* 25 April 1891, 211.

35. For instances from Gilman's press cuttings, see "Stetson Objects to Reform— His Wife's Plans for Bettering the Universe Annoy Him," *San Francisco Examiner,* 20 December 1892; "She Didn't Wear Corsets: Artist C. W. Stetson Seeks Divorce from His Handsome Wife," *World,* 18 December 1893; "Had Ideas of Her Own: Mr. Stetson Cut No Figure with Her," *Boston Globe,* 7 December 1892; and "'Isms' Ruin Wedlock: Divorce Sought because Wife Is Dress Reformer," unidentified newspaper clipping, New York, 18 December 1893. "A Woman Orator's Pet Ambition: She Abandoned Her Family for a Career—a Brilliant Lecturer," *Rochester Democrat,* 14 March 1897; "Has Found Her Benedick: After Denouncing Marriage, Mrs. Charlotte Perkins Stetson Weds Her Cousin," unidentified newspaper clipping, June 1900; and "Famous Mrs. Stetson Married a New York Man," *New York Journal,* 1 June 1900, CPGP, SL 177/282. See also "Wife Charged with Being a Crank," *Chicago Daily Tribune,* 18 December 1892, 1; "Entre Nous," *Milwaukee Journal,* 13 January 1893, 4; "An Odd Divorce Suit," *Washington Post,* 5 March 1894, 1; "In a New Role: Charlotte Perkins Stetson Wants a Divorce," *Los Angeles Times,* 4 March 1894, 10; "Stetson's Woes," *Los Angeles Times,* 5 March 1895, 5; "A Pretty Romance," *Los Angeles Times,* 6 March 1894, 8; "Stetson Will Fight," *Los Angeles Times,* 2 April 1894, 3; "Not Even Her Friends Knew," *Kansas City Star* 20, no. 278 (21 June 1900): 6; "Ambitious Woman Gets Rid of a Husband," *Idaho Daily Statesman,* 9 September 1900, 7.

36. Helen Campbell, "Charlotte Perkins Stetson—a Sketch," *Time and the Hour,* 16 April 1898, 7, clipping, CPGP, SL 177/287. See, for instance, *London Daily Chronicle,* 26 June 1898; and for a full listing of these see Scharnhorst, *Bibliography,* 100–102.

37. "Lecture on Public Ethics: Mrs. C. P. Stetson Addresses the League for Political Education and Urges Self-Sacrifice," *New York Times,* 23 April 1899, 20.

38. It should be noted, however, that the report contained no details of Gilman addressing the issue specifically; instead, she focused on socialism. See "Speaks Out for Woman Suffrage," *Vancouver Evening World,* 23 June 1905, CPGP, SL 177/287. "'The Extension of the Suffrage to Women': Subject of an Interesting Debate before the Outlook Club Last Evening," unidentified clipping, annotated "1903," CPGP, SL 177/266/1. "Charlotte Perkins Gilman: Writer, Public Speaker, Advanced Thinker," *Pictorial Review* 13 (October 1911): 14.

39. Review of *Women and Economics, Boston Evening Transcript* [1898?], CPGP 177/300; "The Ideal Home," *New York Times Saturday Review of Books and Art,* 2

December 1903, 983. For full listing of these articles by or about Gilman, see *Proquest Historical Newspapers,* and see nn. 42 and 44 below.

40. These estimates are derived from a basic search of the electronic database *Proquest Historical Newspapers: The New York Times* (1851–2004). A search of the name, "Stetson, Charlotte Perkins Stetson" yields forty-nine documents, while for "Gilman, Charlotte Perkins," the total is 251. The same search for the *Washington Post, Chicago Daily Tribune,* and *Los Angeles Times* yielded 79, 116, and 159, respectively. The grand total for these four metropolitan dailies then (so far) is 654.

41. See, for instance, "Charlotte Perkins Stetson," *Chicago Daily Inter Ocean,* 8 July 1893, 13; "Personal and Political," *Boston Daily Advertiser,* 14 September 1895, 4; "The Woman Suffragists," *Morning Oregonian,* 27 January 1896, 2; "Mrs. Stetson Is Coming Here," *Columbus (GA) Enquirer-Sun* 11, no. 42 (17 February 1899); "More Than Up to Date," *North American,* 20 November 1899, 6; "Mrs. Stetson's Book," *Denver Evening Post,* 18 December 1899, 3; "A Mistaken Idea of Work," *Minneapolis Journal,* 10 February 1900, 4; "Women's Influence," 7, no. 80 (11 November 1904): 4; "Home No Place for the Baby," *Fort Worth Telegram* 21, no. 151 (3 December 1904); "Is a Wife a Slave?" *Olympia (WA) Morning Olympian* 18, no. 277 (3 February 1909): 3; "No More Dolls: Comments on Recent Views Aired by Mrs. Gilman," *Columbia (SC) State* 8414 (6 April 1914): 4; and "Which Way Are Women Going? America's Leading Feminist" *Montgomery Advertiser* 91, no. 25 (25 January 1920): 1.

42. For extensive evidence of local Gilman reportage, see the electronic database, *America's Historical Newspapers, 1690–1922* (American Antiquarian Society). Based on newspapers indexed to date (the project is incomplete), the search for Charlotte Perkins Stetson/Gilman yielded 439 documents, all in addition to the Proquest Historical Newspapers yield of 654, for a provisional national total of 1,093 documents. Given that such index may still be incomplete, especially for mentions of Stetson/Gilman in "[No headline]" contexts, this is a conservative estimate of press coverage during her lifetime. With the exception of the 1890s Californian press, the bulk of newspapers' coverage occurred in the 1900–1920 period, and most especially 1910–16. Meanwhile, a survey of Proquest periodical articles by or about Gilman during her lifetime yields 452 further articles or items. Again, these indexes too may be incomplete. On discussions of feminism, see, for instance, Ernest Salliere, "The Reaction against Feminism in Germany I and II," *Living Age* 225, nos. 2913 and 2914 (5 and 12 May 1900): 1–12 and 358–66; "Feminism in France," *Sunday Duluth (MN) News Tribune,* 8 April 1900, 13; Emily Stone Whitely, "A Study in Feminism," *Critic* 39, no. 1 (July 1901): 70–72; "A Fine Study in Feminism," *Chicago Daily Tribune,* 25 October 1902, 2; "Feminism in Germany," *Kansas City Star* 24, no. 306 (19 July 1904): 306.

43. Lena Schroder to CPG, 3 September 1899, CPGP, SL 177/137. The epigraph to this section, the quote from Dorothy M. Richardson, n.d. London, can be found in Charlotte Perkins Gilman Papers, SL 177/152.

44. Patricia Cox to CPG, 18 June 1911; Frank B. Patterson to CPG, 13 July 1909, CPGP, SL 177/141/1; 139/1.

45. W. Orinde Stockdale to CPG, 22 April 1904; Clement R. Wood to CPG, 1 April 1912, CPGP, SL 177/138; 141/1.

46. May Glenhauser to CPG, April 1914 and 19 December 1914, CPGP, SL 177/141/2.

47. "Mrs. Charlotte Perkins Gilman. Miles Franklin: An American Letter," *Stock and Station Journal,* 6 December 1912, CPGP, SL 177/266/1.

48. See Nellie S. Bowman to CPG, 27 May 1906, CPGP, SL 177/152; Hill, *Journey from Within,* 210; Tyler Hewett Bennett to CPG, 28 August 1934, Emily E. Keel to CPG, 1 August 1934; William Marion Reedy to CPG, 2 February 1915, CPGP, SL 177/146/2; 141/2.

49. "Box 34, Chicago" to CPG, 24 March 1914, CPGP 177/141/1.

50. Harriet Tebbetts to CPG, 21 January 1915, CPGP, SL 177/142/2.

51. See G. C. Yearling to CPG, 24 May [1907?], CPGP, SL 177/139.

52. Gilman, "Why Are There No Women on the President's Commission?" *Good Housekeeping* 48 (January 1909): 120–22; and L. E. Middlehope to CPG, 14 June 1909, CPGP, SL 177/139/1.

CHAPTER 8

The epigraph to this chapter, Gilman, *His Religion and Hers,* can be found at 83.

1. Gilman, "Old Religions and New Hopes," *Forerunner* 6 (February 1915): 34–36, and Gilman, "With Her in Ourland," *Forerunner* 7 (November 1916): 296.

2. For some indicative examples of commentary on *Herland,* which garners the most Gilman commentary after "The Yellow Wall-paper," see Frances Bartkwoski, "Remembering and Inventing: Charlotte Perkins Gilman's *Herland* and Monique Wittig's *Les Guerilleres,*" in *Feminist Utopias* (Lincoln: University of Nebraska Press, 1989), 161–72; Bridget Bennett, "Pockets of Resistance: Some Notes Towards an Exploration of Gender and Genre Boundaries in *Herland,*" in *A Very Different Story: Studies on the Fiction of Charlotte Perkins Gilman,* ed. Val Gough and Jill Rudd (Liverpool: Liverpool University Press, 1998), 38–53; Martha J. Cutter, "Herstory in Hisland, History in *Herland:* Charlotte Perkins Gilman's Reconstruction of Gender and Language," in *Unruly Tongue: Identity and Voice in American Women's Writing, 1850–1930* (Jackson: University Press of Mississippi, 1999), 111–40; Elizabeth Keyser, "Looking Backward: From Herland to Gulliver's Travels," in *Critical Essays,* 159–72; Kathleen M. Lant, "The Rape of the Text: Charlotte Gilman and the Violation of 'Herland,'" *Tulsa Studies in Women's Literature* 9 (Fall 1990): 291–308; Thomas Galt Peyser, "Reproducing Utopia: Charlotte Perkins Gilman and 'Herland,'" *Studies in American Fiction* 20 (Spring 1992): 1–16; Christopher P. Wilson, "Charlotte Perkins Gilman's Steady Burghers: The Terrain of Herland," in *Woman and Her World,* 173–90.

3. Gilman, "Toward Monogamy," 65.

4. Gilman, *Women and Economics,* 312–317. The epigraph to this section is, in full, "Woman's Weakness due to Education: Girls Do Not Belong to the Weaker Sex Necessarily, Mrs. Gilman Asserts," *New York Times,* 26 March 1914, 10.

5. See, for instance, Gilman, "The Beauty of a Block," 67–72, Gilman, "Why Are There No Women on the President's Commission?" 120–22, Gilman, "A Thousand Farmer's Wives," *Forerunner* 4 (May 1913): 120–21, Gilman, "The 'Nervous Breakdown' of Women," *Forerunner* 7 (August 1916): 202–6, and Gilman, "Applepieville," 365 and 393–95.

6. Gilman, "Feminism and Social Progress," 124 and 119.

7. Gilman, *What Diathna Did,* 36 and 19, Gilman, *His Religion and Hers,* 14, 29, 130; Gilman, *The Home,* 98–100 and 314, Gilman, "His Excuse," *Forerunner* 7 (April 1916): 85–88, Gilman, *Women and Economics,* 297, 240, and 244–47; while this was a common theme in her fiction, its most poignant treatment was in her short story, "The Vintage," *Forerunner* 7 (October 1916): 253–57, discussed in chap. 9.

8. For fuller discussion of some these ramifications of the novel, see Sharon M. Rambo, "What Diantha Did: The Authority of Experience," in *Woman and Her World,* 151–71; and Jill Bergman, "'Amazon of Industry': Maternal Realism in Charlotte Perkins Gilman's *What Diantha Did,*" *Journal of the Association for Research on Mothering* 4 (Fall–Winter 2002): 85–98.

9. Gilman, "Special Education for Women," CPG to James Wood, 23 February 1933, CPGP 177/146/1; Gilman, *The Home,* 125, 330, 331, Gilman, "Homes without Housekeeping: A Present Demand," *Delineator* 69 (May 1907): 875–76, and 955, Gilman, *Women and Economics,* 255–56 and 32, Gilman, "The Home without a Kitchen," *Puritan* 7 (December 1899): 417–22, Gilman, "Private Homes and Common Kitchens," *New Idea Woman's Magazine* 18 (November 1908): 8, Gilman, "Bee Wise," *Forerunner* 4 (July 1913): 169–73, and Gilman, "A Surplus Woman," *Forerunner* 7 (May 1916): 113–18.

10. See Gilman, *The Home,* 334–35, Gilman, *Women and Economics,* 210–12 and 284–92, Gilman, "Why Not Nursery Suites?" *Saturday Evening Post,* 11 November 1899, 382, Gilman, "A Garden of Babies," *Success* (June 1909), 370–71, Gilman, "Groups of Babies," *Forerunner* 7 (April 1916): 104.

11. See "The Ideal Home," *New York Times,* 26 December 1903, 3; and Gilman, *Women and Economics,* 118.

12. For discussion of Gilman's clichéd representation of Tibet in *Moving the Mountain,* see Asha Nadkarni, "Eugenic Feminism: Asian Reproduction in the U.S. National Imaginary," *Novel: A Forum on Fiction* 39 (Spring 2006): 221–44.

13. Gilman, "Moving the Mountain" [chap. 1], *Forerunner* 2 (January 1911): 25.

14. Gilman, "Moving the Mountain" [chap. 2], *Forerunner* 2 (February 1911): 54 and 56.

15. Gilman, "Moving the Mountain" [chap. 10], *Forerunner* 2 (October 1911): 274.

16. Gilman, "Moving the Mountain" [chap. 4], *Forerunner* 2 (April 1911): 112 and 113.

17. Gilman, "Moving the Mountain" [chap. 5], *Forerunner* 2 (May 1911): 136–41.

18. Gilman, "Feminism and Social Progress" 122. The epigraph to this section, Gilman, "Sex and Race Progress," 115.

19. Gilman, *Women and Economics,* 8 and 158–59, and Gilman, "Masculine, Feminine, and Human," *Woman's Journal* 23 (9 July 1892): 220.

20. Gilman, *Human Work,* 72.

21. Ibid., 207, 214, 63–64, 72, 223, and 281–82. Tracy Fessenden is outraged at abolitionist feminists Gilman and Stanton's comparing women's situation with chattel slaves, as a "stunning erosion of the singularity of racial bondage even in this supposed account of strengthened commitment to abolitionism," showing starkly the current unfamiliarity of this deeply felt and widely cited analogy a century ago. Once again this signals the historicity and contingency of the discourses in which feminism has been embedded, nationally and internationally. See further discussion of the problem

of presentism in appraisal of earlier feminists like Gilman in chap. 12; and see also Fessenden, *Culture and Redemption: Religion, the Secular, and American Literature* (Princeton, NJ: Princeton University Press, 2007), 163.

22. CPG to Edward Alsworth Ross, 1 February 1900, Edward Alsworth Ross Collection (EARC), film A526, reel 2, 1892–1900; and Gilman, *Human Work*, 214; for examples of Progressive Era views of "the Orient," see G. W. Knox, "Spirit of the Orient," *Chautauqua* 42 (September 1905): 11–49; F. J. Koch, "Lazy Languor of the East," *Overland Monthly* 49 (April 1907): 321–24; Paul Samuel Reinisch, "Ideal of Oriental Unity," *Atlantic* 102 (July 1908): 23–33; and William I. Thomas, "The Significance of the Orient for the Occident," *American Journal of Sociology* 12, no. 4 (January 1907): 435–69.

23. Gilman, *Human Work*, 213 and 214; CPG to James Wood, 23 February 1933, "Special Education for Women," CPGP 177/146/1, 1–2, and Gilman, *Human Work*, 141–42.

24. Gilman, *Human Work*, 141–42, 124–25, and 126–27.

25. Gilman, *His Religion and Hers*, 77–78.

26. See Gilman, "Comment and Review," *Forerunner* 5 (January 1914): 26–27.

27. See "Married Teachers Not Wanted Here; School Board Committee Finds Their Retention Is against Public Policy," *New York Times*, 23 June 1913, 1–2.

28. "New Fight to Save Teacher Mothers," *New York Times*, 1 October 1914, 20; and see "Teacher Mothers Look to Mitchel," *New York Times*, 17 November 1914, 9.

29. See George MacAdam, "Feminist Apartment House to Solve Baby Problem," *New York Times*, 24 January 1914, 9, reprinted as "Henrietta Rodman: An Interview with a Feminist," in *The New Feminism in Twentieth-Century America*, ed. June Sochen (Lexington, MA: D.C. Heath & Co., 1971), 47–59. See also Schwarz, *Radical Feminists of Heterodoxy*, 17, 27, 32–39, 56, 87, 125; and Sochen, *The New Woman*, 39–42, 52–60, 65–73, 86–88, 92–93, 130–36, and 140–47.

30. See Gilman, "Maternity Benefits and Reformers," 65–66.

31. See CPG to Upton Beale Sinclair, 31 August 1910, Sinclair Manuscripts, Lilly Library, Indiana University.

32. See chap. 12 for further discussion of this criticism.

33. Gilman, "Women in Industry," 45, 26, and 46–47.

34. The epigraph to this section can be found in Charlotte Perkins Gilman Papers, Schlesinger Library 177/122.

35. Gilman, *Herland*, 55 and 56–57.

36. Ibid., 55, 57, 52–53, and 64. On Gilman's approach to Terry's violence, see Kathleen M. Lant, "The Rape of the Text," 303–4.

37. Gilman, *Herland*, 132 and 124–26.

38. See Lisa A. Long, "Charlotte Perkins Gilman's *With Her In Ourland:* Herland Meets Heterodoxy," in *Her Contemporaries*, 184; and Gilman, *With Her in Ourland*, 244.

39. Gilman, "Parasitism and Civilized Vice," 124, Gilman, "New Generation," 285, Gilman, "Progress through Birth Control," 628, Gilman, "Toward Monogamy," 65, and Gilman, "Parasitism and Civilized Vice," 124–26.

40. See Jill Rudd and Val Gough's introduction to *Optimist Reformer*, xii–xvi.

PART 3

The epigraph to part 3, Charlotte Perkins Gilman to George Houghton Gilman, 29 March 1899, can be found in *A Journey from Within*, 264.

CHAPTER 9

The epigraph to this chapter, Gilman, *The Man-Made World*, can be found at 246–59.

1. See, for instance, Barbara Meil Hobson, *Uneasy Virtue: The Politics of Repression and the American Reform Tradition* (Chicago: University of Chicago Press, 1990), 142.

2. See Mara L. Keire, "The Vice Trust: A Reincarnation of the White Slavery Scare in the United States, 1907–1917," *Journal of Social History* 35 (Fall 2001): 5–41; Timothy J. Gilfoyle, *City of Eros: New York City Prostitution and the Commercialization of Sex, 1790–1920* (New York: W. W. Norton, 1992), 291; Ruth Rosen, *The Lost Sisterhood: Prostitution in America, 1900–1918* (Baltimore: Johns Hopkins University Press, 1982), 86–89 and 112–16; Mark Thomas Connelly, *The Response to Prostitution in the Progressive Era* (Chapel Hill: University of North Carolina Press, 1980), 4, 12, 18, 21, 26–27, 125, 128–31 and 144–47.

3. See Hobson, *Uneasy Virtue*, 183 and 175–76.

4. See Gilfoyle, *City of Eros*, 277; and Rosen, *The Lost Sisterhood*, 16–18.

5. Janet Beer and Katherine Joslyn presume, however, that because of Gilman's criticism of the "mixing of races or nations," she would not have used the chattel slavery/sex slavery analogy ("'Diseases of the Body Politic': White Slavery in Jane Addams 'A New Conscience and an Ancient Evil' and Selected Short Stories by Charlotte Perkins Gilman," *Journal of American Studies* 33 [April 1999]: 11). In fact, Gilman closely aligned with exactly this analogy in work on this subject stretching back to the 1880s, for as discussed in chaps. 3 and 4, she saw the sexual enslavement of women as the original or first slavery of human societies, the model from which others derived. This feminist position underpinned not only her own embrace of abolitionism but that of others as well. For a more generous views of abolitionists in Anglophone countries in this period, see David J. Pivar, *Purity and Hygiene: Women, Prostitution, and the "American Plan," 1900–1930* (Westport, CT: Greenwood Press, 2002); Mary Spongberg, *Feminizing Venereal Disease: The Body of the Prostitute in Nineteenth-Century Medical Discourse* (New York: New York University Press, 1997); Sheila Jeffreys, *The Spinster and Her Enemies: Feminism and Sexuality, 1880–1930* (London: Pandora Press, 1985); and Lucy Bland, *Banishing the Beast: Feminism, Sex, and Morality* (London: Tauris Park, 2001).

6. See Susan Kingsley Kent, *Sex and Suffrage in Britain, 1860–1914* (Princeton, NJ: Princeton University Press, 1987), 33.

7. See Gilman, *Man-Made World*, 64, Gilman, "The Oldest Profession in the World," *Forerunner* 4 (March 1913): 63 and 64, Gilman, *The Home*, 97, Gilman, *Human Work*, 253, Gilman, *His Religion and Hers*, 41, Gilman, "Parasitism and Civilized Vice," 110–26; and see Beer, *Kate Chopin, Edith Wharton and Charlotte Perkins Gilman: Studies in Short Fiction* (Basingstoke: Palgrave Macmillan, 2005), 176.

8. CPG, Diary, 9 May 1884, CPGP 177/vol. 19/68; Gilman, "The Oldest Profes-

sion in the World," 64. The epigraph to this section—Charlotte Perkins Gilman, *Women and Economics* (1898)—can be found at 63.

9. See Gilman, "Causes and Cures" (lecture, presented at Pasadena, CA., November 1890), CPGP, 177/10, 2.

10. "A Sociological Study," *Los Angeles Times,* 22 December 1892, 4.

11. Gilman, *Women and Economics,* 72, 33, 28–29, 49, 53, 45, and 72.

12. Ibid., 42 and 96; and Carole Pateman, *The Sexual Contract* (Palo Alto, CA: Stanford University Press, 1988), 199 and 209.

13. Gilman, *Women and Economics,* 93 and 93–4.

14. Gilman, "Comment and Review," *Forerunner* 4 (August 1913): 224.

15. Gilman, "Comment and Review," *Forerunner* 2 (November 1910): 22–24.

16. Gilman, "Comment and Review," *Forerunner* 2 (January 1911): 27.

17. Prince Morrow, *Social Disease and Marriage* (New York: Lea Brothers & Co., 1904), 92.

18. Frederick J. Adams et al., *The Report and Recommendations of the Bridgeport Vice Commission* (Bridgeport, CT: n.p., 1916), 15–16.

19. Gilman, "Comment and Review," *Forerunner* 5 (February 1914): 56; and Morrow, *Social Disease,* 22, 25, 24–25, 30, 103, 27, 32, 34, 52, and 54.

20. Gilman, "In Its Sociological Aspects," *Transactions of the American Society of Sanitary and Moral Prophylaxis* 3 (1910): 141–54. See also Pivar, *Purity and Hygiene,* 148; Gilman, "Comment and Review" (February 1914): 56, Gilman, "Comment and Review" (November 1910): 24.

21. Gilman, "Comment and Review" (February 1914): 56.

22. Gilman, "Comment and Review," *Forerunner* 6 (March 1915): 83; Upton Sinclair, *Sylvia's Marriage: A Novel* (New York: Albert & Charles Boni, 1928), 314, 208–9; and Morrow, *Social Disease and Marriage,* 33.

23. See Richard Hofstadter, *The Age of Reform: From Bryan to FDR* (New York: Vintage, 1955), 174–214; Eugene Brieux, *Damaged Goods (Les avaries): A Play in Three Acts,* trans. John Pollock (New York: Brentanos/Connecticut Society of Social Hygiene, 1912); "Three Won't Back New Coppee Play," *New York Times,* 30 September 1913, 3; Northrup Morse, *Peach Bloom: An Original Play in Four Acts* (New York: Medical Review of Reviews, Sociological Fund, 1913); Gilman, "Comment and Review," *Forerunner* 5 (March 1914): 84; Elizabeth Robins, *My Little Sister* (London: Dodd, Mead, & Co., 1913). See also Harriet Burton Laidlaw, "'My Little Sister,'" *Survey* 30 (May 1913): 199–202.

24. Gilman, "The Oldest Profession in the World," 63–64.

25. Gilman, "Comment and Review," *Forerunner* 3 (November 1912): 308.

26. Gilman, "Comment and Review," *Forerunner* 1 (November 1910): 23–24.

27. See William I. Thomas, *The Unadjusted Girl: With Cases and Standpoint for Behavior Analysis* (Boston: Little Brown, 1923), 70–87 and 222–57. The epigraph to this section, Gilman, *Man-Made World,* is at 62.

28. See Edwin R. A. Seligman, *The Social Evil with Special Reference to Conditions Existing in the City of New York: A Report Prepared (in 1902) under the Direction of the Committee of Fifteen,* 2nd ed. (New York: G. P. Putnam's Sons, 1912), 7 and 8.

29. See Jane Addams, *A New Conscience and an Ancient Evil* (New York: Macmillan, 1912), 27–28, 49, 199, 201, 203, 5–13, 37–46, 49, and 214. Hill justly observes

that Gilman was immensely more feminist and radical in her analysis of women's situations than Addams. See Hill, *Making of a Radical Feminist*, 278–79. Gilman herself wrote to Houghton from a visit to Hull House on 12 December 1898, after she published *Women and Economics:* "I had a nice little chat with Miss Addams last night—but I don't feel at all near her" (Hill, *Journey from Within*, 215). Beer and Joslyn offer a critical account of both Addams and Gilman's stances on prostitution; however, their criticisms chiefly concern issues of class, race, and ethnicity, further addressed in chap. 12. Though the authors identify mutual influence between Addams and Gilman in this area, the implied causal chain may be inaccurate: Gilman's concerns with prostitution, "social purity," and venereal diseases, discussed in chaps. 1–3, long predated meeting Addams and certainly her 1912 treatise, *A New Conscience and an Ancient Evil*. See Beer and Joslyn, "'Diseases of the Body Politic,'" 9 and 11–12.

30. Katharine C. Bushnell, *Plain Words to Plain People* (New York: n. p., 1918), 1–2. See also Virginia Brooks, *My Battles with Vice* (New York: Macaulay Co., 1915), 87–92 and 199–202.

31. Ernest A. Bell, *Fighting the Traffic in Young Girls; or, War on the White Slave Trade* (Chicago: Southern Bible House, 1910), 229.

32. J. W. Walton, "Young Men and Morality," in *National Purity Congress, Its Papers, Addresses, Portraits: An Illustrated Record of the Papers and Addresses of the First National Purity Congress* (New York: American Purity Alliance, 1896), 8, 83, and 85–86; Jessie A. Ackermann, "Plan of Work along Social Purity Lines," *National Purity Congress*, 334.

33. Clifford G. Roe, *What Women Might Do with the Ballot: The Abolition of the White Slave Traffic* (New York: National American Woman Suffrage Association, [1912?]), 8–9; and Roe, *Panders and Their White Slaves* (New York: Fleming H. Revell Co., 1910), 220.

34. Theodore A. Bingham, *The Girl That Disappears: The Real Facts about the White Slave Trade* (Boston: Richard G. Badger, 1911), 62–63; and Robert K. Massie et al., *Report of the Vice Commission of Kentucky* (Lexington: J. L. Richardson & Co., 1915), 47.

35. See Jane Addams, *A Challenge to the Contemporary Church* (New York: The Survey, n.d.), 5–6.

36. Morrow, *Social Diseases*, 340; Lavinia L. Dock, *Hygiene and Morality: A Manual for Nurses and Others, Giving an Outline of the Medical, Social, and Legal Aspects of the Venereal Diseases* (New York: G. P. Putnam's Sons, 1910), 59 and 61–62; O. Edward Janney, "The Medical Profession and Morals," *National Purity Congress*, 161–62; and Chicago Society for Social Hygiene, *For the Protection of Wives and Children from Venereal Contamination* (Chicago: Chicago Society for Social Hygiene, 1900), 4.

37. Others, rather than distinguishing between abolitionists and neo-regulationists, treat all Progressive Era reform as "antiprostitution." Connelly sees the more crucial distinctions as those between reformer texts or representational genres: lurid, vicariously voyeuristic and semipornographic white slave narratives—which he likens to Indian captivity narratives and urban vice commission reports. See Connelly, *The Response to Prostitution*, 6–7, 11–27, 152–53, 116–19, 123–27, and 129; Rosen, *The Lost Sisterhood*, 62–67; and Gilfoyle, *City of Eros*, 309–10.

38. Honolulu Social Survey, *Report of the Committee on the Social Evil* (Honolulu: Honolulu Star-Bulletin, 1914), 16–17, 29, 31, and 36–37; *Municipalities and Vice* (reprinted from *Municipal Affairs*, vol. 5, no. 2 [June 1901]) ([New York, Reform Club, Committee on City Affairs], 1901), 8–10, 9, 10, and 26; and Seligman, *The Social Evil*, 254. In some ways, Katharine Bement Davis exemplified the most pragmatic approach, centered on the prostitute as a correction problem, to which Seligman objected. See, e.g., Davis, "A Study of Prostitutes Committed from New York City to the State Reformatory for Women at Bedford Hills," in *Commercialized Prostitution in New York City*, ed. George J. Kneeland (New York: Century Co., 1917), 163–227.

39. Gilman, "Cleaning up Elita," *Forerunner* 7 (January 1916): 1–4 and 4.

40. Ben L. Reitman, *The Second Oldest Profession: A Study of the Prostitute's Business Manager* (New York: Vanguard Press, 1931), 4–5, 6–7, and 9. Reitman estimates over $700 million for Chicago alone (2009 values).

41. Gilman, "Feminism," in *Nonfiction Reader*, ed. Ceplair, 184–86.

42. Gilman, "The Vintage," *Forerunner* 7 (October 1916): 253–57 and 255–56.

43. Gilman, "His Mother," *Forerunner* 5 (July 1914): 169–73 and 172.

44. Gilman, *Crux*, 41–42.

45. See my "Charlotte Perkins Gilman, Prostitution and Frontier Sexual Contracts," 190–91. And see also Jennifer S. Tuttle, "Gilman's *The Crux* and Owen Wister's *The Virginian*: Intertextuality and 'Woman's Manifest Destiny'" in *Her Contemporaries*, 132–35; and Tuttle, "Rewriting the West Cure," 111–13.

46. See Gilman, *Crux*, 98.

47. Ibid., 131, 134, and 141.

48. Ibid., 172–173.

49. Ibid., 221–22.

50. Ibid., 131, 137, 128, 144, 130, 141, 153, 165, 185–86, 192–94, 192, 222, 225, 203, and 230–35.

51. For instances of studies of prostitution through other frameworks, see Ivan Light, "The Ethnic Vice Industry, 1880–1944," *American Sociological Review* 42 (June 1977): 464–79; and Egal Feldman, "The Prostitute, the Alien Woman, and the Progressive Imagination, 1910–1915," *American Quarterly* 30 (Summer 1967): 192–206; Gilman, *Women and Economics*, 73. See also Bederman, *Manliness and Civilization*, 138; for discussion of regeneration narratives in Gilman's *The Crux*, see Dana Seitler, "Unnatural Selection: Mothers, Eugenic Feminism, and Charlotte Perkins Gilman's Regeneration Narratives," *American Quarterly* 55 (March 2003): 71–76; and see also my *Sex and Secrets*, 60–63, 80–82.

52. The epigraph to this section, Gilman, *The Man-Made World*, is at 247–48.

53. See, for instance, Allan Brandt, *No Magic Bullet: A History of Venereal Disease in the United States Since 1880* (New York: Oxford University Press, 1985), 52–121; Bureau of Social Hygiene, *Commercialized Prostitution in New York City: A Comparison Between 1912 and 1915* (New York: Bureau of Social Hygiene, 1915), 4–5, 6, 10, and 14.

54. Seligman, *The Social Evil*, 148–51.

55. Leonard Dinnerstein, *Uneasy at Home* (New York: Columbia University Press, 1987), 15–18; Gilman, "Prisons, Convicts, and Women Voters," *Forerunner* 4 (April 1913): 92, Gilman, "Humanness," *Forerunner* 4 (February 1913): 52–53, *Gil-*

man, "Sex and Race Progress," 109–126, Gilman, "Is America Too Hospitable?" 1983–9, Gilman, "Progress through Birth Control," 622–9, Gilman, "Divorce and Birth Control," 130–51, Gilman, "Birth Control, Religion, and the Unfit," 108–9; and Gilman, "What May We Expect of Eugenics?" 219–22.

56. Gilman, *Women and Economics,* 38, Gilman, *Man-Made World,* 175, 45–46, Gilman, "The Double Standard," *Woman's Journal* 35 (March 1904): 82, Gilman, "Feminism," in Ceplair, *Nonfiction Reader,* 185.

57. Gilman, *Man-Made World,* 63–64, 169; Honolulu Social Survey, *Report of Committee on Social Evil,* 19; and Jane Addams, "A Challenge to the Contemporary Church," 1.

58. Gilman, *"Mag—Marjorie" and "Won Over": Two Novels* (New York: Ironweed Press, 1999), Gilman, "Moving the Mountain," *Forerunner* 2 (November 1911): 302, 308, and Gilman, *The Crux,* 96.

59. Gilman, *Man-Made World,* 205, 254; and Henry B. Blackwell, "Equal Suffrage versus Prostitution," *National Purity Congress,* 424–26.

60. Honolulu Social Survey, *Report of Committee on the Social Evil,* 15.

61. Christabel Pankhurst's text, originally published in England as *The Great Scourge and How to End It* (London: E. Pankhurst, 1913), was retitled as *Plain Facts about a Great Evil* (New York: Medical Review of Reviews, Sociological Fund, 1913), 7 and 9.

62. Pivar, *Purity and Hygiene,* 211–12, 214–25, and 241. Ethel Dummer, a key financial sponsor of William I. Thomas's research on juvenile prostitutes, confided to him her disgust with entrapment strategies used by wartime and immediate postwar authorities. See Ethel Sturges Dummer to William Isaac Thomas, 17 September 1920, and Thomas to Dummer, 26 September 1920, Ethel Sturges Dummer Papers, SL 1a-127/36/785. See also Hobson, *Uneasy Virtue,* 162–99; and Rosen, *The Lost Sisterhood,* 170–72; and see Pivar, *Purity and Hygiene,* xiv and 224–25.

63. Gilman, "New Generation," 285, Gilman, "Progress through Birth Control," 628, Gilman, "Toward Monogamy," 65; and Gilman, "Parasitism and Civilized Vice," 124–26. See, for instance, Schmalhausen, "The Sexual Revolution," 349; and Smith Ely Jelliffe, "The Theory of the Libido," 456–71, both in *Sex in Civilization,* ed. Calverton and Schmalhausen; G. V. Hamilton, "The Emotional Life of Modern Woman," 207–29; and V. F. Calverton, "Are Women Monogamous?" 475–88, both in *Woman's Coming of Age,* ed. Schmalhausen and Calverton; Floyd Dell, "Can Men and Women Be Friends?" 183–96; and Beatrice M. Hinkle, "Women and the New Morality," 235–49, both in *Our Changing Morality,* ed. Kirchwey.

64. Gilman, "The Oldest Profession in the World," 63.

CHAPTER 10

The epigraph to this chapter, Gilman, "The Women Who Won't Move Forward," can be found in *Physical Culture* 37 (February 1914): 126.

1. For Gilman's own clippings of extensive press coverage of her, see CPGP, SL 177/266.

2. For a useful discussion of the concept of the public intellectual, see Helen Small, ed., *The Public Intellectual* (Oxford: Blackwell, 2002).

3. An exception to the tendency to marginalize Gilman in general histories is McGerr, *Fierce Discontent*, 46, 52, 61, 64, 65, 69, 227, 266, and 315. See also Robert M. Crunden, "Progressivism," in *The Reader's Companion to American History*, ed. Eric Foner and John A. Garraty (Boston: Houghton Mifflin, 1995), 869. Gilman's work receives token mention, for instance, in Sean Dennis Cashman, *America in the Age of Titans: The Progressive Era and World War I* (New York: New York University Press, 1988), 248–49; and David B. Danbom, *The World of Hope: Progressives and the Struggle for an Ethical Public Life* (Philadelphia: Temple University Press, 1987), 186; but in most of the "classic" and debated "revisionist" studies of the Progressive Era, Gilman's name shadows no page at all. Where mentioned, she is often connected with Addams, who declared Gilman's *Women and Economics* (1898), simply a "Masterpiece." See Jane Addams to CPG, 19 July 1898, and Florence Kelley to CPG, 26 July 1898, CPGP, SL 177/137. Most work on Addams predates recent revisionist interpretations of Progressive Era race, ethnic, and sexual politics. The usual contrast drawn between Gilman and Jane Addams (1860–1935) is that the former figures as the most famous feminist of the era, and Addams, its most famous woman. While some of Addams's prolific writings directly concerned women, feminism did not frame her preoccupations in the senses defined by Barrett, Cott, and others examined above—that is, a methodical analysis of women as systematically oppressed largely by, and in, men's interests did not form the axiomatic core of her thinking and animate all or most of her political interventions.

4. The untitled clipping that serves as the epigraph to this section is more completely identified as follows: *Oakland Enquirer*, untitled clipping (n.d., 1900), N.P., CPGP, 177/266.

5. Concerning coverage of her various lectures, see, on "The Mother's World," "The Mother's World," *Geneva Evening World*, 20 December 1902; on "Androcentrism," "Woman Created First," *New York Tribune*, 17 October 1903, 3; on "The Larger Feminism," "Adam the Real Rib Mrs. Gilman Insists," *New York Times*, 19 February 1914, 3; "A Feminist Revision of History," *New York Times*, 3 April 1914, 15; on "The World War and Its Effect on Women," "Great Duty of Women after War," *Boston Post*, 26 February 1918, 7; on "Americans and Non-Americans," "Fiction of America Being a Melting Pot Unmasked by Charlotte Perkins Gilman," *Dallas Morning News*, 15 February 1926, 7–8; "Charlotte Perkins Gilman: The Apostle for Women," unidentified journal offprint, penciled "1905" in Gilman's handwriting, CPGP, 177/266.

6. Hill, *Journey from Within*, 64, 380, 65, 343, 218, and 31.

7. CPG to Mrs. Williams, 17 June 1915; "Charlotte Perkins Gilman, Author and Lecturer," February 1925, CPGP, 177/153, 10. Gilman paid agents 25 percent of the takings. The agent covered publicity, advertising, venue rental, and, often, also travel and accommodation, with all expenses reimbursed by the ticket profits. In the 1910s, her minimum expenses for lecture courses in towns and smaller cities were $45 ($995 in 2009 values), while her minimum "returns" were $445 ($9,837), from which she deducted advance expenses and the agent's 25 percent commission, leaving $289 ($6,388). Large cities involved higher costs for travel, accommodations (including a parlor), a paid assistant, and local travel expenses, accruing over days, even weeks, since Gilman, easily exhausted, spoke only once a day, a policy that maximized in-

come after the considerable time and effort involved in transregional and transcontinental travel. If large urban tour advance costs might be $300 ($6,632), returns anticipated from a successful run were $1,200 ($26,526), split as $300 for the agent and $900 ($19,895) for Gilman.

8. Hill, *Journey from Within*, 224.

9. For insight into her early lectures, I thank Susan Ware for allowing me to read her unpublished paper, "Charlotte Perkins Gilman: The Early Lectures, 1890–1893" (Cambridge, MA: May 29, 1973).

10. Her lecture titles in the 1900s included "The Social Organism," "The Servant Question Answered," "Home, Past, Present, and Future," "Our Unknown Children," "Why We Work," "America's Place Today," "Social Science," "Duties, Domestic and Other," "Child Labor," "The Body, the Dress, and the Health," "Collective Ethics," "Moral Gymnastics," and "The Heroes We Need Now." In 1915, she offered four courses—"The Larger Feminism," "Studies in Masculism," "Brain Training," "War and the World Hope"—with the lectures including "The Biological Base," "The Economic Relation," "'Love,' Love and Marriage," "The Home, Past, Present, and Future," "Motherhood, Personal, and Social," "Our Male Civilization," "Specialization, Its Use and Danger," "Social Parentage," "War, Waste, and Social Economy," "Where Women Come In," "How to Make World Citizens," "Old Religions and New Hopes," "The Wicked Waste of Housework," "The Meaning of Feminism," "The Dress of Women," "A Place for Babies," "A Reasonable Socialism," "Common Sense and Equal Suffrage," "America's Place Today," "Men, Women, and People," "World Federation," and "The World War and Its Effects on Women" (1915 lecture circular) and CPG to Mrs. Roantree, 15 September 1920, CPGP, SL 177/10 and 153; and Cott, *The Grounding*, 3–10.

11. Hill, *Journey from Within*, 144, 147, and 228–29.

12. Ibid., 141, 224, 145, 147, 142, and 144.

13. When Gilman began her lecturing career in 1889–90, 2,682 women and 12,837 men had received bachelor's degrees in the United States, while 194 women and 821 men had received master's degrees, and two women and 147 men had received doctoral degrees. See National Center for Education Statistics, *Digest of Education Statistics* (Washington, DC: Department of Education, Office of Education Research and Improvement, 1995), NCES-95-0291. See Jane Addams, *Twenty Years*, 28; Katharine Bement Davis, "Three Score Years and Ten," *University of Chicago Magazine* 26 (December 1933): 28.

14. This recalls the element of recognizable feminism that criticizes existing femininities, see Cott, *The Grounding*, 6–8.

15. Gilman, "She Who Is to Come" (lecture, 10 March 1891), CPGP, 177/165, 5–6.

16. See, for instance, Gilman, "Washtubs," 152–59; and Bederman, *Manliness and Civilization*, 156–61.

17. This included her work for journals in her California period, *Kate Field's Washington*, 1890–94, *Pacific Monthly*, 1890–91, *Stockton Mail*, 1893, *Pacific Rural Press*, 1891–93, the Pacific Coast Women's Press Association *Bulletin*, 1893, and *Impress*, 1893–95. Some of her later venues were *American Fabian*, 1897–8, the *Saturday Evening Post*, 1899–1900, *Current Literature*, 1899, and *Success*, 1901–3. For full details

of her publication of articles with over thirty journals, magazines, and newspapers by then, see Scharnhorst, *Bibliography,* 75–105. The epigraph to this section, Gilman, *His Religion and Hers,* can be found at 149–51.

18. See the following article by Gilman: "In Duty Bound," *Woman's Journal* 25 (12 January 1884): 14; "Woman's Hour," *Woman's Journal* 47 (9 December 1916): 397; "The 'Right' People," *Independent,* 28 December 1899, 3489–90; "Domestic Economy," *Independent,* 16 June 1904, 1359–63; "The Beauty of a Block," 67–72; "Child Labor in the Schools," *Independent,* 21 May 1908, 1135–39; "Have You Paid Your Board?" *Independent,* 26 November 1908, 1221–23; and "Gum Chewing in Public. Is a National Funeral The Proper Place to Indulge This Habit?" letter to the editor, *New York Times,* 20 May 1914, 2.

19. Gilman, *The Living,* 304; see also Josephine J. Eschenbrenner (National Child Labor Committee) to CPG, 29 October 1913, CPGP, SL 177/141/1; Gilman, "Social Darwinism," *American Journal of Sociology* 12 (March 1907): 713–14, Gilman, "Improving on Nature," *Forerunner* 3 (July 1912): 174, Gilman, "How They Did It," *Forerunner* 6 (January 1915): 7–9, Gilman, "Having Faith in Evolution" *Forerunner* 6 (March 1915): 299–300. See also, for instance, Paul R. Reynolds to CPG, 31 May 1905; *Philadelphia Saturday Evening Post* to CPG, 26 September 1899; Hamilton Holt (*Independent*) to CPG, 31 May 1902; Esther Faber (*Shopping*) to CPG, 17 September 1908; and Elizabeth Jordan (*Harper's Bazaar*) to CPG, 10 December 1908 — CPGP, SL 177/128, 126, 133.

20. C. W. A. Veditz to CPG, 9 November 1906; Ross to CPG, 11 October 1915, CPGP 177/139/1; 141/2. She appreciated Ross's keen "race psychology" in his discussion of "the position of Chinese women past and present" — Gilman, "Comment and Review," *Forerunner* 3 (February 1912): 56. See the following articles by William I. Thomas: "On a Difference in the Metabolism of the Sexes," *American Journal of Sociology* 3 (July 1897): 31–63, "The Relation of Sex to Primitive Control," *American Journal of Sociology* 3 (May 1898): 754–76, "The Psychology of Modesty and Clothing," *American Journal of Sociology* 5 (September 1899): 246–62, "The Psychology of Race-Prejudice," *American Journal of Sociology* 9 (March 1904): 593–611, and "The Mind of Woman and the Lower Races," *American Journal of Sociology* 12 (January 1907): 435–69. See Gilman's "Comment and Review" column in the following issues of *Forerunner:* 1 (December 1909): 26; 1 (October 1910) 26; and 6 (July 1915): 195. Her serialized works included "Our Androcentric Culture or the Man-made World" (1909–10), "Our Brains and What Ails Them" (1912), "Humanness" (1913), "Social Ethics" (1914), "The Dress of Women" (1915), "Growth and Combat" (1916), and "Studies in Social Pathology" (1916).

21. For an excellent discussion of her particular distaste for Hearst newspapers, see Denise D. Knight, "Charlotte Perkins Gilman, William Randolph Hearst, and the Practice of Ethical Journalism," in *Her Contemporaries,* 46–58; and Edelstein, "The Yellow Newspaper," 72–92.

22. See the following *Forerunner* articles: "Animals in Cities," 1 (September 1910): 6; "Dogs, Pigs, and Cities," 7 (May 1916): 137–38; "The Kitchen Fly," 1 (August 1910): 8–10; "Why Make Dust," 3 (March 1912): 62–64; "Interstate Sanitation," 3 (September 1912): 237; "The Milkman and the Public," 7 (November 1916): 285–86; "Beauty from Ashes," 6 (November 1915): 300–301; "How We Waste Three-Fourths of Our

Money," 1 (December 1910): 18–19; "The Cost and Price of Living," 4 (January 1913): 25–26; "Why We Honestly Fear Socialism," 1 (December 1909): 7–10; "Pensions for 'Mothers' and 'Widows,'" 5 (January 1914): 7–8; "The New Faith," 3 (April 1912): 90–91; "The Comfort of God," 4 (March 1913): 61–62; "Two Rooms and a Bath," 3 (March 1912): 76; "Our Sleeping Cars," 4 (September 1913): 231–34; "Our Coal," 5 (July 1914): 185–86; "Standardizing Towns," 6 (February 1915): 52–54; "The Sociologist and the Reformer," 6 (September 1915): 243–44; "Having Faith in Evolution," 6 (November 1915): 299–300; "American Ships," 7 (January 1916): 12–13; "Wanted: A Railroad Cafeteria," 7 (February 1916): 33–34; "From a Hearst Paper," 5 (Septmber 1914): 251; "The Ford Party and the Newspapers," 7 (March 1916): 73–76; "Newspapers and Democracy," 7 (November 1916): 300–303, and 7 (December 1916), 314–18; and "Patriotism and Humanism," 7 (February 1915): 35–37.

23. R. O. Johnson (superintendent, Northern Pacific Railroad Company, Billings, MT) to CPG, 28 October 1916, CPGP, SL 177/142/1; and Gilman, "Comment and Review," *Forerunner* 7 (November 1916): 279.

24. See Gilman, "Comment and Review," *Forerunner* 3 (December 1911): 336. The epigraph to this section, Gilman, "Pernicious Adam: A Study in Ethics," is an unpublished typescript (1930), Charlotte Perkins Gilman Papers, 177/227/162.

25. On Middleton's many plays about the New Woman, see Bettina Friedl, *On to Victory: Propaganda Plays of the Woman Suffrage Movement* (Boston: Northeastern University Press, 1987), 35–36; and see Gilman, "Comment and Review," *Forerunner* 1 (November 1910): 24, vol. 6 (March 1915): 82, and vol. 5 (March 1914): 83–84. See also George Middleton, *These Things Were Mine: The Autobiography of a Journeyman Playwright* (New York: Macmillan, 1947), 125–32, Middleton, *Tradition, with "On Bail," "Their Wife," "Waiting," "The Cheat of Pity" and "Mothers": One Act Plays of Contemporary Life* (New York: Henry Holt & Co., 1913) and Middleton, *Possession, with the Groove, The Unborn, Circles, A Good Woman, The Black Tie: One Act Plays of Contemporary Life* (New York: Henry Holt & Co., 1915).

26. Leroy Scott, *Counsel for the Defense* (Garden City, NJ: Doubleday, 1912), 284–85; and Gilman, "Comment and Review," *Forerunner* 3 (May 1912): 139.

27. Henry Kitchell Webster, *The Real Adventure: A Novel* (Indianapolis: Bobbs Merrill Co., 1916), 120, 502–3; and Gilman, "Comment and Review," *Forerunner* 7 (January 1916): 27.

28. CPG to Upton Beall Sinclair, 31 August 1910, Sinclair Papers, Series 1, Lilly Library, Indiana University; Upton Sinclair, *The Jungle* (1906; reprint, New York: Penguin Books, 1985), 406–7.

29. Sinclair, *Love's Pilgrimage* (New York: Mitchell Kennerley, 1911), 561–62; 562–63.

30. CPG to Upton Beall Sinclair, 31 August 1910, Sinclair Papers, Lilly Library Collections, Indiana University. See, for instance, Sinclair, *Love's Pilgrimage,* 194–97 and 277–80.

31. Gilman, *The Living,* 96–97.

32. Australian promoter of the *Forerunner* in Sydney, Rod McMillen, and editor of the *Stock and Station Journal* wrote to Gilman: "I feel as if I had lost a friend. . . . I for one — and I represent a good many I'm sure — thank you cordially for all you have done for women and the race. We are one people — men and women with one destiny,

and whatever helps one sex is good for the race, and you have helped women greatly" ("Gossip," *Stock and Station Journal* [April 1916], clipping, and Rod McMillen to CPG, 30 April 1916, CPGP 177/Vol.7/8). One of his readers, Bertha S. Pearce called Gilman "one of the World's Great Women and I bless the day I heard of her through yr. journal" (Bertha S. Pearce to Rod McMillen, 25 April 1916, CPGP 177/155). See the following by Gilman: *The Living*, 310; "Poverty and Women," *Proceedings of the National Conference of Social Work* (Chicago: The Conference, 1917), 10–15; "Jane Smith's Life," *Pictorial Review* 18 (May 1917): 2, 82; "The Housekeeper and the Food Problem," *Annals of the American Academy* 74 (November 1917): 123–30; "Concerning Clothes," *Independent*, 22 June 1918, 478 and 483; and "Released Energy of Women," *World Outlook* 4 (September 1918): 3.

33. Gilman, "Killing the Failures," *Louisville Herald*, 13 June 1919, 8.

34. W. E. B. Du Bois (1868–1963), sociologist, founder of the National Association for the Advancement of Colored People (NAACP) in 1909, and editor of its magazine, the *Crisis,* for twenty-five years, before leaving in 1933 to teach at Atlanta University, published *The Philadelphia Negro: A Social Study* (Philadelphia: Published for the University of Pennsylvania, 1899), and *The Souls of Black Folk* (Chicago: A. C. McClurg & Co., 1903). Moorfield Storey (1845–1929) was an attorney who wrote on law and race, including *Charles Sumner* (Boston: Houghton Mifflin, 1900), *Problems of To-Day* (Boston and New York: Houghton Mifflin, 1920), and *The Conquest of the Philippines by the United States* (New York: G. P. Putnam's Sons, 1926). Oswald Garrison Villard (1872–1949), journalist and a grandson of William Lloyd Garrison, authored many articles and several books, including *John Brown, 1800–1859: A Biography Fifty Years After* (Boston and New York: Houghton Mifflin, 1910), and *Fighting Years: Memoirs of a Liberal Editor* (New York: Harcourt, Brace, 1939). William Pickens (1881–1954) authored numerous books, including *The Vengeance of the Gods: And Three Other Stories of Real American Color Line Life* (Philadelphia: A.M.E. Book Concern, 1922), *The New Negro: His Political, Civil, and Mental Status; and Related Essays* (New York: Neal, 1916), *The Heir of Slaves: An Autobiography* (Boston and New York: Pilgrim Press, 1911), and *Lynching and Debt-Slavery* (New York: American Civil Liberties Union, 1921). Linden Wallace Bates, Jr. (1883–1915) authored *The Russian Road to China* (Boston and New York: Houghton Mifflin, 1910). See Gilman, *With Her In Ourland*, 120.

35. Gilman, *The Living*, 310.

36. Cott, Lerner, Sklar, DuBois, and Hewitt, "Considering the State of U.S. Women's History," 153.

CHAPTER 11

The first epigraph to this chapter is Carrie Chapman Catt to CPG, 6 November 1930, and the second is CPG to Carrie Chapman Catt, 22 November 1930, Carrie Chapman Catt Papers, Schlesinger Library, M-27.

1. Gilman's publications of this later period included: "Toward Monogamy," 53–66, "Sex and Race Progress," 109–23, "Feminism and Social Progress," 115–42, "Parasitism and Civilized Vice," 110–26; and *Living*, 317. Examples of Gilman's earlier optimism about immigration can be found in the following articles by her: "Malthu-

sianism and Race Suicide," *Woman's Journal,* 3 September 1904, 282, "The Making of Americans," *Woman's Journal,* 13 August 1904, 258, and "Progress through Birth Control," 622–29. See Department of Commerce, Bureau of the Census, *Fourteenth Census of the United States Taken in the Year 1920,* vol. 3, *Compositions and Characteristics of the Population by States* (Washington, DC: GPO, 1923), 687.

2. See, for instance, Gilman, "Vanguard, Rearguard, and Mudguard," 348–53, Gilman, "Divorce and Birth Control," 130–31, Gilman, "Birth Control, Religion, and the Unfit," 108–9, Gilman, "The Right to Die," 297–30, and Gilman, "Prisons, Convicts, and Women Voters," 91–92; Douglas, *Terrible Honesty,* 6–9; and Grace Ellery Channing Stetson to Katherine Beecher Stetson Chamberlin, 14 February 1936, GECSP, SL Mss. 83-M201/5/141.

3. See Scharnhorst, *Bibliography,* 156–83, 192–93; Golden and Knight, "Afterword," in *Unpunished,* by Gilman, 213–40; and Robinson, "Killing Patriarchy," 273–85.

4. For claims of Gilman's marginality by the war years, see Bederman, *Manliness and Civilization,* 122; and on the demise of Progressivism, see McGerr, *Fierce Discontent,* 315–19. For claims that interwar Gilman no longer worked on feminist issues, see Degler, introduction to Gilman, *Women and Economics* (1966), xiv; and Lane, introduction to Gilman, *Living,* xvii. See Scharnhorst, *Bibliography,* for full details, 55–57, 73, and 157–93. The epigraph to this section is CPG to Lyman Beecher Stowe, 16 July 1928, Beecher-Stowe Collection, Schlesinger Library Mss., 77-M181, reel 3/416.

5. For mentions of her activities in these years, see Gilman, *Living,* 320; "Labor Takes a Stand against Pacifists," *New York Times,* 19 August 1917, 11; "Says Chicago Mayor Let Pacifists Meet," *New York Times,* 27 September 1921, 18; Elmer Bendiner, *A Time For Angels: The Tragicomic History of the League of Nations* (New York: Knopf, 1975), 104 and 149. For examples of Gilman's popular press syndicated articles, see the following articles from *Louisville Herald:* "The Cave Man Theory," 29 April 1919, 7, "The Habit of Being Oppressed," 21 April 1919, 6, "The Unfair Sex," 18 March 1919, 5, "The Strength of Women," 30 December 1919, 6, "Why Women Are Restless," 21 August 1919, 6, "Private Homes with Public Service," 21 October 1919, 6, "Wasted Babies," 16 April 1919, 7, and "Why We Are Going Dry," 17 March 1919, 6. And see her unpublished typescript, "Pernicious Adam: A Study in Ethics" (1930), 94, advocating temperance rather than Prohibition: "Asceticism is not temperance, Prohibition is not temperance, total abstinence is not temperance. Temperance is a wide restraint, which gives due gratification to any appetite not more." See also Gilman, "Killing the Failures," *Louisville Herald,* 13 June 1919, 7; and see her later speech on "Race Prejudice, Antipathy and ??" (handwritten, title illegible), CPGP, SL 177/173; and Gilman, "Race Prejudice in Russia," *Louisville Herald,* 12 May 1919, 4.

6. Gilman, *Living,* 317.

7. Channing Stetson to Chamberlin, 29 January 1923, GECSC, SL Mss. 89-M54/2. The initial problems of incompatibility, political disagreements, money, and divisions of labor only accelerated across the next decade. See CPG to Lyman Beecher Stowe, 16 December 1932: "Things go from bad to worse here; we now plan to have a partition suit and sell the whole place. Houghton cannot 'carry' two families" (Beecher Stowe Family Papers [hereafter BSFP], SL 77-M181, reel 3/416). See Gilman, "Should Women Take Alimony?" *Woman Citizen* (5 February 1921), 953. See also Carl R. Burghardt, *Robert M. La Follette, Sr.: The Voice of Conscience*

(New York: Greenwood Press, 1992), 109–15; and Gilman, *Living,* 332–34. See El-len Chesler, *Woman of Valor: Margaret Sanger and the Birth Control Movement in America* (New York: Simon & Schuster, 1992), 328 and 315. In January 1934, she or-ganized the thousand-person Birth Control and National Recovery conference in Washington DC, at which Gilman spoke (see discussion below). Chesler, *Woman of Valor,* 344–45.

8. CPG to Stowe, 23 April 1935, BSFP, 77-M181, reel 3/416; and CPG to Chan-ning Stetson, 3 March 1935, CPG Letters 1884–1935, mf6/5. Lyman Beecher Stowe (1880–1963) was the grandson of Harriet Beecher Stowe and the great-grandson of Lyman Beecher. His publications included *Saints, Sinners and Beechers* (Indianapo-lis: Bobbs-Merrill Co., 1934), *Harriet Beecher Stowe: The Story of Her Life* (Boston and New York: Houghton Mifflin, 1911), and with his father, Charles Edward Stowe, *Booker T. Washington: Builder of a Civilization* (Garden City, NY: Doubleday, Page & Co., 1916). Channing Stetson, however, believed Gilman too generous toward Thomas at Kate and her children's expense, resolving to urge Gilman to reverse this allocation, promising success. See Channing Stetson to Chamberlin, 29 November 1929, GECSP 83-M201/5/130; Channing Stetson to Chamberlin, 18 September 1922, 30 April 1930, and 25 March 1934, GECSP, 83-M201/1/2; 5/132; 5/138. Ten-sions were especially obvious in Channing Stetson's letters with Gilman's daughter and Channing Stetson's stepdaughter Kate (see Channing Stetson to Chamberlin, 7 December 1929, 25 March 1930, 12 January 1934, GECSP, 83-M201/5/130, 131, and 138). See CPG to Stowe, 23 April 1935, BSFP, SL 77-M181/416.

9. George Houghton Gilman to Channing Stetson, 2 January 1934, GECSP 83-M201/9/281; Hill, *Journey from Within,* 111; and see Channing Stetson to Chamber-lin, 20 May 1934 and 24 June 1934, GECSP, 83-M201/5/138.

10. CPG to Zona Gale, 14 December 1934, CPGP 177/153. Zona Gale (1874–1938) published thirteen novels and numerous short stories, poems, essays, plays, and a biography, winning the Pulitzer Prize in 1921 for the dramatic version of her 1920 novel, *Miss Lulu Bett.* In 1935 she wrote the foreword to Gilman's autobiography. See Deborah Williams Lindsay, *Not in Sisterhood: Edith Wharton, Willa Cather, Zona Gale and the Politics of Female Authorship* (New York: Palgrave, 2001).

11. CPG to Gale, 14 December 1934; and Gilman, "Feminism and Social Prog-ress," 132–33. On 1920s changes in sexual mores, see Leonard Wilcox, "Sex Boys in a Balloon: V. F. Calverton and the Abortive Sexual Revolution," *Journal of American Studies* 23 (1989): 7–26.

12. For fuller discussion of interwar feminism, see Trigg, "'To Work for Ends Larger than Self,'" 52–55; and see Susan D. Becker, *The Origins of the Equal Rights Amendment: American Feminism between the Wars* (Westport CT: Greenwood Press, 1981).

13. Gilman, *Living,* 332–35; Lane, *To Herland,* 19; CPG to Channing Stetson, 13 March 1933, CPG Letters, 1884–1935, SL mf6/5; Channing Stetson to Chamberlin, 6 May 1934, GECSP 83-201/5/138; and see Anne Edwards, *A Remarkable Woman: A Biography of Katharine Hepburn* (New York: William Morrow & Co., 1985), 32–33. For insightful discussions of interwar feminism, see Susan Ware, *Still Missing: Ame-lia Earhart and the Search for Modern Feminism* (New York: W. W. Norton, 1993), 112–43; and Freedman, "The New Woman," 21–42. With Gilman's enthusiasm for

flying, the young aviator could only inspire her approval—see Gilman, "When We Fly," *Harper's Weekly* 35, 9 November 1909, 1650, 1664, CPGP, 177/#1/3. Amelia Earhart (1897–1937) was the first woman to fly across the Atlantic (1928). She wrote three books: *The Fun of It* (New York: Brewer, Warren & Putnam, 1932), *Last Flight* (New York: Harcourt, Brace, Jovanovich, 1968), and *Twenty Hours Forty Minutes: Our Flight in the "Friendship"* (New York: Arno Press, 1979). See Doris L. Rich, *Amelia Earhart: A Biography* (Washington, DC: Smithsonian Institution, 1989), 62, 273. For discussion of movie images of flappers, see Mary P. Ryan, "The Projection of a New Womanhood," in *Decades of Discontent,* ed. Scharf and Jensen, 113–30.

14. See Gilman, "Parasitism and Civilized Vice," 125, and "Feminism and Social Progress," 131.

15. See the following works by Gilman: "Pernicious Adam: A Study in Ethics," unpublished typescript (1930), CPGP 177/227, "Fashion, Beauty, and Brains," *Outlook* 7 (August 1929): 578–79, "Do Women Dress to Please Men?" *Century* 103 (March 1922): 651–55, and *Living,* 318. Ironically, masculist objections to flapper fashions were similar: the shift dress removed the allure of outlined breasts and hips in tight-waisted garments before the 1920s. See also Kenneth Yellis, "Prosperity's Child: Some Thoughts on the Flapper," *American Quarterly* 21 (Spring 1969): 44–64.

16. Gilman, "Comment and Review," *Forerunner* 3 (December 1912): 336; and see Lillie Hamilton French, "Where Are the Old Ladies?" *Century* 84 (October 1912): 824–28; George Frederick (director, Society of Arts and Sciences) to CPG, 26 December 1922, CPGP, SL 177/143/2; Gilman, "New Generation," 731–37, and Gilman, *His Religion and Hers,* 142.

17. Gilman, "Toward Monogamy," 58–59, 57; and Kimmel and Aronson, introduction to Gilman, *Women and Economics* (1998), liii–vi. For instance, criminologist Ethel Dummer saw a dilemma: on the one hand, she adhered to Gilmanite analysis of the "oversexualization" of women as critical in accounting for their subjection; on the other, with "the psychoanalyst's dictum concerning the evils of repressed emotions, truly Adonis seems the god of the moment"—Ethel Sturges Dummer to William I. Thomas, 9 June 1920, Ethel Sturges Dummer Papers, SL A-127/36/285. See also Wittenstein, "Feminist Uses of Psychoanalysis," 38–62.

18. Gilman, "Toward Monogamy," 59, and Gilman, "Women's Achievements since the Franchise," *Current History* 27 (October 1927): 7–14.

19. Gilman, *Man-Made World,* 126–42, Gilman, "Our Brains and What Ails Them," *Forerunner* 3 (July 1912): 189–95, and Gilman, *His Religion and Hers,* vii, 92, 120, 213, 36, and 267.

20. Gilman, *His Religion and Hers,* 217, 111–14, and 179–80.

21. Ibid., 125, 180, and vii–viii.

22. Ibid., 5 and 4.

23. Ibid., 8 and 48. See Barnett, *Foundations of Feminism,* 72–73; and Avrom Barnett to CPG, 6 March 1921, CPGP 177/142/2; and Gilman, *His Religion and Hers,* 10–11.

24. Gilman, *His Religion and Hers,* 93 and 212–13.

25. Ibid., 36, 194, and 217.

26. Ibid., 95 and 54. The 1923 text received few, but mainly favorable, reviews. Some critical responses were due less to her remarks on world religions than those

on sexuality and modern women. See reviews of *His Religion and Hers* in *Christian Register*, 8 November 1923, 1070; *Booklist* 20 (December 1923): 82; Amy Wellington, *Literary Review*, 1 December 1923, 303; *Woman Citizen*, 29 December 1923, 27; Hildegarde Fillmore, *Bookman* 58 (January 1924): 575; *Dial* 76 (March 1924): 290; and William Pepperell Montague, *Birth Control Review* 8 (June 1924): 178. See P. Moriarty to CPG, 10 January 1924, CPGP, SL 177/144/1; Louise Curran Downes to CPG, 24 July 1923, CPGP, 177/143/2; and Charlotte Mix to Mr. Bennett, 13 March 1933, CPGP, 177/155; Elizabeth Fackt (assistant professor of international relations) to CPG, 16 September 1932, CPGP 177/144/1; 143/2; 155; and 146/1.

27. Modern feminist studies of religion include trajectories demonstrating that current formulations are unjustifiably patriarchal, as well as those seeking to extend religions more fully and fairly to women. See, for instance, Mary Daly, "After the Death of God the Father: Women's Liberation and the Transformation of Christian Consciousness," in *WomanSpirit Rising: A Feminist Reader in Religion,* ed. Carol P. Christ and Judith Plaskow (San Francisco: Harper San Francisco, 1992); and Leila Gal Berner, "Hearing Hannah's Voice: The Jewish Feminist Challenge and Ritual Innovation," in *The Daughters of Abraham: Feminist Thought in Judaism, Christianity and Islam,* ed. Yvonne Yazbeck Haddad and John L. Esposito (Gainesville: University Press of Florida, 2001).

28. Correspondence between Gilman and socialist psychoanalyst and cultural critic, Samuel D. Schmalhausen, debated her work warmly and testily. She agreed to write a chapter, "Parasitism and Civilized Vice," for a large anthology he coedited. See Schmalhausen to CPG, 19 June 1930, CPG to Schmalhausen, 23 June 1930, and CPG to Schmalhausen, 24 September 1930, CPGP, SL 177/122.

29. Gilman, "Pernicious Adam," 22; and for the project's earlier prototype, see her "Social Ethics," *Forerunner* 5 (January–December 1914): 20–25, 48–53, 76–82, 102–8, 130–36, 160–66, 187–93, 216–22, 244–49, 271–77, 300–305, and 327–32.

30. Gilman, "Pernicious Adam," 28–29.

31. Ibid., 41, 43, and 42–43.

32. Ross to CPG, 1 December 1927, CPGP, SL 177/145; and CPG to Stowe, 16 July 1928, BSFP, SL 77-M181, reel 3/416.

33. Hill, *Journey from Within,* 214; and Gilman, "Malthusianism and Race Suicide," 282. The epigraph to this section, Gilman, "The Making of Americans," appeared in *Woman's Journal* 35 (13 August 1904): 258.

34. Newman, *White Women's Rights,* 143.

35. Gilman, "Is America Too Hospitable?" 1989.

36. Gilman, "Sex and Race Progress," 111

37. Ibid., 116.

38. Gilman, "Is America Too Hospitable?" 1984–86 and 1989.

39. Ibid., 1984. In the light of her frequent criticisms of Jim Crow practices and the color bar, it is difficult to reconcile this evidence with Bederman's view that Gilman's opposition to lynching was "only lukewarm" (*Manliness and Civilization,* 158).

40. Fredrickson, *Racism,* 110; and Gilman, "With Her in Ourland," *Forerunner* 7 (June 1916): 155 and 154.

41. On abolitionists and race, see John Stauffer, *The Black Hearts of Men: Radical Abolitionists and the Transformation of Race* (Cambridge, MA: Harvard University

Press, 2002); and William H. Pease and Jane H. Pease, "Antislavery Ambivalence: Immediatism, Expediency, Race," *American Quarterly* 17 (Winter 1965): 682–95. And see Gilman, "A Suggestion on the Negro Problem," *American Journal of Sociology* 14 (July 1908): 79.

42. For discussion of this belief in relation to a spectrum of white supremacist rhetoric, see Brian McGee, "Rhetoric and Race in the Progressive Era: Imperialism, Reform, and the Ku Klux Klan," in *Rhetoric and Reform in the Progressive Era,* ed. Hogan, 311–38.

43. Nonetheless, her rare specific address of African Americans displayed the de facto discrimination and negative stereotyping that prevailed in the northern United States between Reconstruction and the 1950s among those otherwise classified politically as liberals or Progressives—see *What Diantha Did,* 160–61. For claims of other subjugationists on topics in articles with titles such as "The Negro Brain," "The Permanence of Racial Characteristics," and "A Defense of Negro Disenfranchisement," see *The Development of Segregationist Thought,* ed. I. A. Newby (Homewood, IL: Dorsey, 1968), 47, 60, and 103. See also A. J. McKelway, "The Atlanta Riots 1: A Southern White Point of View," *Outlook* (3 November 1906), 562; and see Gilman, "A Suggestion on the Negro Problem," 82, 85, 82, and 84.

44. For debate on this, See, for instance, "The Negro Problem in Foreign Eyes," *Nation* 88 (12 February 1909): 158; and Elliott G. Barlow, "On Lynching" (letter to the editor), *Nation* 103 (6 July 1916): 11. See also McGerr, *Fierce Discontent,* 186–87.

45. McGerr, *Fierce Discontent,* 180, 187, 200, and 201–3; see also "Lessons of Coatesville," *Nation* 93 (31 August 1911): 183–84.

46. See, for instance, "The Census and the Colored Population," *Nation* 52 (19 March 1891): 232–33; W. E. B. Du Bois, "The Republicans and the Black Voter," *Nation* 110 (5 June 1920): 757–58; Abram L. Harris, "The Negro Problem as Viewed by Negro Leaders," *Current History* 18 (June 1923): 410–17; Kelly Miller, "The Causes of Segregation," *Current History* 25 (March 1927), 827–31; and see McGerr, *Fierce Discontent,* 192, 194, 199–200.

47. See, for instance, Patrick Wolfe, "Land, Labor, and Difference: Elementary Structures of Race," *American Historical Review* 106 (June 2001): 866–905.

48. "Make the Negro Work," *Literary Digest* (10 October 1908): 500, 499; and McGerr, *Fierce Discontent,* 192.

49. See Knight, "Charlotte Perkins Gilman and the Shadow of Racism," *American Literary Realism* 32 (Winter 2000): 163; W. E. B. Du Bois, "A Negro Schoolmaster in the New South," *Atlantic Monthly* 83 (1892): 99, Du Bois, "The Training of Black Men," *Atlantic Monthly* 93 (1902): 289; Du Bois, "Slavery and Its Aftermath," *Dial* 40 (January–June 1906): 294, Du Bois, "Reconstruction and its Benefits" *American Historical Review* 15 (July 1910): 781–99; Oswald Garrison Villard, "The Objects of the National Association for the Advancement of Colored People," *Crisis* 4 (June 1912): 81; William Pickens, "Jim Crow in Texas," *Nation* 117 (15 August 1923): 155–56.

50. See Jane Addams, "The Progressive Party and the Negro," *Crisis* 5 (November 1912): 30–31; Katharine Bement Davis, "The Negro in Philadelphia," *Journal of Political Economy* 8 (March 1900): 248–60, esp. 257.

51. See Gilman, "American Unity," *Forerunner* 7 (December 1915): 326. See also W. I. Thomas, "The Psychology of Race Prejudice," 597–99 and 603, Thomas, "Race

Psychology with Particular Reference to the Immigrant and Negro," *American Journal of Sociology* 17 (May 1912): 736–37 and 749–56, and Thomas, "The Mind of Woman and the Lower Races," 453–62. And see Gilman, "Is America Too Hospitable?" 1984.

52. John Higham, *Strangers in the Land: Patterns of American Nativism 1860–1925* (New Brunswick, NJ: Rutgers University Press, 1988), 282, 11, and 4.

53. Gilman, *Living,* 316; and Higham, *Strangers in the Land,* 265–66, and 278.

54. Gilman, "Is America Too Hospitable?" 1984–86, 1989, 1983, Gilman, "Progress through Birth Control," 627, and Gilman, "Prisoners, Prisons, and Women Voters," 91–92.

55. Gilman, "Sex and Race Progress," 111.

56. Gilman, "Is America Too Hospitable?" 1986.

57. Higham, *Strangers in the Land,* 273–77.

58. Gilman, "Is America Too Hospitable?" 1986.

59. Higham, *Strangers in the Land,* 305.

60. Du Bois, "The Damnation of Women," in *Darkwater: Voices from within the Veil* (1920; reprint, Amherst, NY: Humanity Books, 2003), 187.

61. Higham, *Strangers in the Land,* 304, 278–86; and see Peyser, *Utopia and Cosmopolis,* 77–78.

62. Newman, *White Women's Rights,* 132–57; and Gilman, "Her 'Natural Protector'" [1926?], CPGP, 177/177/2/5.

63. Katherine Mayo, *Mother India* (New York: Harcourt, Brace, 1927), 22, 27, 33–41. Ross assured her that "Miss Mayo has invented nothing. I rejoice that the damnable system of female subordination—the worst which now exists anywhere, has been shown up.... I rejoice to see their bluff called" (See Ross to CPG, 1 December 1927, CPGP 177/145). For a critical discussion of earlier feminist support for Mayo, see Mrinalini Sinha, *Specters of Mother India: The Global Restructuring of an Empire* (Durham, NC: Duke University Press, 2006). See also Ward: "The androcentric worldview may almost be said to have its headquarters in India" (*Pure Sociology,* 366).

64. Gilman, "Is America Too Hospitable?" 1987. Compare her approach with Frederick Jackson Turner (1861–1932); see his "Pioneer Ideals and the State University," reprinted in John Mack Faragher, *Rereading Frederick Jackson Turner* (New York: Holt, 1994), 109; see also Turner, "Strategy for a Saturated Earth" (research notes 1922–23), and "Birth Control" (research notes 1923), Henry E. Huntington Library, Frederick Jackson Turner Collection, File Drawer 10A(2), and Turner, "Children of the Pioneers," *Yale Review* 226 (July 1926): 667. And see also Hans Voight, "Division and Reunion: Woodrow Wilson, Immigration, and the Myth of Unity," *Journal of American Ethnic History* 13 (Spring 1994): 24–51; and Higham, *Strangers in the Land,* 309.

65. See Schreiner, *Woman and Labour,* 54–55.

66. See Bart Moore-Gilbert, "Olive Schreiner's 'Story of an African Farm': Reconciling Feminism and Anti-Imperialism?" *Women* 14 (Spring 2003): 85–103; and Anne McClintock, *Imperial Leather: Race, Gender and Sexuality in the Colonial Contest* (New York: Routledge, 1995), 258–95. And for a magisterial earlier discussion of these theories of American democratic origins in northern Europe, see Richard

Hofstadter, *Social Darwinism in American Thought* (Boston: Beacon Press, 1944), 143–200.

67. For discussion of this issue, see Ellen Carol DuBois, *Woman Suffrage and Women's Rights* (New York: New York University Press, 1998), 92–95.

68. See Peyser, *Utopia and Cosmopolis*, 74–75. For a scathing critique of suffragist racism, see Douglas, *Terrible Honesty*, 254–99; and see Gilman, "Immigration, Importation, and Our Fathers," 117–19. And see Du Bois, *Harriot Stanton Blatch*, 276–77.

69. Yet that same assimilationism meant that she could breezily endorse an Italian local mayor in Norwich and praise an Irish novel as enlightening. See CPG to Channing Stetson, 5 October 1933, CPG Letters, 1884–1935, mf6/5.

70. Hill ("Feminist's Struggle," 517n31) portrays her as supporting Sanger's campaign from its mid-1910s outset, while Ceplair (*Nonfiction Reader*, 274), noting Gilman's early disapproval of birth control, applauds her arrival at advocacy of it by the 1930s, without interrogating the course and context of her shift. The epigraph to this section, Gilman, *His Religion and Hers*, can be found at 63–64.

71. For examples, see Linda Gordon, "Why Nineteenth-Century Feminists Did Not Support 'Birth Control' and Twentieth-Century Feminists Do: Feminism, Reproduction and the Family," in *Rethinking the Family: Some Feminist Questions*, ed. Barrie Thorne and Marilyn Yalom (New York: Longman, 1982), 40–53; and Kimmel and Aronson, introduction to Gilman, *Women and Economics* (1998), liv–lvii.

72. "Bars Magazine from Mail," *New York Times*, 4 April 1914, 19.

73. For Long's enlightening discussion of this, see her "Charlotte Perkins Gilman's *With Her in Ourland*," in *Her Contemporaries*, ed. Davis and Knight, 173, 191–92.

74. "Want Women to Try Her: Friends Petition Court for Mixed Jury in Mrs. Sanger's Case," *New York Times*, 15 January 1916, 5.

75. In other areas, she saw her work influence contemporaries—for instance, the Feminist Alliance, founded in 1913 to implement her housing and domestic arrangement reforms. See "Feminists Design a New Type Home," *New York Times*, 5 April 1914, C4; and Gilman, "Toward Monogamy," 57.

76. William Josephus Robinson (1867–1936) wrote pamphlets and books on various aspects of sexual intercourse, including contraception, disease, and ethics. See his *Sex Knowledge for Men, Including a Program for Sex Education of the Boy* (New York: Critic & Guide Co., 1916), *Sexual Truths versus Sexual Lies, Misconceptions and Exaggerations* (New York: Eugenics, 1927), *Woman: Her Sex and Love Life* (New York: Eugenics, 1929), and *The Safe Period or the Natural Method of Birth Control* (New York: Eugenics, 1935); and Gilman, "The Perpetuation of the Race," *Forerunner* 5 (July 1914): 174.

77. Gilman, "The Perpetuation of the Race," 175.

78. Gilman, "Birth Control," *Forerunner* 6 (July 1915): 177, 178, 179, and 180.

79. Gilman, "Back of Birth Control," 32.

80. Gilman, "Feminism, College Education, and the Birthrate," *Forerunner* 6 (October 1915): 261.

81. Gilman, "Back of Birth Control," 32, 31, and 32.

82. Ibid., 32–33, Gilman, "New Generation," 736, and Gilman, "Birth Control," 179–80.

83. F. W. Stella Browne, "Birth Control and Sex Psychology: A Reply to 'Back of Birth Control,'" *Birth Control Review* 6 (March 1922): 33, 34. Browne (1882–1955) published several pamphlets and books on aspects of abortion, birth control, and reproduction. See her *Memorandum Regarding Certain Suggestions for the Reform of the Abortion Laws* (London: Abortion Law Reform Association, [1935?]), and *Abortion* (London: George Allen, 1935), with A. M. Ludovic and Harry Roberts. And see Gilman, "Toward Monogamy," 58.

84. Gilman, "Progress through Birth Control," 623. See also Marie Carmichael Stopes, *Enduring Passion: Further New Contributions to the Solution of Sex Difficulties Being the Continuation of Married Love* (London: Putnam & Co. Ltd., 1928); Gilbert Van Tassel Hamilton, *A Research in Marriage* (New York: A. C. Boni, 1929); Katherine Bement Davis, *Factors in the Sex Lives of Twenty-Two Hundred Women* (New York: Harper Bros., 1929); and Robert Latou Dickinson and Lura Beam, *A Thousand Marriages: A Medical Study of Sex Adjustment* (Baltimore: Williams & Wilkins, 1931); and Gilman, *Herland*, 73. And see also Gilman, "The Giant Wisteria," *New England Magazine* 4 (June 1891): 480–85, and "My Poor Aunt," *Kate Field's Washington*, 7 January 1891, 9–11. See also Farrell, *Contraception and Abortion*, 32; Jeffrey Weeks, *Sex, Politics and Society: The Regulation of Sexuality since 1800* (London: Longman, 1981), 48; and my *Rose Scott*, 182.

85. Gilman, "Progress through Birth Control," 626–27 and 629, and Gilman, "Back of Birth Control," 180.

86. Gilman, "Birth Control, Religion, and the Unfit," 109, 108–9.

87. Ross, *Standing Room Only?* (New York: Century Co., 1927), 285; and Gilman, "Progress through Birth Control," 626.

88. Sanger to CPG, 3 November 1931, Margaret Sanger Papers [MSP], 1880–1966, Sophia Smith Collection, Smith College, Northampton, MA, Lamont Library Microfilm A903.2. On two of the days that Sanger, Gilman, and many others were testifying on H.R. 11082 (see below), the former also testified at the hearing for S. 4436, considering legislation to permit importation and distribution through the mails of contraceptives and birth control information. U.S. Congress, Senate, Committee on the Judiciary, *Hearing on Senate Bill 4436, May 12, 19 and 20, 1932, 72nd Congress, 1st Session* (Washington, DC: GPO, 1932). Gilman herself was accused "of making 'an attack on the Catholic Church.'" Both House and Senate bills died in committee. See David M. Kennedy, *Birth Control in America: The Career of Margaret Sanger* (New Haven, CT: Yale University Press, 1970), 234. U.S. Congress, House of Representatives, *Birth Control: Hearings before the Committee on Ways and Means—Seventy-Second Congress, First Session on H.R. 11082, May 19 and 20, 1932* (Washington, DC: GPO, 1932), 54–7. CPG to Sanger, 26 May 1932, MSP, Lamont Library, A903.2/507:0142. See also Gilman, "Birth Control, Religion, and the Unfit," 109.

89. Margaret Sanger, ed., *Biological and Medical Aspects of Contraception: Papers and Discussions Presented at the American Conference on Birth Control and National Recovery at Washington, D.C., January 15, 16, 17, 1934* (Washington, DC: National Committee on Federal Legislation for Birth Control, Inc., 1934), closing speeches by Sanger, Gilman, and William McDougall, 446–74. See also Chesler, *Woman of Valor*, 556; and see CPG to Carrie Chapman Catt, 1 November 1933, CPGP, SL 177/

153/2; CPG to Sanger, 31 January 1934, MSP, A903.2/508:0483; and Sanger to CPG, 4 February 1934, MSP, Lamont Film A903.2/C05: 0704.

90. Compare, for instance, Gilman, "Back of Birth Control," 31–33, and her "Birth Control, Religion, and the Unfit," 108–9. See also CPG to Frederic Palmer, 22 January 1921, CPGP, SL 177/143/1. See Gilman, "Public Library Motion Pictures," *Annals of the American Academy* 128 (November 1926): 144; and CPG to Stowe, 2 November 1933, BSFP, SL 77-M181 [reel 3]/416. The Katharine Hepburn movies released at the time of this letter were her first three films, *A Bill of Divorcement* (1932), *Christopher Strong* (1933), and *Morning Glory* (1933). On her career at this point, see Edwards, *A Remarkable Woman*, 411–12.

91. Gilman would have been surprised at the extensive scholarly attention the story would receive within a century of its publication. In the recently published document collection compiled by distinguished feminist historian, Estelle B. Freedman, the only document included from Gilman's oeuvre is "The Yellow Wall-paper" (*The Essential Feminist Reader* [New York: Modern Library, 2007], 128–44).

92. CPG to Stowe, 27 May 1935, BSFP, SL 77-M181 [reel 3]/416.

93. Gilman, "The Right to Die," 299; Abraham L. Wolbarst, "Legalize Euthanasia!" *Forum* 94 (December 1935): 330–32; James J. Walsh, "Life Is Sacred," *Forum* 94 (December 1935): 333–34; see also Mary R. Beard, Harriot Stanton Blatch, and Carrie Chapman Catt to the editor, *Forum* 94 (December 1935): 323–24. And see Gilman, "The Right to Die," 298–99, Gilman, "Is There a Double Standard in Filial Duty?" *Forerunner* 3 (November 1912): 299–300, Gilman, "The Right to Die," 299, 300, and Gilman, "The Providence Ladies Sanitary Gymnasium," *Providence Journal*, 23 May 1883, 2.

94. CPG to Stowe, 1, 18, 23 February 1933, BSFP, SL 77-M181 [reel 3]/416.

CHAPTER 12

The epigraph to this chapter can be found at 440 of that work.

1. Some indication of the scale of scholarly Gilmaniana emerges from the bibliographies attached to three recent anthologies about her work: Davis and Knight, *Her Contemporaries;* Golden and Zangrando, *Mixed Legacy;* and Rudd and Gough, *Optimist Reformer.* Otherwise, basic academic article search engines and databases such as the Modern Language Association online periodical and bibliography provide clear guides.

2. On third-wave feminist concerns more generally, see Catherine Orr, "Charting the Currents of the Third Wave," *Hypatia* 12 (Summer 1996): 29–45; Sonia Shah, review of *Listen Up: Voices from the Next Feminist Generation,* by Barbara Finlen, *Sojourner* 21 (May 1996): 43; and Deborah L. Siegel, "The Legacy of the Personal: Generating Theory in Feminism's Third Wave," *Hypatia* 12 (Summer 1997): 46–75.

3. See Dale Spender, *There's Always Been a Women's Movement This Century* (London: Pandora, 1983), 112–13; and for an insightful discussion of the paradoxes of the wave metaphor, see "Waves" in Laurel Thatcher Ulrich, *Well-Behaved Women Seldom Make History* (New York: Knopf, 2007), 191–222. See also Newman, *White Women's Rights,* 19.

4. For more precise discussion of these concerns, see Rita Alfonso and Jo Triglio,

"Surfing the Third Wave: A Dialogue between Two Third Wave Feminists," *Hypatia* 12 (Summer 1997): 7–16; Cathryn Bailey, "Making Waves and Drawing Lines: The Politics of Defining the Vicissitudes of Feminism," *Hypatia* 12 (Summer 1997): 22–28; Jennifer Baumgardner and Amy Richards, *Manifesta: Young Women, Feminism, and the Future* (New York: Farrar, Straus & Giroux, 2000); Jennifer Drake, review of *Listen Up: Voices from the Next Feminist Generation,* by Barbara Finlen, *Feminist Studies* 23 (Spring 1998): 97; Barbara Finlen, *Listen Up: Voices from the Next Feminist Generation* (Seattle: Seal Press, 1995); Anastasia Higginbotham, review of *Manifesta: Young Women, Feminism, and the Future,* by Jennifer Baumgardner and Amy Richards, *Women's Review of Books* 18, no. 1: (October 2000): 1.

5. See, for instance, Peyser, *Utopia and Cosmopolis,* 74; Newman, *White Women's Rights,* 132–57; and Weinbaum, *Wayward Reproductions: Genealogies of Race and Nation in Transatlantic Modern Thought* (Durham, NC: Duke University Press, 2004), 62, 77, and 88–89. And see Lenore Karo, "The Racist Legacy of Charlotte Perkins Gilman," Master's thesis, Sarah Lawrence College, 2003.

6. See discussion of this problem in Denise D. Knight, *Charlotte Perkins Gilman: A Study of the Shorter Fiction* (New York: Twayne Publishers; London: Prentice Hall International, 1997), 152. The epigraph to this section, Maureen Egan, "Evolutionary Theory in the Social Philosophy of Charlotte Perkins Gilman," can be found in *Hypatia* 4 (Spring 1987): 116, 119.

7. Lane, *To Herland,* 3–4 and 19.

8. Johnston, "Exploring Lack and Absence," 75–86; Seitler, "Unnatural Selection," 63; Kimmel and Aronson, introduction to *Women and Economics* (1998), xx–xxi, xxiii; Kessler, *Charlotte Perkins Gilman,* 43; and Hausman, "Sex before Gender," 505 and 507.

9. See Oz Frankel, "Whatever Happened to 'Red Emma'? Emma Goldman, from Alien Rebel to American Icon," *Journal of American History* 83 (December 1996): 903. See also the use of "Margaret" throughout Chesler, *Woman of Valor.* Meanwhile, Scharnhorst describes the "Charlotte" usage as "too smug and familiar." See Scharnhorst, *Charlotte Perkins Gilman,* ii. Lane exemplifies such identification in her psychologically sensitive biography of Gilman—see Lane, *To Herland,* xiii, Lane, "What My Therapist," 27–34, and Lane, "Charlotte Perkins Gilman and the Rights of Women: Her Legacy for the 1990s," in *Optimist Reformer,* ed. Rudd and Gough, 3. Other examples are Joanne B. Karpinski, "The Economic Conundrum in the Life-writing of Charlotte Perkins Gilman," in *Mixed Legacy,* ed. Golden and Zangrando, 209–20; Allen, *Building Domestic Liberty,* 5; and Knight, "On Editing Gilman's Diaries," in *Mixed Legacy,* ed. Golden and Zangrando, 55. Recently, Cynthia J. Davis has adopted the use of "Charlotte" on the grounds that Gilman published under three names, "Perkins," "Stetson," and "Gilman," and she uses Gilman's husbands' first names as well. See her "Love and Economics," 257. Though some biographers use her first name to avoid confusion when discussing her and her relatives before and after her marriages, this study of Gilman's feminist theory and reform advocacies adheres throughout to the surname by which she was most known during her life time and after.

10. For instance, see Fessenden, *Culture and Redemption,* 163, 167, and 168.

11. "Presentism"—"A bias towards the present or present-day attitudes, esp. in the

interpretation of history. . . . 1956 *N.Y. Times Bk. Rev.* 8 Jan. 22/3, I think Mr. Nevins' review underscores the danger of 'presentism'; I suggest historians would strengthen their position by applying the chief test of their profession—perspective and caution in contemporary analyses. . . . 1994 *Compass* (Toronto) Mar.–Apr. 19/1 Some critics of the films have accused us of what is called presentism—judging the leaders and policies of the Second World War by today's different standards" (*Oxford English Dictionary*, 2d ed.).

12. See Hayden, *The Grand Domestic Revolution*, 183, 184, and 196, Hayden, "Charlotte Perkins Gilman and the Kitchenless House," 241; Gaudelius, "Kitchenless Houses and Homes," 25; Hill, *Journey from Within*, 32 and 7; Scharnhorst, "Historicizing Gilman," 71; and Hill, *Making of a Radical Feminist*, 172. The epigraph to this section—Gilman, "The Wolf at the Door"—can be found in *In This Our World*, 178.

13. For criticism of these views of Gilman and class, see Ganobcsik-Williams, "The Intellectualism of Charlotte Perkins Gilman," 31 and 35; Lane, introduction to *Gilman Reader*, xxi; and Hill, *Making of a Radical Feminist*, 293. See also Knight, *Diaries*, 2:506–7. And see Gilman, "How Many Poor?" *American Fabian*, 3 April 1898, 8.

14. For examples of Gilman's thoughts on socialism see *The Labor Movement: A Prize Essay Read before the Trades and Labor Unions of Alameda Country, California, September 5, 1892* (Oakland: Alameda Country Federation of Trades, 1893), "Women as a Class," *Impress*, 17 November 1894, 2–3, "What We Are Doing," *Impress*, 8 December 1894, 1–2, "The Review," *Impress*, 22 December 1894, 1–2, "The Solution to the Labor Problem," *Arena*, 14 October 1895, 272–74, "When Socialism Began," *American Fabian* 3 (October 1897): 1–2, "Selfishness and Socialism," *American Fabian* 4 (April 1898): 1–2, "Socialism and Patriotism," *American Fabian* 4 (May 1898): 5–6, "Economic Basis of the Woman Question," *Woman's Journal*, 1 October 1898, 313–14, "Socialism and Women," *Coming Nation*, 11 February 1899, 1, and "Why We Honestly Fear Socialism," *Forerunner* 1 (December 1909): 7–10.

15. See, for instance, Ceplair, *Nonfiction Reader*, 43.

16. In fact Wienen argues that Gilman was just as significant as a socialist thinker, as she was a feminist thinker—see Mark W. Van Wienen, "A Rose by Any Other Name: Charlotte Perkins Stetson (Gilman) and the Case for American Reform Socialism," *American Quarterly* 55 (December 2003): 603–34. See chapters 4, 8, 10, and 11 for earlier discussions of these areas of Gilman's criticisms.

17. Certainly, she portrayed herself as a socialist to her then fiancé Houghton Gilman, discussed in chapter 2: she would not require him also to become a socialist, but she would encourage him to take a more social and collective rather than individualist view of issues. See Hill, *Journey from Within*, 143.

18. For example, Beer and Joslyn snipe that Gilman offered words not deeds, "shrank from direct contact and preferred to get the dirty work done by her fictional heroines," in their more general rejection of her presumption to theorize "the disease of middle class marriage" (a most reductionist reading of Gilman's 1898 *Women and Economics*), complete with her "unpalatable ideological standpoint" instead of Jane Addams–style "social work." See Beer and Joslyn, "Diseases of the Body Politic," 1, 11, and 15.

19. The first epigraph to this section is Lane, "What My Therapist," 34. The second is: Alys Weinbaum, *Wayward Reproductions: Genealogies of Race and Nation in Transatlantic Modern Thought* (Durham, NC: Duke University Press, 2004), 65.

20. For examples of the influential racists of the period, see Madison Grant, *The Passing of the Great Race; or, The Racial Basis of European History* (New York: Scribner's, 1916); Ellsworth Huntington, *The Character of Races* (New York: Charles Scribner, 1924); Lothrop Stoddard, *The Rising Tide of Color against White World Supremacy* (New York: Blue Ribbon Books, 1920); Thomas Dixon, *The Clansman: An Historical Romance of the Ku Klux Klan* (New York: Grosset & Dunlap, 1905); Rebecca Latimer Felton, *My Memoirs of Georgia Politics* (Atlanta: Index Printing Co., 1911); and Charles Carroll, *"The Negro a beast"; or, In the image of God* (St. Louis: American Book & Bible House, 1900).

21. See also See W. E. B. Du Bois, "The Damnation of Women," in *Darkwater,* 186.

22. For discussion of the slightness of her contributions to the marked racialist thinking of her era, see Lane, *To Herland,* 17–19; and Ceplair, *Nonfiction Reader,* 7, 85, and 276; in contrast, others place her closer to "robust" racists of Ross's ilk—see Peyser, *Utopia and Cosmopolis,* 67; and Newman, *White Women's Rights,* 143. Relevant examples of Edward Alsworth Ross's work are *Changing America: Studies in Contemporary Society* (New York: Century, 1914), 36–48, *The Social Trend* (New York: Century, 1922), 7, *Standing Room Only?* (New York: Century, 1927), 230–31, 344–46, and 355. For discussion of his relation to Gilman, see Peyser, *Utopia and Cosmopolis* 78; and Weinbaum, "Writing Feminist Genealogy," 277–79.

23. Fredrickson, *Racism,* 170 and 5–9.

24. *Webster's Third New International Dictionary* , s.v. "racism." For a helpful discussion of racist thought in the period, see McGee, "Rhetoric and Race," 312–15 and 318–22.

25. For instances of Gilman's criticisms of racial prejudice and ethnic discrimination, see Lanser, "Feminist Criticism," 429, 433–35; Allen, *Building Domestic Liberty,* 46–50, 53; and Deegan, introduction to *With Her in Ourland,* 45–46.

26. See *Oxford English Dictionary,* 2d ed., svv. "racism" and "ethnocentricism."

27. See Knight, "Shadow of Racism," 168; and for further discussion of her later years, see chapter 11. See also Newman, *White Women's Rights,* 20.

28. In 1956, Degler noted Gilman's nativist anti-immigration stances, while key biographers, Lane and Hill, called her anti-Semitic and racist. Lane published a 1981 anthology of Gilman short stories excluding "jarring and offensive" racist and anti-Semitic sections. Allen deplored Gilman's "naive collusion" with institutionalized racism, blind to the "social poison of racial segregation." See Lane, introduction to *Gilman Reader,* xxii; Hill, *Making of a Radical Feminist,* 172–73; and Allen, *Building Domestic Liberty,* 173. Meanwhile, the Gilman texts taken to be pertinent to race and ethnicity yield different readings. Some see Gilman's views as typical, or even moderate, compared with subjugationist Jim Crow advocates of racial subjugation and Progressive Era sociologists like Edward Ross. By contrast, others call Gilman a disciple of Ross's "robust racism." See Lane, *To Herland,* 17–19; and Ceplair, *Nonfiction Reader,* 7, 85, and 276; Peyser, *Utopia and Cosmopolis,* 67; and Newman, *White Women's Rights,* 143.

29. For instances of new attention to Gilman's race and ethnic prejudices among established Gilman scholars, see, for instance, Knight, "I could Paint Still Life," 480, and Knight, "Shadow of Racism," 165 and 167.

30. Bederman, *Manliness and Civilization,* 124, 167, 168, 122, 123, 136, 145, and 146–47. Among scholars taking issue with Bederman's characterization of Gilman's racial and eugenic thought, Susan Marie Rensing recently reiterated Kimmel and Aronson's point that race as used by Gilman clearly meant the human not only the "white" races. In her nuanced and perceptive study of the historical relationship between feminism and eugenics, Rensing argues that critical Gilmaniana gives insufficient consideration to Gilman's feminist theory during a period "when eugenics took center stage in popular discussions of women, biology and racial duties," showing little appreciation of the sharp differences in that period between eugenic applications to feminism that sought to constrain women and whose advocates fiercely criticized Gilman and feminist eugenics, and, on the other hand, those which sought to constrain men and empower women, personified by Gilman herself. See Rensing, "Feminist Eugenics in America: From Free Love to Birth Control, 1880–1930," Ph.D. diss., University of Minnesota, 2006, 123–25.

31. Bederman, *Manliness and Civilization,* 142, 143, 149, 158, 162, 164, and 168.

32. See Lane, introduction to *Gilman Reader,* xxxvi; Hill, *Making of a Radical Feminist,* 172–73; Peyser, *Utopia and Cosmopolis,* 180; and Lanser, "Feminist Criticism," 429. Yet, see also, Lanser, "Feminist Criticism," 433–35; Allen, *Building Domestic Liberty,* 46–50, 53; and see Gilman, "Race Pride," *Forerunner* 4 (April 1913): 90. See also Shelley Fisher Fishkin, "Reading Gilman in the Twenty-First Century," in *Mixed Legacy,* ed. Golden and Zangrando, 214; Kessler, *Charlotte Perkins Gilman,* 51–54 and 56; and Mary Moynihan, "*Charlotte Perkins Gilman/The Living of Charlotte Perkins Gilman* (Book Review)," *NWSA Journal* 4 (Fall 1992): 397.

33. Knight, "Shadow of Racism," 159–69, and Knight, "On Editing Gilman's Diaries," in *The Mixed Legacy,* ed. Golden and Zangrando, 61. See, for instance, McGee, "Rhetoric and Race," 332; and Deegan, introduction to *With Her in Ourland,* 45–46.

34. Lloyd's reading here contrasts with others who see in *Herland* proof positive of Gilman's obnoxious racism, an Aryan fantasyland of genetic isolationism, eugenic extremism, and totalitarian, incipient fascism. See Lloyd, "Feminism, Utopian and Scientific," 112; Ganobcsik-Williams, "Confronting the Issues of Race, Class, and Ethnicity in *Herland*" 114–16; and see Kimmel and Aronson, introduction to *Women and Economics* (1998), lvii, lxix, lvi, and lviii; Fredrickson, *Racism,* 161; and Leonard Dinnerstein, *Uneasy at Home* (New York: Columbia University Press, 1987), 15–18. And see Robert D. Johnson, "Re-Democratizing the Progressive Era: The Politics of Progressive Era Political Historiography," *Journal of the Gilded Age and Progressive Era* 1 (January 2002): 68–91.

35. Peyser, *Utopia and Cosmopolis,* 74, 65–67, 71–74, 77, and 89–90.

36. See Newman, *White Women's Rights,* 134 and 136.

37. Ibid., 138–39, 143, and 135.

38. Ibid., 3–8; and see DuBois, *Woman suffrage and women's rights,* 93 and 96.

39. See Bederman, *Manliness and Civilization,* 168. And see "Emmeline Pankhurst," in *Suffrage and the Pankhursts,* ed. Jane Marcus (London: Routledge, 2001),

132; and various discussions of manhood and suffrage in *Defining the Victorian Nation: Class, Race, Gender and the British Reform Act of 1867,* ed. Catherine Hall, Keith McClelland and Jane Rendall (Cambridge: Cambridge University Press, 2000); and see Jo Aitken, "The Horrors of Matrimony among the Masses," *Journal of Women's History* 19 (Winter 2007): 107–31.

40. Fessenden, *Culture and Redemption,* 172. Of course, work on Gilman has not been the only manifestation of this problem. Some scholars find presentism a pervasive problem within "whiteness studies," labor historians being one group particularly vocal in response. See, for instance, Eric Arnesen, "Whiteness and the Historians' Imagination," *International Labor and Working-Class History* 60 (Fall 2001): 3–32, and Arnesen, "Assessing the Whiteness Genre: A Reply to James Barrett, David Brody, Barbara Fields, Eric Foner, Victoria Hattam, and Adolph Reed," *International Labor and Working-Class History,* no. 60 (Fall 2001), 81–92. I especially thank Jim Cronin for bringing this exchange to my attention. And see, for instance, Bederman, *Manliness and Civilization,* 168; and Fessenden, *Culture and Redemption,* 168, 176, and 172.

41. Nadkarni, "Eugenic Feminism," 222. This version of "eugenic feminism" contrasts with the 1912 usage propounded by Fabian socialist and "eugenicist feminist," Dr. C. W. Saleeby (1878–1940), who devoted a whole chapter of his book, *Womanhood,* to Gilman. He denounced her as the dysgenic amaternal enemy of women's emancipation, unlike the laudable maternalist eugenicist feminist Ellen Key, as previously discussed. This is a potent reminder of the historicity and contingency of terms and their meanings. The power of the most astute analysis can be diminished by inattention to context and by anachronism. See also C. W. Saleeby, *Woman and Womanhood: A Search for Principles* (London: Heineman, 1912), 7–8 and 327–47.

42. See, for instance, Jennifer Hudak, "The Social Inventor: Charlotte Perkins Gilman and the (Re) Production of Perfection," *Women's Studies* 32 (June 2003): 458. Here see also Seitler, "Unnatural Selection," 66; and Kaplan, "Manifest Domesticity," 582–84 and 600–602. These conflicting emphases come chiefly from readings of her novels, especially *Moving the Mountain* (1911), *The Crux* (1911), *Herland* (1915), and *With Her in Ourland* (1916); and see Nadkarni, "Eugenic Feminism," 227.

43. See also Weinbaum, *Wayward Reproductions,* 4, 8, and 67. Antiracist critics persistently find scholar's responses to their critiques inadequate, despite their great impact within Gilmaniana and beyond. See Knight, "Shadow of Racism"; Davis, "His and Herland," 82–83; Catherine J. Golden, introduction to *Charlotte Perkins Gilman's "The Yellow Wall-Paper": A Sourcebook and Critical Edition,* ed. Catherine J. Golden (New York: Routledge, 2004), 2; Beth Sutton-Rumpseck, *Raising the Dust: The Literary Housekeeping of Mary Ward, Sarah Grand, and Charlotte Perkins Gilman* (Athens: Ohio University Press, 2004), 80–81, 102, and 192. See also Deutscher, "The Descent of Man," 53–55; Gayle Gullett, *Becoming Citizens: The Emergence and Development of California's Women's Movement, 1880–1911* (Urbana: University of Illinois Press, 2000), 31 and 127; and Rebecca J. Mead, *How the Vote Was Won: Woman Suffrage in the Western United States, 1868–1914* (New York: New York University Press, 2004), 75–76.

44. See Ganobcsik-Williams, "The Intellectualism of Charlotte Perkins Gilman,"

16–41. Alternatively, see Weinbaum, *Wayward Reproductions,* 88, 77, and 65; and Fessenden, *Culture and Redemption,* 173 and 179.

45. Bederman, *Manliness and Civilization,* 122; and Newman, *White Women's Rights,* 134.

46. Fredrickson, *Racism,* 158, 162–63, and 165–66.

47. See Jennifer Putzi, "In Short: Recent Reprints," *Legacy* 22 (2005): 92. See Peter Kolchin, "Whiteness Studies: The New History of Race in America," *Journal of American History* 89 (June 2002): 154–73.

48. See Fredrickson, *Racism,* 162.

49. See Arensen, "Whiteness and the Historians' Imagination," 17.

SELECT BIBLIOGRAPHY

Note on sources: This bibliography is first divided into primary sources and then the secondary sources that are directly page referenced in the text and endnotes. The listing order of primary sources is: (1) unpublished manuscript collections; (2) newspapers and periodicals; (3) cited published works by Gilman arranged chronologically; (4) later collections and reprinting of Gilman's works; and (5) other publications. The secondary sources divide into three sections: (1) those about Gilman; (2) other works cited; and (3) unpublished sources. Multiple works by authors are listed in chronological order; successive essays from edited collections have short titles; while individual periodical clippings cited in the text are not listed.

PRIMARY SOURCES

Unpublished Manuscripts

Arthur and Elizabeth Schlesinger Library on the History of Women in America, Radcliffe Institute, Harvard University

Addams, Jane (1860–1935). Correspondence, 1872–1934. M-34.

Beecher Family (1880–1963). Beecher-Stowe Family Papers, 1798–1956. A-102, A/B414, A5891, B-3, M-118, M-45.

Bureau of Vocational Information (1911–26). Records (New York City), 1908–32. M-34.

Catt, Carrie Chapman (1859–1947). Papers, 1848–1950. M-27.

Dennett, Mary Ware (1872–1977). Papers, 1874–1944. M-138, reels B1-36; MC 392.

Dummer, Ethel Sturges (1866–1954). Papers, 1766–1962. A-127; M-55.

Gilman, Charlotte Perkins (1860–1935). Papers, 1846–1961. Mf-1; A/G487.

———. Papers, 1846–1961: A Finding Aid. Mss. 177.

———. Letters from Grace Ellery Channing Stetson, 1884–1935. Mf-6.

———. Letters to Dr. Silas Weir Mitchell and Zona Gale, 1887–1935. A/G487c.

Kitchelt, Florence Ledyard Cross (1874–1961). Papers, 1885–1961. A-6; M-59/reels 975–76.

Laidlaw, Harriet Burton (1873–1949). Papers, 1851–1958. M-133, reels B1-8, A63.

Littledale, Clara Savage (1891–1956). Papers, 1903–82. A-157, M-99.

Page, Mary Hutcheson (1860–1940). Papers in the Women's Rights Collection, 1892–1943. M-133, reel D29, WRC653-653b.

Potter, Frances Boardman Squire (1867–1914). Papers 1879–1923. 1441-B1-M120.

Solomon, Maida Herman (1891–1988). Papers, 1901–80. MC418.

Stetson, Grace Ellery Channing (1862–1937). Papers, 1806–1973. 83-M201.

———.Correspondence [uncatalogued]. 89-M54.

Henry E. Huntington Library, San Marino, CA

Strong, Harriet Russell (1844–1926). Papers, 1815–1939. Ms.HS-1-938.

Turner, Frederick Jackson (1861–1932). Frederick Jackson Turner Papers. 1857–1932. Mss.MFilm 00452.

John Hayes Brown Library, Brown University

Ward, Lester Frank (1841–1913). Lester Frank Ward Papers, 1866–1913. Ms.90-23

Lamont Library, Harvard University

Ross, Edward Alsworth (1866–1951). Edward A. Ross Correspondence, 1859–1965. Madison: State Historical Society of Wisconsin, Division of Archives and Manuscripts; Teaneck, NJ: Chadwyck-Healy, 1985. Lamont Library Film A 526.

Sanger, Margaret (1879–1966). The Papers of Margaret Sanger, 1900–1965. Library of Congress 16700, Washington, DC. Lamont Library Film A 903.

———. The Margaret Sanger Papers, 1880–1966. Sophia Smith Collection, Smith College, Northampton, MA. Lamont Library Film A903.2.

Lilly Library, Indiana University

Sinclair, Upton Beall (1814–1968). Papers, 1860–1968. Series I.

Rhode Island Historical Society, Manuscripts Division

Charlotte Perkins Gilman (1860–1935). Letters to Martha Luther Lane, 1879–1890. Mss. 437.

Newspapers and Periodicals

Chicago Daily Tribune, 1894–1935.

Los Angeles Times, 1888–1935.

Louisville Herald, 1919–1920.

Nation, 1900–1935.

New York Times, 1890–1938.

Washington Post, 1890–1935

Charlotte Perkins Gilman Published Works

"The Providence Ladies Gymnasium." *Providence Journal,* 23 May 1883, 8.

"In Duty Bound." *Woman's Journal* 15 (12 January 1884): 14.

"One Girl among Many." *Alpha* 1 (February 1884): 15.

"Why Women Do Not Reform Their Dress." *Woman's Journal* 17 (9 October 1886): 336.

"A Protest against Petticoats." *Woman's Journal* 17 (26 February 1887): 60.

"Pungent Paragraphs." *Woman's Journal* 18 (12 March 1887): 88.

Art Gems for the Home and Fireside. Providence, RI: J. A. & R. A. Reid, 1888.

"My Poor Aunt." *Kate Field's Washington,* 7 January 1891, 9–11.

"Pacific Coast Press Notes." *Woman's Journal* 22 (25 April 1891): 130.

"The Giant Wisteria." *New England Magazine* 4 (June 1891): 480–85.

"The Yellow Wall-paper." *New England Magazine* 5 (January 1892): 647–656.

"Masculine, Feminine, and Human." *Woman's Journal* 23 (9 July 1892): 220.

The Labor Movement: A Prize Essay Read before the Trades and Labor Unions of Alameda Country, California, September 5, 1892. Oakland: Alameda Country Federation of Trades, 1893.

"Editorial Notes." *Impress,* 1 June 1894, 1.

"Women as a Class." *Impress,* 17 November 1894, 2–3.

"What We Are Doing." *Impress,* 8 December 1894, 1–2.

"The Review." *Impress,* 22 December 1894, 1–2.

"The Review." *Impress,* 29 December 1894, 1–2.

"The Solution to the Labor Problem." *Arena,* 14 October 1895, 272–74.

"The Washington Convention." *Woman's Journal* 27 (15 February 1896): 49–50.

"Women Do Not Want It." *Woman's Journal* 28 (23 January 1897): 30.

"On the Anti-Suffragists." *Woman's Journal* 28 (26 June 1897): 206.

"When Socialism Began." *American Fabian* 3 (October 1897): 1–2.

Women and Economics: A Study of the Economic Relation between Men and Women as a Factor in Social Evolution. Boston: Small, Maynard & Co., 1898.

"Selfishness and Socialism." *American Fabian* 4 (April 1898): 1–2.

"Socialism and Patriotism." *American Fabian* 4 (May 1898): 5–6.

"Who Will Do the Dirty Work?" *Denver New Nation,* 11 June 1898, 3–4.

"Household Cooking and Intemperance." *Union Signal* 10 (August 1898): 4.

"Economic Basis of the Woman Question." *Woman's Journal* 29 (1 October 1898): 313–14.

"Socialism and Women." *Coming Nation,* 11 February 1899, 1.

"The Flagstone Method." *Saturday Evening Post,* 15 July 1899, 42.

"Why Not Nursery Suites?" *Saturday Evening Post,* 11 November 1899, 382.

"The Home without a Kitchen." *Puritan* 7 (December 1899): 417–22.

"The Great Meeting of Women in London." *Saturday Evening Post,* 27 May 1899, 758.

"The Women's Congress of 1899." *Arena* 22 (September 1899): 342–50.

"The 'Right' People." *Independent,* 28 December 1899, 3489–90.

Concerning Children. Boston: Small Maynard, 1900.

The Home, Its Work and Influence. New York: McClure, Philips, 1903.

"The Home as a Food Purveyor." *Success* 6 (April 1903): 219–20.

Human Work. New York: McClure, Phillips, 1904.

"Shall Suffrage Clubs Work for Anything Besides Suffrage?" *Woman's Journal* 35 (30 January 1904): 34.

"At the Convention." *Woman's Journal* 35 (20 February 1904): 58.

"Why Great Women Are Few." *Woman's Journal* 35 (20 February 1904): 58.

"Suffrage Work." *Woman's Journal* 35 (5 March 1904): 74.

"The Double Standard." *Woman's Journal* 35 (19 March 1904): 82.

"What Shall the Suffrage Clubs Do?" *Woman's Journal* 35 (19 March 1904): 90.

"An Advancing Cause." *Current Literature* 36 (April 1904): 338–39.

"The Model Home." *Woman's Journal* 35 (2 April 1904): 106.

"Apropos of Prof. Ward's Theory." *Woman's Journal* 35 (16 April 1904): 122.

"The Women Do Not Want It." *Current Literature* 36 (May 1904): 4.

"Woman's 'Manifest Destiny.'" *Woman's Journal* 35 (4 June 1904): 178.

"Domestic Economy." *Independent* 56 (16 June 1904): 1359–63.

"From Germany." *Woman's Journal* 35 (25 June 1904): 202.

"The Beauty of a Block." *Independent* 57 (14 July 1904): 67–72.

"Woman's Alleged Inhumanity to Woman." *Woman's Journal* 35 (23 July 1904): 234.

"Feminine Occupations." *Woman's Journal* 35 (30 July 1904): 242.

"Is the Woman Movement Slow?" *Woman's Journal* 35 (30 July 1904): 242.

"The Making of Americans." *Woman's Journal* 35 (13 August 1904): 258.

"Malthusianism and Race Suicide." *Woman's Journal* 35 (3 September 1904): 282.

"The Refusal to Marry." *Woman's Journal* 35 (17 September 1904): 298.

"Public Sins and Private Indifference." *Woman's Journal* 35 (24 September 1904): 306.

"Impure Food." *Woman's Journal* 35 (1 October 1904): 314.

"Over-Marriage." *Woman's Journal* 35 (1 October 1904): 314.

"World Peace and Sex Combat." *Woman's Journal* 35 (8 October 1904): 322.

"An Englishman on American Women." *Woman's Journal* 35 (15 October 1904): 330.

"This Also from the N.Y.Times." *Woman's Journal* 35 (29 October 1904): 346.

"Two 'Natural Protectors.'" *Woman's Journal* 35 (29 October 1904): 346.

"Japan's Reserve." *Woman's Journal* 35 (19 November 1904): 370.

"The Passing of the Home in Great American Cities." *Cosmopolitan* 38 (December 1904): 137–47.

"These 'Municipal Nurseries.'" *Woman's Journal* 35 (10 December 1904): 394.

"The Home and the Hospital." *Good Housekeeping* 40 (February 1905): 192–94.

"Dr. Weininger's 'Sex and Character.'" *Critic* 48 (May 1906): 414–417.

"The Untrained Mother." *National Home Journal* 21 (July 1906): 18.

"Social Darwinism." *American Journal of Sociology* 12 (March 1907): 713–14.

"Homes without Housekeeping: A Present Demand." *Delineator* 69 (May 1907): 875–76, 955.

"Child Labor in the Schools." *Independent* 64 (21 May 1908): 1135–39.

"A Suggestion on the Negro Problem." *American Journal of Sociology* 14 (July 1908): 78–85.

"Private Homes and Common Kitchens." *New Idea Woman's Magazine* 18 (November 1908): 8.

"Have You Paid Your Board?" *Independent* 65 (26 November 1908): 1221–23.

"Woman and the Ballot." *Marsh's Magazine,* 1 October 1908, 5 and 12.

"Woman the Enigma." *Harper's Bazaar* 42 (December 1908): 1193–97.

"Why Are There No Women on the President's Commission?" *Good Housekeeping* 48 (January 1909): 1120–22.

"Song for Equal Suffrage." *Woman's Journal* 40 (13 February 1909): 28.

"The Money Value of Women's Work." *New Idea Woman's Magazine* 19 (May 1909): 6 and 46.

"A Garden of Babies." *Success* 12 (June 1909): 370–71 and 410–11.

"When We Fly." *Harper's Weekly* 35 (9 November 1909): 1650 and 1664.

"Comment and Review." *Forerunner* 1 (December 1909): 23–28.

"Why We Honestly Fear Socialism." *Forerunner* 1 (December 1909): 7–10.

What Diantha Did. New York: Charlton, 1910.

"Kitchen-Mindedness." *Forerunner* 1 (February 1910): 7–11.

"Parlor-Mindedness." *Forerunner* 1 (March 1910): 6–10.

"Nursery Mindedness." *Forerunner* 1 (April 1910): 7–10.

"Comment and Review." *Forerunner* 1 (June 1910): 24–25.

"The Kitchen Fly." *Forerunner* 1 (August 1910): 8–10.

"Animals in Cities." *Forerunner* 1 (September 1910): 6.

"Woman and the State." *Forerunner* 1 (October 1910): 10–14.

"The Socialist and the Suffragist." *Forerunner* 1 (October 1910): 25.

"Comment and Review." *Forerunner* 1 (October 1910): 26–27.

"Comment and Review." *Forerunner* 2 (November 1910): 22–24.

"How We Waste Three-Fourths of Our Money." *Forerunner* 2 (December 1910): 18–19.

The Crux. New York: Charlton, 1911.

The Man-Made World; or, Our Androcentric Culture. New York: Charlton, 1911.

Moving the Mountain. New York: Charlton, 1911.

"Woman Suffrage Would Unsex Women." In *Twenty-Five Answers to the Antis: Five-Minute Speeches on Votes for Women by Eminent Suggragists,* ed. National American Woman Suffrage Association. New York: National Woman Suffrage Publishing, Co., 1912.

"Comment and Review." *Forerunner* 2 (January 1911): 26–28.

"Moving the Mountain" [chap. 1]. *Forerunner* 2 (January 1911): 21–25.

"Moving the Mountain" [chap. 2]. *Forerunner* 2 (February 1911): 51–56.

"Answers to the Antis." *Forerunner* 2 (March 1911): 73–77.

"Moving the Mountain" [chap. 3]. *Forerunner* 2 (April 1911):107–13.

"Moving the Mountain" [chap. 4]. *Forerunner* 2 (May 1911): 136–41.

"Something to Vote For." *Forerunner* 2 (June 1911) 143–53.

"Moving the Mountain" [chap. 5]. *Forerunner* 2 (June 1911): 163–68.

"Moving the Mountain" [chap. 6]. *Forerunner* 2 (October 1911): 274–80.

"The Woman's Party." *Forerunner* 3 (November 1911): 288–91.

"Comment and Review." *Forerunner* 3 (December 1911): 336–38.

"The Work before Us." *Forerunner* 3 (January 1912): 6–9.

"Women and Democracy." *Forerunner* 3 (February 1912): 33–37.

"Miss Tarbell's Uneasy Woman." *Forerunner* 3 (February 1912): 37–39.

"Comment and Review." *Forerunner* 3 (February 1912): 55–56.

"Why Make Dust?" *Forerunner* 3 (March 1912): 61.

"Two Rooms and a Bath." *Forerunner* 3 (March 1912): 76.

"The New Faith." *Forerunner* 3 (April 1912): 90–91.

"Miss Tarbell's Third Paper." *Forerunner* 3 (April 1912): 92–95.

"Comment and Review." *Forerunner* 3 (April 1912): 110–12.

"Miss Tarbell's Homeless Daughter." *Forerunner* 3 (May 1912): 120–21.

"Comment and Review." *Forerunner* 3 (May 1912): 139–40.

"Woman Suffrage and the Average Mind." *Forerunner* 3 (June 1912): 148–53.

"Interstate Sanitation." *Forerunner* 3 (September 1912): 237.

"The New Party." *Forerunner* 3 (September 1912): 252.

"Is There a Double Standard in Filial Duty?" *Forerunner* 4 (November 1912): 299–300.

"Comment and Review." *Forerunner* 4 (November 1912): 307–8.

"Should Women Use Violence?" *Pictorial Review* 14 (November 1912): 11 and 78–79.

"Comment and Review." *Forerunner* 4 (December 1912): 335–36.

"A Platform for Women." *Forerunner* 4 (January 1913): 6–7.

"The Cost and Price of Living." *Forerunner* 4 (January 1913): 25–26.

"On Ellen Key and the Woman Movement." *Forerunner* 4 (February 1913): 35–38.

"Humanness." *Forerunner* 4 (February 1913): 52–53.

"The Comfort of God." *Forerunner* 4 (March 1913): 61–62.

"The Oldest Profession in the World." *Forerunner* 4 (March 1913): 63–64.

"Prisons, Convicts, and Women Voters." *Forerunner* 4 (April 1913): 91–92.

"A Thousand Farmers' Wives." *Forerunner* 4 (May 1913): 120–21.

"Comment and Review." *Forerunner* 4 (June 1913): 165–67.

"Lester F. Ward Is Dead." *Forerunner* 4 (June 1913): 166.

"Bee Wise." *Forerunner* 4 (July 1913): 169–73.

"The Woman Suffrage Congress in Buda-Pest." *Forerunner* 4 (August 1913): 213–14.

"Comment and Review." *Forerunner* 4 (August 1913): 223–24.

"Our Sleeping Cars." *Forerunner* 4 (September 1913): 231–32.

"Education for Motherhood." *Forerunner* 4 (October 1913): 259–62.

"Why I Wrote 'The Yellow Wall-paper.'" *Forerunner* 4 (October 1913): 271.

"Comment and Review." *Forerunner* 5 (November 1913): 303–8.

"Our Wickedest Waste." *Pictorial Review* 15 (November 1913): 18 and 72.

"'The Brute in Man.'" *Forerunner* 4 (December 1913): 316–17.

"Humanness." *Forerunner* 4 (January–December 1913): 20–25, 48–54, 76–81, 105–10, 132–38, 160–65, 190–96, 218–23, 246–51, 272–77, 298–303, and 328–34.

The Man-Made World; or, Our Androcentric Culture. New York: Charlton, 1914.

"Social Ethics." *Forerunner* 5 (January–December 1914): 20–25, 48–53, 76–82, 102–8, 130–36, 160–66, 187–93, 216–22, 244–49, 271–77, 300–305, and 327–32.

"Pensions for 'Mothers' and 'Widows.'" *Forerunner* 5 (January 1914): 7–8.

"Comment and Review." *Forerunner* 5 (January 1914): 26–27.

"As to 'Feminism.'" *Forerunner* 5 (February 1914): 45.

"An Anti-Suffrage Meeting." *Forerunner* 6 (February 1914): 52.

"Comment and Review." *Forerunner* 5 (February 1914): 54–56.

"The Women Who Won't Move Forward." *Physical Culture* 31 (February 1914): 126–28.

"What May We Expect of Eugenics?" *Physical Culture* 31 (March 1914): 219–22.

"The Biological Anti-Feminist." *Forerunner* 5 (March 1914): 64.

"Comment and Review." *Forerunner* 5 (March 1914): 83–84.

"His Mother." *Forerunner* 4 (July 1914): 169–73.

"The Perpetuation of the Race." *Forerunner* 5 (July 1914): 174.

"Our Coal." *Forerunner* 4 (July 1914): 185–86.

"Is Feminism Really So Dreadful?" *Delineator* 85 (August 1914): 6

"From a Hearst Paper." *Forerunner* 5 (September 1914): 251.

"Masculism at Its Worst." *Forerunner* 5 (October 1914): 257–58.

"Feminism or Polygamy?" *Forerunner* 5 (October 1914): 260–61.

"A New Impulse in the Women's Movement." *Forerunner* 5 (December 1914): 313.

"A 'Debate' on Suffrage." *Forerunner* 6 (January 1915): 10–11.

"The Dress of Women." *Forerunner* 6 (January 1915): 20–25.

"Old Religions and New Hopes." *Forerunner* 6 (February 1915): 34–36.

"The Dress of Women." *Forerunner* 6 (February 1915): 46–51.

"An Anti-Suffrage Meeting." *Forerunner* 6 (February 1915): 51–52.

"Standardizing Towns." *Forerunner* 6 (February 1915): 52–54.

"Comment and Review." *Forerunner* 6 (February 1915): 54–55.

"Freedom of Speech in the Public Schools." *Forerunner* 6 (March 1915): 72–74.

"The Dress of Women." *Forerunner* 6 (March 1915): 75–81.

"The Dress of Women." *Forerunner* 6 (May 1915): 132–38.

"The Dress of Women." *Forerunner* 6 (June 1915): 159–65.

"Addressing the New Voters." *Forerunner* 6 (June 1915): 165–67.

"Birth Control." *Forerunner* 6 (July 1915): 177–80.

"Comment and Review." *Forerunner* 6 (July 1915): 195–96.

"The Sociologist and the Reformer." *Forerunner* 6 (September 1915): 243–44.

"Feminism, College Education and the Birthrate." *Forerunner* 6 (October 1915): 259–61.

"Do We Want a Political Party for Women?" *Forerunner* 7 (November 1915): 285–86.

"Having Faith in Evolution." *Forerunner* 7 (November 1915): 299–300.

"Beauty from Ashes." *Forerunner* 7 (November 1915): 300–301.

"American Unity." *Forerunner* 7 (December 1915): 326–28.

"Cleaning up Elita." *Forerunner* 7 (January 1916): 1–4.

"American Ships." *Forerunner* 7 (January 1916): 12–13.

"Comment and Review." *Forerunner* 7 (January 1916): 26–27.

"Wanted: A Railroad Cafeteria." *Forerunner* 7 (February 1916): 33–34.

"Patriotism and Humanism." *Forerunner* 7 (February 1916): 35–37.

"Woman Suffrage and the Woman's Journal." *Forerunner* 7 (February 1916): 45–46.

"Growth and Combat." *Forerunner* 7 (February 1916): 47–53.

"Her Overhearing." *Forerunner* 7 (March 1916): 57–61

"Maternity Benefits and Reformers." *Forerunner* 7 (March 1916): 65–66.

"The Ford Party and the Newspapers." *Forerunner* 7 (March 1916): 73–76.

"Growth and Combat." *Forerunner* 7 (March 1916): 76–82.

"What Feminism Is and Isn't." *Ford Hall Folks* 2 (April 1916): 1–2 and 4.

"With Her in Ourland." *Forerunner* 7 (April 1916): 93–98.

"Dogs, Pigs, and Cities." *Forerunner* 7 (May 1916): 137–38.

"Comment and Review." *Forerunner* 7 (May 1916): 138–40.

"Among Our Foreign Residents." *Forerunner* 7 (June 1916): 145–46.

"With Her in Ourland." *Forerunner* 7 (June 1916): 152–57.

"Comment and Review." *Forerunner* 7 (July 1916): 193–96.

"The 'Nervous Breakdown' of Women." *Forerunner* 7 (August 1916): 202–6.

"The National Woman's Party." *Forerunner* 7 (August 1916): 214–15.

"Obstacles to Suffrage by States." *Forerunner* 7 (August 1916): 215–16.

"What Is Feminism?" *Boston Sunday Herald*, 3 September 1916, magazine section, 7.

"Comment and Review." *Forerunner* 7 (September 1916): 251–52.

"The Vintage." *Forerunner* 7 (October 1916): 253–57.

"Comment and Review." *Forerunner* 7 (October 1916): 279–80.

"The Milkman and the Public." *Forerunner* 7 (November 1916): 285–86.

"A Summary of Purpose." *Forerunner* 7 (November 1916): 286–90.

"With Her in Ourland." *Forerunner* 7 (November 1916): 291–97.

"Newspapers and Democracy." *Forerunner* 7 (November 1916): 314–18.

"Woman's Hour." *Woman's Journal* 47 (9 December 1916): 397.

"Jane Smith's Life." *Pictorial Review* 18 (May 1917): 2 and 82.

"The Housekeeper and the Food Problem." *Annals of the American Academy* 74 (November 1917): 123–30.

"Poverty and Women." In *Proceedings of the National Conference of Social Work*, 10–15. New York: The Conference, 1917.

"Concerning Clothes." *Independent* 22 (June 1918): 478 and 483.

"Released Energy of Women." *World Outlook* 4 (September 1918): 3.

"Why We Are Going Dry." *Louisville Herald*, 17 March 1919, 4.

"The Unfair Sex." *Louisville Herald*, 18 March 1919, 5.

"Wasted Babies." *Louisville Herald*, 16 April 1919, 7.

"The Habit of Being Oppressed." *Louisville Herald*, 21 April 1919, 6.

"Cave Man Theory." *Louisville Herald*, 29 April 1919, 7.

"Race Prejudice in Russia." *Louisville Herald*, 12 May 1919, 4.

"Killing the Failures." *Louisville Herald*, 13 June 1919, 7.

"Why Women are Restless." *Louisville Herald*, 21 August 1919, 6.

"Private Homes with Public Service." *Louisville Herald*, 21 October 1919, 6.

"The Strength of Women." *Louisville Herald*, 30 December 1919, 6.

"Community Conservation of Women's Strength." *Proceedings of the International Conference of Women Physicians* 1 (1920): 257–64.

"Whatever Else We Lose, We Must Keep the Home." *Woman Citizen*, 19 June 1920, 72–74.

"Applepieville." *Independent* 103, 25 September 1920, 365 and 393–95.

"Blunders about Women." *Evening Post Literary Review*, 30 October 1920, 8.

"Women's Outlook for 1921." *San Francisco Chronicle*, 26 December 1920, magazine, 1

"Should Women Take Alimony?" *Woman Citizen*, 5 February 1921, 953–54.

"Making Towns Fit to Live In." *Century* 102 (July 1921): 361–66.

"Back of Birth Control." *Birth Control Review* 6 (March 1922): 31–33.

"Do Women Dress to Please Men?" *Century* 103 (March 1922): 651–55.

"Vanguard, Rearguard, and Mudguard." *Century Magazine* 104 (July 1922): 348–53.

"The Problem of the Unhappy Woman." *Beautiful Womanhood* 1 (October 1922): 10 and 64.

"Cross-Examining Santa Claus." *Century* 105 (December 1922): 169–74.

His Religion and Hers: A Study of the Faith of Our Fathers and the Work of Our Mothers. New York: Century Co., 1923.

"Do You Know Beauty When You See It?" *Beautiful Womanhood* 2 (March 1923): 12–13 and 68.

"His Religion and Hers." *Century* 105 (March 1923): 676–83.

"His Religion and Hers." *Century* 105 (April 1923): 855–61.

"If You Are Queer and Know It." *Survey,* 15 March 1923, 773–74.

"The New Generation of Women." *Current History* 18 (August 1923): 731–37.

"Is America Too Hospitable?" *Forum* 70 (October 1923): 1983–89.

"New Morals for Old: Toward Monogamy." *Nation* 118 (6 November 1924): 671–73.

"Toward Monogamy." In *Our Changing Morality,* ed. Freda Kirchwey, 53–66. New York: Albert & Charles Boni, 1924.

"Washtubs and Women's Duty: Is A Mother's Business Child Culture or Housework?" *Century* 110 (June 1925): 152–59.

"The Nobler Male." *Forum* 74 (July 1925): 19–21.

"What Our Children Might Have." *Century* 110 (October 1925): 706–11.

"Mind-Stretching." *Century* 111 (December 1925): 217–24.

"These Too, Too Solid Ghosts." *Forum* 75 (February 1926): 238–44.

"American Radicals." *Jewish Daily Forward* 1 (August 1926): 1.

"Public Library Motion Pictures." *Annals of the American Academy* 128 (November 1926): 143–45.

"Women's Achievements since the Franchise." *Current History* 27 (October 1927): 7–14.

"Progress through Birth Control." *North American Review* 224 (December 1927): 622–29.

"Divorce and Birth Control." *Outlook* 125 (25 January 1928): 130–31.

"Thrills, Common and Uncommon." *Forum* 80 (July 1928): 97–102.

"Sex and Race Progress." In *Sex in Civilization,* ed. Samuel D. Schmalhausen and V. F. Calverton, 109–26. New York: Macaulay, 1929.

"Feminism and Social Progress." In *Problems of Civilization,* ed. Brownell Baker, 115–42. New York: Van Nostrand, 1929.

"Fashion, Beauty, and Brains." *Outlook* 7 (August 1929): 578–79.

"Unity is Not Equality." *World Unity* 4 (August 1929): 418–20.

"Parasitism and Civilized Vice." In *Woman's Coming of Age,* ed. V. F. Calverton and Samuel D. Schmalhausen, 110–26. New York: Liveright, 1931.

"Birth Control, Religion, and the Unfit." *Nation,* 27 January 1932, 108–9.

"The Right to Die." *Forum* 94 (November 1935): 297–300.

The Living of Charlotte Perkins Gilman. New York: Appleton-Century, 1935.

Selected Collected and Reprinted Gilman Works

Women and Economics: A Study of the Economic Relation between Men and Women as a Factor in Social Evolution. Edited by Carl N. Degler. San Francisco: Harper Torchbooks, 1966.

The Forerunner (1909–1916). Edited by Madeline B. Stern. New York: Greenwood Reprint Corp., 1968.

The Living of Charlotte Perkins Gilman: An Autobiography. New York: Arno Press, 1972.

The Yellow Wallpaper. Edited by Elaine Hedges. New York: Feminist Press, 1973.

In This Our World. New York: Arno Press, 1974

His Religion and Hers: A Study of the Faith of Our Fathers and the Work of Our Mothers. Westport, CT: Hyperion Press, 1976.

Herland. Edited by Ann J. Lane. London: Women's Press, 1979.

The Charlotte Perkins Gilman Reader: The Yellow Wallpaper and Other Fiction. Edited by Ann J. Lane. London: Woman's Press, 1980.

Herland and Selected Short Stories by Charlotte Perkins Gilman. Edited by Barbara H. Solomon. New York: Signet, 1992.

The Yellow Wallpaper. Edited by Thomas Erskine and Connie Richards. New Brunswick, NJ: Rutgers University Press, 1993.

"The Yellow Wall-paper" and Selected Stories of Charlotte Perkins Gilman. Edited by Denise D. Knight. Newark: University of Delaware Press; London: Associated University Presses, 1994.

Benigna Machiavelli: A Novella by the Author of "The Yellow Wallpaper." Edited by Joan Blake. Santa Barbara: Bandana Books, 1994.

The Yellow Wall-Paper, and Other Stories. Edited by Robert Shulman. The World's Classics. Oxford; New York: Oxford University Press, 1995.

With Her In Ourland—the Sequel to Herland. Edited by Mary Jo Deegan and Michael R. Hill. Westport, CT: Praeger, 1997.

Unpunished: A Mystery. Edited by Catherine J. Golden and Denise D. Knight. New York: Feminist Press, 1997.

"The Yellow Wallpaper": And Other Stories. Dover Thrift Editions. New York: Dover, 1997.

The Yellow Wall-paper. Edited by Dale M. Bauer. Boston: Bedford Books, 1998.

Women and Economics: A Study of the Economic Relation between Men and Women as a Factor in Social Evolution. Edited by Michael Kimmel and Amy Aronson. Reprint, Berkeley: University of California Press, 1998.

Charlotte Perkins Gilman's "The Yellow Wall-Paper" and the History of Its Publication and Reception: A Critical Edition and Documentary Casebook. Edited by Julie Bates Dock. University Park: Pennsylvania State University Press, 1998.

Charlotte Perkins Gilman's Utopian Novels: "Moving the Mountain," "Herland" and "With Her in Ourland." Edited by Minna Doskow. Madison, NJ: Fairleigh Dickinson University Press; London: Associated University Presses, 1999.

Charlotte Perkins Gilman's "The Yellow Wallpaper." Edited by Peter Leigh. London: Hodder & Stoughton, 1999.

"Herland," "The Yellow Wallpaper," and Selected Writings. Edited by Denise D. Knight. New York: Penguin, 1999.

Mag—Marjorie: Two Novels by Charlotte Perkins Gilman. Forest Hills, NY: Ironweed Press, 1999.

The Man-Made World. Edited by Mary A. Hill. Amherst, NY: Humanity Books, 2001.

The Dress of Women: A Critical Introduction to the Symbolism and Sociology of Clothing. Edited by Michael R. Hill and Mary Jo Deegan. Westport, CT: Greenwood Press, 2002.

The Home, Its Work and Influence. Edited by Michael Kimmel. 1903. Reprint, Walnut Creek, CA: AltaMira Press, 2002.

The Crux: A Novel. Edited by Jennifer S. Tuttle. Newark: University of Delaware Press, 2002.

The Crux. Edited by Dana Seitler. Durham, NC: Duke University Press, 2003.

Charlotte Perkins Gilman's "The Yellow Wall-Paper: A Sourcebook and Critical Edition. Edited by Catherine Golden. New York: London: Routledge, 2004.

Human Work. Edited by Michael S. Kimmel and Mary M. Moynihan. Walnut Creek, CA: Altamira Press, 2005.

Social Ethics: Sociology and the Future of Society. Edited by Mary Jo Deegan and Michael R. Hill. Westport, CT: London: Praeger, 2004.

The Yellow Wallpaper. Edited by Crystal Cawley. Portland, ME: Wolfe Editions, 2004.

What Diantha Did. Edited by Charlotte J. Rich. Durham, NC: Duke University Press, 2005.

"The Yellow Wall-Paper" by Charlotte Perkins Gilman: A Dual-Text Critical Edition. Edited by Shawn St. Jean. Athens: Ohio University Press, 2006.

Other Publications

Ackermann, Jessie A. "Plan of Work along Social Purity Lines." In *National Purity Congress, Its Papers, Addresses, Portraits: An Illustrated Record of the Papers and Addresses of the First National Purity Congress.* New York: American Purity Alliance, 1896.

Adams, Frederick J., et al. *The Report and Recommendations of the Bridgeport Vice Commission.* Bridgeport, CT: n.p., 1916.

Addams, Jane. *A New Conscience and an Ancient Evil.* New York: Macmillan, 1912.

———. "The Progressive Party and the Negro." *Crisis* 5 (November 1912): 30–31.

———. *Twenty Years at Hull House.* New York: Signet, 1961.

———. *A Challenge to the Contemporary Church.* New York: The Survey, n.d.

Anthony, Katharine. *Feminism in Germany and Scandinavia.* New York: Henry Holt & Co., 1915.

Barnett, Avrom. *Foundations of Feminism: A Critique.* New York: Robert M. McBride & Co., 1921.

Bell, Ernest A. *Fighting the Traffic in Young Girls; or, War on the White Slave Trade.* Chicago: Southern Bible House, 1910.

Bingham, Theodore A. *The Girl That Disappears: The Real Facts about the White Slave Trade.* Boston: Richard G. Badger, 1911.

Black, Alexander. "The Woman Who Saw It First." *Century Magazine* 107 (November 1923): 33–42.

Blackwell, Henry B. "Equal Suffrage versus Prostitution." In *National Purity Congress, Its Papers, Addresses, Portraits: An Illustrated Record of the Papers and Addresses of the First National Purity Congress.* New York: American Purity Alliance, 1896.

Brooks, Virginia. *My Battles with Vice.* New York: Macaulay Co., 1915.

Browne, F. W. Stella. "Birth Control and Sex Psychology: A Reply to 'Back of Birth Control.'" *Birth Control Review* 6 (March 1922): 33–34.

Bureau of Social Hygiene. *Commercialized Prostitution in New York City: A Comparison between 1912 and 1915.* New York: Bureau of Social Hygiene, 1915.

Bushnell, Katherine C. *Plain Words to Plain People*. New York: n.p., 1918.

Cape, Emily Palmer. *Lester Frank Ward: A Personal Sketch*. New York: Putnam's, 1922.

Channing-Stetson, Grace Ellery. *The Fortune of a Day*. Chicago: Stone, 1900.

"Charlotte Perkins Gilman: Writer, Public Speaker, Advanced Thinker." *Pictorial Review* 13 (October 1911): 14.

"Charlotte Perkins Gilman's Dynamic Social Philosophy." *Current Literature* 51 (July 1911): 67–70.

"Charlotte Perkins Gilman's Reply to Ellen Key." *Current Opinion* 54 (March 1913): 220–21.

Chicago Society of Social Hygiene. *For the Protection of Wives and Children from Venereal Contamination*. Chicago: The Society, 1900.

"The Conflict between 'Human' and 'Female' Feminism." *Current Opinion* 56 (April 1914): 291–92.

Creighton, Louise. *The Social Disease and How to Fight It: A Rejoinder*. New York: Longman's, Green & Co., 1914.

Davis, Katharine Bement. "The Negro in Philadelphia." *Journal of Political Economy* 8 (March 1900): 248–60.

———. "A Study of Prostitutes Committed from New York City to the State Reformatory for Women at Bedford Hills." In *Commercialized Prostitution in New York City*, ed. George J. Kneeland, 163–227. New York: Century Co. 1917.

———. "Three Score Years and Ten." *University of Chicago Magazine* 26 (December 1933): 58–62.

Dell, Floyd. *Women as World Builders: Studies in Modern Feminism*. Chicago: Forbes, 1913.

Dock, Lavinia L. *Hygiene and Morality: A Manual for Nurses and Others, Giving an Outline of the Medical, Social, and Legal Aspects of the Venereal Diseases*. New York: G. P. Putnam's Sons, 1910.

Du Bois, W. E. Burghardt. "A Negro Schoolmaster in the New South." *Atlantic Monthly* 83 (January 1899): 99–104.

———. "The Training of Black Men." *Atlantic Monthly* 90 (1902): 289–97.

———. "Reconstruction and Its Benefits." *American Historical Review* 15 (July 1910): 781–99.

———. "The Damnation of Women." In *Darkwater: Voices from within the Veil*, 163–86. 1920. Amherst, NY: Humanity Books, 2003.

"Ellen Key's Revaluation of Woman's Chastity." *Current Literature* 52 (February 1912): 200–202.

"Ellen Key's Reply to Her Critics." *Current Opinion* 52 (March 1912): 317–19.

"Ellen Key's Attack on 'Amaternal' Feminism." *Current Opinion* 54 (February 1913): 138–39.

Fite, Warner. "Birth-Control and Biological Ethics." *International Journal of Ethics* 27 (October 1916): 50–66.

———. "The Feminist Mind." *Nation* 96 (6 February 1913): 123–26.

———. "Psycho-Analysis and Sex-Psychology." *Nation* 103 (10 August 1916): 127–29.

French, Lillie Hamilton. "Where Are the Old Ladies?" *Century* 84 (October 1912): 824–28.

Gale, Zona. "Charlotte Perkins Gilman." *Nation* 141 (25 September 1935): 350–51.

Hartley, Catherine Gasquoine. *The Truth about Women*. New York: Dodd Mead, 1913.

Hepburn, Katharine Houghton. *Woman Suffrage and the Social Evil*. New York: National Woman Suffrage Publishing Co., Inc., 1914.

———. "The Revolution in Women's Work Makes Votes for Women a Practical Necessity." New York: National American Woman Suffrage Association, 1918.

Hinkle, Beatrice M. "Woman and the New Morality." *Nation* 119 (19 November 1924): 541–43.

———. "Why Feminism?" *Nation* 125 (6 July 1927): 8–9.

Honolulu Social Survey. *Report of the Committee on the Social Evil*. Honolulu: Honolulu Star Bulletin, 1914.

Hooker, Edith Houghton. "Charlotte Perkins Gilman." *Equal Rights Independent Feminist Weekly* 1 (31 August 1935): 202.

Howe, Harriet. "Charlotte Perkins Gilman—as I Knew Her." *Equal Rights*, 5 September 1936, 211–16.

"Ida Tarbell Answered." *Woman Voter* 3 (June 1912): 7–13.

"Is Woman Making a Man of Herself?" *Current Literature* 52 (June 1912): 682–84.

Janney, O. Edward. "The Medical Profession and Morals." In *National Purity Congress, Its Papers, Addresses, Portraits: An Illustrated Record of the Papers and Addresses of the First National Purity Congress*. New York: American Purity Alliance, 1896.

Key, Ellen S. *Love and Marriage*. New York: G. P. Putnam's Sons, 1911.

———. "Education for Motherhood." *Atlantic Monthly* (July 1913): 49–50.

———. *The Woman Movement*. New York: G. P. Putnam, 1912.

Kipling, Rudyard. *Many Inventions*. New York: D. Appleton & Co., 1893.

Knapp, Adeline E. *An Open Letter to Mrs. Carrie Chapman Catt*. New York City: New York State Association Opposed to Woman Suffrage, 1899.

Laidlaw, Harriet Burton. "My Little Sister." *Survey* 30 (May 1913): 199–202.

Lippman, Walter. *Drift and Mastery: An Attempt to Diagnose the Current Unrest*. New York: Kennerley, 1914.

"Make the Negro Work." *Literary Digest* 10 (October 1908): 499–500.

Martin, John M., and Prestonia Mann Martin. *Feminism: Its Fallacies and Follies*. New York: Dodd, Mead & Co., 1916.

Massie, Robert K., et al. *Report of the Vice Commission of Kentucky*. Lexington: J. L. Richardson & Co., 1915.

Mayo, Katherine. *Mother India*. New York: Harcourt, Brace, 1927.

McKelway, A. J. "The Atlanta Riots 1: A Southern White Point of View." *Outlook* 84 (3 November 1906): 557–62.

McLennan, John Ferguson. *Primitive Marriage: An Enquiry into the Origin of the Form of Capture in Marriage Ceremonies*. Edinburgh: Adam & Charles Black, 1865.

McManis, John T. *Ella Flagg Young and a Half Century of the Chicago Public Schools*. Chicago: A. C. McClurg & Co., 1916.

Middleton, George. *These Things Were Mine: The Autobiography of a Journeyman Playwright*. New York: Macmillan, 1947.

Mighels, Ella Sterling Cummis. *The Story of the Files: A Review of California Writers and Literature.* Issued under the auspices of the World's Fair Commission of California, Columbian Exhibition, 1893. [San Francisco: Cooperative Print. Co.], 1893.

Morrow, Prince. *Social Disease and Marriage.* New York: Lea Brothers & Co., 1904.

"Mrs. Charlotte Perkins Gilman." *Current Literature* 36 (May 1904): 511.

Municipalities and Vice. [New York: Reform Club, Committee on City Affairs], 1901.

National American Woman Suffrage Association (NAWSA). *Eminent Opinions on Woman Suffrage.* Warren, Ohio: NAWSA, n.d.

"A New Conception of Maternity." *Current Opinion* 54 (March 1913): 220–21.

"News from the Clubs." *New Nation* (25 April 1891), 211.

Pankhurst, Christabel. *Plain Facts about a Great Evil.* New York: Sociological Fund of the Medical Review of Reviews, 1913.

Pickens, William. "Jim Crow in Texas." *Nation* 117 (15 August 1923): 155–56.

Reitman, Ben L. *The Second Oldest Profession: A Study of the Prostitute's Business Manager.* New York: Vanguard Press, 1931.

Roe, Clifford G. *Panders and Their White Slaves.* New York: Fleming H. Revell Co., 1910.

———. *What Women Might Do with the Ballot: The Abolition of the White Slave Traffic.* New York: National American Woman Suffrage Association [1912?].

Ross, Edward Alsworth. *Changing America: Studies in Contemporary Society.* New York: Century Co., 1912.

———. *The Changing Chinese: The Conflict of Oriental and Western Cultures in China.* New York: Century Co., 1911.

———. *The Social Trend.* New York: Century, 1922.

———. *Standing Room Only.* New York: Century, 1927.

———. *Seventy Years of It: An Autobiography.* New York: D. Appleton-Century, 1936.

Saleeby, C. W. *Woman and Womanhood: A Search for Principles.* London: Heineman, 1912.

Sanger, Margaret. *The Case for Birth Control.* New York: Modern Art Printing Co, 1917.

———. *Family Limitation.* New York: Margaret Sanger, 1918.

———. *Debate on Birth Control: Margaret Sanger and Winter Russell; and Shaw vs. Roosevelt on Birth Control.* Girard, KS: Haldeman-Julius, 1921.

———. *Biological and Medical Aspects of Contraception: Papers and Discussions Presented at the American Conference on Birth Control and National Recovery, at the Mayflower, Washington, D.C., January 15, 16, 17, 1934.* [Closing speeches by Margaret Sanger, Charlotte Perkins Gilman and William McDougall, 446–74]. Washington, DC: National Committee on Federal Legislation for Birth Control, 1934.

———. *Biological and Medical Aspects of Contraception.* Washington, DC: National Committee on Federal Legislation for Birth Control, Inc., 1934.

Schreiner, Olive. "Three Dreams in a Desert." In *Dreams.* London: G. P. Putnam's Sons, 1890.

———. "The Woman Question." *Cosmopolitan* 28 (November 1899): 45–54.

———. "The Woman Question." *Cosmopolitan* 28 (December 1899): 182–92.

———. *Woman and Labour.* New York: F. A. Stokes, 1911.

Scott, Leroy. *Counsel for the Defense.* Garden City, NY: Doubleday, 1912.

Seligman, Edwin R. A. *The Social Evil with Special Reference to Conditions in New York: A Report Prepared (in 1902) under the Direction of the Committee of Fifteen.* 2d ed. New York: G. P. Putnam's Sons, 1912.

Sinclair, Upton. *The Jungle.* 1906. Reprint, New York: Penguin Books, 1985.

———. *Love's Pilgrimage.* New York: Mitchell Kennerley, 1911.

———. *Sylvia's Marriage: A Novel.* 1915. Reprint, New York: Albert & Charles Boni, 1928.

Stanton, Elizabeth Cady. "The Matriarchate; or, Mother-Age." In *Transactions of the International Council of Women,* ed. Rachel Avery, 218–27. Philadelphia: Lippincott, 1891.

Stevens, Doris. *Jailed for Freedom.* New York: Boni & Liveright, 1920.

———. "Wages for Wives." *Nation* 122 (27 January 1926): 81–83.

———. "Birth Control and Women's General Advance." *Birth Control Review* 10 (April 1926): 122–23.

———. "Is a Uniform Marriage and Divorce Law Desirable? Pro." *Congressional Digest* 6 (June–July 1927): 203–5.

Thomas, William I. *Sex and Society: Studies in the Social Psychology of Sex.* Boston: Richard G. Badger, 1907.

———. *The Unadjusted Girl: Cases and Standpoint for Behavior and Analysis.* Boston: Little Brown, 1923.

Turner, Frederick Jackson. "Pioneer Ideals and the State University." Reprinted in John Mack Faragher, *Rereading Frederick Jackson Turner.* New York: Holt, 1994.

United States, Department of Commerce, Bureau of the Census. *Fourteenth Census of the United States Taken in the Year 1920.* Vol. 3, *Compositions and Characteristics of the Population by States.* Washington, DC: GPO, 1923.

United States, Congress, House of Representatives. *Birth Control: Hearings Before the Committee on Ways and Means—Seventy-Second Congress, First Session on H. R. 11082, May 19 and 20, 1932.* Washington, DC: GPO, 1932.

United States Congress, Senate, Committee on the Judiciary. *Hearing on Senate Bill 4436, May 12, 19 and 20, 1932, 72nd Congress, 1st Session.* Washington, DC: GPO, 1932.

Villard, Oswald Garrison. "Objectives of the Association for the Advancement of Colored People." *Crisis* 4 (June 1912): 81.

Walling, William English. *The Larger Aspects of Socialism.* New York: MacMillan, 1913.

Walsh, Correa Moylan. *Feminism.* New York: Sturgis & Walton, 1917.

Walsh, James J. "Life Is Sacred." *Forum* 94 (December 1935): 333–34.

Walton, J. W. "Young Men and Morality." In *National Purity Congress, Its Papers, Addresses, Portraits: An Illustrated Record of the Papers and Addresses of the First National Purity Congress.* New York: American Purity Alliance, 1896.

Ward, Lester Frank. "The Social Evil." *Iconoclast,* 4 September 1871. Reprinted in Ward, *Glimpses of the Cosmos,* 1:238–41.

———. "On Male Sexual Selection." *Transactions of the Anthropological Society of Washington* 1 (May 1881): 37–39. Reprinted in Ward, *Glimpses of the Cosmos* 3:75–76.

———. *Dynamic Sociology.* 2 vols. New York: Appleton, 1883.

———. "Our Better Halves." *Forum* 6 (November 1888): 266–75.

———. "Genius and Women's Intuition." *Forum* 9 (June 1890): 401–8.

———. *The Psychic Factors of Civilization.* Boston: Ginn & Co., 1893.

———. "Weissman's Concessions." *Popular Science Monthly* 45 (June 1894): 175–84.

———. "Collective Telesis." *American Journal of Sociology* 2 (March 1897): 801–22.

———. *Pure Sociology: A Treatise on the Origin and Spontaneous Development of Society.* New York: Macmillan, 1903.

———. "The Past and Future of the Sexes." *Independent* 60 (8 March 1906): 541–47.

———. "Social Darwinism." *American Journal of Sociology* 12 (March 1907): 709–10.

———. "The Historical View of Women." *Independent* 68 (16 June 1910): 1326–28.

———. "Eugenics, Euthenics, and Eudemics." *American Journal of Sociology* 18 (May 1913): 737–54.

———. *Glimpses of the Cosmos,* 6 vols. (New York: Putnam's, 1913–18).

Webster, Henry Kitchell. *The Real Adventure: A Novel.* Indianapolis: Bobs Merrill Co., 1916.

Wister, Owen. "The Pentecost of Calamity." *Saturday Evening Post* 188, 3 July 1915, 3–5 and 26–29.

Wolbarst, Abraham L. "Legalize Euthanasia!" *Forum* 94, no. 6 (December 1935): 330–32.

"Woman's Growing Revolt against 'Coercive' Marriage." *Current Opinion* 56 (February 1914): 132–33.

Woolf, Virginia. *A Room of One's Own* [1929]. New York: Harcourt, 1985.

———. *Three Guineas.* London: Hogarth Press, 1938.

SECONDARY SOURCES

Selected Books and Articles on Gilman

Allen, Judith A. "Charlotte Perkins Gilman, Prostitution and Frontier Sexual Contracts." In *Charlotte Perkins Gilman: Optimist Reformer,* ed. Jill Rudd and Val Gough, 173–99. Iowa City: University of Iowa Press, 1999.

———. "Charlotte Perkins Gilman, Feminism, and Progressivism." In *Rhetoric and Reform in the Progressive Era,* ed. Hogan, 427–69.

———. "The Overthrow of Gynaecocentric Culture: Charlotte Perkins Gilman and Lester Frank Ward." In *Charlotte Perkins Gilman and Her Contemporaries: Literary and Intellectual Contexts,* ed. Cynthia J. Davis and Denise D. Knight, 59–86. Tuscaloosa: University of Alabama Press, 2004.

Allen, Polly Wynn. *Building Domestic Liberty: Charlotte Perkins Gilman's Architectural Feminism.* Amherst: University of Massachusetts Press, 1988.

Bederman, Gail. *Manliness and Civilization: A Cultural History of Gender and Race in the United States, 1880–1917.* Chicago: University of Chicago Press, 1995.

Beer, Janet. *Kate Chopin, Edith Wharton and Charlotte Perkins Gilman: Studies in Short Fiction.* Basingstoke: Palgrave Macmillan, 2005.

Beer, Janet, and Katherine Joslyn. "Diseases of the Body Politic: White Slavery in Jane Addams' 'A New Conscience and an Ancient Evil' and Selected Short Stories by Charlotte Perkins Gilman." *Journal of American Studies* 33 (April 1999): 1–18.

Berkin, Carol Ruth. "Private Woman, Public Woman: The Contradictions of Charlotte Perkins Gilman." In *Critical Essays on Charlotte Perkins Gilman,* ed. Karpinski, 150–73.

Ceplair, Larry. *Charlotte Perkins Gilman: A Nonfiction Reader.* New York: Columbia University Press, 1992.

Davis, Cynthia J. "His and Herland: Charlotte Perkins Gilman 'Re-presents' Lester F. Ward." In *Evolution and Eugenics in American Literature, 1880–1940: Essays on Ideological Conflict and Complicity,* ed. Claire Roche and Lois Cuddy, 73–88. Lewisburg: Bucknell University Press, 2003.

———. "The Two Mrs. Stetsons and the 'Romantic Summer.'" In *Charlotte Perkins Gilman and Her Contemporaries,* ed. Davis and Knight, 1–16.

———. "Love and Economics: Charlotte Perkins Gilman on 'The Woman Question.'" *American Transcendental Quarterly* 19 (December 2005): 243–58.

De Simone, Deborah. "Charlotte Perkins Gilman and Educational Reform." In *Charlotte Perkins Gilman: Optimist Reformer,* ed. Rudd and Gough, 127–47.

Deegan, Mary Jo. *Jane Addams and the Men of the Chicago School, 1892–1918.* New Brunswick, NJ: Transaction Books, 1988.

———. Introduction to *With Her in Ourland.* Edited by Mary Jo Deegan and Michael R. Hill, 1–57. Westport, CT: Greenwood Publications, 1997.

Degler, Carl N. "Charlotte Perkins Gilman and the Theory and Practice of Feminism." *American Quarterly* 8 (Spring 1956): 21–39.

———. Introduction to *Women and Economics: A Study of the Economic Relation between Men and Women as a Factor in Social Evolution.* 1898. Reprint, San Francisco: Harper Torchbooks, 1966.

Deutscher, Penelope. "The Descent of Man and the Evolution of Woman." *Hypatia: A Journal of Feminist Philosophy* 19 (Spring 2004): 35–55.

Doskow, Minna. "Charlotte Perkins Gilman: The Female Face of Social Darwinism." *Weber Studies: An Interdisciplinary Humanities Journal* 14 (Fall 1997): 9–22.

Edelstein, Sari. "Charlotte Perkins Gilman and the Yellow Newspaper." *Legacy* 24, no. 1 (2007): 72–92.

Egan, Maureen L. "Evolutionary Theory in the Social Philosophy of Charlotte Perkins Gilman." *Hypatia* 4 (Spring 1987): 102–19.

Eldredge, Charles C. *Charles Walter Stetson, Color and Fantasy.* Lawrence: Spencer Museum of Art, University of Kansas, 1982.

Fessenden, Tracey. "Race, Religion, and the New Woman in America: The Case of Charlotte Perkins Gilman." *Furman Studies* 37 (June 1995): 15–25.

———. *Culture and Redemption: Religion, the Secular, and American Literature.* Princeton, NJ: Princeton University Press, 2007.

Fishkin, Shelley Fisher. "Reading Gilman in the Twenty-First Century." In *The Mixed Legacy of Charlotte Perkins Gilman,* ed. Golden and Zangrando, 209–20.

Fleenor, Juliann E. "The Gothic Prism: Charlotte Perkins Gilman's Gothic Stories and Her Autobiography." In *Charlotte Perkins Gilman: The Woman and Her Work,* ed. Sheryl L. Meyerling, 117–31. Ann Arbor: University of Michigan Research Press, 1988.

Ganobcsik-Williams, Lisa. "The Intellectualism of Charlotte Perkins Gilman: Evolutionary Perspectives on Race, Ethnicity, and Gender." In *Charlotte Perkins Gilman: Optimist Reformer,* ed. Rudd and Gough, 16–41.

———. "Confronting Issues of Race, Class, and Ethnicity in Herland." In *Approaches to Teaching Gilman's "The Yellow Wall-paper" and Herland,* ed. Knight and Davis, 111–17.

Gaudelius, Yvonne. "Kitchenless Houses and Homes." In *Charlotte Perkins Gilman: Optimist Reformer,* ed. Rudd and Gough, 111–26.

Gilbert, Sandra, and Susan Gubar. "'Fecundate! Discriminate!' Charlotte Perkins Gilman and the Theologizing of Maternity." In *Charlotte Perkins Gilman: Optimist Reformer,* ed. Rudd and Gough, 200–216.

Golden, Catherine J., and Joanna Schneider Zangrando, eds. *The Mixed Legacy of Charlotte Perkins Gilman.* Newark: University of Delaware Press, 2000.

Hausman, Bernice L. "Sex before Gender: Charlotte Perkins Gilman and the Evolutionary Paradigm of Utopia." *Feminist Studies* 24 (Fall 1998): 488–509.

Hayden, Dolores. "Charlotte Perkins Gilman and the Kitchenless House." *Radical History Review* 21 (Fall 1979): 225–47.

———. *The Grand Domestic Revolution: A History of Feminist Designs for American Homes, Neighborhoods, and Cities.* Cambridge, MA: MIT Press, 1981.

Hedges, Elaine. "Out at Last: 'The Yellow Wall-paper' after Two Decades of Feminist Criticism." In *The Captive Imagination: A Casebook on The Yellow Wallpaper,* ed. Catherine J. Golden, 319–33. New York: Feminist Press, 1992.

Hill, Mary Armfield. "Charlotte Perkins Gilman: A Feminist's Struggle with Womanhood." *Massachusetts Review* 21 (Fall 1980): 503–26.

———. *Charlotte Perkins Gilman: The Making of a Radical Feminist, 1860–1896.* Philadelphia: Temple University Press, 1980

———, ed. *Endure: The Diaries of Charles Walter Stetson.* Philadelphia: Temple University Press, 1988.

———. *A Journey from Within: The Love Letters of Charlotte Perkins Gilman, 1897–1900.* Lewisburg, PA: Bucknell University Press, 1995.

———. "'Letters Are Like Morning Prayers': The Private Work of Charlotte Perkins Gilman." In *The Mixed Legacy of Charlotte Perkins Gilman,* ed. Golden and Zangrando, 47–52.

———. Introduction to *The Man-Made World,* 7–21. Amherst, NY: Humanity Books, 2001.

Hill, Michael, and Mary Jo Deegan. "Introduction: Charlotte Perkings Gilman on the Symbolism and Sociology of Clothing." In *The Dress of Women,* ed. Michael R. Hill and Mary Jo Deegan, lx–xxvii. Westport, CT: Greenwood Publications, 2002.

Hobbs, Margaret. "The Perils of 'Unbridled Masculinity': Pacifist Elements in the Feminist and Socialist Thought of Charlotte Perkins Gilman." In *Women and Peace: Historical and Practical Perspectives,* ed. Ruth Roach Peirson, 149–69. London: Groom Helm, 1987.

Hogan, J. Michael, ed. *Rhetoric and Reform in the Progressive Era, 427–69. A Rhetorical Historical History of the United States,* vol. 6. East Lansing: Michigan State University Press, 2003.

Hudak, Jennifer. "The Social Inventor: Charlotte Perkins Gilman and the (Re) Production of Perfection." *Women's Studies* 32 (June 2003): 455–77.

Johnston, Georgia. "Exploring Lack and Absence in the Body/Text: Charlotte Perkins Gilman Prewriting Irigaray." *Women's Studies* 21 (1992): 75–86.

Karpinski, Joanne. "The Economic Conundrum in the Lifewriting of Charlotte Perkins Gilman." In *The Mixed Legacy of Charlotte Perkins Gilman,* ed. Golden and Zangrando, 209–20.

———, ed. *Critical Essays on Charlotte Perkins Gilman.* New York: G. K. Hall & Co., 1992.

Kessler, Carol Farley. *Charlotte Perkins Gilman: Her Progress toward Utopia with Selected Writings.* Syracuse, NY: Syracuse University Press, 1995.

Kimmel, Michael S., and Amy Aronson. Introduction to *Women and Economics: A Study of the Economic Relation between Men and Women as a Factor in Social Evolution.* Berkeley: University of California Press, 1998.

Kirkpatrick, Frank G. "'Begin Again!' The Cutting Edge of Charlotte Perkins Gilman's Gentle Religious Optimism." In *Critical Essays on Charlotte Perkins Gilman,* ed. Karpinski, 129–43.

Knight, Denise D. "The Reincarnation of Jane: Gilman's Companion to 'The Yellow Wallpaper.'" *Women's Studies* 20, nos. 3–4 (1992): 287–302.

———, ed. *The Diaries of Charlotte Perkins Gilman.* Volume 1, *1879–87* and Volume 2, *1890–1935.* Charlottesville: University Press of Virginia, 1994.

———. *The Later Poetry of Charlotte Perkins Gilman.* Newark: University of Delaware Press; London: Associated University Presses, 1996.

———. *Charlotte Perkins Gilman: A Study of the Short Fiction.* New York: Twayne Publishers; London: Prentice Hall International, 1997.

———. "'But O My Heart': The Private Poetry of Charlotte Perkins Gilman." In *Charlotte Perkins Gilman: Optimist Reformer,* ed. Rudd and Gough, 267–84.

———. "The Dying of Charlotte Perkins Gilman." *American Transcendental Quarterly* 13, no. 2 (1999): 137–59.

———. "Charlotte Perkins Gilman and the Shadow of Racism." *American Literary Realism* 32 (Winter 2000): 159–69.

———. "On Editing Gilman's Diaries." In *The Mixed Legacy of Charlotte Perkins Gilman,* ed. Golden and Zangrando, 53–64.

———. "Charlotte Perkins Gilman's Lost Book: A Biographical Gap." *ANQ: A Quarterly Journal of Short Articles, Notes, and Reviews* 14 (Winter 2001): 26–29.

———. "'Only a Husband's Opinion': Walter Stetson's View of Gilman's 'The Yellow Wall-Paper'—an Inscription." *American Literary Realism* 36 (Fall 2003): 86–87.

———. "'All the Facts of the Case': Gilman's Lost Letter to Dr. S. Weir Mitchell." *American Literary Realism* 37 (Spring 2005): 259–77.

———. "'I am getting angry enough to do something desperate': The Question of Female Madness in 'The Yellow Wall-paper.'" In *"The Yellow Wall-paper" by Charlotte Perkins Gilman: A Dual Critical Edition,* ed. Shawn St. Jean, 73–87. Athens: Ohio University Press, 2006.

———. "'I could Paint Still Life as well as any one on Earth': Charlotte Perkins Gilman and the World of Art." *Women's Studies* 35 (July–August 2006): 475–92.

Knight, Denise D., and Cynthia J. Davis, eds. *Approaches to Teaching Gilman's "The Yellow Wall-paper" and Herland,* 111–17. New York: Modern Language Association of America, 2003.

Lane, Ann J. Introduction to *Herland.* Edited by Ann J. Lane, v–xxiv. New York: Women's Press, 1979.

———. Introduction to *The Charlotte Perkins Gilman Reader.* Edited by Ann J. Lane, ix–xlii. London: Women's Press, 1981.

———. Introduction to *The Living of Charlotte Perkins Gilman.* Edited by Ann J. Lane, xi–xxiv. Madison: University of Wisconsin Press, 1991.

———. *To Herland and Beyond: A Life of Charlotte Perkins Gilman.* New York: Meridian, 1991.

———. "Charlotte Perkins Gilman and the Rights of Women: Her Legacy for the 1990s." In *Charlotte Perkins Gilman: Optimist Reformer,* ed. Rudd and Gough, 3–15.

———. "What My Therapist, My Daughter, and Charlotte Taught Me While I Was Writing the Biography of Charlotte Perkins Gilman." In *The Mixed Legacy of Charlotte Perkins Gilman,* ed. Golden and Zangrando, 27–34.

Lanser, Susan S. "Feminist Criticism, 'The Yellow Wallpaper,' and the Politics of Color in America." *Feminist Studies* 15 (Fall 1989): 415–41.

Lloyd, Brian. "Feminism, Utopian and Scientific: Charlotte Perkins Gilman and the Prison of the Familiar." *American Studies* 39 (Spring 1998): 93–114.

Long, Lisa A. "Charlotte Perkins Gilman's *With Her in Ourland:* Herland Meets Heterodoxy." In *Charlotte Perkins Gilman and Her Contemporaries,* ed. Davis and Knight, 171–93.

Magner, Lois N. "Darwinism and the Woman Question: The Evolving Views of Charlotte Perkins Gilman." In *Critical Essays on Charlotte Perkins Gilman,* ed. Karpinski, 115–28.

Moynihan, Mary M. "Book Review: Charlotte Perkins Gilman / *The Living of Charlotte Perkins Gilman.*" *NWSA Journal* 4 (Fall 1992): 395–98.

———. "'All Is Not Sexuality That Looks It': Charlotte Perkins Gilman and Karen Horney on Freudian Psychoanalysis." In *Charlotte Perkins Gilman and Her Contemporaries,* ed. Davis and Knight, 194–218.

Nadkarni, Asha. "Eugenic Feminism: Asian Reproduction in the U.S. National Imaginary." *Novel: A Forum on Fiction* 39 (Spring 2006): 221–44.

Newman, Louise M. *White Women's Rights.* New York: Oxford University Press, 1999.

Nies, Judith. *Portraits from the Radical Tradition.* New York: Viking Press, 1977.

O'Brien, Mary M. "Autobiography and Liminality: Which Story Does Charlotte Perkins Gilman Choose to Tell?" *Women's Studies* 20 (October 1991): 37–50.

Palmeri, Ann. "Charlotte Perkins Gilman: Forerunner of a Feminist Social Science." In *Discovering Reality: Feminist Perspectives on Epistemology, Metaphysics, Methodology and Philosophy of Science,* ed. Sandra Harding and Merrill B. Hintikka, 97–119. Dordrecht: Reidel, 1983.

Peyser, Thomas Galt. *Utopia and Cosmopolis: Globalization in the Era of American Literary Realism.* Durham, NC: Duke University Press, 1998.

Purinton, Marjean D. "Reading Marital Relationships: The Wallpaper in *A Room of One's Own.*" In *The Pedagogical Wallpaper: Teaching Charlotte Perkins Gilman's "The Yellow Wall-Paper,"* ed. Jeffrey A. Weinstock, 94–111. New York: Peter Lang; 2003.

Putzi, Jennifer. "In Short: Recent Reprints." *Legacy* 22 (2005): 91–94.

Robinson, Lillian S. "Killing Patriarchy: Charlotte Perkins Gilman, the Murder Mystery, and Post-Feminist Propaganda." *Tulsa Studies in Women's Literature* 10 (Fall 1991): 273–85.

Scharnhorst, Gary. *Charlotte Perkins Gilman.* Boston: Twayne, 1985.

———. *Charlotte Perkins Gilman: A Bibliography.* Metuchen, NJ: Scarecrow Press, 1985.

———. "Historicizing Gilman: A Bibliographer's View." In *The Mixed Legacy of Charlotte Perkins Gilman,* ed. Golden and Zangrando, 65–76.

———. "The Intellectual Context of Herland: The Social Theories of Lester Ward." *Approaches to Teaching Gilman's "The Yellow Wall-Paper" and Herland,* ed. Knight and Davis, 111–24.

Seitler, Dana. "Unnatural Selection: Mothers, Eugenic Feminism, and Charlotte Perkins Gilman's Regeneration Narratives." *American Quarterly* 55 (March 2003): 61–88.

Sutton-Ramspeck, Beth. *Raising the Dust: The Literary Housekeeping of Mary Ward, Sarah Grand, and Charlotte Perkins Gilman.* Athens: Ohio University Press, 2004.

Tuttle, Jennifer S. "Rewriting the West Cure: Charlotte Perkins Gilman, Owen Wister, and the Sexual Politics of Neurasthenia." In *The Mixed Legacy of Charlotte Perkins Gilman,* ed. Golden and Zangrando, 103–21.

———. "Gilman's *The Crux* and Owen Wister's *The Virginian:* Intertextuality and 'Woman's Manifest Destiny.'" In *Charlotte Perkins Gilman and Her Contemporaries,* ed. Davis and Knight, 127–38.

Upin, Jane S. "Charlotte Perkins Gilman: Instrumentalism Beyond Dewey." *Hypatia* 8 (Spring 1993): 38–63.

Veeder, William. "Who Is Jane? The Intricate Feminism of Charlotte Perkins Gilman." *Arizona Quarterly* 44 (Autumn 1988): 40–79.

Weinbaum, Alys Eve. "Writing Feminist Genealogy: Charlotte Perkins Gilman, Racial Nationalism and the Reproduction of Maternalist Feminism." *Feminist Studies* 27 (Summer 2001): 271–302.

———. *Wayward Reproductions: Genealogies of Race and Nation in Transatlantic Modern Thought.* Durham, NC: Duke University Press, 2004.

Wienen, Mark W. Van. "A Rose by Any Other Name: Charlotte Perkins Stetson (Gilman) and the Case for American Reform Socialism." *American Quarterly* 55 (December 2003): 603–34.

Zauderer, Naomi B. "Consumption, Production, and Reproduction in the Work of Charlotte Perkins Gilman." In *Charlotte Perkins Gilman: Optimist Reformer,* ed. Rudd and Gough, 151–72.

Other Books and Articles Cited

Allen, Judith A. *Sex and Secrets: Crimes Involving Australian Women since 1880.* Melbourne: Oxford University Press, 1990.

———. "Contextualizing Late Nineteenth-Century Feminism: Problems and Comparisons." *Journal of the Canadian Historical Association* 1, no.1 (1990): 17–36.

———. "Frameworks and Questions in Australian Sexuality Studies." In *Rethinking Sex: Social Theory and Sexuality Research,* ed. R. W. Connell and Gary Dowsett, 5–31. Melbourne: Melbourne University Press, 1992.

———. *Rose Scott: Vision and Revision in Feminism, 1880–1925.* Melbourne: Oxford University Press, 1994.

Arnesen, Eric. "Whiteness and the Historians' Imagination." *International Labor and Working-Class History* 60 (Fall 2001): 3–32.

Barrett, Michele. *Women's Oppression Today.* London: Verso, 1981.

Beauvoir, Simone de. *The Second Sex.* New York: Penguin, 1953.

Bendiner, Elmer. *A Time For Angels: The Tragicomic History of the League of Nations.* New York: Knopf, 1975

Berkman, Joyce Avrech. *Olive Schreiner: Feminism on the Frontier.* St. Albans, VT: Eden Press Women's Publications, 1979.

Bland, Lucy. *Banishing the Beast: English Feminism and Sexual Morality, 1885–1914.* London: Penguin, 1995.

Borda, Jennifer L. "Woman Suffrage in the Progressive Era: A Coming of Age." In *A Rhetorical History of the United States,* 339–86.

Brandt, Allan. *No Magic Bullet: A History of Venereal Disease in the United States since 1880.* New York: Oxford University Press, 1985.

Buhle, Mari Jo. *Feminism and Its Discontents: A Century of Struggle with Psychoanalysis.* Cambridge, MA: Harvard University Press, 1998.

Burgchardt, Carl R. *Robert M. La Follette, Sr.: The Voice of Conscience.* New York: Greenwood Press, 1992.

Cashman, Sean Dennis. *America in the Age of Titans: The Progressive Era and World War I.* New York: New York University Press, 1988.

Chesler, Ellen. *Woman of Valor: Margaret Sanger and the Birth Control Movement in America.* New York: Simon & Schuster, 1992.

Connelly, Mark Thomas. *The Response to Prostitution in the Progressive Era.* Chapel Hill: University of North Carolina Press, 1980.

Cott, Nancy F. *The Grounding of Modern Feminism.* New Haven, CT: Yale University Press, 1987.

———. "What's in a Name? The Limits of 'Social Feminism,' or Expanding the Vocabulary of Women's Political History." *Journal of American History* 76 (December 1989): 809–29.

Cott, Nancy F., Gerda Lerner, Kathryn Sklar, Ellen DuBois, and Nancy Hewitt. "Considering the State of U.S. Women's History." *Journal of Women's History* 15 (Spring 2003): 145–63.

Coward, Rosalind. *Patriarchal Precedents: Sexuality and Social Relations.* London: Routledge & Kegan Paul, 1983.

Crunden, Robert M. "Progressivism." In *Reader's Companion to American History,* ed. Eric Foner and John A. Garraty, 869. Boston: Houghton Mifflin, 1991.

Danbom, David B. *The World of Hope: Progressives and the Struggle for an Ethical Public Life.* Philadelphia: Temple University Press, 1987.

Deegan, Mary Jo. *Jane Addams and the Men of the Chicago School, 1892–1918.* New Brunswick, NJ: Transaction Books, 1988.

Delap, Lucy. *The Feminist Avant-Garde: Transatlantic Encounters of the Early Twentieth Century.* Cambridge: Cambridge University Press, 2007.

Dinnerstein, Leonard. *Uneasy at Home.* New York: Columbia University Press, 1987.

Douglas, Ann J. *Terrible Honesty: Mongrel Manhattan in the 1920s.* New York: Farrar, Straus & Giroux, 1995.

DuBois, Ellen Carol. *Harriot Stanton Blatch and the Winning of Woman Suffrage.* New Haven, CT: Yale University Press, 1997.

———. *Woman Suffrage and Women's Rights.* New York: New York University Press, 1998.

Edwards, A. *A Remarkable Woman: A Biography of Katharine Hepburn.* New York: William Morrow & Co., 1985.

Fitzpatrick, Ellen. *Endless Crusade: Women Social Scientists and Progressive Reform.* New York: Oxford University Press, 1990.

Frankel, Oz. "Whatever Happened to 'Red Emma'? Emma Goldman, from Alien Rebel to American Icon." *Journal of American History* 83 (December 1996): 903–42.

Fredrickson, George M. *Racism: A Short History.* Princeton, NJ: Princeton University Press, 2002.

Friedl, Bettina. *On to Victory: Propaganda Plays of the Woman Suffrage Movement.* Boston: Northeastern University Press, 1987.

Frye, Marilyn. *The Politics of Reality: Essays in Feminist Theory.* Trumansburg, NY: Crossing Press, 1983.

Garton, Stephen. *Histories of Sexuality: Antiquity to Sexual Revolution.* London: Equinox, 2004.

Geertz, Clifford. *The Interpretation of Cultures.* New York: Basic Books, 1973.

Gilfoyle, Timothy J. *City of Eros: New York City Prostitution and the Commercialization of Sex, 1790–1920.* New York: W. W. Norton, 1992.

Gordon, Linda, and Ellen Carol DuBois. "Seeking Ecstasy on the Battlefield: Danger and Pleasure in Nineteenth-Century Feminist Sexual Thought." *Feminist Studies* 9 (Spring 1983): 17–38.

Grosz, Elizabeth. *The Nick of Time: Politics, Evolution and the Untimely.* Sydney: Allen & Unwin, 2004.

Gullett, Gayle. *Becoming Citizens: The Emergence and Development of California's Women's Movement, 1880–1911.* Urbana: University of Illinois Press, 2000.

Harel, Kay. "When Darwin Flopped: The Rejection of Sexual Selection." *Sexuality and Culture* 5 (December 2001): 29–42.

Heilbrun, Carolyn. *Writing a Woman's Life.* London: Women's Press, 1981.

Higham, John. *Strangers in the Land: Patterns of American Nativism, 1860–1925.* New Brunswick, NJ: Rutgers University Press, 1988.

Hobson, Barbara Meil. *Uneasy Virtue: The Politics of Repression and the American Reform Tradition.* Chicago: University of Chicago Press, 1990.

Jablonsky, Thomas J. *The Home, Heaven, and Mother Party: Female Anti-Suffragists in the United States, 1868–1920.* Brooklyn: Carlson Publications, 1994.

Johnson, Robert D. "Re-Democratizing the Progressive Era: The Politics of Progressive Era Political Historiography." *Journal of the Gilded Age and Progressive Era* 1 (January 2002): 68–91.

Kaplan, Amy. "Manifest Domesticity." *American Literature* 70 (September 1998): 581–606.

Keire, Mara L. "The Vice Trust: A Reincarnation of the White Slavery Scare in the United States, 1907–1917." *Journal of Social History* 35 (Fall 2001): 5–41.

Kent, Susan Kingsley. *Sex and Suffrage in Britain, 1860–1914.* Princeton, NJ: Princeton University Press, 1987.

Kolchin, Peter. "Whiteness Studies: The New History of Race in America." *Journal of American History* 89 (June 2002): 154–73.

Kraditor, Aileen S. *The Ideas of the Woman Suffrage Movement, 1850–1920.* New York: Columbia University Press, 1965.

———. *Up from the Pedestal: Selected Writings in the History of American Feminism.* Chicago: Quadrangle Books, 1968.

Levine, Philippa. *Victorian Feminism, 1850–1900.* London: Hutchinson, 1987.

Lovett, Laura L. *Conceiving the Future: Pronatalism, Reproduction, and the Family in the United States, 1890–1938.* Chapel Hill: University of North Carolina Press, 2007.

MacKinnon, Catharine A. "Feminism, Marxism, Method and the State: An Agenda for Theory." *Signs* 7 (Spring 1982): 515–45.

McGee, Brian. "Rhetoric and Race in the Progressive Era: Imperialism, Reform, and the Ku Klux Klan." In *Rhetoric and Reform in the Progressive Era,* 311–38.

McClintock, Anne. *Imperial Leather: Race, Gender and Sexuality in the Colonial Contest.* New York: Routledge, 1995.

McGee, Brian. "Rhetorical Race in the Progressive Era: Imperialism, Reform, and the Ku Klux Klan." In *Rhetoric and Reform in Progressive Era,* ed. Micharl Hogan. East Lansing: Michigan State University Press, 2003.

McGerr, Michael. *"A Fierce Discontent": The Rise and Fall of the Progressive Movement in America, 1870–1920.* New York: Free Press, 2003.

McMahon, Sean H. *Social Control and Public Intellect: The Legacy of Edward A. Ross.* New Brunswick: Transaction, 1999.

Mead, Rebecca J. *How the Vote Was Won: Woman Suffrage in the Western United States, 1868–1914.* New York: NYU Press, 2004.

Moore-Gilbert, Bart. "Olive Schreiner's 'Story of an African Farm': Reconciling Feminism and Anti-Imperialism?" *Women* 14 (Spring 2003): 85–103.

Morantz, Regina. "The Lady and Her Physician." In *Clio's Consciousness Raised: New Perspectives on the History of Women,* ed. Mary S. Hartman and Lois Banner, 38–53. New York: Harper & Row, 1974.

Morris, Edmund. *Theodore Rex.* New York: Random House, 2001.

Newby, I. A., ed. *The Development of Segregationist Thought.* Homewood, IL: Dorsey, 1968.

Pateman, Carole. "Defending Prostitution: Charges against Ericsson." *Ethics* 93 (April 1982): 557–62.

———. *The Sexual Contract.* Palo Alto, CA: Stanford University Press, 1988.

Pivar, David J. *Purity and Hygiene: Women, Prostitution, and the "American Plan," 1900–1930.* Westport, CT: Greenwood Press, 2002.

Rafferty, Edward C. *Apostle of Human Progress: Lester Frank Ward and American Political Thought.* New York: Rowman & Littlefield, 2003.

Rich, Doris L. *Amelia Earhart: A Biography.* Washington, DC: Smithsonian Institution, 1989.

Rickard, John. *Class and Politics: Victoria, New South Wales, and the Early Commonwealth.* Canberra: Australian National University Press, 1976.

Rodgers, Daniel. T. *Atlantic Crossings: Social Politics in a Progressive Age.* Cambridge, MA: Harvard University Press, 1998.

Roe, Jill. *Stella Miles Franklin: A Biography.* Sydney: HarperCollins, 2008.

Rosen, Ruth. *The Lost Sisterhood: Prostitution in America, 1900–1918.* Baltimore: Johns Hopkins University Press, 1982.

Rosenberg, Rosalind. *Beyond Separate Spheres: Intellectual Roots of Modern Feminism.* New Haven, CT: Yale University Press, 1982.

Rupp, Leila J. "Feminism and the Sexual Revolution in the Early Twentieth Century: The Case of Doris Stevens." *Feminist Studies* 15 (Summer 1989): 289–309.

———. "Sexuality and Politics in the Early Twentieth Century: The Case of the International Women's Movement." *Feminist Studies* 23 (1997): 577–605.

Schwarz, Judith. *Radical Feminists of Heterodoxy: Greenwich Village, 1912–1940.* Norwich, VT: New Victoria Publishers, 1986.

Scott, Clifford H. *Lester Frank Ward.* Boston: Twayne, 1976.

———. "A Naturalistic Rationale For Women's Reform: Lester Frank Ward on the Evolution of Sexual Relations." *Historian* 33(November 1970): 54–67.

Sochen, June. *The New Woman in Greenwich Village, 1910–1920.* New York: Quadrangle, 1972.

Stansell, Christine. *American Moderns: Bohemian New York and the Creation of a New Century.* New York: Metropolitan Books, 2000.

Trigg, Mary. "'To Work Together for Ends Larger Than Self': The Feminist Struggles of Mary Beard and Doris Stevens in the 1930s." *Journal of Women's History* 7 (Summer 1995): 52–85.

Trimberger, Ellen Kay. Introduction to *Intimate Warriors: Portraits of a Modern Marriage, 1899–1944 — Selected Works by Neith Boyce and Hutchins Hapgood.* New York: Feminist Press, 1991.

Valverde, Mariana. "'When the Mother of the Race is Free': Race, Reproduction, and Sexuality in First Wave Feminism." In *Gender Conflicts: New Essays in Women's History,* ed. Franca Iacovetta and Mariana Valverde, 3–26. Toronto: University of Toronto Press, 1992.

Ware. Susan. *Still Missing: Amelia Earhart and the Search for Modern Feminism.* New York: Norton, 1993.

Weeks, Jeffrey. *Sex, Politics and Society: The Regulation of Sexuality since 1800.* London: Longmans, 1981.

Wilcox, Leonard. "Sex Boys in a Balloon: V. F. Calverton and the Abortive Sexual Revolution." *Journal of American Studies* 23 (1989): 7–26.

Wittenstein, Kate. "The Feminist Uses of Psychoanalysis: Beatrice M. Hinkle and the Foreshadowing of Modern Feminism in the United States." *Journal of Women's History* 10 (Summer 1998): 38–62.

Wolfe, Patrick. "Land, Labor, and Difference: Elementary Structures of Race." *American Historical Review* 106 (June 2001): 866–905.

Unpublished Sources

Allen, Judith A. "Aspects of the Public Career of Rose Scott, 1890–1920." B.A. Honors diss., University of Sydney, 1978.

Bederman, Gail. "Naked, Unfettered, and Unashamed: Charlotte Perkins Gilman, Anti-Feminism, and the Figure of the Savage Rapist." Paper presented at the Second International Charlotte Perkins Gilman Conference. Skidmore College, Saratoga Springs, NY, June 26–29, 1997.

Kennedy, Adelaide M., Jane S. Knowles, and Lucy Thoma. Channing, Grace Ellery, 1862–1937. Papers, 1806–1973: A Finding Aid, Arthur and Elizabeth Schlesinger Library on the History of Women Radcliffe College May 1985. Radcliffe College, 1985—OASIS, Harvard University, Cambridge, MA.

Mosley, Eva. Gilman, Charlotte Perkins, 1860–1935. Papers, 1846–1961: A Finding Aid. [177 (mf1)]. Arthur and Elizabeth Schlesinger Library on the History of Women in America, Radcliffe College, Cambridge, MA, December 1972.

Rensing, Susan Marie. "Feminist Eugenics in America: From Free Love to Birth Control, 1880–1930." Ph.D. diss., University of Minnesota, 2006.

Ware, Susan. "Charlotte Perkins Gilman: The Early Lectures, 1890–1893." Manuscript. Cambridge, MA, May 29, 1973.

ethology, 11
eugenics, 198, 244, 321–22, 348, 427n30

A Fallen Sister (Gilman), 48
feminism, 5, 12, 132, 338; "amaternal,"
176, 199; Anglo-American, 178, 181,
359; "biological basis" for, 76, 171,
201; eugenic, 343, 428n41; "feminine," 176; history and historicity
of, 347–49, 361; human/humanist,
177–78, 298; reform Darwinist, 5, 12, 263, 270, 349; Teuto-
Scandinavian, 178–80; "waves"
("first," "second," or "third"), 6, 238,
327–29, 343–44, 423n2
"Feminism" (Gilman), vii, 1
Feminist Alliance, 225
feminist theory and theorists, 2, 4, 327,
349, 362
Fessenden, Tracy, 328, 343, 403n21
Field, Kate, 51
Fite, Warner, 152–53
flappers, xiv, 214, 291, 294, 417n15
Flynn, Elizabeth Gurley, 128
food, 108, 213, 318; adulteration, 157,
280; agriculture, 213; cooking, 54,
105–6, 118–19, 217; distribution,
157; milk, 158, 388n13; nutrition, 106
The Forerunner (Gilman), 281, 287, 289,
291, 388n17
Foucault, Michel, 10
Frankel, Oz, 330
Franklin, Stella Miles, xiii, 144, 164,
168–69, 208–9
Fraser, Nancy, 10
Frederickson, George M., 307, 336–37,
340, 344
Freud, Sigmund, 7, 187, 267
Friedan, Betty, 6, 364n12
Fuller, Margaret, 17, 37, 138
Fuller, Meta, 286–87

Gage, Matilda Joslyn, 9
Gale, Zona, 294, 416n10
Ganobcsik-Williams, Lisa, 344
gender, 329, 344, 346–47, 359, 362;

androgyny, 44, 223, 295, 362; femininity and feminization, 106, 221;
masculinity and masculinization,
221, 342, 358
George, W. L., 182
Germany, xiv, 127–28; androgyny, relative, 312; Ellen Key's influence in,
178; war and atrocities, 290
Gilbert, Sandra, and Susan Gubar, 10
Gilman, Charlotte Perkins; as an
abolitionist, 236, 250; and Adeline
E. Knapp, 50–62, 72; on "American unity," and exceptionalism,
300–301, 419n51; ancestors and
family of, 205, 363n3; on androcentric culture, 1, 74, 99, 109, 334;
anger and depression of, 20, 31–34,
48, 62–63, 65; art and artworks of,
8, 35–36, 43; as an assimilationist,
310, 421n69; audiences, 93, 110, 271,
275–80, 410n7; birth control work
and writings, 314–23; breakdown
and recurrences, 25–27, 54, 67,
139, 241; breast cancer of, 44, 294;
as celebrity, 192–93, 203–11; and
Charles Walter Stetson, 19, 43–44,
69–70; correspondents of, 192,
207–11; and courtship and suitors,
27, 51–56, 64–69, 73, 375n34; on
demand for prostitution, 237, 244,
262; diaries of, 26, 31–34, 40, 61,
371n28; on differential rates of
evolution, 120; divorce of, 40–50,
54–58, 204–5, 296; editorial work,
59, 61, 280–89; education, vii, 360;
as erotophilic, 42–43, 46, 64–65;
as erotophobic, 4, 35, 41, 73; on
ethics, 120; and Eugene Hough, 58,
62; on "feminism," 1, 164–90; "the
larger feminism," 154, 168, 182, 232,
321; fiction and nonfiction writing,
8–11, 43, 203, 237, 366n20; and
George Houghton Gilman, 63–73,
270, 294; and George O. Virtue,
62–63; and Grace Ellery Channing
Stetson, 47, 57, 70; on "growth," 123,

League for Political Education, 205
League of Women Voters, 162, 189, 293
Lerner, Gerda, 12, 414n36
Life and Labor, xiii
Lindsay, Estelle Lawton, 179–80
Lippmann, Walter, 184
Littledale, Clara Savage, 183–84, 189
The Living of Charlotte Perkins Gilman
 (Gilman), 3, 23–24, 53
Lloyd, Brian, 340, 427n34
Love and Marriage (Key), 175
Love's Pilgrimage (Sinclair), 286–87

"Mag-Marjorie" (Gilman), 265
Magner, Lois, 344
"The Making of Americans" (Gilman),
 300
The Man-Made World (Gilman), 3, 102,
 195, 205–6; epigraphs from, 87, 115,
 156, 239
Mann Martin, Prestonia, 167, 179, 191–97,
 224–26, 332; antisuffragism and
 antifeminism of, 193–94, 354
Markham, Edwin, 44, 58
Marriot-Watson, H. B., 153
Martin, John, 191, 194–97, 224–26, 354,
 398n5
masculism and masculists, xiv, 42, 73,
 152, 353; and antisuffragism, 137; and
 racism, 339; and war, 17, 121, 127
matriarchate, and matrifocal cultures,
 xv, 78, 80, 84, 88–89
McGerr, Michael, 305–6, 410n, 419n
McMillen, Rod, 413n32
Mead, Margaret, 10, 164
men, 111, 123, 125. *See also* sexuality and
 masculism and masculists; aggression and combativeness, 121–23;
 combat and war, 106, 111, 121–24,
 150, 180; European, 73, 176, 261;
 letters to Charlotte Perkins Gilman,
 191–92; as work-averse, 96
Mendel, Gregor, 17
Menken, H. L., 128, 283
Middleton, George, 191, 283–84, 316,
 413n25

Mighels, Ella Sterling Cummis, 56
Mill, John Stuart, 2, 17, 138, 197
misandry, 84, 195
misanthropy, 84
misogyny, 36, 117, 152, 195, 354
Mitchell, Alice, 52
Mitchell, Silas Weir, 20–22, 25, 27, 40
Morris, William and May, 332
Morrow, Prince, 245, 247, 254–55
Mother India (Mayo), 311
"Moving the Mountain" (Gilman),
 218–20, 228, 236, 265, 352; criticism
 of, 403n12
Moynihan, Mary, 340, 396n43
Mumford, Lewis, 10

NAACP (National Association for the
 Advancement of Colored People),
 288, 305
Nadkarni, Asha, 343–44, 428n41–42
Nation, 152
National Woman's Party, 158–61
native Americans, 123, 141, 221
nativism, xiv, 8, 291, 340, 360
A New Conscience and an Ancient Evil
 (Addams), 250, 252
"New Woman" and younger women,
 181, 185, 224, 360
New York Times, 3, 148, 153–55, 160–61;
 antisuffragism of, 167, 205, 269;
 coverage of Gilman, 169–70, 183,
 315, 332
New York Tribune, 288, 292, 415n5
Newman, Louise M., 338, 341, 343–44,
 346
newspaper press, 166, 192, 202, 269,
 356
Noblesse Oblige (Channing and Gilman), 45

Okin, Susan Moller, 10
"On the Anti-Suffragists" (Gilman),
 148
"On Male Sexual Selection" (Ward),
 82–83
"One Girl among Many" (Gilman), 19

demand for, 76–77, 316–20; coitus: rates of, reported, 422n84; conjugal rights, men's, 14–15, 38, 40–42, 46, 70; conjugal rights, men's: women's submission to, 69–70, 123, 231, 316–18, 320; conjugality, 26–27, 32, 199, 225, 230; "free love," 165–66, 180–82, 184, 316, 349; heterosexuality, 1, 29, 44, 63, 72–73; homophobia, 186; homosexuality and lesbianism, 44, 52, 56, 76, 375n26; male, as excessive and "hydraulic," 83, 184, 242, 251–56, 357; men's inherent sex instincts, 254, 256; monogamy, 240, 243, 314, 318; polygamy, 42; polygyny, voluntary matriarchal, 96, 100–101; as separated from reproduction, 182, 358, 359

sexualization and hypersexualization, xiv, 68, 108, 180, 243

Shaw, George Bernard, 2, 196, 332, 364n9

"Similar Cases" (Gilman), 89–90, 93

Simmons, Jim, 38–39

Sinclair, Upton, 247–48, 269, 285–86, 332, 352

Sklar, Kathryn Kish, 414n36

slavery, 81, 150, 222, 280, 297–98; abolitionists, 236, 418n39; chattel, and sex slavery analogy, 107, 222, 403n21, 405n22

"Social Ethics" (Gilman), 3

social hygiene, 35, 240

socialism and socialists, 9, 44, 68, 332, 352; Fabian socialism, 3, 64, 67, 196, 226; Marx, Karl, and Marxism, 7, 12, 292, 349, 352; Nationalism (Californian socialism), 3, 4, 44, 51, 55, 332, 333; and revolution, 333

sociology, xiv, 6–11, 256, 281–82, 361, 366n21

"Something to Vote For" (Gilman), 157–58

Stansell, Christine, 9

Stanton, Elizabeth Cady, 9, 78, 84, 146–49, 327

Stetson, Charles Walter, 14, 19–26, 63; and art patrons, 33, 40; Bohemian persona of, 26; and Charlotte Perkins Gilman, 20, 35–50, 70, 205, 241; diaries of, 26–28, 31–33; female nudes of, 25, 28–36, 42; German Romanticism, espousal of, 30; and Grace Ellery Channing, 46–49; on mistresses and prostitutes, 25–30, 35, 40–42, 242, 357

Stetson, Charlotte Anna Perkins: see Gilman, Charlotte Perkins

Stetson, Grace Ellery Channing, 14, 45, 47–48, 57, 325; miscarriage of, 70; resentment and criticisms of Charlotte Perkins Gilman, 70–72, 416n8; widowhood and poverty of, 24–25, 293, 324; writings and publications of, 373n12

Stevens, Doris, 185–87

Stevenson, Karen, 10

Stoddard, Lothrop, 336, 426n20

Stokes, Rose Pastor, 128

Stopes, Marie Carmichael, 376

Storey, Moorfield, 288

Stowe, Harriet Beecher, 2, 203, 387n13

Stowe, Lyman Beecher, 324, 416n8

Strong, Harriet Russell, 23, 370n12

"Studies in Masculism" (Gilman), 206

"Studies in Social Pathology" (Gilman), 3

"Study in Ethics" (Gilman), 361

The Subjection of Women (Mill), 2

"A Suggestion on the Negro Problem" (Gilman), 303–7, 344

Survey (1915), 195–96

Sylvia's Marriage (Sinclair), 247–48

Tarbell, Ida M., 4, 111, 148, 152–53, 164, 352

"teacher mothers" dispute, 224–27

The Theory of the Leisure Class (Veblen), 90, 112, 358

Thomas, William I., 4, 102, 282, 343, 358

"Toward Monogamy" (Gilman), 296